FLORENCE, VENICE, & MILAN ACCESS®

Orientation

Italy has a long history of conflicts—between city-states, between noble families, and, in recent times, between political parties. In fact, the nation was only unified some 130 years ago. Rivalry could be said to be a defining characteristic of the country, responsible for molding **Florence**, **Venice**, and **Milan** into three remarkably individual cities.

Shaping the character of Florence is its magnificent artistic heritage, of which the city is justly proud. It was here, after all, that **Brunelleschi**, Donatello, and Masaccio shook off the weight of the Middle Ages and started the Italian Renaissance. During the height of the Renaissance the city also produced some of the greatest writers, philosphers, and scientists since the ancient Greeks; Dante, Machiavelli, and da Vinci all helped define the Florentine character. But the power of Florence was not limited to its artists and thinkers; under Medici rule the city was a force to be reckoned with—not just in Italy but throughout Europe as well.

Venice also influenced events in Europe, but its eminence derived more from its mastery of eastern trade routes than the power of any one family. Although its luster may have faded some since it held the title "Queen of the Adriatic," this radiant city remains one of the world's most tempting tourist destinations. The vast wealth of its once-powerful court is still here, preserved in the palaces lining the **Canal Grande (Grand Canal)**, and in the great achievements of its master artists, Bellini, Titian, and Tintoretto. Venice is still

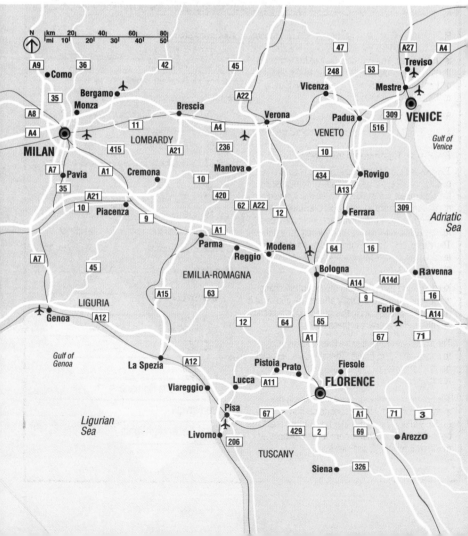

a city of merchants—from purveyors of designer clothing to hawkers of tacky souvenirs—the inheritors of a tradition that goes back to a time when the city brought Europe the sumptuous silks and exotic spices of the Far East.

The mantle of mercantile preeminence in Italy has long since passed to Milan, an economic force creating modern-day braggadocios in the arenas of business and finance. This modern city may venerate its past less than Florence or Venice, but Milan's history is evident nearly everywhere: in the spikey profile of the **Duomo**; in the Sforza's family fortress; in the streets tracing the paths of ancient canals; and even in the city's very modernity, a product of heavy bombing during World War II. Rather than rest on past laurels, though, the citizens of Milan choose to seek new ones, setting trends in fashion and design that can be found in the exclusive boutiques of its shopping district.

Those who are weary of the sameness of western mall culture can find refuge in these three cities, still more notable for their differences than for their similarities. Among them, Florence, Venice, and Milan hold some of Italy's— and the world's—most famous works of art and architecture, alongside some of its finest hotels and restaurants. The tourist who sees all three, the lucid Renaissance grace of Florence, the incredible Byzantine lightness of Venice, and the sophisticated Lombard dynamism of Milan, will come to love the crucible of human achievement known as Italy.

How To Read This Guide

FLORENCE/VENICE/MILAN ACCESS® is arranged so you can see at a glance where you are and what is around you. The numbers next to the entries in the following chapters correspond to the numbers on the maps. The text is color-coded according to the kind of place described:

Restaurants/Clubs: Red　　**Hotels:** Blue
Shops/ Outdoors: Green　**Sights/Culture:** Black

Rating the Restaurants and Hotels

The restaurant star ratings take into account the quality, service, atmosphere, and uniqueness of the restaurant. An expensive restaurant doesn't necessarily ensure an enjoyable evening; however, a small, relatively unknown spot could have good food, professional service, and a lovely atmosphere. Therefore, on a purely subjective basis, stars are used to judge the overall dining value (see the star ratings at right).

Keep in mind that chefs and owners often change, which sometimes drastically affects the quality of a restaurant. The ratings in this guidebook are based on information available at press time.

The price ratings, as categorized at right, apply to restaurants and hotels. These figures describe general price-range relationships among other restaurants and hotels in the area.

The restaurant price ratings are based on the average cost of an entrée for one person, excluding tax and tip. Hotel price ratings reflect the base price of a standard room for two people for one night during the peak season.

Restaurants

★	Good	
★★	Very Good	
★★★	Excellent	
★★★★	Extraordinary Experience	
$	The Price Is Right	(less than $25)
$$	Reasonable	($25-$45)
$$$	Expensive	($45-$70)
$$$$	Big Bucks	($70 and up)

Hotels

$	The Price Is Right	(less than $90)
$$	Reasonable	($90-$125)
$$$	Expensive	($125-$225)
$$$$	Big Bucks	($225 and up)

Map Key

City/Town ●

1 Entry Number
M Milan Metro Station
■ Point of Interest

37 Autostrada
Tunnel
Main Road
Secondary Road
Pedestrian Area
Trail
Railroad

Ferry
Venice Vaporetto Stop

Getting to Italy
Airlines

The main gateways to Italy are Milan and Rome; connecting flights may be made to Florence and Venice on Italy's domestic airline, **ATI**. See the orientation chapters of the individual cities for specific airline and airport information.

Getting Around Italy
Buses

Two bus services connect most of Italy. They are: **ANAC** (Piazza Esquilino 29, Rome, 06/463383) and **SITA** (Viale dei Cadorna 105, Florence, 055/278611). See the orientation chapters of the individual cities for more information.

Driving

Members of the European Economic Community can use their countries' drivers' licenses in Italy. US citizens can get by with a photo-ID driver's license, but you may want to get an International Driver's Permit from the **American Automobile Association (AAA);** (check your local yellow pages or write to 1000 AAA Dr., Heathrow, FL, 32746-5080, 407/444.7000; fax 407/444.7380) to be 100 percent official. Car rental is almost always cheaper when arranged in advance from abroad. Emergency service is provided by the **Automobile Club Italiano (ACI);** simply dial 116 from any phone in the country.

Trains

The Italian state railway is known as **Ferrovie dello Stato**, or **FS**. Though the trains do not always run on time (as they allegedly did during Mussolini's day), train travel can be a pleasure in Italy, although strikes can sometimes mar the experience. The fastest train is the *Pendolino*, which is first class only and links Milan, Florence, and Rome. The other trains have first- and second-class tickets: In order of efficiency they are the *EuroCity (EC)*, an international train; *InterCity (IC)*, its domestic equivalent, which operates between major cities with minimal stops; express *(espresso)*, which is considerably slower than the *IC* and *Pendolino;* direct *(diretto)*, which

stops at most stations; and local *(locale)*, which stops at all stations. *EC* and *IC* trains require the payment of a supplement *(supplimento)*.

A wide variety of special passes is available and deals on train tickets are constantly changing—check with a travel agent about them. Leave plenty of time to buy a ticket at the station, or purchase it in advance from a local travel agency (be sure to specify if you are traveling on an *EC* or *IC* train in order to pay for and receive the appropriate supplement; there is a stiff penalty if either the ticket or supplement is purchased on board). Another word of caution: Before boarding the train, be sure to validate your ticket in the machine located at the head of the track to avoid paying a hefty penalty.

A seat reservation *(prenotazione)* is almost always recommended during the busy summer months and is included in the cost of an *EC* or *IC* supplement (it may be optional or obligatory on other trains and will cost extra). Nonsmoking seats are available on first-class trains, but they are the first to disappear, so be sure to reserve them well in advance.

A word of warning—travelers are occasionally robbed on overnight trains, especially those traveling from north to south. A simple security measure is to ask the conductor to lock your compartment from the outside (the door can still be opened from the inside in case of an emergency).

CIT (Compagnia Italiana Turismo), owned by **FS,** has two offices in the US and two in Canada. They can help with rail schedules and ticket costs:

- 342 Madison Ave, New York, NY 10173, 800/CIT.RAIL, 800/248.8687; 212/697.2100, 697.1482 in New York; fax 212/697.1394.

- 6033 W Century Blvd, Los Angeles, CA 90045, 800/CIT.RAIL, 310/338.8620 in Los Angeles; fax 310/670.4269.

- 1450 City Councillors, Montreal, Quebec H3A 2E6, Canada, 514/845.9101.

- 111 Avenue Rd, Toronto, Ontario M5R 3J8, Canada, 416/927.7712.

Information is also available from **Rail Europe** (800/4.EURAIL; fax 800/432.1329).

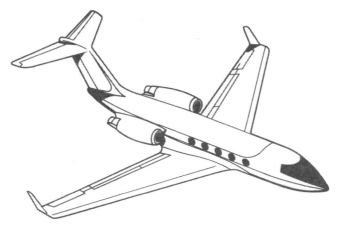

FYI

City Maps

Individual city maps, collectively called *Tutto Città,* cover extensive ground off the beaten track. Most hotels and bars have a copy on hand. Less detailed maps are readily available at most hotels and all tourist information offices (see individual city orientations for locations).

Climate

Northern Italy has a fairly moderate climate (see the individual city orientations for average temperatures and weather conditions); you should dress accordingly and comfortably (but take note that Italians are fairly formal). Bare shoulders and skimpy shorts are considered inappropriate dress for churches and the street. Classic, conservative attire has long been considered quite chic in Italy. A casual look, for both sexes, of polo shirts in warm weather, quilted jackets in the cooler weather, and Timberland shoes year-round will help you to pass for a local.

Customs and Immigration

A valid passport is required to enter and leave Italy; no inoculations are needed. Visas are not necessary for stays of less than six months (for stays of six months or more, contact the nearest Italian consulate). Those visiting for more than three months are required to register with the local police station once in Italy. Hotels generally ask for your passport on arrival and will take care of this formality for you. If you are not staying in a hotel, you are expected to register yourself each time you change residences, though the Italian authorities are usually fairly lax about enforcing this requirement.

Visitors are allowed to bring in up to 1,000,000 lire in Italian currency; two still cameras and 10 rolls of film for each; one movie camera and 10 rolls of film for it; one video camera and one cassette for it; 400 cigarettes and 500 grams of cigars or pipe tobacco; and two bottles of wine and one bottle of hard liquor. When bringing in any other special equipment or prescription medicines, be sure to have documentation to back them up. From the US, contact the **US Customs Service** (202/927.2095) about obtaining the proper forms for equipment; a physician can provide a letter about medications.

Check with your local customs service about what may be brought back from Italy.

Drinking

Though having wine with meals is common, hard liquor is rarely consumed outside of tourist bars and TV ads, and drunkenness is considered extremely bad form *(brutta figura).* There is no minimum drinking age in Italy. Bars are typically open Monday through Saturday from 8AM to 8PM, although some bar/cafes that attract after-dinner patrons will stay open later. Some bars are open on Sunday from 8AM until lunchtime.

Drugs

Italy has stiff penalties for possession of any amount of narcotics.

Etiquette

Italians love titles, the most popular being *dottore (dottoressa* for women) for anyone with a university degree. More specific titles good for both sexes are *ingegnere* (engineer), *architetto* (architect), and *avvocato* (attorney). When in doubt, *dottore* or *dottoressa* will take you further than a simple *signore* or *signora.*

Within such a formal culture, it is surprising how aggressive Italians can be in public situations. Be prepared for inconsiderate drivers, pushing and shoving at lines in banks and post offices (and no lines at all at bus stops or in similar situations), and the sharp *gomitata* (elbow thrust) from innocent-appearing seniors in food markets. A stern look accompanied by a firm *"Prego?"* (what gives?) will usually be met with feigned incomprehension on the part of the offender, but he or she will usually back down.

Italian men seem to have no rules of etiquette when it comes to foreign women, and catcalling on the street is common. Squeezing and pinching on crowded buses are referred to as *mano morta* (dead hand—but where it shouldn't be) and *mano lesta* (molesting hand). Use a sharp elbow jab or a good heel kick to get rid of unwelcome attention. Ignore the man in the street who tries to pick you up. A firm *"Vada via!"* (go away!) will usually suffice. Unfortunately, this is a national male pastime.

Hours

In 1993 the Ministry of Culture announced a revolutionary rescheduling of state-run museum hours, all of which are to be open Tuesday through Saturday from 9AM to 7PM and Sunday from 9AM to 1PM. They are to close only on such important holidays as Christmas and Easter. City museums and smaller, privately owned or operated museums will continue to have confusing and ever-changing schedules. Refer to local listings or ask a hotel concierge for a more definitive answer.

See the individual city orientations for information about dining, bank, and shop hours.

Holidays

There are a number of religious and state holidays when everything closes down. Expect massive delays, if not complete lack of services, on:

Capo d'Anno (New Year's Day), 1 January

Befana (Epiphany), 6 January

Pasqua (Easter) 7 April 1996, 30 March 1997

Pasquetta (Easter Monday) 8 April 1996, 31 March 1997

Liberazione (Liberation Day) 25 April

Festa del Lavoro (Labor Day) 1 May

Ferragosto (Feast of the Assumption) 15 August

Tutti Santi (All Saints' Day) 1 November

Festa della Madonna Immacolata (Feast of the Immaculate Conception) 8 December

Natale (Christmas) 25 December

Santo Stefano (St. Stephen's Day) 26 December

Each city also celebrates the feast day of its patron saint (see individual city orientations for more information).

Medical Care

The **International Association for Medical Assistance to Travelers (IAMAT)** provides a list of English-speaking physicians throughout the world as well as a number of useful publications. Membership is free; sign up by contacting the organization at 417 Center St, Lewiston, NY 14092, 716/754.4883; 40 Regal Rd, Guelph, Ont. N1K 1B5, Canada, 519/836.0102; PO Box 5049, Christchurch 5, New Zealand.

Travelers with special medical needs should check with their doctors about the latest health precautions; in the US, call the **Centers for Disease Control** travel information line (404/639.2572) for up-to-date information. Your physician can provide generic prescriptions.

In nonemergency situations ask a hotel concierge or contact the appropriate consulate (see individual city orientations for listings) for help in finding a doctor or dentist.

Money

The Italian monetary unit is the lira. Bills come in denominations of 100,000, 50,000, 20,000, 10,000, 5,000, 2,000, and 1,000 lire; coins in 500, 200, 100, and 50 lire.

Avoid changing money at the currency exchange offices *(cambio)* in airports and train stations, since they often charge exorbitant fees (information about these should be posted; be sure to read it). If there's no other alternative, change only enough to make it through the day. As a general rule, the state-owned travel agency **(CIT)** and American Express offices offer good rates and minimal fees. Money may also be exchanged in travel agencies, banks, and hotels at varying exchange rates and for a fee.

Automated teller machines (ATMs) are common-place in Florence, Venice, and Milan and most are connected to international networks such as CIRRUS and PLUS; machines that accept Visa or MasterCard are also common. Your bank or credit card company can provide additional information.

Most hotels, shops, and restaurants accept major credit cards, but be aware that most credit card companies charge one percent of the transaction amount as a fee for converting foreign currencies. Moreover, the rate of exchange depends not on the date of purchase but the date the transaction is processed.

Personal Safety

Watch your belongings on crowded streets, markets, train stations, and public transportation; purse-snatching and pickpocketing occurs, usually without violence. Panhandlers, often accompanied by children, approach people with astounding tenacity, one of them begging while the others pick your pocket.

In case of trouble, call 113, the emergency number throughout Italy. Any one of the various Italian police can also be helpful. First choice should be the well-educated and courteous *carabinieri,* who wear dark blue uniforms. *Polizia,* who wear navy jackets and lighter pants or skirts, have a reputation for being a little hard-boiled. *Vigili urbani,* who wear navy outfits and white bobby's hats, usually concern themselves only with traffic violations and petty crime.

Postal Service

The Italian postal service (called *Ufficio Postale*) is considered the most expensive and least efficient in Europe. Post offices provide mail, telex, telegram, and fax services (except to the US; to send faxes there, use a hotel or private fax service); use a courier for anything important. Tobacconists also sell stamps. To receive mail at a post office, have the sender mark it *fermo posta* (c/o the post office or *ufficio postale)* in the city where it will be picked up (for a small fee).

American Express offices will hold mail for clients without charging a fee. Federal Express and DHL have courier services throughout Italy, and though they strive to meet American standards, they are still working out such bugs as on-time pickup and delivery.

Publications

Such periodicals as the *International Herald Tribune,* the *Financial Times, USA Today, Time, Newsweek,* and *The Economist* are available on newsstands throughout Italy. **Telemontecarlo** (a Monte Carlo–based private television network accessible throughout Italy) rebroadcasts the *CBS Evening News* and **CNN** at various times. The pricier hotels carry live broadcasts of **CNN, Skychannel,** and other cable networks. **Radio Vaticano,** the Vatican radio station, periodically broadcasts the news in English.

Restaurants

Dating from the time when restaurants were primarily family run, Italian law states that all such establishments must observe one closing day per week (hotel retaurants are exempt from this regulation). Tacked on to restaurant bills are a charge for *pane e coperta* (bread and cover) and a separate service charge. Although most dining is à la carte, some restaurants offer a fixed-price *menù turistico,* a "one from column A, one from column B" affair of two or three courses. It's

a good idea to make a reservation, although it is not required in most cases. Lunch is usually served between 1 and 3PM; dinner between 8 and 10:30PM.

Smoking

Italians still think smoking is smart, even though it is prohibited on buses, in the subways, on domestic air flights, and in public offices. Nonsmoking sections in restaurants and smoke-free rooms in hotels are a rarity, but ask anyway.

Taxes

Taxes are always included in hotel room rates, meals, and merchandise. The European Economic Community levies a sales tax (Value Added Tax, called IVA in Italy) of about 18 percent (much higher for jewelry) on merchandise sold in Italy. Non-EEC visitors can request partial exemption on purchases of 300,000 lire or more made in any one store, and any tax paid can be refunded by mail or credited to your credit card. Getting a check refund by mail, however, often takes many weeks and sometimes months. Italian customs officials at refund counters in the major airports will ask to see a special form filled out by the merchant, an official receipt, and the merchandise when you are leaving the country.

Telephones

Calling local or long distance from your hotel room usually costs at least twice as much as it would on the outside. The cheapest way to phone the US is to call collect (dial 170 and the international operator will arrange it) and have someone call you back. AT&T calling card users can dial 1721011 to be connected to an AT&T operator in the US. MCI users can dial 1721022; Sprint Express members, 1721877. Otherwise, go to the phone company offices known by the acronyms of SIP-Telecom or ASST, and pay cash.

There are three kinds of coin phones in Italy, all of which offer international direct dialing. The few remaining small green ones take only a *gettone* (phone slug), available at many tobacconists and newsstands. The larger, metallic phones and the orange ones take a *gettone*, a 200- or 500- lire coin, or two 100-lire coins. When a phone is not working, a red light comes on. A sign reading *guasto* means out of order, although likely as not the shop owner just doesn't feel like letting people use the phone; try it anyway.

Five-thousand- and 10,000-lire prepaid phone cards, which fit into the metal boxes adjacent to the coin phones in many public places, are sold at SIP-Telecom and ASST offices as well as at bars and tobacconists (ask for a *carta telefonica* or *scheda telefonica).* The card loses value each time it is used, and when it is used up, it will not be returned. Clip off the top corner along the dotted line the first time you use it.

Italy is at long last bringing its telephone system into the late 20th century. It was not long ago that parties were required to share "duplex" lines or waited up to a year to have a telephone installed. Modernization, of

Porcellino, Mercato Nuovo, Florence

course, means that there is a growing number of new telephone listings and new numbers. Recordings of the new numbers (often no more than the addition of a single digit to the old number) are sometimes offered in English as well as Italian, but don't count on it.

Time Zone

Florence, Venice, and Milan are all in the same time zone, Greenwich Mean Time plus one hour (six hours ahead of US Eastern Standard Time). Clocks in Italy are set ahead one hour in the spring and back one hour in the fall, but it does not coincide with daylight saving time in the US or elsewhere in Europe. Italian timetables use the 24-hour clock, denoting 3:15PM, for example, as 15:15.

Tipping

In restaurants the tip (usually around 15 percent) has been included when the words *servizio compreso* or *servizio incluso* appear on the bill, but you may choose to leave a bit more to bring it up to 17 or 18 percent. Otherwise, adding 15 percent is generous and should be greatly appreciated. Italians themselves generally leave an additional 1,000 to 2,000 lire per diner on the table. Taxi drivers get 10 percent. Tip porters, hotel maids, and concierges according to the quality of service. Theater and cinema ushers expect a nominal tip for showing you to your seat.

Toilets

There are few public bathrooms in Italy. An air of self-confidence and a good sense of direction will help get you to the facilities available in the more upscale hotels; otherwise the price of a coffee at the counter will entitle you to ask for *la toiletta* or *il gabinetto* in a coffee bar, although the hygiene is often not the best and you may want to bring your own tissue paper.

The Main Events

Traditional festivals are celebrated in most Italian towns in commemoration of local historical or religious events. The most notable in Florence, Venice, and Milan are listed here; some draw such large crowds that it's a good idea to make reservations in advance.

January

On the 6th, **Epiphany** is celebrated with a parade of the Three Kings proceeding from the **Duomo** to the **Chiesa di Sant'Eustorgio.**

February

While **Carnevale** officially starts about two weeks before **Ash Wednesday,** Venetians really don't begin festivities until about a week before. Officially revived by the mayor of Venice in the late 1970s, this pre-**Lenten** festival is celebrated with masks and costumes, theatrical entertainment, masked balls, and an air of gaiety and lightheartedness. With crowds topping 100,000, **Piazza San Marco** and the neighboring streets become extremely crowded and noisy, while back-street routes, restaurants, and hotels remain relatively tranquil. The grand finale includes fireworks over the lagoon on **Shrove Tuesday.**

March

Scoppio del Carro, literally "explosion of the cart," takes place in Florence on **Easter Sunday** in celebration of a Christian victory during the Crusades, and culminates in a great fireworks

display. At high mass, when the bells announce the Resurrection of Christ, the Cardinal Archbishop of Florence sets off a dove-shaped rocket (with flints said to have been brought back from Jerusalem during the Crusades) that runs along a metal wire into the piazza and into a large cart drawn by white oxen. When the cart explodes, the spectators cheer with joy, taking the event and the flight of the "dove" as a good omen for the future.

April

Festa di San Marco, on the 25th, is the feast day of Venice's beloved patron saint, when loved ones exchange red roses and a special high mass is celebrated in the **Basilica di San Marco** at 10AM.

Fiera di Milano, held annually in late April since the 1920s, is the city's biggest trade fair and has put Milan squarely on the international business map. (For information about other fairs, get a copy of the useful bilingual periodical *In Fiera* and a year-round calendar of events from the main **Trade Fair** office at 1 Largo Domodossola; (49971).

May

On **Ascension Day,** in early May, Florentine children celebrate the **Festa del Grillo** by going to the **Cascine,** a park along the **Arno** at the edge of the center, buying crickets in cages and setting them free.

In mid-May (usually on a Sunday), Venetians of all ages and in all kinds of boats participate in the annual **Vogalonga,** a local regatta second only in popularity and color to the **Regata Storica** (see page 9). The regatta starts at 9AM at the **Molo** off Piazza San Marco.

The **Maggio Musicale** takes place in Florence from early May through the end of June. This festival, featuring classical music, dance, and opera, draws renowned performers from all over the world.

June

On the first Sunday in June, the **Festa dei Navigli** (Canal Festival) takes place on Milan's two *navigli* (canals) and in **La Darsena**—Milan's port—with music, food, and folklore.

Florence is bathed in medieval splendor during the **Festa di San Giovanni Battista** (Feast of St. John the Baptist) on 24 June. The celebration includes a parade of more than 500 Florentines wearing colorful 16th-century costumes, followed by an extremely rough game of soccer. (Three games are actually played—two preliminaries and a final—within two weeks of 24 June. Four teams of 27 people play, each representing the old rival neighborhoods of San Giovanni, Santo Spirito, Santa Croce, and Santa Maria Novella.)

From June through October, in odd-numbered years, the important **Esposizione Internazionale d'Arte Moderna** (International Exposition of Modern Art), better known as **Biennale d'Arte,** takes place in Venice in a small park beyond the **Riva dei Sette Martiri.**

July

On the third Saturday of July, Venice commemorates the end of a deadly 16th-century plague with **Festa del Redentore** (Feast of the Redeemer). A bridge of pontoons is built across the **Canale della Giudecca,** from the door of the **Chiesa del Redentore** to **Zattere.** The church, designed by **Palladio** and built as an offering of thanks for the end of the terrible plague, is open that Saturday and Sunday for visiting and mass. Boats of all sizes and degrees of luxury (from ports far and near) arrive in the morning, their passengers opening bottles of wine, and setting out food, flowers, and lounge chairs. As dusk approaches, boats take their places, and celebrants eat, drink, and greet their neighbors. At 11PM the sky explodes for a half hour of spectacular fireworks, followed by the tooting of hundreds of horns. As the frenzy dies down, the great pontoon "bridge" opens, and for the next 24 hours, boats

make the trek across the water. Spectators on land crowd the canalside *fondamente* to watch the festivities and then keep San Marco's restaurants busy into the wee hours of the morning.

August

Venice's annual **Mostra Internazionale di Cinematografica** (International Film Festival) is a 10-day festival held on the **Lido** in late August and early September.

September

In Venice, on the first Sunday of the month, gondola races and a magnificent procession of decorated barges and gondolas filled with Venetians in Renaissance dress highlight the **Regata Storica** (Historic Regatta) on the **Canal Grande.**

The **Festa delle Rificolone,** on the 7th, is celebrated in Florence with a procession along the Arno and across the **Ponte San Niccolò** with colorful paper lanterns and torches.

Also in Florence is the **Mostra dell'Antiquariato,** a prestigious international antiques fair, held in odd-numbered years in September and October at the **Palazzo Strozzi.**

October

Every October, a marathon starts along the Veneto's **Brenta Canal** and follows the tow paths, passing Palladian villas and ending in the center of Venice at the **Basilica di San Marco.** Runners who want information about competing can contact the **Venice Marathon Secretariat** at 34 Via Felisati, Mestre; (940644; fax: 940349).

During the third week of the month, at the **Fortezzo del Basso** in Florence, the **Mostra Mercato degli Antiquari Toscani** showcases regional Tuscan antiques dealers selling everything from Etruscan relics to 19th-century antiques.

In Milan, **Via Ripamonti** is the site of a truffle festival on the last Sunday of the month.

November

Venice celebrates the **Festa della Salute** on 21 November, forming a "bridge" of boats from **Santa Maria del Giglio** to the **Chiesa di Santa Maria della Salute.**

December

On the 7th, the feast day of Milan's patron saint, Saint Ambrose, festivities take place throughout the city. Drawing many of opera's greatest fans and performers on this day is the opening of **Teatro alla Scala**'s (more commonly known as **La Scala**) opera season. Milan's most important antiques fair, the annual **Fiera di Sant'Ambrogio,** also begins on the 7th—and goes on for 15 days—in **Piazza Sant'Ambrogio** and adjoining streets.

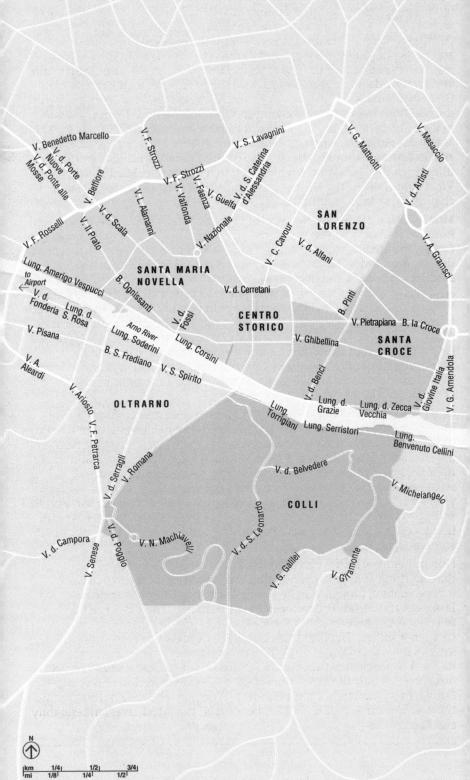

Florence Orientation

Of all of Italy's glorious tourist destinations, Florence is perhaps its most popular stop. As the birthplace of the Renaissance, the city's primary attraction is the wealth of artistic and architectural treasures produced during that period. In the **Centro Storico** (Historical Center), behind the harsh stone of the city's numerous churches and patrician palazzi, lie some of the greatest works of art in the western world. This, after all, is the city of Michelangelo, Botticelli, and Ghirlandaio, and their works are here in profusion—in the **Galleria degli Uffizi** (Uffizi Gallery), **Palazzo Pitti** (Pitti Palace), and **Galleria dell'Accademia.** Some of the buildings themselves are architectural wonders known to every student of the humanities in the world—most notably **Brunelleschi's** dome for **Santa Maria del Fiore** (the **Duomo**). Renaissance Florence was not just about art and architecture though; the city also boasted some of the great writers and thinkers of the age: Dante Alighieri, Petrarch, Boccaccio, Machiavelli, da Vinci, and Galileo. The *Divine Comedy* and *The Prince* are two of Western civilization's classic writings.

Much of what made Florence a preeminent cultural force as Europe emerged from the Middle Ages was due to the wealth and power of a single aristocratic family, the Medici, whose influence (and coat of arms) is visible throughout the city even today. From the 14th to 16th centuries, the merchants and bankers of the Medici clan controlled not only the city's purse strings but also its government. They used their power to install family members in the Vatican and intermarry with other European nobility. They used their wealth to commission architectural works and to support the city's greatest artists. Among the most influential of the family's art patrons, Lorenzo il Magnifico (1449-92), put Florence in the forefront of the Italian Renaissance by supporting the work of Botticelli, Ghirlandaio, Filippino Lippi, and Michelangelo. His patronage resulted in such glorious masterpieces as *Spring* and *David.*

While the glory days may be long past, there is a sense of continuity here. The fashionable courtiers in the city's Renaissance paintings are kin to today's stylishly attired Florentines (the meter maids wear Pucci uniforms). Modern-day merchants like Gucci have built international empires that could rival their Renaissance counterparts, and the city offers some of the finest shopping that can be found anywhere in Europe. The Florentines' infallible sense of style is evident even in the touristy open-air **Mercato di San Lorenzo** where, bypassing the Taiwan-made dross, the determined shopper can still find accessories and souvenirs of excellent quality, made in Italy and for sale at moderate prices.

Florentines have sometimes been faulted for refusing to acknowledge that anything of note happened after the golden age of the Renaissance (or even before, though the site was probably settled by the ancient Etruscans and certainly developed by the Romans). There is, in fact, a reserved self-assurance about the place and its people that might support such an assertion. The Florentine character, though, has been criticized at least as far back as Dante, whose native dialect was adopted as the official Italian language when the country was unified in the last century. And if you listen hard to how the Florentines speak the modern version of *la lingua di Dante*—in an aspirated, countrified way—you may even begin to appreciate the down-to-earth quality that lies beneath all that Machiavellian ceremony and Gucci gloss.

City code is 55 unless otherwise noted. To call Florence from the US, dial 011-39-55, followed by the local number. When calling from inside Italy, dial 055 and the local number.

Getting to Florence

Airports

Aeroporto Galileo Galilei
The closest international airport to Florence is **Aeroporto Galileo Galilei** in **Pisa,** a distance of 85 kilometers (53 miles).

Airport Services
Airport Emergencies	050/500707
Currency Exchange	050/41288
Customs	050/26280
Ground Transportation	050/44325
Information	050/500707
Lost Baggage	050/582400
Lost and Found	050/29329
Police	050/29329
Traveler's Aid	050/582460

Airlines
Air France	284304; 800/237.2747
Alitalia	27888; 800/223.5730
Lufthansa	238.1450;800/645.3880

Getting to and from Aeroporto Galileo Galilei
By Car
To get to Florence from the airport, follow the signs out of the airport to **Route 67** east. This becomes **Via Baccio da Montelupo** in Florence, and crosses the **Arno** at **Piazza Taddeo Gaddi**. From there, either continue on to the **Piazza della Stazione** or turn right onto **Lungarno Amerigo Vespucci**. An alternative route (though not as scenic) is to take the **A11** autostrada east to Florence. Then take **Route 66** east into the city, turn right on **Via Francesco Baracca**, which becomes **Via del Ponte alle Mosse** on the opposite side of **Piazza Giacomo Puccini.** At the **Piazzale di Porta al Prato,** go right to the **Piazza della Stazione** or left to **Lungarno Amerigo Vespucci,** which runs along the banks of the Arno River.

Rental Cars
The following rental car agencies have offices at **Galileo Galilei** airport:
Avis	050/42028; 800/331.1084
Budget	050/45490; 800/472.3325
Hertz	050/49187; 800/654.3001
Europcar (National)	050/41017; 800/227.3876

By Taxi
Taxi service to and from Florence is extremely expensive (about $120 at press time). The taxi stand is just outside the airport and the trip takes about an hour.

By Train
Trains between the airport and the Florence train station run hourly; the trip takes about one hour on the direct train. Passengers departing from the airport on **Alitalia** may check in directly at **Stazione Centrale di Santa Maria Novella,** Florence's main train station. All other passengers should be sure to ask for *Pisa Aeroporto* when purchasing train tickets and verifying track information.

Aeroporto Amerigo Vespucci
Service at **Aeroporto Amerigo Vespucci** (formerly called **Aeroporto Peretola**), located 4 kilometers (2.5 miles) from Florence, is generally limited to domestic flights. There are, however, daily flights to major European cities, where connections to US destinations can be made.

Airport Services
Currency Exchange	315642
Customs	3061610
Information	373498
Lost Baggage	3061606
Police	3061627; 3061628

Getting to and from Aeroporto Amerigo Vespucci
By Bus
Bus service to and from Florence's **Stazione Centrale di Santa Maria Novella** operates daily at approximately 30-minute intervals. The trip takes about 15 minutes.

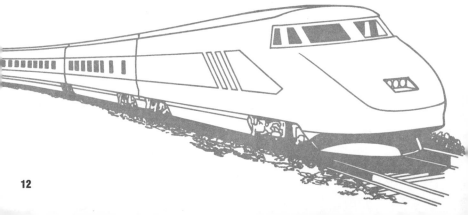

By Car

To get from the airport to the center of Florence, follow the "Centro" signs out of the airport to A11 east to Florence. Take Route 66 east into the city, turn right on Via Francesco Baracca, which becomes Via del Ponte alle Mosse on the opposite side of **Piazza Giacomo Puccini.** At the **Piazzale di Porta al Prato,** go right to the **Piazza della Stazione** or left to Lungarno Amerigo Vespucci, which runs along the banks of the Arno River.

Rental Cars

The following rental car agencies have offices at **Aeroporto Amerigo Vespucci:**

Avis 315588; 800/331.1084

Europcar (National) 318609; 800/227.3876

By Taxi

Taxis to downtown Florence are available outside the airport. The trip takes about 15 minutes.

Bus Station (Long-Distance)

Two private bus companies, **SITA** (Via Santa Caterina da Siena 15r, west of the train station, 483651), and **Lazzi** (Piazza della Stazione 4-6, east of the train station, 215154), serve the Tuscany region.

Train Station (Long-Distance)

Florence's main train station, **Stazione Centrale di Santa Maria Novella** (Piazza della Stazione, 288785), is right in the center of town. When buying a ticket to Florence, make sure the train stops at that station (also called "Firenze S.M.N.") and not the **Campo di Marte** or **Rifredi** stations, which are in inconvenient locations outside of the town center. There's a taxi stand in front of the **Santa Maria Novella** station.

Getting Around Florence

Bicycles and Mopeds

It's easy to see Florence on foot, but cycling to its sights is an attractive alternative. Many locals have adopted this mode of transport, especially now that most of the Centro Storico is closed to traffic (even mopeds). To rent a bicycle or moped contact **Alinari** (Via Guelfa 85r, at Via Nazionale, 280500); **Motorent** (Via San Zanobi 9r, at Via Guelfa, 490113); or **Vesparent** (mopeds only; Via Pisana 103r, between Via Chiesino and Via Monticelli, 715691).

Buses

Florence's orange **ATAF** city buses run frequently and efficiently. Bus routes are published in the yellow pages of the telephone directory. Tickets, which are good for one hour, are available at most newsstands, tobacconists, and bars/cafes, and must be purchased before boarding the bus (get on at the rear door, as the center one is for getting off). Once on the bus, validate the ticket in a little orange machine. A special seven-day *Carta Arancio* permits unlimited travel on all city buses, as well as other buses and trains throughout the province of Florence. This pass can be purchased at the **ATAF** office at 115 Viale dei Mille (near Piazza Cure, 56501). **ATAF** also has an information office at the entrance to the **Santa Maria Novella** train station (5650222). Both offices are open daily.

Driving

Because of the Dantesque rings of traffic zones in Florence, getting around by car is not recommended. An ever-expanding *zona blu* (pedestrian zone) in the Centro Storico is completely closed to private vehicles (except those of residents) Monday through Saturday from 9AM to 6:30PM. This can get tricky if your hotel lies within the restricted area. If traffic police stop you in this section, mention the hotel's name and address, and show a confirmation.

Parking

Street parking is hard to find and towing of illegally parked cars is frequent, costly, and a major hassle. Private and public garages throughout the city often give weekly rates. A new multilevel parking lot beneath the train station has increased the parking possibilities near the center.

Taxis

Cabs are plentiful and drivers pleasant in Florence. They wait at strategic locations around town (usually in or near the principal squares), may be called by dialing 4390, 4798, or 4242, and may occasionally be hailed on the street when their "taxi" sign is illuminated. Ask about additional charges for evening, Sunday, and holiday service, and for luggage.

Tours

Half- and full-day tours of the city and nearby Tuscan towns are arranged through **American Express** (Via Dante Alighieri 22r, at Via Cimatori, 50981; Via Guicciardini 49r, near Piazza de' Pitti, 288751) and **SITA** (Via Santa Caterina da Siena 15r, west of the train station, 483651). Private guides are expensive, but a luxurious way to splurge for history or art buffs; the **Informazione Turistica** booths (see "Visitors' Information," below) have lists of qualified guides. **Laura Kramer** (Via di Piazza Calda 1A, 689530) arranges customized daylong walking or driving tours in Florence or Tuscany.

Walking

Florence's Centro Storico is fairly small and quite self-contained. With the help of a city map, most principal sites of interest are within walking distance. In fact, much of it is a *zona blu.*

FYI

Accommodations

Reserving a hotel ahead of arrival is suggested in Florence, particularly during the busiest times of year (Easter through June; September through October; and the Christmas holidays). Travelers who arrive without reservations should inquire at the **Informazione Turistica** booth (see "Visitors' Information Office," below) for assistance.

A pleasant alternative to conventional hotel accommodations is renting an apartment. **Suzanne Pitcher** (2 Via Pietro Thouar, off Viale della Giovine Italia, 2343354; fax 2347240), an independent real estate agent, rents apartments, farmhouses, and villas by the week or month.

Addresses

Residence addresses are posted in black numerals on the streets and written as simple numbers; business addresses are posted in red numerals and written by a number followed by an "r" for *rosso* (red). To add to the confusion, these two series of numbers usually do not run in parallel order. For example, Via Sant'Andrea 129 (black) may be found adjacent to Via Sant'Andrea 5r (red). At press time, there were plans to make all numerals black.

Climate

Located in a valley on the banks of the Arno River, Florence is hot and humid in summer. The average low temperature in July and August is 65 degrees Fahrenheit and the average high is 87. Late October and November can be rainy, and winters are cold and damp. The average low temperature in January is 35 degrees, the average high is 48. The most ideal weather is in May, June, September, and October.

Months	Average Temperature (°F)
January	45
February	47
March	50
April	60
May	67
June	75
July	77
August	70
September	64
October	63
November	55
December	46

Embassies and Consulates

British Consulate Lungarno Corsini 2 (between Ponte San Trinita and Ponte alla Carraia) 284133

The nearest US and Australian consulates are in Milan. The nearest US and Canadian embassies are in Rome.

Holidays

In addition to the national holidays (see "Northern Italy Orientation"), Florence shuts down on 24 June to celebrate the feast day of San Giovanni, the city's patron saint.

Hours

The lengthy midday break is a fact of life in Italy. In the off-season, stores and businesses are generally open Monday only from 3:30 until 7:30PM; and Tuesday through Saturday they are open from 9AM to 7:30PM, but with a midday break from 1 to 3:30PM. In peak season (June through September), stores and businesses are open Monday through Friday from 9AM until 7:30PM (with a midday break from 1 to 3:30PM), and on Saturday from 9AM until 1PM. Certain tourist-oriented stores in the Centro Storico eschew the midday break in high season, and some are even open on Sunday. Food markets keep roughly the same hours, but are closed on Wednesday afternoons. Most churches are open for viewing Monday through Friday and on Saturday mornings; Sunday visits are discouraged. Most museums are open Tuesday through Saturday and on Sunday mornings. Opening and closing times are listed by day(s) only if normal hours apply; in all other cases, specific hours are given (e.g., 8AM-3:30PM, noon-5PM).

Medical Emergencies

Contact the **Tourist Medical Service** (Via Lorenzo il Magnifico 59, between Piazza della Libertà and Fortezza da Basso, 475411) in the event of a medical emergency. It's open 24 hours a day and has English-speaking operators to handle incoming calls. The **Misericordia** (Piazza del Duomo 19, south side of piazza, 212222) also provides medical assistance, and the **Associazione Volontari Ospedalieri** (403126), a volunteer organization, offers free interpreting services for travelers needing medical care.

In nonemergency situations ask your hotel concierge for help in finding a doctor or dentist.

Money

Banks are open Monday through Friday from about 8:30AM to 1:30PM, and reopen for an hour or so (usually 3:30 to 4:30PM) in the afternoon. **American Express** (Via Dante Alighieri 22r, at Via Cimatori, 50981; Via Guicciardini 49r, near Piazza de' Pitti, 288751) and **Universalturismo** (Via Speziali 7, off Piazza della Repubblica, 217241) are also good places to exchange money. Avoid changing money at the airports and train station; the agencies there charge high commissions.

Personal Safety

It is remarkably safe to walk the streets of Florence at night—to visit the **Duomo** or **Piazza della Signoria,** to window shop on the **Ponte Vecchio,** or just to stroll the city streets, armed only with an ice-cream cone in hand. But take elementary precautions—using common sense will outwit most bag, camera, and wallet snatchers. Never carry more than you can afford to lose—i.e., keep your passport and larger amounts of cash in the hotel safe or well concealed in a money purse—and don't leave any valuables visible in a rented car.

Be alert for pickpockets who operate on the buses in Florence and in crowded tourist sites. Panhandlers harass locals and visitors alike in front of the train station and the outdoor market of **San Lorenzo.**

Pockets of drug dealing have shifted from neighborhood to neighborhood over the years. For quite some time the dealers' hangout of choice was the lovely **Piazza Santo Spirito,** which has since been cleaned up and is now the most popular evening hangout for the city's youth. Its temporary replacement, the charming pedestrian **Via dei Neri,** has also been cleaned up, relocating the illegal drug market to the small piazzetta in front of the well-known **Gelateria Vivoli.** At press time, police surveillance was being used to drive them, yet again, elsewhere.

Pharmacies

The following drugstores are open 24 hours:

Farmacia Comunale Stazione Santa Maria Novella (Piazza della Stazione) 289485

Farmacia Molteni Via Calzaiuoli 7r (between Piazza del Duomo and Orsanmichele).......................215472

Farmacia Taverna Piazza San Giovanni 20r (near Via dei Cerretani) 284013

Postal Service

The main post office, **Poste e Telecommunicazioni,** is at Via Pellicceria 3 (in Piazza della Repubblica). It's open Monday through Friday 8:15AM to 7PM and Saturday 8:15AM to 12:30PM.

Publications

English-language listings of cultural events include the monthly *Florence Concierge Information,* available at the better hotels, and *Florence Today,* available at the tourist information office (see "Visitors' Information Office," below). *Firenze Avvenimenti* and *Un Ospite a Firenze (A Guest in Florence),* two Italian-language publications, are also available at the tourist information office. The local daily newspaper, *La Nazione,* and the national daily, *La Repubblica,* are other good sources of information.

Restaurants

Most restaurants close one or two days a week (the day varies for each establishment), usually a week or so in August (often the entire month), and between Christmas and New Year's Eve. Lunch is served from 12:30 to 2PM. Peak dinner time is 8:30PM; kitchens close around 10:30PM.

Reservations, while not required, are suggested and may be essential at the most expensive or popular restaurants. When calling to make a reservation, inquire about a dress code; although no restaurant is likely to keep you out because of your attire, you may feel uncomfortable
if you are underdressed. Major credit cards are accepted at all of the most expensive restaurants.

Shopping

Florence, Italy's fashion capital in the 1960s, still has some of the most wonderful shopping on the continent. For designer clothing, head for **Via Tornabuoni, Via della Vigna Nuova, Via Calzaiuoli,** or **Via Roma.** Since 1593 the **Ponte Vecchio** has been the destination of choice for gold jewelry (though some former residents have now moved elsewhere in the city). The **Mercato di San Lorenzo** and **Mercato Nuovo** are crowded, colorful, and lively; they are good places to pick up souvenirs, leather and wool goods, and table linens.

Street Plan

Florence is divided by the Arno River. Most of the major tourist sites are on the right bank, or north side, of the river. From west to east the neighborhoods on the right bank are **Santa Maria Novella, San Lorenzo,** Centro Storico, and **Santa Croce.** The left bank, called **Oltrarno** (meaning "beyond the Arno"), is home to the **Palazzo Pitti** and the **Giardino di Boboli** (Boboli Gardens), but is somewhat less touristy.

Telephones

At the **Telecom Cavour** office (Via Cavour 21, San Lorenzo, near Piazza del Duomo; phone: 212910), you can make phone calls using American calling cards, credit cards, or paying afterward in cash. It is open daily from 8AM to 9:45PM.

Visitors' Information Office

Every visitor's first stop should be the **Informazione Turistica** booth in the train station or at Via Cavour 1r, north of Via dei Gori (290832/3). Information is also available from the **Ente Provinciale per il Turismo (EPT,** Via Alessandro Manzoni 16, at Via G.B. Niccolini, 23320; or Chiasso Baroncelli 17/19r, south of Piazza della Signoria, 2302124). All offices are open Monday through Saturday from 8:30AM to 1:30PM.

Phone Book

Emergencies

Ambulance	113
Fire	115
Police Emergency	113
24-hour Medical Service	475411

Visitors' Information

Bus	580528
Taxi	4390, 4798, 4242
Train	288785

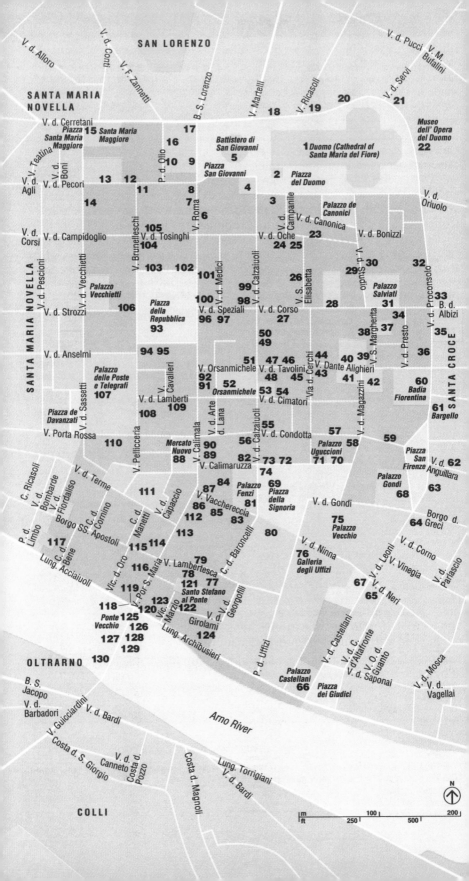

Centro Storico

The old city center of every Italian town is called Centro Storico (literally, historical center), but the term is especially meaningful in Florence. While not the palimpsest that Rome is, Florence offers varying and vivid impressions of all periods from its rich history within its small Centro Storico. To begin with, ancient Roman colonials gave many of the streets their grid pattern. Though only a rare column or capital remains from those days, some streets have taken on the names of the Roman buildings that once stood on them—the baths were on **Via delle Terme,** the capitol was on **Via del Campidoglio.** Still, what is most noticeable in this part of Florence is its medieval aspect. The powerful guilds, predecessors of modern-day unions, were active and influential in governing the city during that period. The enclaves in which their workshops were clustered gave the names to streets you can still find, among them **Via Pellicceria** (furriers), **Via dei Calzaiuoli** (cobblers), **Via dell' Arte della Lana** (woolmakers), and **Via delle Ruote** (wheelmakers). **Palazzo Vecchio,** the **Bargello,** and **Ponte Vecchio,** and what remains of the medieval churches and towers, evoke the era of Florence's first stirrings as a powerful force in international commerce. That wealth made possible construction of the great **Duomo**—ushering in the Renaissance—and financed the building of majestic private palazzi. In the 17th century, a local version of the Baroque took its place in a few churches alongside the great works of the Renaissance.

The next great building boom happened in the 19th century, when Florence became, albeit briefly, the capital of a newly united Italy. Inspired by Haussmann in France, the city fathers strived for a monumental look, knocking down old buildings and replacing them with more grandiose edifices. Finally, the postwar phenomenon of Italian design has brought about some exciting interior spaces in shops right in the center of Florence. And it's all as easy to see as it is enjoyable, now that the Centro Storico is largely a pedestrian zone (though buses, taxis, and vehicles making deliveries or belonging to residents may still enter), just as it was in the centuries before the advent of the automobile.

Campanile

There are still plenty of cars and Vespas zooming around the cathedral, though, giving the Duomo's full-time team of restorers more than enough to keep them busy. But even more intense than the traffic is the concentration of art and architecture, the densest in the Western world. Its effect on visitors is so overwhelming that a Florentine psychiatrist coined the term Stendhal syndrome (named after the Grand Tour–era French traveler and connoisseur) to describe the dizziness she observed in one bewildered tourist after another.

Fortunately, there are a number of antidotes close at hand. Besides the legacy of Leonardo and Michelangelo, a vital part of Florence's heritage is the commercial skill that helped amass the fortunes of the Medici and other merchant families. So even here in the Centro Storico, things that appeal to the purse and palate are interspersed with things that engage the eye and the mind. Past and present, it's all Florence.

1 Duomo (Cathedral of Santa Maria del Fiore) Though construction of this cathedral began in 1296 following the plans of **Arnolfo di Cambio,** continued from 1334 under **Giotto,** and from 1357 under **Francesco Talenti** and **Lapo Ghini, Filippo Brunelleschi**'s dome constructed in 1436 is what most people notice and remember. The octagonal, red-tile cupola soars above Florence's *duomo*, or cathedral (see plan at right), overwhelming the city and dominating the countryside for miles around. According to Renaissance chronicler Giorgio Vasari's *Lives of the Artists,* **Brunelleschi** won the commission to erect a dome on the base of the candy-colored cathedral by challenging his competitors to make an egg stand up on a flat piece of marble. "So an egg was procured and the artists in turn tried to make it stand on end; but they were all unsuccessful," the account goes. "Then Filippo was asked to do so, and taking the egg graciously he cracked its bottom on the marble and made it stay upright. The others complained that they could have done as much, and laughing at them Filippo retorted that they would also have known how to vault the cupola if they had seen his model or plans. And so they resolved that Filippo should be given the task of carrying out the work. . . ." That kind of *egg-o*, and the boldness of Filippo's feat (the first dome in Italy since the Pantheon, which **Brunelleschi** studied) helped usher in the Renaissance. Other greats of the era to have their say about the dome were **Andrea Verrocchio,** who designed the bronze globe and cross for the top of its lantern, and Michelangelo, whose remark that **Baccio d'Agnolo**'s balcony at its base was a "cricket cage" halted construction after only one of its eight sides had been so embellished.

Brunelleschi's cracks and wisecracks were as portentous as they were pretentious. A half-millennium later, the dome is riddled with fissures, some due to age and others because modern restorers filled in holes with concrete, blocking the built-in safeguards for expansion and contraction from temperature changes. No one quite knows what to do about it, but should Humpty Dumpty have a great fall, all the authorities' lasers, plumb lines, and other measuring devices (some 300 of them make it the most closely watched structure in the world) will be there to duly record, if not prevent, the event.

The dome overpowers the confection of Tuscan marble (red from Maremma, white from Carrara, and green from Prato—also the colors of the Italian flag) facing the building beneath it. Its original Gothic facade by **Arnolfo di Cambio,** never completed, was demolished in 1587. The current Neo-Gothic version was put up in the late 19th century, part of the frenzy of construction and destruction when Florence became the capital

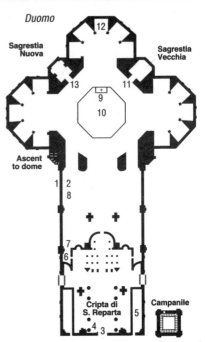

Duomo

of the newly united kingdom of Italy. But the richly ornamented *Porta della Mandorla* **[1]** (numbers refer to the floor plan above) on the north side, with an *Assumption of the Virgin* **[2]** by Nanni di Banco in its pediment, dates from the late-Gothic period. Much of the rest of the decoration—indoor and outdoor—is now in the **Museo dell'Opera del Duomo.**

The cathedral has been taken as a metaphor for the Florentine character—showy on the outside, austere on the inside—for despite the directive that it be *più bello che si può* (as beautiful as can be), the interior remains remarkably spartan. The entrance wall **[3]** has three stained-glass windows made to the designs of **Lorenzo Ghiberti,** better known for (and represented by) the three-dimensionality of his bronze door reliefs on the **Baptistry;** also on the entrance wall is Paolo Uccello's giant clock with the heads of four prophets and the hands going backwards. Just to the left is Tino da Camaino's almost minimalist monument to Bishop Antonio d'Orso **[4].**

In the right aisle, under a bust of **Brunelleschi** by his adopted son, Buggiano, is the architect's tomb slab **[5]**, found just beneath its current location during the excavation of the **Cripta,** or **Crypt of Santa Reparata.** The earlier church, built on Roman foundations in the fourth or fifth century, occupied the western third of the present cathedral's nave. The entrance to the site, which has Roman early Christian relics as well as Gothic tombs and frescoes, is at the first pillar of the right aisle.

Farther ahead, across the nave in the left aisle, are two works of art taken as tributes to

Florentine parsimony, Andrea del Castagno's to Niccolò da Tolentino [6] and Uccello's monument to Sir John Hawkwood [7]. Presumably commissioned as monumental equestrian sculptures, they were instead executed in paint to resemble marble as trompe l'oeil frescoes. Beyond them is a more straightforward, albeit complicated, Florentine subject, Domenico di Michelino's *Dante Explaining the Divine Comedy* [8].

Inside the cupola are newly restored frescoes of *The Last Judgment* [9] by Vasari and Federico Zuccari. Beneath them is a choir by Bandinelli and a crucifix (over the high altar) [10] by Benedetto da Maiano. The entrance to the **Sagrestia Vecchia** (Old Sacristy) [11], to the right of the altar, is topped by a terra-cotta lunette of the *Ascension* by Luca della Robbia. Della Robbia was also responsible for the two terra-cotta angels in the chapel at the extreme end of the nave [12] (the nave also contains a bronze urn by Ghiberti, which holds the relics of St. Zanobius; for the terra-cotta *Resurrection* above the doors to the **Sagrestia Nuova** (New Sacristy) [13] to the left of the altar; and for the bronze doors themselves, a unique example of della Robbia's use of this medium. The doors played a significant role on a dark day in Florentine history—the Pazzi Conspiracy. On Sunday, 26 April 1478, a group of mad assassins led by the Pazzi family (the name means crazies) attempted to seize power from the Medici family by murdering them in the cathedral at the ringing of the bells at the most sacred moment of the mass. Giuliano died after receiving 29 dagger blows; Lorenzo (a.k.a. Il Magnifico, or The Magnificent) fought off his attackers and took shelter behind della Robbia's doors, which slammed shut with a clang that echoed through the enormous space.

Works by Renaissance masters (though admittedly not masterpieces) and *più bello che si può* notwithstanding, the real beauty of the cathedral interior is its expansive space. As a cathedral, it is surpassed only by St. Peter's in Rome, St. Paul's in London, and the **Duomo** in Milan—and it is less cluttered than any of them. If not exactly intimate, at least its empty grandeur is evocative: Above the quiet shuffling of the tourists, it is easy to imagine the Pazzi Conspiracy, or, just a few years later, the fanatic preacher Girolamo Savonarola railing at a packed house for being more worshipful of the ancients than of the saints. Today the crowds gather outdoors in the piazza on Easter Sunday to watch *Lo Scoppio del Carro* (the explosion of the cart), a medieval folk event in which an ornately decorated cart is drawn by white oxen into the piazza. At the Gloria of the mass, a rocket in the shape of a dove is lit inside at the high altar, then, traveling the length of the church along a wire attached to the cart, it sets off a riot of fireworks. The event is meant to recall the days when a flame ignited during the Gloria was then distributed to the townspeople.

The cathedral's enormous size and height provide the perfect opportunity to view some of the world's most famous indoor and outdoor spaces. And now there's even more great art on display here—4,000 square feet of frescoes by Vasari have recently been restored. The 463-step climb to the top along the catwalks and spiral staircases used by the builders provides close-up views of **Brunelleschi**'s dome-within-a-dome structure, and the lantern offers panoramas of Florence's sea of terra-cotta roofs and monuments in *pietra forte* (strong stone), the local golden-brown stone. ♦ Duomo: free. Cupola and Crypt of Santa Riparata: admission. Duomo: daily. Cupola and Crypt: M-Sa. Piazza del Duomo (between Via dell' Oriuolo and Via de' Cerretani)

2 **Campanile** Known locally as "Il Campanile di Giotto," the tower (pictured on page 17) was actually a collaborative effort. **Giotto** designed the first story and **Andrea Pisano** and **Francesco Talenti** finished it, creating visual harmony by using the same three colors of marble that cloak the cathedral. (Musical harmony is provided by the bells, named *Grossa, Beona, Completa, Cheirica,* and *Squilla*—Big, Tipsy, Finished, Priestling, and Shrieker.) The ascent offers views of the city and surroundings, as well as a dumbfounding view of **Brunelleschi**'s dome. ♦ Admission. Daily. Piazza del Duomo (at Via dei Calzaiuoli)

3 **Arciconfraternità della Misericordia** Continuing a Florentine tradition established in 1294 and secured during the 14th-century plague years, this charitable organization of volunteers from all walks of life tends to the sick and needy free of charge, supported entirely by contributions. To preserve their anonymity, members cloak themselves in hooded black robes, a custom adopted during the plague of 1630. The organization is housed inside the **Palazzo della Misericordia** where statues of *St. Sebastian* and the *Madonna* by Benedetto da Maiano, as well as a tabernacle by Andrea della Robbia, can be found. Architect **Alfonso Parigi** began work on the structure in 1575 and was later asssisted by **Stefano Diletti**. ♦ Piazza del Duomo 19 (at Via dei Calzaiuoli)

4 **Loggia di Santa Maria del Bigallo** Originally part of the **Misericordia**, the loggia by **Alberto Arnoldi** dates back to 1352-58. The organization occupying the palazzo now takes care of beggar children and runs a rest home for the aged. Frescoes depicting religious subjects and acts of charity adorn the inside. ♦ Piazza San Giovanni 1 (at Via dei Calzaiuoli)

Battistero di San Giovanni

5 Battistero di San Giovanni (Baptistry of San Giovanni) Dante fondly referred to this church dedicated to Florence's patron saint as "*bel San Giovanni*" (beautiful St. John). Florentines once flattered themselves by believing it to be an ancient Roman temple of Mars dating to the fifth century, but although there are Classical elements in the decoration of the green-and-white marble facade and authentic Roman columns inside (see drawing above), it dates from much later. The **Baptistry** is best known for the gilded bronze doors on three of its eight sides. The original doors, now replaced by copies, are gradually being restored and are displayed in the **Museo dell'Opera del Duomo.** The doors were made in the 14th and 15th centuries, the first such work since the ancients. The south doors (1330), by **Andrea Pisano,** combine the Gothic style with the Neo-Realism of Giotto. The upper 20 panels tell the story of the life of John the Baptist; the lower eight, the cardinal and theological virtues. The north doors (1403-24) are by **Lorenzo Ghiberti,** who beat **Brunelleschi** in a famous competition held for them in 1401 (their entries are on display in the **Bargello**). The upper 20 panels depict scenes from the *New Testament* (the artist also cast his self-portrait, the hooded head on the left door); the lower eight panels represent the four evangelists and the four doctors of the church. Artistically the most important, the east doors (1424-52), also by **Ghiberti,** were called "The Gates of Paradise" by the usually cryptic Michelangelo. The 10 panels illustrate scenes from the *Old Testament* and are surrounded by playful animal motifs and portrait heads (another one of the artist is on the left door, the fourth from the top on the right side, next to a portrait of his son Vittorio).

The vault inside contains mosaics made to the designs of Cimabue and other artists. A marble pavement of the zodiac surrounds the baptismal font, and the hands of Donatello and Michelozzo may be seen in the tomb of Cardinal Baldassare Coscia. ◆ Admission. M-Sa afternoon; Su 9AM-1PM. Piazza San Giovanni (between Via de' Pecori and Via de' Cerretani)

6 Eredi Chiarini Men may want to do their one-stop shopping at these two adjacent locations, where the taste in suits, jackets, shirts, trousers, sweaters, and accessories winningly combines Anglo-American conservatism with Italian stylishness. ◆ M-F, Sa morning Mar-Oct; M afternoon, Tu-Sa Nov-Feb. Via Roma 16r and 18-22r (between Via de Tosinghi and Piazza del Duomo). 284478

7 Luisa Via Roma Florence's most international boutique by far, this is the one place in town you're guaranteed to find Kenzo and Comme des Garçons alongside such Italian sartorial maestros as Dolce & Gabbana or Moschino for both sexes. ◆ M-F, Sa morning Mar-Oct; M afternoon, Tu-Sa Nov-Feb. Via Roma 19-21r (between Via de Tosinghi and Piazza del Duomo). 217826

8 Raspini The biggest names in Italian and international clothing and shoe design for the whole well-heeled family are here, next to the store's own prestigious label of Florentine leather goods. There are three shops in town, but none outside of Florence, so if a well-designed and well-crafted style works with yours, this is the best place to take out your wallet. ◆ M-F, Sa morning Mar-Oct; M afternoon, Tu-Sa Nov-Feb. Via Roma 25r (off Piazza del Duomo). 213077. Also at: Via Martelli 1-5r (at Piazza del Duomo). 2398336; Via Por Santa Maria 72r (at Via Vaccereccia). 215796

9 Palazzo Arcivescovile (Archbishop's Palace) The facade of this palace, built from 1573-84 by **Giovanni Antonio Dosio,** was sliced off to enlarge the piazza in 1895. Its interior courtyard leads to the tiny church of **San Salvatore al Vescovo,** built on the site of a Romanesque church and completely frescoed like a pastry from **Scudieri** (see page 21). For a lower-calorie treat, go around the corner to see the Romanesque facade of the original church, which is part of the palazzo wall facing **Piazza dell'Olio.** ◆ Piazza del Duomo 3 (between Via de' Pecori and Via de' Cerretani)

10 San Salvatore al Vescovo The facade is all that's left of a 13th-century Romanesque church (the rest was remodeled and incorporated into the surrounding **Palazzo Arcivescovile**). Its green-and-white marble matches that of the **Baptistry** and **San Miniato al Monte.** ♦ Piazza dell'Olio (between Via de' Pecori and Via de' Cerretani)

11 MaxMara This fashion house appeals to discerning women, who appreciate its stylish and well-made line of suits, sweaters, separates, shoes, and accessories. ♦ M-F, Sa morning Mar-Oct; M afternoon, Tu-Sa Nov-Feb. Via de' Pecori 23 (at Via Brunelleschi). 287761. Also at: Via dei Tornabuoni 89r (near Via Strozzi). 214133

12 Casa dei Tessuti You'll find bolts and bolts of beautiful wools, silk, and linens here by Italian designers from A (Armani) to Z (Zegna), as well as other European names, who more than likely had their goods produced in Italy anyway. ♦ M-F, Sa morning Mar-Oct; M afternoon, Tu-Sa Nov-Feb. Via de' Pecori 20-24r (at Via Brunelleschi). 215961

13 Palazzo Orlandini del Beccuto This massive palazzo, redesigned in 1679 by **Antonio Maria Ferri** and owned by a succession of noble Florentine families, has housed the local branch of the **Monte dei Paschi di Siena,** the world's oldest bank, since the beginning of this century. The bank has restored the palazzo to something of its original splendor, visible indoors in the terracotta floor, white stucco walls, and *pietra serena* details, including the only 15th-century wall fountain in Florence. ♦ M-F. Via de' Pecori 6-8 (at Via dei Vecchietti)

"OLD ENGLAND STORES"

14 Old England Stores Florentines, already mad for local knockoffs of English style, go gaga for the real thing at this shop, stocked with such exotic items as port, sherry, biscuits, and a full line of American breakfast cereals, as well as a fine selection of British woolens in the back. Expatriate Anglophones may be seen here during the holidays stocking up on plum pudding and cranberry sauce. ♦ M-F, Sa morning Mar-Oct; M afternoon, Tu-Sa Nov-Feb. Via de' Vecchietti 28r (between Via de Campidoglio and Via de' Pecori). 211983

15 Santa Maria Maggiore One of the oldest churches in Florence (built in the 11th century and reconstructed in the 13th), this one has a plain stone facade like many in the city. High up on its old Romanesque bell tower on the Via de' Cerretani side is a late-Roman bust of a woman. The interior, redesigned by **Bernardo Buontalenti,** contains a number of artworks, most notably a 13th-century painted wood sculpture of the *Madonna and Child* attributed to Coppo di Marcovaldo. ♦ Vicolo di Santa Maria Maggiore 1 (off Via de' Cerretani)

16 Fiaschetteria Torrini This kind of hole-in-the-wall wine shop is an ancient Florentine tradition (historian Giovanni Villani says that there were 86 such places in the city in the 14th century) and an ideal place for a quick pick-me-up of a glass of Chianti with *crostini* (chicken liver pâté on bread rounds) and other snacks. ♦ M-Sa 7AM-10PM. No credit cards accepted. Piazza dell'Olio 15r (between Via de' Pecori and Via de' Cerretani). 2396616

17 Scudieri Sample homemade pastry, including perhaps the best plum cake in Florence. Florentines have come here for centuries for the *schiacciata alla fiorentina* (a flat sweet cake dusted with confectioners' sugar). Stop by for tea indoors or sit at one of the outdoor tables and gaze at the **Baptistry** and the endless crowds encircling it. ♦ M-Tu, Th-Su 7:30AM-9PM. Piazza San Giovanni 21r (at Via de' Cerretani). 210733

18 Lo Sport This is the place to pick up that last-minute tennis outfit or clothes for the slopes, Italian-style. This shop also has the widest possible selection of sporting goods and an ever-popular inventory of Italian-made imitations of English and Austrian woolens (we prefer the soft Italian loden coats to the real thing). ♦ M-F; Sa morning Mar-Oct. M afternoon; Tu-Sa Nov-Feb. Piazza del Duomo 7-8r (at Via Martelli). 284412. Also at: Lo Sport Due, Piazza dell'Olio 5-7r (off Via de' Pecori). 292163

19 Torrini This expensive Florentine jeweler carries international brands such as Rolex, as well as their own ultimate souvenir—a reproduction of the florin (the deutsche mark or yen of the Middle Ages), with the lily symbol of Florence on one side and the city's patron saint, John the Baptist, on the other. ♦ M-F; Sa morning Mar-Oct. M afternoon; Tu-Sa Nov-Feb. Piazza del Duomo 10r (near Via Ricasoli). 2302401

20 Fratelli Favilli Florence's finest engravers, the Favilli also specialize in signet rings. They offer etched gold jewelry in their own patterns and will craft practically any design you bring them. ♦ M-F, Sa morning Mar-Oct; M afternoon, Tu-Sa Nov-Feb. Piazza del Duomo 13r (between Via dei Servi and Via Ricasoli). 211846

Restaurants/Clubs: Red   **Hotels:** Blue
Shops/ ♦ **Outdoors:** Green   **Sights/Culture:** Black

21 Il Papiro The so-called Florentine or marbleized-paper revival began right here with simple sheets of wrapping paper, pencils, and boxes. It now extends to desk sets, picture frames, even Venetian masks—a parti-colored paper chase. ♦ M-F, Sa morning Mar-Oct; M afternoon, Tu-Sa Nov-Feb. Piazza del Duomo 24r (near Via dei Servi). 215262. Also at: Via Cavour 55r (near Via Guelfa). 215262; Lungarno Acciaiuoli 42r (west of Ponte Vecchio). 215262.

IL PAPIRO

22 Museo dell'Opera del Duomo The town fathers perhaps anticipated the destructive effects of fume-belching traffic buzzing around the **Duomo** when they began relegating works from the **Cathedral, Campanile,** and **Baptistry** to the administrative headquarters of this museum, open to the public since 1891. A grandiose coat of arms of Cosimo I de' Medici, almost opportunistically trying to fill in the void left by the removed sacred decoration, marks the entrance. The courtyard has two Roman sarcophagi from the **Baptistry,** which no doubt fueled the conceit that the building was an ancient Roman temple. The vestibule contains a marble bust of **Duomo** architect **Filippo Brunelleschi** (attributed to Buggiano). The main sculpture room, the **Sala dell'Antica Facciata del Duomo** (Room of the Old Facade of the Duomo) has a drawing of **Arnolfo di Cambio**'s original facade of the **Duomo,** as well as many sculptures from it by him, Nanni di Banco, Donatello, and others. Two rooms on the ground floor display **Brunelleschi** memorabilia, including his death mask and model for the dome. On the mezzanine is Michelangelo's *Pietà,* a late work designed for his own tomb (Vasari says that the face of Nicodemus is a self-portrait); this work was later smashed by the master and then restored by his pupil Tiberio Calcagni, who completed the figure of Mary Magdalene. Upstairs are two joyous *cantorie* (choir lofts), one by Luca della Robbia and the other by Donatello, whose horrifying *Mary Magdalene*—again, a late work—repents below. The next room contains statues from the **Campanile,** ending with Donatello's *Habakkuk,* known locally as "Lo Zuccone," which translates roughly as Pumpkin Head. The **Sala delle Formelle** (Room of the Panels) houses relief panels from the **Campanile** illustrating spiritual progress. Four of the bronze panels from **Ghiberti**'s famous **Baptistry** east doors ("the Gates of Paradise") are on display here; six are still being restored. The **Baptistry** now displays copies of these masterworks. Finally, the **Sala dell'Altare** (Room of the Altar) displays a silver altar for the **Baptistry** (made by members of the goldsmiths' guild such as Verrocchio and Antonio Pollaiuolo) and needlework panels for a tapestry made by craftsmen of the cloth importers' guild to the designs of artists such as Pollaiuolo, Andrea Pisano, and Jacopo della Quercia. ♦ Admission. Daily 9AM-7:30PM Mar-Oct; M-Sa 9AM-6PM Nov-Feb. Piazza del Duomo 9 (between Via dell' Oriuolo and Via dei Servi). 2302885

23 Torre degli Adimali During the Middle Ages, Florence was filled with towers like this 13th-century example and even higher ones, as can be seen in the Tuscan town of San Gimignano even today. In 1250, however, the Commune passed what amounted to a zoning law requiring that the height of no tower surpass 100 feet and that those exceeding that height be truncated. ♦ Via delle Oche (at Via Santa Elisabetta)

Within the Torre degli Adimali:

Ottorino ★★$$ Situated in an expansive space within the tower, this popular restaurant has an equally expansive menu of Tuscan specialties like *stracotto al Chianti* (beef cooked in Chianti wine), vegetarian dishes (*melanzane alla parmigiana,* the Italian eggplant-and-mozzarella classic), and such original dishes as *portafoglio Ottorino,* a delicious slice of veal stuffed with parmesan cheese and truffles. ♦ M-Sa lunch and dinner. Via delle Oche 12-16r (at Via Santa Elisabetta). 215151

24 Store The American concept of close-out discounts is a relatively new approach to designer-label shopping in this country, but one that has caught on quickly. Here, in a tastefully turned-out stock house, is an unpredictable selection from some of Italy's high priests and priestesses of the fashion world (items by Moschino and Byblos might appear) for both men and women. Bargain-basement prices they're not, but the savings can be substantial. ♦ M-F, Sa morning Mar-Oct; M afternoon, Tu-Sa Nov-Feb. Via delle Oche 9-11r (off Via dei Calzaiuoli). 288335

25 Alessi This Orsanmichele of gastronomy offers something different on each of its two levels. The store's ground floor caters to the sweet tooth, selling such seasonal goodies as the dove-shaped Easter cake called *colomba* and the Christmas confections *pandoro* and *panettone,* along with syrups and liqueurs. Downstairs is the best commercial wine cellar in town, displaying vintages by region, with a decided emphasis on Tuscany. Pick up a bottle of your favorite Brunello here. ♦ M-F, Sa morning Mar-Oct; M afternoon, Tu-Sa Nov-Feb. Via delle Oche 27r (at Via Santa Elisabetta). 214966

★ ★ ★

26 Hotel Brunelleschi $$$ Partially housed in a medieval church and a semicircular Byzantine tower, which was once used as a women's prison, this hotel combines the best of early Christian architecture with the upscale ambience of postmodern style in its own secret little piazza. The 94 rooms are tastefully decorated, some incorporating architectural details from the ancient tower, a few with views of the **Duomo.** The restaurant is open daily for breakfast, lunch, and dinner. ♦ Piazza Santa Elisabetta 3 (between Via del Corso and Via delle Oche). 562068; fax 219653

27 Albergo Firenze $ This is one of the most popular of the small, cheap hotels in the Centro Storico. Half of its 60 rooms have private baths, many of them recently renovated. The hotel has lately taken to renting rooms on a long-term basis to American students, so book well in advance. There's no restaurant. No credit cards accepted. ♦ Piazza Donati 4 (on Via del Corso between Via dei Cerchi and Via dei Calzaiuoli) 214203; fax 2312370

28 Santa Margherita in Santa Maria de' Ricci The facade by **Gherardo Silvani** dates from 1611, but the interior of this elaborately porticoed little church was redone in Baroque style in 1769 by **Zanobi del Rosso.** The *Madonna de' Ricci* on the altar is a venerated image. It is an evocative setting for frequent organ concerts. ♦ Via del Corso 10 (between Via dello Studio and Via Santa Elisabetta)

29 Zecchi You'll find the city's best selection of artists' materials here, from paints and brushes to a rainbow of pigments—carmine red made from insects, amber varnish made from fossilized amber, malachite green made exclusively by Zecchi from the mineral, and lapis lazuli imported from Afghanistan. ♦ M-F, Sa morning Mar-Oct; M afternoon, Tu-Sa Nov-Feb. Via dello Studio 19r (between Via del Corso and Via delle Oche). 211470

30 Pegna This Uffizi of food shops has window after window and rack upon rack of Italian delicacies, from olive oil to sun-dried tomatoes to porcini mushrooms, laid out in well-organized, spacious, mouth-watering displays. ♦ M-Tu, Th-Sa; W morning. Via dello Studio 8r (between Via del Corso and Via delle Oche). 282701

31 Palazzo Salviati This imposing 16th-century palazzo was built on the site of the houses of the Portinari family, whose daughter Beatrice captured Dante's heart. Today it houses the **Banca Toscana,** and inside are a 14th-century fresco of the *Madonna and Child with Saints* and 16th-century frescoes by Alessandro Allori, including a lively cycle taken from *The Odyssey.* ♦ M-F. Via del Corso 6 (between Via del Proconsolo and Via dello Studio)

32 Le Mossacce ★★$$ The rustic Tuscan cuisine here is served up family style on communal tables covered with paper tablecloths. Among the menu items worth sampling are such relative rarities in Florence as good lasagna and *spezzatino* (veal in tomato sauce). ♦ M-F lunch and dinner. Via del Proconsolo 55r (between Via del Corso and Piazza del Duomo). 294361

33 Palazzo Nonfinito (Unfinished Palace) Begun for Alessandro Strozzi in 1593 by **Bernardo Buontalenti,** the palace was never completed to its original scheme. **Buontalenti** was responsible for the ground floor, **Giovanni Battista Caccini** completed the next two floors to the designs of **Vincenzo Scamozzi,** and **Ludovico Cardi da Cigoli** designed the courtyard. Part of the palazzo houses Italy's first anthropological museum **(Museo Nazionale di Antropologia ed Etnologia),** established in 1869 while Florence was still the capital. These days it might as well be called the "unopened museum," since access to its magnificently musty collection of shrunken heads and the like is more erratic than at any other of Florence's cultural institutions. ♦ Admission. Th-Sa, third Su of month 9AM-1PM. Via del Proconsolo 12 (at Borgo degli Albizi). 2396449

The area that includes the Duomo and its Baptistry, today considered the very heart of Florence, stood outside the circuit of city walls until the eighth century. At that time new walls were built to include this grand architecture within the newly fortified town.

34 Cucciolo *Bomboloni*—freshly deep-fried pastries *con crema* (stuffed with custard) or *con mermellata* (filled with jam) and dusted with sugar—are the specialty of this unassuming pasticceria, which in turn is always stuffed with appreciative Florentines. ♦ M-Sa 8AM-9PM. Via del Corso 25r (betweeen Via del Presto and Via Santa Margherita). 287727

35 Palazzo Pazzi-Quaratesi This rustic 15th-century palazzo was designed by **Giuliano da Maiano** for Jacopo de' Pazzi, who lived here but died up the street at the **Bargello,** where he was hung in 1478 for his instigative role in the Pazzi Conspiracy. Step inside for a look at the arcaded courtyard. ♦ Via del Proconsolo 10 (at Borgo degli Albizi)

36 Grand Hotel Cavour $$$ This splendid, tastefully modern hotel is housed in the renovated 14th-century **Palazzo Strozzi-Ridolfi.** Located smack in the center of town (its small roof garden has a breathtaking 360° view of the Centro Storico), the 90-room hotel preserves an air of quiet—thanks to the double-paned windows—despite the fact that it is located on a busy street. The theatrical **Ristorante Beatrice** next door (2398123) offers drama in both its menu and setting. ♦ Via del Proconsolo 3 (between Via Dante Alighieri and Via del Corso). 282461; fax 218955

37 San Martino del Vescovo In 1285 Dante supposedly married Gemma Donati in the original church, built in 989 and rebuilt 1479, which apparently faced in the opposite direction. Inside is lots of "school of" art—school of Ghirlandaio frescoes, school of Desiderio da Settignano terra-cotta candelabra, school of Perugino *Madonna and Child.* This is one of several places Dante is said to have first spied his beloved Beatrice; both she and his wife Gemma are buried in the church. ♦ Piazza San Martino (on Via Santa Margherita)

38 Taddei Many leather-goods shops in Florence somehow feel obliged to sell gaudy reproductions of medieval and Renaissance designs, or to dispense with the so-called "Made in Italy" label altogether. Not so at this third-generation, family-run business, where the taste in beautifully hand-crafted leather boxes and desk accessories is at as high a level as the craftsmanship. ♦ M-F, Sa morning Mar-Oct; M afternoon, Tu-Sa Nov-Feb. Via Santa Margherita 11 (between Via Dante Alighieri and Via del Corso). 2398960

When the Black Death hit Florence in 1348, the population was swiftly cut in half. In order to increase the local work force, slavery was legalized in 1363, and Tartars, Russians, Moors, and Ethiopians were purchased in the nearby ports of Venice and Genoa.

39 Casa e Museo di Dante (Dante House and Museum) Reopened in 1994, this shrine to Dante Alighieri, whose family owned the group of houses (heavily restored) in which this museum of memorabilia has been installed, is typically Florentine in its parsimony. The lean collection—a few portraits, reproductions of Botticelli's illustrations for *The Divine Comedy,* photos of places associated with Dante, editions of his work—makes one wonder whether the Florentines ever forgave the poet for reviling them. According to tradition, he was born here in 1295. ♦ Admission. M, W-Su. Via Santa Margherita 1 (between Via Dante Alighieri and Via del Corso). 283962

40 Pennello ★★$$ Besides the usual Tuscan specialties, here is an *abbon-dante* (pun intended—the place is also known as "Casa di Dante") antipasti table groaning with olives, salami, prosciutto, and other delectables that offer a complete meal in themselves. The decor is typical of Florentine trattorie—plain walls decorated only with wine bottles. ♦ Tu-Sa lunch and dinner; Su lunch. No credit cards accepted. Via Dante Alighieri 4r (between Via Santa Margherita and Via dei Cerchi). 294848

41 Pretura Take a peek into the 13th-century courtyard here, the former convent of the **Badia Fiorentina** (Florentine Abbey) and now the magistrate's court, for a look at the original facade of the **Badia Fiorentina** by **Arnolfo di Cambio.** ♦ Piazza San Martino 2 (on Via Dante Alighieri)

42 Torre della Castagna This *pietra forte* medieval tower dating to 1282, once the home of the supreme magistrate of the *Priori delle Arti* guild, now houses the *Associazione Nazionale Veterani e Reduci Garibaldini,* veterans of the Garibaldi campaigns, whose numbers must certainly be dwindling.
♦ Piazza San Martino 1 (on Via Dante Alighieri)

43 Da Ganino ★★$$ This was one of the first of the younger-generation places in Florence to bring back the tradition of *cucina genuina,* in the sense of unpretentious (an understated sign says simply *Vini e Olii*—  okay, so it's just a little pretentious). It offers a seasonal menu along with such year-round items as *risottino verde* (rice infused with spinach) and *strozzapreti strascicati* (literally, choked priests; a fusilli-like pasta in ragout sauce), served in a simple setting of just seven communal paper-covered tables. A few more spill out into the tiny piazza during the warmer months. ♦ M-Sa lunch and dinner. No credit cards accepted. Piazza dei Cimatori 4r (at Via dei Cerchi). 214125

44 Tripperia "*A Firenze c'è una trippaia,*" went a popular love song to a fetching *venditrice* of tripe, a Florentine specialty and a favorite street eat. The delicacy (cow's stomach), stewed in an herb broth, is sold along with *lampredotto,* the fattiest part of the poor beast's intestine, at this spotless stainless-steel outdoor stand. Both are eaten served on waxed paper or in sandwich form, accompanied by the traditional garnish of salt and pepper, ground red pepper, or *salsa verde* (a green sauce of parsley). Blue- and white-collar types alike stop by for a snack of either innard; you may just want to look. ◆ M-Sa. No credit cards accepted. In front of Via Dante Alighieri 16 (at Via dei Cerchi). No phone

45 I Maschereri The long-dormant Venetian art of mask-making has its Florentine counterpart in this shop, which the owners claim opened in Florence even before Carnevale was revived in Venice. The masks go well beyond the traditional commedia dell'arte characters and include imaginative designs based on Florentine Renaissance patterns, as well as the kitsch icon of Michelangelo's *David* and rather psychedelic variations on sun and moon themes. ◆ M-F, Sa morning Mar-Oct; M afternoon, Tu-Sa Nov-Feb. Via dei Tavolini 13r (between Via dei Cerchi and Via dei Calzaiuoli). 213823

46 Paoli ★★$$ Vaulted ceilings frescoed in Neo-Gothic abandon set the amusingly kitsch scene for "atmospheric" dining in the former storerooms of a 15th-century palazzo. It's a bit a matter of style over substance, though the food is substantial enough, and best appreciated if one happens to be in a Gothic kind of mood, say, having just come from the highly Gothic **Orsanmichele**. The basically Tuscan menu offers such dishes as *pollastrino alla griglia* (grilled chicken), supplemented by Italian staples like *scaloppine alla boscaiola* (veal scaloppine in a spicy tomato sauce) and its very own *taglierini alla Paoli* (pasta with prosciutto, peas, and mushrooms in a cream sauce). ◆ M, W-Su lunch and dinner. Via dei Tavolini 12r (between Via dei Cerchi and Via dei Calzaiuoli). 216215

The period we now know as the Renaissance was first called a *rinascità* (rebirth) by Vasari in 1550. People living at that time certainly were aware that something new was happening, but the word had no wide currency until used by Swiss historian Jacob Burchardt in his classic *The Civilization of the Renaisance in Italy* (1860).

47 Cantinetta dei Verrazzano ★★$$ This ambitious and immediately successful eating establishment is operated by the Cappellini family, whose 50 hectares of Chianti farmland provide this handsome wood-and-marble decorated wine-bar–cum–bread-store with its simple and rustic fare. A wood oven constantly churns out heavenly focaccia (used to make a variety of sandwiches), which, when enjoyed with a glass of wine from their extensive selection at one of the small tables here, will recharge your batteries in a most uplifting Tuscan manner. A small store selling their food items has recently opened next door. ◆ M-Sa 8AM-8PM. Via dei Tavolini 18-20r (between Via dei Cerchi and Via dei Calzaiuoli). 268590

48 Perchè No! . . . And why not, indeed, have a morning or midnight ice cream in one of Florence's oldest *gelaterie?* Myriad flavors of creamy gelati and the mousselike *semifreddi* include zuppa inglese (trifle) and *riso* (rice). There are a few stools, but the ritual is to bring it with you for a stroll through **Piazza della Signoria**. ◆ Daily 11AM-midnight. No credit cards accepted. Via dei Tavolini 19r (off Via dei Calzaiuoli). 2398969

49 Hotel Calzaiuoli $$ Location is the byword of this small, handsomely furnished 45-room hotel (a dignified 19th-century palazzo) in the very heart of the Centro Storico. There is a breakfast room, and each guest room has a mini-bar. ◆ Via dei Calzaiuoli 6 (between Via dei Tavolini and Via del Corso). 212456; fax 268310

50 Coin The Florence branch of Italy's largest department store provides a change of pace from the local mercantile tradition of specialty shops. While not on a par with Macy's or Harrod's, it's a cut above other large local emporiums, offering a wide selection of its own label of medium-priced quality clothing as well as accessories, cosmetics, and household items. ◆ M-F, Sa morning Mar-Oct (no midday closing); M afternoon, Tu-Sa Nov-Feb. Via dei Calzaiuoli 56r (between Via dei Tavolini and Via del Corso). 280531

51 Beltrami This shop and its namesake across the street (at Via dei Calzaiuoli 44r, 212418) are the two original gleaming links in the Italian chain featuring high-fashion shoes and leather goods for men and women (the clothing is not as interesting). Its Florentine origin sets the tone for excellent quality of leather and craftsmanship, as well as some surprisingly imaginative designs. ♦ M-F, Sa morning Mar-Oct; M afternoon, Tu-Sa Nov-Feb. Via dei Calzaiuoli 31r and 44r (near Via Orsanmichele). 214030. Also at: Via dei Tornabuoni 48r (between Via Porta Rossa and Via Anselmi). 216321

52 Orsanmichele Talk about mixed-use architecture. This odd Gothic box, built on the site of the eighth-century garden and oratory of Orto di San Michele (the origin of its name), had an even odder function when it was built in 1337 by **Neri di Fioravante, Benci di Cione,** and **Francesco Talenti** (all of whom also worked on the **Duomo**). The ground floor, which had become a covered market, was converted into an oratory; the upstairs housed a communal granary. The ruling Guelph party assigned the decoration of the exterior, begun in the next century, to various guilds.

The edifice combines the essence of much of Florence in this guilded cage: the practicality of using a house of worship to store grain, the glorification of mercantilism in the guilds' sponsorship of the decoration, and the early-Renaissance genius of the decoration itself. (Not to mention the city's trick of moving its sculptures around in a gargantuan sleight-of-hand game. Many of the originals are now indoors in museums, with copies in the niches here.) Counterclockwise from the far end of Via dei Calzaiuoli, the sculpture in the 14 niches is as follows: Via dei Calzaiuoli side: Ghiberti's *St. John the Baptist* for the *Calimala* (cloth importers); Verrocchio's *Doubting Thomas,* with medallion by Luca della Robbia above, for the *Mercantazia* (merchants' tribunal); Giambologna's *St. Luke* for the *Guidici e Notai* (judges and notaries). Via Orsanmichele side: Ciuffagni's *St. Peter* for the *Beccai* (butchers); Nanni di Banco's *St. Philip* for the *Conciapelli* (tanners); Nanni di Banco's *Four Crowned Saints,* with medallion by Luca della Robbia above, for the *Maestri di Pietre e Legname* (masons and carpenters); a bronze copy of Donatello's *St. George* (marble original in the **Bargello**) sculpture and relief for the *Corazzai* (armorers). Via dell'Arte della Lana side: Ghiberti's *St. Matthew* for the *Cambio* (bankers); Ghiberti's *St. Stephen* (it replaced the statue by Andrea Pisano now in the **Duomo Museum**) for the *Lana* (wool guild); Nanni di Banco's *St. Eligius* for the *Maniscalchi* (smiths). Via dei Lamberti side: Donatello's *St. Mark* for the *Linaiuoli e Rigattieri* (linen drapers); Niccolò di Piero Lamberti's *St. James the Great* for the *Pellicciai* (furriers); Piero Tedesco's or Niccolò di Piero Lamberti's *Madonna della Rosa,* with medallion by Luca della Robbia above, for the *Medici e Speziali* (doctors and druggists); Baccio da Montelupo's *St. John the Evangelist* (it replaced a 14th-century statue now in the **Innocenti Gallery**), with medallion by Andrea della Robbia above, for

the *Setaiuoli e Orafi* (silk merchants and goldsmiths).

The interior, still used as a church, has stained-glass windows based on designs by Lorenzo Monaco and an elaborate 14th-century tabernacle by **Andrea Orcagna,** surrounding a *Madonna* completed by Bernardo Daddi in 1348. For access to the granary, go to the 14th-century **Palagio dell'Arte della Lana** (the exquisite palazzo that once housed the Wool Guild) next door. A connecting bridge, often closed, leads you back to the rooms known as the **Saloni di Orsanmichele,** which offer marvelous views of the heart of Florence. ♦ Daily. Entrances on Via dei Calzaiuoli or Via dell'Arte della Lana (between Via dei Lamberti and Via Orsanmichele)

53 San Carlo dei Lombardi This simple 14th-century church, its facade cut into golden *pietra forte* like a giant Romanesque cookie, is an oasis of serenity amid the bustle of the pedestrian traffic outside. Inside, its *Deposition* by Niccolò di Pietro Gerini was borrowed from **Orsanmichele** across the street. ♦ Via dei Calzaiuoli (opposite Orsanmichele at Via dei Cimatori)

54 Vini del Chianti Another of Florence's typical watering holes—and among its nicest—this place is run by two brothers whose Chianti is accompanied by a wide selection of sandwiches. Souvenir Chianti flasks, wrapped in rice straw as in days of old, are also on sale in many sizes. ♦ M-Sa 8AM-8PM. No credit cards accepted. Via dei Cimatori 38r (between Via dei Cerchi and Via dei Calzaiuoli). 2396096

55 Caffè Italiano ★★$ With the dust settling from the success of his restaurant **Alle Murate,** young Umberto Montano recently opened this immediately popular bar/cafe. The handsome turn-of-the-century decor is an alluring ambience for a Manhattan, a snack, or some of the best coffee in town. Upstairs, an inexpensive buffet lunch comes straight from the acclaimed kitchen of **Alle Murate** (be sure to try one of the delicious soups), while must-sample desserts are made on the premises. One of the nicest spots in town to sit for a moment or an hour. ♦ Bar: M-Sa 8AM-1AM. Upstairs: M-Sa lunch and dinner. No credit cards accepted. Via della Condotta 56r (at Via dei Calzaiuoli). 291082

56 Farmacia Molteni The neon sign in the window of this ancient building says "Sempre Aperta," meaning if one needs a quick fix of pharmaceuticals at any time of the day or night, this is the place to come. And a lovely one it is, with 19th-century ceiling frescoes and gilding intact. The *dottoressa* behind the counter says Dante studied here when the place was part of the university. ♦ Daily 24 hours. Via dei Calzaiuoli 7r (at Via Porta Rossa). 289490, 215472

57 Alessandro Bizzarri The old jars in the shop window (not to mention its name) are an intriguing invitation to Florence's only spice and mineral shop, a musty, family-run business that has been selling a medieval mix of spices, gums, extracts, and essences since 1842. ♦ M-F, Sa morning Mar-Oct; M afternoon, Tu-Sa Nov-Feb. Via della Condotta 32r (between Via dei Magazzini and Via dei Cerchi). 211580

57 Wanda Nencioni This shop's seemingly endless selection of antique prints of Florentine scenes are sold singly or in sets. In addition to Italian prints there are also English, French, and German prints, all from the 1500s to the early 1900s. Some of the simplest botanical or rural scenes become attention-getting art when expertly mounted in made-to-measure artisanal reproductions of classic frames which, unfortunately, the store cannot ship. ♦ M afternoon; Tu-Sa. Via Della Condotta 36r (between Via dei Magazzini and Via dei Cerchi). 215345

Libreria Condotta 29

58 Libreria Condotta 29 In addition to the usual tourist fare, this recently expanded shop carries an intelligent selection of art books, as well as tasteful prints, posters, and postcards and a number of books in English, including art books and the classics. ♦ M-F (no midday closing); Sa. Via della Condotta 29r (between Via dei Magazzini and Via dei Cerchi). 213421

59 Cravatte & Dintorni The diversity of this small shop's stylish tie selection—the perfect gift that weighs little and won't break—will keep you in knots. This accessories heaven is stocked with quality names such as Moschino, Byblos, and Dolce & Gabbana. In addition to ties, there are scarves, belts, vests, and umbrellas. Or check out their second shop, **Mr. Aramis,** a few blocks away at Via dei Leoni 22r (near Via dei Neri), 2396978. ♦ M-F, Sa morning Mar-Oct; M afternoon, Tu-Sa Nov-Feb. Via della Condotta 22r (off Piazza San Firenze). 282881

60 Badia Fiorentina (Florentine Abbey) Whether or not Dante first saw Beatrice in this Benedictine church (built in the 10th century; remodeled in the 13th), it was here in the Pandolfini Chapel, then the site of the church of **Santo Stefano,** that Boccaccio delivered his lectures on the great poet. The abbey was rebuilt in the 17th century by **Matteo Segaloni,** who frescoed its ceiling. Also inside are Filippino Lippi's *St. Bernard's Vision of the Madonna* and works by Mino da Fiesole, including his monument to Count Ugo. ♦ Temporarily closed for restoration. Via del Proconsolo and Via Dante Alighieri

61 Bargello This fearful 14th-century palace (see illustration below) was originally Florence's first Town Hall, then it became the residence of the city's chief magistrate, or *Podestà,* later the residence of its police chief, or the *Bargello.* It was also the site of public hangings, and to make sure the people learned their lesson, artists frescoed gruesome scenes of the executions on the outside walls. Sometimes artists were even given public commissions, as when Andrea del Sarto was granted the task of depicting the hanging of the Pazzi conspirators (see page 19) here (Botticelli got to decorate the **Palazzo Vecchio** with the same subject). Leonardo da Vinci made a famous drawing (now in Bayonne, France) of one of the conspirators hanging from the window, whose fashion statement was carefully noted: tawny cap; black satin vest; black, lined sleeveless coat; turquoise blue jacket lined with fox; collar appliquéd with black and red velvet; black hose.

Bargello

Today the museum houses the most important collection of Renaissance sculpture in the world. Have a look at the arcaded courtyard before going into the ground-floor gallery. The gallery contains Michelangelo's *Pitti Tondo*, *Brutus*, and *Drunken Bacchus*, as well as Jacopo Sansovino's *Bacchus* made in response. The colorful Mannerist sculptor-goldsmith Benevenuto Cellini (whose *Autobiography* is a delightful definition of the pseudo-Italian word "braggadocio") is here represented by his model for the *Perseus* in **Piazza della Signoria** as well as *Perseus and Andromeda* from the actual sculpture's base. He attributed the shape of *Narcissus* to a flaw in the marble rather than to an artistic conceit. The exquisitely grandiose bust of *Cosimo I* by Cellini and *Victory of Florence over Pisa* by Giambologna are also on display.

Upstairs in the loggia are Giambologna's *Mercury* and his bronze menagerie made for the Medici. The **Salone del Consiglio Generale** has two panels from the competition to design the **Baptistry** doors, *The Sacrifice of Isaac* as interpreted by **Filippo Brunelleschi** and **Lorenzo Ghiberti** (the latter won). Among the Donatellos are *St. George* from the church of **Orsanmichele** and two Davids, one in marble and the other in bronze; the latter was the first nude sculpted since ancient times and reflects the classical appreciation of young male beauty. Young female beauty is represented by Desiderio da Settignano's *Pensive Girl;* equally enchanting are the various della Robbias (Luca and Andrea), here and in the rooms on the next floor. Before ascending, take a look at the large collection of decorative art.

The first room on the next floor has Cellini's *Ganymede,* as well as the Roman Baroque sculptor Gian Lorenzo Bernini's bust of *Costanza Bonarelli*. The **Sala di Verrocchio** contains that artist's *David*, a less willowy solution than Donatello's treatment of the same subject. In addition to Antonio Pollaiuolo's *Hercules and Antaeus*, the room contains a number of memorable portrait busts, Mino da Fiesole's *Piero de' Medici* being the first in the genre since Roman times. Finally, as its name implies, the **Sala del Camino o dei Bronzetti** houses Italy's finest collection of small bronzes, displayed before a *pietra serena* chimney piece by Benedetto da Rovezzano. ♦ Admission. Tu-Su. Via del Proconsolo 4 (at Via Ghibellina). 23885

62 **Vinaio Carlo** Here's yet another tiny, old-fashioned wine shop where you can stop for a little tipple with the locals if your elbow is so inclined. ♦ M-Sa 9:30AM-7:30PM. No credit cards accepted. Via dell'Anguillara 70r (at Piazza San Firenze). No phone

63 **San Filippo Neri and San Firenze** Is it any wonder that the proud natives of Florence would corrupt "San Fiorenzo" to "San Firenze?" The saint's ancient oratory stood on the spot now occupied by the 18th-century church of **San Filippo Neri,** a rare and rather restrained example of Baroque architecture in Florence. On its right and connected to it by a Neo-Classical palazzo, is **San Firenze**, built as an oratory for the monastic order known as the Filippini, who commissioned the ensemble. Today the palazzo and oratory are occupied by the Law Courts, hence the armed police always outside. ♦ Piazza San Firenze (between Borgo dei Greci and Via della Condotta)

64 **Hotel Bernini Palace** $$$ Some of the hotel's 83 guest rooms have views of the **Palazzo Vecchio**, and members of parliament used to meet in the frescoed breakfast room when Florence was the capital of Italy. These are two of the niceties of this centrally located Old World hotel attracting an upscale crowd of businesspeople and tourists. There is no restaurant and the guest rooms are due for a face-lift. ♦ Piazza San Firenze 29 (at Borgo dei Greci). 288621; fax 268272

65 **Loggia del Grano** As you might have guessed by the bust in the middle arch, this space by **Giulio Parigi** was commissioned in 1619 by Cosimo II. It was originally a granary, but Florentines know it best as the entrance to the movie theater, **Capitol Cinema**. ♦ Temporarily closed. Via de' Castellani (at Via dei Neri)

66 **Palazzo Castellani** This medieval palace once housed the *Accademia della Crusca* (literally, the Bran Academy, or Academy of Letters), one of those typically esoteric Florentine societies, in this case a linguistic fraternity dedicated to separating the wheat from the chaff in the Italian language. (They would certainly have their work cut out for them in modern-day Florence, home of shops operating "no stop" and "self-service" restaurants selling "cheeseburghers" and "wurstel.") The palazzo now houses the **Istituto e Museo di Storia della Scienza** (Institute and Museum of the History of Science), which displays the Medici family's large collection of scientific instruments, including the lens with which Galileo discovered the moons of Jupiter, which he dutifully named after his Medici patrons. ♦ Admission. M-Sa. Piazza dei Giudici 1 (on Lungarno dei Medici). 293493

67 **Piccolo Vinaio** The young owners who recently bought this tiny 19th-century wine bar (said to be Florence's first) proudly point to the faded photograph of a horse-drawn *vinaio* (wine seller), the original incarnation of this wine stop. Pull up one of the stools outside, order some of the simple and traditional finger foods like *bruschetta* and

---

Restaurants/Clubs: Red   **Hotels:** Blue
Shops/ ♥ **Outdoors:** Green   **Sights/Culture:** Black

crostini, and check out the die-hard habitués.
♦ Daily Mar-Oct; M-Sa 11AM-11PM Nov-Feb.
Via de' Castellani 25r (at Via dei Neri). No
phone

68 Palazzo Gondi Designed by **Giuliano da
Sangallo,** this is another fine 15th-century
monumental Renaissance palace in private
hands. Peek into the courtyard to see the
fountain and Roman statue, perhaps the
spoils from the Roman amphitheater that
formerly stood nearby. ♦ Piazza San Firenze 2
(between Via dei Gondi and Via della
Condotta)

Within Palazzo Gondi:

Bar-Pasticceria San Firenze One of the
oldest pastry shops in Florence, this one has a
tantalizing display of pastries and cookies,
including fresh fruit tarts in the warmer
months. ♦ M-Sa 7AM-8PM. 211426

69 Piazza della Signoria The piazza has
been the center of civic life for centuries, and
there's nothing like the sight of two elegantly
dressed Florentines walking arm-in-arm in
deep discussion here to catapult one's spirit
back to the Middle Ages. Called an "open-air
museum" (though what isn't in outdoor
Florence?), the piazza and the **Loggia dei
Lanzi** are filled with an impressive collection
of monumental sculpture celebrating the
schizoid Florentine fascination with tyrants,
both in life and in death. From north to south,
the assemblage in the piazza begins with
Giambologna's equestrian monument to
Cosimo I and his attributed bronze figures
decorating the base of **Bartolommeo
Ammannati**'s **Neptune Fountain.** Much
derided by Florentines, it gave rise to the taunt
*"Ammannato, Ammannato, che bel marmo hai
rovinato!"* (What beautiful marble you've
ruined!) and to this day is known locally as *"Il
Biancone"* (The Great White One). Then come
copies of Donatello's *Judith and Holofernes*
(the original is inside the **Palazzo Vecchio**)
and his *Marzocco,* the heraldic lion of Florence
(original in the **Bargello**), Michelangelo's
David (the original is in the **Accademia**), and
Bandinelli's *Hercules and Cacus* (the original
is here—the town fathers don't seem to feel
it's worth sheltering from the elements; most
art historians seem to agree).

The piazza was the subject of a recent uproar
when it became an open-air quarry. What
began as a routine cleaning of its paving
stones led to an archeological excavation
of Roman and medieval sites beneath. When
it came time to repave the piazza in 1993,
most of the stones had disappeared, allegedly
into the driveways of some wealthy local
residents. Furthermore, the remaining
stones had been ruined in the cleaning
(shades of Ammannati) and no longer fit
in place. Florentines wanted to take the
opportunity to pave the space in a redbrick

and gray *pietra serena,* as it appears in 15th-
and 16th-century paintings, but instead the
authorities gave them a literal cover-up—too-
perfect, brand-new rectangular *pietra serena*
paving stones, which hardly live up to their
name. This is the hottest scandal since
Savonarola was burned in the piazza in 1498
(a granite disk marks the spot), just a few
years after he incited the Florentines to make
the original bonfires of their vanities in the
piazza. ♦ Via Calimaruzza and Via dei
Calzaiuoli

70 Palazzo Uguccioni **Mariotto di Zanobi**
built this palazzo in 1550, according to
tradition, to the designs of **Michelangelo**
or **Antonio da Sangallo.** From the balcony,
a bust of *Cosimo I* oversees the piazza,
including his equestrian monument just
below. ♦ Piazza della Signoria 7 (between
Via dei Magazzini and Via dei Cerchi)

71 Il Cavallino ★★$$ Right on **Piazza della
Signoria** near Giambologna's equestrian
monument, convenient to the surrounding
sights, is one of the better restaurants in
town. It serves reliable Tuscan specialties,
such as the ribboned *pappardelle* pasta and
the juicy steak called *bistecca alla fiorentina,*
to a clientele of discriminating locals and
tourists. It is also one of the few good
restaurants in Florence open on Sunday or
with outdoor dinng in such a remarkable
setting. ♦ M-Tu, F-Su lunch and dinner; Th
dinner. Via delle Farine 6r (in Piazza della
Signoria). 215818

**72 Raccolta Alberto della Ragione Arte
Italiana del '900 (Alberto della Ragione
Collection of Italian Art of the 1900s)**
This small museum features modern Italian
art by artists of local and international
reputation. The former include Ottone
Rosai, beloved by Florentines for his
charming views of Via San Leonardo
(for tourists, the paintings serve as a nice
enticement to stroll down the lovely country
road); among the latter are a few works by
Giorgio De Chirico, Giorgio Morandi, and
Marino Marini. ♦ Free Sa 9AM-2PM. Piazza
della Signoria 5 (between Via dei Cerchi and
Via dei Calzaiuoli). 283078

73 Bar Perseo If **Caffé Rivoire** (see page 35)
is closed or crowded, this is a reliable
alternative (it is operated by **Rivoire**'s
owners) for coffee or *gelato.* It also sells
Brazilian cigarrillos and stamps for the
postcards purchased at the newsstand in
front. ♦ Daily 8AM-8PM Mar-Oct; M-Sa
Nov-Feb. Piazza della Signoria 16r (at Via
dei Calzaiuoli). 2398316

74 Newsstand Besides selling an ample
selection of international newspapers and
magazines to the tourist throngs, this
understandably mercurial *giornalaio*
(newsstand) also has a nice souvenir video

about Florence and stocks the best and widest selection of postcards in the city. There are cards of everyone's favorite Florentine scenes and works of art here, from risqué details of David's anatomy to stigmata on the most pious of saints. ♦ M-Sa 8AM-8PM; Su 8AM-1PM. Piazza della Signoria (at Via dei Calzaiuoli). No phone

75 Palazzo Vecchio (Old Palace or Palazzo della Signoria) This embodiment of the imposing, rustic side of the Florentine character was originally built in 1298 by

Palazzo Vecchio

Arnolfo di Cambio to house and protect the ministry of the republican government, the *Signoria.* In 1540, Cosimo I brazenly set up house here, moving in from the **Medici Palace**. After 10 years, wife Eleanor of Toledo talked him into transferring the official residence to the **Pitti Palace.** Ever since, it has been known as the **"Palazzo Vecchio,"** or Old Palace (see drawing at left). Under Cosimo's reign, it was decorated with sycophantic alacrity by Giorgio Vasari, who virtually became the court painter. He indiscreetly mythologized the entire Medici line with help from some of the finest artists available, primarily late Mannerists. The modern visitor should exercise more discretion in visiting the palazzo, since, unless you're a specialist, it is a waste of energy to try to sample all the often overripe fruits of Vasari's labors.

The courtyard contains a copy of Verrocchio's bronze *Putto* in the fountain (the original is upstairs in the **Cancelleria**), surrounded by frescoes of Austria, which Vasari commissioned to honor Francesco de' Medici's marriage to Joanna of Austria. If you're wondering why the throngs here don't seem to be admiring the works of art but passing through with disgruntled looks on their faces, it's because the palace now serves its original function as **City Hall**—a more immediate function might be use of the public toilets in this area.

Upstairs are the **Quartieri Monumentali** (Historical Rooms). Visit the **Salone dei Cinquecento,** a gigantic room frescoed with Florentine battle scenes—all victorious, of course. Of more interest are the statues: In the center of the longest wall is Michelangelo's *Victory;* on the opposite wall is Giambologna's *Virtue Overcoming Vice;* and scattered throughout are the almost comically labored *Labors of Hercules* by Vincenzo de' Rossi. A door to the right of the entrance leads to the **Studiolo di Francesco I,** which Vasari provided as a hideout for Cosimo I's son Francesco. The walls represent the four elements—earth, air, fire, and water. (It was Pope Boniface who remarked that the world is made up of five elements—the above, plus Florentines.) Bronzino's portraits of Francesco's parents, *Cosimo I* and *Eleanor of Toledo,* face each other from either end of the room. They presumably kept an eye on young Francesco as he meditated over his paintings and bronzes on the subject of science.

Of interest on the next floor are the private apartments of Eleanor of Toledo, among which is a chapel frescoed by Bronzino. The **Cappella della Signoria** contains an *Annunciation* by Ridolfo Ghirlandaio, whose father, Domenico, frescoed the **Sala dei Gigli.** (The *giglio,* which means lily but actually depicts an iris, is a symbol of the city, and **City Hall** marriages downstairs always end with a bouquet of them for the bride.) The **Sala dei Gigli** dates from before the Medici occupation of the palace and sticks to mere classical and religious subjects. Outside this room are the sculptures *Judith and Holofernes* by Donatello (in the **Sala dell'Udienza**) and Verrocchio's original *Putto* (in the **Cancelleria**). Before leaving, take the stairs in the **Sala dei Gigli** to the tower for a guard's-eye view of the **Piazza della Signoria. ♦** Courtyard: free. Palazzo: admission. M-W, F-Sa; early closing Su. Piazza della Signoria (at Via dei Gondi). 27681

76 Galleria degli Uffizi (Uffizi Gallery) In 1560, Grand Duke Cosimo I commissioned **Giorgio Vasari** to design a building for offices (*uffici* in Italian, corrupted to "uffizi" by the Florentines). Construction was completed by **Bernardo Buontalenti** under Francesco I, who turned the top floor into a museum of art and curiosities and installed artists' and artisans' studios there. **Vasari**'s first architectural commission, the building is a masterful blend of Classical elements with the Tuscanisms of *pietra dura* (a semiprecious lead-colored stone from nearby Fiesole) and white stucco walls. The Medici family put together the collection, whose unrivaled strong points are paintings from the Florentine Renaissance as well as works by Flemish and Venetian masters, and an impressive array of antique sculpture. The last of the Medici line, Anna Maria Ludovica, donated it to the people of Florence in 1737.

The most important single museum in Italy, it is suprisingly manageable, laid out more or less chronologically in a series of human-scale rooms. It is also the most crowded museum in the country. To avoid the squeeze, try to visit it during the lunch hour or late afternoon. Otherwise, be resigned to packs of raucous and enraptured Italian schoolchildren gathered for indoctrination in the national trait of living intimately with great works of art, and, at the other end of the scale, university students clustered around pompous and pedantic art historians—both engaging if distracting subsidiary exhibits in their own right. As with most Italian museums, but particularly frustrating at this one, don't expect every room to be open (the principal rooms, however, almost always are).

Stop for a look at Andrea del Castagno's frescoes of *Illustrious Men* (mostly Florentines) next to the ticket office in the remains of the 11th-century church of **San Piero Scheraggio,** which Vasari incorporated into his building. Across from the elevator is a fresco of the *Annunciation* by Botticelli. **Vasari**'s monumental staircase leads to the prints and drawings department, which usually has an exhibition or two mounted from its rich collection. (If climbing the staircase seems too monumental a task, take the elevator to the right of it, pretending not to understand the sign that says it's for staff only.)

The painting galleries are on the top floor (see floor plan on page 32). Walking from *sala* to *sala* (room to room), don't overlook what may seem to be decorative background elements—lively ceiling frescoes, Flemish tapestries, antique sculpture. This gallery is the place in Florence most conducive to the Stendhal syndrome, so take a break now and then to gaze out the windows at Florence and the surrounding countryside, or into the courtyard when it is filled with a flower show in the spring.

To recuperate from the following tour, go to the museum bar at the end of the corridor, overlooking **Piazza della Signoria** from the roof of the **Loggia dei Lanzi.** In 1993, a car bomb allegedly set by the Mafia damaged 15 rooms in the west wing of the **Uffizi.** Some rooms and galleries in the wing have since been closed and many works of art are still awaiting restoration. Temporary exhibits scattered throughout the museum illustrate the bomb damage and ongoing restoration work.

Highlights of the Uffizi Gallery (*sala* numbers refer to floor plan on page 32):

Sala II Three imposing altarpieces depicting the Madonna enthroned (*Maestà* in Italian) open the show with deserving majesty. On the right side of the room is the earliest version, by Cimabue, considered the father of modern painting, though his panel still shows close ties to Byzantine painting in the classical stylization of its angels and drapery. In the center of the room is the more realistic (and, for its day, revolutionary) interpretation by Cimabue's alleged pupil, Giotto. ("Cimabue thought that he held the field in painting, but now Giotto is acclaimed and his fame obscured," writes Dante in *Purgatory.*) To the left is a work by Cimabue's contemporary from nearby Siena, Duccio di Buoninsegna, whose attention to graceful humanity, rich color, and surface pattern was seminal to the Sienese school.

Sala III What Duccio sowed may be seen here in this room of Sienese pictures. Simone Martini's *Annunciation* is full of grace, whereas Pietro Lorenzetti's *Madonna in Glory* and his

GALLERIA DEGLI UFFIZI

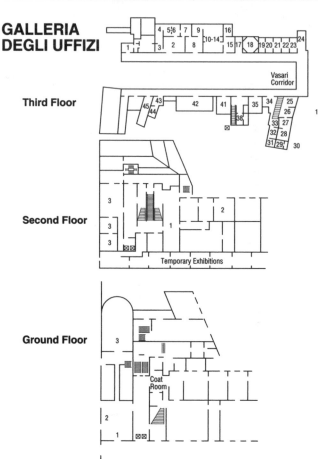

Third Floor

Second Floor

Vasari Corridor

Temporary Exhibitions

Ground Floor

Coat Room

Third Floor
1 Archaeology Room
2 Tuscan School of the 13thC and Giotto
3 Sienese School of the 14th C
4 Florentine School of the 14th C
5-6 International Gothic
7 Early Renaissance
8 Filippo Lippi
9 Antonio del Pollaiulo
10-14 Botticelli
15 Leonardo da Vinci
16 Map Room
17 Hermaphrodite Room
18 The Tribuna
19 Perugino and Signorelli
20 Dürer and the German School
21 Gianbellino and Giorgione
22 Flemish and German Masters
23 Correggio and Mantegna
24 Miniature Room
25 Michelangelo and Florentine Masters
26 Raphael and Andrea del Sarto
27 Pontormo and Rosso Fiorentino
28 Titian and Sebastiano del Piombo
29 Parmigianino and Dosso Dossi
30 16th C Paintings in Emilia
31 Paolo Veronese
32 Tintoretto
33 16th C Paintings (Italian & foreign)
34 Lombard School
35 Baroccio
38 Temporary Exhibitions
41 Rubens
42 Niobe Room
43 Caravaggio
44 Rembrandt
45 18th C Paintings

Second Floor
1 Exhibition Room - Prints and Drawings
2 Reading Room - Prints and Drawings
3 Library and Reading Rooms

Ground Floor
1 Entrance
2 Ticket Office
3 Church of St. Pier Scheraggio

brother Ambrogio Lorenzetti's *Presentation in the Temple* and *Story of St. Nicholas* continue the Sienese preoccupation with surface pattern, here combined with an awareness of Giotto's sense of space and solidity.

Sala IV Here you'll find an assemblage of what used to be referred to as "Primitives." What these panels by followers of Giotto lack in artistic innovation they make up for by capturing the intimate and intense spirituality of the era (the 14th century), their saints performing various empassioned acts before gently glowing goldleaf backgrounds.

Sala V-VI These two rooms bring the Gothic period to a close with Lorenzo Monaco's *Coronation of the Virgin* and *Adoration of the Magi*. In Gentile da Fabriano's treatment of the same subject *(Adoration of the Magi)* across the room, the Gothic marches out with charming pageantry.

Sala VII Recently reevaluated and acclaimed because of the restoration of their frescoes for the **Brancacci Chapel** in Florence's **Carmine** church, Masaccio and Masolino, whose work

is seen here in the collaborative *Madonna with Child and St. Anne*, are the most sought-out 15th-century artists in this room. But there are other masterpieces, namely a rare picture by Domenico Veneziano (*Sacra Conversazione*), *Federico da Montefeltro and Battista Sforza* by Veneziano's pupil Piero della Francesca, and the epic *Battle of San Romano* by Paolo Uccello. Uccello was obsessed with perspective, a fact that becomes all the more frightening when you consider that this busy picture, bristling with lances and fantastically colored horses, is but one of three panels that once decorated the **Medici Palace.** The other two sections are now in the Louvre and London's National Gallery.

Sala VIII Paintings by Masaccio's pupil, Filippo Lippi, indicate a return to the tender and decorative style of the Gothic period.

Sala IX Paintings by the brothers Antonio and Piero Pollaiuolo, particularly *The Feats of Hercules* by Antonio, show a strong interest in the Renaissance study of human anatomy. Botticelli's *Finding of the Body of Holofernes* has some of Antonio's energy, though his

Return of Judith derives more from his master Filippo Lippi.

Sala X-XIV Botticelli's—and the museum's—most famous paintings are in these rooms, which have been joined into one large space. They are *The Birth of Venus* and *Primavera* (Spring). The former masterpiece is a fairly straightforward representation of the goddess of the sea, received by a nymph and the personified wind. *Primavera* is a flowery Renaissance interpretation of classical mythology (depicting from right to left, Zephyr, Chloe, Flora, the Three Graces, and Mercury). In addition to the other Botticellis in the rooms, there are two Flemish masterpieces—Hugo van der Goes's Portinari *Altarpiece* and Roger van der Weyden's *Entombment of Christ*—as well as works by Domenico Ghirlandaio, Filippino Lippi, and Lorenzo di Credi.

Sala XV Tuscany's own Leonardo da Vinci is represented by his sketch for the *Adoration of the Magi*, as well as by an attributed *Annunciation* and a confirmed angel (the one in profile) in his master Verrochio's *Baptism of Christ*. Other noteworthy works are Luca Signorelli's *Crucifixion* and the *Pietà* by Perugino, Raphael's master.

Sala XVII The "Room of the Hermaphrodite," as it is also known, is often closed. Inside (enter from **Sala XVIII**) is the Hellenistic sculpture that gives the room its name as well as other bits of classical sculpture.

Sala XVIII Buontalenti designed this octagonal (like the **Baptistry**) room, known as **"La Tribuna"** (The Tribune). It is made of lavish materials that represent the four elements—lapis lazuli for air, mother-of-pearl for water, red walls for fire, and green *pietra dura* (semiprecious stone) floors for earth. It was meant to showcase the gems of the Medici collection, especially the *Medici Venus,* a Roman copy of a Greek original, which caused longing sighs during the Grand Tour era. It is a veritable temple to Mannerist portraiture, with Medici likenesses by Vasari, Bronzino, and Jacopo Pontormo. Another Mannerist, Rosso Fiorentino, painted the delightful little *Musical Angel,* a popular image that graces everything from postcards and calendars to T-shirts.

Sala XIX Notice Luca Signorelli's *Holy Family* (there's a similar composition by Michelangelo in **Room 25**) and Perugino's *Madonna* and *Portrait of Francesco delle Opere.*

Sala XX German Renaissance painting in all its intensity is exemplified by Lucas Cranach's *Adam and Eve,* not to mention Dürer's treatment of the same subject, as well as Cranach's *Adoration of the Magi* and *Portrait of the Artist's Father.*

Sala XXI The beginnings of important Venetian painting are seen here in Giovanni Bellini's *Sacred Allegory.*

Sala XXII Works by more northern Europeans are on view in this room, including Hans Holbein the Younger's *Portrait of Sir Richard Southwell* and Albrecht Altdorfer's *Martyrdom of St. Florian* and *Departure of St. Florian.*

Sala XXIII Spend some time with Correggio's *Rest on the Flight to Egypt* and religious works by his master, the northern Italian painter Andrea Mantegna.

Sala XXIV The *Cabinet of Miniatures* is an example of the kind of curiosities collectors favored in times past.

Sala XXV This houses Michelangelo's only painting in Florence, the *Doni Tondo* (a *tondo,* or round painting, of the Holy Family made for the Doni family), which through its strongly modeled and muscular forms of figures of both sexes shows the artist's clear preference for sculpture. Its garish colors, which were meant to disturb, inspired Florentine painters Fiorentino (his violent *Moses Defending the Daughters of Jethro* is in this room) and Pontormo to begin working in the style known as Mannerism.

Sala XXVI Enjoy a moment of serenity here with Raphael's *Madonna of the Goldfinch,* which owes its restful pyramidal composition to Leonardo. The other Virgin, *Madonna of the Harpies,* is by Andrea del Sarto. Raphael is also represented by the *Portrait of Pope Leo X,* a Medici.

Sala XXVII A high-pitched frenzy of early Florentine Mannerism is reached in this room with Pontormo's vivid *Supper at Emmaus* and Bronzino's *Holy Family.* The movement's counterpart in Siena is also represented, albeit weakly, by Domenico Beccafumi's *Holy Family.*

Sala XXVIII This salon of Titians is invitingly presided over by the sensuous *Venus of Urbino. Flora* and *Eleanora Gonzaga della Rovere* are part of the lustrous and illustrious company.

Sala XXIX Central Italian Mannerism, certainly less spiritual than the Tuscan but equally contorted and distorted, is here typified by Parmigianino's *Madonna of the Long Neck.*

Sala XXX Emilian painting, with works by Battista Dossi and Dosso Dossi, is the focus here.

Sala XXXI-XXXIV These rooms showcase Venetian and French painting.

Sala XXXIV is the **Corridoio Vasariano** (Vasari Corridor), built in five months with **Vasari**'s usual fast hand to link the gallery with the **Pitti Palace** via the **Ponte Vecchio**. The corridor, which houses a display of 17th- and 18th-century works, as well as a gallery of self-portraits extending to the 20th century, is closed indefinitely due to damage incurred in the 1993 bombing.

Sala XXXV While admiring the Umbrian and Venetian painters on display here, don't miss the Venetian-trained El Greco.

Exit Hall Peek in for a look at the *Wild Boar,* a Roman copy of a Greek original. It was copied again by Pietro Tacca for his fountain at the **Mercato Nuovo.** Come back here at the end of the visit for a grand descent down **Buontalenti**'s staircase.

Sala XLI Don't overlook this room, home to works by Van Dyck and Rubens, among them the latter's *Portrait of Isabella Brant.*

Sala XLII The **Sala della Niobe** is named after the Roman sculptures of *Niobe and Her Children,* here ogled incongruously by a collection of 20th-century self-portraits by artists from around the world.

Sala XLIII Return to 17th-century Italy to view some of Caravaggio's earthy and realistic responses to the squeamishness of Mannerism—the mad *Medusa,* decadent *Bacchus,* and emotionally charged *Sacrifice of Isaac.* There are also the more bucolic *Summer Diversion* by Guercino and *Seaport with Villa Medici* (this villa is at the top of the Spanish Steps in Rome) by Claude Lorraine.

Sala XLIV The Dutch paintings here, including two self-portraits by Rembrandt from his early and later years, are worth the long walk.

Sala XLV The collection ends with a Rococo flourish of paintings by Tiepolo, Canaletto, Guardi, Chardin, and Goya. ♦ Admission. Tu-Sa; Su 9AM-1PM. Piazzale degli Uffizi (between Piazza della Signoria and Lungarno Archibusieri). 23885

77 Antico Fattore ★★$$ The "old farmer" of the name doesn't really exist, but his spirit lives on in the rustic country cooking (try the classic Tuscan white-bean soup, *ribollita*) in an informal setting to match. At press time, the restaurant was closed due to heavy damage from the 1993 bombing of the **Uffizi** and is not scheduled to reopen until late1996 at the earliest. ♦ Tu-Sa lunch and dinner. Via Lambertesca 1-3r (near Chiasso dei Baroncelli). 2381215

78 Il Vecchio Armadio This store is well named (the old closet), if your boudoir consists of clothes of the army surplus or *American Graffiti* variety. If that's the look you like—currently quite stylish among gilded Florentine youth and increasingly difficult to obtain in its country of origin— you're in for some "Happy Days" here. There are also a few European goods on occasion. ♦ M-F, Sa morning Mar-Oct; M afternoon, Tu-Sa Nov-Feb. Via Lambertesca 19r (between Chiasso dei Baroncelli and Via Por Santa Maria). 217286

Loggia dei Lanzi

79 Matassini Friends who have an eye for Bulgari, Cartier, and the like tip their hats to the Matassini sisters, who have a knack for knocking off the spirit rather than the letter (hence the lawsuits) of the big-name jewelry designers. ♦ M-F, Sa morning Mar-Oct; M afternoon, Tu-Sa Nov-Feb. Via Lambertesca 18r (between Chiasso dei Baroncelli and Via Por Santa Maria). 212897

80 Loggia dei Lanzi Located on the south side of **Piazza della Signoria,** this arcaded space (see page 34) was designed by **Benci di Cione** and **Simone di Francesco Talenti** for public ceremonies in the 14th century and last used as such to receive Queen Elizabeth II. **Michelangelo,** with the same eye for symmetry he used to rework Piazza Campidoglio in Rome, once suggested that the loggia be continued around **Piazza della Signoria.** What a wonderful piazza it would have been. The loggia has been under restoration for years, but most of the scaffolding is down, revealing the statues within. Of interest are Cellini's *Perseus* (the base panels and statuary are in the **Bargello**), which he touchingly writes about making in his autobiography; a classical lion and its 16th-century copy; and Giambologna's *Rape of the Sabine Women* and *Hercules Slaying the Centaur.* A lineup of Roman priestesses brings up the rear. ♦ Piazza della Signoria (at Via Vacchereccia)

81 Rivoire ★★$$ This was Florence's first chocolatier, founded by a Piedmontese who acquired the sweet vice from French sources. It remains the most elegant such emporium in town. Take the harsh edge off the **Piazza della Signoria** with a cup of hot chocolate topped with luscious whipped cream, or in warmer weather—at the most coveted tables in the piazza—iced tea or cappuccino dusted with rich cocoa. For those who can't afford to find the tiny boxed Rivoire chocolates on their pillows at the **Hotel Excelsior,** they are also available here. ♦ Tu-Su 8AM-midnight. No credit cards accepted. Piazza della Signoria 5 (at Via Vacchereccia). 214412

82 Pineider When Italians present their calling cards, they like to draw a line through their titles to show how modest and well-bred they are, a charming if disingenuous gesture that somehow sums up the Janus-faced Italian culture in one swift stroke. The best-bred (and made) cards in the country come from this stationery store founded in Florence in 1774 and recently purchased by a Japanese concern. There are branches throughout the country, but this is the flagship store. Through the ages, notables from heads of state to Hollywood stars have had their names engraved here. ♦ M-F, Sa morning Mar-Oct; M afternoon, Tu-Sa Nov-Feb. Piazza della Signoria 13r (at Via dei Calzaiuoli and Via Calimaruzza). 284655. Also at: Via Tornabuoni 76r (near Piazza Antinori). 211605

83 Erboristeria Palazzo Vecchio This shop offers one of the widest selections of medicinal herbs in one of the most convenient locations in Florence. Also available are hair-restoring shampoos and tanning creams (so that's what accounts for all those strangely apricot juice–faced Florentines), and for gifts, there are charmingly packaged aromatic soaps, candles, Tuscan herbs, and more. ♦ M-F, Sa morning Mar-Oct; M afternoon, Tu-Sa Nov-Feb. Via Vacchereccia 9r (in Piazza della Signoria). 2396055

84 Tabasco Since 1974 the town's chic rendezvous spot for the gay crowd is a stone's throw from Michelangelo's *David,* whose "camp" aspect has been adopted as the restaurant's logo. Local male gay life as witnessed in this deconsecrated church consists of that combo of refined surface and provincial substance that permeates the Florentine genius loci, and it doesn't come cheap. ♦ Tu-F, Su 10PM-3AM; Sa 10PM-4AM. Piazza Santa Cecilia 3r (off Via Vacchereccia behind Piazza della Signoria). 213000

85 Oliver This just may be the place to find the trendiest men's clothing and shoes this side of Milan. Major Italian designers are represented, along with the shop's own line of wool and cotton trousers. ♦ M-F, Sa morning Mar-Oct; M afternoon, Tu-Sa Nov-Feb. Via Vacchereccia 15r (between Piazza della Signoria and Via Por Santa Maria). 2396327

86 Benetton In case you've had the wool over your eyes for the past decade, this chain is to sheep hair what McDonald's is to cow meat. The Benetton siblings devised a way to make finished woolen goods before applying the dye, thus guaranteeing that their garments could be given the trendiest possible colors in conjunction with the latest market research. This particular shop is geared toward women, but there is a veritable flock of them through-out Florence (eight locations in all) and indeed the world. ♦ M-F, Sa morning Mar-Oct; M afternoon, Tu-Sa Nov-Feb. Via Por Santa Maria 68r (at Via Vacchereccia). 287111

87 Prada Miuccia Prada has infused the fresh breath of youth into her family's already successful leather-goods empire. One of the first to prove that a bag made from synthetic fabric could be every stitch as chic as leather, she has recently turned her infallible design sensibility to women's clothing. ♦ M-F, Sa morning Mar-Oct; M afternoon, Tu-Sa Nov-Feb. Via Vacchereccia 26-28r (between Piazza della Signoria and Via Por Santa Maria). 213901

88 Mercato Nuovo (New Market) This "new market," designed by **Giovanni Battista del Tasso,** was a 16th-century annex to the old one in what is now **Piazza della Repubblica.** Today it still functions as such, although filled with stalls selling tourist trinkets, leather bags, and linen-embroidered tablecloths (manufacture of the old Italian straw hat, alas, has been moved to Asia). The Florentines call the market the "Porcellino" (piglet) after their nickname for Pietro Tacca's bronze statue, *Wild Boar,* at its south end. Tradition dictates that if one rubs the beast's nose or tosses it a coin, it ensures a return to Florence, preferably not to buy a fat pig but rather some cow innards from the nearby tripe stand (in the southwest corner). Of course there's no dearth of goods to purchase in this fair city. ♦ Daily Mar-Oct; Tu-Sa Nov-Feb; no midday closing. Piazza del Mercato Nuovo (Via Porta Rossa at Via Calimala). No phone

89 Libreria del Porcellino Dare to browse in this bookshop, a welcome respite in a heavily trafficked part of town, since the management doesn't discourage it and the selection of books about all aspects of Italian culture—art, food, history, travel, etc., in many languages—warrants a long stay. ♦ M-F, Sa morning Mar-Oct; M afternoon, Tu-Sa Nov-Feb. Piazza del Mercato Nuovo 6-8r (at Via Calimaruzza). 212535

90 Antica Farmacia del Cinghiale This *erboristeria* (herbalist's shop) claims to be more than 300 years old. It sells herbal teas for the inside, herbal fragrances for the outside, and herbal potpourris for the homesite. There's also a pharmacy. ♦ M-F, Sa morning Mar-Oct; M afternoon, Tu-Sa Nov-Feb. Piazza del Mercato Nuovo 4r (on Via Calimala). 282128

91 Pollini Their name may mean chicks, but chic is the word for the footwear designed by the four Pollini siblings, who hatch sophisticated shoes for both sexes. Be sure to check out the classic men's loafer or the more stylish women's pumps and boots. ♦ M-F, Sa morning Mar-Oct; M afternoon, Tu-Sa Nov-Feb. Via Calimala 12r (at Via Orsanmichele). 214738

Unlike its five neighboring bridges, the Ponte Vecchio was spared bombing by the Germans in World War II—some say this was because Hitler admired it.

92 Brioni The medieval palazzo that once housed the *Arte della Lana* (Wool Guild) is now the splendid setting for the Florence home of the famous Roman tailor, whose classic made-to-measure and ready-to-wear men's and women's clothing adds a bit of conservative theatricality to the rational Florentine silhouette. ♦ M-F; Sa morning Mar-Oct. M afternoon; Tu-Sa Nov-Feb. Palagio Arte della Lana, Via Calimala 22r (at Via Orsanmichele). 210646

93 Piazza della Repubblica This open space is not named after the neon sign at one end proclaiming "La Repubblica," which is Italy's best newspaper. The piazza was the site of the ancient Roman forum, which later became the **Mercato Vecchio** (Old Market), bordering on Florence's Jewish ghetto at its north end. Florentines still bemoan the 1887 demolition of what was one of the city's most picturesque piazzas, as seen in displays in the **Museo di Firenze Com'Era,** in spite of the plaque on the piazza's grand arch referring to the *secolare squallore* (centuries of squalor) that the restoration eradicated. The visitor may like to conjure up those centuries past while walking in the piazza, surrounded by historical cafes. Going about your business at the post office beneath the Classical-style loggia paved in colored marbles along the piazza's western edge, you can wonder whether patrons of Diocletian's baths might have enjoyed similarly imperial diminishing perspectives. (The baths of ancient Roman Florence were, in fact, nearby on Via delle Terme.) On Thursday, the flower market is reminiscent of the piazza's earlier commerce. And the ever-present save-the-animals woman and her minions collect donations with as much devotion as any medieval mendicant. ♦ Via degli Speziali at Via Roma

94 Giubbe Rosse ★$$ This has to be the most historic of the piazza's cafes, named after the red jackets still worn by the waiters, whose antecedents served Florence's intellectuals a century ago. The atmosphere today is rather more lightweight, with a mediocre restaurant in the back, which serves a convincing approximation of American-style breakfast for the homesick. ♦ M-Tu, Th-Su 8AM-1AM breakfast, lunch, and dinner. Piazza della Repubblica 13-14r (at Via Pellicceria). 212280

95 Donnini ★$$ The best sandwiches and pastry, including a nice *budino di riso* (the custardy Florentine version of rice pudding), are yours for the asking at the smallest of the piazza's cafes. ♦ Daily until 1AM Mar-Oct; M, W-Su 7AM-9PM Nov-Feb breakfast, lunch, and dinner. Piazza della Repubblica 15r (between Via Calimala and Via Pellicceria). 211862

96 UPIM Floor upon floor of middle-priced merchandise fills this branch of the nationwide Italian department store owned by the upscale chain **La Rinascente.** The clothing is middlebrow (with the occasional find), but there is a wide selection of well-designed housewares upstairs. ♦ M-F, Sa morning Mar-Oct; M afternoon, Tu-Sa Nov-Feb. Piazza della Repubblica 1r (at Via degli Speziali). 216924

97 Universalturismo This busy travel agency looks like a discreet bank but acts like the trading floor of Wall Street. Besides having the best exchange rate in town at no commission, it provides a full line of travel services. It also serves as box office for some of the city's cultural events. ♦ M-F; Sa morning. Via degli Speziali 7r (between Via dei Calzaiuoli and Piazza della Repubblica). 217241

98 Profumerie Aline Those who simply can't go on without their favorite European, American, or Japanese brand of cosmetics will most likely find what they are looking for in this *profumeria.* Locals were amused when the American men's cologne, Tuscany, made its European debut here. ♦ M-F, Sa morning Mar-Oct; M afternoon, Tu-Sa Nov-Feb. Via dei Calzaiuoli 53r (at Via degli Speziali). 215269. Also at: Via Vacchereccia 11r (in Piazza della Signoria). 294976

99 Il Granduca This *gelateria,* or ice-cream parlor, is an atonal symphony of harsh brass and stone design, sweetened by 32 wonderful flavors made fresh daily. Among them is a rare Florentine appearance of Sicilian *cassata siciliana,* a creamy white *gelato* dotted with candied fruits and bits of chocolate. ♦ M-Tu, Th-Su 10AM-11PM. Via dei Calzaiuoli 57r (off Via degli Speziali). 2398112

100 Romano This is one of the major Florentine leather firms, associated for generations with luxury men's and women's shoes, accessories, and leather clothing. Other designer names are also represented, but it is primarily Romano's wares that reign beneath the gilded reliefs and frescoed ceilings. ♦ M-F, Sa morning Mar-Oct; M afternoon, Tu-Sa Nov-Feb. Piazza della Repubblica 22-24r (at Via degli Speziali). 2396890

101 Savoy $$$$ Though its name was changed from **Savoia** after Italy's rulers from that royal house were politely requested to abdicate (just as **Piazza della Repubblica** was changed from **Piazza Vittorio Emanuele II**), this 100-room hotel retains some of its former glory. It is the oldest and most centrally located, if not the grandest, of Florence's luxury hotels, with loyal and subdued business travelers retiring within its reserved and faded fin de siècle facilities. There is no restaurant. ♦ Piazza della Repubblica 7 (at Via Roma). 283313; fax 284840

102 Gilli ★★$$ The most elegant of the piazza's many cafes preserves the glory days from when it moved here in 1910. Stained-glass windows, stucco walls, and marble-top tables are matched by Florence's trendiest cocktails

and creamiest *coppa gelato* (the delicious *coppa fiorentina* is concocted out of coffee pudding, chocolate ice cream, and whipped cream). When seating moves outside these are some of the most coveted tables in the piazza. ♦ M, W-Su 7:30AM-midnight Mar-Oct; M, W-Su 7:30AM-9PM Nov-Feb. Piazza della Repubblica 39r (at Via Roma). 2396310

103 Paszkowski ★★$$ Under the same ownership as **Gilli,** yet with its own identity, this is the liveliest of the piazza's cafes by night, especially in the warmer months, when it offers crowd-gathering music. The crowd is a friendly mix of locals and tourists, and the music ranges from Julio Iglesias to Tony Bennett classics. ♦ Tu-Su 7AM-1:30AM breakfast, lunch, and dinner. Piazza della Repubblica 6r (at Via Brunelleschi). 210236

104 Ricordi Here you'll find the best selection of records, tapes, CDs, and sheet music in this part of town. The helpful, young staff is not above naming that tune for you if it's slipped your mind and you hum a few bars. ♦ M-F, Sa morning Mar-Oct; M afternoon, Tu-F, Sa morning Nov-Feb. Via Brunelleschi 8r (at Via de' Tosinghi). 214104

105 Gianfranco Ferrè Boutique The Milanese designer's Florence boutique is also one of the most striking contemporary spaces in the city. A steel spiral staircase connects the stark-white men's and women's floors, both framed by the tall arched windows of a 19th-century palazzo. Oh, yes, there are Ferre's well-known clothes and accessories, too. ♦ M-F, Sa morning Mar-Oct; M afternoon, Tu-Sa Nov-Feb. Via de' Tosinghi 52r (at Via Brunelleschi). 292003

106 Pendini $$ This 42-room hotel has been in operation for more than 100 years. Currently undergoing a refurbishment, the lodging continues to offer old-fashioned charm and unrivaled value, considering its simple but spacious rooms and its central location on the **Piazza della Repubblica.** On summer nights, the piazza's six outdoor cafes beckon young Florentines, which can make piazza-side rooms too noisy for some. If you're a couple with a young child or two you'll find the rooms are large enough to accommodate a cot. There is no restaurant. ♦ Via degli Strozzi 2 (in Piazza della Repubblica). 211170; fax 210156

107 Palazzo delle Poste e Telegrafi The Renaissance-style post office was built in 1917 by **Rodrigo Sabatini** and **Vittorio Tognetti.** It's the place to buy stamps; to send mail, telegrams, and faxes (the latter to anywhere but the US); and to make telephone calls if you're not taking care of such business at your hotel. There are tables for writing postcards, though chairs are always disappearing. ♦ M-F; Sa morning. Via Pellicceria 3 (entrance near Via Porta Rossa). 2382101

108 Caffè La Posta If the post office across the way is crowded, go to this friendly neighborhood bar for your stamps. They also sell simple stationery and tasteful cards and make their own sandwiches fresh daily. The house aperitif (ask for the *aperitivo della casa*—it's made with Spumante, Martini rosso, Campari bitter, and gin) is guaranteed to send you special delivery. ◆ M-Sa 7AM-7:30PM. Via Pellicceria 24r (at Via dei Lamberti). 214773

109 Hotel Pierre $$$ Located in a 19th-century building done in a 13th-century style, this refurbished hotel has 39 contemporary rooms with double-paned Neo-Gothic windows, ensuring monastic quiet in the center of town. There is no restaurant. ◆ Via dei Lamberti 5 (between Via Calimala and Via Pellicceria). 217512; fax 2396573

110 Passamaneria Valmar This shop is jam-packed with home-decorating trimmings that make lovely gift items. You'll find everything from fat twisted cords and decorative borders to silk tassels in every color combination, all made with exemplary Italian textiles and workmanship. ◆ M-F, Sa morning Mar-Oct; M afternoon, Tu-Sa Nov-Feb. Via Porta Rossa 53r (between Via Pellicceria and Piazza de Davanzati). 284493

111 Palagio dei Capitani di Parte Guelfa The Guelph party called in the best artists and architects of the day to work on its 14th-century headquarters, the earliest Renaissance palazzo in Florence. It discreetly dominates a tiny piazza where one can easily picture political intrigues of the day taking place. **Filippo Brunelleschi** was responsible for the high-ceilinged interior during a 15th-century remodeling, topped with a coffered ceiling by **Giorgio Vasari**, who was also responsible for the loggia in 1589. ◆ Piazza di Parte Guelfa 1 (Via delle Terme at Via Pellicceria). No phone

112 C.O.I. There's nothing coy about the **Commercio Oreficeria Italiana**, a bustling gold market with the largest imaginable selection of merchandise at some of the best prices in town (and you don't have to bargain for them). Prices are quoted in US dollars. ◆ M-F, Sa morning Mar-Oct; M afternoon, Tu-Sa Nov-Feb. Via Por Santa Maria 8r (between Via Lambertesca and Via Vaccereccia), Upstairs. 283970

> A 16th-century chronicler reported that Catherine de' Medici, a member of Florence's most famous family and a notorious glutton, ate so heavily at the marriage of Mademoiselle de Martigues that she "just missed kicking the bucket."

113 Cirri The delicate Florentine art of hand embroidery is alive and well in this shop. It's well stocked with thousands upon thousands of table linens, collars, kerchiefs, and lingerie in cotton, silk, and linen, as well as exquisite outfits for infants and toddlers. ◆ M-F, Sa morning Mar-Oct; M afternoon, Tu-Sa Nov-Feb. Via Por Santa Maria 38-40r (between Via Lambertesca and Via Vaccereccia). 2396593

MANDARINA DUCK

114 Mandarina Duck The Florence branch of this Italian chain is known for trendy, heavy-duty rubber bags and briefcases and smaller accessories. ◆ M-F, Sa morning Mar-Oct; M afternoon, Tu-Sa Nov-Feb. Via Por Santa Maria 23r (between Borgo SS. Apostoli and Via delle Terme). 210380

115 Il Gatto Bianco A visit is worth a thousand words! The highly individualistic jewelry featured here, exquisitely crafted by a master silversmith on the premises, is for both the bold and the artistic of soul. Some classic pieces can be found, but this is primarily a treasure trove for those who lean toward innovative design and the unusual combination of precious and common materials. ◆ M-F, Sa morning Mar-Oct; M afternoon, Tu-Sa Nov-Feb. Borgo SS. Apostoli 12r (between Via Por Santa Maria and Corso dei Manetti). 282989

115 La Torre Guelfa $$ Housed in a 14th-century historical landmark palazzo on a cobblestoned street in the heart of the Centro Storico, this hotel has a devoted following. Enter the lobby and you'll most likely find guests relaxing in overstuffed armchairs discussing where they ate dinner the night before (the hotel does not have a restaurant, but apparently no one minds) or where to find the best buys. The decor of the 14 rooms leans toward the, well, creative, with idiosyncratic combinations of colors and patterns (the new Belgian owners may see to some changes). Still, the rooms have rudimentary comfort and the bathrooms are clean and modern. The top-floor mansard has its own terrace and a view that rivals the best of them. ◆ Closed in August. Borgo SS. Apostoli 8 (between Via Por Santa Maria and Corso dei Manetti). 2396338; fax 2398577

116 Casa-Torre degli Amadei This 14th-century tower, rebuilt after it—like most of the immediate vicinity—was destroyed during World War II, now houses the conservative jeweler **Ugo Piccini**. Once upon a time, it was the residence of one of the most reactionary families of medieval Florence. The Amadei (the name, ironically, means love of God) arranged for the murder of Buondelmonte dei Buondelmonti, who had jilted their daughter (see Ponte Vecchio, page 40). The Florentines affectionately call this tower "La Bigonciola," meaning the tub—only Amadei knows why. ♦ Via Por Santa Maria 9-11r (between Lungarno Acciaiuoli and Borgo SS. Apostoli)

117 Santi Apostoli Legend (and legend only) has it that this small 11th-century church (rebuilt in the 15th to 16th centuries) was founded by Charlemagne. Within its Romanesque interior, partially built with material from the nearby Roman baths, is a 16th-century *Immaculate Conception* by Vasari. ♦ Piazza del Limbo (between Lungarno Acciaiuoli and Borgo SS. Apostoli)

117 Giorgio Vanini This young designer's hidden location does not hinder his word-of-mouth following: Florence's well-heeled ladies love the finely tailored chic silhouettes of suits made from designer Italian fabrics. Prices are reasonable considering the quality of limited artisanal production and keen choice of gabardine, linen, and silk. ♦ M afternoon; Tu-Sa. Piazza del Limbo 2r (between Lungarno Acciaiuoli and Borgo SS. Apostoli). 293037

118 Torre dei Donati Consorti Located near the **Casa-Torre degli Amadei,** this little 12th-century tower was affiliated with the Guelph family whose daughter Buondelmonte chose and who murdered him for jilting her. Talk about unfriendly neighbors. The atmosphere here is warmer these days, since it houses part of the **Hotel Continental.** ♦ Lungarno Acciaiuoli 2 (at Ponte Vecchio)

118 Hotel Continental $$$ Owned by the Ferragamo family, this is one of the few hotels in the area that looks out on the Arno—a mixed blessing since the soundtrack to that gorgeous view of the river and the Ponte Vecchio is a racket of cars, Vespas, and an endless stream of tourists. The windows in the 48 modern, comfortable rooms are double-paned, which helps cut down on the noise (recent new traffic regulations also help). The guest rooms all have mini-bars, and there is a breakfast room. ♦ Lungarno Acciaiuoli 2 (at Ponte Vecchio). 282392; fax 283139

119 Bijoux Cascio This shop specializes in well-crafted imitations—sincerely flattering gold-plated designs (both classic and contemporary) set with ersatz stones that look remarkably like the real thing. ♦ M-F,

Sa morning Mar-Oct; M afternoon, Tu-Sa Nov-Feb. Via Por Santa Maria 1r (at Ponte Vecchio). 294378

CAFFE' delle CARROZZE

120 Caffè delle Carrozze Silvia, the friendly Italian-Canadian proprietor, knows her co-continentals' tastes. Lick your cups clean of the berry flavors (all natural, made only with fruit and water) and the sinfully delicious, *semifreddo* specialty of *nocciolato* (a cool, creamy chocolate mousse-like concoction). ♦ M-Tu, Th-Su; closed in January. No credit cards accepted. Piazza del Pesce 3-5r (at Ponte Vecchio). 2396810

121 Santo Stefano al Ponte The lower part of the Romanesque green-and-white marble facade of this church dates from 1233, though records claim it was built in 1116 or earlier. The interior was rebuilt in the 17th century by **Ferdinando Tacca** and includes his bronze relief *The Stoning of St. Stephen*. (The church itself was reduced to rubble during the German retreat during World War II, damaged in the 1966 flood, and again in the 1993 bombing of the **Uffizi Gallery**.) Much of the interior was originally made for other churches—the elaborate marble staircase by **Bernardo Buontalenti** stood in **Santa Trinita,** and the altar by Giambologna was in **Santa Maria.** The church is usually open only for noteworthy concerts and occasional exhibitions. ♦ Piazza Santo Stefano al Ponte (off Via Por Santa Maria near Ponte Vecchio)

122 Buca dell'Orafo ★★$$ Its name notwithstanding, one doesn't have to be a goldsmith to afford this typical Florentine trattoria (many such restaurants have the typically self-effacing *buca,* meaning hole, in their names). This one is known for its *frittata di carciofo* (artichoke omelette) among other simple dishes. ♦ Tu-Sa lunch and dinner. Reservations recommended. No credits cards accepted. Volta de' Girolami 28r (near Ponte Vecchio). 213619

122 Casa Artigiana dell'Orafo In this goldsmith's house you can watch more than 30 jewelers go about their timeless craft, producing what's in store for you in the elite shops on the **Ponte Vecchio**. ♦ M-F, Sa morning Mar-Oct; M afternoon, Tu-Sa Nov-Feb. Vicolo Marzio 2 (at Ponte Vecchio). 292382

123 Archibusieri $$ Sharing the same spectacular location (and rooftop breakfast terrace) with the slightly more expensive **Hermitage,** this seven-room hotel has recently undergone a thorough face-lift. The guest rooms are small and simple, and all have private showers and are nicely furnished with terra-cotta floors. There's no restaurant. ♦ Vicolo Marzio 1 (Piazza del Pesce, near Lungarno Achibusieri). 282380; fax 212208

Above the Archibusieri:

Hotel Hermitage $$ It's somewhat pricier than its sister hotel (see above), but a recent restoration, spectacular views, and a lovely roof-garden have kept this 22-room hotel a favorite. Housed in the top three floors of a medieval tower two steps from the **Ponte Vecchio,** the view of the bridge and the Arno River are all the reason you need to stay here. Rooms are of average size, tastefully done, with new bathrooms; units in the back, facing the **Duomo,** are quieter. There's no restaurant. ♦ 287216; fax 212208

124 Morè This well-known Piedmontese candy manufacturer founded in 1886 has found a sweet reception in a city that recognizes artisanal gems when it sees them. Lovely packaging enhances century-old recipes and molds for hard candies that appease every imaginable taste (and with nary an artificial flavor). In addition to marmelades and preserves, there are more than 40 types of pralines and white chocolates flavored with everything from raspberries to lemons. ♦ M afternoon; Tu-Sa. Lungarno Archibusieri 6r (between the Uffizi Gallery and Ponte Vecchio). 2382411

Maledetta e sventurata fossa—cursed and unlucky ditch—is what Dante called the Arno River, which has overflown its banks some 70 times since its first recorded flood in 1177. The worst flood ever was the most recent: On 4 November 1966 the Arno rose 4.92 meters—more than 16 feet. The aftermath of mud mixed with fuel oil flushed out from basement storage tanks engulfed paintings, sculptures, books, manuscripts, and other objects. Thousands of such items were extracted from the morass by teams of local and international volunteers the Florentines dubbed "angels of the mud" in an atypical fit of gratitude, if with a characteristically ambivalent moniker.

125 Ponte Vecchio Florence's 12th-century "Old Bridge" was so named to distinguish it from the **Ponte alla Carraia** upstream, built in thoroughly modern 1220. The Ponte Vecchio crosses the Arno at its narrowest point in the city. It was probably where the Romans built a bridge for the Via Cassia, the ancient road that ran through Florence on its way from Rome to what are now Fiesole and Pisa, much more important cities in those days. A statue of *Mars* once stood at the northern end of the bridge, the scene of a seminal event in the history of Tuscany. There, on Easter Sunday in 1215, assassins killed Buondelmonte dei Buondelmonti, who had spurned his fiancée of the Amadei family in favor of a more attractive member of the rival Donati clan.

The present bridge and its shops replaced a 12th-century structure swept away in a flood in 1333. Although **Vasari** writes that **Taddeo Gaddi** reconstructed it in 1354, **Vasari** may have been trying to reinforce his own link with Florentine artistic tradition, since he himself designed the corridor running over it, buying up property on either side of the bridge to do so. (For all his power, he was not able to persuade the Manelli family to let him run it through their residence, however, so it twists briskly around the Manelli tower at the Pitti end of the bridge.) The **Ponte Vecchio**'s medieval character persists, albeit dazzling with the glint of gold in its shops. (Medieval spectacle can be fully appreciated by watching the *Calcio Storico* parade march over the bridge, with participants in full period garb, each 24 June and two other days in June, varying each year.) After **Vasari** built his corridor, Ferdinand I de' Medici, annoyed at having to pass over the shops of butchers, tanners, and other practitioners of the "vile arts," as he called them, rousted the low-rent tenants and raised the rates. In came the goldsmiths and jewelers whose professional descendants line the bridge today. A tribute to their craft is the bust of the goldsmith/sculptor Benvenuto Cellini in the middle of the bridge.

During the German retreat of World War II, this was the only bridge Hitler's troops did not blow up. Instead, they reduced the buildings on either side of it to rubble (which is why Via Por Santa Maria is so modern looking), effectively blocking passage across the Arno. In 1966, the **Ponte Vecchio**'s jewelers were among the first to witness the river's most recent flood, and they played a crucial role in alerting the townspeople. Their shops and **Vasari**'s corridor suffered some damage, but the bridge beneath them remained intact.

These days the Ponte Vecchio bustles with upscale shoppers—particularly tourists. At night during the warmer months, however, the last hippies in Italy (who seem to have somehow become embedded in the structure in the 1966 flood) congregate in the two terraces in the middle of the bridge, twanging guitars and performing street theater. Jewelers on the **Ponte Vecchio** come and go (talking not of Michelangelo, but no doubt of Cellini), but the current crop is likely to stay put for a while. ♦ At Via Por Santa Maria and Via Guicciardini

T.RISTORI

126 T. Ristori Unlike the trinkets of the former tenant (**Settepassi,** now on Via dei Tornabuoni) of this prime space at the foot of the bridge, the jewelry here has a contemporary feel, though timeless in the cut (and price tag) of its precious stones. The semiprecious stock is equally inventive and, naturally, more reasonably priced, and many settings make bold use of both precious and semiprecious sparklers. ♦ M-F, Sa morning Mar-Oct (no midday closing); M afternoon, Tu-Sa Nov-Feb. Ponte Vecchio 1-3r (on the Ponte Vecchio). 215507

Rajola

127 Rajola The precious metals and stones in contemporary designs this inventive jeweler produces are so of-the-moment that they sometimes startle. ♦ M-F, Sa morning Mar-Oct (no midday closing); M afternoon, Tu-Sa Nov-Feb. Ponte Vecchio 24r (on the Ponte Vecchio). 215335

128 U. Gherardi Having corralled the coral market in Florence (most of it is produced in Naples), this jeweler sells buckets of the stuff in pale white, blushing pink, and beet red. Check out the cultured pearls and cameos, but beware of the tortoiseshell, since it won't pass through customs in some countries. ♦ M-F, Sa morning Mar-Oct (no midday closing); M afternoon, Tu-Sa Nov-Feb. Ponte Vecchio 5r (on the Ponte Vecchio). 211809

In the 12th century, interfamily feuds were widespread, and more than 150 square stone towers—built for defense by influential families right next to their homes—dominated Florence's skyline.

. . . Giotto's tower, the lily of Florence blossoming in stone.

FRATELLI PICCINI

129 Fratelli Piccini The Piccini brothers have been crowning heads ever since Queen Elena married Vittorio Emanuele III at the turn of the century. Their current designs are on the street level; upstairs are antique pieces that the descendants of the king and queen could easily have pawned on their abdication. ♦ M-F, Sa morning Mar-Oct (no midday closing); M afternoon, Tu-Sa Nov-Feb. Ponte Vecchio 23r (on the Ponte Vecchio). 294768

Cassetti
gioielli antichi

130 Cassetti Among the most creative of the bridge's jewelers, the Cassetti family were among the first Florentine jewelers to mix precious and semiprecious stones in the same pieces, as well as to come up with Rolex-like combinations of steel and gold. They are particularly known for their selection of antique jewelry. ♦ M-F, Sa morning Mar-Oct (no midday closing); M afternoon, Tu-Sa Nov-Feb. Ponte Vecchio 52r (on the Ponte Vecchio). 2396028

Bests

Amerigo Franchetti
Hotelier/Owner, Torre de Bellosguardo

When it is raining, sleep as long as possible.

At twilight sit on the **Ponte Santa Trinita** and dream while the lights go on along the **Arno** and on the **Ponte Vecchio.**

Eat a memorable sandwich of boiled beef with green sauce at **Nerbone** in the central **San Lorenzo** food market. Then go upstairs and wallow in the fruit and vegetable stands.

Admire the 18th-century looms still clattering away, weaving wonderfully patterned cloths at the **Antico Setificio Fiorentino.**

Bribe the guardian of the **Chiostro dello Scalzo** to open the little door and let you see the wonderful chiaroscuro frescoes of Andrea del Sarto on all four sides of the cloister.

Restore your energy at my favorite trattoria, **Alla Vecchia Bettola**—wonderful *penne alla Bettola* and the best steaks.

Colli

Even before Luca Pitti built his palazzo at the foot of what are now the **Boboli Gardens**, Florentines have been heading for the hills—*colli* in Italian—across the **Arno**. According to a medieval legend, one of the first to do so was the martyr Saint Minias, who in AD 250 carried his severed head from Florence's Roman amphitheater to the **Mons Florentinus**, now the site of the beloved church of **San Miniato**.

Many have followed through the ages, including **Michelangelo**, who built fortifications around San Miniato to protect Florence from a siege, and the Medici, who greatly expanded the already grandiose palazzo begun by Pitti. Others have been great Florentine families such as the Guicciardini, Torrigiani, and Serristori, who built palazzi from the Middle Ages onward, and 20th-century plein air painters such as Ottone Rosai, who immortalized the landscape of **Via San Lorenzo**, the Florentines' favorite country road.

The Colli continue to provide a bit of country in the city, on **Via di San Leonardo** as well as in the panoramic **Boboli Gardens**, the **Forte di Belvedere**, and **Piazzale Michelangiolo**, all ideal spots for a picnic. Even the

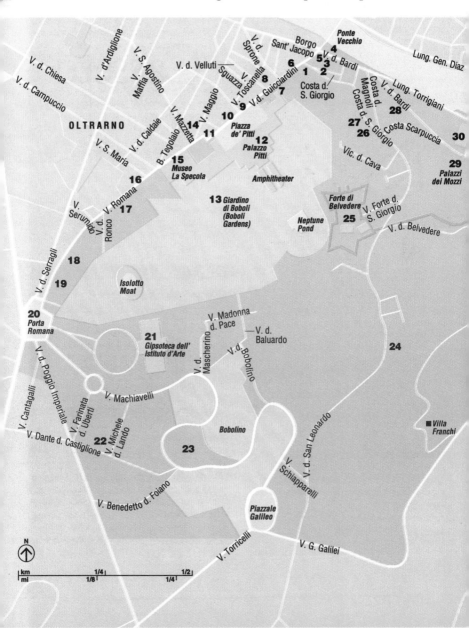

most famous museum in the area, **Palazzo Pitti,** is uncrowded (though the arrangement of the art is not) compared with other Florentine institutions.

So as not to lose your head like Saint Minias, be forewarned that much of Colli is as hilly as its name implies. Before you begin to explore it, put on some sturdy walking shoes. If they're trendy Timberlands, you may even pass for a native!

1 Santa Felicità The present Neo-Classical structure, built in 1736 by **Ferdinando Ruggieri,** is a remodeling of a Gothic church, though there has been a church on this choice site since the early Christian era. The column in its piazza dates from 1381; **Giorgio Vasari** built the portico to support the corridor he designed to run between the **Uffizi** and **Palazzo Pitti** in 1564. Inside, the most important sight is the **Capponi Chapel,** which may have been built by **Brunelleschi.** It houses Jacobo da Pontormo's Mannerist masterpiece, *The Deposition,* as well as his *Annunciation* and tondos of the *Evangelists,* worked on in collaboration with his pupil, Agnolo Bronzino. ♦ Piazza Santa Felicità (on Via Guicciardini near Ponte Vecchio)

1 Celestino ★★$$ Smallish and chic, this bright eatery offers an Italian menu of such dishes as *ravioli rose* (in a tomato-and-cream sauce), *scaloppine alla boscaiola* (veal with tomato and mushroom), and *scampi alla pescatore* (shrimp with tomato and garlic). In warm weather, a few tables spill out into the little piazza for dining *all'aperto*—don't ask to eat *al fresco,* since the expression has now come to mean "in the slammer." ♦ M-Sa lunch and dinner. Piazza Santa Felicità 4r (on Via Guicciardini near Ponte Vecchio). 292185

2 Mannelli This well-known jewelry store, once on the **Ponte Vecchio,** is now in a beautiful location replete with frescoed ceilings. The owners are descendants of the former inhabitants of the eponymous medieval tower in *pietra forte* at the end of the **Ponte Vecchio,** noteworthy because the family refused to let **Vasari** run his corridor through it. These days they are more concerned with *pietra dura,* the semiprecious stones they set along with *pietre preziose* (precious stones) in bracelets, necklaces, and rings. They are also more obliging than their ancestors, crafting jewelry in whatever designs the client desires. ♦ M-F, Sa morning Mar-Oct; M afternoon, Tu-Sa Nov-Feb. No midday closing. Piazza de' Rossi 1r (off the Via Guicciardini behind Piazza Santa Felicità). 213759

2 Le Volpi e L'uva This refined wine bar is run by Emilio and Riccardo, two young wine enthusiasts who have created a stylish, relaxing niche for a sip and snack. Dozens of changing wines-by-the-glass are posted daily, with small sandwiches and a good cheese selection as an aside. Most interesting are the lesser known Italian wines and those of small producers—and the chance to sample them all at a few outdoor tables when nice weather arrives. ♦ M-Sa. Piazzi de' Rossi 1r (off the Via Guicciardini behind Piazza Santa Felicità). 2398132

3 La Porcellana Bianca White porcelain is the specialty of this housewares shop. Spots of color among the sea of white dishes, cups, and platters include lovely country dish towels and brass-handled stainless-steel cookware. ♦ M-F, Sa morning Mar-Oct; M afternoon, Tu-Sa Nov-Feb. Via de' Bardi 53r (between Via Guicciardini and Costa di San Giorgio). 211893

4 Kenny ★$ Fast food is served here with a slow view. Besides the price, the saving grace of the grease here—not-bad Italian burgers with names like Kennyburger, Superkenny, Cheesekenny, and Fishkenny—is that it's right on the Arno, looking out over the Ponte Vecchio to the **Uffizi**. Less culturally shocking is the **Old Bridge Gelateria** in the same space. It prides itself on its *coppa Firenze* (custard ice cream with whipped cream, strawberries, and pineapple) and its *coppa Ponte Vecchio* (a banana split the likes of which you'd never find at Dairy Queen). ♦ Daily 11AM-midnight Mar-Oct; Tu-Sa Nov-Feb. Via de' Bardi 64r (between Costa di San Giorgio and Via Guicciardini). 212915

5 Madova This is Florence's prime glove emporium, hands down. The firm makes its own gloves of various leathers, linings, and colors—including custom-made sizes—and will ship anywhere free of charge. ♦ M-F, Sa morning Mar-Oct; M afternoon, Tu-Sa Nov-Feb. Via de' Guicciardini 1r (at Via de' Bardi). 2396526

6 Quaglia e Forte The late Enzo Quaglia was from Naples, a city renowned for its delicately carved corals and cameos. Master craftsmen continue that tradition today, as well as reproducing historical jewelry for museums throughout the world. ♦ M-F, Sa morning Mar-Oct; M afternoon, Tu-Sa Nov-Feb. Via de' Guicciardini 12r (between Via dello Sprone and Borgo Sant' Jacopo). 294534

7 Pasticceria Maioli ★$ This glitzy modern establishment offers a selection of pizzas and sandwiches. ♦ Pizza ♦ M, W-Su Via de' Guicciardini 43r (near Piazza de' Pitti). 214701

7 Palazzo Guicciardini This 15th-century palazzo was the birthplace of the historian Francesco Guicciardini, who lived here from 1482 to 1540. Rebuilt in 1620-25 to designs of **Cigoli** by **Gherardo Silvani**, its elegant courtyard contains a stucco representation of Hercules in the style of Antonio Pollaiuolo. ♦ Via de' Guicciardini 15 (near Piazza de' Pitti)

8 Freon In this shop's high-tech setting you'll find some of the most creative costume jewelry in Florence. Most recently they were showing large, frankly fake stones, following the trends of the fashion runway. ♦ M-F, Sa morning Mar-Oct; M afternoon, Tu-Sa Nov-Feb. Via de' Guicciardini 118r (near Via dello Sprone). 2396504

9 Giulio Giannini & Figlio Beautifully marbleized Florentine paper goods are the specialty of this fifth-generation shop, which has also been doing custom bookbinding for some of those generations. ♦ M-F, Sa morning Mar-Oct; M afternoon, Tu-Sa Nov-Feb. Piazza de' Pitti 37r (near Via dei Velluti). 212621. Also at: Via Porta Rossa 99r (between Piazza Davanzati and Via Tournabuoni). 215448

Pitti Mosaici

10 Pitti Mosaici It's rare to see the younger generations continuing the Florentine tradition of *artigianato* (craftsmanship), but Elio de Filippis has taken up the 16th-century Florentine specialty of *pietra dura*, the inlay of precious and semiprecious stones in jewelry, artwork, and furniture. ♦ M-F, Sa morning Mar-Oct; M afternoon, Tu-Sa Nov-Feb. Piazza de' Pitti 16r (near Via de' Pitti). 282127. Showroom at: Piazza de' Pitti 17r

11 Il Caffè ★$ This warm, inviting cafe is as old-fashioned in its dark old European-style decor as in its long list of such mixed drinks as Cuba *libres*, grasshoppers, and stingers.

Restaurants/Clubs: Red **Hotels:** Blue
Shops/ ❦ Outdoors: Green **Sights/Culture:** Black

Palazzo Pitti

Snacks, such light lunches as daily-changing pastas or salads, or a simple cappuccino are most enjoyed when the tables move outside. Filled by day with discriminating tourists and by night with the closest thing in Florence to cafe society. ♦ Tu-Su 11AM-1AM. Piazza de' Pitti 9r (near Via de' Marsili). 2396241

11 Caffè Bellini ★$ This bright, sparkling, expansive option for coffee in **Piazza de' Pitti** offers some of the best cappuccino in Florence as well as a scrumptious *budino di riso,* the local rice pudding tart. ♦ M-Sa 7AM-8PM. Piazza de' Pitti 6a-r (near Via de' Marsili). 212964

12 Palazzo Pitti Florence's largest if not most beloved palazzo was commissioned circa 1457-70 for Luca Pitti, a wealthy importer of French cloth who was trying to keep up with the Joneses, in his day named Medici and Strozzi. Legend has it that Pitti's pitiless ambition called for a plan with windows larger than the doors of the **Palazzo Medici** and a courtyard that could contain the entire **Palazzo Strozzi.** (Though the former palazzo was under construction at the time, the latter existed only as a plot of land.) Somewhere between legend and fact is the story that architect **Luca Fancelli** built the palazzo according to a grandiose plan his master **Brunelleschi** had presented to Cosimo il Vecchio. According to Vasari, when the Medici rejected it, **Brunelleschi** "tore the drawing into a thousand pieces in disdain." The original palazzo consisted of only the seven central bays of the present structure, built— as were later additions—out of rough-hewn golden *pietra dura* stone quarried from the **Boboli Gardens** behind it. Even so, it was

most imposing. Machiavelli called the palazzo "grander than any other erected in the city by a private citizen," and **Vasari** wrote that the view from it was "*bellissima,*" commenting that the surrounding hills in the Boboli made it "almost a theater."

Work on the palazzo had been at a standstill for decades when Cosimo I's wife, Eleanor of Toledo, bought it from Pitti's impoverished heirs in 1549. From then on, the palazzo became the official residence of the rulers of Florence. The Medici brought in **Bartolommeo Ammannati,** who added the wings toward the **Boboli** and the courtyard in 1558-77. (He did not ruin any marble here, as the Florentines say of his statue of Neptune in **Piazza della Signoria,** but instead enlarged the palace with more stone from the **Boboli** brought with the help of a mule, whose efforts are commemorated on a plaque in the courtyard.) After **Ammannati**'s interventions, the estate, with its grounds, was the most magnificent in Europe, a rustic and rambling precursor to Versailles. (It was this version of the palace that Eleanor's homesick granddaughter, known as Marie de Médicis when she was married off to Henry IV of France, tried to recall when she commissioned the Palais du Luxembourg in Paris.)

During the 17th century, at the behest of the Medici, **Giulio Parigi** added the three bays on either side of the original seven, and his son **Alfonso** extended the two lower floors to their present dimensions. The two porticos reaching into the **Piazza de' Pitti** were added in the 18th century under the house of Lorraine, giving the palazzo the exterior aspect you see today (see drawing above).

Meanwhile, as the Florentine genius loci that brought about the Renaissance and the Medici began to wane, the royal rulers looked increasingly beyond the city to embellish the palace with suitably magnificent paintings and decoration. The **Pitti** became the residence of the Italian royal family when Florence was the capital of Italy in the last century. In this century, Victor Emmanuel III gave it to the state. It now houses no fewer than seven museums (many of which have erratic hours or are indefinitely closed from time to time).

Centuries after Luca Pitti commissioned the palazzo, his name lives on in another Florentine institution—the trade shows collectively known as *Pitti Immagine.* These Italian fashion shows, which originally took place in the palazzo's **Sala Bianca,** are now held at the **Fortezza da Basso** and market everything from housewares to international fashion, including the latest versions of those French textiles Luca used to import over half a millennium ago.

Ammannati's monumental 140-step staircase leads to the most famous museum in the palazzo, **Galleria Palatina** (Palatine Galleries; floor plan at right).

The first five rooms are decorated with Pietro da Cortona's allegorical ceiling frescoes, which give the rooms their names. In the **Sala di Venere [1]** (Venus Room; numbers refer to floor plan at right) are *Titian's Concert, La Bella,* and *Portrait of Pietro Aretino,* as well as Rubens's *Landscape with the Wreck of Ulysses* and Salvator Rosa's *Harbor View.* The **Sala di Apollo [2]** (Apollo Room) has more rich Titians (notably a *Mary Magdalene*) and works by Rosso Fiorentino, Andrea del Sarto, and the maudlin Guido Reni, considered the greatest painter of all time during the Grand Tour days. In the **Sala di Marte [3]** (Mars Room), look for Tintoretto's *Portrait of Luigi Cornaro* and numerous Rubens paintings. The **Sala di Giove [4]** (Jove Room), used as the throne room, contains one of the most famous paintings in the gallery, Raphael's *La Velata.* There are also important works by his master, Perugino, as well as by Fra Bartolommeo and Andrea del Sarto. The **Sala di Saturno [5]** (Saturn Room) houses the painting most singularly identified with the Pitti, Raphael's *Madonna della Seggiola,* as well as his other Madonnas and portraits.

Of particular interest in the remaining rooms are Raphael's *La Gravida* in the **Sala dell'Iliade [6]** (Iliad Room); Cristofano Allori's *Judith,* a sensual exception to the cloying 17th-century Florentine school; and Pietro da Cortona's flamboyant Baroque frescoes depicting *The Four Ages of Man* in the **Sala della Stufa [7]** (Hot Bath Room); *stufa* has no mythological significance—it means stove—but the subjects were taken

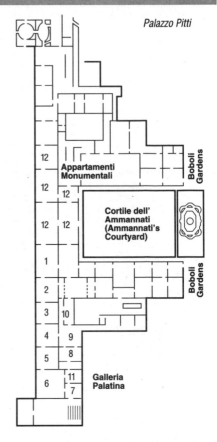

Palazzo Pitti

from Ovid's *Metamorphoses.* Also look for Cigoli's *Ecce Homo* in the **Sala di Ulisse [8]** (Ulysses Room); Filippo Lippi's *Madonna and Child* in the **Sala di Prometeo [9]** (Prometheus Room); and Francesco Furini's *Hylas and the Nymphs,* another exceptional example of the Florentine Baroque, in the **Galleria Poccetti [10]** (Poccetti Gallery). More Florentine Baroque paintings are in the **Sala Volterrano [11]** (Volterrano Room).

On the same floor as the **Palatina, Appartamenti Monumentali [12]** (State Apartments) is often closed. It contains 17th-century portraits of the Medici by Justus Sustermans, 18th-century Gobelins tapestries, and 19th-century decorations commissioned by the Lorraine.

Don't be misled by the name **Galleria d'Arte Moderna** (Galleries of Modern Art) one flight up, which contains mostly uninteresting 19th- and 20th-century Tuscan paintings. The quite notable exceptions are the *macchiaioli.* These plein air painters, whose name means stainers or blotters, were long considered to be the Italian counterpart (if not predecessors) of the French Impressionists, but are becoming increasingly appreciated abroad in their own right.

Museo degli Argenti (Silver Museum) too, is a bit of a misnomer since, rather than silver, the museum (accessible from the courtyard) is primarily a "camp" glorification of the Medici. It is also known for Lorenzo de' Medici's collection of precious-stone vases. They spawned a vogue for *pietra dura,* or precious-stone work, so associated with Florence during the days of the Grand Tour that it became known in English as Florentine mosaic. There are some examples of it on display here; it reaches its apotheosis in the **Medici Chapel.**

Dwarfed by the **Pitti, La Meridiana** (see map below) was where King Victor Emmanuel chose to stay instead of in the more imposing palace. Its *Collezione Contini-Bonacossi* (Italian and Spanish paintings and decorative art) is also dwarfed by that of the Pitti, but works by such artists as Giovanni Bellini, Paolo Veronese, Tintoretto, Gian Lorenzo Bernini, Goya, and El Greco are more than rewarding for those with the stamina. It also houses the *Galleria del Costume,* a costume collection of largely Italian fashion from the mid-18th to the mid-20th centuries.

The **Museo delle Carrozze** (Carriage Museum), often closed, is in the portico extending into the **Piazza de' Pitti** to the right facing the palazzo. It has 18th- and 19th-century carriages, primarily from the house of Lorraine. ♦ Admission. Tu-Su. Piazza de' Pitti (south of Ponte Vecchio, off Via de' Guicciardini). 213440

13 Giardino di Boboli (Boboli Gardens)
Providing the *bellissima* view Vasari enthused about, the gardens were laid out in 1550 by Niccolò Tribolo on the hilly slopes behind the **Palazzo Pitti.** Probably named after a family that owned property on the site, the park combines a formal, groomed appearance with

whimsical Mannerist statuary. It was once the private property of the Medici and other courts, but now its expanses provide fresh air and soothing views for one and all. Matrons, young lovers, foreign au pairs with babies, and hippies, who seem even more anachronistic than the statues, all pass their afternoons in the park with its resident legion of feral cats.

The main entrance is on the left side of the **Palazzo Pitti** facing it from its piazza. Just inside to the left (see map below) is Valerio Cioli's statue of Cosimo I's favorite dwarf, *Pietro Barbino Riding a Turtle,* whose image is almost as popular as that of David. A gravel path leads to the **Grotto,** which was designed by **Vasari** and **Buontalenti** and contains copies of Michelangelo's *Slaves* and the original of Giambologna's *Venus.* As in much of the gardens, the Venus room once contained *giochi d'acqua* (surprise jets of water), which were the Mannerist equivalent of water pistols. The **Amphitheater,** which extends behind **Ammannati**'s courtyard (both were used to stage court frolics), was modeled on an ancient Roman circus and contains such authentic Roman relics as a granite basin from the Baths of Caracalla and part of an Egyptian obelisk brought to the Eternal City. To the left towers the red **Kaffeehaus,** a semicircular structure with a fanciful dome, built by **Zanobi del Rosso** during the reign of the Lorraine. It offers refreshments and a terrace with nice views of Florence and Fiesole. From here, a path leads up to the **Neptune Pond,** which surrounds a bronze statue by Stoldo Lorenzi. Above it, completing the perspective down to the **Pitti,** is a colossal statue of *Abundance* designed by Giambologna and finished by the workshop of Piero Tassi. Near it is the **Giardino del Cavaliere,** where the **Museo delle Porcellane,** a museum of

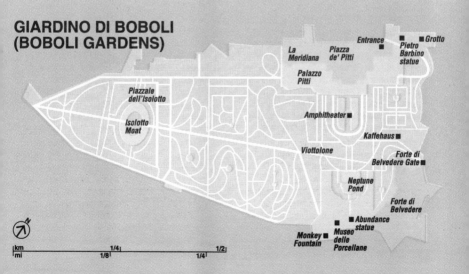

GIARDINO DI BOBOLI
(BOBOLI GARDENS)

La Meridiana
Piazza de' Pitti
Entrance
Pietro Barbino statue
Grotto
Palazzo Pitti
Piazzale dell'Isolotto
Isolotto Moat
Amphitheater
Kaffehaus
Viottolone
Forte di Belvedere Gate
Neptune Pond
Forte di Belvedere
Monkey Fountain
Museo delle Porcellane
Abundance statue

km mi
1/4
1/8
1/2
1/4

European porcelain, has been installed. Its playful **Monkey Fountain** is by Pietro Tacca, and its terrace has lovely views of the surrounding slopes. From here a path leads to the Viottolone, a magnificent cypress alley studded with classical and neo-classical statues. The spectacular path leads downhill to the **Piazzale dell'Isolotto,** the centerpiece of which is Giambologna's **Ocean Fountain,** containing a copy of his *Oceanus.*
♦ Admission. Daily 9AM-dusk. Piazza de' Pitti (behind Palazzo Pitti). 213440

14 Casa Guidi The poets Robert and Elizabeth Barrett Browning lived and held court on the first floor of this 15th-century palazzo for 15 years. Here their son, Pen, was born, and this was where Elizabeth developed her romanticized support of the unification of Italy. She died here in 1861 and is buried in Florence's **English Cemetery.** All that's left of the Brownings' sojourn in this house is a plaque. The **Casa Guidi Windows,** immortalized in Elizabeth's poem of the same name ("a little child go singing . . . " O bella libertà, etc.), remain intact.
♦ Piazza San Felice 8 (at Via Maggio)

14 San Felice **Michelozzo** may have designed the facade of this 13th-century medieval church in 1457. Inside are a crucifix and many delapidated frescoes by Giotto's school.
♦ Piazza San Felice (at Via Maggio)

15 Museo La Specola This ancient palazzo was acquired from the Torrigiani family in 1771 by Grand Duke Peter Leopold, who added an astronomy observatory (*specola*), giving the palazzo and museum its name. It houses a monument to Galileo, the **Tribuna di Galileo,** built in 1841 on the occasion of a scientific conference. Its main attraction, however, is the morbid part of the **Zoological Museum** (also founded by the Grand Duke) that contains graphic wax models of every imaginable part of the human anatomy by Clemente Susini and Felice Fontana, as well as memento mori wax tableaux by Gaetano Zumbo representing such upbeat subjects as *The Plague, The Triumph of Time, Decomposition of Bodies,* and *Syphillis.*
♦ Donation suggested. Zoological Museum: M, Tu, Th-Sa, second Su of month. Anatomical Museum: Tu-Sa. Via Romana 17 (near Piazza de' Pitti). 222451

16 Annalena $$ This former pensione is housed in a 15th-century *pietra serena* and stucco palazzo given by Cosimo de' Medici to a woman named Annalena, something of a tragic heroine in Florentine history. Having lost her husband in a political intrigue and then her son, she became a nun and turned her palazzo into a convent that gave refuge to Caterina Sforza, herself the widow of Giovanni di Lorenzo de' Medici, and to her infant son. The tradition continued under Fascism, when the place harbored political refugees. These days it simply lodges a loyal clientele that appreciates its antiques-furnished rooms and the quiet of the former **Giardino d'Annalena,** now a plant nursery, which some of the 20 rooms and their adjoining terraces overlook. There is no restaurant. ♦ Via Romana 34 (near Piazza de' Pitti). 222402; fax 222403

Giardino di Boboli

17 Hotel Boboli $ This is a clean if rather plain option for lodgings in the area. Some of its 30 rooms overlook a bit of green in the back. There is no restaurant. ♦ Via Romana 63 (between Porta Romana and Piazza de' Pitti). 2298645, 2336518

18 Ficalbi & Balloni Trompe l'oeil painting is the specialty of Stefano Ficalbi and Maurizio Balloni, who decorate everything from large murals to tiny boxes in neo-classical style. ♦ M-F, Sa morning Mar-Oct; M afternoon, Tu-Sa Nov-Feb. Via Romana 49r (between Porta Romana and Piazza de' Pitti). 2337697

19 Il Barone di Porta Romana ★$$$ Although there's nothing baronial about this restaurant, it offers a very good Florentine menu in a comfortable country setting, with dining in an outdoor garden in the warmer months—a real treat in Florence. Start with the *antipasto caldo* (hot antipasto) or *spaghetti al granchio* (spaghetti with a delicate crab sauce). ♦ M-Sa lunch and dinner. Via Romana 123r (near Porta Romana). 220585

20 Porta Romana This and a few other gates to the city are remnants of the medieval walls that once surrounded Florence. They lasted from the end of the 12th century until 1865, when, in an effort to modernize the short-lived capital of Italy, they were largely demolished. The *viali* (boulevards) now follow their outline. (The longest sections of remaining walls extend on either side of the **Porta Romana.**) The road here led to Rome, hence the gate's name. Its portal and fresco of the *Madonna with Child and Saints* date from the 14th century. The large white statue on the grass outside the portal is by Michelangelo Pistoletto. ♦ Piazzale di Porta Romana and Via Romana

21 Gipsoteca dell'Istituto d'Arte To get to this curious little museum, follow the gravel path from the gate next to a tripe stand popular with students from the art school in which the museum is housed. Walk through the run-down park filled with dogs and their walkers to the building at the end of the path, formerly the royal stables. The collection consists of plaster casts of famous sculptures (Michelangelo's *David* and *Prisoners*), quite dusty but supposedly used for didactic purposes by the art academy surrounding it. ♦ Temporarily closed for renovations. Call for updated information. Piazzale di Porta Romana 9 (off Porta Romana). 220521

22 Villa Carlotta $$ This 27-room hotel, housed in a modernized 19th-century palazzo, suits the needs of those who want to stay away from the hustle and bustle of the center yet remain within pleasant walking distance of the Porta Romana. There is a small restaurant for hotel guests only. ♦ Via Michele di Lando 3 (near Via del Poggio Imperiale). 2336134; fax 2336147

23 Grand Hotel Villa Cora $$$$ A larger (with 48 rooms), much more luxurious version of the above (in addition to lavish 19th-century decorations and a private garden, it has a strictly 20th-century swimming pool), this hotel attracts a business clientele and local passersby who have come to dine at its restaurant, **Taverna Machiavelli.** ♦ Viale Machiavelli 18 (off Via Dante di Castiglione). 2298451; fax 229086

Within the Grand Hotel Villa Cora:

Taverna Machiavelli ★★★$$$ International cuisine is the rule here, supplemented with Tuscan specialties. Carpaccio is a popular choice among the many first courses, as are the simple Tuscan soups *ribollita* (made with bread, white beans, and vegetables) and *pappa al pomodoro* (rich, thick tomato soup). Good old-fashioned lobster thermidor goes well with the lavish decor of the restaurant, which opens out onto the pool in the summer. ♦ Daily lunch and dinner. 2298451

24 San Leonardo This little 11th-century church gave its name to the street where it stands, Via di San Leonardo, every Florentine's favorite country road, lined with olive orchards and stone walls. The Romanesque church, restored in 1899 and 1921, contains a lovely pulpit of the same period moved here from the demolished church of **San Piero a Scheraggio** in 1782. ♦ Via di San Leonardo 23 (between Viale Galileo Galilei and Via di Belvedere)

25 Forte di Belvedere Entered from Costa San Giorgio and occasionally from the **Boboli Gardens,** the fort—constructed from 1590-95 by architect **Bernardo Buontalenti**—affords beautiful panoramic views of Florence and the vicinity from all sides, as its name promises. The rustic fortress was designed to fortify Grand Duke Ferdinando I de' Medici's ego more than anything else—notice the heavy-handed Medici coat of arms. The star-shaped bastions are topped by the **Palazzetto di Belvedere,** designed by **Buontalenti** in the Mannerist style, with windows set on the sides and decreasing in size on the higher stories; it was the temporary residence of Grand Duke Ferdinando II de' Medici during the plague of 1633. The **Porta San Giorgio** entrance to the fort has a fresco of the *Madonna and Saints* by Bicci di Lorenzo and a relief of St. George. There are often indoor and outdoor exhibitions at the site, which also hosts outdoor film screenings in the summer. ♦ Free; admission for exhibitions. Daily 9AM-dusk. Via di San Leonardo (off Costa di San Giorgio). 2342425

26 Spirito Santo Despite its heavy outward appearance, this Baroque church (erected in the 14th century and remodeled in 1705 by **Gian Battista Foggini)** is one of the lightest in Florence on the inside. It is filled with 17th-century paintings, including Alessandro

Gherardini's *The Glory of St. George* (the church is also known as "San Giorgio," after this ceiling fresco). To the right of the altar is *Madonna and Child with Two Angels,* considered an early work by Giotto. ♦ Costa di San Giorgio 31 (off Lungarno Torrigiani)

27 Casa di Galileo Galilei Galileo lived in this palazzo, now covered with faded frescoes and closed to the public. Grand Duke Ferdinando II de' Medici used to stop by on his morning walks from the family residence in the **Palazetto di Belvedere.** ♦ Costa di San Giorgio 19 (off Lungarno Torrigiani)

28 Il Torchio This *torchio* (printing press) produces some of the loveliest (and more moderately priced than at centrally located stores) marbleized paper in Florence, applied to notebooks, boxes, picture frames, and other gift items. ♦ M-F, Sa morning Mar-Oct; M afternoon, Tu-Sa Nov-Feb. No credit cards accepted. Via dei Bardi 17r (off Lungarno Torrigiani). 23428627

29 Palazzi dei Mozzi These adjacent 13th-century medieval palazzi, now private residences, were originally owned by the now-extinct Mozzi family, wealthy bankers who belonged to the Guelph party. Pope Gregory X stayed here in 1273 to negotiate a peace, albeit temporary, between the Guelphs and Ghibellines. ♦ Not open to the public. Piazza dei Mozzi (at Via dei Bardi)

30 Centro Di Situated in the basement of the **Palazzo Torrigiani,** this hip art bookshop stocks material from many periods in many languages and has a distinguished small press of its own, specializing in museum and exhibition catalogs. ♦ M-F, Sa morning Mar-Oct; M afternoon, Tu-Sa Nov-Feb. Piazza dei Mozzi 1r (at Via dei Renai). 2342666

31 Museo Bardini A precursor to Bernard Berenson, dealer-connoisseur Stefano Bardini (1836-1922) built this palazzo out of bits and pieces of other buildings (tearing down a 13th-century church in the process) and filled it with an eclectic collection to match. The result would make a good spread in *Architectural Digest* today, consisting of artworks from classical and Etruscan pieces to 17th-century Florentine paintings, all thrown together with the unfailing eye of an uptown interior decorator. ♦ Admission. M-Tu, Th-Su. Piazza dei Mozzi 5 (at Via dei Renai). 2342427

32 Silla $$$ This small (32 rooms) hotel in a 15th-century palazzo is just far enough away from the center of town to be relaxing (the greenery helps too), yet within convenient walking distance to most of the major sights. It also has a lovely terrace with a view for breakfast or afternoon tea; there is no restaurant. ♦ Via dei Renai 5 (on Piazza Nicola Demidoff). 234288; fax 2341437

33 Piazza Nicola Demidoff This piazza is named after the wealthy Russian ambassador and philanthropist who lived in Florence from 1773 to 1828 and died in the nearby **Palazzo Serristori.** The main feature of the piazza is an elaborate monument to Nicola Demidoff, covered with a glass canopy to protect it from the elements. The monument, by the neo-classical sculptor Lorenzo Bartolini, is composed of allegorical figures of the virtues that Demidoff was said to personify. ♦ Between Via dei Renai and Lungarno Serrestori

34 San Niccolò sopr'Arno This 12th-century church has a simple facade, to which the portal and rose window were added during the Renaissance. The interior contains numerous 15th- and 16th-century paintings by minor local artists. ♦ Between Via di San Niccolò and Via del Giardino

34 Le Sorelle ★★$$ This typically Tuscan restaurant has a seasonal menu, but you can always depend on the *spaghetti al pomodoro* here, prepared perfectly al dente and smothered in rich tomato sauce. ♦ M-W, F-Su lunch and dinner. Via di San Niccolò 30r (near Porta San Miniato). 2342722

35 Palazzo Serristori This 16th-century palazzo, rebuilt in 1873 by **Mariani Falcani,** takes its name from one of Florence's most distinguished noble families, the Serristori, who gave Italy numerous men of state, from 15th-century soldiers to a 20th-century senator. (It is now best known for its wines, among them Chianti Classico Machiavelli, named for Niccolò Machiavelli, a clever marketing ploy that would undoubtedly have pleased him.) In the 19th century, family members also became landlords, renting to Russian ambassador Nicola Demidoff, King of Westphalia Jerome Bonaparte, and King of Naples and Spain Joseph Bonaparte, who died here in 1844. Gone are the days of the *grandes fêtes* given by Countess Ortensia Serristori. Severely damaged during the 1966 flood, the palazzo is of interest to the passerby today who can peek into its vast garden (also visible from Piazzale Michelangiolo). ♦ Not open to public. Lungarno Serristori 21-23 (at Via dell' Olmo)

> Renaissance Florence was ". . . the perfect center of man's universe."
>
> D.H. Lawrence

Restaurants/Clubs: Red **Hotels:** Blue
Shops/ Outdoors: Green **Sights/Culture:** Black

Tuscan Treats

A typical Tuscan repast starts with an antipasto of *crostini* (toasted bread rounds spread with a chicken liver pâté) or *fettunta* (garlic bread such as you've never tasted), followed by such cured meats as *prosciutto crudo* (a salty prosciutto), *finocchiona* (a salami seasoned with fennel seeds), and *salsiccia di cinghiale* (sausage made from wild boar). Simplicity is perfection in *bruschetta*, a slab of toasted bread rubbed with garlic and drizzled with olive oil.

Primi piatti (first courses) can consist of excellent local versions of risotto or variations of pasta dishes available throughout Italy. Particularly Florentine, however, are such soups as *pappa al pomodoro* (tomatoes, bread, olive oil, onions, and basil), *ribollita* (white beans, bread, black cabbage, and onions), *carabaccia* (a sweet-and-sour onion soup) and, in the summer, *panzanella* (a salad of tomatoes, onions, vinegar, olive oil, and bread). Before they are eaten, these dishes are often christened with un *C d'olio*—a generous C-shaped pouring of the local olive oil from the ever-present tabletop cruet.

Second to none among the *secondi piatti* (main courses) is *bistecca alla fiorentina*— a thick slab of, ideally, local Chianina beef (though these days most comes from Eastern Europe), grilled over charcoal, seasoned with olive oil, salt, and pepper, and served rare. It is usually charged in units of 100 *grammes* called an *etto*—one *bistecca* can be quite costly but often feeds two. Inquire first. *Trippa alla fiorentina* (tripe stewed with tomatoes in a meat sauce) is also a regional specialty. For the fainthearted, there's *vitello* (veal) or *arrista* (loin of pork), roasted meats that go especially well with Chianti. Tuscany's hills provide a yearlong appearance of *cacciagione* (game) on the menu. Main courses are usually served with a *contorno* (side dish) of white beans, sautéed greens, or such seasonal vegetables as artichokes, all of which can be drizzled with more of that wonderful olive oil.

Florentine desserts are typically parsimonious. The cheese is the hard pecorino (made from ewe's milk), and locals like to go for the even tougher almond cookies called *biscotti di Prato*, which provide an excuse to dunk them in the potent sweet dessert wine called *vin santo*. A delicious hot dessert is the Piedmontese import *panna cotta*—literally, cooked cream. At its best it is nothing more than just that, although it is often thickened with some sort of starch and dressed up with chocolate sauce. Dessert time is also a good opportunity to try some of the seasonal sweets made in Florence—*schiacciata con l'uva* (a grape-covered bread) in the fall, *castagnaccio* (a chestnut-flour cake) in the winter, and *schiacciata alla fiorentina* (a sweet sprinkled with powdered sugar) during carnival time.

Tripe stands (the one in **Piazza Dante** is a favorite) scattered throughout town offer snacks of tripe and the more delicate *lampredotto* (cow's intestine); other places, such as **Luisa** on Via Sant'Antonino, serve salty snacks of fried polenta (cornmeal); pastry shops, including **Cucciolo** on Via del Corso, serve fresh *bomboloni* (deep-fried doughnuts filled with vanilla or chocolate custard or jam).

As soon as you've ordered, start right in on the local wine—Chianti, *naturalmente*. Don't be surprised if the waiter brings an entire bottle or straw-covered flask to the table. You'll be charged only for what you consume (*a consumo*, the arrangement is called), but you may wish to ask for a flask or bottle to be opened then and there, because leftover wines are often mixed. Be prepared to pay a higher price, though, as the only available unopened wine may be of a higher quality.

Chianti Classico, with the black rooster symbol on the neck of the bottle, is the best known and most common type of the various Chianti wines. Some of the other fine local vintages include the robust red Brunello di Montalcino, Carmignano, and Vino Nobile di Montepulciano. Of the whites, the dry Vernaccia di San Gimignano is the traditional choice, though the light Galestro has become increasingly popular in recent years.

36 Porta San Niccolò An imposing three-story medieval tower, built not as a residence but for defense purposes in 1324. ♦ Piazza Giuseppe Poggi (at Pescaia San Niccolò)

37 Trattoria del Granducato ★★$$ The Grand Dukes would have felt right at home in this antiques-furnished trattoria, where the decor dates from the 15th century. Natalia and Gianni's dishes are equally noble, such as *tortellini tartufati* (tortellini stuffed with truffles) and *tortellini fagiano* (stuffed with pheasant). ♦ Tu-Su lunch and dinner. Via di San Niccolò 8r (near Porta San Niccolò). 2345037

38 Il Rifrullo ★★$$ This loungy bar/cafe isn't as trendy as it once was, making it all the more pleasant (particularly when the warm weather arrives and tables are moved out into the garden) for those who find Florentine nightlife a bit of a yawn. Instead, it's settled into the comfortable role of one of the few decent places in town for a late-night drink, ice cream, light sandwich, crepes, or dessert—including some fine renditions of British and American fare. ♦ M-Tu, Th-Su breakfast, lunch, and dinner. Via di San Niccolò 57r (near Porta San Miniato). 2342621

38 Gelateria Frilli All the climbing in this part of town will doubtless make you appreciate the mounds of homemade ice cream the Frilli family produces daily in its little grocery store. Flavors change according to the season, but year-round treats include *caffè* (coffee), *mousse al cioccolato* (chocolate mousse), and *crema* (vanilla custard). An upstairs, outdoor terrace is open in warm weather. ♦ M-Tu, Th-Su. Via San Miniato 5r (at Via di San Niccolò). 2345014

39 Porta di San Miniato A relatively small medieval city gate that for centuries provided passage from Florence to the church of **San Miniato,** these days via the long staircase at the end of the street just outside it. ♦ Connecting Via San Miniato with Via del Monte alle Croci

EnotecaBar 'FuoriPorta' ♀

39 EnotecaBar FuoriPorta The name of this wine bar refers to its location just outside the old city gates, which is particularly enjoyable when tables move outside and you can sip while gazing at the ancient ramparts. The bar sells hundreds of wines by the bottle (from as far afield as Chile and South Africa or as close as the Chianti vineyards), but it is most popular for wines sold by the glass and a wide range of *crostini* or *crostoni* (small or large slabs of toasted bread) served up with a choice of toppings: mushrooms, cheese, cold cuts, vegetables—and toasted. ♦ M-Sa 10:30AM-1AM. Via Monte Alle Croci 10r (at Porta di San Miniato). 2342483

40 La Beppa ★★$$ This homey trattoria offers home-style cooking—if your home is in the Tuscan countryside. Particularly good are the simple first-course soups (*ribollita, pappa al pomodoro*, minestrone). ♦ M-Tu, Th-Su lunch and dinner. Via dell' Erta Canina 6r (near Porta San Miniato off Via del Monte alle Croci). 2342906

Piazzale Michelangiolo

41 Piazzale Michelangiolo *Piazzale* means big piazza, and *Michelangiolo* is a corruption of Michelangelo, to whom this panoramic piazza is dedicated. It could just as easily be dedicated to Cupid, given the amorous Florentines who park their cars in the postcard-perfect scenic overlook of the city, famous for its sunsets that silhouette the cypresses and major monuments and render the Arno golden as it passes beneath a succession of bridges. Michelangelo was originally supposed to be commemorated here with a museum of all his works in Florence brought together under one roof in **La Loggia** (see page 52). As if that idea weren't ill-advised enough, in 1873 architect **Giuseppe Poggi** devised as a monument an odd bronze hybrid of some of Michelangelo's most famous works in Florence—*David* and the sculptures from the Medici tombs—the end result of which some have called a giant paperweight. Under the olive trees to the right of the piazza is an iris garden. The flower, which (originally in a stylized white and later in a red version) became the symbol of Florence, is celebrated in the piazza each May with an international iris show. ♦ At Via del Monte alle Croci and Viale Michelangelo

42 La Loggia ★★$$$ Instead of architect **Giuseppe Poggi**'s originally planned Michelangelo museum, this space is now occupied by a restaurant. At press time new owners had taken over and the menu was undergoing some changes. One thing that won't change though is the unbeatable view—ask for an outdoor table, or a window seat in cooler weather. ♦ M-Tu, Th-Su lunch and dinner. Piazzale Michelangiolo 1 (at Via Michelangelo, south of the piazzale). 2342832

43 Gelateria Michelangiolo If it's hot or if you've hiked all the way up to the piazzale and need some refreshment, have one of the numerous homemade ice creams here, a hangout for young Florentine roadsters, who also appreciate its pinball parlor. ♦ M, W-Su. Viale Galileo Galilei 2r (near Piazzale Michelangiolo). 2342705

44 San Salvatore al Monte Michelangelo called this simple late 15th-century Franciscan church, high on the hills overlooking Florence, "my pretty little country girl." No doubt he appreciated the three windows on the facade, which used alternating triangular and curved pediments (a Roman convention) for the first time in Florence, just as the columns in the simple interior used alternate orders for the first time locally. ♦ Piazza di San Salvatore al Monte (just south of Piazzale Michelangiolo)

45 San Miniato al Monte Florence's most beloved church (and a favorite wedding site) crowns the highest hill in the vicinity and is well worth a detour. It was built circa 1018-1207 on the spot where, according to legend, an early martyr, known in English as Minias, carried his head from the Roman amphitheater across the Arno and up the hill. The geometric green-and-white marble facade (the green is from Prato, the white from Carrara; see drawing above), which ranks with the **Baptistry** among the finest examples of Romanesque architecture in Florence, is embellished with a 13th-century mosaic of Christ and the Virgin and San Miniato above the central window. Inside is a 13th-century mosaiclike marble pavement with signs of the zodiac (considered one of the prettiest of its kind); **Michelozzo**'s 15th-century **Crucifix Chapel;** the 15th-century **Chapel of the Cardinal of Portugal,** with a monument to the cardinal, who died in Florence, by Antonio Rosellino; an Annunciation by Alesso Baldovinetti; angels by Antonio Pollaiuolo; a terra-cotta ceiling by Luca della Robbia; and a pulpit alive with Romanesque animals. In the crypt, along with the *Reliquary Altar of Saint Minias,* are ancient columns and frescoes by Taddeo Gaddi. Benedictine monks sing vespers in Gregorian chant followed by a mass here each day at 4:30PM. The adjoining cemetery offers a remarkable selection of gravestones and tombs, including that of Carlo Lorenzini, a.k.a. Carlo Collodi, author of *Pinocchio.* On the church grounds are **Andrea dei Mozzi**'s 1295 **Palazzo Vescovile,** built for the bishop of Florence as a summer residence; a bell tower, built on a preexisting structure in 1523 by architect **Baccio d'Agnolo** and never finished; and fortifications put up by **Michelangelo** barely in time for the 1529 siege of Florence and finished by **Francesco da Sangallo** and others in 1553. ♦ Daily. Via del Monte alle Croci 34 (off Viale Galileo Galilei, south of Piazzale Michelangiolo)

Santa Maria Novella

Tourism is nothing new to this part of town. As a plaque in **Piazza Santa Maria Novella** states, the area was once called *la Mecca degli stranieri*—the mecca of foreigners. Indeed, as the plaque reads, Henry Wadsworth Longfellow stayed here, as did numerous others. Henry James wrote *Roderick Hudson* in a house on **Via della Scala**. John Ruskin took his inspiration for *Florentine Mornings* from Francesca Alexander, who stayed in a hotel on the piazza. And William Dean Howells, Ralph Waldo Emerson, and Percy Bysshe Shelley all sojourned here as well.

Today the most conspicuous contingent of foreigners is made up of Third World immigrants who congregate in the piazza on weekends. At all times,

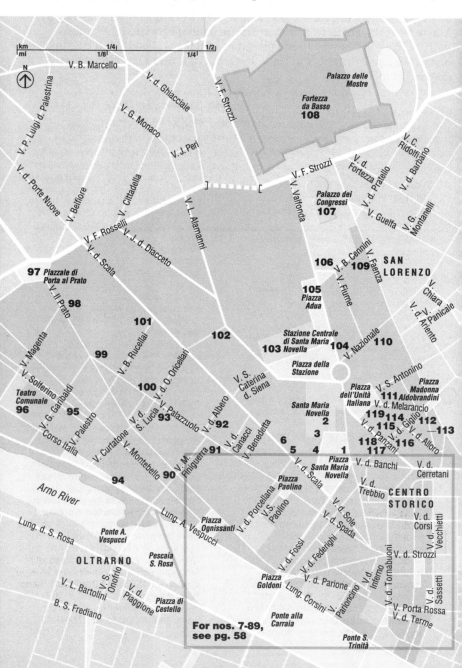

For nos. 7-89, see pg. 58

however, foreigners continually pour out of the nearby train station (a masterpiece of Functionalist architecture), named after the church of **Santa Maria Novella**, to see the sights or attend conferences at the **Palazzo dei Congressi**, the **Palazzo degli Affari**, or the nearby **Forteza da Basso**.

Almost as if deliberately designed to accommodate foreigners, many of the streets are broad avenues. It is no accident that **Via dei Tornabuoni**, Italy's most elegant shopping street, is filled with shops in the best Florentine mercantile tradition. It is the widest and most welcoming (if you can call the somewhat sinister lineup of palazzi welcoming) expanse in the historical part of the city. Almost as wide, if not quite as welcoming because of their barrackslike buildings funneling a barrage of Vespa mopeds and car traffic, are many of the other streets near **Santa Maria Novella**. But at least they are more easily negotiated than most parts of Florence, having been laid out as straight and oddly intersecting, just as the lances intersect in Paolo Uccello's painting *The Battle of San Romano* in the **Uffizi**.

Another aspect of the area seems almost to have been predestined to attract a certain group of foreigners. It is the legacy of its former residents, the Vespucci family, who as merchants and Medici civil servants had a great deal of contact with outsiders. A bridge over the **Arno**, a stretch of street along it, and chapels in the church of the **Ognissanti** were all named after them. And one of its members, Amerigo, gave his name not only to the New World but to the Americans, who continue to return to this part of Florence to their consulate and their church, not to mention to some fine deluxe hotels and **Harry's Bar**.

---

1 Piazza Santa Maria Novella Once used by the Dominicans of the church of **Santa Maria Novella** for preaching to the multitudes, this piazza was later adapted for public spectacles, including jousts and horse races run around the giant obelisks resting on Giambologna's bronze turtles. Today its pervading calm is enlivened at sunset, when the Hitchcockian starlings swoop down into the cypresses in the church cemetery and chatter endlessly into the night. It is the only piazza in town with grass, and it has a few benches where you can sit and take it all in.
♦ Between Via della Scala and Piazza della Stazione

2 Santa Maria Novella In 1246, the town fathers erected the present church on the site of a 10th-century oratory for the dogmatic, inflammatory Dominican preaching order. The colored-marble facade was begun in the 14th century by **Fra Jacopo Talenti**. In 1470, **Leon Battista Alberti**, a true Renaissance man (in addition to being an architect and architectural theorist, he was a painter, scientist, musician, and playwright), finished the Romanesque-Gothic facade (see drawing at right) in Renaissance style, complete with a plug for his patron Giovanni Ruccellai emblazoned in Latin along with the date of completion beneath the pediment. **Alberti** wrote the first Renaissance treatise on architecture (*De re aedificatoria*), and his design for the facade

was the first Renaissance use of his theories of harmonic proportions. The system was remarkably well named; despite the theorizing, the facade remains pleasingly undogmatic, if a bit two-dimensional and Dodge City–like, with what appears to be a false front, like so many Florentine church facades. **Alberti** was the first to use those scroll-like shapes, known as volutes, on either side of the upper portion of the facade. In this case they were meant to mask the nave aisles. Not inappropriately, given Alberti's scientific bent, astronomical instruments were added to the facade in 1572 by the Dominican Egnazio Danti, astronomer to Cosimo I de' Medici. The pointed *pietra forte* bell tower to the left of the facade (attributed to **Fra Jacopo Talenti**) is complemented in visual volume and often

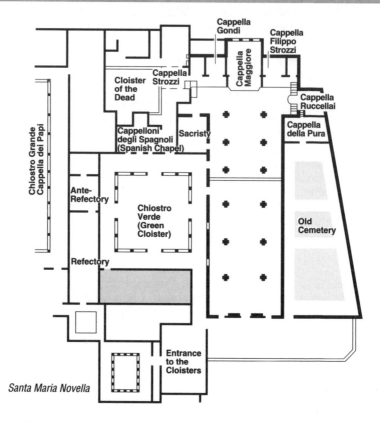

Santa Maria Novella

surpassed in acoustical volume by the starling-filled cypresses above the old cemetery niches to the right, which are called *avelli* and give their name to the short street along the side.

The vast Gothic interior (see floor plan above) was richly decorated in the early Renaissance and later refurbished by **Giorgio Vasari,** who characteristically whitewashed over a number of frescoes. In the second bay on the right aisle is the 15th-century tomb of Beata Villana by Bernardo Rossellino. At the end of the right transept is the **Cappella Ruccellai** (Ruccellai Chapel), which has a 14th-century statue of the Virgin by Nino Pisano and the 15th-century bronze tomb of Leonardo Dati by **Lorenzo Ghiberti.** To the right of the altar is the **Cappella Filippo Strozzi,** with a 15th-century tomb of Filippo Strozzi by Benedetto da Maiano and frescoes from the same period by Filippino Lippi. Boccaccio chose the chapel (before it was given its present embellishment) as the fictitious meeting-place of the young storytellers at the beginning of *The Decameron.* The high altar has a bronze crucifix by Giambologna. Behind it, in the **Cappella Maggiore,** is an important 15th-century fresco cycle by Domenico Ghirlandaio, allegedly depicting the lives of the Virgin and St. John the Baptist, but

actually a delightful document of everyday life in Florence at the time. The **Cappella Gondi** to the left of the high altar, designed by Giuliano da Sangallo in the early 16th century, has a 15th-century crucifix by Brunelleschi, his only work in wood. The **Cappella Strozzi** at the left end of the transept is frescoed with 14th-century scenes of *The Last Judgment, Paradise,* and *Hell* by Nardo di Cione, and has an altarpiece by Orcagna from the same period. Behind it in the sacristy is a 13th-century crucifix by Giotto. Down the left aisle off the entrance, the next-to-last pilaster is adorned with a 15th-century pulpit designed by Brunelleschi and executed by his adopted son, Buggiano. Just behind it is the most popular work in the church, the 15th-century fresco *Holy Trinity with the Virgin, St. John the Evangelist, and Donors* by Masaccio.
♦ Piazza Santa Maria Novella (between Via della Scala and Piazza della Stazione)

3 Chiostri di Santa Maria Novella (Cloisters of Santa Maria Novella) The **Chiostro Verde,** or Green Cloister (circa 1350, **Fra Giovanni Bracchetti** and **Fra Jacopo Talenti**), takes its name from the green tint that predominates in Paolo Uccello's 15th-century masterpiece fresco cycle of the *Universal Deluge* (ironically, it was badly damaged during the 1966 flood), which is as concerned with movement and perspective as his *Battle of San Romano* in the **Uffizi**, but is more charged with emotion. The **Refectory** has a 16th-century *Last Supper* by Alessandro Allori. The **Chiostro Grande** (Great Cloister) is now part of the noncommissioned officers' school of the *carabinieri* (police) and is closed to the public. Still, the guards sometimes honor a visitor's request to see the cloister's **Cappella dei Papi** (Chapel of the Popes), frescoed in the 16th century by Jacopo Pontormo and Ridolfo del Ghirlandaio. The **Cappelloni degli Spagnoli** (Spanish Chapel, so called because Eleanor of Toledo, wife of Cosimo I de' Medici, gave her fellow Spaniards burial privileges there) is completely covered with 14th-century frescoes by Andrea da Firenze glorifying the Dominican order founded by the Spaniard St. Dominic. Note the symbolic pooches (*domini cane*, Latin for "dogs of God," is a play on the name of the order) and the famous Dominican saints Dominic, Thomas Aquinas, and Peter Martyr (all of whom preached at **Santa Maria Novella**) refuting heretics. ♦ Admission. M-Th, Sa-Su. Piazza Santa Maria Novella (between Via della Scala and Piazza della Stazione). 282187

4 Grand Hotel Minerva $$$ The unassuming facade conceals a pleasant, recently renovated hotel, many of whose 100 rooms have views of **Piazza Santa Maria Novella** or the church cloisters. Other amenities include the **Sala Garden** restaurant serving Tuscan and international food and overlooking a quiet private garden, and a small rooftop swimming pool for those who want to cool off amid a sea of terra-cotta roofs and Florentine monuments. ♦ Piazza Santa Maria Novella 16 (near Via della Scala). 284555; fax 268281

5 Aprile $$ In a palazzo once owned by the Medici, complete with faded traces of frescoes, high vaulted ceilings, and a small breakfast courtyard, this 30-room hotel has a graceful air of antiquity. Rooms are kept simple (not all have air-conditioning or color TV) and all have private baths. Some have a limited view of the **Piazza Santa Maria Novella.** There is no restaurant. ♦ Via della Scala 6 (at Via della Porcellana). 2162371; fax 280947

6 Officina Profumo-Farmaceutica di Santa Maria Novella This centuries-old *erboristeria* (herbalists' shop) was opened to the public in 1612 by Dominican monks from the church of **Santa Maria Novella**, who prepared medicinals for local hospitals and clients such as Catherine de' Medici. Today the tradition continues with all sorts of exotic products, such as handmade soaps, skin creams, shampoos, liqueurs (the Medici's own is still sold as *liquore mediceo*), and pungent smelling salts called *aceto dei sette*

ladri ("seven thieves' vinegar," from the plague days when corpse robbers, each knowing one of its secret ingredients, used it to protect themselves on their gruesome rounds). The monks are gone, but the knockout Neo-Gothic salesroom is presided over with Dominican astringency by the white-coated high priests and priestesses of Florentine *erboristerie*. ♦ M-F, Sa morning Mar-Oct; M afternoon, Tu-Sa Nov-Feb. Via della Scala 16 (near Via della Porcellana off Piazza Santa Maria Novella). 216276

7 Hotel Croce di Malta $$$ This pleasant 98-room hotel in a former convent conserves a feeling of privacy and simplicity in its understated and serene decor, with a touch of modernity in the small plunge swimming pool located in a shady, tranquil garden. Its restaurant, **Il Cocodrillo**, has a Tuscan and international menu. ♦ Via della Scala 7 (between Piazza Santa Maria Novella and Via della Porcellana). 218351, 282600; fax 287121

8 Loggia di San Paolo Fronting the **Hospital of San Paolo**, this late 15th-century loggia was built in the style of **Brunelleschi**'s loggia for the **Hospital of the Innocenti** in **Piazza Santissima Annunziata.** Its medallions, by Luca and Andrea della Robbia, depict saints and include a lunette by Andrea illustrating *The Meeting of St. Francis and St. Dominic,* which supposedly took place in the hospital. **Il Quadrifoglio,** a florist in a former chapel of the loggia (No. 9-B, 283010), sells little sachets of long-lasting Florentine lavender, which make lovely gifts or souvenirs. ♦ Piazza Santa Maria Novella (at Via della Scala)

9 Hotel Roma $$$ A major restoration of this 16th-century palazzo brought this hotel into the 21st century with modern-day comforts amidst stained-glass windows, frescoed ceilings, and inlaid marble floors. Many of the 51 simply furnished rooms overlook the piazza and church of **Santa Maria Novella.** ♦ Piazza Santa Maria Novella 8 (at Via del Sole). 210366; fax 215306

The prized symbol of Florence since ancient times is referred to as *il giglio* (the lily) when it is, in fact, an iris. The Florentine iris (chosen because of the pale blue irises that continue to grow wild throughout Tuscany) is often mistaken for the similar French fleur-di-lis symbol which does appear, to add to the confusion, on the shield of Florence's powerful Medici family. This was because the privilege of displaying the French symbol was granted to Cosimo the Elder, grandfather of Lorenzo il Magnifico, for his role in maintaining a steadfast political alliance between France and Florence.

Restaurants/Clubs: Red **Hotels:** Blue
Shops/ ♦ Outdoors: Green **Sights/Culture:** Black

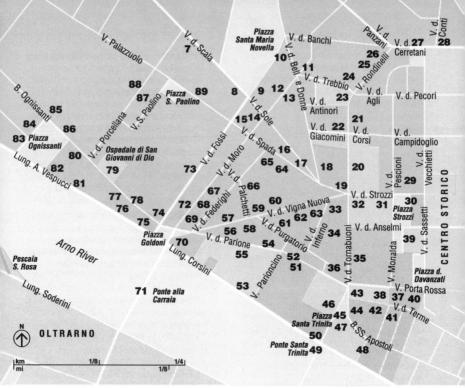

10 Palazzo Pitti Luca Pitti lived in this relatively humble palazzo (renovated in 1994) before his family went bankrupt building their more famous digs across the river. A plaque on the facade recalls Giuseppe Garibaldi's sojourn when it was a hotel in 1867. Here the unifier of Italy stirred the crowds with the words, "Rome or die." While not in keeping with the piazza's tradition as a mecca for foreigners, the speech was in line with the great Dominican preachers who once filled the piazza. ♦ Piazza Santa Maria Novella 21 (near Via delle Belle Donne)

11 Croce al Trebbio In 1308, this cross was erected at the intersection of three narrow streets (now five) where Dominicans inflamed by the preaching of St. Peter Martyr at nearby **Santa Maria Novella** battled heathen heretics. ♦ Via del Moro (at Via delle Belle Donne)

12 Latteria/Bar Ponticelli This *latteria* (dairy shop) is one of the few places open on Sunday for a limited selection of last-minute grocery items and wine. ♦ M, W-Su. Via del Moro 61r (at Via delle Belle Donne). 216903

Under Cosimo I (16th century), Jewish men were forced to wear a yellow badge on their hats and the women the same ornament on the sleeves of their coats or dresses. Their business privileges were curtailed and they were forbidden to deal in the wholesale market or in art objects. It was Cosimo who first confined Florentine Jews to the Old Market area where the Piazza della Repubblica now stands.

13 Franco Maria Ricci This small publishing house is the very definition of esoteric, with book titles such as *Lost Florence, Ertè,* and *Casanova.* ♦ M-F, Sa morning Mar-Oct; M afternoon, Tu-Sa Nov-Feb. Via delle Belle Donne 41r (at Via del Moro). 283312

14 Cellerini Silvano Cellerini, one of Florence's master leather craftsmen, prides himself on his original creations. In his shop you'll find exquisitely handmade handbags, wallets, and suitcases, as well as a limited selection of men's and women's shoes and a collection of Hermès look-alikes. ♦ M-F, Sa morning Mar-Oct; M afternoon, Tu-Sa Nov-Feb. Via del Sole 37r (at Via del Moro). 282533

15 Buca Mario ★★$$ This downstairs restaurant draws largely a tourist crowd, but if you're comfortable in such surroundings, try the reliable versions of Tuscan soups and *bistecca alla fiorentina* (a slab of steak grilled with olive oil). ♦ M-Tu, F-Su lunch and dinner; Th dinner. Piazza degli Ottaviani 16 (south of Piazza Santa Maria Novella). 214179

16 Rafanelli The Bronze Age is going strong at the showroom of master *bronzisti* (bronze workers) Enzo and Renato Rafanelli, whose workshop is in the artisans' quarter across the river. Bedsteads, fireguards, doorknobs, knockers, and other handcrafted bronze and copper objects are the dazzling inventory of this unusual shop. ♦ M-F, Sa morning Mar-Oct; M afternoon, Tu-Sa Nov-Feb. Via del Sole 7r (between Via della Spada and Via del Moro). 283518

17 Ideabooks Here you'll find a nice selection of art, photography, design, and fashion books, as well as posters and postcards, in a light and lively contemporary bookstore, whose official name is **Assolibri.** An archaic municipal law won't let them remove the old neon sign outside! ♦ M-F, Sa morning Mar-Oct; M afternoon, Tu-Sa Nov-Feb. Via del Sole 3r (Via Via della Spada and Via del Moro). 284533

18 Belle Donne ★★$$ The name is not visible from the outside, but this hole-in-the-wall eatery is named after its street, which translates "beautiful women," hinting at its shady past. The restaurant is popular with younger professionals who stop in for a light lunch of soup and salad, or more innovative dinners, eaten communally and followed by some of the best desserts in town. ♦ M-Sa lunch and dinner. Via delle Belle Donne 16 (off Via della Spada). 262609

19 Giacosa Count Camille Negroni invented the Negroni cocktail (one-third Campari bitter, one-third Martini & Rossi sweet vermouth, and one-third gin) here in the 1920s. Today this elegant cafe attracts an upscale crowd of young Florentines for cocktails, coffee, tea, and snacks at the bar or the tiny tables. ♦ M-Sa 7:30AM-8:30PM. No credit cards accepted. Via dei Tornabuoni 83 (at Via della Spada). 2396226

20 Palazzo Corsi This rambling palazzo, built in the 19th century to a design by **Telemaco Bonaiuti,** replaced a 15th-century palazzo by **Michelozzo,** whose courtyard stands invitingly intact within. ♦ Via dei Tornabuoni 76 (between Via del Strozzi and Piazza Antinori)

Within Palazzo Corsi:

Seeber Florence's oldest and most respected bookshop (founded in 1865) is one of the few in town staffed by actual bibliophiles; it is especially good for books on Florentine and Tuscan subjects, many of which are in English. ♦ M-Sa. Via dei Tornabuoni 70r (between Via del Strozzi and Piazza Antinori). 215697

Procacci Since 1885, this family-run stand-up snack emporium has been famed for its *panini tartufati* (truffle sandwiches). It also offers delicate concoctions made with salmon, anchovies, and cheese, served with local wines and fresh-pressed tomato juice. Chianti wines and vinegars, as well as limited-edition balsamic vinegar from Modena, are also available for purchase as gifts or souvenirs. ♦ M-F, Sa morning Mar-Oct; M afternoon, Tu-Sa Nov-Feb. No credit cards accepted. Via dei Tornabuoni 64r (between Via del Strozzi and Piazza Antinori). 211656

21 San Gaetano Though originally erected in the 11th century, this church has the truest-to-form of Florence's few Baroque church facades—the 17th-century work of **Matteo Nigetti, Gherardo Silvani,** and **Pier Francesco Silvani**—complete with billowy statues and imposing coats of arms (Medici, of course). Among the works of art within are *The Martyrdom of St. Lorenzo* by Pietro da Cortona and *Crucifix with Saints Mary Magdalene, Francis, and Jerome* by Filippo Lippi. Unfortunately, it has been closed to the public for years with no reopening in sight. ♦ Piazza Antinori (at Via degli Agli)

22 Hotel de la Ville $$$$ A handsome hotel in a stylish location, this top establishment is quiet and discreet, with an intimate after-hours bar that closes at 1AM. Most desirable for its Via dei Tornabuoni address, the hotel has 75 totally renovated rooms. ♦ Piazza Antinori 1 (at Via degli Antinori). 261805; fax 2381809

23 Palazzo Antinori This rustic 15th-century palazzo by **Giuliano da Maiano** is now the property of the Marchesi Antinori, known internationally for their wines. In the lovely porticoed courtyard is the **Cantinetta Antinori,** where, Monday through Friday, you can sample those vintages along with a light meal of soup or salad at lunch, or with more substantial Florentine fare at dinnertime. ♦ M-F. Piazza Antinori 3 (at Via degli Antinori). 292234

23 Pomellato A rarefied setting, replete with frescoed ceilings, is indicative of the guaranteed top-of-the-line quality and prices of Via dei Tornabuoni's jewelry stores. A newcomer to Florence, but for years a household name in Milan, this shop follows the spirit and fashion of the times, yet is classic enough to resist the ephemeral tides of trends. ♦ M-F, Sa morning Mar-Oct; M afternoon, Tu-Sa Nov-Feb. Piazza Antinori 8-9r (at Via degli Antinori). 213200

23 Buca Lapi ★★$$ This restaurant is located downstairs on the north side of the **Palazzo Antinori.** *Buca* is a typically self-deprecating restaurant name meaning hole. This one, founded in 1880 and papered with faded travel posters, prides itself on its *bistecca* *alla fiorentina* and its various preparations of artichokes. ♦ M dinner; Tu-Sa lunch and dinner. Via del Trebbio 1r (between Piazza Antinori and Via del Moro). 213768

23 Loretta Caponi Exquisite hand embroidery is the forte of this well-known designer, whose creations embellish aristocratic kitchens, presidential dining rooms, sumptuous baths, and bedrooms. These dramatic new quarters deservingly showcase her handmade creations under 19th-century frescoes (one of the two adjoining palazzi dates back to the 13th century), and additional space allows for the display of her special collections for infants and children, men's lounge- and sleepwear, and matchless women's lingerie. ♦ M-F, Sa morning Mar-Oct; M afternoon, Tu-Sa Nov-Feb. Piazza Antinori 4r (at Via degli Antinori). 213668

24 Il Tricolore The *tricolore* refers to the three colors of the Italian flag, and true to its name, this patriotic boutique sells Italian military and police uniforms and accessories. Much more chic than most such gear, the merchandise ranges from the plumed hats of the *bersaglieri* corps to a selection of artfully designed pins and medals, and Italian military watches. ♦ M-F, Sa morning Mar-Oct; M afternoon, Tu-Sa Nov-Feb. Via del Trebbio 4r (between Piazza Antinori and Via del Moro). 210166

24 Grandi Firme This new store's name refers to the "big names" whose fashion for men and women are heavily discounted here. Big names carry big prices even when discounted, so don't expect any "giveaway" bargains. But the merchandise is current, rarely damaged, and nicely displayed. The arrivals are erratic—you might happen upon a Valentino—but more probably the likes of Versace, Moschino, Thierry Mugler, or Montana. In all, it's a bargain hunter's paradise. ♦ M afternoon; Tu-Sa. Via del Trebbio 10 (between Piazza Antinori and Via del Moro). 2381527

25 Richard Ginori The Ginori line of porcelain began in the 18th century, merging in 1896 with the Milanese ceramic firm, Richard, to create the present partnership, the most famous porcelain manufacturer in Florence, indeed in Italy. Over the years this firm has become a veritable household name in the US. Most of its current production is based on historical patterns; other internationally known names such as Waterford and Lalique are on sale as well. ♦ M-F, Sa morning Mar-Oct; M afternoon, Tu-Sa Nov-Feb. Via Rondinelli 17 (between Piazza Antinori and Via de' Panzani). 210041

26 Bojola Walking sticks, umbrellas, bags, and luggage are manufactured with an eye to modern style by this Florentine institution, over a century old. ♦ M-F, Sa morning Mar-Oct; M afternoon, Tu-Sa Nov-Feb. Via Rondinelli 25r (at Via de' Panzani). 211155

27 Hotel Sofitel $$$$ Opened in 1992, this 82-room hotel (a cool and calm oasis, despite its main-drag address) was immediately popular for its unbeatable location and clean, contemporary design. The **Il Patio** restaurant offers a full American breakfast as well as other meals. Many amenities usually associated with five-star luxury are offered, but if you're looking for European charm, you won't want to hang your hat here. ♦ Via dei Cerretani 10 (near Via dei Conti). 2381301, 800/221.4542 in US; fax 2381312

28 Feltrinelli This is Florence's first megabookstore, the largest of its kind in Tuscany. If they don't have it (there's a good chance they will) they'll place a special order for you and ship it anywhere in the world. Foreign visitors will appreciate the architecture, art, and history departments; fully stocked travel section with guidebooks for all destinations; and wide selection of English-language fiction and nonfiction. The ambience is one of friendly browsing beneath 19th-century frescoes and industrial lighting; the schedule is "no-stop," making this a great place to spend an air-conditioned lunch hour when the city shuts down. ♦ M-Sa (no midday closing). Via dei Cerretani 30/32r (between Piazza Duomo and Via dei Conti). 2382652

29 Hotel Helvetia & Bristol $$$$ This stately 19th-century hotel (where Gabriele D'Annunzio, Igor Stravinsky, Luigi Pirandello, and Giorgio De Chirico, among others, stayed) is rich in character and remains one of Florence's—and Italy's—finest hotels. Paintings and antiques give the public and guest rooms individual character. The **Giardino d'Inverno** restaurant is a bright, airy space for breakfast, lunch, or snacks. ♦ Via dei Pescioni 2 (at Via degli Strozzi). 287814; fax 288353

Restaurants/Clubs: Red   **Hotels:** Blue
Shops/ ♥ Outdoors: Green   **Sights/Culture:** Black

Within Hotel Helvetia & Bristol:

The Bristol ★★$$$ This elegant restaurant produces equally elegant versions of local classics such as *piccione alle olive nere* (squab with black olives) and *baccalà alla livornese* (dried cod with a spicy tomato sauce), as well as other simple albeit sophisticated Tuscan classics. ◆ Daily dinner. 287814

di FIRENZE

30 Principe One of the top clothing stores in Florence, this large emporium specializes in Italian imitations of classic English fashion for men, women, and children; it is also the exclusive agent for Missoni knitwear. ◆ M-F, Sa morning Mar-Oct; M afternoon, Tu-Sa Nov-Feb. No midday closing. Via degli Strozzi 21-29r (in Piazza Strozzi). 292764

31 Palazzo Strozzi Florence's most beautiful Renaissance palazzo was begun in 1489 as the private residence of merchant Filippo Strozzi, and construction (under architect **Benedetto da Maiano**) continued intermittently as the family was exiled. Though work was completed in 1504 under **Cronaca** and **Jacopo Rosselli,** the great cornice atop the heavily rusticated building was never finished, as can be seen from the Via degli Strozzi side. The palazzo now houses a number of organizations (such as the Gabinetto Vieusseux, a private library and reading room) and is used for exhibitions. The most prestigious of these is the *Mostra-Mercato Internazionale dell'Antiquariato,* an international antiques biennial held in September on odd years. A fire at an antiques fair in Todi occasioned the hideous practicality of the fire stairs in the otherwise harmonious courtyard. ◆ Piazza Strozzi (at Via degli Strozzi)

32 La Residenza $$ This charming 24-room hotel reflects the personality of the deep-voiced *signora* who oversees a multilingual staff and a good kitchen, should you choose to elect the old *pensione* or meal option (strongly encouraged during high season). Some of the top-floor rooms have balconies overlooking Via dei Tornabuoni; all guests can enjoy intimate glimpses of the *centro storico* from the third-floor lounge and of Via dei Tornabuoni from the roof garden. ◆ Via dei Tornabuoni 8 (between Via degli Anselmi and Via degli Strozzi). 284197; fax 284197

33 Gucci The world's most famous fashion statement started right here in the firm's flagship store, where the full line of loafers, scarves, bags, luggage, and men's and women's clothing are displayed before the admiring eyes of status-conscious shoppers and the famously condescending raised eyebrows of the sales help. ◆ M-F, Sa morning Mar-Oct; M afternoon, Tu-Sa Nov-Feb. Via dei Tornabuoni 73r (between Via del Parione and Via della Vigna Nuova). 264011.

33 Mario Buccellati The Florence branch of this Milanese designer, whose talents were praised in the poetry of Gabriele D'Annunzio, is still known for delicately handcrafted jewelry and sterling silver objects. ◆ M-F, Sa morning Mar-Oct; M afternoon, Tu-Sa Nov-Feb. Via dei Tornabuoni 71r (between Via del Parione and Via della Vigna Nuova). 2396579

34 Tanino Crisci This family-run business has been crafting fine classic footwear for the well-heeled of both sexes for three generations. ◆ M-F, Sa morning Mar-Oct; M afternoon, Tu-Sa Nov-Feb. Via dei Tornabuoni 43-45r (between Via del Parione and Via della Vigna Nuova). 214692

34 Casadei The hallmark of this elegant women's shoe store is that many of its heels stand proudly high in spite of the highs and lows of trends in footwear. ◆ M-F, Sa morning Mar-Oct; M afternoon, Tu-Sa Nov-Feb. Via dei Tornabuoni 33r (between Via del Parione and Via della Vigna Nuova). 287240

35 Ugolini The firm that once gloved the hands of the Italian royal family continues to provide high-quality merchandise in all types of leather for all types of clients, provided they can afford the price that once obliged the noblesse. ◆ M-F, Sa morning Mar-Oct; M afternoon, Tu-Sa Nov-Feb. Via dei Tornabuoni 20-22r (between Via del Parione and Via della Vigna Nuova). 216664

36 Beacci Tornabuoni $$ This charming former *pensione* (much improved by a recent renovation) on the top three floors of a 15th-century palazzo is decorated like a house in the Tuscan countryside. It's just as welcoming, and the roof garden is just as sunny. A clientele of regulars makes it necessary to reserve well in advance. ♦ Via dei Tornabuoni 3 (near Via del Parione). 212645; fax 283594

36 Faraone-Settepassi Florence's oldest jewelry store (today owned by Tiffany's), transplanted from the **Ponte Vecchio**, has been known since the time of the Medici as the most exclusive such enterprise in town. Diamonds, rubies, emeralds, and silver all glitter here; in addition, its jewelers are the only ones in Italy to use Oriental pearls. ♦ M-F, Sa morning Mar-Oct; M afternoon, Tu-Sa Nov-Feb. Via dei Tornabuoni 25r (at Via del Parione). 215506

37 Hotel Porta Rossa $$ The decadent setting of smoked glass and antique furnishings draws a like crowd of English and French. Its 81 rooms are cavernous, perfect for large families, but they're in need of refreshing. Part of the **Palazzo Bartolini Salimbeni,** its history as a hotel dates back to the 14th century. ♦ Via Porta Rossa 19 (between Via dei Sassetti and Via dei Tornabuoni). 287551; fax 282179

38 La Bussola ★$$ One of the nicest things about this comfortably modern-looking restaurant is that it's the only place in the center of town open until the wee hour of 2AM. Such dishes as *spaghetti allo scoglio* (made with a fresh seafood sauce) and the grilled meats almost make it worth staying up late. ♦ Tu-Su lunch and dinner. Via Porta Rossa 58r (between Piazza dei Davanzati and Via dei Tornabuoni). 293376

39 Palazzo dello Strozzino Filippo Strozzi lived in this palazzo (begun 1458 by **Michelozzo** and completed by **Giuliano da Maiano** in 1462-65) while overseeing construction of his big place across the piazza. Its three "layers," or stories, were built in three periods and styles. ♦ Piazza Strozzi 2 (at Via Monalda)

40 Museo dell'Antica Casa Fiorentina (Florentine House Museum) The 14th-century medieval **Palazzo Davanzati** houses displays of everyday objects used in Florence from the Gothic to the Renaissance periods. From the small courtyard, an elegant staircase leads upstairs to numerous Madonnas (including Lorenzo Monaco's *Madonna and Child with Saints*), textiles, tapestries, chests, and other furniture and decorations evocative of the domestic life of the wealthy Florentine merchant class. ♦ Admission. Tu-Su. Via Porta Rossa 13 (at Piazza dei Davanzati). 2388608

41 Casa-Torre dei Buondelmonti This 13th-century medieval tower belonged to the Buondelmonti family, whose scion's fickleness touched off the Guelph-Ghibelline conflicts in Tuscany. Its street, Via delle Terme, preserves some of the aspects it had in the Middle Ages, when it was a mini-Manhattan bursting with towers for that "riv vw" of the Arno, as an apartment listing in *The New York Times* would say. ♦ Via delle Terme 13r (at Chiasso delle Misure)

Oliviero

42 Oliviero ★★★$$$ This elegant restaurant offers both well-prepared Tuscan specialties and more creative dishes in a comfortably elegant, toney atmosphere. Piano music, top-notch service, banquettes, and candlelight create an appropriate backdrop for a special evening. The kitchen is directed by Francesco Altomare, who is largely responsible for the continuing fame of this historical restaurant frequented by a global Who's Who. Even such classic dishes as *minestra di farro* (a barleylike soup) and *risotto di zucca gialla* (risotto with pumpkin) are given special and delicate interpretation. Among the entrées you'll also find some of the city's finest fresh fish preparations. Accompany your choice with a selection from the impressive wine collection. ♦ M-Sa lunch and dinner. Reservations required for lunch, suggested for dinner. Via delle Terme 51r (off Via Tornabuoni). 287643

42 Al Lume di Candela ★★$$$ A romantic, candlelit atmosphere for a pricey dinner for two, with a menu based on seasonal ingredients, including some of the freshest fish in town. ♦ M dinner, Tu-Sa lunch and dinner. Reservations required for lunch, suggested for dinner. Via delle Terme 23 (off Via Por Santa Maria). 294566

43 Palazzo Bartolini Salimbeni This 16th-century palazzo by **Baccio d'Agnolo,** was the first in Florence to embody the principles of the High Renaissance used by Raphael and **Bramante** in Rome. The palazzo was initially criticized for looking more like a church than a residence (note the cross-shaped window sashes). The Salimbeni family motto, "Per Non Dormire" (not to sleep—they were no slouches, it seems), and its counterpoint, poppies, appear throughout the palazzo. The small courtyard is decorated with ebullient sgraffiti, the two-tone designs drawn in stucco on many Renaissance palazzi. ♦ Piazza Santa Trinita 1 (at Via Porta Rossa)

44 La Nandina ★★$$ One of Florence's oldest restaurants has changed hands only twice in the last hundred years. In addition to an international menu, there are daily Tuscan specials and such staples as *ricotta arrostita* (baked ricotta cheese) and *gallina in odori* (chicken stewed in basil, tomato, and other herbs). There is a huge antipasto table. ◆ M-Sa lunch and dinner. Borgo Santissimi Apostoli 64r (at Via dei Tornabuoni). 213024

45 Colonna della Giustizia This ancient granite "column of justice," taken from the Baths of Caracalla in Rome, was given to Cosimo I de' Medici by Pope Pius IV after Medici forces had won the battle of Montemurlo (1537) and established the family's absolute power. The statue on top (1581) is by Francesco del Tadda. ◆ Piazza Santa Trinita (at Via dei Tornabuoni)

46 Santa Trinita This Gothic church, dating from the 11th century, was rebuilt in the 14th century (possibly by **Neri di Fioravante**). Behind its Renaissance facade (erected in 1593-94 by **Bernardo Buontalenti**) are a number of important 15th-century works of art. In the fourth chapel along the right aisle are an altarpiece and frescoes by Lorenzo Monaco. The **Cappella Sassetti** (Sassetti Chapel), in the right transept, has frescoes of *The Life of St. Francis* and *The Adoration of the Shepherds* by Domenico Ghirlandaio, filled with rich scenes of 15th-century Florence, including portraits of *Lorenzo the Magnificent* and his sons Piero, Giovanni, and Giuliano (to the right, in front of the Piazza della Signoria). The second chapel in the left transept contains the tomb of Bishop Benozzo Federighi by Luca della Robbia, and in the left aisle is a wooden statue of *Mary Magdalene* by Desiderio da Settignano. ◆ Piazza Santa Trinita (at Via del Parione)

47 Palazzo Spini-Ferroni Built as the residence of a family of wool merchants in 1289, this greatest of the medieval palazzi in Florence today houses the shops and offices of their contemporary counterparts. ◆ Piazza Santa Trinita 2 (at Borgo Santissimi Apostoli)

Within Palazzo Spini-Ferroni:

Salvatore Ferragamo This is the flagship store of the famous family-run shoe firm begun by Naples-born Salvatore Ferragamo, who came to Florence after a stint in Hollywood, where he became known as "shoemaker to the stars" by shoeing the feet of the likes of Mary Pickford and Douglas Fairbanks. Ever since, Americans have appreciated his family's understanding of their podiatric peculiarities. The rest of the body can also be clad in equally exquisite Ferragamo clothing and accessories, including silk scarves and ties. ◆ M-F, Sa morning Mar-Oct; M afternoon, Tu-Sa Nov-Feb. Via dei Tornabuoni 16r (at Borgo Santissimi Apostoli). 292123

47 Museo Salvatore Ferragamo In response to the worldwide success of a traveling exhibit of the designer's choicest creations, the Ferragamo family recently opened this museum showcasing the history of shoes and their company. Also featured is a research center, library, and archives. ◆ M, W, F; closed 23 December-6 January. Visits by appointment only. Via dei Tornabuoni 2 (at Borgo Santissimi Apostoli). 3360456

48 Hotel Berchielli $$$ Don't be put off by this hotel's lobby, a Postmodern apotheosis of polished marble. The 80 rooms upstairs are quieter in all senses (all of them are sound-proofed) and many have views of the Arno. All rooms are air-conditioned and have televisions and mini-bars. There is no restaurant. ◆ Piazza del Limbo 6r (on Borgo Santissimi Apostoli; there is another entrance at Lungarno Acciaiuoli 14). 264061; fax 218636

49 Ponte Santa Trinita Graceful curves make this the most beautiful bridge in Florence, maybe even the world. Designed by **Bartolommeo Ammannati** in the 16th century using the curves from Michelangelo's tombs in the **Cappelle Medicee**, it was built of stone from the **Boboli Gardens.** The bridge was blown up during the German retreat at the end of World War II, and has been painstakingly reconstructed from as many of the original pieces as could be salvaged and from new stone taken from the original quarry, using the original plans and 16th-century stonecutting tools. The original statues at either end represent the four seasons, the head of Spring having been retrieved from the river only in 1961 and replaced with great fanfare. ◆ Between Piazza Santa Trinita and Piazza Frescobaldi

50 Caffè Tornabuoni ★★$$$ If you'll take Manhattan—or a Black Russian or Singapore Sling—this is the most tasteful and relaxing ambience in which to do so. Appealing to an upscale, discerning clientele that prefers popping in here rather than in the nearby **Harry's Bar,** this cafe–piano-bar–restaurant offers it all; from light (or not) meals to perhaps just tea and live jazz piano music every evening after 9PM. The polylingual barman-and-hostess team of Luigi and Trudy Brizzi has created a welcoming respite from culture overload and marathon shopping. ◆ Tu-Su 11AM-2AM lunch, dinner, and late-night meals. Lungarno Corsini 12-14r (between Piazza San Trinita and Via Parioncino). 210751

51 Chiostro del Convento di Santa Trinita (Cloister of the Convent of the Holy Trinity) This former cloister, constructed in 1584 by **Alfonso Parigi** to designs by

Bernardo Buontalenti, is now occupied by the **University of Florence Law School.** In the refectory are 17th-century frescoes of *The Story of Christ* by Giovanni da San Giovanni and Nicodemo Ferrucci. ♦ Via del Parione 7 (between Via dei Tornabuoni and Via del Parioncino)

Within the Chiostro del Convento di Santa Trinita:

Alimentari Orizi There's something comfortably down-to-earth about Mariano's invitingly simple downstairs grocery store in a neighborhood of lavish shops, whether it's the barrel seats at the side counter, or the lunch itself, which consists of sandwiches made to order out of such cheeses as mozzarella and *stracchino* and such cold cuts as *prosciutto crudo* (cured) or *cotto* (baked) and *bresaola* (dried salted beef). ♦ M-Tu, Th-Su; W morning. No credit cards accepted. Via del Parione 19r (between Via dei Tornabuoni and Via del Parioncino). 214067

52 Il Barretto This night spot, popular with Florence's older professionals, offers light piano music in dark-wood surroundings. ♦ M-Sa 6PM-2AM. Via del Parione 50 (off Via dei Tornabuoni). 2394122

52 Coco Lezzone ★★★$$ Though the name of this small restaurant is Florentine dialect for big, smelly cook, the food is great and aromatic in nothing but a positive sense. The sight of well-heeled Florentines and foreigners packed into the simple white-tile surroundings of this much-frequented restaurant is an amusing lesson in radical chic eating. Tuscan specialties (the full range of peasant soups, roast meats accompanied by cannellini beans or cooked or fresh vegetables, pecorino cheese, and an extensive selection of Chianti wines) predominate. ♦ M, W-Sa lunch and dinner; Tu lunch. Via del Parioncino 26r (between Via del Parione and Via del Purgatorio). 287178

53 Palazzo Corsini A bit of the Baroque adorns the Renaissance underpinnings of this palazzo, built in the 17th century by **Pier Francesco Silvani** and **Antonio Maria Ferri,** the grandest of the many palazzi associated with the Corsini family in Florence. Its balustrades and statuary are not quite as buoyant and ecstatic as their Roman counterparts would be, but even the Corsinis, it seems, felt obliged to make concessions to Florentine parsimony. ♦ Lungarno Corsini 10 (near Via dei Parioncino)

54 Silvio ★★$$ Typical Tuscan dishes such as *ribollita* and roast meats make this small restaurant a neighborhood favorite. ♦ M-Sa lunch and dinner. Via del Parione 74r (between Via del Parioncino and Piazza Goldoni). 214005

55 Galleria Corsini Here you'll find the greatest private art collection in Florence, put together by Lorenzo Corsini (nephew of Pope Clement XII—the family has produced a number of religious figures, including a saint), whose idiosyncratic arrangement (à la **Palazzo Pitti**) includes important works by Antonello da Messina, Pontormo, Signorelli, and Raphael. ♦ Admission. By appointment only. Call at least 10 days in advance. Via del Parione 11 (between Via del Parioncino and Piazza Goldoni). 211976

55 Il Bisonte Tanned, undyed leather in casual designs was once the hallmark of this shop, which has since added an array of bright colors as well as sheepskin jackets and coats. ♦ M-F, Sa morning Mar-Oct; M afternoon, Tu-Sa Nov-Feb. Via del Parione 31r (between Via del Parioncino and Piazza Goldoni). 215722

55 Bazzanti If you've ever harbored a perverse Pygmalion-like desire to appreciate a statue for more than strictly aesthetic reasons, now is your chance. This shop sells high-quality replicas of the world's most famous sculpture. While the prices are considerably higher than picture postcards, it's still less of an investment than breaking into the **Bargello.** ♦ M-F, Sa morning Mar-Oct; M afternoon, Tu-Sa Nov-Feb. Via del Parione 37-39r (between Via del Parioncino and Piazza Goldoni; other entrance at Lungarno Corsini 44-46-48r). 215649

56 Emilio Pucci This tiny store, dedicated to the timeless technicolor fabrics of the late Marchese Emilio Pucci, displays the designer's geometric patterns in the signature colors first shown in 1950. The **Palazzi Pucci,** owned by his family for centuries and housing his offices and a store that sells his family's Chianti products, is located at Via de' Pucci 6. ♦ M-F, Sa morning Mar-Oct; M afternoon, Tu-Sa Nov-Feb. Via della Vigna Nuova 97r (near Piazza Goldoni). 294028

57 Minetta Here you'll find the best selection of hosiery for women in Florence—every color, pattern, and fabric imaginable. ♦ M-F, Sa morning Mar-Oct; M afternoon, Tu-Sa Nov-Feb. Via della Vigna Nuova 70r (between Via dei Palchetti and Piazza Goldoni). 287984

58 Caffè Amerini ★★$$ This comfortable, Postmodern-looking cafe attracts a like crowd of chic shoppers and equally chic shop clerks. A great place for a quick sandwich at lunch, it

---

Restaurants/Clubs: Red   **Hotels:** Blue
Shops/ 🌳 Outdoors: Green   **Sights/Culture:** Black

becomes something of a tearoom in the afternoon, offering dozens of brews and tasty pastries. ♦ M-Sa. Via della Vigna Nuova 63r (at Via Palchetti). 284941

58 Ermenegildo Zegna This elite menswear manufacturing firm, known for its luxurious fabrics and stylishly conservative tailoring, offers what Italians call the "total look," that is, everything from top to toe. ♦ M-F, Sa morning Mar-Oct; M afternoon, Tu-Sa Nov-Feb. Piazza Rucellai 4-7r (on Via della Vigna Nuova at Via del Purgatorio). 283011

58 Desmo A front-runner in high-quality, high-fashion leather manufacturing, this boutique carries bags in strong, bright colors and materials ranging from fine calfskin and stamped leather to trendy nylon. Women's bags are the highlight, but it's worth a visit to check out the beautifully made accessories, travel bags, attaché cases, and a small line of leather clothing. ♦ M-F, Sa morning Mar-Oct; M afternoon, Tu-Sa Nov-Feb. Piazza Rucellai 10r (on Via della Vigna Nuova at Via del Purgatorio). 292395

59 Palazzo Rucellai This is one of the most handsome of Florence's Renaissance palazzi, built in 1446-51 by **Bernardo Rossellino** to designs of **Leon Battista Alberti** for textile merchant Giovanni Rucellai. The family emblem, "Fortune's Sail," can be seen on the building's facade, a classicized and refined version of the rusticated architecture prevalent at the time this palazzo was built. ♦ Via della Vigna Nuova 18 (Piazza Rucellai at Via Palchetti)

Within the Palazzo Rucellai:

Alinari The Alinari archives, primarily known for sepia views of late 19th-century–early 20th-century Italy and Italian works of art photographed at that time, provide the evocative stock of this small shop. Its reasonably priced prints of period photos, loose or mounted, make souvenirs reminiscent of those of Miss Lavish in E.M. Forster's *A Room with a View.* ♦ M-F, Sa morning Mar-Oct; M afternoon, Tu-Sa Nov-Feb. Via della Vigna Nuova 16 (Piazza Rucellai at Via Palchetti). 218975

Museo di Storia della Fotografia Alinari (Alinari Museum of the History of Photography) Temporary photo exhibitions here draw on the extensive collection of the Alinari brothers (whose shop and archives are in the same building); the museum also displays the work of acclaimed international photographers. ♦ Admission. M-Tu, Th-Su;

special exhibitions, call to confirm. Via della Vigna Nuova 16 (Piazza Rucellai at Via Palchetti). 213370

60 Emilio Paoli Though the Florentine art of straw work has all but died out, this shop offers some genuine Florentine goods in an otherwise Asian haystack, namely straw place mats and animals, natural and colored. ♦ M-F, Sa morning Mar-Oct; M afternoon, Tu-Sa Nov-Feb. Via della Vigna Nuova 26r (between Via dei Tornabuoni and Via Palchetti). 214596

61 Loggia dei Rucellai This loggia was built in 1460-66 on the occasion of the marriage of Giovanni Rucellai's son Bernardo to Cosimo Il Vecchio's granddaughter Nannina. Now glassed in, it is used for art exhibitions sponsored by the Società Alberto Bruschi. ♦ Via del Purgatorio 12 (at Via della Vigna Nuova)

61 Naj Oleari This Milanese firm specializes in fancifully printed fabrics, which appear on a kaleidoscopic selection of jackets, bags, and toys ideal for spoiling your favorite child or teenager. ♦ M-F, Sa morning Mar-Oct; M afternoon, Tu-Sa Nov-Feb. Via della Vigna Nuova 37r (between Via dei Tornabuoni and Via Purgatorio). 210688

62 Giorgio Armani This is the Florence home of the revered Milanese designer, known for his sophisticated interpretations of classic American tailoring, loosely cut in luxury fabrics. ♦ M-F, Sa morning Mar-Oct; M afternoon, Tu-Sa Nov-Feb. Via della Vigna Nuova 51r (between Via dei Tornabuoni and Via del Purgatorio). 219041

63 Enrico Coveri Florence's late native son's line of imaginative clothing continues under his famous label in this flagship store. The designer's clothes and accessories brightly cover adults and children alike. ♦ M-F, Sa morning Mar-Oct; M afternoon, Tu-Sa Nov-Feb. Via della Vigna Nuova 27-29r (between Via dei Tornabuoni and Via del Purgatorio). 2381769. Also at: Via dei Tornabuoni 81r (at Via della Vigna Nuova). 211263

63 Alex One of the few women's boutiques in Florence with a wide selection of Italian designers as well as international ones. Non-Italians spotlighted are Claude Montana, Jean-Paul Gaultier, and Thierry Mugler. ♦ M-F, Sa morning Mar-Oct; M afternoon, Tu-Sa Nov-Feb. Via della Vigna Nuova 19r (between Via dei Tornabuoni and Via del Purgatorio). 214952

64 Cappella Rucellai Within this chapel, once part of the church of **San Pancrazio,** is **Leon Battista Alberti**'s 1467 funerary monument to Giovanni Rucellai. Called *The Aedicule of the Church of the Holy Sepulchre,* it is a scaled-down version of the eponymous church in Jerusalem. ♦ Via della Spada (between Via dei Tornabuoni and Via Federighi)

65 Museo Marino Marini A permanent one-man show is housed within the deconsecrated 14th-century church of **San Pancrazio.** The man is Marino Marini (1901-1980), who though he was born and died in Tuscany (in Pistoia and Viareggio, respectively) became an international figure in 20th-century art. The show features 179 works, many examples of his most famous subject, the horse and rider, which he treated with almost Cycladic simplicity and abstraction in bronze and wood sculptures. ♦ Admission. M, W-Su. Piazza San Pancrazio (at Via della Spada). 219432

66 Il Latini ★★★$$ Giovanni, the delightful and diminutive owner of this former *fiaschetteria* (tavern), provides personable companionship to delectable Tuscan dishes that set the standard for the genre, from soup (*ribollita, pappa al pomodoro, zuppa di porri*) to nuts (the almonds in the *biscotti di Prato* cookies offered with the *vin santo* dessert wine at the end of the meal). In between is a Lucullan cavalcade of grilled and roasted meats, best accompanied by the white cannellini beans or fresh greens sautéed in oil and garlic. The house wine is an Il Vivaio Chianti, specially bottled for this trattoria. ♦ W-Su lunch and dinner. Reservations recommended. Via dei Palchetti 6r (between Via della Vigna Nuova and Via Federighi) 210916

67 Garga ★★★$$$ While Florentine-born owner Giuliano has contributed such items as *spaghetti ai carciofi* (spaghetti with artichokes) and *agnello saltato in padella* (sautéed lamb) to the menu of this lively little restaurant, his Canadian wife Sharon's contribution—cheesecake—needs no translation, even to the local contingent of the polyglot crowd that has come to appreciate the creative cuisine of this innovative restaurant. ♦ Tu-Sa lunch and dinner; Su dinner. Via del Moro 48r (near Via Palchetti). 2398898

68 Osteria Numero Uno ★★$$$ As the write-ups from American and Japanese periodicals proudly displayed at the entrance indicate, this place attracts wealthy tourists. The vault-ceilinged rooms are elegant and upscale, the multilingual service is patient and professional, and the Tuscan-based cuisine is very good. If you're not dieting, start your meal with the *stogliatino di ricotta al basilico* (ricotta cheese pastry with basil sauce), move on to the *vitello con prosciutto e funghi e formaggio* (veal roll with prosciutto, mushrooms and cheese in a truffle sauce), and finish off with the *torta di crema con pesche* (cream torte with peaches). ♦ M-Sa lunch and dinner. Via del Moro 22 (between Piazza Goldoni and Via Palchetti). 284897

69 Antico Caffè del Moro Known locally (and even internationally) as "the Art Bar," this small cafe has the best mixed drinks in town, discreetly served in an upscale ambience. ♦ M-Sa 10PM-1AM. No credit cards accepted. Via del Moro 4r (between Piazza Goldoni and Via Palchetti). 287661

70 Palazzo Ricasoli This 15th-century palazzo, built for the Ricasoli family, had the strange name of **Hotel de New York** in the 19th century, when this part of town was known as the "mecca of foreigners." ♦ Closed to the public. Piazza Goldoni 2 (at Lungarno Corsini)

71 Ponte alla Carraia Originally called the **Ponte Nuovo,** or New Bridge, to distinguish it from the **Ponte Vecchio,** the bridge (built and rebuilt) on this spot was washed away in a flood in 1274, crushed by a crowd watching a spectacle on the Arno in 1304, destroyed in another flood in 1333, reconstructed by **Ammannati** in 1557, and blown up by the Germans in 1945—sort of a bridge over troubled waters in reverse. The current version was put up in the old style after World War II. ♦ Between Piazza N. Sauro and Piazza Goldoni

72 Zi Rosa ★★$$ Tuscan fare is the basis of the menu in these antiques-filled rooms, but if you'd like a change from all that, try *scampi al curry* (curried shrimp) or the *paglia e fieno al prosciutto e panna* (straw and hay, i.e., yellow and green pasta in a cream-and-prosciutto sauce). ♦ M-W, F-Su lunch and dinner. Via dei Fossi 12r (between Piazza Goldoni and Piazza Ottaviani). 287062

73 Lisio Tessuti d'Arte In this landmark tower setting you'll find handwoven luxury furnishings and precious fabrics in a variety of antique patterns, made in silks and blends that are less expensive but just as finely worked. Silk tassels are available, too. ♦ M-F, Sa morning Mar-Oct; M afternoon, Tu-Sa Nov-Feb. Via dei Fossi 45r (between Piazza Goldoni and Piazza Ottaviani). 212430

74 BM Bookshop The wide selection of English-language books (many on Florence and Italy, many others Italian fiction in translation) may be more expensive here than at home, but you can't think of every-thing. Happily, the owners of this place just might well have—there are guidebooks, cookbooks, and children's books in English and Italian. ♦ M-F, Sa morning Mar-Oct; M afternoon, Tu-Sa Nov-Feb. Borgo Ognissanti 4r (near Piazza Goldoni). 294575

75 Bruzzichelli One of Florence's most respected antiques dealers, Giovanni Bruzzichelli has a range of paintings, furniture, and objects spanning the centuries. ♦ M-F, Sa morning Mar-Oct; M afternoon, Tu-Sa Nov-Feb. Borgo Ognissanti 31 (between Piazza Goldoni and Piazza Ognissanti). 292307

76 Palazzo alla Rovescia The story goes that Alessandro de' Medici, when asked if he would approve the plans for a balcony on this palazzo, remarked sarcastically "Yes, in reverse." To many, that would mean "no," but the literal-minded builder interpreted it as a go-ahead to design it upside-down, as it remains today. ♦ Borgo Ognissanti 12 (between Piazza Goldoni and Piazza Ognissanti)

77 Fallani Best Art Nouveau (called *liberty* in Italian) and Art Deco (called Art Deco in Italian) are among the best; among the rest are 19th-century European antiques. ♦ M-F, Sa morning Mar-Oct; M afternoon, Tu-Sa Nov-Feb. Borgo Ognissanti 15r (between Piazza Goldoni and Piazza Ognissanti). 214986

78 Paolo Romano Antichità Signor Romano, a third-generation antiques dealer whose Neapolitan grandfather started the *Fondazione Salvatore Romano* of Romanesque sculpture, extends the tradition with his stock of primarily Italian furniture from the 17th to 19th centuries. ♦ M-F, Sa morning Mar-Oct; M afternoon, Tu-Sa Nov-Feb. Borgo Ognissanti 20r (between Piazza Goldoni and Piazza Ognissanti). 293294

79 Ospedale di San Giovanni di Dio Designed and built by **Carlo Andrea Marcellini** in the early 1700s, this hospital, connected with the nearby church of **Ognissanti,** was funded by the Vespucci family. It incorporated the family houses, in one of which Amerigo (the Florentine cartographer after whom America was named) was born in 1454. It contains a fresco by Vincenzo Meucci in the vault. Attached to it is **Marcellini**'s remodeled church, **Santa Maria dell'Umiltà.** ♦ Borgo Ognissanti 20 (between Piazza Goldoni and Piazza Ognissanti)

80 Baccus ★★$ This gleaming modern restaurant is perfect for a light plate of pasta (they have 30 kinds), if you're not in the mood for a serious meal. ♦ Tu-Su lunch and dinner until 12:30AM. Borgo Ognissanti 45r (between Via Porcellana and Piazza Ognissanti). 283714

The Medici line became extinct in 1737 with the death of Grand Duke Gian Gastone de' Medici, whose fondness for the grape and dissolute young boys (called *ruspanti*) caused court scandals.

81 Harry's Bar ★★$$$

The name is the only thing this place shares with the higher-priced Harry's in Venice. This one's good for the best burger in town, as well as a variety of more classic Italian dishes. Also the quintessence of what Italians are fond of calling an "American bar," that is, it's a place that serves mixed drinks. Bartender Leo Vadorini is justly proud of his martinis. ♦ M-Sa lunch and dinner. Lungarno Amerigo Vespucci 22r (near Piazza Ognissanti). 2396700

82 Excelsior $$$$ This grandest of Florence's grand hotels combines Old World elegance with the relaxed but efficient management of the CIGA chain, now part of ITT Sheraton's Luxury Collection. The grandeur is made to feel human-scale by the highly professional staff. The 135 guest rooms boast a balance of antique furnishings and such modern conveniences as towel warmers and hair dryers. Ask for one of the recently renovated rooms. ♦ Piazza Ognissanti 3 (at Lungarno A. Vespucci). 264201, 800/325.3589 in US; fax 210278

Within the Excelsior:

Il Cestello ★★★$$$ This is one of the few restaurants in Florence open daily and it's also one of the best, particularly in the warm-weather months when meals are served on the terrace overlooking the river. The international menu changes with the seasons, but you'll often find local delicacies such as carpaccio with truffles and *mille foglie di manzo con parmigiano e pistacchie* (an elaborate dish of beef, parmesan cheese, and pistachio nuts). ♦ Daily lunch and dinner. Piazza Ognissanti 3 (at Lungarno A. Vespucci). 264201

83 Grand Hotel $$$$ This hotel has been restored to its former grandeur by the CIGA chain (recently purchased by ITT Sheraton) after a long dormant spell. Its 107 luxurious rooms overlooking the Arno have since acquired a roster of regulars, who claim the hotel's smaller size makes for more personalized service than its sister hotel across the piazza. The guest rooms are decorated either in 15th-century Florentine style or fin de siècle imperial style, and all are air-conditioned. There is a restaurant and a lounge. ♦ Piazza Ognissanti 1 (at Lungarno A. Vespucci). 288781, 800/325.3589 in US; fax 217400

84 Palazzo Lenzi This Renaissance palazzo, built in 1470, is covered with intricate two-tone stucco designs (called *sgraffiti*) by

Andrea Feltrini. It is the home of the **Istituto Francese**, the Florence branch of the **University of Grenoble**, which sponsors a variety of cultural activities, including art exhibitions and film series. ◆ Piazza Ognissanti 2 (at Borgo Ognissanti)

Within the Palazzo Lenzi:

Giotti Bottega Veneta Florence's only outlet for the prestigious leather chain is known for its distinctive woven treatment of butter-soft hides. ◆ M-F, Sa morning Mar-Oct; M afternoon, Tu-Sa Nov-Feb. Piazza Ognissanti 2 (at Borgo Ognissanti). 294265

85 Ognissanti This church (dating from 1256 and rebuilt in 1627 by **Bartolomeo Pettirossi**) has one of the earliest Baroque facades in Florence (built in 1637 by **Matteo Nigetti**). Inside, above the second altar on the right, is Domenico Ghirlandaio's fresco *The Madonna of Mercy Protecting the Vespucci Family*. The Vespucci were parishioners, and the boy to the right of the Madonna is probably the young Amerigo Vespucci, whose later voyages (and boastful, perhaps apocryphal, writings about them) gave the New World the name America. In the sacristy is a fresco of the *Crucifixion* by Taddeo Gaddi and a crucifix by a follower of his father, Giotto. In the left transept is a monk's robe believed to be the one St. Francis was wearing when he received the stigmata. ◆ Piazza Ognissanti 38 (at Borgo Ognissanti)

85 Refettorio della Chiesa di Ognissanti (Refectory of the Church of Ognissanti) The refectory houses three important paintings. *The Last Supper,* a fresco by Domenico Ghirlandaio, was painted for the space, as can be seen by the clever use of the room's real window as a light source. The other two paintings, *St. Jerome* by Ghirlandaio and *St. Augustine* by Botticelli, originally hung in the church of **Ognissanti**. ◆ Piazza Ognissanti 42 (at Borgo Ognissanti)

86 Palazzo Liberty Nothing patriotic and no English snobbery was intended by the name of this building, built in the early 20th century by **Giovanni Michelazzi**. It is one of the few examples of florid Art Nouveau (called *liberty* in Italian, as in Liberty of London, the store that helped introduce the style in Italy) in Florence. ◆ Borgo Ognissanti 26 (in Piazza Ognissanti)

87 Gianfaldoni On this street a cluster of artisans still work in centuries-old *bottegas* (workshops). The 18th-century art of *sciagliola* is alive and well in this workshop, where the chalklike stone by that name is pressed into artful designs for tabletops and wall hangings that make unique keepsakes. ◆ M-F, Sa morning Mar-Oct; M afternoon, Tu-Sa Nov-Feb. Via della Porcellana 6r (between Borgo Ognissanti and Via Palazzuolo). 2396336

88 Sostanza ★★★$$ Known to Florentines as "Il Troia" (the pigsty, or more colorfully, a loose woman), this restaurant—another of the city's radical chic eateries—is hardly bigger than a pigsty, so expect a pretty tight squeeze. Bloomingdales buyers sit at communal tables alongside the workers who still make up a small fraction of the clientele at this former butcher's shop. Better than the people watching, however, is the food itself, which still includes the best *bistecca* in town. Non-carnivores might want to try the excellent *omelette di carciofi* (artichoke omelette). ◆ M-F lunch and dinner. Reservations required. No credit cards accepted. Via della Porcellana 25r (between Borgo Ognissanti and Via Palazzuolo). 212691

89 Amon ★★$ One of the happier (and cheaper) options for ethnic dining in town, this tiny stand-up sandwich shop serves Egyptian specialties on pita bread, freshly baked twice a day (whole wheat only). One room has a counter where you can order a *shauerma* (like a Greek gyro but served, if you want, with a spicier sauce) or a falafel (owner Elkarsh's version is made with a puree of Tuscan white beans instead of chick peas). You can then dig into your Egyptian find in the adjoining room, decorated with tongue-in-cheek tomb paintings. ◆ M-Sa lunch and dinner. Via Palazzuolo 28r (between Via dei Fossi and Via della Porcellana). 2393146

90 Il Profeta ★★$$ A small, discreet restaurant with an Italian menu of dishes such as *pennette di crema di pomodoro del Profeta* (pasta in a creamy tomato sauce) and *scalloppine campagnola* (veal scallops in a robust tomato sauce). ◆ M-Sa lunch and dinner. Borgo Ognissanti 93r (near Via Melegnano Finiguerra). 212265

91 Il Contadino ★★$ Good, cheap home cooking is the order of the day here, as witnessed by the fact that the two spotless, modern dining rooms are always packed with handsome young men who've just left home to do their military service. ◆ M-Sa lunch and dinner. Via Palazzuolo 69-71r (near Via Melegnano Finiguerra). 2382673

92 Il Biribisso ★★$$ This small restaurant makes a good *zuppa di cipolla* (onion soup), followed nicely by *pennette al Barolo* (pasta in a red wine sauce). ◆ M-Sa lunch and dinner. No credit cards accepted. Via dell'Albero 28r (between Via Palazzuolo and Via della Scala). 288670

93 Baldini The *bottega* of this master *bronzista* (bronze worker) is where upper-crust Florentines have their antique furniture refitted with metal accoutrements, but it also offers such items as doorknobs, towel racks, and other elegant decorations. ◆ M-F, Sa morning Mar-Oct; M afternoon, Tu-Sa Nov-

Feb. Via Palazzuolo 99-105r (near Via di Santa Lucia). 210933

94 Hotel Principe $$$ This small, 20-room hotel is a favorite with visiting Americans, who appreciate its river views and garden. It is just far enough off the beaten track to be convenient (and within walking—well, hiking—distance of the major sites) and relatively quiet. There is no restaurant. ◆ Lungarno Amerigo Vespucci 34 (near Ponte Amerigo Vespucci). 284848; fax 283458

95 Hotel Kraft $$$ One of the few Florentine hotels with a small swimming pool, this peaceful place offers 77 guest rooms with efficient service and a pleasant roof garden and restaurant, all relatively removed from the buzzing traffic of the city. ◆ Via Solferino 2 (between Via Palestro and Via G. Garibaldi). 284273; fax 2398267

96 Teatro Comunale This 19th-century theater by **Telemaco Bonaiuti** was burned in 1863, firebombed in 1944, and flooded in 1966. But the show goes on, the big one being the annual *Maggio Musicale Fiorentino,* an international (and internationally renowned) music and dance festival held between May and early July. ◆ Corso Italia 12 (at Via Magenta). 2779236

97 Porta al Prato Built in 1284, this is one of the ancient gates to the city left standing after the walls were knocked down to make way for the *viali* (broad avenues) now running in their stead. ◆ Piazzale di Porta al Prato (at Via il Prato)

98 Il Gourmet ★★$$ This basically Tuscan restaurant lives up to its name, offering refined versions of such specialties as *crostini* (bread rounds spread with a rough chicken-liver pâté or a vegetable puree), ravioli or tortellini pasta stuffed with spinach, and the ubiquitous *bistecca alla fiorentina,* here served as it should be with Tuscan cannellini beans drizzled in olive oil. ◆ M-Sa lunch and dinner. Via Il Prato 68r (near Porta al Prato). 294766

99 Hotel Villa Medici $$$$ This peaceful and luxurious 107-room hotel is partially housed within the **Palazzo Corsini,** which was built for Alessandro Acciaiuoli by **Bernardo Buontalenti** in the 16th century. Within walking distance of the center of town (only for those who enjoy walking!), the hotel is rather self-contained, equipped with its own garden, shops, swimming pool, bar, and an elegant restaurant, **Lorenzo de' Medici,** serving an international menu. ◆ Via Il Prato 42 (at Via Bernardo Rucellai). 2381331; fax 2381336

100 La Carabaccia ★★$$ The menu here changes according to season and to what's available in local markets. Besides the titular dish, a type of sweet-and-sour onion soup, such items as *crespelle con funghi o asparagi* (mushroom or asparagus crepes) and *sformato di carciofi* (a vegetable casserole prepared with artichokes) make regular appearances, as do fish and roasts. As for desserts, the place offers some of the smoothest mousses in town. ◆ Tu-Sa lunch and dinner. Via Palazzuolo 190r (near Via Bernardo Rucellai). 214782

101 St. James Long-term visitors to Florence appreciate this Neo-Gothic church—which serves the American community—for its weekly rummage sales, where they can either pick up the odd appliance they won't be able to use elsewhere or unload one of their own. During its annual Christmas sale, volunteers serve enough burgers and hot dogs to make the city seem like Kansas City–on-the-Arno. On Wednesday evenings during the academic year, cultural talks are followed by a home-cooked meal. ◆ Via Bernardo Rucellai 13 (between Via Palazzuolo and Via della Scala). 294417

102 Otello ★★$$ This large restaurant, whose wood decor gives it a rustic feel, has a large menu of all the classic Tuscan dishes, from soups to the steak called *bistecca alla fiorentina,* as well as a rare selection of fresh fish dishes. ◆ M, W-Su lunch and dinner. Via degli Orti Oricellari 36r (off Via della Scala). 215819

103 Stazione Centrale di Santa Maria Novella Florence's central train station—built in 1935 by the late **Giovanni Michelucci** and other members of the *gruppo toscano,* **Piero Berardi, Nello Baroni, Italo Gamberini, Baldassare Guarnieri,** and **Leonardo Lusanna**—was the first example of Functionalist architecture in Italy and has been granted the status of a national monument. It is so functional looking, in fact, that when its plans were first made public one critic wrote, "The papers made a mistake, careful! They published the packing crate. The model is inside." Instead, inside and out the station is filled with intelligent references to the

Florentine vernacular, from its *pietra forte* skin to its striped marble pavement and the landscape paintings by Ottone Rosai in the cafeteria. Other functional aspects of the station include its always-open pharmacy (just inside the entrance, to the left) as well as a mailbox outside the always-open postal dispatch center (behind *Binario 1*, or Track 1) where you can shave a few days off delivery of those important cards and letters.

More recent criticism was caused by the *pensilina* (1990, **Cristiano Toraldo di Francia** and **Andrea Noferi**), a covered platform in front of the station. Its detractors say that, unlike the station, it is functionless, since it apparently serves mainly to block the view of the entrance to the station (it actually houses newspaper stands and booths selling bus tickets). When **Michelucci** died in 1990, a few pundits wanted to honor him by blowing up the *pensilina*. But the platform lingers on, an almost deliberately discordant Postmodern appropriation of such Florentine architectural traditions as marble stripes, impassably narrow sidewalks, and a Vasarian propensity to blot out previous architects' work. The final insult to **Michelucci**'s Functionalism is the fact that the platform severely limits station access to a single opening—a convention of military architecture reinforced by a siren that goes off each time pedestrians are given the green light. In its favor, one can say that it sort of looks like a train . . . boat? . . . Renaissance spaceship? The architects also designed a less assertive small station, the **Terminal di Via Valfonda** (1991), adjacent to the main station. Via Valfonda, incidentally, is bridged by an overpass designed by **Gae Aulenti** (1991).

A major, multilevel parking area beneath the station was completed in 1994. This makes a convenient, central, and safe spot to leave your car when visiting the Centro Storico area, which is almost entirely closed to traffic. ◆ Piazza della Stazione.

104 Italy & Italy ★$ This was one of the first and the slickest of the *fast* (Italian for "fast food") chains to open in Florence. Designed with a trendy Anglo logo (suspiciously similar to Coca-Cola's), tons of travertine, and yards of high-tech tubing, it microwaves up the fastest of American and Italian foods. The burgers here are freshly thawed rather than fresh, but they can sometimes serve to nip that onslaught of homesickness in the bun. Pizza (frozen) and pasta (fresh) are also available, and smoking is not allowed, a rarity in the land of Vesuvius. ◆ Daily 10AM-1AM July-Aug; M, W-Su 10AM-1AM Sept-June lunch and dinner. No credit cards accepted. Piazza della Stazione 25r (near Via Nazionale). 282885

105 Fountain This marble depiction of *The Arno and Its Valley* by Italo Griselli, set before the linear **Sala d'Onore** (Reception Hall), is a rare and outstanding example of Roman-style Fascist-era art and architecture in Florence. Opposite it, at the end of the covered platform, is a contemporary fountain representing the river Mugnone, which flowed into the Arno near this spot before it was diverted. ◆ Piazza Adua (east wall of station)

106 Palazzo degli Affari Another rare example of modern architecture in Florence, this palazzo—built in 1974 by **Pierluigi Spadolini**—has a prefabricated white cement exterior pierced with upside-down arched windows in dark glass. The modular structure of its insides can be adapted to everything from large receptions to small exhibition spaces. ◆ Piazza Adua 1 (near Piazza della Stazione at Via Cennini)

107 Palazzo dei Congressi This 19th-century Neo-Classical villa by **Giuseppe Poggi** was refashioned by **Pierluigi Spadolini**, brother of the late prime minister of Italy Giovanni Spadolini, into a 20th-century meeting center. His splendid 1,000-seat underground auditorium is celebrated for its perfect acoustics and is used for concerts and recording sessions. ◆ Piazza Adua 1 (near Piazza della Stazione)

108 Fortezza da Basso Alessandro de' Medici commissioned this imposing fortress, built by **Antonio Sangallo** in 1534-35. Some four-and-a-half centuries later its extensive grounds now defend the **Padiglione Espositivo** (1975, **Pierluigi Spadolini**), a modern space hosting trade shows throughout the year, many of them (such as *Firenze a Tavola*, a culinary show) interesting and open to the public. ◆ Viale Filippo Strozzi 1 (at Via Valfonda). 49721

109 Hotel Mario's $$ This spotless and tasteful 16-room hotel conveniently located near the station (cleanliness is next to gaudiness) is popular with Americans who are in town to see the sights or to attend the trade shows held in the nearby **Fortezza da Basso**. There is no restaurant. ◆ Via Faenza 89 (at Via Cennini). 216801; fax 212039

Restaurants/Clubs: Red	**Hotels:** Blue
Shops/ 🍴 **Outdoors:** Green	**Sights/Culture:** Black

La Lampara

110 La Lampara ★★$ Over 80 types of pizza are the hottest ticket at this rambling restaurant, which prepares it by the orthodox method in a wood-burning oven as opposed to the sea of microwaves on which other Florentine pizzerias navigate. ◆ Daily lunch and dinner Mar-Oct; M, W-Su lunch and dinner Nov-Feb; closed last two weeks in December. Via Nazionale 36r (near Via Fiume). 215164

111 Hotel Majestic $$$$ An unobtrusively modern facade in a primarily 19th-century piazza fronts this efficient, modern 103-room hotel. Its piano bar–restaurant is a popular late-night watering hole with the business travelers that make up most of the hotel's clientele. The **Majestic** is also a popular destination for tourist groups that are more concerned with location than charm. ◆ Via del Melarancio 1 (in Piazza dell'Unità Italiana). 264021; fax 268428

112 Ganesh ★★$$ This Indian restaurant takes itself seriously, as attested by the reliably high quality of the food and service and by this ethnic restaurant's success in a city not known for its all-embracing acceptance of things not Italian. If you can't look another tortellini in the face and are curious to know where the locals go for a change of pace, stop by for the exotic aroma of chicken or beef curry that will transport you even farther east. Vegetarians will also appreciate the creative menu offerings geared to their particular tastes. ◆ Tu-Su lunch and dinner. Via del Giglio 26-28r (between Via Panzani and Piazza Madonna Aldobrandini). 289694

113 Bellettini $ Set in a handsomely restored Renaissance building, this place is a well-kept secret in Florence, so hope for an available room and then don't tell a soul about it. It offers a central location (quiet nonetheless), optional air-conditioning, tiled bathrooms, and frescoed breakfast room (there is no restaurant); some of the 27 rooms even overlook the **Duomo.** The staff speaks fluent English. ◆ Via dei Conti 7 (between Via dei Cerretani and Via de' Zannetti) 213561; fax 283551

114 De' Medici ★$$ Don't be put off by the expanse of this restaurant, which seems to do things in a big way, beginning with its specialty, *bistecca alla fiorentina,* a slab that you know immediately will demand a doggie bag. One room is devoted to a wine bar and offers a large selection of light lunches, such as pasta or pizza; the other offers an even bigger menu of Florentine favorites. Stick with the simple stuff. ◆ Tu-Su lunch and dinner. Via del Giglio 49r (between Via dei Panzani and Via Melarancio). 218778

115 Astoria Hotel $$$ This centrally located hotel, primarily favored by business travelers and tour groups, is in a grand 16th-century palazzo. Its 100 rooms have recently been renovated. Breakfast is served in a theatrical salon-ballroom with a frescoed ceiling. The restaurant, less dramatic in effect, was closed at press time but upon opening will serve lunch and dinner. ◆ Via del Giglio 9 (between Via dei Panzani and Via Melarancio). 2398095; fax 214632

116 Hotel Delle Tele $$ Given its central location and recent top-to-toe renovation, this hotel is surprisingly at the very low end of its category. Double-paned windows ensure quiet, even for the eight rooms in the front (seven others face a side street or courtyard). Terra-cotta floors, air-conditioning in each room, trompe l'oeil decoration, and a number of large reproductions of Renaissance works (the hotel's name makes reference to these canvas paintings) are handsome touches uncommon in two-star hotels. There is no restaurant. ◆ Via dei Panzani 10 (near Via del Giglio and Via dei Conti). 2382419; fax (same as phone)

117 Standa This grand 16th-century palazzo by **Bartolommeo Ammannati** has been converted into a *grande magazzino,* Italian for department store. The chain does best in the housewares department and is conveniently open no-stop (Italian for nonstop), if for some reason you need to pick up a cheese grater or some other item when other stores are closed. ◆ M-F, Sa morning Mar-Oct; M afternoon, Tu-Sa Nov-Feb. No midday closing. Via dei Panzani 31r (at Via del Giglio). 2398963

118 Sabatini ★★★$$$$ The formal "Old World charm" of this dean of Florentine restaurants makes it the kind of place where men feel jacket and tie are in order whether required or not (they're not), where the service is polished and professional, and where Japanese tourists feel compelled to eat. The extensive international menu is ambitious and generally successful. Begin with the house specialty *spaghetti alla Sabatini* (a variation of carbonara). Best choices are such Tuscan classics as *bistecca alla fiorentina* and generic Italian dishes such as osso buco (veal shank) and saltimbocca (veal and prosciutto). ◆ Tu-Su lunch and dinner. Via dei Panzani 9a (between Via del Giglio and Piazza dell'Unità Italiana). 282802

119 Hotel Baglioni $$$ This large, once grand hotel is popular with visiting business travelers. Its rooftop restaurant, **Brunelleschi,** is a popular and convenient spot for a business lunch, offering an international menu amidst sweeping views. Its 193 rooms could use sprucing up. ◆ Piazza dell'Unità Italiana 6 (at Via dei Panzani). 23580; fax 2358895

San Lorenzo

The area around **San Lorenzo**, the Medici parish church, is something of a Medici theme park. Cosimo Il Vecchio, founder of the dynasty, had **Michelozzo** build the imposing **Palazzo Medici-Riccardi** here, embellished with playful frescoes of the family by Benozzo Gozzoli and sycophantic ones by Luca Giordano (commissioned by later owners). Around the same time, Cosimo commissioned **Michelozzo** to build the monastery of **San Marco**, keeping aside two cells within it for his personal use. Cosimo also founded the manuscript collections that are kept in the library of San Marco as well as in the **Biblioteca Mediceo-Laurenziana**, a library specially commissioned by Medici Pope Clement VII. The church of **San Lorenzo** itself, greatly expanded by the Medici and housing the family's last remains in its chapels, the **Cappelle Medicee**, epitomizes the beginning and end of the entire dynasty.

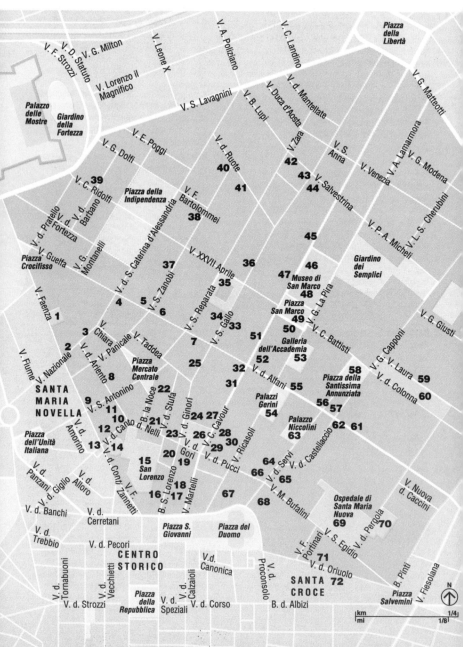

The Medici legacy lives on in a number of noble palazzi that were built in the area over the centuries. It also continues in the surrounding streets, from the numerous coats of arms (they have any number of balls on them—usually six—giving rise to predictable jokes about Medici anatomy) above palazzo entrances to names of cafes and restaurants. Sadly, the family's original profession as bankers has its modern counterpart in the increasing commercialization of the area with tacky boutiques and pizza parlors. Still, one can't help thinking that Lorenzo Il Magnifico (who wrote such lines in praise of love and youth as the famous *"quant'è bella giovinezza/che si fugge tuttavía,"* roughly, "how beautiful is youth/which quickly flees") would have enjoyed the large number of university students in the area, and that the livelier members of the Medici family would have appreciated the spirit of the bustling indoor food market and the outdoor vendors' stalls in the shadow of **San Lorenzo** today.

1 Cenacolo di Foglino (Last Supper)
Similar in composition to the Florentine Last Suppers by Andrea del Castagno and Domenico Ghirlandaio, this treatment of the subject by Raphael's master, Perugino, contains a background depicting the Sermon in the Garden set in the Umbrian hills. ♦ By appointment only. Via Faenza 42 (between Via Nazionale and Piazza Crocifisso). 286982

2 Il Triangolo delle Bermude
This splashy *gelateria,* named after the Bermuda Triangle, offers such adventurous ice cream flavors as rose, whiskey, peanut, and coffee crunch. ♦ Tu-Su 11AM-midnight. Closed 1-20 January. No credit cards accepted. Via Nazionale 61-63r (near Via Faenza). 287490

3 Le Fonticine ★★★$$
When proudly parochial Italians are pressed as to which of their regional cuisines is best, that of Emilia-Romagna usually wins by a nose over Tuscany's. This restaurant (named after the 16th-century fountain by Luca della Robbia on the street outside) offers the best of both worlds, as all Italian regions are truly worlds apart. Bruna Grazia is from Emilia-Romagna, and each day she makes her famous pasta (such as tortellini) fresh, with help from daughter Gianna. Gianna's husband, Silvano, sees to it that Tuscany is well represented with such standard-setting classics as *bistecca alla fiorentina* (steak), rivaled in season by the almost-as-meaty *funghi porcini* (a type of mushroom prepared in a variety of ways). A well-balanced regional menu and wine list make this one of the better general Italian restaurants in Florence. ♦ Tu-Su lunch and dinner. Via Nazionale 79r (at Via dell'Ariento). 282106

4 Giuseppe Bianchi
Italian bicycles of all shapes and sizes, with a decided emphasis on the house brand of Florence's oldest manufacturer, are the stock and trade of this shop. If you've been swept up in the national cycling craze, this is your best bet in Florence. Its cyclers' caps, shirts, and sweaters make nice gifts, too. ♦ M-F, Sa morning Mar-Oct; M afternoon, Tu-Sa Nov-Feb. No credit cards accepted. Via Nazionale 130r (near Via Guelfa). 216991

5 Arte Cornici
If you're a fan of fans, this is the place for you. Caterina Carola repairs and restores antique fans and mounts them in frames worthy of the art objects these fashion accessories have become. ♦ M-F, Sa morning Mar-Oct; M afternoon, Tu-Sa Nov-Feb. No credit cards accepted. Via Guelfa 88r (near Via San Zanobi). 499452

6 i' Toscano ★★$$
This clean, modern restaurant bases its food on old Florentine recipes. First-course soups are good here, as are the tripe and *bistecca alla fiorentina.* ♦ M, W-Su lunch and dinner. Via Guelfa 70r (near Via San Zanobi). 215475

7 Cafaggi ★$$
In the same family for decades, this roomy restaurant specializes in fresh fish, offering such dishes as *spaghetti allo scoglio* (spaghetti in a seafood sauce) and *frittura di pesce* (breaded and fried fish and shellfish). ♦ Tu-Sa lunch and dinner; Su lunch. Via Guelfa 35r (between Via San Gallo and Via Santa Reparata). 294989

Restaurants/Clubs: Red	Hotels: Blue
Shops/♥ Outdoors: Green	Sights/Culture: Black

8 Mercato Centrale (Central Market) *Bei harshofini!* is how the greengrocers here sing the praises, in their aspirated Florentine accents, of their beautiful little *carciofi,* or artichokes. The market's hangarlike iron structure was designed in 1874 by **Giuseppe Mengoni,** the architect of Milan's stylish Galleria Vittorio Emanuele II. This being Florence, however, it draws a more rustic assemblage of shops and shoppers than its stylish Milan counterpart. Downstairs are butcher shops selling all types of meat (their proud displays of skinned rabbits, dead pheasants, and decapitated boars' heads are inevitable gross-outs for first timers), grocers' shops, and an open-air (and what air—both fish and foul!) fish market; many fish vendors still use their booths' original 19th-century marble counters. Upstairs are endless displays of fruits, vegetables, and local color. ♦ M-Sa 7AM-2PM. No credit cards accepted. Entrances on Via dell'Ariento and Piazza Mercato Centrale (betweeen Via Sant'Antonino and Via Panicale)

Within the Mercato Centrale:

Nerbone ★$ If you can't find this restaurant on the ground floor of the bustling San Lorenzo market, just ask: Everyone knows it as the best place around for a quick bite and a glass of local wine. Alessandro, the amiable owner, is the son of well-known local restaurateurs. Try his grilled vegetables, daily soup and pasta specials, or the typically Tuscan *bollito* (beef chunks boiled in broth). Rub elbows with the market merchants and enjoy the high spirits and low prices. ♦ M-Sa lunch. No credit cards accepted. Ground floor. 219949

9 Fiaschetteria Zanobini This is one of only two wine shops in Florence that sell wine from their own vineyards by the bottle or the glass. Its label, *Le Lame,* appears on *Chianti classico* and *vin santo,* a sweet dessert wine. In exceptional years (most recently, 1985), the Zanobini family also produces a *Chianti classico riserva* called *Sorripa,* named after one small tract of its tiny vineyard. ♦ Daily (no midday closing). No credit cards accepted. Via Sant'Antonino 47r (between Via dell'Ariento and Via Faenza). 2396850

9 Palle d'Oro ★★$ This inexpensive restaurant is popular with neighborhood office workers who pack the stand-up lunch counter in the front, so try to come early or late unless you'd like to sit

in the back, where table-service is available. The daily *primi piatti* (first courses) are your best bets for a light but filling lunch, and usually include some sort of pasta, risotto, and minestrone. On Friday the special is

cacciucco, the tomatoey seafood stew of nearby Livorno. ♦ M-Sa lunch and dinner. Via Sant'Antonino 43-45r (between Via dell'Ariento and Via Faenza). 288383

10 Sieni A bit of gloss amid the dross of the San Lorenzo market, this family-run *pasticceria* (pastry shop) is the best in the area and one of the best in Florence. Try any (or better, all) of its cream puffs—*cioccolato* (chocolate), *caffè* (coffee), *nocciola* (hazelnut), *zabaglione* (custard and liqueur), or *crema* (plain custard)—or such seasonal treats as *l'orange* (a flat orange sponge cake drizzled with orange glaze). ♦ M afternoon; Tu-Sa 8AM-7:30PM. No credit cards accepted. Via dell'Ariento 29r (between Piazza San Lorenzo and Via Sant'Antonino). 213830

FRIGGITORE Nº 34

FRIGGITORIA · LUISA

11 Friggitoria Luisa ★$ This is one of Florence's last remaining *friggitorie,* hole-in-the-wall eateries that offer fried snacks. (There were once at least a few dozen, as the marble slab above the entrance, "Friggitore No. 34," indicates.) Luisa has made-to-order sandwiches inside, but her best foods are deep-fried street eats available over the curb-side counter. To sooth an aching sweet tooth, try the voluptuous *bomboloni* (sugar-dusted, custard-filled doughnuts), *cimballe* (plain doughnuts), or *crochette di riso* (rice croquettes); for saltier fare try the rectangles of polenta. ♦ M-Sa. No credit cards accepted. Via Sant'Antonino 50-52r (at Via dell'Ariento). 211630

12 Palazzo Riccardi-Mannelli This little palazzo was one of many in Florence that were covered with frescoes in the 16th century; at that time it was known as **Palazzo Benci.** The bug-eyed bust above the entrance is a sycophantic tribute to Francesco I de' Medici, who is buried in the colorful mausoleum chapel across the piazza. According to tradition, Giotto, the father of modern painting, was born in one of the simple houses from which the palazzo was built. ♦ Piazza Madonna degli Aldobrandini 4 (at Via Faenza)

13 Trattoria Antellesi ★★$$ Janice is from Arizona; her husband Enrico is from a line of respected Florentine restaurateurs. Together they are the spirit of this popular and comfortable trattoria in the shadow of the **Cappelle Medicee.** With the central food *mercato* just around the corner, a meal here is guaranteed to be fresh, delicious, and a memorable, authentically Tuscan dining experience. Janice will guide you to an appropriate selection from the wine list to accompany the seasonally changing menu of good homemade pastas, grilled meats, and desserts made on the premises. ♦ M-Sa lunch and dinner. Reservations recommended. Via Faenza 9r (off Piazza Madonna Aldobrandini). 216990

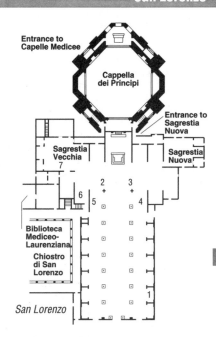

Entrance to Capelle Medicee

Cappella dei Principi

Entrance to Sagrestia Nuova

Sagrestia Vecchia 7

Sagrestia Nuova

2 + 3 +

6 5 4

Biblioteca Mediceo-Laurenziana

Chiostro di San Lorenzo

1

San Lorenzo

14 Cappelle Medicee (Medici Chapels) The entrance to these chapels leads to the **Cappella dei Principi** (Chapel of the Princes), built in 1604 by **Giovanni de' Medici** and **Matteo Nigetti** and home of the Medici mausoleum, which once ranked among the must-see monuments in Florence—the Graceland of its day (see drawing above). Despite the proto-psychedelic brightness of the mother-of-pearl, lapis lazuli, coral, and other *pietra dura* (semiprecious stone) materials, the chapel leaves the modern eye cold, a frozen object lesson in grandiosity. Note the octagonal plan (see floor plan at right), similar in style to the **Baptistry,** the **Tribune room** in the **Uffizi,** and the cupola of the **Duomo.** By contrast, the **Sagrestia Nuova** (New Sacristy) begun by **Michelangelo** in 1521 and completed by **Vasari** and **Ammannati** in 1555, seems almost restful, though **Michelangelo** designed it as an uneasy response in part to **Brunelleschi's Sagrestia Vecchia** (Old Sacristy). It contains the tombs of four more members of the Medici family—two Lorenzos and two

Giulianos. Lorenzo Il Magnifico (the Magnificent) and his brother Giuliano (killed in the **Duomo** during the Pazzi Conspiracy) lie in the simple tomb opposite the altar. On top of it is Michelangelo's *Madonna and Child.* The remains of the more grandiose, but less important, 16th-century Lorenzo and Giuliano de' Medici are in the more elaborate tombs to the left and right, from which **Ammannati** took the unusual curve for his Ponte Santa Trinita. The tomb of Lorenzo, Duke of Urbino, on the left of the altar, is crowned with Michelangelo's reclining allegorical statues *Dawn* and *Dusk;* opposite, the tomb of Giuliano, Duke of Nemours, has *Night* and *Day.* Michelangelo is said to have been brooding about the decline of the Florentine Republic when he made these sculptures; it's unclear what he was thinking when he painted the remarkably spontaneous frescoes in a room beneath the sacristy; discovered in 1976, the room is now open to the public. ♦ Admission. Tu-Su. Piazza Madonna degli Aldobrandini (Via dei Conti at Via del Canto de' Nelli). 23885

15 San Lorenzo Built on the site of a church consecrated in 393 by St. Ambrose and enlarged in the Romanesque era, the present exterior (which was begun in 1419, continued in 1442 by **Filippo Brunelleschi,** and completed 1447-60 by **Antonio Manetti**), though lacking a finished facade, is one of the handsomest piles of brick and stone in Italy. When viewed by day from a few paces behind the shoulders of the overlooked 16th-century monument to Giovanni delle Bande Nere (by Baccio Bandinelli) in **Piazza San Lorenzo,** its jumble of curves and angles seems almost Byzantine, a Florentine Hagia Sophia looming over a veritable souk, a rich visual backdrop for the heartbreaking bells that ring from **Ferdinando Ruggieri**'s Baroque campanile. When the piazza is deserted on Monday morning and at night, it is easy to imagine the cloaked Medici and their minions hurrying off to attend to affairs of state or even affairs of the heart.

Financed by the Medici, the great cake of **San Lorenzo** was never iced (they rejected **Michelangelo**'s model for the facade, now on display at **Casa Buonarroti**) but filled instead with the fruits of the best artists of the era, which became almost too candied for the contemporary palate in the *pietra dura* extravaganza of the **Cappella dei Principi. Brunelleschi**'s interior magnificently lives up to the name of the *pietra serena* (literally "serene stone," a warm-colored stone) used throughout. The inside wall of the facade is by **Michelangelo.** In the second chapel on the right is the 16th-century *Marriage of the Virgin* [1] (numbers refer to floor plan on page 75) by Rosso Fiorentino. Just before the transept are two 15th-century bronze pulpits [2, 3] designed by Donatello; behind the right one is a 15th-century marble tabernacle [4] by Desiderio da Settignano, and behind the left one is the 16th-century fresco *The Martyrdom of St. Lawrence* [5] by Bronzino. In a chapel in the left transept is Filippo Lippi's 15th-century *Annunciation* [6]; **Brunelleschi**'s harmonious **Sagrestia Vecchia** (Old Sacristy), based on the architectural convention of a circle within a square, is just ahead. It was decorated by Donatello in the 15th century with medallions depicting the life of St. John the Evangelist, roundels of the Evangelists, and doors of the Apostles and Martyrs. To the left of the **Old Sacristy** entrance is Andrea Verrocchio's 15th-century monument to Piero and Giovanni de' Medici [7]. ♦ Piazza San Lorenzo (Borgo San Lorenzo at Via del Canto de' Nelli)

Within San Lorenzo:

Chiostro di San Lorenzo (Cloisters of San Lorenzo) A remarkably tranquil break from the bustling market outside, the cloisters (note the views of the **Duomo** and the dome of the **Cappella dei Principi**) lead to the **Biblioteca Mediceo-Laurenziana (Laurentian Library),** which was begun in 1524 by **Michelangelo** and completed in 1578 by **Vasari** and **Ammannati**. The *pietra serena* is less serene here in the Mannerist vestibule, which gives a dramatic slant on the Classical elements rediscovered during the Renaissance in anticipation of the Baroque. Things settle down once again inside the library, where the Medici motifs on the wooden ceiling are echoed on Tribolo's marble floor. Michelangelo designed the reading benches. Works on display from the

rare book collection (begun by Cosimo Il Vecchio) include the *Medici Virgil* and autographs of Petrarch, Poliziano, Machiavelli, and Napoleon. ♦ Free. M-Sa morning. 210760

16 Moradei This is a middle-priced clothing store for middle-class Florentines—but in a city where the bus drivers wear jacket-and-tie and the meter maids' outfits were designed by Emilio Pucci, that's saying something. The sprawling space has the city's widest selection of the tastefully conservative Anglo-American look (with some real UK and US labels mixed in for good measure) that has long fascinated the Florentines. ♦ M-F, Sa morning Mar-Oct; M afternoon, Tu-Sa Nov-Feb. Borgo San Lorenzo 15r (between Via dei Cerretani and Piazza San Lorenzo). 211468

17 Bata On a street of discount shoe stores, this Italian chain (with 160 locations in Italy alone) is a step ahead. Inexpensive renditions of this season's trends keep pace with more traditional classics for both sexes. ♦ M-F, Sa morning Mar-Oct; M afternoon, Tu-Sa Nov-Feb. Borgo San Lorenzo 34r (between Via dei Cerretani and Piazza San Lorenzo). 211309

Nuti

18 Nuti ★★$$ It's nothing much to look at, but this is one of the few places in Florence that serve continuously and don't discourage clients from eating only what they want instead of a full-course meal; perhaps the only real reason to eat here! Some things to want are *penne alla Nuti* (pasta in a sauce of prosciutto, peas, and mushrooms) and, when in season, *cinghiale alla maremma* (a wild boar stew). There is a vast choice of other dishes, but most locals come for the pizza. ♦ Tu-Su lunch and dinner. Borgo San Lorenzo 24r (between Via dei Cerretani and Piazza San Lorenzo). 210145

19 San Giovanni Evangelista This small neighborhood church, begun in 1579 by **Bartolommeo Ammannati** and finished in 1661 by **Alfonso Parigi the Younger,** was restored after World War II along with **Ammannati**'s Santa Trinita Bridge. ♦ Via de' Gori (at Via Martelli)

Man About Town

Ever concerned with triumph over tyranny, Florentines often commissioned artists to address subjects such as Perseus and Hercules, but it was David—slayer of Goliath—who is most closely associated with this city and most often represented here. The **Museo del Bargello** has a large number of Davids. Donatello's two treatments there are a marble sculpture from 1408 and a bronze form made around 1430. Verocchio's version is also bronze and dates from earlier than 1476, when it was documented that it had been acquired to decorate **Palazzo Vecchio.** Also at the **Bargello** is a marble statue begun around 1531 by Michelangelo, alternately known as *David* and *Apollo*.

Michelangelo's 1501-1504 *David* at the **Galleria dell'Accademia** is considered the definitive version (and perhaps one of the greatest pieces of sculpture in the world). To the endless stream of visitors who come to stare in quiet awe, the sheer perfection of proportion and flawless comprehension of the human anatomy are even more astonishing in light of the fact that Michelangelo was barely 26 years old when he threw himself into the four-year project. Eventually the artist was given the privilege of going directly to Carrara's marble caves to select the piece of stone within which he believed his next figure was "trapped." For David, however, he inherited a long columnlike stone that had been nicknamed "il Gigante." It had been worked, spoiled, and then abandoned by Agostino di Duccio in the courtyard of the **Opera del Duomo;** Michelangelo considered himself lucky to attempt what he thought of as the ultimate challenge.

The *David* established Michelangelo as one of the leading sculptors of the Renaissance and secured his favor with wealthy art patrons and popes, whose commissions kept him busy and (solvent) in the years that followed. Having finished the *Pietà* (now on view in the Vatican's St. Peter's Basilica) just one year before his commission to create *David*, Michelangelo was hardly an unknown fledgling. But even with the completion of *David*, his success was hindered by the predicted scandal of having been the first to depict this biblical figure in all his anatomical perfection. Lacking a fig leaf, *David*, which D.H. Lawrence would much later call "the genius of Florence," was nearly forbidden occupation of his original location in the **Piazza della Signoria,** where a life-size replica stands today.

The victim of jeers and egg-throwing, the sculpture elicited strong reactions from those who hated it. William Hazlitt, an early 19th-century Grand Tourist and drama critic, described it as "an awkward overgrown actor at one of our minor theatres, without his clothes." Perhaps it was more an actor looking for the appropriate stage: *David* was moved in 1873 (to protect it from the elements) by being slowly rolled on logs to a special hall built for its display in the **Galleria dell'Accademia,** where it stands proudly today, representative of Italy's unrivaled artistic patrimony.

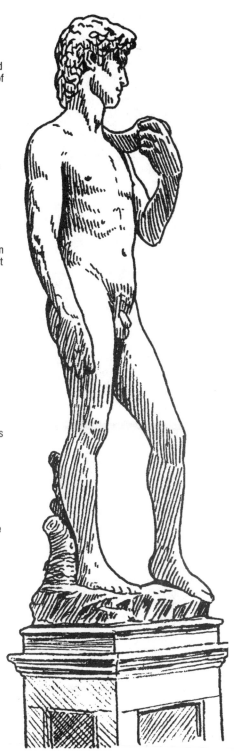

20 Mercato di San Lorenzo (San Lorenzo Market) Don't be fooled by the low-rent, almost souklike air of this outdoor clothing and souvenir market, which snakes through a number of streets. The simple canvas-covered vendors' stalls, called *bancarelle*, are equipped with electricity, cellular phones, and charge card machines. (Many of the free-spirited vendors also have near-perfect American accents, one product of their nocturnal trysts with junior-year–abroad coeds who, along with Italian and foreign tourists, make up the market's clientele.) Best buys are woolens, scarves of all sizes and designs, gloves of all leathers and linings, and other leather goods. Also be on the lookout for (besides pickpockets) unusual trends in T-shirts and sweaters. And unlike most other Florentine merchants, they occasionally bargain here, particularly with cash customers buying more than one item. ♦ M-Sa Mar-Oct; Tu-Sa Nov-Feb. No midday closing. Piazza San Lorenzo, Via dell'Arrento, and surrounding streets

21 Palazzo Inghiarini More interesting than its more rusticated neighbor, **Palazzo Bonaluti,** this 16th-century palazzo boasts a bust of Cosimo I by Baccio Bandinelli, whose monument to Giovanni delle Bande Nere stands in the piazza below and whose descendants once lived here. ♦ Piazza San Lorenzo 2 (at Borgo la Noce)

Within the Palazzo Inghiarini:

Sergio ★★$ This is another typical neighbor-hood trattoria in one of the most typical of Florentine neighborhoods. Open for lunch only, it features daily pasta specialties and grilled meats and caters to market vendors with serious appetites. Don't expect to linger (they make their *lire* on fast turnover), but do try the house wine from the Gozzi family's Chianti vineyard. ♦ M-Sa lunch. No credit cards accepted. Piazza San Lorenzo 8r (at Borgo La Noce). 281941

Back in the 16th century, Catherine de' Medici married King Henry II of France, and her cousin Maria de' Medici married Henry IV. The women took their cooks, their recipes for creams, sauces, pastries, provisions of olive oil and ice cream, and the Italian invention of the *forchetta* (the fork) to the French court—along with their trousseaus. As an Elizabethan poet said, "Tuscany provided creams and cakes and lively Florentine women to sweeten the taste and minds of the French."

22 Zà-Zà ★★$$ This family-run trattoria is one of the most popular neighborhood places among Florentines and visitors alike. Tuscan classics such as *ribollita* (soup made with white cannellini beans, bread, and black cabbage) is served in an informal setting of communal wooden tables and faded movie-star posters. ♦ M-Sa lunch and dinner. Piazza Mercato Centrale 26r (at Via Rosina). 215411

23 Palazzo della Stufa The Stufa family (the name means Hot Bath) made enough money running medieval saunas to build this 14th-century palazzo, where a 16th-century loggia and the modern stovepipe openings in the windows one floor below apparently still help let off steam. ♦ Piazza San Lorenzo 4 (between Via de' Ginori and Via della Stufa)

Within the Palazzo della Stufa:

Passamaneria Toscana The best and most extensive selection of home-decor trimmings in Florence can be found here, including fabrics, borders, and the ever-popular cord tassels (one of the city's most versatile gifts). ♦ M-F, Sa morning Mar-Oct; M afternoon, Tu-Sa Nov-Feb. Piazza San Lorenzo 12r (between Via de' Ginori and Via della Stufa). 214670. Also at: Via della Vigna Nuova (at Via Federighi). 2398047

24 La Ménagère This purveyor of housewares, one of the best in Florence, looks like an old-fashioned general store, with worn wooden floors, a long counter, and a vintage cash register. The shop sells everything from the traditional Tuscan glass *fiasco* (flask) for cooking beans to Richard Ginori ovenware and china, highly designed Alessi stovetop espresso makers, and Guzzini plastic items. ♦ M-F, Sa morning Mar-Oct; M afternoon, Tu-Sa Nov-Feb. Via de' Ginori 8r (between Piazza San Lorenzo and Via Taddea). 213875

GIRaFFA
il mondo per casa

24 Giraffa A group of young design-conscious Florentines created this contemporary souk that sells an eye-catching array of hand-crafted goods from around the world. The bright, tastefully mounted space creates a comfortable environment for browsing among the artisanal glass, ceramics, and rugs. Lighting is a specialty here, and two Italian-made products are highlights: replicas of old Murano glass–and-iron ceiling fixtures; and terra-cotta sconces made in Puglia.

Restaurants/Clubs: Red   **Hotels:** Blue
Shops/ 🍴 Outdoors: Green   **Sights/Culture:** Black

M afternoon; Tu-Sa. Via de' Ginori 20r (between Piazza San Lorenzo and Via Taddea). 283652

25 After Dark Of all Florence's English-language bookshops, this one has the largest selection of Italy-related material in English. Norman Grant, the affable Scottish proprietor, is expanding his stock of English-language magazine titles (he already carries over 200) and English-language videocassettes. The videos may make thoughtful gifts for your Anglophone Florentine friends, especially if they understand the expression "couch potato." But unless you have a VCR that can play European PAL system cassettes, don't take these videos home! There are also lots of tasteful, artistic cards and postcards. ♦ M-F, Sa morning Mar-Oct; M afternoon, Tu-Sa Nov-Feb. Via de' Ginori 47r (between Via Taddea and Via Guelfa). 294203

26 Palazzo Medici-Riccardi This palazzo by **Michelozzo,** (see drawing below) was commissioned in 1444 by Cosimo de' Medici for the Medici family, who received such visitors as Emperor Charles VIII and Charles V of France. The corner arches were originally an open loggia, filled in with the first examples of the bracketed kneeling windows (designed by **Michelangelo**) that became all the rage on Florentine palazzi and to this day enrage tourists who bump into them. In the 18th century, the Riccardi family had the facade lengthened by seven windows on the **Via Camillo Cavour** side. All that remains of the extensive Medici art collection once installed in the palazzo is in the **Cappella di Benozzo Gozzoli,** also referred to as **"Cappella dei Magi."** The chapel contains frescoes by 15th-century artist Benozzo Gozzoli depicting the *Journey of the Magi,* in which various members of the Medici family take part in a delightful procession through the Tuscan countryside. Upstairs is a 17th-century fresco by Luca Giordano, *The Apotheosis of the Medici,* commissioned by the Riccardi family to commemorate the original owners of the palazzo. ♦ Admission. M-Tu, Th-Sa; Su morning. Via Camillo Cavour 1 (at Via dei Gori). 27601

27 Casci $ A recent restoration has put this former 15th-century convent in prime shape, further enhanced by the accommodating Lombardi family. The 18 rooms all have private showers as well as such amenities as color TV, **CNN,** and telephones. It's more than one could hope for in a budget hotel—particularly the 17th-century frescoed ceilings in some of the public rooms. There's no restaurant. ♦ Via Camillo Cavour 13 (between Via dei Gori and Via Guelfa). 211686; fax 2396461

28 Colomba $ Great for the young at heart, this hotel is as plain and neat as they come and sparkles with a fresh coat of paint. It is most memorable for the gracious hospitality of its young, English-speaking owners. Some of the 17 large, tiled rooms (15 with private baths) are spacious enough to sleep four. There's no restaurant. ♦ Via Camillo Cavour 21 (between Via dei Gori and Via Guelfa). 289139

29 Frette This Milan-based firm has been supplying the world with luxury bed, bath, and table linens and lingerie for more than 125 years. Traditional, classic, and contemporary prints appear on beautiful quality cottons,

Palazzo Medici-Riccardi

silks, and linens. ♦ M afternoon; Tu-Sa. Via Camillo Cavour 2 (at Via dei Pucci). 292367

30 Viceversa There is a sleek, often humorous touch of Milanese design evident here in the tabletop objects that look like they belong in a modern art museum. A back room is dedicated to designs by Alessi for the kitchen and home, one of the better-known labels in this signature-obsessed consumer culture. ♦ M-F, Sa morning Mar-Oct; M afternoon, Tu-Sa Nov-Feb. Via Ricasoli 53r (between Via dei Pucci and Via Guelfa). 2398281

31 Il Papiro This is one of four locations of the shop whose specialty is Florence's trademark marbleized paper, sold in sheets or decorating an array of desk and other accessories. ♦ M-F, Sa morning Mar-Oct; M afternoon, Tu-Sa Nov-Feb. Via Camillo Cavour 55r (near Via Guelfa). 215262. Also at: Piazza del Duomo 24r (between Via dell'Oriuolo and Via dei Servi). 215262

32 Il Guelfo Bianco $$ After an extensive refurbishment this 29-room hotel is contemporary, efficiently run, and nicely decorated. Pluses include location (midway between the **Duomo** and the **Piazza San Marco**), beautiful bathrooms, a helpful staff, and a peaceful courtyard. There are an additional eight rooms in the adjacent **Cristallo** annex. There's no restaurant. ♦ Via Camillo Cavour 57 (at Via Guelfa). 288330; fax 295203

33 Palazzo Marucelli Go through the bizarre doorway of this 17th-century palazzo by **Gherardo Silvani** to see 18th-century frescoes by Sebastiano Ricci depicting *Scenes from Roman History, The Labors of Hercules,* and *Hercules Ascending Olympus*. The palazzo now serves as seat of the **University of Florence Law School.** ♦ Via San Gallo 10 (between Via Guelfa and Via XXVII Aprile)

34 Monastero di Sant'Appollonia This former monastery (begun in the 11th century and remodeled in the 14th century), which now houses various departments of Florence's university, has a lovely portal (attributed to **Michelangelo**) that leads to a cloister and on to Poccetti's fresco of the *Last Supper* in the former refectory. ♦ Via San Gallo 25-A (between Via Guelfa and Via XXVII Aprile)

35 Cenacolo di Sant'Appollonia Andrea del Castagno's 15th-century *Last Supper* fresco unfolds dramatically beneath three scenes of the Passion. ♦ Tu-Su. Via XXVII Aprile 1 (between Via San Gallo and Via Santa Reparata). 23885

36 Miró ★★$$ This eatery's stylized design in a large space creates an ambience not usually associated with Tuscan food. In fact,

the menu often emphasizes inventive fish preparations such as *pesce spada con capperi e ricotta* (swordfish with fresh capers and ricotta cheese). More conventional Tuscan specialties and meat dishes are also served. ♦ M-Sa lunch and dinner. No credit cards accepted. Via San Gallo 57-59r (near Via XXVII Aprile). 481030

37 San Zanobi ★★$$ Mariangela and Delia, the two sisters who operate this restaurant, pride themselves on their elegant preparations of Florentine dishes old and new, such as the classic *pappardelle al sugo di coniglio* (homemade pasta with rabbit sauce), one of the rarest and best regional pasta dishes. ♦ M-Sa lunch and dinner. Via San Zanobi 33r (between Via Guelfa and Via XXVII Aprile). 475286

38 Cose Buone ★★$ A Milanese-style *paninoteca* (sandwich shop), unusual for Florence, this pretty place offers more than 100 interesting and tasty sandwich combinations as well as crepes and ice cream. ♦ M-Sa 7AM-1AM. No credit cards accepted. Via San Zanobi 63r (near Via XXVII Aprile and Via F. Bartolommei). 473160

39 Don Chisciotte ★★★$$$ Owner Walter Viligiardi's mother was a cook for descendants of the Corsini princes, and he carries on the princely tradition with such dishes as *risotto dell'ortolano* (risotto with garden vegetables) and *filetto al sale con salsa alle erbe aromatiche* (filet of beef with herb sauce). ♦ M dinner; Tu-Sa lunch and dinner. Via C. Ridolfi 4-6r (near Via di Barbano). 475430

40 La Macelleria ★★$$ The husband-and-wife team of Danilo and Daniela does marvelously refined justice to this space's past as a butcher shop with such dishes as *tagliata al pepe verde e rosemarino* (beef with green pepper and rosemary), and they extend their talents to land and sea in *riso verde con pignoli al burro di salmone* (green risotto with pine nuts and salmon butter). ♦ M-Sa lunch and dinner. Via San Zanobi 97r (near Via della Ruote). 486244

41 Taverna del Bronzino ★★★$$$ Set in a 16th-century historical landmark palazzo, this antiques-filled restaurant offers such palatial dishes as *tortelloni al cedro* (pasta with lime) and *involtini di vitella al sedano e gorgonzola* (veal rolls with celery and gorgonzola, a pungent blue cheese). There is a large selection of local and international wines and grappa, the Italian aquavit. ♦ M-Sa lunch and dinner. Via delle Ruote 25r (between Via San Santa Reparata and Via San Zanobi). 495220

42 Hotel Cimabue $$ At the very low end of this category, yet offering amenities of a more expensive category (attentive service, tasteful decor, color TVs, etc.), this 15-room hotel is a delightful alternative when the better-known ones are booked. Named after Giotto's master teacher, artistic touches can be found in the preserved ceiling frescoes, hand-painted and decorated furniture, and the recent (and tasteful) refurbishment of this 19th-century palazzo. The friendly and professional Rossi family make their presence known. There's no restaurant. ♦ Via Bonifacio Lupi 7 (at Via Santa Reparata). 475601; fax 471989

43 Residenza Johanna $ Its location—just slightly outside the "hub" of town, yet within easy walking distance—explains the low prices of this lovely *pensione*-like residence. Of the 12 rooms, only one double has a private bath. The well-furnished library, enthusiastic English-speaking proprietors, attention to detail (all rooms have electric kettles for a tea break or simple breakfast), and special weekly and monthly rates make this a home-away-from-home for an interesting clientele of foreign guests. There's no restaurant. No credit cards accepted. ♦ Via Bonifacio Lupi 14 (at Via San Gallo). 481896; fax 482721

44 Palazzo Pandolfini Based on designs by Raphael, this elegant 16th-century palazzo (see drawing below) was built by **Giovanni Francesco** and **Aristotle da Sangallo** for bishop Giannozzo Pandolfini, as the strange inscription under the cornice indicates. Peek through the iron gate to see the statue-studded garden, in which the bishop presumably contemplated the pressing theological issues of the day. ♦ Via San Gallo 74 (near Via Salvestrina)

45 Chiostro dello Scalzo Andrea del Sarto's 16th-century frescoes here include remarkable representations of scenes from the life of St. John the Baptist, such as *The Visitation, Charity,* and *Justice.* ♦ Admission. Tu-Su. Via Camillo Cavour 69 (between Via XXVII Aprile and Via Salvestrina). 2388603

46 Antica Farmacia di San Marco Like the Dominicans of **Santa Maria Novella,** the Dominicans of **San Marco** founded a pharmacy, and the variety of pampering products at this one would have made Savonarola start a pharmaceutical bonfire of the vanities. Commercial creams, soaps, shampoos, and eau de cologne seem even more appealing amid the antique fixtures. You can also fill real prescriptions here. ♦ M-F, Sa morning Mar-Oct; M afternoon, Tu-Sa Nov-Feb. No credit cards accepted. Via Camillo Cavour 146r (between Piazza San Marco and Via Dogana). 210604

47 Casino di San Marco Built in 1574 as a laboratory for Francesco I de' Medici by **Bernardo Buontalenti,** today this large palazzo is the headquarters of the Court of Appeals. ♦ Via Camillo Cavour 57 (between Via XXVII Aprile and Via Salvestrina)

Palazzo Pandolfini

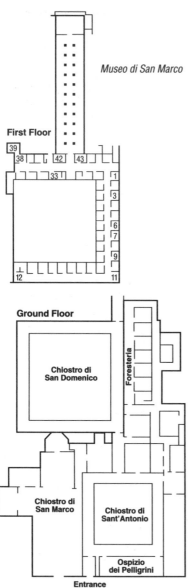

Museo di San Marco

First Floor

39
38 · 42 · 43
33 · 1
3
6
7
9
12 · 11

Ground Floor

Chiostro di
San Domenico

Foresteria

Chiostro di
San Marco

Chiostro di
Sant'Antonio

Ospizio
dei Pellegrini

Entrance

48 Museo di San Marco (San Marco Museum) or Museo dell'Angelico (Fra Angelico Museum) The church and convent of San Marco were built in 1299 on the site of Vallombrosian (later, Sylvestrine) monasteries. Dominicans from the nearby town of Fiesole took it over in the 15th century (Savonarola became Prior of **San Marco** before he was dragged from it to his death in **Piazza della Signoria**). Cosimo Il Vecchio financed its expansion in 1437-53 by **Michelozzo,** setting apart two cells for his own meditations. The decorations of those cells by Fra Angelico and his assistants, along with other works by the 15th-century Dominican friar-painter, are what

still draw visitors inside beyond the almost generic facade designed in 1780 by **Giocchino Pronti.**

Michelozzo's **Chiostro di Sant'Antonino** (Cloister of Sant'Antonino) is reached through the entrance vestibule to the right of the church (see floor plan on left). The **Ospizio dei Pellegrini** (Pilgrim's Hospice), which once hosted religious pilgrims, now houses 20 paintings by Fra Angelico, among them *The Madonna of the Linen Guild* and the San Marco altarpiece, which, in addition to the church's patron saint, Mark, represents the Medici patron saints Cosmas and Damian. The **Sala Capitolare** (Capitolary Room) across the courtyard has Fra Angelico's *Crucifixion* and a *Last Supper* by Domenico Ghirlandaio. Upstairs is Fra Angelico's *Annunciation* and the monks' cells frescoed by the friar and his assistants. Fra Angelico's hand is most evident in the cells on the left side of the corridor, especially cell **Nos. 1** *(Noli Me Tangere),* **3** *(Annunciation),* **6** *(Transfiguration),* **7** *(The Mocking of Christ),* and **9** *(Coronation of Mary).* Savonarola stayed in **No. 11** (his portrait, by Fra Bartolommeo, is on the right side of the vestibule of **No. 12**), Fra Angelico in cell **No. 33,** and old Cosimo de' Medici in **Nos. 38** and **39.** The passage between **Nos. 42** and **43** is where the crowd nabbed Savonarola; beyond it is **Michelozzo**'s harmonious library, today displaying the manuscript collection started by Cosimo. ♦ Admission. Tu-Su 9AM-2PM. Piazza San Marco 3 (entrance on northeast side of piazza). 23885

49 Piazza San Marco This Italian provincial piazza looks like a hundred others of its ilk in Italy. And like the others, it is a pleasant place to rest, with the requisite trees, benches, and cumbersome monument to an obscure war hero. The administration building of the **University of Florence,** many buildings of which are in the vicinity, is in the southeast corner of the piazza at **No. 4.** ♦ Between Via G. La Pira and Via Camillo Cavour at Via XXVII Aprile

50 Setteclavo For the *appassionato* of classical music this shop has more than 50,000 titles available on vinyl, tape, and CD. A knowledgeable but respectful staff advises in a multitude of languages and may be further consulted by mail through the store's members' club. ♦ M-F, Sa morning Mar-Oct; M afternoon, Tu-Sa Nov-Feb. Piazza San Marco 10r (south side of piazza). 287017

51 Biblioteca Marucelliana (Marucelli Library) This library, founded in 1752 with the collection of Francesco Marucelli, contains over 400,000 works, among them rare books, manuscripts, and prints. ♦ M-F (no midday closing); Sa morning. Via Camillo Cavour 43 (between Via Guelfa and Piazza San Marco). 210602

Dynasty, Italian-Style

The one family most closely associated with Florence is the Medici, which held power without interruption from the 15th through the 18th centuries and whose ball-studded coats of arms still hang with varying degrees of pomp around the city.

The Medici fortune originally came from the banking business founded by Giovanni di Bicci (1360-1429). His son Cosimo il Vecchio (1389-1464) rose to power in the Florentine Republic. Cosimo's son Piero il Gottoso (Piero the Gouty, 1416-69) further enhanced the family fortune by marrying Lucrezia Tornabuoni, daughter of another wealthy Florentine banker, and enriched the family prestige when his illegitimate grandson, Giulio (1478-1534), became Pope Clement VII. Piero and Lucrezia's legitimate son, Lorenzo il Magnifico (Lorenzo the Magnificent, 1449-92), began the family tradition of wedding nobility with his marriage to Clarice Orsini of the patrician Roman family. Lorenzo continued the tradition of commissioning great works of art and was a distinguished man of letters; his powerful presence in the Neoplatonic Academy brought together the best minds of his day and laid the groundwork for the rediscovery of classical ideals, which led to the Renaissance. The family's association with the church was strengthened when Lorenzo's son Giovanni (1475-1521) became Pope Leo X, and its noble aspirations were further advanced when Il Magnifico's grandson, Lorenzo II (1492-1519), became Duke of Urbino and Lorenzo II's daughter Catherine (1518-89) married Henry II of France. After a period of unrest, the family reestablished itself when Cosimo I (1519-74) became Duke of Florence and then Grand Duke of Tuscany. While his marriage to Eleanor of Toledo and the marriages of their son Francesco I (1541-87) to Joanna of Austria and of their granddaughter Maria (1573-1642) to Henry IV of France strengthened the family's ties to royalty, court life was growing increasingly dreary under Medici absolute power. On the death of the decadent Gian Gastone (1671-1737), the Medici line came to a disappointing finish.

Reminders of the dynasty, in addition to the numerous works of art and architecture made under their rule, are the numerous Medici coats of arms displayed throughout Florence. The ball motif probably came from the coins on the coat of arms of the bankers' guild with which the family was once linked, reinterpreted as pills in a play on the Medici name (which means doctors). One of the balls is often decorated with a French symbol of nobility, the fleur-de-lis, a prophetic privilege Louis XI granted Piero the Gouty early on in the Medici line.

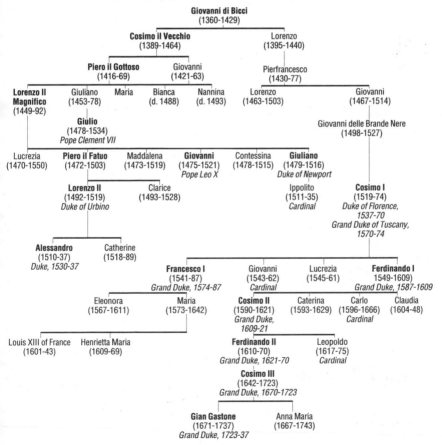

52 Calamai Of the four Florence branches of this novelty-housewares outlet, this one has the largest selection of merchandise. The children's stuff on the ground floor is a bit too cute for words, but downstairs are colorful plastic items for use throughout the home. ♦ M-F, Sa morning Mar-Oct; M afternoon, Tu-Sa Nov-Feb. No midday closing. Via Camillo Cavour 74r (at Via degli Alfani). 214452

53 Galleria dell'Accademia Michelangelo's *David* is the highlight of this gallery. You'd best see it right away, to dispel the tension. The towering masterpiece is at the far end of the gallery, standing majestically in its own room, which was built for it in the 19th century when it was moved indoors from **Piazza della Signoria** (where a full-size replica now stands in its place). Carved from a block of white Carrara marble that had been worked and abandoned by another sculptor, *David* is a mature representation of the Biblical subject, which had been portrayed more youthfully (some say effeminately) by Donatello and Verrocchio, and also represented Michel-angelo's coming of age as a sculptor (he was barely 26 when he began it). A clear Plexiglas screen was placed around the base of statue in early 1992, after a deranged devotee smashed *David*'s toe (it was restored within weeks). After you catch your breath, head back to see the other works by Michelangelo: *Slaves, St. Matthew, The Palestrina Pietà*. The gallery also has a good collection of primitive painting, as well as works by Alesso Baldovinetti and Botticelli. ♦ Admission. Tu-Sa; early closing Su. Via Ricasoli 60 (between Via degli Alfani and Piazza San Marco). 23885

54 Palazzi Gerini These two fused palazzi dominate the street's architecture. The first was designed by **Bernardo Buontalenti** and reworked in the 19th century; the other is attributed to **Gherardo Silvani.** ♦ Via Ricasoli 40-42 (near Via degli Alfani)

55 Opificio Pietre Dure Florentine mosaic, or *pietre dure,* is the art of inlaying semiprecious stone that was so popular during the days of the Medici Grand Dukes, as seen in the **Cappelle Medicee.** Here you can see it in a museum. Though these mosaics seem precious indeed to modern eyes, it is amusing to see them depict views of Florence like grandiose postcards. There are also examples of *pietre dure* used in various types of furniture. The museum was closed since 1991 for renovation and was scheduled to reopen as we went to press; call first. ♦ Admission. M-Sa. Via degli Alfani 78 (near Via Ricasoli). 210102

The real cause of the Renaissance was not the fall of Constantinople, the invention of printing, or the discovery of America, though these were phases in the process; it was, quite simply, money.

55 Biblioteca del Conservatorio di Musica Luigi Cherubini (Luigi Cherubini Library of the Conservatory of Music) Among the collection of the library of Florence's prestigious music academy are ancient instruments as well as violins, violas, and cellos by Stradivarius and other famed Italian instrument makers. ♦ By appointment only. Via degli Alfani 80 (near Via Ricasoli). 292180

56 La Mescita *Mescita* is another Tuscan term for wine shop (like *fiaschetteria*), and this one has quite a mix of wines, Tuscan and otherwise, including fizzy Lambrusco from Emilia-Romagna. Cheese, salami, and a hot dish-of-the-day are also served on inviting granite-topped wooden tables. ♦ M-Sa lunch and dinner (shop opens at 8AM). No credit cards accepted. Via degli Alfani 70r (near Via dei Servi). 2396400

57 Robiglio Florence's most revered *pasticceria,* it has been known for over half a century for such goodies as its *torta campagnola,* a rich torte stuffed with fresh and candied fruit. Unfortunately, there are no tables. ♦ M-Sa 8AM-8PM. Via dei Servi 112r (between Via degli Alfani and Piazza della Santissima Annunziata). 212784

58 Piazza della Santissima Annunziata

Florence's most perfectly proportioned piazza is surrounded by loggias on three sides (see engraving at right). Within it is some rather less harmonious sculpture—two strange fountains by Pietro Tacca depicting sea creatures (they were destined for the Medici port of Livorno, but were so well liked they remained in Florence) and a pompous equestrian statue of *Fernando I de' Medici,* begun by Giambologna and finished by Tacca. The piazza has been the center of folkloric activity in the city for many centuries. Its church's namesake image of the Annunciation, according to legend begun by a monk and finished by an angel, was a popular pilgrimage destination. Annunciation Day used to mark the beginning of the Florentine calendar and is still commemorated with a celebration by city officials and a little fair in the piazza on 25 March. On 8 September children carry lanterns to the piazza from the **Duomo** down **Via dei Servi,** which becomes an open-air candyland for the Festa delle Rificolone, or Lantern Festival. ♦ Between Via dei Servi and Via C. Battisti

Santissima Annunziata

58 Palazzo della Regione (Palazzo Riccardi-Mannelli) This imposing 16th-century palazzo by **Bartolommeo Ammannati,** an administrative building shared by the province of Florence and the region of Tuscany, is unusual in Florence for its exposed brick. ♦ Piazza della Santissima Annunziata (southwest corner of piazza)

58 Ospedale degli Innocenti Since 1988, part of this facility has been used as a research center by UNICEF. The facade of the foundlings' hospital is by **Brunelleschi,** with medallions by Andrea della Robbia. Inside is the **Galleria degli Innocenti,** a gallery that contains works by Piero di Cosimo, Filippo Lippi, and Domenico Ghirlandaio. ♦ Admission. M-Tu, Th-Su. Piazza della Santissima Annunziata 12 (at Via della Colonna). 2479317

58 Santissima Annunziata Long one of the Florentines' favorite churches, this is the first choice for society weddings. The entrance to the 13th-century church, rebuilt in 1444-81 by **Michelozzo** (see floor plan at right), called the "*Chiostrino dei Voti*" (Cloister of the Ex-Votos), once held wax votive offerings (ex-votos) left by pilgrims. It has lovely 16th-century Mannerist frescoes. On the right portico wall are a *Visitation* [1] (numbers refer to floor plan) by Jacopo Pontormo (he is buried in the **Cappella di San Luca,** as is Benvenuto Cellini) and an *Assumption* [2] by Rosso Fiorentino. At the end of the right wall is Andrea del Sarto's *Birth of the Virgin* [3]. An earlier work, Alesso Baldovinetti's *Nativity* [4] (containing one of the earliest landscapes in Italian painting), is to the left of the nave entrance. Inside the nave, immediately to the left, is **Michelozzo**'s *tempietto,* which houses the miraculous image of the *Annunciation*

[5]. The nave itself is a Baroque extravaganza relieved by Andrea del Castagno's 15th-century *Vision of St. Julian* [6] above the altar and his *Holy Trinity* [7] in the second chapel on the left. At the far end of the circular presbytery is a chancel [8] decorated in the late 16th century by Giambologna as the tomb for the sculptor and his fellow Flemish artists working in Florence; to its left is a 16th-century *Resurrection* [9] by Bronzino. The **Chiostro dei Morti** (Cloister of the Dead), to the left of the church,

Santissima Annunziata

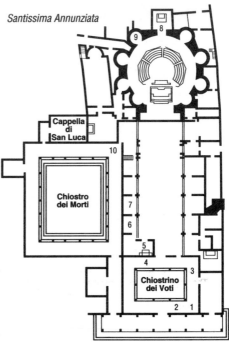

contains Andrea del Sarto's masterpiece, the *Madonna del Sacco* **[10]**, which takes its name from the sack on which St. Joseph is leaning in this representation of the Holy Family. ♦ Piazza della Santissima Annunziata (north side of piazza)

58 Loggiato dei Serviti $$$ Like **Due Fontane,** this even smaller and far more charming hotel faces Florence's most architecturally satisfying piazza. Originally a 16th-century convent, this 29-room hotel offers some of the more tastefully decorated lodgings in town, with period wrought-iron beds and terra-cotta floors. It's almost always full, so book well in advance. There's no restaurant. ♦ Piazza della Santissima Annunziata 3 (southwest corner of piazza). 289592; fax 289595

58 Le Due Fontane $$$ This small, modern hotel with 50 rooms takes its name from the two fountains by Pietro Tacca that it faces. Rooms and views (they'll try to accomodate your request for a view of the square) are a nice balance of cleanliness and pleasantness, and this is a particularly quiet location for being just five minutes from the **Duomo.** There's no restaurant. ♦ Piazza della Santissima Annunziata 14 (southeast corner of the piazza). 280086; fax 294461

Morandi alla Crocetta
Firenze

59 Morandi alla Crocetta $$$ This quiet nine-room hotel is furnished with antiques, paintings, icons, and medieval manuscripts. The latter accoutrements are quite fitting, considering the place is housed in a former convent dating from the 16th century. (**Room 29** still has original frescoes filling one wall.) The genteel Anglo-Italian owners make guests feel they have been welcomed into a private home. There's no restaurant. ♦ Via Laura 50-52 (between Via della Pergola and Via Gino Capponi). 2344747; fax 2480954

60 Museo Archeologico The highlights of this museum include the *François Vase,* a fifth-century BC Greek vase signed by Kleitias and Ergotimus; a mother figure from the Etruscan town of Chianciano; an important Egyptian collection; a fourth-century bronze chimera restored by Benvenuto Cellini; and a first-century BC Etruscan orator statue. The top floor contains a jumble of Greek and Etruscan material. ♦ Admission. Tu-Su. Via della Colonna 36 (between Via della Pergola and Via Gino Capponi). 2478641

61 Palazzo Giugni **Bartolommeo Ammannati**'s palazzo, built about 1577, has a lovely fresco, *Allegory of Art,* in its courtyard.

♦ Via degli Alfani 48 (near Via dei Fibbiai)

62 Rotonda di Santa Maria degli Agnoli This rather academic-looking octagonal church was begun by **Brunelleschi** some time after he went to Rome in 1433. He completed his trip, but not the church, which was restored to its original nonsplendor in this century. It now houses the **University of Florence**'s **Centro Linguistico.** ♦ Via degli Alfani (at Via del Castellaccio)

63 Palazzo Niccolini This 16th-century palazzo by **Baccio d'Agnolo** is decorated with 19th-century sgraffiti, the two-tone stucco designs popular during the Renaissance. Go inside to see the two courtyards, and if the *portiere* will let you in, you can also admire the 17th- and 18th-century frescoes. ♦ Via dei Servi 15 (between Via de' Pucci and Via degli Alfani)

64 Fior di Loto ★$$ None of the Chinese restaurants in Florence are on a par with those in the rest of the West—or with this one. The names of some of the dishes have been Italianized (the spring rolls appear on the menu as cannelloni), but the Beijing specialties remain the same. Finish your meal with some *frutta fritta* (fried bananas, apples, pears, or pineapple) and a grappa (aquavit) called *mautai,* made with millet. By the way, the Italian word for chopsticks is *bastoncini.* ♦ Tu-Su lunch and dinner. Via dei Servi 35r (near Via de' Pucci). 2398235

65 Dino Bartolini This shop stocks a vast array of Italian housewares and unabashedly displays high-tack cookie jars alongside genuinely high-tech contemporary designs by Alessi and others. ♦ M-F, Sa morning Mar-Oct; M afternoon, Tu-Sa Nov-Feb. Via dei Servi 30r (at Via Bufalini). 211895

66 Palazzi Pucci Historians have attributed the design of these connected palazzi to **Bartolommeo Ammannati** and **Paolo Falconieri.** Note the coats of arms of Cardinal Pucci and Leo X (a Medici pope), the latter badly deteriorated. ♦ Via de' Pucci 2-6 (between Via dei Servi and Via Ricasoli)

Within the Palazzi Pucci:

Pucci The Marchese Emilio Pucci, who died in 1992, was famous for his bright silk patterns, which began adorning the jet set almost as soon as there were jets. Apparently loving a woman in uniform, he then extended his line to brighten the costumes of airline stewardesses and Florence's meter maids. His silk scarves have become the colorfully un-uniform uniforms of young-minded old money and the new rich alike. Scarves are but the most classic and accessible items available in his boutique, which sells blouses, dresses, and palazzo pajamas—the designer's contribution to the evening wear of the 1960s. ♦ M-F, Sa morning Mar-Oct; M afternoon, Tu-Sa Nov-Feb. Via de' Pucci 6. 283061. Also at: Via Vigna Nuova 97-99r (in Piazza Goldoni). 294028

Perry Bond This is the source for striking costume jewelry by the designer who adorns the necks, wrists, and ears of luminaries the likes of Elizabeth Taylor and Princess Caroline. The affable Bond has transplanted American designs and painstakingly produces each piece of glittering fantasy by hand. Swarovski crystals come together with semi-precious stones in combinations that are meant to be seen and not described. Most pieces are formal and elegant, but many are more casual and even classic for the timid and less ostentatious; the prices are surprisingly approachable. ♦ M-F; Sa morning. Via de' Pucci 4. 2302995

67 **Teatro Niccolini** This 17th-century theater, modern on the inside, is one of the most active in Florence. ♦ Via Ricasoli 5 (between Piazza del Duomo and Via de' Pucci). 213282

68 **San Michelino** Inside this Baroque-style church, designed in 1660 by **Michele Pacini,** at the second altar on the right, is *Holy Family with Saints* by Florentine Mannerist Jacopo Pontormo. ♦ Via dei Servi (at Via Bufalini)

69 **Ospedale di Santa Maria Nuova** Florence's oldest hospital was founded in 1287 by Folco Portinari (the father of Beatrice, Dante's beloved). Its portico, perhaps designed by **Bernardo Buontalenti,** contains busts of the Medici; inside the portico are frescoes by the 16th-century artist Taddeo Zuccari and the 17th-century artist Pomarancio. Within the hospital complex itself are the 15th-century church of **Sant'Egidio** and the former monastery of **Santa Maria degli Angeli,** as well as a 15th-century fresco of the *Crucifixion* by Andrea del Castagno. ♦ Piazza Santa Maria Nuova 1 (Via Sant'Egidio at Via F. Portinari)

70 **Teatro della Pergola** Court spectacles took place in a wooden theater built on this spot by **Ferdinando Tacca** in 1656. Subsequently rebuilt more than once, the present 18th-century structure by **Giulio Mannaioni** was heavily altered in the 19th century. It is still one of the city's busiest theaters. ♦ Via della Pergola 12-32 (between Via Sant'Egidio and Via degli Alfani). 2479651

71 **Museo di Firenze Come'Era** This museum recounts the history of the city's growth from the Renaissance on, displaying topographical maps, prints, and paintings. Its grounds, the **Giardino delle Oblate,** are peaceful proof that Florence hasn't grown by too many leaps and bounds. ♦ Admission. M-W, F-Su. Via dell'Oriuolo 4 (between Piazza Salvemini and Via F. Portinari). 2398483

72 **Teatro dell'Oriuolo** Another one of Florence's theaters, this one primarily presents plays in Italian. The theater and its street take their name from an old Florentine word for clock. ♦ Via dell'Oriuolo 31 (between Piazzas Salvemini and del Duomo). 2340507

Child's Play

Have the kids seen one too many Michelangelos? Though the art and architecture of the Renaissance can be aesthetically pleasing and culturally enriching, some of the following activities—with a focus on fun—might well be your children's (and perhaps your) most vivid recollection of travel in Italy.

In Florence

Enjoy a picnic in the farthermost reaches of the **Boboli Gardens,** behind the **Palazzo Pitti,** then stroll the gardens, stopping along the way to pose like the statues. (Keep an eye out for the more grotesque ones!) From the eastern confines of the gardens, you can reach **Forte Belvedere** by foot, another perfect grassy venue-with-a-view.

Pick up everyone's spirits at any of the city's well-known *gelaterie,* perhaps the world-famous **Vivoli.** There are dozens of flavors to pick from (coconut! melon! black cherry!): A large cup can accommodate half a dozen creamy wonders.

Rub the nose of the *Porcellino* in **Mercato Nuovo.**

Roam the **Mercato San Lorenzo,** an open-air market just north of the **Duomo,** in search of everything from souvenir "Firenze" T-shirts and Italian football banners to leather jackets and silk scarves.

In Venice

Cruise the small back canals of Venice on a meandering gondola. Or try a far less expensive *vaporetto* ride down the **Canal Grande:** The *No. 1* will transport you past the hundreds of proud palazzi lining the *Canalazzo* (patrician homes of the wealthy merchants who once made the Venetian Republic one of the most powerful in Europe).

Take a trip to **Murano**'s glass-blowing *fornaci* (furnaces), where you'll learn about Venice's thousand-year history as an unrivaled leader in the glass industry, and see firsthand the local masters perfecting this delicate art.

Climb the steep steps inside the **Basilica di San Marco** up to the **Museo,** where you'll get a close-up view of the famous *quadriga* (four horses) kept here, protected from the elements; while outside on the open loggia, you'll find copies of the horses standing guard over the piazza, the bell tower, and the lagoon to your left, sparkling in the sun.

Build sandcastles on the **Lido.**

In Milan

Ride to the roof of the white gothic **Duomo** and spend some time amidst the forest of marble pinnacles and hundreds of statues, while taking in the view of the busy piazza and surrounding neighborhood.

Visit the armor exhibit at **Castello Sforzesco.**

Santa Croce

The church of **Santa Croce** is where Lucy Honeychurch becomes flustered in E.M. Forster's novel *A Room with a View*, not having brought along her *Baedeker*. These days, most of the frustration in Santa Croce comes from tourists not having brought along their credit cards to the area's numerous leather and souvenir stores, while others object to the presence of tourists and shops here in the first place.

Since Lucy Honeychurch's time (not to mention that of Michelangelo, who lived in the neighborhood as a boy), Santa Croce has changed from a place of lowlife to a place of hard sell. Shady ladies used to operate in the area between the churches of **Santa Croce** and **Sant'Ambrogio,** and the debtors' prison once

occupied the site of the **Teatro Verdi**. While much has remained the same (prisons still occupy its eastern end, and minor drug dealing in Florence currently occurs around the otherwise wonderfully animated **Via dei Neri** and **Piazza San Piero Maggiore**), the area continues to be gentrified. Little antiques shops have sprung up around **Piazza dei Ciompi** and, throughout the area, **Via Ghibellina** has become something of a restaurant row for all budgets; other entrepreneurs are opening shops and restaurants in the surrounding streets. Once one is off the well-trodden tourist track between the parking lots on the *viali* and the leather shops surrounding **Piazza Santa Croce**, the area can still be a rather pleasant place for a stroll, with or without a guidebook.

RUGGINI

1 Ruggini This *pasticceria* is known for its *crostate* (pies) and *millefoglie* (the rough Italian version of the French pastry mille-feuilles, a.k.a. Napoleon). ♦ Tu-Sa. No credit cards accepted. Via dei Neri 76r (near Via dei Leoni). 214521

2 Mario ★$ This trattoria-*rosticceria* is an informal place where you can stand up and eat at the counter or sit beneath the ancient brick vaults. ♦ Tu-Su lunch and dinner. No credit cards accepted. Via dei Neri 74r (between Via della Mosca and Via dei Leoni). 2382723

3 Eito ★$$ One of Florence's two Japanese restaurants, this one maintains strict standards, not because the city is so gastronomically cosmopolitan (Florentines, in fact, are notoriously unadventurous in their eating habits), but because of the large groups of Japanese tourists who eat here. Specialties are sushi and *yakizakan* (grilled fish). ♦ Tu-Su lunch and dinner. Via dei Neri 72r (between Via della Mosca and Via dei Leoni). 210940

4 San Remigio Founded on the site of an 11th-century inn for French pilgrims, this Gothic church dating from the 13th and 14th centuries has a *Madonna and Child* by a follower of Cimabue, who was known as the "Master of San Remigio." ♦ Piazza San Remigio, at Via de' Magalotti and Via Vinegia

5 Da Benvenuto ★$ Yet another typically Florentine neighborhood trattoria, the fare here includes wonderful first-course soups and good *bollito misto* (or boiled meats) served with *salsa verde*, a sauce made with parsley and olive oil. ♦ M-Tu, Th-Sa lunch and dinner. No credit cards accepted. Via della Mosca 16r (at Via dei Neri). 214833

6 Fiaschetteria Vecchio Casentino This inviting neighborhood watering hole, with its old marble tables and wood bar, offers a large selection of prepared foods against a background of soothing classical music. ♦ M-Sa 11AM-3PM, 6PM-midnight. No credit cards accepted. Via dei Neri 17r (between Via dei Benci and Via della Mosca). 217411

7 Piccolo Slam If you're wondering where fashion-conscious *bambini* get their threads, look no farther. This high-toned boutique outfits children from six to 16 years old in Italian-made fashions by Armani, Simonetta, and C.P. All the design sensibility, workmanship, and quality fabrics that have set Italian adult fashion apart from the rest is available here for the younger set. Party outfits for special occasions (*da cerimonia*) will make you sigh, while across the street at **No. 9/11r**, newborn to six-year-old customers can be outfitted in mostly French labels. ♦ M afternoon; Tu-Sa. Via dei Neri 10 (between Via dei Benci and Via della Mosca). 294610

8 Hotel Balestri $$$ The rooms in this family-run hotel (30 facing the Arno and 20 facing a quiet courtyard) are a good choice within walking distance of all major sites. ♦ Piazza Mentana 7 (at Lungarno Generale Diaz). 214743; fax 2398042

9 CarLie's This elegant incarnation of an American-style bakery produces authentic cupcakes, cheesecake, and chocolate chip cookies hot from the oven. Best of all, in a concession to baking *all'italiana*, the brownies are made with Perugina chocolate. ♦ M-F afternoon; Sa-Su morning. No credit cards accepted. Via delle Brache 12r (between Via dei Neri and Piazza dei Peruzzi). 292664

10 Piazza dei Peruzzi This evocative little piazza retains the original residences and the name of the medieval banking family, the Peruzzi, whose descendants run leather shops in the vicinity. ♦ At Via delle Brache and Via Bentaccordi

11 Osteria da Quinto ★★$$ Though this downstairs restaurant seems a bit garish and touristy at first, the food makes up for it. "Quinto" could stand for quintessence, since the eponymous owner's menu is a paragon of Florentine and Tuscan cooking. Classics such as *baccalà alla livornese* (dried salt cod Livorno-style in a tomatoey stew) are paired with such simple yet inventive dishes as *incavolata*, Quinto's warming concoction of polenta (cornmeal) with *cavolo nero* (black cabbage). ♦ Tu-Su lunch and dinner. Piazza dei Peruzzi 5r (east side of piazza, off Via dei Verdi). 213323

Restaurants/Clubs: Red	**Hotels:** Blue	
Shops/ ♦ Outdoors: Green	**Sights/Culture:** Black	

Palazzo Corsini

12 Migliori This shop stocks a colorful array of terra-cotta and ceramic housewares and decorative objects from Tuscany and other parts of Italy. ♦ M-F, Sa morning Mar-Oct; M afternoon, Tu-Sa Nov-Feb. No credit cards accepted. Via dei Benci 39 (between Via dei Neri and Piazza Santa Croce) 283681

Ristorante del Fagioli
Zucchini - Ceroni s.d.f

13 Ristorante del Fagioli ★★$$ Named after "Beans," a famous buffoon of the Grand Ducal court who used this spot as his watering hole when it was a simple *fiaschetteria* (tavern), this rustic restaurant preserves other Florentine traditions in its cuisine. It offers all the usual Tuscan soups, as well as such dishes as osso buco (roast veal shank) and, on Friday, *baccalà alla livornese* (a Tuscan stew of dried salt cod and tomatoes). ♦ M-F Mar-Oct; M-Sa Nov-Feb; lunch and dinner. No credit cards accepted. Corso dei Tintori 47 (near Via dei Benci). 244285

13 Museo Horne Housed in the late 15th-century Renaissance **Palazzo Corsi,** which was designed by **Cronaca,** the collection of 19th-century British art historian Herbert Percy Horne includes a number of paintings by the so-called Primitives (Agnolo Gaddi, Bernardo Daddi, Pietro Lorenzetti, Filippo Lippi) as well as some interesting Mannerist art (by Domenico Beccafumi and Dosso Dossi). There are also some appealing pieces of decorative art scattered throughout the museum. ♦ Admission. M-Sa. Via dei Benci 6 (between Lungarno Generale Diaz and Corso dei Tintori). 244661

14 Plaza Lucchesi $$$ This comfortable, stylish hotel is just far enough away from the hustle and bustle of the center of town to be quiet (with the help of soundproof windows), yet still an easy walk to most tourist attractions. Its 100 rooms, some with room-length terraces, have views of the Arno in front and **Santa Croce** in the rear. Its restaurant, **La Serra,** is a spacious and serene spot for breakfast, lunch, or dinner. ♦ Lungarno della Zecca Vecchia 38 (east of Piazza dei Cavalleggeri). 26236; fax 2480921

15 Biblioteca Nazionale (National Library) The core of the national library's collection includes one of the greatest assemblages of incunabula and illuminated manuscripts in the world. On public view in this imposing early 20th-century building by **Cesare Bazzani** are early editions of Dante's *Divine Comedy* as well as sculpture by Giovanni della Robbia and Antonio Canova. ♦ M-F; Sa morning. Piazza dei Cavalleggeri 1 (at Corso dei Tintori). 244443

16 Palazzo Corsini The elegant (and elegantly barred from public access) courtyard of yet another palazzo belonging to the Corsini family (this one dates from the Renaissance) has 19th-century frescoes by Gasparro Martelli. ♦ Borgo Santa Croce 6 (between Santa Croce and Via dei Benci)

17 Palazzo Spinelli-Rasponi The facade and interior courtyard of this Renaissance palazzo are decorated with the two-tone stucco work known as *sgraffiti*. ♦ Borgo Santa Croce 10 (between Santa Croce and Via dei Benci)

18 Palazzo dell'Antella The colorful frescoes on the facade of this 17th-century palazzo by **Giulio Parigi** were applied by a team of artists in an astounding 20 days. The current restoration of the delicate facade took much longer. ♦ Piazza Santa Croce 21 (south in piazza)

19 Piazza Santa Croce This large, open piazza is lined with stately corbelled palazzi on one side and their gawky poor relations on the other. Both sides are more interesting than the green-and-white marble church facade, which was added just in the last century, as was the campanile. As the Dominicans preached in the piazza in front of **Santa Maria Novella,** so the Franciscans preached in the piazza before **Santa Croce.** This piazza was also used for public spectacles, including jousts in honor of such noble families as the Visconti, Sforza, and Medici. As in centuries past, it is still used as a soccer field by the local urchins (the marble disk dated 1565 in front of the palazzo at **No. 21** marks the center line), who daily reenact the ancient rite as if hired by the city to do so. In June a more deliberately historical spectacle, Calcio in Costume, takes place in the piazza. Played in costume and by medieval rules, the game ends up resembling less its modern equivalent than a Renaissance drawing by Antonio Pollaiuolo, as it degenerates into a giant wrestling match with balletic overtones. ♦ Bounded by Via Magliabechi and Via dei Benci

20 Cappella Pazzi and Museo dell'Opera di Santa Croce (Pazzi Chapel and Santa Croce Museum) Here in the freestanding 15th-century chapel, **Filippo Brunelleschi** used the same harmonious circle-in-a-square idea that he had used in the **Old Sacristy** in the church of **San Lorenzo.** Despite the chapel's name (it means "crazies" and actually derives from the family name of its patrons, also known for their role in the notorious Pazzi Conspiracy), it is one of the most peaceful spots in Florence, as are the surrounding cloisters (see drawing below) Decoration of the chapel is by Luca della Robbia, who was responsible for the 15th-century tondos of St. Andrew over the door and the Apostles in the chapel. **Brunelleschi** may have made the tondos of the Evangelists. In the museum, Cimabue's *Crucifixion* has become somewhat of a symbol of the 1966 flood, which totally submerged it and lifted huge patches of paint from its surface. It has since been restored.

Cappella Pazzi and Museo dell'Opera di Santa Croce

Also on display are Donatello's 15th-century *St. Louis of Toulouse* and a 14th-century *Last Supper* by Taddeo Gaddi. ◆ Admission. M-Tu, Th-Sa. Piazza Santa Croce 16 (south of church). 244619

21 Santa Croce Begun in 1294 by **Arnolfo di Cambio,** with additions made in 1560 by **Giorgio Vasari,** and a facade finished in 1863 by **Niccolò Matas,** this vast church is not quite in keeping with the humble practices of St. Francis. The town fathers erected it (on the site of an earlier church) as a showplace for the glory of Florence as much as for the gentle preaching order of the Franciscans. In the former function, the church contains the tombs and cenotaphs of many of the city's illustrious citizens, a sort of Gothic (then Neo-Gothic) Pantheon. Franciscan principles come through in its fresco decoration by Giotto and his pupils, at once vivid and faded.

Within the vast, simple space are an equally vast number of tombs, cenotaphs, and works of art (see floor plan below). At the first pilaster in the right aisle is Antonio Rossellino's 15th-century tomb of Francesco Nori **[1]** (numbers refer to floor plan), topped by his *Madonna and Child.* In front of it is Vasari's 16th-century monument to Michelangelo **[2]** (buried here). Just ahead is Stefano Ricci's belated 19th-century cenotaph to Dante Alighieri **[3]** (not buried here, although he is also commemorated by a statue outside). Farther on is Benedetto da Maiano's 15th-century pulpit with marble reliefs of *Scenes of the Life of St. Francis* **[4]**; on the wall behind it is Antonio Canova's 19th-century monument to poet Vittorio Alfieri **[5]**. Farther along is Innocente Spinazzi's 18th-century monument to Niccolò Machiavelli **[6]** (buried here), followed by Donatello's 15th-century *Annunciation* **[7]**, in the unusual medium of gilded *pietra serena,*

and Bernardo Rossellino's elaborate 15th-century tomb of Leonardo Bruni **[8]**, a Florentine statesman. The right transept has the **Cappella Castellani [9]**, frescoed with scenes from the lives of saints in the 14th century by Agnolo Gaddi and his pupils; and the **Cappella Baroncelli [10]**, with wonderfully human 14th-century frescoes of scenes from the life of the Virgin, the masterpiece of Taddeo Gaddi, who also did the crucifix in the sacristy. The two chapels to the right of the chancel, the **Cappella Peruzzi [11]** and the **Cappella Bardi [12]**, have 14th-century frescoes by Giotto, damaged in the course of having been whitewashed, uncovered, and restored. Another **Cappella Bardi [13]**, in the left transept, contains a 15th-century crucifix by Donatello. The left aisle has Desiderio da Settignano's 15th-century lavish tomb of Carlo Marsuppini **[14]**, a Florentine statesman, and Giulio Battista Foggini's monument to Galileo **[15]** (buried here). ◆ Piazza Santa Croce (east side)

22 I Francescano ★★$$ Named after the humble Franciscan monks who built the nearby church of **Santa Croce,** this stylishly rustic restaurant serves simple Tuscan cuisine to a young, professional crowd. Among the first courses is the house specialty, *risotto di erbe,* a soupy rice dish made with herbs and spinach. Second courses include *spezzatino* (veal with potatoes) and *bresaola* (smoked beef). ◆ M-Tu, Th-Su lunch and dinner. Largo Bargellini 16 (east of Piazza Santa Croce). 241605

23 Arte del Mosaico This workshop continues the art of *pietra dura,* the inlay of semiprecious stone, so popular during the days of the Medici grand dukes. Although elaborate tables and wall-hangings are available (at prices only a grand duke could afford), more portable (and affordable) items are the attractive jewelry boxes and cigarette cases. ◆ M-F, Sa morning Mar-Oct; M afternoon, Tu-Sa Nov-Feb. Largo Bargellini 2-4 (east of Piazza Santa Croce). 241647

The great Escoffier was moved to admit, "The French cuisine is an enriched capitulation of Tuscan cooking."

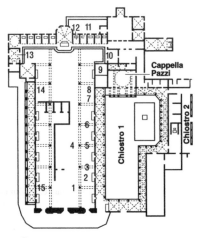

Santa Croce

24 Peruzzi The mercantile tradition of the medieval Peruzzi family continues in this spacious store, laid out to accommodate bewildered tour groups paraded in like cattle to peruse an array of leather goods—bags, clothing, wallets, etc. Groups and goods both would put the Chicago stockyards to shame. Quality increases significantly upstairs, with designer labels such as Armani, Valentino, and Moschino. ♦ Daily. Borgo dei Greci 8-14r, other entrance at Via dell'Anguillara 7-15r (west of Piazza Santa Croce). 289039

25 Palazzo Serristori The studied Classical elements of this Renaissance palazzo built from 1469 to 1474, more Roman than Florentine, have given rise to various attributions as to its architect, among them **Baccio d'Agnolo** and **Giuliano da Sangallo.** ♦ Piazza Santa Croce 1 (at Via dell'Anguillara)

26 Leo in Santa Croce ★★$$ Constructed on the site of the former Roman amphitheater, this restaurant retains original columns and capitals from that era and the early Renaissance. Even the atmosphere is somewhat theatrical, with a large international menu catering to tourists. Reliable choices include *risotto ai funghi* (a creamy rice and mushroom dish) and *bocconcini di vitello* (veal with peas and tomato). ♦ Tu-Su lunch and dinner. Via Torta 7r (west of Piazza Santa Croce). 210829

27 San Simone This 14th-century Gothic church was redone Baroque-style by **Gherardo Silvani** in 1630, but it retains some medieval frescoes as well as a terra-cotta garland in the style of the della Robbia family. ♦ Piazza San Simone (on Via Isola delle Stinche)

27 Cinema Astro In the not-too-distant past, practically the only movies shown at Florence's English-language uniplex were scratchy prints of *Midnight Cowboy* and *The Graduate.* Happily, though not first-run, the pix now seem to play around the same time as their release in the States. Consult local newspapers for films and show times. ♦ Tu-Su. Piazza San Simone (on Via Isola delle Stinche)

28 Il Pallottino ★★$$ The eponymous first course of this restaurant, penne Pallottino, is made with seven p's—penne, *porri,* pancetta, *pomodoro, peperoncino, panna,* and *parmigiano* (tubular pasta, leeks, Italian bacon, tomato, hot pepper, cream, and parmesan cheese). Expect good renditions of all the Florentine classics, from the typical soups (*ribollita, pappa al pomodoro, zuppa di farro*) to the *bistecca alla fiorentina.* The inexpensive lunchtime *menu turistico* is the latest draw. ♦ Tu-Su lunch and dinner. Via Isola delle Stinche 1r (between Via della Burella and Via della Vigna Vecchia). 28952573

28 Vivoli One of Florence's best, and certainly its best-known, this *gelateria* can be found by following the discarded paper cups to their well-lit and jam-packed point of origin, a third-generation family business that prides itself on its ability to make lip-smacking ice cream out of the freshest ingredients. ♦ Tu-Su 8AM-1AM. Closed January. No credit cards accepted. Via Isola delle Stinche 7r (between Via della Burella and Via della Vigna Vecchia). 292334

29 Acqua al Due ★★$$ This unique, forever-crowded restaurant features *assaggi* (tastings) as well as a full menu. First-course *assaggi* may be rice with gorgonzola cheese, artichokes, or *sugo verde* made with green vegetables; or pasta paired with salmon, pumpkin, mushrooms, and eggplant. Desserts are given the same treatment. ♦ Tu-F dinner, Sa-Su lunch and dinner. Reservations required. Via della Vigna Vecchia 40r (near Via dell'Aqua). 284170

30 Teatro Verdi The neighborhood's ancient theatrical tradition is alive and well here. (The outlines of the Roman amphitheater may be traced by following the curves of Via Torta and Via Bentaccordi a block away.) The modern entrance to Florence's most popular theater leads to a 19th-century interior with a capacity of 3,000. ♦ Via Ghibellina 99 (at Via Verdi). 2396242

31 La Maremma ★★$$ Tuscany's Maremma area prides itself on its rough and independent spirit, as the rustic decoration of this restaurant, complete with Maremma wagon wheels, bears out. Game in season is the specialty here (*salsiccia* and prosciutto made from *cinghiale,* or wild boar; partridge, etc.), as are the many dishes based on the more generic *tartufo,* or truffle. ♦ M-Tu, Th-Su lunch and dinner. Via Giuseppe Verdi 16r (north of Piazza Santa Croce). 244615

32 Palazzo Quaratesi Look up at the lovely loggia with Doric columns in this 14th-century medieval palazzo. ♦ Via Matteo Palmieri and Via Ghibellina

LIBRERIA SALIMBENI

33 Salimbeni One of the best art and antiquarian bookshops in the country (with many titles in English), it also operates a small press that produces Italian-interest books. ♦ M-F, Sa morning Mar-Oct; M afternoon, Tu-Sa Nov-Feb. Via Matteo Palmieri 14-16r (between Via Ghibellina and Via Pandolfini). 2340904

34 Danny Rock ★$$ This "pub," besides gathering a crowd of Florence's gilded youth, is one of the few places in the neighborhood for late-night crepes, pizza, and hamburgers. ♦ Tu-Su lunch and dinner until 1:30AM. Via dei Pandolfini 13r (at Via Palmieri). 2340307

Restaurants/Clubs: Red   **Hotels:** Blue
Shops/ ♥ Outdoors: Green   **Sights/Culture:** Black

35 Palazzo degli Alessandri Built in the 14th century, this is one of the oldest and most distinguished of the palazzi in this palazzo-populated area. ♦ Borgo degli Albizi 15 (between Via Palmieri and Via delle Seggiole)

36 Palazzo Altoviti The portrait busts of famous Florentines (Dante, Petrarch, Boccaccio, Amerigo Vespucci, etc.) adorning the facade of this 16th-century palazzo attributed to **Baccio Valori** earned it the name "Palazzo dei Visacci" (of the ugly faces). ♦ Borgo degli Albizi 18 (between Via delle Seggiole and Via Giraldi)

37 Palazzo degli Albizi This is considered the most imposing of the palazzi of the Albizi family, one of many Medici rivals. Built in the 16th century, it is attributed to **Gherardo Silvani.** ♦ Borgo degli Albizi 12 (between Via Palmieri and Via delle Seggiole)

38 Il Viaggio Florence's best shop for maps and travel guides for all destinations is worthy of the land of Christopher Columbus. ♦ M-F, Sa morning Mar-Oct; M afternoon, Tu-Sa Nov-Feb. Borgo degli Albizi 41r (near Piazza San Pier Maggiore).

38 Fornasetti Painter, sculptor, interior decorator, and creator of thousands of articles, each covered with his whimsical designs and fantasy, the late Milanese artist is represented here by a large number of his creations. Furniture, china, fabrics, trays, and ties are transformed by the genius that made Fornasetti famous throughout the world. ♦ M afternoon, Tu-Sa. Borgo degli Albizi 70r (near Piazza San Pier Maggiore). 2347398

39 I Ghibellini ★★$ This clean and modern place—nicest when you can eat outdoors in the small and lovely piazza—is useful for its large selection of inexpensive and decent pizzas. ♦ M-Tu, Th-Su lunch and dinner. Piazza San Pier Maggiore 8 (at Borgo degli Albizi). 214424

40 Loggia di San Pier Maggiore This piece of real estate (it can hardly be called a building) is all that remains of the **Matteo Nigetti**-designed 17th-century church of **San Pier Maggiore.** (It's also called "San Piero"; Piero is a Tuscan diminutive for Pietro, or Peter.) The church was demolished in 1784, and its former loggia was subsequently altered with uncharacteristic architectural insouciance. Two of its arches were filled in (the one on the left now houses a butcher shop), and a string of flats was built on top of it, the overall effect being rather more like devil-may-care Baroque Rome than rigid

Renaissance Florence. The *piazzetta* is still one of the more colorful corners of the city, with a daily produce stand and outdoor tables at **I Ghibellini.** ♦ Piazza San Pier Maggiore (at Borgo degli Albizi)

41 Natalino ★★$$$ This fish restaurant (one of only a handful in Florence) is especially good for such dishes as *spaghetti alle vongole* (spaghetti with clams), *risotto seppie nero* (creamy black rice made with squid ink), and *cannelloni di pesce* (tubes of pasta stuffed with fish). ♦ Tu-Su lunch and dinner. Borgo degli Albizi 17r (in Piazza San Pier Maggiore). 289404

42 Sbigoli Terrecotte Terra-cotta—plain, glazed, and painted—is the specialty of this shop, which stocks earthenware from all over Tuscany. Reliable shipping can be arranged, though it can double the price. ♦ M-F, Sa morning Mar-Oct; M afternoon, Tu-Sa Nov-Feb. Via Sant'Egidio 4r (at Borgo Pinti). 2479713

43 L'Enoteca Pinchiorri ★★★★$$$$ This elegant restaurant and *enoteca* (wine cellar) provides the most refined dining experience in Florence and is one of only a few restaurants in Italy to deviate successfully from its tried-and-true regional formula. It is also one of the few in the country to be awarded two Michelin stars. Given the sumptuous setting in a Renaissance palazzo (tables are set with Gambellara linen, Ricci di Alessandra silver, Riedel crystal, and delicate flowers) and Giorgio Pinchiorri's palate-boggling selection of thousands of vintages, Annie Féolde's cuisine manages to come off with a minimum of pretense while maintaining a healthy sense of adventure. The various *menu di degustazione* (inspired by fish, Tuscan regional cuisine, or simply by the chef herself, who comes from a long line of French restaurateurs), which present each course accompanied by a different wine, are the best way of sampling the legendary Pinchiorri cellar. ♦ M dinner; Tu-Sa lunch and dinner. Via Ghibellina 87 (between Via dei Pepi and Via Verrazano). 242777

The neighborhood today known as Santa Croce was once a suburb of early Florence. During its Renaissance heyday, this district was the center of the working-class wool and silk businesses. The dyeing, rinsing, stretching, and drying of fabric was a messy, smelly acitivity, and the damp and noisy workshops were confined to neighborhoods far from the elegant center of Florence so as not to offend the upper classes.

44 Casa Buonarroti (Michelangelo Museum)

Michelangelo did not live here (but rather in a house on the corner of Via dell'Anguillara and Via Bentaccordi west of **Piazza Santa Croce**), but he did buy the land for his nephew Leonardo, whose son Michelangelo Il Giovane (the Younger) had it decorated. On the death of Cosimo Buonarroti, the last of the line, in 1858, it was left to the state, which waited until 1964 to restore it. The space is sometimes used for interesting temporary exhibitions. Of special note in the permanent collection are Michelangelo's relief sculptures, *Madonna della Scala* (1490-92, his earliest known work) and *Battle of the Centaurs*. Other works by the master on display are a wooden crucifix (attributed) and his wooden model for the never-completed facade of **San Lorenzo.** ♦ Admission. M, W-Su. Via Ghibellina 70 (at Via Buonarroti). 241752

45 Alle Murate ★★★$$

Chef Umberto Montano designed the menu for the restaurant at the Metropolitan Opera in New York City, and the one at his restaurant in Florence is just as triumphant. *Orecchiette con le rape* ("little ears" of pasta with turnip greens) is an adaptation of a dish from his native Basilicata; more local in inspiration are his various *sformati di verdura* (a kind of mousse made with vegetables) or *di parmigiana* (with cheese). Light and refined are the operative words for the desserts (don't miss the "Armstrong," made with dense dark chocolate and fresh whipped cream). Experts will appreciate the fine wine list and the budget-minded should investigate the adjacent *vineria* (wine bar), which offers a more informal, less expensive menu from the same talented kitchen. ♦ Tu-Su dinner. Reservations recommended. Via Ghibellina 52r (between Borgo Allegri and Via Buonarroti). 240618

46 La Baraonda ★★★$$

The hearty and varied dishes here are prepared by Elena and served by husband Duccio in a refined dining room. There are always six first courses, including homemade tagliatelle pasta, often served with *ragù alla fiorentina* (made with chicken liver). Of the six main courses, you're always sure to find a vegetarian dish and the house specialty, *polpettone in umido* (meatloaf made from scratch). Desserts include a *torta di mela* (apple pie) like mother never made, topped with cream. Unusual, and delightful, is the *digestif nocino,* the walnut liqueur from Emilia-Romagna. ♦ M dinner; Tu-Sa lunch and dinner. Via Ghibellina 67r (at Borgo Allegri). 2341171

47 Dino ★★★$$$

A modernized Renaissance palazzo sets the tone for such historical dishes such as the house specialty, *stracotto del granduca* (beef with garlic, rosemary, almonds, pine nuts, mint, and cinnamon); each dish is paired with the owner's selection of fine Italian wines. ♦ Tu-Sa lunch and dinner; Su lunch. Via Ghibellina 51r (between Via dei Macci and Borgo Allegri). 241452

48 Piazza dei Ciompi

Woolworkers in medieval Florence, called *ciompi,* were a frustrated and rebellious lot who finally revolted in 1378, winning themselves the right to organize into guilds like the other professions. Their modern counterparts, in a sense, surly flea market vendors as opposed to full-fledged antiques dealers, occupy this piazza today, and on the last Sunday of the month they hold an outdoor market. At one end of the piazza is **Vasari**'s **Loggia del Pesce** (1567). It once housed a fish market in the center of Florence, but it was salvaged from the ill-advised urban renewal that created **Piazza della Repubblica** in the last century, and was reconstructed here in 1955. ♦ Tu-Sa; last Sunday of the month. No midday closing. Via Martiri del Popolo (between Via Buonarotti and Borgo Allegri)

49 Caffè Cibrèo ★★★$$

An old-fashioned cafe atmosphere prevails in Cibreo's latest enterprise. Coffee and cocktails may be sampled here along with such desserts as homemade cheesecake topped with marmalade made from Sicilian oranges. ♦ Tu-Sa 8AM-1AM. Via Andrea del Verrochio 5r (at Via dei Macci near Piazza Ghiberti). 2345853

50 Cibrèo Alimentari

Wines from the restaurant and olive oil from throughout Tuscany are sold here along with products from all over Italy (balsamic vinegar, dried porcini mushrooms, sun-dried tomatoes) and the world (the sight of Paul Newman's salad dressing is always good for a dash of culture shock). ♦ M-Tu, Th-Sa; W morning. Via Andrea del Verrocchio 4r (near Piazza Ghiberti at Via dei Macci). 2341094

50 Il Cibrèo ★★★$$$

Named for an old Florentine dish made of chicken giblets and cockscombs, this restaurant typifies more deliciously than any other in Florence the relatively recent move to let grandma's recipes out of the closet (or kitchen) and on to the plate. No country bumpkins, Fabio Picchi and wife Benedetta Vitali have attracted an international clientele (and opened a place in Tokyo) by basing their menu on Tuscan country cooking. Regularly occurring antipasti include chicken liver pâté and tripe and chick-pea salad. Of the excellent soups (there are no pastas), the one made with *peperoni gialli* (yellow bell peppers) is a favorite. If you don't like stuffed chicken necks, there are plenty of other dishes to choose from, such as rabbit, lamb, and pigeon boned and stuffed with seasonal vegetables, then proudly presented on sparkling white Ginori china in a refined trattoria setting. Behind the kitchen (entrance at Piazza Ghiberti 35r) is a no-frills, no-reservations restaurant **Il Cibreino,** where many of the same dishes are served on different plates (institutional rather than museum quality), at much lower prices. ♦ Tu-Sa lunch and dinner. Via dei Macci 118r (west of Piazza Ghiberti). 2341100

51 Le Campane ★★$$ This bustling place beneath the bells of the church of **Sant'Ambrogio** prides itself on its homemade ravioli (stuffed with everything from cheese to pumpkin) and a huge selection of main courses from all over Italy and the world, including *gran pezzo* (standing rib roast) and *scampi al cognac* (shrimp with cognac). ♦ Tu-Su lunch and dinner. Borgo la Croce 87r (between Via della Mattonaia and Piazza Sant'Ambrogio). 2341101

52 Mercato di Sant'Ambrogio Intended for neighborhood rather than citywide use, this market is more functional than its flamboyant counterpart in San Lorenzo. It houses a few inexpensive stand-up lunch counters along with stands where staples cost less than in other shops. Just outside are a number of stalls selling fresh farm produce and a ragtag assemblage of housewares and clothing. ♦ M-Sa 8AM-1PM. Piazza Ghiberti (between Via della Mattonaia and Via dei Macci)

53 Cose Cosi This housewares shop carries a full line of classic porcelain Tuscan ovenware made by Linea Tuscia. It features such items as a *fagioliera* for making beans, a boar's head–shaped dish for stews, and numerous baking dishes and casseroles. It's a nice shop, but perhaps not worth a detour unless you happen to be in the neighborhood. ♦ M-F, Sa morning Mar-Oct; M afternoon, Tu-Sa Nov-Feb. No credit cards accepted. Borgo la Croce 53r (east of Via della Mattonaia). 2343474

54 Sant'Ambrogio This site has had churches on it since well before the 13th century, from which the present structure dates. The plain facade was applied in 1888. The interior, redone in 1716, contains a tabernacle by Mino da Fiesole housing some miraculous blood, a 15th-century fresco by Cosimo Rosselli depicting a procession in front of the original church facade, and a 15th-century panel by Alesso Baldovinetti, *Angels and Saints.* ♦ Piazza Sant'Ambrogio (at Borgo la Croce and Via dei Macci)

55 Hotel J&J $$$ Housed in a 16th-century monastery, this hotel still provides an air of peace and tranquillity in a just-off-the-beaten-track part of town. In the public areas as well as in the 20 guest rooms, soft modern furnishings, including plenty of pillows, play off the solid wooden ceilings and stonework.

There's no restaurant. ♦ Via di Mezzo 20 (between Via dei Pepi and Piazza Sant'Ambrogio). 240951; fax 240282

56 Alessi ★★★$$ Giuseppe Alessi's stated aim is to reinterpret Tuscan food classics at prices everyone can afford. He does so with an almost missionary zeal in this monastic setting, preaching his culinary gospel to devoted initiates while also dishing out exquisite and ever-changing dishes. Technically the doors are closed to non-members, but if you hold up under strict scrutiny, you may be accepted on the spot (for a nominal membership fee). ♦ M-Sa lunch and dinner. No credit cards accepted. Via di Mezzo 24-26r (between Piazza Sant'Ambrogio and Via dei Pepi). 241808

57 Osteria il Chiasso ★★★$$ Though its name means uproar, the noise at this bistro-type restaurant is restricted to the groaning antipasto table and the bubbling *prosecco* wine (served on tap, as it is in Venice). Three comfortable dining rooms offer a menu that changes every two weeks but maintains such staples as *nicchette del Chiasso* (pasta with carrots, tomato, and onion) and *petto di pollo del Chiasso* (breast of chicken in white wine with onion). Desserts are all made on the premises and should be followed by a glass of one of 60 different kinds of grappa, the potent Italian aquavit. ♦ M dinner; Tu-Sa lunch and dinner. Via Fiesolana 13r (between Via di Mezzo and Piazza Salvemini). 242241

58 Hotel Monna Lisa $$$ This is one of the nicest small hotels in town (although some of the 30 guest rooms tend to be cramped). It is housed in the 14th-century palazzo belonging to the Neri family, whose most famous member, St. Philip Neri, was supposedly born in room **No. 19.** The palazzo, with terra-cotta floors, white stucco walls, and *pietra serena* details, is now property of the Duprè family, whose ancestor Giovanni's sculptures are displayed throughout. There is also some typically Florentine noise on the street side, so ask for a room with a view of the courtyard or the garden. There's no restaurant. ♦ Borgo Pinti 27 (between Via di Mezzo and Via dei Pilastri). 2479751; fax 2479755

59 Paperback Exchange As its name implies, this is the place to trade your English-language paperback book (as well as war stories about your travels in Italy) for one of thousands of well-thumbed volumes. Credit for your book is applied to the already-discounted price of your selection. Half of the stock of books is new with an emphasis on "Italianistica": Florentine and Italian art, culture, and history. ♦ M-F, Sa morning Mar-Oct; M afternoon, Tu-Sa Nov-Feb. Via Fiesolana 31r (at Via Pilastri). 2478154

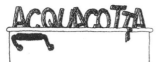

60 Acquacotta ★★$$ The signature dish of this warm Tuscan trattoria is *acquacotta*—not cooked water, as its name translates, but thick slices of toasted Tuscan bread smothered in vegetable soup and topped with a poached egg. New management has done little to disturb the traditional Tuscan menu and atmosphere of this comfortable restaurant. ♦ M, Th-Su lunch and dinner; Tu lunch. No credit cards accepted. Via dei Pilastri 51r (near Via Fiesolana). 242307

61 Tempi Futuri

Italians are great fans of comic books, to which the curious sight of grown men and women avidly reading them on trains and buses bears witness. Here you may begin to see why, as this shop is devoted to rack upon rack of such titles as *Topolino* (the little mouse, none other than Mickey), *Braccio di Ferro* (iron arm, or Popeye), *Superman* (Superman), and more esoteric Italian characters with cutesy and/or erotic overtones. Books, posters, and postcards on comic book themes are also available. ♦ M-F, Sa morning Mar-Oct; M afternoon, Tu-Sa Nov-Feb. No credit cards accepted. Via dei Pilastri 20-22r (between Via dei Pepi and Via Luigi Carlo Farini). 242946

62 Vainio Personalized stationery and calling cards in an imaginative array of colors are the specialty of this print shop. ♦ M-F, Sa morning Mar-Oct; M afternoon, Tu-Sa Nov-Feb. No credit cards accepted. Via dei Pilastri 18r (between Via dei Pepi and Via Luigi Carlo Farini). 243301

63 Tempio Israelitico (Jewish Synagogue) The first stone laid for Florence's synagogue came from Jerusalem; the rest is a fanciful Neo-Moorish pile of intricately carved, parti-colored stone topped with a copper dome. It was constructed 1874-82 to the designs of **Mariano Falcini, Marco Treves,** and **Vincenzo Micheli.** ♦ M-F, Su. Via Luigi Carlo Farini 4 (between Via dei Pilastri and Piazza Massimo d'Azeglio). 245252

64 Santa Maria Maddalena dei Pazzi The highlight of this church—rebuilt 1480-92 by **Giuliano da Sangallo,** and dedicated to a saint from Florence's own Pazzi family—is Perugino's fresco of the *Crucifixion* in the chapter house. In the church itself are paintings by 17th-century Neapolitan artist Luca Giordano (on either side of the high altar) and a modern stained-glass window by Isabella Rouault (in the fourth chapel on the right), which is a hint that the church is now in the hands of French Franciscans. ♦ Donation. Tu-Su. Borgo Pinti 58 (between Via dei Pilastri and Via della Colonna). 2478420

65 Palazzo Panciatichi Ximenes Enlarged in 1620 by **Gherardo Silvani,** Napoleon slept here in 1796, but long before that it was the residence of the architects **Giuliano** and **Antonio da Sangallo,** who built it circa 1499. ♦ Borgo Pinti 68 (at Via Giuseppe Giusti)

66 Hotel Regency $$$$ There's something almost volatile about the air of respectability suffusing this elegant, 33-room hotel in a 19th-century palazzo: It could be that the colors of the decor have taken William Morris to an almost psychedelic extreme, or that the tranquil green expanse of the shady **Piazza Massimo d'Azeglio** outdoors is disturbingly rare for Florence. But if you need to relax, there can hardly be a better place to do so without leaving the city. ♦ Piazza Massimo d'Azeglio 3 (north side of piazza). 245247; fax 2342938

Within the Hotel Regency:

Relais Le Jardin ★★★$$$ In two dazzlingly decorated dining rooms (one over-looking a garden that offers warm-weather seating, the other with a zodiac painted on the ceiling), chef Paolo Bisogno offers refined regional cooking from all over Italy and quality well above what you'd expect from a hotel restaurant. Some recurrent examples are *risotto alla milanese* (a creamy rice and saffron dish from Milan) and *orecchiette con broccoli* (ear-shaped pasta and broccoli, a specialty of Apulia). ♦ M-Sa lunch and dinner. Piazza Massimo d'Azeglio 5 (north side of piazza). 245247

67 Hotel Liana $ Housed in a 19th-century palazzo once occupied by the British embassy and now decorated in Art Nouveau style, this hotel has 26 peaceful rooms (all but three with private baths), many of them facing a garden planted with lonesome pines. There's a breakfast room but no restaurant. ♦ Via Vittorio Alfieri 18 (between Piazza Massimo D'Azeglio and Viale Antonio Gramsci). 245303; fax 2344596

68 Cimitero degli Inglesi (English Cemetery) This Protestant burial ground contains the mortal remains of such immortals as Elizabeth Barrett Browning, Frances Trollope, and the American preacher and abolitionist, Theodore Parker. ♦ Piazzale Donatello (at Viale Antonio Gramsci)

Oltrarno

For centuries Florentines have made a distinction between the *Arno di quà* (*this* side of the **Arno River**, spreading from its more developed north bank) and the *Arno di là* (*that* side of the Arno, along the south bank), also known as the Oltrarno, or the *other side* of the Arno. Perhaps because of that enduring distinction, based more on attitude than on actual distance, the Oltrarno has largely been spared the myriad shops and high-volume pizzerias that have sprung up across the river.

The Oltrarno embodies Florence in both its most palatial and most popular aspects. **Via Maggio** (from *maggiore*, or major), historically its most important street, is lined with noble palazzi housing elegant antiques shops. The **San Frediano** area, quite different in character, is a tight-knit neighborhood appreciated by outsiders who have strolled its colorful streets or read about it in the late Vasco Pratolini's book *Le ragazze di Sanfrediano* (The Girls of Sanfrediano), which beautifully captured the everyday drama of its working-class residents. In between is the **Santo Spirito** neighborhood, where the high- and low-rent aspects of the Oltrarno come together in perfect harmony.

It is easy to see why Florentines have a soft spot for the Oltrarno. Here you can still hear the hammering of craftsmen in their workshops (take a stroll down **Via Toscanella**) and the peal of bells from the campanile of **Santo Spirito**. Workshops and palazzi somehow take on a friendlier air, and even the pace seems slower and quieter in the Oltrarno.

---

1 Pitti Palace $$ This refurbished former *pensione*, while offering an excellent location and modern facilities, has, alas, very little character. The views from many of the 70 smallish rooms—you can almost reach out and touch the Ponte Vecchio—and the lovely roof terrace come close to making up for it. ◆ Via Barbadori 2 (at Ponte Vecchio). 2398711; fax 2398867

2 La Luna e le Stelle The women's blouses, dresses, suits, and coats here are beautifully custom-made by talented seamstress Anna Cei in the styles of big-name designers. ◆ M-F, Sa morning Mar-Oct; M afternoon, Tu-Sa Nov-Feb. Borgo San Jacopo 17r (between Ponte Vecchio and Via dei Ramaglianti). 214623

3 Hotel Lungarno $$$ Half of the 66 rooms at this contemporary hotel owned by the Ferragamo family, equipped with modern—albeit plain—accommodations amid ancient surroundings, have views of the Arno between its two loveliest bridges, and some even have balconies; others are comfortably installed in an adjacent medieval tower. There is no restaurant. ◆ Borgo San Jacopo 14 (at Via dei Ramaglianti). 264211; fax 268437

4 Giancarlo Giachetti Peek into Florence's past and its patrimony of artisanal masters with a visit to this young sculptor's *bottega* (workshop). He uses horseshoes, black-smith's nails, and other oddities to create a modern-day menagerie of crescent-taloned eagles and fanciful fish. ◆ M-F, Sa morning Mar-Oct; M afternoon, Tu-Sa Nov-Feb. No credit cards accepted. Via Toscanella 3-5r (between Via dello Sprone and Borgo San Jacopo). 218567

5 Nava & Nencini These silversmiths specialize in small birds and animals, but they also do custom work and will faithfully etch each feature of Felix or Fido should you wish a tony tribute to the family pet. ◆ M-F, Sa morning Mar-Oct; M afternoon, Tu-Sa Nov-Feb. No credit cards accepted. Via dello Sprone 4-4r (at Via Toscanella). 283224

6 Mamma Gina ★★★$$$ This elegant Tuscan trattoria is set in a vaulted 15th-century palazzo. Its extensive menu is based on Tuscan classics. Particularly good are the *minestrone di riso* (a vegetable soup) and *delizie alla Mamma Gina* (beef rolls in a creamy mushroom sauce). There is also an extensive wine list. ◆ M-Sa lunch and dinner. Borgo San Jacopo 37r (between Via Toscanella and Via Maggio). 2396009

7 Flos This is the Florence branch of the prestigious Italian lighting firm. The store sells its own brand of high-design fixtures, including such signatures as Achille Castiglione and Tobia Scarpa as well as lighting fixtures by Arteluce. ◆ M-F, Sa morning Mar-Oct; M afternoon, Tu-Sa Nov-Feb. Borgo San Jacopo 62r (between Via Toscanella and Via Maggio). 284509

8 Osteria del Cinghiale Bianco ★★★$$ The *cinghiale* (wild boar) in the name of this friendly restaurant (set dramatically and charmingly in a medieval tower and candlelit in the evening) appears in such items as antipasti made with gamy boar's sausage and prosciutto, and the main course of *cinghiale con la polenta* (boar with cornmeal). Another dish appropriate to the setting is *carabaccia*, a sweet-and-sour onion soup. There are also choices that allow for that rarity in Florence, a light lunch, such as the *insalata dello chef*, a chef's salad made with prosciutto, mozzarella, olives, and hard-boiled eggs. If you're in love, ask to be seated at table seven, in a romantic upstairs alcove. ◆ M, Th-Su lunch and dinner. No credit cards accepted. Borgo San Jacopo 43r (between Via Toscanella and Via Maggio). 215706

8 Cammillo ★★$$ The owners of this family-run restaurant pride themselves on the homemade pasta and dishes based on porcini mushrooms and truffles (when in season), which appear in such dishes as *taglierini* pasta (narrow flat noodles) with mushrooms and carpaccio (thinly sliced raw beef) with truffles. Other Tuscan dishes, from wild boar to beet greens, round out the menu. ◆ M-Tu, F-Su lunch and dinner. Borgo San Jacopo 57-59r (between Via Toscanella and Via Maggio). 212427

9 San Jacopo sopr'Arno This 13th-century Romanesque church has been altered through the ages, giving it a strange Romanesque-Baroque aspect today. At the entrance to the presbytery are two 14th-century frescoes, a *Pietà* and *Angels Holding the Monstrance*. ◆ Borgo San Jacopo (between Via Toscanella and Via Maggio)

Mannerist architect Bernardo Buontalenti is credited with creating in 1565 the first gelato for the court of Francesco I de' Medici.

Restaurants/Clubs: Red   Hotels: Blue
Shops/ ♥ Outdoors: Green   **Sights/Culture:** Black

9 Lo Spillo As its name implies, the point of this tiny specialty shop is pins, which come in all sizes and varieties (brooches, tiepins, lapel pins, stickpins, hat pins, etc.)—in case you're stuck for an unusual gift idea. ♦ M-F, Sa morning Mar-Oct; M afternoon, Tu-Sa Nov-Feb. No credit cards accepted. Borgo San Jacopo 72r (between Via Toscanella and Via Maggio). 293126

9 Angela Caputi If you've just bounced a check buying a designer dress, come here for accessories to the crime. The eponymous owner's imaginative costume jewelry coordinates conspiratorially with the strongest of fashion statements; she also sells her own line of clothes in an adjacent shop. ♦ M-F, Sa morning Mar-Oct; M afternoon, Tu-Sa Nov-Feb. Borgo San Jacopo 82r (between Via Toscanella and Via Maggio). 212972

10 Palazzo dei Frescobaldi Dating back to the 13th century, this is the oldest of the palazzi associated with the Frescobaldis. The family gave birth to a number of distinguished members, including ambassadors, composers, writers, and—currently—vintners. ♦ Piazza Frescobaldi 2r (at Borgo San Jacopo)

Within Palazzo dei Frescobaldi:

Vera This shop has the best (and most expensive) Tuscan takeout in town, with a full selection of regional cheeses and lunch meats, soups, prepared foods and pasta salads, breads, a broad wine selection, and mineral waters ideal for an idyllic picnic. ♦ M-Tu, Th-Sa; W morning. 215465

Giorgio Albertosi Neo-classical antiques, called *impero,* from "French Empire," are the specialty of this dealer, whose stock usually includes pieces from throughout Europe with a heavy Italian accent. ♦ M-F, Sa morning Mar-Oct; M afternoon, Tu-Sa Nov-Feb. 213636

11 Caffè Santa Trinita ★$ A pleasant, modern, and unhurried place for a coffee or sandwich break during or after a day's stroll. ♦ M-Sa 7:30AM-8PM. No credit cards accepted. Via Maggio 2r (in Piazza Frescobaldi at Via Santo Spirito). 214558

12 Bartolozzi e Maioli Fiorenzo Bartolozzi, Italy's finest wood-carver, is best known for his restoration of the famed choir stalls in the Benedictine abbey of Monte Cassino outside of Naples after it was destroyed during World War II. These days he and his workshop of master craftsmen continue to carve and gild practically anything imaginable for churches, palaces, and other distinguished clients. His two-floor showroom is filled with his creations great and small, from smiling cupids to fanciful life-size pythons and ostriches. ♦ M-F, Sa morning Mar-Oct; M afternoon, Tu-Sa Nov-Feb. No credit cards

accepted. Via Maggio 13r (south of Piazza Frescobaldi). 282675

13 Guido Bartolozzi One of Florence's leading and most exclusive antiques dealers, Signor Bartolozzi presides over a rambling space filled with furniture, paintings, and objets d'art ranging from the times of the Medici to those of Mussolini. ♦ M-F, Sa morning Mar-Oct; M afternoon, Tu-Sa Nov-Feb. Via Maggio 18r (south of Piazza Frescobaldi). 215602

14 Luciano Ugolini Signor Ugolini makes exquisite copper tubs and jugs in patterns inspired by the collection of the **Museo degli Argenti** in the **Palazzo Pitti.** The pieces are ideal as planters, since their timeless quality works well with practically any kind of decor. ♦ M-F, Sa morning Mar-Oct; M afternoon, Tu-Sa Nov-Feb. No credit cards accepted. Via del Presto di San Martino 23 (between Piazza Santo Spirito and Via Santo Spirito). 287230

15 Casa di Bianca Cappello This ancient palazzo, covered with delicate and recently restored sgraffiti decoration by Poccetti, was altered by **Bernardo Buontalenti** between 1570 and 1574 for the mistress (and later wife) of Francesco I de' Medici, the Venetian Bianca Cappello, whose family's coat of arms (featuring a *capello,* or hat) appears above the entrance. ♦ Via Maggio 26 (between Piazza San Felice and Frescobaldi)

16 Franceschi Frames from stately Renaissance style to Minimalist modern are the specialty of this shop. Though meant for paintings, they can also be used to make mirrors pretty as a picture. Even those weary of shopping should seek out this narrow street full of artisans whose *bottegas* (workshops) and skills are often centuries old. ♦ M-F, Sa morning Mar-Oct; M afternoon, Tu-Sa Nov-Feb. No credit cards accepted. Via Toscanella 34-38r (between Sdrucciolo de' Pitti and Via dei Velluti). 284704

The nations which have put mankind and posterity most in their debt have been small states—Israel, Athens, Florence, Elizabethan England.

Dean Inge

In the days before the Renaissance, Florence was ruled and governed by its merchants' and craftmen's guilds, progressive associations that organized everyone from butchers, bakers, and silkweavers to moneylenders (who were to become known as the first bankers of Europe, having invented the international letter of credit and established the first stable international currency, the 13th-century florin stamped with the Florentine lily).

17 Le Quattro Stagioni ★★$$ This restaurant, popular with the neighborhood's better-heeled antiques dealers, prides itself on its Italian and international menu. Homemade gnocchi (tiny potato dumplings) with spinach and ricotta, and *gran pezzo* (standing rib roast) are reliable choices here. ◆ M-Sa lunch and dinner. Via Maggio 61r (north of Piazza San Felice). 218906

18 Il Maggiolino One of the nicest things about the Art Deco items in this shop is that most of them (jewelry, tableware, toiletries) will fit neatly into your carry-on luggage. ◆ M-F, Sa morning Mar-Oct; M afternoon, Tu-Sa Nov-Feb. Via Maggio 80r (north of Piazza San Felice). 216660

19 Prezzemolo Some of the young and the restless (and rich) Florentines come to this nightspot to play board games (and bored games) in an unusual setting of catacomblike rooms divided up Italian-style into little seating areas for the local lounge lizards. ◆ Tu-Sa 9PM-2AM; Su 3:30PM-2AM. No credit cards accepted. Via delle Caldaie 5r (at Via della Chiesa). 211530

20 Piazza Santo Spirito This piazza, which extends before the Augustinian church bearing the same name, is as down-to-earth as **Piazza Santa Maria Novella** and **Piazza Santa Croce** are grand. A peaceful oasis, it is shaded by trees, cooled by a fountain, and enlivened by vendors who sell produce on weekday mornings. On the second Sunday of the month, there is a small open-air flea market here. This is also Florence's current favorite nighttime hangout for young people during the warm months. ◆ Via Mazzetto and Via delle Caldaie

21 Bandini $ This is one of the last old-fashioned *pensioni* in Florence, installed on the third floor of the Renaissance **Palazzo Guadagni** (attributed to **Cronaca** or **Baccio d'Agnolo**). Only three of its 10 large, simply furnished rooms have private baths, but all have views, either of peaceful **Piazza Santo Spirito** or of the historic neighborhood and nearby Tuscan hills. ◆ Piazza Santo Spirito 9 (at Via Mazzetta). 215308; fax 282761

22 Fondazione Salvatore Romano The only part of the Gothic monastery of **Santo Spirito** spared by the fire of 1471 is this foundation, established by a Neapolitan antiques dealer who worked in Florence. Housed in the former refectory just west of the church, it is also known as **"Cenacolo Santo Spirito."** Among the works on display are a *Last Supper* and a *Crucifixion* attributed to Andrea Orcagna, as well as Romanesque sculpture and other pieces attributed to Jacopo della Quercia, Donatello, and Bartolommeo Ammannati. ◆ Admission. Tu-Sa morning. Piazza Santo Spirito 29 (west of the church). 287043

22 Chiesa di Santo Spirito The church's 17th-century facade, almost Postmodern in its simplified line, rises like a pale plaster Holy Ghost. Inside is one of Florence's finest 15th-century Renaissance interiors, fairly faithful to **Filippo Brunelleschi**'s original design. (**Vasari**, however, remarked that had it not been for the alterations, this church would have been "the most perfect temple of Christianity," a surprising statement for a man who made such sweeping changes in so many of Florence's interior spaces.) In the right transept is Filippino Lippi's 15th-century *Nerli Altarpiece*, which depicts the nearby Porta San Frediano; the left transept has Andrea Sansovino's **Cappella Corbinelli**, which also contains some of his pieces of sculpture. A door beneath the organ leads to **Cronaca**'s 15th-century vestibule and **Giuliano da Sangallo**'s 15th-century sacristy, whose octagonal shape is based on the **Baptistry of San Giovanni**. ◆ M-Tu, Th-Su. Piazza Santo Spirito (north side of the piazza)

23 Zona This home-furnishings and lifestyle store, the first of its kind in Italy, is the fourth (and perhaps most beautiful) in the growing international chain. A painstakingly edited assemblage of handmade crafts marries the American Southwestern with the Italian in an aesthetically arresting display. ◆ M-F, Sa morning Mar-Oct; M afternoon, Tu-Sa Nov-Feb. Via Santo Spirito 11 (between Via Maggio and Via degli Serragli). 2302272

24 Arredamenti Castorina Florence's antiques dealers and restorers come here for the little bits of sculpted wood they use to mend and embellish their frames and furniture. Many of the pieces—putti, or geometrical shapes—are lovely objects in and of themselves, and make unusual souvenirs, gifts, and even Christmas tree ornaments. ◆ M-F, Sa morning Mar-Oct; M afternoon, Tu-Sa Nov-Feb. Via Santo Spirito 13-15r (between Via Maggio and Via degli Serragli). 212885

"Firenze, the most damned of Italian cities, wherein is place neither to sit, stand, nor walk . . ."

Ezra Pound

25 Angiolino ★★$$ This atmospheric Tuscan restaurant has a varnished-wood, yellowed-wall ambience that could have been painted by an Italian Frans Hals. This is the place to try classic Tuscan dishes and grilled meats (the grill is charcoal fired). The owner is the Florentine representative of the Sommeliers' Association, so there are over 50 wines to choose from—a rarity for an Italian trattoria! ♦ Tu-Su lunch and dinner. No credit cards accepted. Via Santo Spirito 36r (between Via Maggio and Via degli Serragli). 2398976

26 Marino There are two shifts of fresh-baked bliss at this *pasticceria* (pastry shop). Croissants, plain or filled with jams and custards, emerge from the oven each morning until noon, and then again after 4PM, into the eager hands of waiting Florentines. ♦ Tu-Sa; Su 8AM-1PM. Piazza Nazario Sauro 19r (at Ponte alla Carraia). 212657

27 Lamberto Banchi Master bronze worker Lamberto Banchi makes intricate tiny objects (frames, paperweights, candlesticks) and larger items (lamps, tabletops) in bronze and copper. He also repairs antiques made of those metals. ♦ M-F, Sa morning Mar-Oct; M afternoon, Tu-Sa Nov-Feb. No credit cards accepted. Via dei Serragli 10r (between Via Santa Monaca and Borgo San Frediano). 2394694

Gozzini e Restelli

28 Gozzini e Restelli Silver shines in this craftsman's workshop, where affordable small objects such as frames and "toilettes" (brush and mirror sets) are among the handcrafted items for sale. ♦ M-F, Sa morning Mar-Oct; M afternoon, Tu-Sa Nov-Feb. No credit cards accepted. Via dei Serragli 44r (between Via della Chiesa and Via Sant'Agostino). 284650

29 Vino Olio Renzo and Luana Salsi stock a full line of Italian wines and olive oils by such famous names as Antinori, Frescobaldi, and Villa Banfi. Other delicacies include truffled olive oil, aged balsamic vinegars, and vinegars made with champagne and fermented apples. ♦ M-Tu, Th-Sa; W morning. No credit cards accepted. Via dei Serragli 29r (between Via della Chiesa and Via Sant'Agostino). 2398708

30 Cinema Goldoni Want to know where to find Mel Gibson, Michelle Pfeiffer, Richard Gere, and Arnold Schwarzenegger during your stay in Florence? The Anglo-American community (and with 32 junior year–abroad university programs, it's large and growing) lives for Monday night showings of English-language movies (including films from England and Australia). Now, if they'd only break out the popcorn and Milk Duds. ♦ M 3:30PM-10:45PM. Via dei Serragli 109 (north of Porta Romana). 222437

31 Diladdarno ★★$$ This is the local option for local cuisine in a typical trattoria. Tuscan first-course soups (minestrone, *ribollita, pappa al pomodoro*) and Florentine main courses (*trippa alla fiorentina, baccalà*, osso buco) are available here. ♦ W-Su lunch and dinner. No credit cards accepted. Via dei Serragli 108r (between Via del Campuccio and Via della Chiesa). 225001

32 Trattoria I Raddi ★★$$ The Raddi family, which owns and operates this trattoria, serves up a special sauce, *ardiglione* (made with sausage and a secret blend of herbs), on *taglierini* pasta as a first course. The featured main course, *pepposo,* is a hearty beef stew with tomatoes, garlic, and wine. ♦ Tu-Sa lunch and dinner; M dinner. Via d' Ardiglione 47r (south of Via Santa Monaca). 211072

33 Santa Maria del Carmine The "Carmine," as it is known locally, was built in 1268 for the Carmelite nuns and suffered a devastating fire in 1771. Though the fire destroyed most of the church (it was rebuilt in 1782 by **Giuseppe Ruggieri** and **Giulio Mannaioni**), the **Cappella Brancacci (Brancacci Chapel)** was untouched. Recently restored, the chapel contains 15th-century frescoes begun by Masolino, continued by Masaccio, and completed by Filippino Lippi. Masaccio's contribution was a watershed in the history of art—combining perspective, chiaroscuro, and the vivid rendering of emotions with unprecedented boldness, seminal to the painters of the later Renaissance. Two of Masaccio's sections dominate the cycle—the agonizing *Expulsion from Paradise* on the extreme upper-left wall, and the serene and noble *The Tribute Money* just to its right. Below it, *St. Peter Enthroned* contains a portrait of Masaccio, the figure gazing out at the viewer in the group of four men at the right of the composition. If you feel like looking at anything else ever again, the left transept of the church contains the 17th-century **Cappella di Sant'Andrea Corsini,** with three relief sculptures by Giovanni Battista Foggini, and the dome has Luca Giordano's 17th-century fresco *The Apotheosis of St. Andrew Corsini.* ♦ Brancacci Chapel: admission. Church: daily. Chapel: M, W-Su. Piazza del Carmine (south side of piazza). 2382195

34 Dolce Vita Named after the Fellini film about the good life in Rome in the 1960s, this modern-looking nocturnal hangout for

Florentine and foreign youth brings a sweet smile, especially when its clientele's earnest and urgent interactions take over the parking lot in true Roman fashion. ♦ M-Sa 11AM-1:30AM. No credit cards accepted. Piazza del Carmine (at Borgo Stella). 284595

35 Carmine ★★$$ One of the most popular trattorie among Florentines and visitors alike (especially during the warmer months when its tables move outside), this warm and friendly restaurant serves a substantial *tagliatelle a funghi porcini* (ribbons of pasta with porcini mushrooms) and filet of beef given the same tasty treatment. ♦ M-Sa lunch and dinner. Piazza del Carmine 18r (at Borgo San Frediano). 218601

36 San Frediano in Cestello This rare Florentine-Baroque church, constructed 1680-89 by **Antonio Maria Ferri** with designs by **Cerutti**, is best admired from a distance, where its cupola adds a nice shape to the city's profile. *Cestello* in Italian means crate, though in Florence it was a corruption of Cistercense or Cistercians, the monks who once inhabited the site. The church's interior decorations, primarily by 18th-century Florentine painters, are inoffensive if uninspiring, though the third chapel on the left has a blissed-out 13th-century smiling *Madonna.* ♦ South side of Piazza di Cestello (on Lungarno Soderini)

37 Granaio di Cosimo III Built as a granary under the Medici, this wheat bin (constructed in 1695 by **Ciro Ferri** and **Gian Battista Foggini**) is now used as a military building. ♦ Piazza di Cestello 10 (on Lungarno Soderini)

38 Antico Ristoro di' Cambi ★★$$ The Cambi family has been running this rustic restaurant in an old *fiaschetteria* (wine shop) for decades. All the Tuscan soups are well prepared here. If you're feeling adventurous, try the *trippa* (tripe) or *lampredotto* (cow intestine); otherwise, there is an excellent *spezzatino* (beef stewed with tomatoes, potatoes, and herbs). There's outdoor seating in warm weather. ♦ M-Sa lunch and dinner. Via Sant'Onofrio 1r (between Borgo San Frediano and Lungarno Soderini). 217134

39 Antico Setificio Fiorentino This 500-year-old silk manufacturing mill, revived years ago by the late Marchese Emilio Pucci, is currently run by his son, who was anxious to keep alive this important element of local history. Exquisite fabrics woven on 17th-century wooden looms are available in precious quantities. A retail outlet is located down the block at Via Bartolini 16 (2381557), but serious customers can visit this small factory (by appointment only with director Aldo Marzucchi). ♦ M-F. Via L. Bartolini 4 (at Via Sant'Onofrio). 213861

40 Brandimarte Brandimarte Guscelli specializes in fanciful silver. The semiprecious

metal is exquisitely handcrafted into his signature goblets as well as such ordinary objects as cheese graters for the person who has everything. ♦ M-F, Sa morning Mar-Oct; M afternoon, Tu-Sa Nov-Feb. Via L. Bartolini 18 (west of Via Sant'Onofrio). 218791

41 Porta San Frediano This towering ancient city gate (part of the old wall is still attached) was built in 1332-34 by **Andrea Pisano** and still sports its original wood and ironwork, to which visitors once hitched their horses. ♦ Piazza di Verzaia (at Borgo San Frediano)

42 Ugolini Romano Ugolini carries on a long family tradition as a *bronzista* (bronze worker). His specialty is lamps of all types, with a minimum order of four. ♦ M-F, Sa morning Mar-Oct; M afternoon, Tu-Sa Nov-Feb. No credit cards accepted. Via del Drago d'Oro 25r (between Via dell'Orto and Borgo San Frediano). 215343

43 Alla Vecchia Bettola ★★$$ A *bettola* was a sort of prototypical lunch counter in old Florence, a place where peasants ate and ran. Perhaps you'll want to linger, though, in this ceramic-tiled trattoria. The atmosphere is warm; communal tables are understandably for lovers of fun, and the specialties of tripe and the like are for lovers of the heartiest of Florentine food. The less ambitious will be happy with the classic standbys that change daily. ♦ Tu-Sa lunch and dinner. No credit cards accepted. Viale Ludovico Ariosto 32-34r (at Piazza Torquato Tasso). 224158

In the 13th century, one third of Florence's population was engaged in either wool or silk trades, responsible for a period of extraordinary prosperity.

"Of course it is very dead in comparison [with Paris] but it's a beautiful death. . . "

Elizabeth Barrett Browning

Medieval Florence was surrounded by fortified walls—there was nowhere to build except up. As families expanded, one room was built atop the other until some towers stretched as high as 240 feet, comparable to a 10- or 12-floor apartment building!

Additional Florence Highlights

1 Museo Stibbert The **Villa Stibbert** houses the eclectic collection of Frederick Stibbert, a Scotch-Italian who was active in the unification of Italy during the 19th century. That aspect of his life is easily inferred from room after room of displays of arms and armor from East and West, enough to glut any *Camelot* or *Shogun* fantasies. Besides arms, the man also collected furniture, paintings, porcelain, clocks, and objects of every sort—most of which are not collecting dust in this oddball, slightly out-of-the-way museum, sure to appeal to obsessive-compulsives of all ages. ♦ Admission; free on Sunday. M-W, F-Su. Via Federico Stibbert 26 (near Via Bolognese). 475520

2 Le Cascine Florentines of all ranks have long loved their public park, named after the Medici dairy farms, or *cascine*, that once occupied the area, extending almost two miles along the Arno west of the city center. Though the park saw its heyday as center of the carriage trade in the last century, the well-heeled still make use of its private tennis courts and swimming pool (as can foreigners). At the other end of the social scale are the ladies of the night (and the men who dress like them), plying their trade along its alleys. Children can ride merry-go-rounds year-round, or take part in the *Festa del Grillo* on Assumption Day (15 August), a festival of crickets, which chirp away in tiny cages. On Tuesday morning a large open-air market offering everything from live chickens to antique embroidered linens extends west of **Piazza Vittorio Veneto.** Though few visitors seem to take advantage of the breezy expanses of the farm, one who did was Shelley, who was inspired to write "Ode to the West Wind" here. At the west end of the park is the **Piazzaletto dell'Indiano,** a little piazza named after the Indian maharaja Raiaram Cuttaputti, who died in Florence in 1870 and was cremated in accordance with the Brahmanic rite and laid to rest nearby, where the Mugnone River joins the Arno. ♦ North bank of the Arno (between Piazza Vittorio Veneto and Piazzaletto dell'Indiano)

3 Torre di Bellosguardo $$$ Escape the seasonal crush while being a guest at the remarkable home of the charming Barone Amerigo Franchetti, the nicest of Florence's historical villas-turned-hotels (after the far

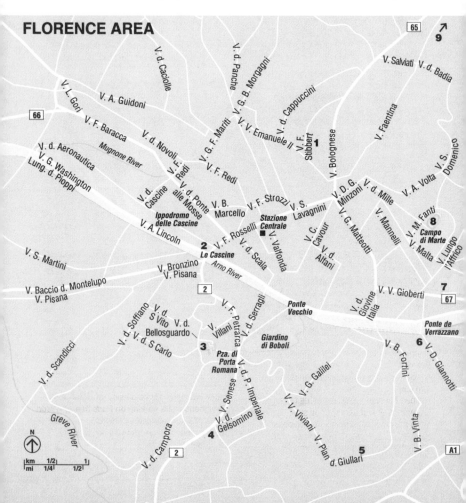

FLORENCE AREA

costlier **Villa San Michele** on the other side of town). Guests bask in any of 16 handsomely renovated rooms, common areas, and groomed gardens, all fraught with history and decorated with impeccable taste. One of the many attractions of this Renaissance time capsule is the landscaped pool with views of Florence seemingly light-years away. There is no restaurant. ◆ Via Roti Michelozzi 2 (follow signs heading southwest out of Piazza Torquato Tasso to Piazza Bellosguardo). 2298145; fax 229008

4 Ruggero ★★★$$ Owned by a former cook from the tongue-in-chic **Coco Lezzone** restaurant off Via de' Tornabuoni, the ambience of this rustic eatery is somehow more authentic in its location just outside the city gate. Tuscan first courses take first place here—*pappa al pomodoro* (a thick tomato soup), *ribollita* (a hearty vegetable soup thickened with day-old bread), and *zuppa di farro* (soup made with wheat). ◆ M, Th-Su lunch and dinner. No credit cards accepted. Via Senese 89 (south of Porta Romana). 220542

5 Omero ★★★$$ A healthy hike or a short cab ride from **Piazzale Michelangiolo** or **Porta Romana,** this rustic country restaurant with large windows looking out over the countryside offers strictly Tuscan cuisine, from the salami antipasti to pasta with *ceci* (chick peas) and *strascicata* (literally, dragged in meat sauce) to fried chicken, rabbit, and brain. The restaurant opens its garden terrace for dinner in the warmer months. ◆ M, W-Su lunch and dinner. Via Pian dei Giullari 11r, Acetri (5 km—3 miles south of Florence). 220053

6 La Capannina di Sante ★★★$$$
Florence's best fish restaurant, Signor Sante's modestly named little shack is appropriately located along the Arno, with tables outdoors during the warmer months. His offerings change according to what he finds at the market that day, but you can always depend on top quality (and top dollar). Wines are good, and the kitchen stays open past midnight, when the dining rooms are packed to the gills. ◆ Tu-Sa lunch and dinner; M dinner. Piazza Ravenna (at Ponte de Verrazzano). 688345

7 Cenacolo di San Salvi This *cenacolo* (muraled refectory) in the former monastery of San Salvi, now an asylum, houses a magnificent *Last Supper* by Andrea del Sarto. The fresco, painted between 1519 and 1525, represents the apogee of the High Renaissance in Florence, as do Leonardo da Vinci's *The Last Supper* (painted between 1495 and 1498) in Milan and Raphael's *School of Athens* and *Disputa* (painted between 1509 and 1511) in Rome. Though del Sarto is less well-known than the other two painters, Michelangelo is said to have warned Raphael, "There is a little fellow in Florence who would make you sweat if ever he got a great commission to do." *The Last Supper* was del Sarto's greatest commission and is his masterpiece, embodying the Renaissance principles of solid composition and movement in its figures and drapery. It was painted at the moment in art history shortly before del Sarto's Florentine contemporaries, Jacopo Pontormo and Rosso Fiorentino, were to take movement and color to a disconcerting extreme in the style that became known as Mannerism. ◆ Admission. Tu-Su. Via Andrea del Sarto 16 (east of Via Lungo l'Affrico and Piazza di San Salvi). 23885

8 Stadio Comunale Florence's soccer stadium (seating capacity 40,000) is a 1932 Modernist masterpiece of reinforced concrete by **Pier Luigi Nervi,** master of the medium, who designed for it an expansive cantilever roof and widely flying spiral staircase. Beside the stadium rises his **Torre di Maratona** (Marathon Tower). ◆ Open during soccer matches. Viale Manfredo Fanti (in Campo di Marte). 572625

9 Villa San Michele $$$$ Just far enough outside of Florence (in Fiesole) for peace and quiet, with views of the distant **Duomo** anchored above a sea of terra-cotta roofs, this luxury hotel with 26 rooms and two suites is named after the former 15th-century monastery in which it is installed. One of its suites is named after **Michelangelo,** who is said to have designed the villa (though certainly not the Jacuzzi and pool). Ask for one of the rooms with a view of Florence and its monuments, unless you're content to look out onto the bucolic countryside or the hotel itself. The recently added luxurious suites are housed in an 18th-century *limonaia,* a building that was used to house plants in the winter. It's surrounded by oak trees and graced with the same awe-inspiring vistas of Florence. Request the upper-level suite—its private terrace is the perfect venue for a private candlelight dinner; guests on the lower floor have a private garden. The restaurant serves upscale Tuscan fare. Half- or full-pension is strongly suggested. The hotel often closes for a short period in winter, so be sure to call ahead. ◆ Via Doccia 4, Fiesole (follow signs for Fiesole from Piazza le Cure, heading northeast). 59451; fax 598734

Bencistà $$ Just below the **Villa San Michele** in location and well below it in price, this hotel and its 42 rooms have the same magnificent views of Florence, here in a country-villa setting where guests are asked to take one meal of good home cooking per day. ◆ Via Benedetto da Maiano 4, San Domenico (follow signs for Fiesole from Piazza le Cure, heading northeast). 59163; fax 59163

Mark Twain, who lived outside of Florence in Settignano while working on *Pudd'nhead Wilson* in the 1890s, said he wrote more there in four months than he could in two years at home.

Laguna Veneta

San Michele

Canale delle Fondamenta Nuove

S. Pietro di Castello

S. Elena

CASTELLO

Canale di San Marco

S. Giorgio Maggiore

Canale delle Navi

■ Piazza San Marco

CANAL GRANDE

SAN MARCO

CANNAREGIO

SAN POLO

SANTA CROCE

DORSODURO

Canale della Giudecca

GIUDECCA

■ Stazione Ferroviaria Santa Lucia

■ Piazzale Roma

Canale delle Sacche

Ponte della Libertà

11

Porto Commerciale

Bacino di Marittima

Nuova Isola del Tronchetto

↙ to Mostre

N ←

| km | | 1/2 | | 1 |
| mi | 1/4 | | 1/2 | |

Venice Orientation

A dazzling, fabled link between East and West, Venice remains one of the world's most exciting cities to discover, albeit one that thrives on tourism. Seen on foot in the sparkling sunlight of a summer's day or through the brooding mist of a winter's morning, from a gondola in the moonlight or a *vaporetto* drifting down the gently curving **Canal Grande** (Grand Canal), Venice has the power to enchant. The greatest tour in town is aboard the *No. 1 vaporetto*, cruising past weathered palazzi and ancient piazze. While the effects of age, pollution from nearby **Mestre**, and ever-increasing *acqua alta* (high water from the **Adriatic Sea**) take their toll, the theatricality of these Gothic palaces and the absence of automobiles give the city an ageless quality reminiscent of its former epithet, *La Serenissima*, or Most Serene.

This unique city, built on 117 islands separated by 177 small canals, started life as a swampy refuge from the violent barbarian invasions of the fifth century. By the time of the Crusades, Venice had become a major power on the Adriatic and its merchants gradually tightened their control of the major trade routes to the Levant. The most famous of all the merchants of Venice was Marco Polo, who grew wealthy selling silks and spices collected on his oriental adventures to the rest of Europe. In the heyday of *La Serenissima*, the riches brought from the East made the Venetian court one of the most luxurious and influential in Europe. Among other things the Venetians take credit for is the introduction of coffee and the use of the fork. Of more interest to visitors, though, this vast wealth made it possible to commission great works of art from the likes of Titian, Tintoretto, and Veronese, and of architecture from **Palladio** and **Longhena**—a priceless legacy.

The artistic heritage of Venice draws tourists by the millions, resulting in negatives for visitors and residents alike. Myriad masks and kitsch glass are displayed in every shop window and prices only occasionally correspond to quality. Yet the magic remains, and through it all, the Venetians somehow remain hospitable and enthusiastic, and eager to direct visitors who get lost in the maze of their city's streets. But getting lost is one of the best parts of a Venetian experience. After all, how else can one find the special tranquillity of a tiny *campo* filled with the sounds of children's laughter and golden sunlight, a picturesque but forgotten canal, and the legendary romance of Venice?

City code is 41 unless otherwise noted. To call Venice from the US, dial 011-39-41, followed by the local number. When calling from inside Italy, dial 041 and the local number.

Getting to Venice

Airport
Aeroporto Marco Polo
The closest international airport to Venice is in **Tessera,** 13 kilometers (8 miles) from the city.

Airport Services
Airport Emergencies	2606470
Currency Exchange	5415471
Customs	2606810
Ground Transportation	5415084
Information	2609260; 2606111
Lost and Found	2606436

Police	2606824
Traveler's Aid	2606425; 2606420

Airlines
Air France	5229111; 800/237.2747
Alitalia	2581333; 800/223.5730
British Airways	049660444; 800/247.9297
KLM	5416200; 800/274.7747

Getting to and from Aeroporto Marco Polo

By Bus

The least expensive way to travel between the city and the airport is on the **ACTV** *No. 5* bus that travels across the mainland between the airport and **Piazzale Roma** (the 20-minute ride costs about $3.50). Tickets are available at the newsstand in the airport lobby. Schedules for the service are available from the tourist information office (see "Visitors'

Information," below) and in *Un Ospite a Venezia* (A Guest in Venice). Local water transportation to destinations throughout the city is available outside the bus terminal in **Piazzale Roma.**

By Car

While it is possible to rent a car at the airport, automobiles are not allowed in Venice. There are only two places to park: **Piazzale Roma** and on the **Lido.** Therefore, unless Venice is one of many stops on a trip, it's not advisable to bring a car here.

To get from the airport to Venice, follow the signs out of the airport to **Route 14.** In Mestre, go east on **Route 11** over the bridge to **Piazzale Roma.**

Rental Cars

The following rental car agencies have offices at the airport:

Avis 5415030; 800/331.1084

Budget.................................5415299; 800/472.3325

Hertz 5416075; 800/654.3001

Europcar (National) 5415654; 800/227.3876

By Boat

The most efficient mode of transport to and from the airport is by *motoscafo* (motor launch). The service is loosely coordinated with arriving and departing flights (leave yourself plenty of time) and connects the airport to **Piazza San Marco** and the Lido. The trip to **Piazza San Marco** takes about a half hour. Service to the Lido runs hourly, and the trip takes about 40 minutes.

By Taxi

Taxi acquei (water taxis) from the airport take passengers as close as possible to their hotels. Many hostelries have their own landings, and those that don't will send a porter to the dock to collect luggage. The taxi landing is outside of the arrivals building; the trip to **Piazza San Marco** takes about 20 minutes, and at press the time cost was about $70.

Bus Station (Long-Distance)

The main bus station for Venice (5287886) is at **Piazzale Roma.**

Train Station (Long-Distance)

Venice's central train station is **Santa Lucia** (Piazza Stazione, on the Fondamenta Santa Lucia, 715555) and is located directly on the Canal Grande. Be sure to buy a ticket to that station and not to the Mestre station across the lagoon on the mainland. (There are, however, shuttle trains that run between the two stations every 15 minutes.) *Vaporetto* and *taxi acqueo* service to other points in the city is available on the pier outside the station.

Those looking to tour in the grand manner of the romantic era of rail travel can hop a ride on the fabled **Venice-Simplon Orient Express.** It starts (or ends) in London, and stops in Paris, Venice, Florence, Rome, Salzburg, Vienna, Budapest, and Istanbul. For more information, contact the **Venice-Simplon Orient Express** (c/o **Abercrombie & Kent,** 1520 Kensington Rd., Oak Brook, IL 60521; 800/524.2420, 708/954.2944; fax: 708/954.3324).

Getting Around Venice

Gondolas and Traghetti

The gondola is the classic way of seeing Venice. Gondoliers gather at strategic places in the city (in front of the train station and the **Hotel Danieli,** for example) and offer 50-minute tours for about $60 at press time (a supplement is charged after sundown). It comfortably accommodates six.

Traghetti (also called gondolas by Venetians) are less luxurious but highly functional; they are the best way to cross the Canal Grande if you are not near one of the three bridges. Follow signs for *traghetto* or gondola, pay, and hop aboard for the short ride across the canal.

Motoscafi and Vaporetti

Motoscafi are enclosed, black-and-white express water buses that stop only at a few places along the canals and cost a bit more than *vaporetti*. Tickets are sold at **ACTV** booths at all stops.

Vaporetti are partially open-air local water buses. The stops, indicated on the maps in this book with a "T", are usually named for a nearby church or landmark. Nos. *1* and *82* travel the entire length of the Canal Grande. Tickets are sold at **ACTV** booths at the stops. If a booth is closed, purchase a ticket on board; passengers caught traveling without tickets are subject to hefty fines. *Vaporetto* lines

and stops change occasionally, so always check the schedule and be sure the boat is heading in the direction you want to go.

Taxi Aqueo

Private water taxis are expensive but will take you anywhere in Venice. There are stands all around town.

Tours

The **Associazione Guide Touristiche** (Calle delle Bande 5267, near Campo di Santa Maria Formosa in Castello, 5209038; fax 5210672) has a list of multi-lingual tour guides whose fixed rates are approved by the local tourist board. Many agencies offer walking and boat tours and day trips to the outer islands or to the **Veneto.** Two of the most reliable are **Ital Travel** (Ascensione San Marco 72B, west of Piazza San Marco, 5236511) and **Kele & Teo** (Ponte dei Bareteri 4930, near Piazza San Marco, 5208722; fax 5208913).

Walking

The best way to truly enjoy Venice is to begin walking. It is nearly impossible not to get lost in the city's labyrinth of *campi* (squares), *calle* (streets), and *fondamente* (canal-side piers). In fact, getting lost is highly recommended. Some of the most pleasant discoveries can be made this way, and obliging Venetians are always willing to help wayward tourists find their way back to a familiar landmark.

VENICE VAPORETTO STOPS

Laguna Veneta

N

LIDO

Punta Sabbioni
14 17

Lido San Nicolò
17, 14

S. Maria Elisabetta
1 6 14 52 82

to Mazzorbo/Burano/Torcello/Treporti 12

to S. Servolo/S. Lazzaro 20

S. Erasmo
13

13

13

Vignole
13

S. Elena
1, 14, 52

G. Biennale
1, 82

Navagero
52

Musso
52

Venier
52

Faro
12, 13, 52

Colonna 52

Serenella 52

Tana
52

to Grazia/S. Clemente 10

Cimitero
52

Celestia
52

Arsenale
1

S. Zaccaria
1, 6, 10, 14, 20, 52, 82

Ospedale
52

S. Giorgio
82

S. Marco
1, 82

VENICE

Fond. Nove
52, 12, 13

Ca' D'Oro
1

S. Maria del Giglio
1

Zitelle
82

GIUDECCA

Rialto
1, 82

S. Angelo
1

Salute
1

S. Giacomo
82

S. Marcuola
1, 82

Madonna dell'orto
52

S. Stae
1

S. Silvestro
1

S. Samuele
82

Accademia
1, 82

Guglie 52

Riva di Biasio
1

S. Toma
82

Ca' Rezzonico
1

Traghetto
16, 52

Tre Archi
52

Zattere
82

S. Eufemia
82

Ferrovia
1, 52, 82

Piazzale Roma
1, 52, 82

S. Basilio
82

Sacca Fisola
82

S. Marta
52, 82

Tronchetto A
82

Tronchetto B
17

Terminal Fusina 16

Legend:
1
6
10, 20
12
13
14
16
17
52
82

Note: Routes subject to change.

FYI

Accommodations

In high season, making reservations ahead is essential. Hotels follow a high-season calendar of their own. Maximum rates are in effect at *Carnevale* (the two weeks preceding Ash Wednesday); from 15 April to 1 July; in September and October; and for the Christmas/New Year's season. Reserve directly or through Venetian travel agencies, such as **CIT Viaggi** (Via Mestrina 65, Mestre, 5040150; fax 5040174) or **Kele & Teo** (Ponte dei Bareteri 4930, near Piazza San Marco, 5208722; fax 5208913). If you arrive without reservations, visit one of the **Azienda di Promozione Turistica (APT)** offices (see "Visitors' Information," below). During the summer months, many houses owned by religious orders open their doors to paying visitors.

Climate

Good times to visit are May, when temperatures stay in the agreeable 60 degrees Fahrenheit range, and September and October, when they don't drop below the mild 50 degrees Fahrenheit. Summers bring high heat and humidity; winter months are chillingly damp and the piazze sometimes flood. It rains often in November/December and in March/April. That said, don't stay away on account of the weather—Venice enchants no matter what the season.

Months	Average Temperature (°F)
January	43
February	48
March	53
April	60
May	67
June	72
July	77
August	74
September	68
October	60
November	54
December	44

Embassies and Consulates

British Consulate Dorsoduro 1051
(at Ponte dell'Accademia).........................5227207

The nearest Australian, Canadian, and US consulates are in Milan.

Holidays

In addition to the national holidays (see "Northern Italy Orientation"), Venice celebrates the feast day of San Marco, its patron saint, on 25 April.

Hours

Most businesses are open Monday through Saturday 9AM-1PM, and 3:30-7:30PM from March through October; from November through February they are also closed on Monday mornings. Food shops are open Monday, Tuesday, and Thursday through Saturday 9AM-1PM and 3:30-7:30PM; Wednesday 9AM-1PM; and closed Wednesday afternoons and Sunday. Churches are generally open daily 8AM-12:30PM and 3:30-7:30PM, with many exceptions. Most museums close on Tuesday, although that too varies. Opening and closing times are listed by day(s) only if normal hours apply; in all other cases, specific hours are given (e.g., 8AM-3:30PM, noon-5PM).

Medical and Legal Emergencies

In a medical emergency, call **Assistenza** (5230000); for legal emergencies contact **Ufficio Stranieri** (5203222).

Money

Banks are open Monday through Friday from about 8:30AM to 1:30PM, and reopen for an hour or so (usually 3:30 to 4:30PM) in the afternoon. A good place to change money is at **American Express** (Campo San Moisè 1471, west of Piazza San Marco, San Marco, 5200844). Another choice would be **Guetta Viaggi** (Calle II dell'Ascensione 1289, west of Piazza San Marco, San Marco, 5208711), or any of the principal banks displaying the "Cambio" sign. Change money at the airport, train station, and private *cambios* around town only as a last resort; these agencies charge high commissions.

Personal Safety

It is remarkably safe to wander the streets of Venice at night—to visit **Piazza San Marco** or the church of **Santa Maria della Salute,** to window shop along the **Mercerie,** to walk back to your hotel after the opera, or have a romantic stroll along a moonlit canal. But take elementary precautions—using common sense will outwit most bag, camera, and wallet snatchers. Never carry more than you can afford to lose—i.e., keep your passport and larger amounts of cash in the hotel safe or well concealed in a money purse—and don't leave any valuables visible in a rented car. Be particularly alert on crowded *motoscafi* and *vaporetti*, especially on the tourist routes.

Pharmacies

Pharmacies in Venice take turns operating on a 24-hour schedule. Your hotel concierge can tell you who has the responsibility during your stay; the information is also published weekly in *Un Ospite a Venezia* (A Guest in Venice).

Postal Service

The main post office, **Poste e Telecommunicazioni (PTT),** is near the **Ponte di Rialto** (Fondaco dei Tedeschi 5554, San Marco, 5299111); it's open Monday through Saturday from 8:15AM to 6:45PM. There's a more centrally located branch at **Calle Larga dell'Ascensione,** just off **Piazza San Marco;** it's open Monday through Friday from 8:10AM to 1:40PM and Saturday from 8:10AM to noon.

Publications

The tourist information office carries copies of the monthly *L'Agenda,* an exhaustive list of nightlife possibilities. (There are also posters plastered about town advertising concerts and the like.) English-language cultural-events listings can be found in *Un Ospite a Venezia* (A Guest in Venice); it is available at most hotels and tourist information offices (see "Visitors' Information," below).

Restaurants

Lunch is served between 12:30 and 2PM; dinner hours are usually from 7:30 until 9:30PM. Most bars and cafes open in the early morning and follow their own particular midday-break schedule; closing time varies from 8PM to midnight. Many eateries close in January, February, before *Carnevale,* or in August, as well as between Christmas and New Year's. Reservations, while not required, are suggested and may be essential at the most expensive or most popular restaurants. When calling to make a reservation, inquire about a dress code; although no restaurant is likely to turn away a customer because of attire, you may feel uncomfortable if you are underdressed. Most restaurants accept major credit cards.

Shopping

The main shopping districts are the area surrounding **Piazza San Marco** and the zigzag maze of streets known as the **Mercerie,** which lead from **San Marco** to the **Ponte di Rialto.** The area west of the piazza is home to most of the high-priced boutiques selling designer clothing and leather goods. Prices drop considerably off the main tourist drags at the shops hidden in Venice's backwater alleyways.

Venetian glass is everywhere, but much of it is of poor quality and design. To get an idea of what to look for, visit the museum and factories on **Murano.** Papier-mâché *Carnevale* masks are also abundant and range from the traditional to the phantasmagorical. Handmade lace can be fabulously expensive, but simple, affordable pieces can be found (here, again, it's best to be educated—visit the lace school on the island of **Burano**).

Street Plan

Venice is divided into six *sestieri* (literally "sixth"), or districts: **San Marco, Dorsoduro, San Polo, Santa Croce, Cannaregio, Castello,** and **Giudecca.** At the base of a Byzantine system that gets even the locals confused is the duality of all addresses: each location has a specific street address and a different mailing address. The street address may be, for example, Calle Santo Stefano 240, while its mailing address is San Marco 240. The latter refers to the *sestiere* in which the place is located, and not to its actual *calle* (street).

When giving directions, Venetians will usually use a church, a *campo,* or a number of bridges as a reference. For example: "When you cross the next *campo,* keep going straight ahead and after crossing two bridges . . . " Seeing the bewilderment in the visitors' eyes, and realizing the language difficulties, some kindhearted Venetians have been known to simply show the way.

Telephones

The **SIP-Telecom** office near the central post office and the **Ponte di Rialto** (Fondaco dei Tedeschi 5551, San Marco, 5333111) is open daily from 8AM until 7:45PM. Telephone calls can be made here using American calling cards or credit cards, or by paying afterward in cash.

Visitors' Information Offices

There are two locations of **Azienda di Promozione Turistica (APT):** at **Palzzetto Selva** (5226356) between the **Giardini Reale** and **Harry's Bar** in San Marco; and in the **Santa Lucia** train station (719078) in Cannaregio. Both offices are open Monday through Saturday from 8:30AM until 7PM.

The **Institute of Architecture of the University of Venice** publishes *Veneziapertutti,* a free map and guide to Venice designed specifically for travelers with disabilities. Write to **Assessorato Sicurezza Sociale, Ufficio Inserimenti Sociali** (Ca' Farsetti, Commune di Venezia, 30100 Venezia, Italy) for a copy.

Phone Book

Emergencies

Ambulance	113
Fire	115
Police	113
Police Nonemergency	703222
24-hour Medical Service	5230000

Visitors' Information

Bus	5207886
Customs	2606810
Postal Information	5299111
Train	715555

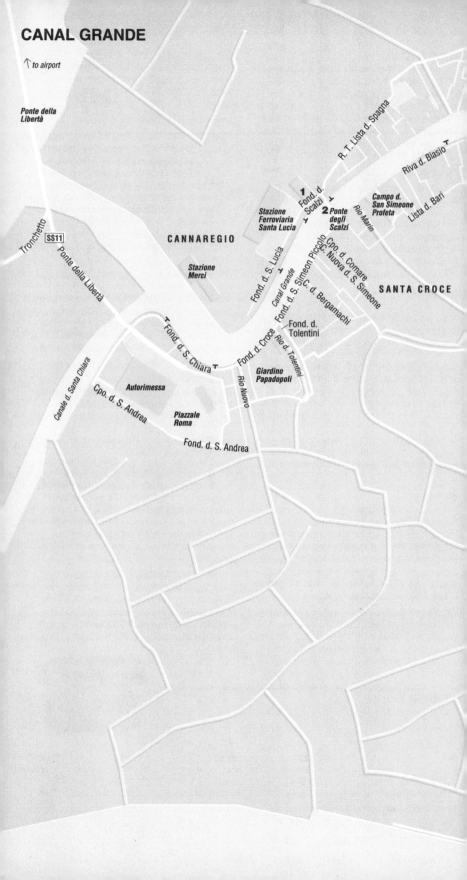

CANAL GRANDE

↑ to airport

Ponte della
Libertà

R. T. Lista d. Spagna

Riva d. Biasio

1 Fond. d.
Scalzi

Campo d.
San Simeone
Profeta

Lista d. Bari

Stazione
Ferroviaria
Santa Lucia

2 Ponte
degli
Scalzi

Rio Marin

Tronchetto

SS11

Ponte della Libertà

CANNAREGIO

Stazione
Merci

Fond. d. S. Lucia

Canal Grande

Cpo. d. Comare

C. Nuova d. S. Simeone

SANTA CROCE

Fond. d. S. Simeon Piccolo

C. d. Bergamachi

Fond. d.
Tolentini

Canale d. Santa Chiara

Fond. d. S. Chiara

Fond. d. Croce

Rio d. Tolentini

Rio Nuovo

Giardino
Papadopoli

Autorimessa

Cpo. d. S. Andrea

Piazzale
Roma

Fond. d. S. Andrea

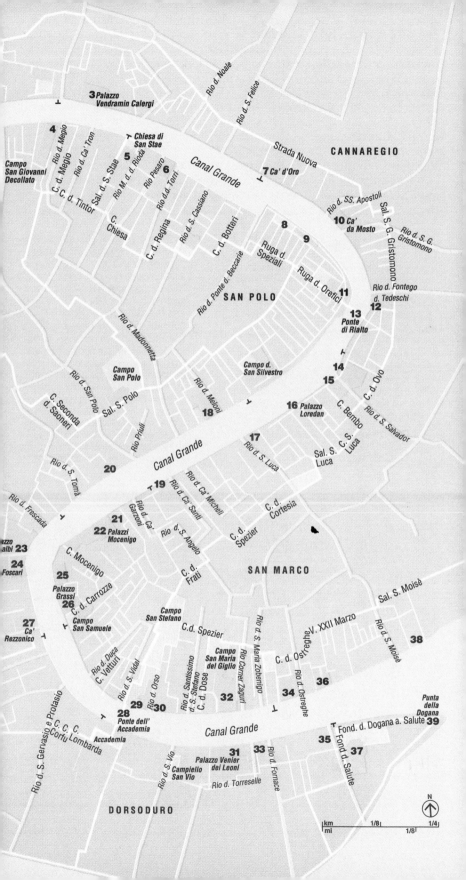

Canal Grande

Whether in high style in a gondola (which will cost you) or on the cheap in *vaporetto No. 1,* a ride on the Canal Grande (Grand Canal) is the perfect, dreamlike introduction to the magic of Venice. The best time to make the trip from **Piazza San Marco** toward **Piazzale Roma** is very early in the morning, from 6AM to 8AM, when the boats are almost empty and the light is perfect; take it in the opposite direction in the late afternoon. The first time around, just let the fantastic palazzi reflected in the water drift by as you absorb the beauty of the city, just as countless visitors from foreign lands and distant times have done before you. Don't worry about identifying the individual sights on your initial visit—once you've seen the Canal Grande you're sure to return. (Many of the places in this chapter are described in further detail elsewhere in this book; check the index for page numbers.)

1 **Chiesa degli Scalzi** This church, a fine example of Roman Baroque architecture, was built in the 17th century from plans by **Baldassare Longhena,** one of the most celebrated architects of the day (he also designed **La Salute,** the church in Dorsoduro at the eastern entrance to the canal). The facade was added a few decades later by **Giuseppe Sardi.**

2 **Ponte degli Scalzi** A team of city architects built the present bridge in 1934, replacing the one built in 1841 by French architect **A.E. Neville** in a style that was later judged to be at odds with the rest of the Canal Grande.

3 **Palazzo Vendramin Calergi** This imposing palazzo, just after the San Marcuola *vaporetto* stop, was one of the first Renaissance buildings in Venice. It was built in the 15th century by **Mauro Codussi,** who abandoned the Gothic tradition to introduce the new style derived from Florence and Rome. Richard Wagner was a guest here when he died in 1883. In winter the palazzo is the seat of the **Casino.**

4 **Fondaco dei Turchi (Turks' Warehouse)** The elongated supports of this splendid, oriental-looking building's arches and the round medallions in carved stone between them (*patere*) are typical elements of the Byzantine style in Venice. Built in the 12th and 13th centuries and originally the home of the Pesaro family, it was then used by the Turkish community. The facade was rather clumsily restored in the 19th century. The palazzo now houses the **Museo di Storia Naturale** (Museum of Natural History).

Ca' d'Oro

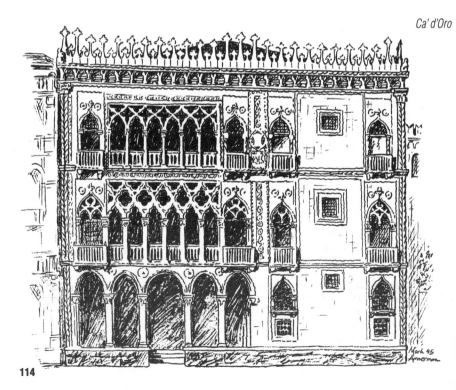

Ponte di Rialto

5 Chiesa di San Stae This fine 18th-century Baroque facade by **Domenico Rossi** is remarkable for its balanced architectural and sculptural harmony. The three statues at the top represent *Christ, Faith,* and *Charity*. This is one of the few churches facing the Canal Grande, with a small, simple piazza opening in front of it.

6 Ca' Pesaro One of the most imposing palazzi (particularly since its restoration) on the Canal Grande, Ca' Pesaro is exquisitely Baroque and conveys an obvious message of wealth and power. The stark-white palazzo, begun 1657 by **Baldassare Longhena,** was also built out of the characteristically Venetian love for ample loggias. On the top floors the facade is mostly columns and arches. Notice the long facade on the side canal—a real luxury, and not a frequent one, even among the wealthy patricians of Venice. It houses the **Museo d'Arte Moderna** (Museum of Modern Art) and the **Museo d'Arte Orientale** (Museum of Oriental Art).

7 Ca' d'Oro This 15th-century palazzo (pictured on page 114) by **Matteo Raverti** is the most admired example of Venetian Gothic in the city. In Venice, Gothic means pointed arches and elaborate—at times flamboyant—stone decorations, as opposed to the austere Gothic cathedrals in Northern Europe. The top two floors here offer an irresistible impression of lightness and grace, in perfect harmony with the water environment. The facade was accurately restored in the 1980s; only the original blue, red, and gold trimmings could not be replaced. Another extensive restoration of the facade was recently completed and the effect is spectacular.

8 Pescheria (Fish Market) Notice the open loggia, built in the Venetian Gothic style in 1907. A gondola service ferries people across the Canal Grande to shop at this important fish market and the adjacent *erberia*, the local fresh produce market.

9 Fabbriche Nuove di Rialto This long, narrow palazzo was erected from 1552 to 1555 as part of a general plan to reorganize the Rialto area around the new stone bridge over the Canal Grande. Designed by **Jacopo Sansovino,** the palazzo now houses government offices.

10 Ca' da Mosto This is one of the oldest palazzi on the Canal Grande. The facade dates from the 13th century (the top floors were added later). The second-floor balcony is one of the finest examples of Byzantine architecture in Venice (narrow arches supported by thin columns, round medallions with stone bas-reliefs). Since the early 1980s, the palazzo has been for sale, but potential buyers have been discouraged by the enormous restoration costs.

11 Palazzo dei Camerlenghi Right at the foot of the Ponte di Rialto, this elegant 16th-century Renaissance palazzo by **Guglielmo Bergamasco** houses government offices.

12 Fondaco dei Tedeschi (Germans' Warehouse) In its heyday, the Republic of Venice had close commercial ties with Northern Europe. German merchants would buy goods imported from the East by Venetian merchants and would then store them here before shipping them to their homeland. The palazzo was rebuilt in the Renaissance style after a fire in 1508; the facade was originally covered with frescoes by Titian and Giorgione. Today the palazzo houses the Venice post office.

13 Ponte di Rialto (Rialto Bridge) In the 16th century, the Republic decided to replace the old drawbridge (the only one over the Canal Grande) with a permanent stone structure designed by **Antonio da Ponte.** The arcades on top were necessary in order to strengthen the structure (illustrated above). Heavy buildings were added on both sides of the bridge to keep the foundations in place.

14 Palazzo Dolfin Manin The ground floor portico of this imposing 16th-century Renaissance palazzo by **Jacopo Sansovino** is a pedestrian walkway. Today the palazzo houses offices of the Banca d'Italia.

15 Palazzo Bembo A delightful Gothic facade was added late in the 15th century, changing the original Byzantine look of this old palazzo. As is the case with many similar buildings, the top floor of the structure was added much later.

16 Palazzo Loredan To many a lover of Venice, this 13th-century palazzo and the one next door (the 12th-century **Ca' Farsetti**) epitomize the beauty of the Canal Grande as it appeared before the Renaissance moved in with heavier, more imposing facades. The rows of narrow arches supported by thin columns (a Byzantine feature) created a rare impression of lightness and grace, now partly impaired because of the top floors, which were added later. Today the two buildings house municipal offices.

17 Palazzo Grimani Begun in 1556 and designed by **Michele Sanmicheli,** this imposing Renaissance structure was built for one of the leading Venetian families. It is now occupied by the offices of the *Corte d'Appello* (Court of Appeals).

18 Palazzo Papadopoli This 16th-century palazzo by **Giangiacomo dei Grigi** used to belong to the Tiepolo family and contained four paintings by Veronese that are now in a museum in Dresden. It was acquired by the Counts Papadopoli, but now belongs to the Italian Department of Education.

19 Palazzo Corner-Spinelli A masterwork of the Venetian Renaissance, this palazzo was built in 1490 by **Mauro Codussi,** who also designed the **Palazzo Vendramin Calergi.**

20 Palazzo Pisani-Moretta A fine example of Venetian Gothic, this privately owned, 15th-century palazzo is currently used for meetings, conferences, and *Carnevale* balls.

21 Palazzo Garzoni This 15th-century palazzo now belongs to the **University of Venice** and is used by its department of foreign languages.

22 Palazzi Mocenigo The powerful Mocenigo family had these twin palazzi built in the 16th century. The controversial monk Giordano Bruno lived here in 1592, and Lord Byron in 1818. Two more palazzi, one on each side, completed the properties of the Mocenigo in this stretch of the Canal Grande. All four palazzi are privately owned residences.

23 Palazzo Balbi Dating from the late Renaissance, this 16th-century palazzo belongs to the state and is currently used for administrative offices.

24 Ca' Foscari This palace, one of the most sumptuous 15th-century Gothic buildings on the Canal Grande, has a great view because of its location at the canal's curve (illustrated on page 117). It belongs to the **University of Venice.**

25 Palazzo Moro-Lin Built by **Sebastiano Mazzoni,** this 17th-century structure is also known as the "palazzo with 13 windows." The top floor is a later addition.

26 Palazzo Grassi This building, designed by **Giorgio Massari,** one of the foremost artists of early 18th-century Venice, was only completed after the architect's death. In the 1980s it was acquired and restored by the Fiat Corporation to be used as a cultural center. It houses expensively mounted art and historical exhibitions and is visited by thousands each day—the highest number of visitors to any building in Venice except for the **Palazzo Ducale.**

27 Ca' Rezzonico The wealth of the Rezzonico family is evident in this sumptuous 17th-century building, designed by **Baldassare Longhena** and completed by **Giorgio Massari** (top floor). It now houses the **Museo del Settecento Veneziano** (Museum of the Venetian 18th Century).

28 Ponte dell'Accademia (Accademia Bridge) As it is now, this wooden bridge is a "temporary" structure, built around 1930 to replace a previous iron bridge too reminiscent of the industrial architecture of the 19th century for the tastes of the time. The temporary structure was restored in the 1980s, and most Venetians are convinced that it will remain here for at least a few generations.

29 Palazzo Franchetti This originally Gothic building was heavily and not very accurately restored in the 19th century.

30 Palazzo Barbarigo The structure dates from the early Renaissance; the striking mosaics on the facade were added in the 19th century.

31 Palazzo Venier dei Leoni The Venier family intended to compete with the **Palazzo Corner della Ca'Grande** across the canal but was never able to go beyond the ground floor. Peggy Guggenheim found the unfinished, 18th-century building fascinating and bought it for herself to live in. At her death, it became a museum of modern art, home to the **Peggy Guggenheim Collection.**

32 Palazzo Corner della Ca' Grande The tallest building on the Canal Grande, erected in 1537, was also one of the first buildings in Venice to express the grandiose ideas of **Jacopo Sansovino,** who soon became the official architect of the Venetian Republic.

33 Palazzo Dario A delightful example of early Venetian Renaissance architecture by **Pietro**

Lombardo, this dangerously slanted palazzo (built in 1487) was acquired in the 1980s by the late Raoul Gardini, an Italian industrialist, as his Venice residence. Gardini was popular in Venice because of his sailboat, *The Moor of Venice,* which competed in the **Americas' Cup** in 1992. In 1994, Gardini was implicated in an unprecedented nationwide scandal involving bribes and kickbacks and he committed suicide while in jail. Woody Allen has since leased the palazzo for his brief stays in Venice during the annual film festival.

34 Palazzo Gritti The somber Gothic facade was slightly modified in the 19th century. It is one of the great luxury hotels of Venice, offering terrace dining right on the canal.

35 Abbazia di San Gregorio This former abbey, of which only a Gothic portal has survived, is now a luxury condominium.

36 Palazzo Contarini-Fasan Also known as "Desdemona's palazzo" as in Shakespeare's *Othello,* this small, beautiful building is noted for its carved stone balcony. Built in the 15th century in Gothic style, it was restored in the late 1980s and is now a private residence.

37 Santa Maria della Salute (La Salute) This is the 17th-century masterwork of **Baldassare Longhena,** the great Baroque architect who redesigned the whole complex at the entrance of the Canal Grande. The statue at the very top represents the *Virgin Mary* dressed as a Venetian admiral. Merchant ships used to stop here for customs upon arrival from all over the Mediterranean and the North Atlantic.

38 Ca' Giustinian The Giustinian family, one of the oldest and wealthiest in Venice, lived in this 15th-century Gothic mansion (*ca'* in old Venetian dialect), the first to appear on the Canal Grande outside of the San Marco area (the next, now **Hotel Monaco,** was built in the 19th century). The palazzo belongs to the city of Venice and houses the offices of the *Biennale,* including the headquarters of the *Venice Film Festival.*

39 Punta della Dogana (Customs Point) In the 15th century, this was the customs center for all Venetian ships. The long, low building was rebuilt in the 17th century and finished in the 19th. At the very tip of the tower is a large sphere representing the world, supported by two bronze giants; the statue over the sphere represents *Fortune.*

Ca' Foscari

117

San Marco

The most-visited *sestiere* of Venice is San Marco. It centers around **Piazza San Marco**, the only square the Venetians deign to call a piazza (the others are called *campi*). Napoleon supposedly called the piazza "the best drawing room in Europe." Just as in the heyday of the Republic of *La Serenissima* (the Most Serene, as Venice was called), **Piazza San Marco** today is a drawing room for people of every nationality. Some stroll, others sit, but all gaze spellbound at the sights surrounding the **Basilica di San Marco**, about which Henry James wrote, "If Venice, as I say, has become a great bazaar, this exquisite edifice is now the biggest booth." But there's more to see in San Marco than that exquisite edifice: the **Campanile**, the **Palazzo Ducale**, the **Museo Correr**, the **Florian** and **Quadri** *caffès,* the shops on the **Frezzeria** and along the **Mercerie.** You may be tempted never to leave the piazza itself, caught up in the comings and goings of the bedazzled crowds that flock here as if they were mimicking the legion of pigeons.

1 Piazza San Marco This square is surely one of the most beautiful and harmonious architectural spaces in the world. Those qualities can be appreciated even while standing amid the bustling hordes of midsummer tourists, though there are special times when the sight is even more breathtaking—in the mist of the early morning, the silence late at night, the light fog that often sets in during the winter, or even during the *acqua alta* (high water) when wooden planks are needed in order to cross the piazza without getting one's feet wet. But at all times, the square symbolizes and traces the history of Venice, from the ninth century (when the **Basilica** was begun and the original **Campanile** was erected) through the Renaissance (when **Jacopo Sansovino** devised the plan for the piazza) to the Neo-Classical (when the addition called the **Ala Napoleonica** was built under Bonaparte). Through it all the pigeons continue to swoop (and pollute the monuments), merchants continue to ply their wares, Venetians pause for refreshments at **Caffè Florian,** and bedazzled visitors gaze in awe at the wonder that is Venice. ♦ Vaporetto stops: San Marco (1, 82); San Zaccaria (1, 52, 82)

2 Basilica di San Marco Originally begun in the ninth century as the doges' private chapel, the **Basilica**—Mark Twain's "vast warty bug taking a meditative walk"—is a complex conglomeration of Medieval, Classical, Byzantine, and Romanesque architectural styles (see drawing on page 120). It was built to house the bones of St. Mark, stolen from their Egyptian tomb in Alexandria and smuggled to Venice in a barrel of pickled pork so that Muslim officials would not search its contents. This event, known as the *tranlatio,* is depicted in a 13th-century mosaic on the exterior of the church over the far left arch. Also noteworthy on the exterior are Romanesque relief carvings on the three receding arches of the main entrance, as well as the copies of the four 2,000-year-old gilded bronze horses (the originals are in the church museum) carted off by Napoleon and returned to the city in 1815, and the Gothic carvings of religious figures on the roof. The interior is a beautifully murky and mysterious space, paved with an intricately patterned undulating mosaic floor and walls and ceilings covered with mosaics dating from the 12th to the 18th centuries. The most important are the 13th-century Old Testament scenes in the vaults, the 13th-century *Ascension* in the central cupola, and the *Christ, Madonna,* and *Prophets* on the walls of the nave aisles. Also in the **Basilica** is the *Pala d'Oro* (golden altarpiece), made between the 10th and 12th centuries of enamels and precious stones; the **Tesoro** (Treasury), containing loot from Constantinople (the 10th-century icon of St. Michael was a real prize); the 15th-century *iconostasis* (choir screen) by the Masegne brothers, located in front of the altar; and the **Cappella dei Mascoli** to the left of the main altar, where there is a bejeweled 10th-century icon known as the *Madonna Nicopeia.* The highlights of the second-floor **Basilica Museum** (the entrance is in the portico) are the original four bronze horses, believed to be about 2,000 years old, and the cover for the *Pala d'Oro,* which was painted by Paolo Veneziano in 1345. Newly instituted rules permit only 20 visitors per minute in the **Basilica,** so you may have to wait to enter. ♦ Admission: Pala d'Oro, Tesoro, and museum. Museum and Basilica: daily. Piazza San Marco (in the northeast corner). Vaporetto stops: San Marco (1, 82); San Zaccaria (1, 52, 82). 5225205

Rio d. Fontego
Rio d. Miracoli
81 — S. d. Fontego d. Tedeschi
80 *Campo San Bartolomeo*
82
Rio d. Paradiso
CASTELLO
Sal. d. S. Lio
Rio d. S. Maria Formosa
ercerie
2 Aprile
C. d. Stagneri
mpo n Salvador
78
C. S. Antonio
C. Cassellaria Bande
4
Rio d. Guerra
C.
83
Rio d. Baratta
84
—Campo d. A. g. Guerra
Campiello d. Piovan
88
oacamini Rio d. Ferai
Rio d.
86
Mercerie d. Orologio
87 C. L. S. Marco
6 C. d. Canonica
C. Fiubera
85
allo
7
Rio d. Palazzo o d. Paglia
mo Gallo
Rio d. Cavalletto
2 *Basilica di San Marco*
25
24
8 *Campanile di San Marco*
11
3 *Palazzo Ducale (Doges' Palace)*
5 *Ponte dei Sospiri (Bridge of Sighs)*
9
1 *Piazza San Marco*
12 *Piazzetta San Marco*
10
13
21
14 **4**
20
Rio d. Zecca
18 **15** *Giardinetti Reali*
Molo
—Calle Vallaresso
16

Bacino di San Marco

N

km | 1/8 | 1/4
mi | 1/8 |

Restaurants/Clubs: Red   **Hotels:** Blue

Shops/ Outdoors: Green   **Sights/Culture:** Black

119

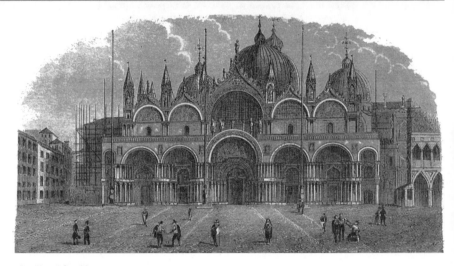

Basilica di San Marco

3 Palazzo Ducale (Doges' Palace) More than just the residence of the doge, this opulent palace (see drawing on page 121) was both a symbol and a seat of power. Behind its pink-and-white confectionery facade were the meeting halls of government and the offices of the dreaded secret police and inquisitors. Construction of the building began in the ninth century, and it was enlarged and modified many times, reaching its present state in the 15th century, when the facade facing the **Piazzetta San Marco** and the monumental door on the **Basilica** side were built. The facade on the lagoon side is the oldest: A column at the southwest corner bears the date 1344 (marking the completion of the ground floor loggias).

Remarkable sculptures adorn the palazzo's corners: near the bridge on the southeast corner is *Drunkenness of Noah,* and on the southwest corner is *Adam and Eve,* both by unknown artists; on the northwest corner is *The Judgment of Solomon,* attributed to Jacopo della Quercia. Over the columns, the capitals are decorated with animals, warriors, men, women, and representations of vices and virtues and human activities. The **Porta della Carta,** the entrance to the palace adjacent to the **Basilica,** is a Venetian-Gothic masterwork by **Giovanni** and **Bartolomeo Bon.** The figure over the door, on his knees in front of *St. Mark's Lion,* is Doge Francesco Foscari, who led the Republic in the acquisition of new territories on the Italian mainland from 1423 to 1457.

In the courtyard, the facades on the south (lagoon side) and west have 14th-century loggias on the second floor; the ground floors were originally just brick walls. In 1602, city architect **Bartolomeo Monopola** performed the amazing feat of replacing those walls with arches and columns by temporarily supporting the structure during construction. The two bronze wellheads at the center of the courtyard were cast in the 16th century. Patricians entered the building by ascending the monumental **Scala dei Giganti** (Giant's Staircase), flanked at the top by statues of *Mars* and *Neptune,* symbols of Venetian power over land and sea.

The interior of the palazzo dates from the 16th century. A fire in 1574 destroyed the original woodwork, ceilings, and walls as well as important paintings by Carpaccio, Giorgione, and Titian. The imposing staircase, **Scala d'Oro [1]** (numbers refer to floor plan on page 121), leads to the **Primo Piano Nobile** (actually the second floor), the location of the doges' apartments, which are now only open for temporary exhibitions. Two small rooms here lead to the **Sala dei Filosofi [2],** where another staircase leads to the doges' chapel. Notice the fresco of *St. Christopher* by Titian over the door at the stairs. The **Sala delle Volte** contains three Venice insignias, among them a famous *St. Mark's Lion* by Vittore Carpaccio.

From the **Scala d'Oro,** continue to the **Secondo Piano Nobile** (third floor). Through the **Atrio Quadrato** (Square Atrium) **[3]** and the **Sala delle Quattro Porte** (Room of Four Doors) **[4]** is the small **Anticollegio [5].** In this room (rebuilt in the 16th century to plans by **Palladio** and **Alessandro Vittoria**), ambassadors and delegations from subject territories would wait to be received by the doge's cabinet. Here, beside the doors, are four paintings by Jacopo Tintoretto. On the wall opposite the window is *Rape of Europa* by Paolo Veronese. The next room is the **Sala del Collegio [6],** where the doges' cabinet would meet to deliberate and to receive its visitors. The ceiling was painted by Paolo Veronese with allegories of virtues and with the famous *Venice Enthroned with Justice an d Peace* (center of ceiling, at the far end). The paintings over the entrance are by Jacopo Tintoretto, and those on the right wall are from his workshop. The one over the cabinet's seats, *Doge Sebastiano Venier Offering Thanks for the Victory of Lepanto,* is by Paolo Veronese. The Venice Senate met in the next room—the **Sala del Senato [7]**. The Senate was a body of elected patricians in charge of foreign policy and some domestic affairs. With about 150 members, it was a more agile body than the *Maggior Consiglio,* the 1,200-member legislative assembly that included all male patricians who were of age. The paintings on the walls and ceiling of the Senate's chamber are minor works by Tintoretto and his workshop, Jacopo Palma il Giovane, and other Mannerist painters. Through the **Sala delle Quattro Porte** and a small atrium is the **Sala del Consiglio dei Dieci** (Room of the Council of Ten) **[8].** This much-feared assembly was in charge of the secret police and of the prosecution of members of the patrician class. Like most secret police, those of Venice acquired enormous power, particularly in the last days of the Republic's life. Three paintings by Paolo Veronese adorn the ceiling in correspondence with the curved woodwork at the back. The central oval is a copy of *Jupiter Striking Vices with Lightning,* also by Veronese (the original is in the Louvre).

The **Sale d'Armi del Consiglio dei Dieci** (Armory Room of the Council of Ten) **[9],** up a few steps from the council's assembly room, contains a large collection of weapons, mostly from the 16th and 17th centuries.

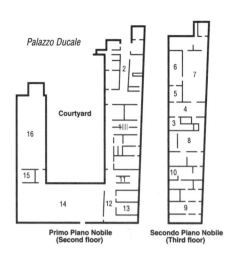

Palazzo Ducale

**Primo Piano Nobile
(Second floor)**

**Secondo Piano Nobile
(Third floor)**

The **Saletta dei Tre Inquisitori** (Three Inquisitors' Office) **[10],** off the **Room of the Council of Ten,** can be seen only as part of a guided tour. The Three Inquisitors, selected from among the 10 council members, were the real terror of Venice, particularly in the 18th century. Their trials of real and supposed political criminals were held in secret without the chance of appeal. A small staircase led directly from this room to the torture chamber, while a secret corridor led to the **Ponte dei Sospiri** (Bridge of Sighs) and the prisons. Inquire at the ticket window for guided tours of these rooms. These tours, called *Itinereri Segreti* (Secret Itineraries) must be booked at least one day in advance and are conducted, unfortunately, only in Italian. (Tours in English

Palazzo Ducale

were planned as we went to press. Check upon arrival.)

Downstairs, at the armory's entrance **(Scala dei Censori) [11],** are the south and west wings of the **Primo Piano Nobile.** Through the **Andito del Maggior Consiglio [12],** the tour proceeds to the *lagò,* a veranda with statues of Adam and Eve by Antonio Rizzo, considered to be among the best works of the early Renaissance in Venice. A door on the left wall leads to the **Sala dell' Armamento [13].** The large, much-damaged fresco here is all that is left of *Paradise,* painted by Guariento in 1367. After the 1574 fire, a new *Paradise* was commissioned from Tintoretto; it is now in the **Sala del Maggior Consiglio** (Great Assembly Hall). The remnants of Guariento's work were discovered when Tintoretto's canvas was removed for restoration. Back in the **Andito,** two doors open into the grandiose **Sala del Maggior Consiglio** (Great Assembly Hall) **[14].** It was in this hall that the patricians, whose numbers varied from 1,200 to 2,000, regularly met to run the Republic. They sat in nine double rows parallel to the long walls of the hall. The doge and his cabinet sat on the dais at the entrance wall. Of the 35 paintings encased in gilt frames on the ceiling the most noteworthy is Paolo Veronese's *Apotheosis of Venice Crowned by Victory* (at the central oval near the dais). The workshops of Veronese and Tintoretto produced most of the other canvases. Behind the dais is Tintoretto's great *Paradise*—the largest painting in the world. It is one of the painter's last works, and his son Domenico and Palma il Giovane helped him complete it. A frieze at the top portrays the first 76 doges of Venice, up to Francesco Venier, who died in 1556. The view from the windows here is spectacular.

A door at the far right leads through the **Sala della Quarantia Civil Nova [15]** to the last great hall of the palace, the **Sala dello Scrutinio** (Ballot Counting Room) **[16],** richly decorated with paintings by Palma il Giovane, Andrea Vicentino, Aliense, and other Mannerist artists. The room is often used for temporary exhibitions. The *Last Judgment* above the dais is by Palma il Giovane. Back in the **Sala del Maggior Consiglio,** a door at the left of Tintoretto's *Paradise* leads back to the staircase and, through a loggia, to the **Ponte dei Sospiri** (Bridge of Sighs), which connects the palazzo with the prisons across the canal. A visit to the prisons is included in the admission ticket.

A high-tech audio guided tour, called Lightman, is now available in English and other languages for visitors to the **Palazzo Ducale.** The portable infrared system offers detailed information about the artwork in the palace and the history of the Republic. Lightman can be rented at the palazzo entrance and is well worth the additional

charge. ♦ Admission. M-Sa Mar-Oct; M afternoon, Tu-Sa Nov-Feb. Piazzetta San Marco (southeast corner of the piazzetta). 5224951. Vaporetto stops: San Marco (1, 82); San Zaccaria (1, 52, 82)

4 Molo di San Marco This quay on the south side of the **Piazzetta de San Marco,** opening toward the lagoon, was once the main entrance to the city. Patricians, merchants, and others having business in the city landed here. The two huge columns marking its sides like an imaginary portal were transported on boats from Byzantium in the 12th century. They support the statues of *St. Theodor* (the original protector of Venice, later replaced by St. Mark) and a puzzling winged animal, accepted as *St. Mark's Lion,* although it is probably a chimera made in China or Persia (the wings were added in Venice). The most charming aspect of the pier today is the row of gondolas parked along it, furiously rocking all day long from the waves created by the heavy motorboat traffic. In fact, only a few courageous gondoliers (and their unsuspecting passengers) still brave the rough waters of St. Mark's basin. ♦ Piazzetta San Marco (south in piazza). Vaporetto stops: San Marco (1, 82); San Zaccaria (1, 52, 82)

5 Ponte dei Sospiri (Bridge of Sighs) This elegant bridge owes its melancholy name (probably invented by 19th-century travelers) to the fact that it connected the **Palazzo Ducale** with the prisons across the canal. It was built in 1602, and has since figured prominently in countless tales, paintings, and movies. ♦ East of the Palazzo Ducale. Vaporetto stops: San Marco (1, 82); San Zaccaria (1, 52, 82)

6 Venini When it was founded in 1921, the Venini glass factory immediately distinguished itself with its innovations in the ancient Venetian glass-making tradition. The firm introduced new types of glass, and contemporary artists produced new shapes. In the 1980s, Venini vases made in the 1950s fetched as much as a half million dollars at auction. ♦ M-Sa Mar-Oct; M afternoon, Tu-Sa Nov-Feb. Piazzetta Leoncini 314 (north side of the Basilica). 52240452. Vaporetto stops: San Marco (1, 82); San Zaccaria (1, 52, 82)

Around 1750, Venice experienced its first *acqua alta,* or flooding of the canals and the lagoon (the low area around St. Mark's Square is especially afflicted). Over time, the frequency of these ephemeral floods has increased drastically; according to current accounts it is now approaching 50 times a year. The worst flood by far was in 1966, the same year Florence was devastated by water, when the tide rose nearly six and a half feet above normal sea level and deluged the city.

7 Torre dell'Orologio (Clock Tower)

Mauro Codussi, one of the fathers of the Venetian Renaissance, probably designed this structure (pictured below) at the end of the 15th century. Its dual purpose was to hold a large clock (which replaced the one that had been on the **Basilica**) and to mark the entrance to Venice's main wholesale and retail streets, appropriately called the *Mercerie* (from the old Venetian word for haberdashers). Every hour on the hour the two bronze statues on the top of the tower hit the large bell with their long-handled hammers, thanks to a 15th-century mechanism that is still a source of wonder. For a moment, life in the square comes to a halt as everyone watches the two Moors—so-called because of the dark color of the bronze they are cast in—majestically pivot around to strike the hour. The tower is closed indefinitely for renovations. ♦ Merceria dell'Orologio 147 (north side of Piazza San Marco). Vaporetto stops: San Marco (1, 82); San Zaccaria (1, 52, 82)

8 Procuratie Vecchie

With your back to the **Basilica,** the building you see on the right is the **Procuratie Vecchie.** This building, along with the **Procuratie Nuove** directly across the piazza to your left, served an important function during the Venetian Republic. The procurators (after whom the edifices were named) were high government officials, and their headquarters next to the **Palazzo Ducale** made **Piazza San Marco** the center of civic life in Venice. The building, attributed to **Mauro Codussi** and erected at the beginning of the 16th century, replaced an earlier Byzantine structure and retains some Byzantine influence in the first-floor arcade. **Jacopo Sansovino,** the official architect of the Republic, created the building's final shape by adding the second floor in 1532. ♦ Piazza San Marco (north side of piazza). Vaporetto stops: San Marco (1, 82); San Zaccaria (1, 52, 82)

8 Caffè Lavena

★★$$$ This historical cafe is forever in the shadow—some pun intended—of the world-famous **Caffè Florian** across the piazza. But Richard Wagner preferred this 18th-century *pasticceria* (pastry shop)/bar, perhaps because he could almost touch the nearby **Basilica** from his outdoor table. Or perhaps it was the **Procuratie**'s cool shade that inspired him in the same way it will move you on a lazy

Torre dell'Orologio

Mark Ammerman 95

summer day, when the cafe's *orchestrina* plays daily from afternoon to midnight. Enjoy the light brunches, light lunches, and not-so-light *coppa Lavena* ice-cream extravaganza. ♦ Daily 8AM-midnight Mar-Oct; M, W-Su Nov-Feb. Piazza San Marco 133 (north side of piazza). 5224070. Vaporetto stops: San Marco (1, 82); San Zaccaria (1, 52, 82)

8 Missiaglia Since 1864 the Missiaglia family has been supplying wealthy Venetians and visitors with the best in jewels and gold. Definitely one of the most reliable goldsmiths in town (most items are crafted in their own workshop), this jeweler excels in sober, classic objects, but keeps an accurate eye on the newest trends in design. ♦ M-Sa Mar-Oct; M afternoon, Tu-Sa Nov-Feb. Piazza San Marco 125 (north side of piazza). 5224464. Vaporetto stops: San Marco (1, 82); San Zaccaria (1, 52, 82)

8 Caffè Quadri ★★$$$ This establishment boasts a rather historic "first": It was this very cafe that allegedly introduced Venetians (and therefore Europeans and North and South Americans) to Turkish coffee in 1725. Other accounts say it had already been imported to the city in the 17th century. No matter—it tastes pretty wonderful here regardless of where it came from or when. So thought Stendhal, Dumas, Byron, and Proust, and so think the myriad modern-day habitués who prefer this setting over its rivals in the piazza. The upstairs restaurant, with a setting befitting a doge (and prices to match), is the only restaurant with windows directly on the square. The food is excellent, but the formal ambience is most appealing to serious diners or expense-account *Biennale* celebs. ♦ Tu-Su 8AM-midnight. Piazza San Marco 120 (north side of piazza). 5289299. Vaporetto stops: San Marco (1, 82); San Zaccaria (1, 52, 82)

9 Ala Napoleonica In 1797 young Napoleon Bonaparte brought about the end of the Republic of Venice after its millennium of glory with a simple letter in which he asked Doge Ludovico Manin to resign and open the way for a new, democratic constitution. Pressed by Napoleon's armies at the Republic's borders, the doge and his men decided to oblige. It was an inglorious end, the only justification for which was that a war would most certainly have ended in defeat for Venice. During their occupation, the French undertook important public works, among them the restructuring on the side of the piazza opposite the **Basilica.** The **Ala Napoleonica,** designed by Italian architect **Giuseppe Maria Soli** in 1814, includes a grand staircase and the so-called royal apartments, with a ballroom that is today part of the **Museo Correr.** ♦ Piazza San Marco (west side of piazza). Vaporetto stops: San Marco (1, 82); San Zaccaria (1, 52, 82)

9 Museo Correr This museum is comprised of three sections: the **Collezioni Storiche** (Historical Collections), consisting of 22 rooms on the second floor at the top of the grand staircase, with material related to the history of Venice; the **Museo del Risorgimento e dell'Ottocento Veneziano** (Museum of 19th-Century Venice) on the third floor; and the **Quadreria** (Collection of Paintings), also on the third floor.

The **Collezione Storiche** include maps and views of Venice (in the **Galleria**); works by Antonio Canova, the Neo-Classical sculptor **(Room 1)**; marbles with various effigies of St. Mark's Lion **(Room 4)**; documents and images related to the doges **(Rooms 5-7)**, with some fascinating bound *commissioni* (instructions sent by the doges to Venetian ambassadors and other high officers); clothes and portraits of patricians **(Rooms 8-10)**; Venetian coins from the 12th century **(Room 11)**; a scale model of the *Bucintoro*, the gilded boat used by the doges for ceremonies and parades **(Room 14)**; material related to the history of the **Arsenale** and to Venetian navigation techniques **(Rooms 15-16)**; weapons **(Rooms 17-18)**; and documents pertaining to Doge Francesco Morosino **(Rooms 19-22)**.

The **Museo del Risorgimento e dell'Ottocento Veneziano** covers the history of Venice from 1797 to 1866, focusing on the unsuccessful attempt to gain independence from Austria in 1848-49. In the **Quadreria,** a large collection of minor paintings documents the evolution of Venetian art from the 13th to the 16th centuries. Included are works by great masters, such as Antonello da Messina's *La Pietà*, painted in Venice; four paintings by Giovanni Bellini (exhibited next to works by Jacopo, his father, and Gentile, his brother); and two portraits by Vittore Carpaccio—*The Courtesans* (though the women portrayed were most likely members of the Venetian upper class) and the striking *Young Man in a Red Beret.* Also here are the original wood dies of Jacopo de'Barbari's famous *Map of Venice in 1500,* an extremely detailed drawing and a valuable resource for reconstructing the shapes of buildings at that time. ◆ Admission. M, W-Su. Piazza San Marco 52 (west side of piazza). 5225625. Vaporetto stops: San Marco (1, 82); San Zaccaria (1, 52, 82)

9 Nardi You may be able to afford nothing more than the window shopping here, but take a peak at the displays of one of Venice's oldest, premier jewelry stores. The more elaborate pieces studded with precious stones are worth a doge's ransom, particularly the museum-quality antique pieces. ◆ M-Sa. Piazza San Marco 69 (west side of piazza). 5225733. Vaporetto stops: San Marco (1, 82); San Zaccaria (1, 52, 82)

9 Pauly Located right under the open porticoes of the **Museo Correr,** this cluster of shops offers a wide selection of exquisite glass objects, mostly produced in its own Murano furnace. Vases, chandeliers, drinking glasses, and statues come in an incredible variety of shapes. While some pieces would be right at home in a museum, others are less elaborate and relatively more affordable. Glass masters since 1866, this firm has an excellent reputation for reliability when shipping abroad. A salesperson at any of the three small shops in the piazza will direct you to their principal location at the end of Calle Larga San Marco, which is open by appointment only. ◆ M-Sa Mar-Oct; M afternoon, Tu-Sa Nov-Feb. Piazza San Marco 72-77 (west side of piazza). 5209899. Vaporetto stops: San Marco (1, 82); San Zaccaria (1, 52, 82)

10 Procuratie Nuove Notice that this facade is heavier and more imposing than its older counterpart on the other side of the square (the **Procuratie Vecchie**). These administrative headquarters were started by **Vincenzo Scamozzi** in the late 16th and early 17th centuries. It was completed a hundred years later by the Venetian-Baroque architect **Baldassare Longhena.** Napoleon designated this building his Royal Palace and had it connected to the **Procuratie Vecchie** with the

Ala Napoleonica. ◆ Piazza San Marco (south side of piazza). Vaporetto stops: San Marco (1, 82); San Zaccaria (1, 52, 82)

10 Caffè Florian ★★★$$$ This most famous of the Venetian cafes was one of the first places in Europe to serve that new and exotic drink—coffee. Today it is still patronized by upper-class Venetians, particularly for afternoon tea inside in the winter where the original 18th-century decor has been preserved. In the summer, a small orchestra plays popular tunes for guests sitting at the outdoor tables, sipping expensive coffee and cappuccino. Those concerned with budgets can take refuge at the counter inside, where they can sip a Bellini cocktail or glass of *prosecco* wine, away from the strains of *"O sole mio"* and *"Volare."* Despite the high prices, this distinguished institution is losing money and may soon close its doors, unless the city finds a way to save it. ◆ M-Tu, Th-Sa 8AM-midnight. Piazza San Marco 56-59 (south side of piazza). 85338. Vaporetto stops: San Marco (1, 82); San Zaccaria (1, 52, 82)

10 Biblioteca Correr (Correr Library) Next to **Caffè Florian,** a doorway leads to one of the inner courtyards of the **Procuratie Nuove,** where an elevator takes scholars and students to the pleasant reading rooms of this library. A friendly staff of librarians helps them find their way through the ancient catalogs, many of which are handwritten. The rich collection of documents and manuscripts was bequeathed in 1830 by the patrician Teodoro Correr. A collection specializing in Venetian art history was more recently acquired by the library. ◆ M-Sa 8:30AM-1:30PM. Piazza San Marco 52 (south side of piazza). 5225625. Vaporetto stops: San Marco (1, 82); San Zaccaria (1, 52, 82)

10 Museo Archeologico This important collection of archaeological pieces, housed in part of the **Biblioteca Marciana,** will eventually be moved to a permanent home in a palazzo under restoration in **Campo Santa Maria Formosa.** From the 16th to the 18th centuries, many of Venice's patrician families assembled archaeological pieces from Rome, Greece, and the Roman-settled territories bordering on the lagoon (Aquileia, Eraclea, and Altinum). The

Grimani family bequeathed its collection to the Republic in the 16th century; other donations followed. The assortment of coins, epigraphs, bas-reliefs, and statues here include many exquisite originals from Greece, particularly from the fifth century BC, and from Rome. Among the most interesting pieces are a statue of *Demetra* and one of *Athena* **(Room 4)**; the *Ara Grimani* (Grimani Altar), with magnificent sculptures from the first century BC **(Room 6)**; and three statues of Gallic warriors, sculpted in Pergamus around the year 200 BC. ♦ Admission. Daily. Piazza San Marco 52 (south side of piazza). 5225978. Vaporetto stops: San Marco (1, 82); San Zaccaria (1, 52, 82)

11 Campanile di San Marco (St. Mark's Bell Tower) Since the ninth century there has been a campanile in the piazza. The design of the current one, the highest monument in Venice (325 feet), dates back to the early 16th century, when **Bartolomeo Bon** gave it its final shape. Nearly three centuries later, on the morning of 14 July 1902, the structure collapsed into the piazza. Miraculously no one was injured and none of the other buildings in the piazza were damaged. Many shops around Venice sell what purports to be a photographic record of the event. Unfortunately, no film at the time was fast enough to have captured it, so the image is a picturesque fake. The replica that was built in its place and dedicated in 1912 used many of the same bricks and one of the original bells. Don't miss the wonderful view of Venice from the top. ♦ Admission. Daily. Piazza San Marco (center of piazza). 5224064. Vaporetto stops: San Marco (1, 82); San Zaccaria (1, 52, 82)

11 Loggetta di San Marco **Jacopo Sansovino** designed this structure at the base of the **Campanile** that was built between 1539 and 1549. The terrace and balustrade in front were added later. The four bronze statues in the niches, executed by Sansovino, represent *Minerva, Apollo, Mercury,* and *Peace* as symbols of good government. Over them is *Venice Clad as Justice,* accompanied by bas-reliefs representing Cyprus and Crete, then part of Venice's empire. Together with the **Procuratie** and the **Biblioteca Marciana,** the **Loggetta** symbolizes the majesty of the Venetian Republic. ♦ Piazza San Marco (center of piazza). Vaporetto stops: San Marco (1, 82); San Zaccaria (1, 52, 82)

12 Piazzetta San Marco This "little piazza," an extension of the **Piazza San Marco** between the south side of the **Basilica** and the lagoon border, is separated from its larger neighbor by the **Campanile**. The white marble pavement was used by the patricians to pace back and forth while Parliament was deliberating inside the **Palazzo Ducale.** When a young patrician came of age, he was taken here on the family gondola and officially admitted into the community of rulers. ♦ Between the Campanile and the lagoon. Vaporetto stops: San Marco (1, 82); San Zaccaria (1, 52, 82)

13 Biblioteca Marciana (St. Mark's Library) **Jacopo Sansovino** started constructing this Renaissance masterpiece in 1537, but left it to be completed by his pupil **Vincenzo Scamozzi** in 1588. The facade was designed to be a continuation of the **Procuratie Nuove,** thus emphasizing the architectural unity of the whole compound. The Roman-inspired solemnity of the exterior was intended to visually represent the power and wealth of the Venetian Republic. Be sure to see the two large caryatids that support the vault flanking the library's monumental door. The library itself contains a collection of incunabula (precious manuscripts and early printed books). General readers (those who arrive before the room fills with high school and college students) are received in a large room on the ground floor. A smaller room on the left is reserved for scholars to consult ancient books or manuscripts (permission must be granted by the library). The library's best architecture and its most precious collection of manuscripts are up the grand staircase. Unless temporary exhibitions are being held, permission to visit the rooms upstairs must be obtained from the director's office. ♦ M-Sa. Piazza San Marco 13; entrance for general public at Piazza San Marco 7 (south side of piazza). 5208788. Vaporetto stops: San Marco (1, 82); San Zaccaria (1, 52, 82)

14 Caffè Chioggia ★★★$$ If you're looking for a splendid way to end an evening in Venice, relax at one of this cafe's outdoor tables and enjoy the romantic music in the company of the **Palazzo Ducale** in front and the lagoon at the side. This is the only one of the piazza's cafes with a view of the water. The music is more consistently good here (from quartets to a solo pianist) and the waiters have less attitude, even encouraging you to linger. ♦ M-Sa 8:30AM-1:30AM Apr-Oct. Piazza San Marco 11 (south side of piazza). 5285011. Vaporetto stops: San Marco (1, 82); San Zaccaria (1, 52, 82)

15 Giardinetti Reali Napoleon's architects razed a building and put a small park in its place to permit a view of the lagoon from the Royal Apartments they had created in the **Procuratie Nuove**. Although far from living up to its name (Royal Gardens), the park offers welcome respite—a rare spot of green in a city of stone and water. ♦ West of Piazzetta San Marco. Vaporetto stop: San Marco (1, 82)

16 Harry's Bar ★★★$$$$ Made famous by Hemingway, **Harry's Bar** originally was just a bar, but has now become Venice's most reliable (and expensive) restaurant as well. Distinguished owner Arrigo Cipriani, son of the original owner, claims that many Venetian specialties were created here—the Bellini (a peach nectar and *prosecco* wine cocktail) and carpaccio, for instance. Both were named after Venetian painters, and are at their best here. Another recommended dish is *risotto primavera* (with a variety of seasonal vegetables). The see-and-be-seen scene is at its most active at the downstairs bar during late afternoon tea or *aperitivo* hour between 6 and 8PM. If you're staying for dinner, ask for a table in the upstairs restaurant for a great view of the Canal Grande. ♦ Tu-Su lunch and dinner. Calle Vallaresso 1323 (west of the Molo). 5285777. Vaporetto stop: San Marco (1, 82)

17 Hotel Monaco and Grand Canal $$$ This is one of the most attractive hotels in town, in part because the ground floor public rooms (and many of the 70 guest rooms) have large windows looking out on the Canal Grande and the church of **Santa Maria della Salute**. In the evening, the public area becomes a piano bar that attracts many Venetians who appreciate the quiet, relaxing atmosphere. Equally popular is the lovely waterfront dining terrace of the hotel's acclaimed **Grand Canal Restaurant**. ♦ Calle Vallaresso 1325 (west of the Molo). 5200211; fax 5200501. Vaporetto stop: San Marco (1, 82)

18 Missoni The latest colorful designs created by the Milanese team of Ottavio and Tai Missoni for men and women are available here. Particular items to look for include cardigans, coats, skirts, and dresses. Venetians watch for the sales at the end of each season. ♦ M-Sa Mar-Oct; M afternoon, Tu-Sa Nov-Feb. Calle Vallaresso 1312B (west of Piazza San Marco). 5205733. Vaporetto stop: San Marco (1, 82)

19 La Bottega Veneta This famous high-fashion leather accessories firm started in New York City before returning to its homeland. Their trademark woven-leather skins come in the season's favorite colors. ♦ M-Sa Mar-Oct; M afternoon, Tu-Sa Nov-Feb. Calle Vallaresso 1337 (west of Piazza San Marco). 5228489. Vaporetto stop: San Marco (1, 82)

19 Camiceria San Marco A large selection of fabrics and years of experience draw customers here for the city's best custom-made shirts, blouses, and pajamas for men and women. Whatever you select, it will be ready in 24 hours, at prices comparable to those at high-end department stores. ♦ M-Sa Mar-Oct; M afternoon, Tu-Sa Nov-Feb. Calle Vallaresso 1340 (west of Piazza San Marco). 5221432. Vaporetto stop: San Marco (1, 82)

LUNA HOTEL BAGLIONI

20 Luna Hotel Baglioni $$$ This elder statesman of Venetian hotels, recently renovated from top to toe, is as handsome as it is historical. Some of the 118 rooms and all of the suites have original 18th-century furnishings. The **Tiepolo Suite** has a terrace with a splendid view over the St. Mark's basin; the **Giorgione Suite** has a terrace with a view over the city rooftops. The main conference hall is a masterwork of 18th-century interior decoration, and the **Canova** restaurant is elegant but relaxed. ♦ Calle Vallaresso 1243 (west of Piazza San Marco). 5289840; fax 5287160. Vaporetto stop: San Marco (1, 82)

21 Vogini Just barely outside of **Piazza San Marco** is one of Venice's oldest and most respected leather goods stores. Three elegant shops under the Vogini name carry men's and women's accessories from wallets and bags to attaché cases and luggage, belts and stylish outerwear. The shops carry other designer collections (including the hard-to-find local house of Roberta di Camerino), but the private, classic Vogini label matches them in quality of craftsmanship and materials. ♦ M-Sa. Calle II dell'Ascensione 1257A, 1301, and 1305 (west of Piazza San Marco). Vaporetto stop: San Marco (1, 82)

Whether or not Venetian blinds originated here will depend upon whom you ask. The supposed ancestors found here are called *veneziane,* and are often used together with outer slatted wooden shutters, curiously called *persiane.*

Restaurants/Clubs: Red   **Hotels:** Blue

Shops/ ♦ Outdoors: Green   **Sights/Culture:** Black

Venetian Victuals

Venice, the city that brought pepper and coffee to the West, and such civilized eating utensils as the fork and glassware to the table, has a distinguished culinary tradition. Today, the main legacy that lives on in Venice's restaurants is the sea.

A full Venetian meal begins with a selection of seafood antipasto, bits of *seppia* (cuttlefish), *scampi* (shrimp), *bottarga* (tuna eggs), or *ostriche alla veneziana* (oysters with caviar). Even risotto dishes have a special sealike texture in Venice. Locals like them *ondoso*—literally "wavy," meaning creamier than you'll encounter in other parts of Italy. The most famous of the Venetian *primi piatti* (first courses) is *risi e bisi*, dialect for rice and peas. After that there are risotto dishes made with any of the local fish—or practically all of them, which is what *risotto di mare* is. One of the most unusual risotto dishes is the black *risotto di seppie* or *risotto nero*, which gets its color from the ink of the cuttlefish. Pasta dishes can be rare in Venice.

The best-known *secondo piatto* (main course) in Venice is *fegato alla veneziana*, liver and onions, prepared with a delicacy matched nowhere else and often accompanied by pale polenta from the nearby Friuli region. Carpaccio is another popular dish. As served at **Harry's Bar** (proprietor Arrigo Cipriani claims to have invented it), the dish is thinly sliced raw beef topped with parmesan cheese, though fish and other ingredient variations have sprung up all over.

Of course, seafood is a natural choice in Venice, and local restaurants do wonders with the humble dried salt cod, called *baccalà*. *Baccalà alla veneziana* is made with onions and anchovies, *baccalà alla vicentina* adds milk and parmesan cheese, and *baccalà mantecata* is made with olive oil and parsley. *Seppie alla veneziana* is cuttlefish cooked in white wine and its own black ink; *bisato* is eel, served *alla veneziana* (sautéed in olive oil with bay leaves and vinegar) or *sull'ara* (baked with bay leaves). There are also seemingly endless local fish, all with unfathomable dialect names. Among the most popular of these are *bransin* (or *branzino*, a type of sea bass) and the tiny soft-shelled crabs called *moleche*.

The most popular wines in Venice are the white Pinot Bianco and Pinot Grigio, which make excellent accompaniments for the seafood, and the dry red Merlot, which goes well with meat dishes. Before, during, and after meals, however, most Venetians sip *prosecco*— a light, sparkling white. Meals are often finished with a grappa (the Italian aquavit) or *sgroppino*, a refreshing combination of lemon ice cream, vodka, and *prosecco* wine.

Inexpensive eating options are the taverns known as *bacari*, which serve a wine pick-me-up called an *ombra*, along with *cicchetti*, or appetizers. These little plates of seafood, vegetables, cheese, and prosciutto are filling, and *bacari* can be great places to meet the locals.

---

valentino

22 Valentino Here you'll find a stylish boutique of the Roman high priest of ready-to-wear fashion. Impeccable tailoring, draping, and choice of luxurious fabrics set these elegant suits and separates apart. ♦ M-Sa Mar-Oct; M afternoon, Tu-Sa Nov-Feb. Salizzada San Moisè 1473 (between Piazza San Marco and Campo San Moisè). 5205733. Vaporetto stop: San Marco (1, 82)

23 Antiquità M This antiques store has its own workshop for the production of precious velvets hand-printed in the style of Mariano Fortuny, the Venice-based artist who was all the rage during the 1920s and 1930s. Both the antiques and the velvets are of the highest quality. ♦ M-Sa Mar-Oct; M afternoon, Tu-Sa Nov-Feb. Frezzeria 1690 (off Calle II dell'Ascensione). 5235666. Vaporetto stop: San Marco (1, 82)

23 Marco Polo, Vetro d'Arte What a welcome relief to enter this cool, gallerylike store of carefully selected glassware, an interesting sampler of the millennium-old Murano industry as it approaches the 21st century. Attractive small-gift ideas fill the front half of the store, while a wide selection of exquisite drinking glasses (from the sleek and modern to the fanciful and historical) fill the back showcases. Head upstairs for "art glass" and the prices escalate: These are the striking limited editions or singular masterworks as interpreted by the premier craftspeople working on Murano today. ◆ M-Sa. Frezzeria 1644 (off Calle II dell'Ascensione). 5229295. Vaporetto stop: San Marco (1, 82)

24 Libreria del Sansovino Art books, including rare and out-of-print copies, and a wide selection of books on Venice in English are the specialties at this bookstore. It also carries current English-language best-sellers—the owner calls them "jet lag" books. ◆ M-Sa Mar-Oct; M afternoon, Tu-Sa Nov-Feb. Fondamenta Orseolo 84 (northwest behind Piazza San Marco). 5222623. Vaporetto stop: San Marco (1, 82)

25 Bacino Orseolo Behind the **Procuratie Vecchie** a canal opens onto this small basin, the main gondola landing for **Piazza San Marco**. Whether you take a ride or not, it is fun just to watch the gondoliers and their customers. ◆ Northwest behind Piazza San Marco. Vaporetto stop: San Marco (1, 82)

26 Osvaldo Böhm Antique prints (originals and reproductions), historic photographs, prints, and watercolors (many of Venetian themes) are available at this shop a few steps from **Piazza San Marco.** ◆ M-Sa Mar-Oct; M afternoon, Tu-Sa Nov-Feb. Salizzada San Moisè 1349-50 (between Piazza San Marco and Campo San Moisè). 5222255. Vaporetto stop: San Marco (1, 82)

27 Calzature Fratelli Rossetti High quality and high style are the hallmarks of the men's and women's shoe collections sold by this worldwide retailer. If you can afford it, treat your feet to something special. ◆ M-Sa Mar-Oct; M afternoon, Tu-Sa Nov-Feb. Salizzada San Moisè 1447 (between Piazza San Marco and Campo San Moisè). 5220819. Vaporetto stop: San Marco (1, 82). Also at: Campo San Salvador 4800. 5230571. Vaporetto stop: Rialto (1, 82)

27 Fendi Luxury leather goods are the specialty here, but this boutique also carries clothes, umbrellas, and gift items. ◆ M-Sa Mar-Oct; M afternoon, Tu-Sa Nov-Feb. Salizzada San Moisè 1474 (between Piazza San Marco and Campo San Moisè). 5205733. Vaporetto stop: San Marco (1, 82)

28 L'Isola The museum-quality glass objects in this store are made in Murano by the famed Carlo Moretti team, which specializes in clean,

sometimes whimsical, modern designs. ◆ M-Sa Mar-Oct; M afternoon, Tu-Sa Nov-Feb. Campo San Moisè 1468. 5231973. Vaporetto stop: San Marco (1, 82)

29 Chiesa di San Moisè Venice is probably the only city in the world with Catholic churches consecrated to prophets of the Old Testament (technically included among the saints): There are churches for Daniel, Zacharias, and the Archangel Raphael. St. Moses was built in 1668 in full Baroque style by **Alessandro Tremignon** with funds from the Fini family. As in many other Venetian churches, statues of the donors were installed over the portals. Here the family's coat of arms is also sculpted on the pediment. The lavish decorations on the facade have often been compared with stage sets for Baroque operas. Equally controversial is the surprising and sumptuous high altar, with a dark and complex sculpture—*Moses Receiving the Tablets on Mount Sinai.* ◆ Campo San Moisè. Vaporetto stop: San Marco (1, 82)

30 Hotel Bauer Grünwald $$$
In addition to the modern entrance on **Campo San Moisè,** this 215-room hotel has a Gothic facade on the Canal Grande, with a restaurant and bar on a splendid terrace over-looking the water. Most suites and some rooms are decorated with antiques. ◆ Campo San Moisè 1459. 5207022; fax 5207557. Vaporetto stop: San Marco (1, 82)

31 Frette This renowned Milan-based company produces high-quality linens for tables, beds, and clothing. The Venice shop is one of a dozen throughout the world, including outlets in London, New York, Paris, and Beverly Hills. ◆ M-Sa Mar-Oct; M afternoon, Tu-Sa Nov-Feb. Calle Larga XXII Marzo 2070A (west of Campo San Moisè). 5224914. Vaporetto stop: San Marco (1, 82)

32 Libreria Sangiorgio This is one of the best bookstores in Venice for English-language reading materials. They have a seemingly endless supply of John Ruskin's *The Stones of Venice* and Mary McCarthy's delightful *Venice Observed,* along with Jan Morris's *Venice* and Toby Coles's collection of quotations on Venice from English and American writers. ◆ M-Sa Mar-Oct; M afternoon, Tu-Sa Nov-Feb. Calle Larga XXII Marzo 2087 (west of Campo San Moisè). 5238451. Vaporetto stop: San Marco (1, 82)

33 Hotel Europa and Regina $$$ Right on the Canal Grande, **Hotel Europa** and **Regina** belongs to the CIGA chain (recently purchased by ITT Sheraton). Its prices, however, are slightly more affordable than at its sister hotels—the **Danieli** and the **Excelsior**— perhaps because the decor is less opulent and its 192 rooms could use refurbishing. The service, however, is at the same level and the view from the canal-side windows even more attractive. The hotel has three terraces for dining along one of the most panoramic points on the Canal Grande. ◆ Calle Larga XXII Marzo 2159 (west of Campo San Moisè). 5200477, 800/325.3589 (US); fax 5231523. Vaporetto stop: San Marco (1, 82)

34 Ristorante La Caravella ★★★$$$$ Its elegant nautical decor and somewhat formal atmosphere make this restaurant one of the fanciest dining spots in Venice. The kitchen specializes in fish dishes, such as *bigoli in salsa*, an old Venetian recipe for homemade pasta with a light sauce based on anchovies, and *branzino alle erbe*, sea bass poached with fragrant herbs, one of its most popular entrées. Accompany your meal with a selection from the restaurant's refined wine list. ◆ M-Tu, Th-Su lunch and dinner. Calle Larga XXII Marzo 2397 (west of Campo San Moisè). 5208901. Vaporetto stops: San Marco (1, 82); Santa Maria del Giglio (1)

35 Hotel Flora $$ This charming hotel, true to its name, offers breakfast in a beautiful garden. Many of its 44 rooms are furnished with antiques, while others can be quite plain, but all enjoy spotless housekeeping. The Romanelli family oversees one of the friendliest, most competent staffs in town. ◆ Calle Larga XXII Marzo 2283A (west of Campo San Moisè). 5205844; fax 5228217. Vaporetto stops: San Marco (1, 82); Santa Maria del Giglio (1)

36 Venetia Studium This exquisite store specializes in items created with hand-printed fabric and accordion-pleated silks in the style of Mariano Fortuny. The lamps, scarves, and handkerchiefs are delightful. In addition, this shop carries the famous Delphos clothes, also created after designs by Fortuny in gem-colored silk. ◆ M-Sa Mar-Oct; M afternoon,

Tu-Sa Nov-Feb. Calle Larga XXII Marzo 2403 (near Calle delle Ostreghe). 5229281. Vaporetto stops: San Marco (1, 82); Santa Maria del Giglio (1)

37 Libreria Antiquaria Cassini This dealer, who specializes in old books and prints, has a large clientele and a solid reputation. ◆ M-Sa Mar-Oct; M afternoon, Tu-Sa Nov-Feb. Calle Larga XXII Marzo 2424 (at Calle delle Ostreghe). 5231815. Vaporetto stops: San Marco (1, 82); Santa Maria del Giglio (1)

38 Ristorante da Raffaele ★★$$ Perhaps a bit too large for attentive service, this restaurant is still recommended because of its location along a charming canal, as well as for its informal and friendly atmosphere bubbling with the local color of a typical trattoria. All the classic Venetian fish specialties are served here. ◆ M-W, F-Su lunch and dinner. Ponte delle Ostreghe 2347 (at Calle delle Ostreghe). 5232317. Vaporetto stop: Santa Maria del Giglio (1)

39 Hotel Gritti $$$$ One of the most exclusive of the luxury hotels in Venice (and a member the CIGA chain, recently purchased by ITT Sheraton), the Gritti has a chaste Gothic facade on the Canal Grande with a waterside terrace for drinks and dining. Most of the 93 rooms and suites are handsomely furnished with valuable antiques. The atmosphere is one of quiet, understated wealth and old European style. ◆ Campo Santa Maria del Giglio 2467 (south in *campo*). 794611, 800/325.3589 (US); fax 5200942. Vaporetto stop: Santa Maria del Giglio (1)

40 Hotel Ala $$ Furnished with all the modern necessities, this comfortable hotel in a renovated building is conveniently located near the city's major sights. The downside is that the 93 rooms are small, a little worn, and the walls paper-thin. ◆ Campo Santa Maria del Giglio 2494 (west of *campo*). 5208333; fax 5206390. Vaporetto stop: Santa Maria del Giglio (1)

41 Chiesa di Santa Maria del Giglio This fine example of a Venetian-Baroque church, completed in 1683 by **Giuseppe Sardi,** carries to an extreme the Venetian habit of immortalizing on the facade the patrician families who financed the construction. Here the Barbaros are represented by four statues in the deep niches, while Antonio Barbaro, the dynasty's patriarch, looms over the portal between the statues of *Honor* and *Virtue*. The bas-reliefs on the lower facade represent the maps of cities under Venetian domination. Inside, the organ's doors were painted by Jacopo Tintoretto with figures of the four evangelists. ◆ Campo Santa Maria del Giglio (north side of *campo*). Vaporetto stop: Santa Maria del Giglio (1)

42 Vino Vino ★★$$ Originally a wine bar with snacks, this place quickly became a preferred restaurant for light, informal meals (one or two pastas daily and a changing choice of vegetables and simple entrées) in a casual atmosphere. Choose from an excellent selection of wine by the glass or bottle. It is also one of the few places in Venice open until midnight (though the food runs out earlier). ◆ M-W, F-Su lunch, dinner, late-night meals. Calle delle Veste 2007A (near Campo San Fantin). 5224121. Vaporetto stop: Santa Maria del Giglio (1)

43 Bar Al Teatro ★★$$ Most of the cozy Campo San Fantin is filled in the summer with tables from this old, established restaurant that stays open late. The service is professional and the pasta is available with a large variety of sauces—try the *tagliolini al salmone e caviale* (wide pasta with smoked salmon and caviar). Among the entrées, a specialty is *cartoccio al Theatro* (a whole fish wrapped in paper and baked with shrimp and clams). ◆ Tu-Su lunch and dinner. Campo San Fantin 1916. 5221052. Vaporetto stop: Santa Maria del Giglio (1)

44 Teatro La Fenice A sober Neo-Classical facade characterizes this theater (illustrated above), designed by **Giannantonio Selva** and built on the initiative of a group of patricians in 1792. Unfortunately, the facade is all that remains of the historic opera house and concert hall after an electrical fire destroyed its elegant interior in January 1996. This was the second fire in "The Phoenix's" history—the first occurred in 1836 (the house reopened a year later). At press time, officals were unsure when the building would rise again from the ashes, but architects will be guided by the plans of the 1836 restoration that were kept in a bank. ◆ Campo San Fantin 1365. Vaporetto stop: Santa Maria del Giglio (1)

44 Antico Martini ★★★$$$ The most renowned of Venetian restaurants is next to **La Fenice.** This grande dame of fine dining, in operation since 1720 and decked out in Belle Epoque finery, serves a peerless menu of classic Venetian dishes and international specialties. In addition to excellent simple preparations of fresh fish, this restaurant's light, delicious *fegato alla veneziana* (liver and onions) is the best you'll find anywhere in Venice. There is a fine wine list as well, and the kitchen accepts orders until 11:30PM (and even later when the opera is performing). In warm weather watch the comings and goings of the theater crowd from one of the few outdoor tables. ◆ M, Th-Sa lunch and dinner; W dinner. Campo San Fantin 1983. 5224121. Vaporetto stop: Santa Maria del Giglio (1)

45 Hotel La Fenice et des Artistes $$$ Long a favorite with theatergoers and performers, this well-known hotel is located across the *campiello* from the legendary **Teatro La Fenice.** Visitors return year after year—it's one of the few hostelries in this bustling and popular neighborhood—drawn no doubt by the beamed ceilings, Murano chandeliers, red-damask wall-papered guest rooms, and lovely garden. Two separate buildings are connected at the lobby, and the 69 rooms vary widely in size, decor, elegance, and ambience; only a few have been renovated. There's no restaurant, but excellent dining is right next door. ◆ Campiello de la Fenice 1936. 5232333; fax 5203721. Vaporetto stops: Santa Maria del Giglio (1); Sant'Angelo (1)

45 Taverna La Fenice ★★★$$$ If you come here after the theater there's a very good chance that the diva or tenor who brought the audience to its feet will be sitting at the table next to you. Self-effacingly called a *taverna,* the restaurant's service and menu are lyrical in themselves, from the *fettuccine alla Pavarotti* (with a light cream base, black truffles, and slivers of tongue and chicken breast) to the fresh fish specialties that change daily. In warm weather, the tables move outdoors, bringing the elegance with them into the lovely little piazzetta. ◆ M dinner; Tu-Sa lunch and dinner. Campiello de la Fenice 1939. 5223856. Vaporetto stops: Santa Maria del Giglio (1); Sant'Angelo (1)

46 Legatoria Piazzesi Originally a bookbinding business, this shop branched out decades ago into marbled paper and other fancy paper objects. There are now many such shops in Venice, but this one remains one of the most professional and elegant. Notebooks, address and appointment books, desktop items, and a large selection of wrapping paper with old Venetian prints make great gifts and souvenirs. ◆ M-Sa Mar-Oct; M afternoon, Tu-Sa Nov-Feb. Campiello della Feltrina 2511C (west of Chiesa di Santa Maria del Giglio). 5221202. Vaporetto stop: Santa Maria del Giglio (1)

47 Palazzo Zaguri While most Venetian palazzi have only one facade, the supremely elegant 15th-century palazzo of the Zaguri family has two, one on **Campo San Maurizio** and another along the canal in back. Pietro Zaguri, the last of his clan to live here, was an intellectual, a free thinker, and a close friend of Giacomo Casanova, who was often a guest here, as was Mozart's librettist Lorenzo da Ponte, who for a time worked as Zaguri's private secretary. When Zaguri was on his deathbed, his brother, a stern Catholic bishop, had to make a deal with the family creditors in order to keep the palazzo until his death. Today it is occupied by a public grade school. ♦ Campo San Maurizio 2668 (on south side of *campo*). Vaporetto stop: Santa Maria del Giglio (1)

ANTICHITÀ

V. Trois

TESSUTI ARTISTICI FORTUNY

48 Antichità V. Trois In business since 1911, this tiny store specializes in home-furnishing fabrics and objects from 18th-century Venice, including lamps, ceramics, and paintings. Most important, it is also the exclusive agent for the precious textiles produced by the Mariano Fortuny workshop, still operating on Giudecca with the original machinery invented by Fortuny. ♦ M-Sa Mar-Oct; M afternoon, Tu-Sa Nov-Feb. Campo San Maurizio 2666 (on north side of *campo*). 5222905. Vaporetto stop: Santa Maria del Giglio (1)

49 Chiesa di San Maurizio The Neo-Classical facade of this church was one of the last construction projects undertaken by the Venetian Republic before its fall in 1797. It was designed by **Pietro Zaguri**, a patrician and intellectual who lived in a palazzo on the same *campo*. The interior is a fine example of Neo-Classical architecture, designed by **Giannantonio Selva,** who was also responsible for the **Teatro La Fenice.** ♦ Campo San Maurizio (north side of *campo*). Vaporetto stop: Santa Maria del Giglio (1)

50 Il Papiro The resurgence of marbleized paper originated in Florence and spread throughout Italy. This branch of the Florentine-owned retailer is a large store with a huge selection of items made of the paper, including desktop items, lamps, picture frames, and even *Carnevale* masks. ♦ M-Sa Mar-Oct; M afternoon, Tu-Sa Nov-Feb. Calle del Piovan 2764 (between Campo San Maurizio and Campo Santo Stefano). 5223055. Vaporetto stop: Santa Maria del Giglio (1); Accademia (1, 82)

IL PAPIRO
VENEZIA

51 Pasticceria Marchini Marchini is a name that makes Venetians' mouths water. The most delicious sweets—from small pastries to large cakes for celebrations—are offered at this shop. Be sure to stop in for a cream-filled *cannolo*. ♦ M-Sa Mar-Oct; M afternoon, Tu-Sa Nov-Feb. Calle del Piovan 2769 (between Campo San Maurizio and Campo Santo Stefano). 5229109. Vaporetto stops: Santa Maria del Giglio (1); Accademia (1, 82)

52 Nalesso Friedrich Nietzsche once wrote: "If I seek another word to say *music*, I always and only find the word *Venice*." Today, he might also find the word *Nalesso*, the name of the city's best-stocked classical music shop. Let the strains of Vivaldi's music wafting from the store lead you to its otherwise hidden location off a small courtyard near **Campo Santo Stefano**. Inside you'll find rare scores and recordings of classical music of all sorts, but the real specialty here is 18th-century Venetian music. The accommodating and knowledgeable staff will assist you with special requests, and help you choose a Vivaldi souvenir by one of the city's world-famous Baroque ensembles: **Interpreti Veneziani, Le Putte Venete,** or **Solisti Veneti.** ♦ M-Sa. Calle Spezier 2765 (east of Campo Santo Stefano). 5203329. Vaporetto stops: Santa Maria del Giglio (1); Accademia (1, 82)

53 Chiesa di Santo Stefano The facade of this 15th-century church is adorned with two rose windows and a handsome Gothic portal. Inside, the carved wooden ceiling has the uniquely Venetian shape of an inverted ship's hull (local master carpenters most likely learned their craft in the shipyards). The church contains many monuments to illustrious Venetians, the most remarkable being *Domenico Contarini* (1650) over the portal; *Antonio Zorzi* (1588) on the left side; and *Giacomo Surian* (1493) on the right side. In the **Sacristy** (enter from the right nave), three large canvases by Jacopo Tintoretto hang on the right wall: *The Last Supper, The Agony in the Garden,* and *Christ Washing the Disciples' Feet.* On the same wall is a *Crucifixion* by Paolo Veneziano (1348). ♦ Campo Santo Stefano (north side of campo). Vaporetto stops: Santa Maria del Giglio (1); Accademia (1, 82)

54 Campo Santo Stefano Ringed with cafes and landmark palazzos, **Santo Stefano** is one of the largest and loveliest squares in Venice. It is also the crossroads for the streets leading from the **Ponte dell' Accademia** to the **Rialto** (north side) and to **Piazza San Marco** (east side), making it one of the busiest public spaces. On the east side at **Nos. 2802-3** is **Palazzo Morosini,** built in the 17th century for one of the local families of wealth and influence; opposite it at **No. 2945** is **Palazzo Loredan,** probably the last Gothic palazzo built in Venice. Locals still meet at **Paolin** (the *gelateria* at the northwest corner, opposite the entrance to **Chiesa di Santo Stefano**) for drinks in the late afternoon and for cappuccino on Sunday mornings. ♦ Vaporetto stop: Accademia (1, 82)

55 Conservatorio Benedetto Marcello
This imposing structure was built between the 17th and 18th centuries for the Pisani family. Today its official name and occupant is the well-known **Venice Conservatory.** The interior contains two courtyards and a handsome ballroom, now used for concerts by the conservatory's teachers and students. Inquire at the headmaster's office about visiting the palazzo. ♦ Campo Pisano (southeast extension of Campo Santo Stefano). Vaporetto stop: Accademia (1, 82)

56 Bottega de l'Indorador Gianni Cavalier is one of the best among the few Venetians who still practice the art of gilding wood. He creates 17th-century–style frames, chandeliers, and sculpture using the technique of that era and can accommodate special requests. ♦ M-Sa Mar-Oct; M afternoon, Tu-Sa Nov-Feb. Campo Santo Stefano 2863A (southwest corner of *campo*). 5238621. Vaporetto stop: Accademia (1, 82)

57 Palazzo Grassi This 18th-century palace, designed by **Giorgio Massari** along Classical lines, was acquired by Fiat in the 1980s. Venetian architect **Antonio Foscari,** and Milanese architect **Gae Aulenti** (designer of a number of international museums, including Paris's Musée d'Orsay) subsequently restored it as a center for international exhibitions. Major shows here have featured such well-known modern artists as Andy Warhol, Marcel Duchamp, and Modigliani, but also have included important exhibits of ancient Celtic art, Renaissance architecture, and the lost world of the Phoenicians. Supported by powerful advertising and by the exceptionally high quality of the exhibitions, it has become the second most visited site in Venice (after the **Palazzo Ducale**), with more than 2,000 visitors a day during exhibitions. The quality of Foscari's and Aulenti's remodeling of the interior is worth a visit in itself. The palazzo has a wonderful view over the Canal Grande and a comfortable cafeteria, run by **Harry's**

Bar owner Arrigo Cipriani. ♦ Admission. Open only during exhibitions. Salizzada San Samuele 3231 (on the north side of Campo San Samuele). 5231680. Vaporetto stop: San Samuele (82)

SCULTURE DI **LIVIO DE MARCHI**

58 Livio De Marchi Signor De Marchi doesn't consider himself a wood-carver, but rather a sculptor who works in wood. His whimsical creations on display here are inspired by the most exact, painstaking realism and there is a powerful sense of movement and life in his objects. The wood clothes hanging on a clothesline seem to move with the wind; and the giant asparagus, the stove, and the draped tablecloth are a source of wonder for those who pass by the windows of his workshop and store. ♦ M-Sa Nov-Feb; M afternoon, Tu-Sa Nov-Feb. Salizzada San Samuele 3157A (east of Campo San Samuele). 5285694. Vaporetto stops: San Samuele (82); Accademia (1, 82); Sant'Angelo (1)

58 Venice Design Art Gallery This gallery specializes in one-of-a-kind objects by contemporary designers, including glass objects by artist Luciano Vistosi. ♦ M-Sa Mar-Oct; M afternoon, Tu-Sa Nov-Feb. Salizzada San Samuele 3146 (east of Campo San Samuele). 5207915. Vaporetto stops: San Samuele (82); Accademia (1, 82); Sant'Angelo (1)

59 Al Bacareto ★★$$ One of the few good Venetian restaurants serving inexpensive meals, this pleasant, informal place attracts a predominantly local crowd. A pasta dish and a salad, or a local specialty like *fegato alla veneziana* (sautéed liver with onions), make a great meal that won't cause your wallet to ache. ♦ M-F lunch and dinner; Sa lunch. Salizzada San Samuele 3447 (north of Campo Santo Stefano). 5289336. Vaporetto stops: San Samuele (82); Accademia (1, 82); Sant'Angelo (1)

60 G (Gaggio) Venice's millennium of trade with faraway Cathay introduced luxurious oriental silks and fabrics to Europe, eventually spawning a fabric industry here that took its influence from the Far East. Precious textiles can still be found in limited quantities today; this store is one of the best places to find rich printed velvets. The workmanship is impeccable, so you'll pay handsomely for these high-quality silk and silk/cotton velvets, all hand-stamped and beautifully hand-finished. Home-design articles for sale here include decorative pillows and bolsters of all sizes and colors, whose designs complement sumptuous throws and romantic bedding in gemlike colors. The store also carries a collection of women's clothing and accessories including shawls, scarves, vests, and jackets appropriate for both day and evening wear. ◆ M-Sa. Calle delle Botteghe 3451-3441 (north of Campo Santo Stefano). 5228574. Vaporetto stops: San Samuele (82); Accademia (1, 82); Sant'Angelo (1)

60 Osteria Alle Botteghe ★★$$ This bar/tavern specializes in panini (Italian-style sandwiches). Choose one of the fillings on display at the counter—eggplant, local salami, a variety of cheeses, or ask for a mixture. More than a dozen varieties of pizza are also made to order. Hot meals and a few tables in the back offer more conventional dining. ◆ M-Sa 7AM-8PM. Calle delle Botteghe 3454 (just north of Campo Santo Stefano). 5228181. Vaporetto stops: San Samuele (82); Accademia (1, 82); Sant'Angelo (1)

61 Ceramiche Rigattieri
A wide variety of ceramics, produced in the famous center of Bassano del Grappa an hour north of Venice are offered at this shop. The Bassano style has a long and successful tradition to which contemporary artists are very attached. The pieces are typically decorated with flowers, fruits, vegetables, and leaves, either in plain white or brightly colored. Look for the reproductions of animals in all sizes and the charming plates decorated with bas-reliefs. ◆ M-Sa Mar-Oct; M afternoon, Tu-Sa Nov-Feb. Calle dei Frati 3532 (between Campo Sant' Angelo and Campo Santo Stefano). 5231081. Vaporetto stop: Sant'Angelo (1)

62 Campo Sant'Angelo (or Sant'Anzolo)
This wide square is characterized, like few others in Venice, by an elevated floor in the center, built in order to enlarge an underground cistern that collected rainwater for domestic use. The wells at the center (with original wellheads from the 15th century) reached the cistern's bottom, where the water gathered after being filtered by layers of sand and pebbles; they are no longer used. Composer Domenico Cimarosa died at the Gothic **Palazzo Duodo** at **No. 3585**. ◆ Vaporetto stop: Sant'Angelo (1)

Sixteenth-century correspondence from the Venetian ambassador to Constantinople, Gian Francesco Morosini, makes mention of "boiling black water": Coffee was introduced to Europe thanks to the Serenissima's first shipments from Turkey in the 17th century.

Restaurants/Clubs: Red   **Hotels:** Blue
Shops/ ☂ Outdoors: Green   **Sights/Culture:** Black

63 Ottica, Danilo Carraro Eyeglass designer/optometrist Dr. Danilo Carraro is one of Venice's more unconventional artisans. If you've spotted distinctive, stylish, and striking glasses in eye-catching colors being sported about town, there is a good chance they came from Carraro's limited-edition collection. His two dozen classic-to-hip models come in a wide range of serious-to-fun colors, from 14 variations on faux tortoise to 35 bold shades of celluloid, all guaranteed for life and at surprisingly reasonable prices. Carraro can fill any prescription or have any model made up as nonprescription sunglasses. ◆ M-Sa. Calle della Mandola 3706 (east of Campo Sant'Angelo). 5204258. Vaporetto stop: Sant'Angelo (1)

64 Museo Fortuny Mariano Fortuny was a multitalented artist from Catalonia who established himself in Venice, where he acquired this palazzo in the early 1900s. A painter, set designer, clothing designer, and textile printer, he charmed all of Europe with his elegant creations. Among his admirers was Marcel Proust. The museum illustrates his many activities with a number of paintings and a precious collection of textiles, but it is most interesting during special exhibits. ◆ Admission. Tu-Su. Campo San Beneto 3780 (between Campo Manin and Campo Sant'Angelo, off Calle della Mandola). 5200995. Vaporetto stop: Sant'Angelo (1)

65 Scala del Bovolo Freshly restored in 1994, this staircase is often seen in paintings and photographs of Venice because of its unusual and elegant snail shape. It was added to the courtyard of **Palazzo Contarini** at the end of the 15th century in order to permit access to the top floors without the necessity of going through the interior stairs. ◆ Calle della Vida 4299 (south of Campo Manin). Vaporetto stop: Sant'Angelo (1)

66 Ristorante da Ivo ★★★$$$ The small number of tables here allows Ivo to receive his guests personally and describe the day's menu to each. Its size and decor (the walls are decorated with paintings of Venice, many by friends of Ivo) give the place an intimacy that makes it an good spot for romantic dining. Venetian cooking, based on fish, is the specialty. But Ivo is originally from Tuscany, and he can cook meat like no one else in Venice. He prepares the only genuine *bistecca alla fiorentina* (a thick grilled steak drizzled with olive oil) in a town in love with the sea. ◆ Tu-Sa lunch and dinner. Ramo dei Fuseri 1809 (north of Frezzeria). 5205889. Vaporetto stop: San Marco (1, 82)

67 Il Prato Begun as a refined, expensive outlet for the sale and rental of elaborate Carnevale clothes and masks, this place has quickly become a successful curiosity shop, as its owner calls it. Its latest successes are automatons: groups of exquisitely crafted figures that move to the sound of a carillon. Their creator is Monsieur Camus, who won a World Championship of Automaton Builders in Switzerland. Other marvels include hand-painted eggs and miniature furniture handmade by craftspeople of the highest caliber. ♦ M-Sa Mar-Oct; M afternoon, Tu-Sa Nov-Feb. Frezzeria 1770 (northwest of Piazza San Marco). 5203375. Vaporetto stop: San Marco (1, 82)

68 Fantoni Libri Arte Originally an outlet of the Electa publishing company (a major Italian art book publisher), this is the best bookstore in Venice for art publications in all languages. ♦ M-Sa Mar-Oct; M afternoon, Tu-Sa Nov-Feb. Salizzada San Luca 4119 (between Campo San Luca and Campo Manin). 5220700. Vaporetto stop: Rialto (1, 82)

69 Leon Bianco ★★$ If you can put it between two slabs of bread, this well-stocked sandwich bar probably has it. Accompany your selection with finger food (especially tasty are the potato, rice, or cheese croquettes) and a glass of wine from the large wine list. ♦ M-Sa. No credit cards accepted. 4153 Salizzada San Luca (west of Campo San Luca). 5221180. Vaporetto stop: Rialto (1, 82)

70 Riva del Carbon This is one of the few stretches of the Canal Grande flanked by a street and allowing pedestrian passage. The name comes from its use as a pier for unloading coal. The presence of **City Hall,** the **Bank of Italy,** and other offices guarantees that the street will be crowded with Venetians, particularly in the morning (most state and city employees work from 8AM to 2PM). Some of the oldest and most charming palazzi in Venice are located here and can be closely inspected from the pier. At **No. 4792** is **Palazzo Bembo,** a Gothic building with remnants of an original Byzantine structure (the frieze on the lower floor); at **No. 4172** is **Palazzo Dandolo,** an early-Gothic building with a stone inscription in memory of Doge Enrico Dandolo, who headed the Fourth Crusade in 1204; and at **Nos. 4137** and **4136** are the two palazzi **Loredan** and **Farsetti** (City Hall offices), which have the original Byzantine ground and first floors (the top floors are later additions). ♦ West of Ponte di Rialto. Vaporetto stop: Rialto (1, 82)

71 Campo San Luca Strategically located between the **Rialto Bridge** and **Piazza San Marco,** this is one of the busiest squares in Venice. During the day it is a traditional meeting place for those who crowd the **Bar Torino** (known for the quality and variety of its *tramezzini*—small sandwiches eaten while standing at the counter) and the **Caffè Rosa Salva,** one of the best pastry shops in town. Before and after dinner, the *campo* is crowded with young men and women—mostly college students—who meet here to gossip and plan their evenings. ♦ Vaporetto stop: Rialto (1, 82)

72 Teatro Goldoni Named after the great Venetian playwright of the 18th century, this is the same theater where Carlo Goldoni enjoyed some of his successes before moving on to Paris. It was entirely rebuilt in the 1970s, and little of the original structure remains. While the fire-damaged **La Fenice** is primarily an opera house, this place is used for other Italian-language theatrical performances. ♦ Calle del Teatro 4650B (near Calle dei Fabbri). 5205422; Tickets: 5207583. Vaporetto stop: Rialto (1, 82)

73 Domus This is the most attractive and best-stocked of Venice's decorative housewares stores. Versace's recent foray into colorful place settings is represented here in all its theatrical glory, but equal attention is given to Alessi's wide array of popular kitchen and home collectibles and to Guzzini, the Italian trend-setter in plastics who first made the word "functional" synonymous with "attractive." ♦ M-Sa. Ponte del Lovo 4753 (west of Campo San Salvador). 5226662. Vaporetto stop: Rialto (1, 82)

74 In Guanotto This very busy *pasticceria-*bar-*gelateria,* well known in Venice for its mixed drinks and cocktails, is the best place to try a before-dinner spritz (the Venetian mixture of white wine, bitters, and seltzer water). A stairway leads to the second floor, one of the few places in Venice where you can sit and enjoy a chocolate or cappuccino at ease. You'll find this a handy address in winter and on rainy days. ♦ M-Sa 7AM-9PM. Ponte del Lovo 4819 (west of Campo San Salvador). 5208439. Vaporetto stop: Rialto (1, 82)

75 Marzato Amalia and Giuliana Marzato are the hat and accessory wizards of Venice. They personally design their creations in the workshop upstairs, working from antique and modern materials (feathers, pearls, ribbons, and lace). In addition to their regular lines, they produce the best tricornes and fantasy *Carnevale* hats in town. ♦ M-Sa Mar-Oct; M afternoons, Tu-Sa Nov-Feb. Calle del Lovo 4813 (west of Campo San Salvador). 5226454. Vaporetto stop: Rialto (1, 82)

76 Scuola di San Teodoro (School of Saint Theodore) A Baroque facade by **Giuseppe Sardi** decorates this early 17th-century building, now used for temporary exhibitions. ◆ Campo San Salvador. Vaporetto stop: Rialto (1, 82)

76 Fantin This is one of the best and most prestigious florists in Venice, and a good address to keep in mind for farewell gifts for your Venetian friends. ◆ M-Sa Mar-Oct; M afternoon, Tu-Sa Nov-Feb. Campo San Salvador 4805. 5226808. Vaporetto stop: Rialto (1, 82)

77 Chiesa di San Salvador The facade of this church, designed by **Giuseppe Sardi** in 1663 and cleaned and restored in 1991, is a fine example of Venetian-Baroque architecture. The interior, begun by **Giorgio Spavento** in 1506 and completed by **Jacopo Sansovino**, is of great interest because of the attempt to divide the space into perfectly regular 15-foot-square modules. The space between the entrance and the first two columns is made of four such squares, aligned to form a rectangle. Two identical rectangles, separated by a square, form the side naves. In the central nave, four modules form squares under the domes. Multiples of the square's sides also regulate the length of the columns. The result is a perfectly geometrical space—a bit too abstract when compared with the emotional impact of Gothic or Romanesque churches. The third altar in the right nave contains one of Titian's last works, an *Annunciation* painted with a revolutionary, almost impressionistic, technique. At the bottom of the painting he wrote "Titianus fecit fecit," the repetition of the phrase "he did it" perhaps being his answer to the criticism he expected. ◆ Campo San Salvador. Vaporetto stop: Rialto (1, 82)

78 Mercerie This series of narrow, zig-zagging streets connecting the **Rialto** with **Piazza San Marco** has long been the retail center of Venice and it is still lined with shops—both fancy and tacky. Most of the buildings along the streets date back to the 14th and 15th centuries. ◆ Between the Rialto and Piazza San Marco. Vaporetto stops: Rialto (1, 82); San Marco (1, 82)

79 Rialto $$$ Half of this aptly named hotel's 77 rooms look out on the world-famous bridge (the view is particularly good from the two rooms with small wrought-iron balconies). The location is ultraconvenient and double-paned windows and air-conditioning keep the street noise to a minimum. The decor is a mixture of modern and 18th-century Venice; beamed ceilings give some of the rooms a cozy feel. The restaurant next door is affiliated with the hotel. ◆ Ponte di Rialto 5149 (at the Rialto Bridge). 5209166; fax: 5238958. Vaporetto stop: Rialto (1, 82)

80 Campo San Bartolomeo One of the busiest centers of Venetian life, this *campo* is enlivened by a graceful, 19th-century statue of playwright Carlo Goldoni. Every evening the square fills with young men and women stopping for long chats and making it difficult to pass through—a sign that TV has not completely wiped out social life in Venice. ◆ Vaporetto stop: Rialto (1, 82)

80 Osteria Ai Rusteghi ★$ The constant flux of back-slapping locals and neighboring merchants come here for the 40 varieties of freshly made panini sandwiches as a light snack, lunch, and an excuse to meet and exchange news. Join the local scene and order an *ombra* (glass of house red wine), or choose from the dozens of wines by the glass, and pull up a stool. Try the grilled vegetables with smoked ricotta cheese or fresh arugula with locally made salami. Stock up on panini to go (*da portare via*) if you're leaving town by train. ◆ M-Sa 9:30AM-3PM; 5-7:30PM. No credit cards accepted. Campo San Bartolomeo 5529 (east corner of campo). 5232205. Vaporetto stop: Rialto (1, 82)

81 Fondaco dei Tedeschi (Germans' Warehouse) Venice's central post office is headquartered in this Renaissance building designed by **Scarpagnino** in 1505. In the heyday of the Republic it housed the offices and storerooms of German merchants, hence its name. The facade on the Canal Grande was originally frescoed by Renaissance artists, including Titian and Giorgione (some very faded remnants of the frescoes are visible at the **Franchetti Gallery** in the **Ca d'Oro**). ◆ Daily. Salizzada del Fontego dei Tedeschi 5554 (north of the Rialto and Campo San Bartolomeo). Vaporetto stop: Rialto (1, 82)

82 Rosticceria San Bartolomeo ★★$$ Right at the end of the narrow Sotoportego de la Bissa, this is the best place in Venice for prepared foods, either to be taken out or eaten at the counter (more formal dining upstairs). Pasta, risotto, roast chicken, *baccalà* (salt cod), and grilled fish keep coming from the kitchen and are quickly consumed by the many customers. The quality is good, much higher even than in some more expensive restaurants. ◆ Tu-Su lunch and dinner until 8:30PM. Calle de la Bissa 5424 (southeast of Campo San Bartolomeo). 5223569. Vaporetto stop: Rialto (1, 82)

83 Al Duca D'Aosta A Venice institution, this shop carries high-quality women's casual clothing sporting Italian and international designer labels. Menswear is across the street at **No. 4946**. ◆ M-Sa Mar-Oct; M afternoon, Tu-Sa Nov-Feb. Merceria dell'Orologio 4922 (southeast of Chiesa di San Salvador). 5204079. Vaporetto stops: Rialto (1, 82); San Marco (1, 82)

84 Jesurum The ancient art of making lace used to have its center on the nearby island of Burano. After a long period of decline, it was resurrected on the same island through the efforts of Michele Jesurum in the second half of the 19th century. **Jesurum** continues to be Venice's premier purveyor of deluxe household linens. In addition to intricate and expensive laces, this shop sells more affordable items, all handmade or—beware!—hand-*finished*. ♦ M-Sa Mar-Oct; M afternoon, Tu-Sa Nov-Feb. Mercerie del Capitello 4857 (between Piazza San Marco and Campo San Salvador). 5206177. Vaporetto stops: Rialto (1, 82); San Marco (1, 82)

85 Valdese For generations the Valdese family of *bronzisti* (bronze craftspeople) have provided gondolas with their *ferri* (seahorse fittings) and virtually every patrician palazzo in Venice with its massive door knockers. Visitors are more than welcome at the Canarregio foundry of Gianni and Mario Valdese (720234), but shoppers should come directly to this shop presided over by their English-speaking sister Loredana. Many of the store's offerings—drawer pulls, knobs, handles, door stops, bookends, sconces, and ceiling fixtures sold here in bronze, copper, brass, pewter, and wrought iron—are perfect historical replicas. The Valdese family is accustomed to shipping worldwide—they've even shipped to the White House. ♦ M-Sa. Calle Fiubera 793 (between the Mercerie and Campo San Gallo). 5227282. Vaporetto stops: Rialto (1, 82); San Marco (1, 82)

86 Eredi Giovanni Pagnacco This unusual store specializes in original, minuscule objects created by the best local craftspeople in glass and ceramics. Its windows are a constant surprise for Venetians, as they

exhibit ever-changing glass reproductions of scenes from life: An orchestra with hundreds of tiny players and instruments is one of the most memorable tableaux, along with the lilliputian reproduction of a religious procession in **Piazza San Marco.** ♦ M-Sa Mar-Oct; M afternoon, Tu-Sa Nov-Feb. Merceria dell'Orologio 231 (near Calle Fiubera). 5223704. Vaporetto stops: Rialto (1, 82); San Marco (1, 82)

Élite

87 Elite Business attire and sportswear are both offered here at one of the most exclusive stores in town for men's clothing. ♦ M-Sa Mar-Oct; M afternoon, Tu-Sa Nov-Feb. Calle Larga San Marco 284 (northwest of Piazza San Marco). 5230145. Vaporetto stop: San Marco (1, 82)

88 Montecarlo $$$ Small enough to offer guests personalized service, this freshly renovated family-run hotel has 48 contemporary rooms done up in flowered prints with tiled bathrooms, and a restaurant, **Antico Pignolo.** While most hotels claim to be a stone's throw from the **Piazza San Marco,** this one actually is conveniently close by, on a popular store-lined street. ♦ Calle degli Specchieri 463 (north of Piazza San Marco). 5207155; fax 5207789. Vaporetto stops: San Marco (1, 82); San Zaccaria (1, 52, 82)

Bests

Ennio Montagnaro
Gondolier, Venice

Usually considered a tourist attraction, the gondola is still very important for Venetian people on their wedding day, when it carries the bride to the church. The gondola, beautifully decorated and furnished for this occasion, together with the elegant dress of the bride, takes Venice back to the 18th century—and the old Venice is, for me, the real one.

The sophisticated **Caffè Florian,** with its frescoes and old furniture, offers elegant meals to the Venetian upper class and to wealthier tourists. One can spend hours there, delighted by live music.

Ristorante Da Romano on the island of **Burano** (famous all over the world thanks to the lace made there) is a typical restaurant where Venetians have parties with family and friends and where everybody can taste excellent dishes of fresh fish.

To eat characteristic Venetian dishes, go to **La Corte Sconta** or **Trattoria Da Remigio** (both in the *sestiere* of **Castello**). Try *risi e bisi* (rice and peas), *sarde in saor* (marinated sardines), and *fegato alla Veneziana* (liver with onions and white wine): You'll never forget them.

If you can afford it, go to the **Hotel Danieli,** the former residence of the Doge Dandolo. Personally, I'd love to spend a night in this hotel.

Venice is romantic, fascinating, and elegant . . . but sometimes it is also fun. Kids and grownups love the phenomenon of the "high water," which is actually a serious problem for the city. In spite of this, nobody can stop laughing when others slip and take a salty bath.

If you're looking for adventure, rent a small motorboat, go visit the islands (**Murano,** Burano, **Torcello**), and have a little swim in the middle of the journey.

Dorsoduro

While the throngs of visitors pouring across the **Ponte dell'Accademia** are usually drawn to Dorsoduro for its art museums, the **Galleria dell' Accademia** and the **Peggy Guggenheim Collection**, others have long preferred this largely residential area as a place for their own Venetian homes. Poet Ezra Pound lived here, and his tiny house is still occupied by Olga Rudge, his lifelong companion. It stands a few steps from the palazzo where Peggy Guggenheim spent the last decades of her life hosting a parade of international literati and glitterati. In keeping with the times, in recent years Dorsoduro has become home to wealthy industrialists. Susanna Agnelli, sister of Fiat president Gianni, keeps a place here, as did industrialist Raoul Gardini. But simple folk will enjoy just strolling around, especially along the three small canals with walkable banks, to take in such unassuming sights as the **Campiello Barbaro**, a tiny square that has inspired artists for years.

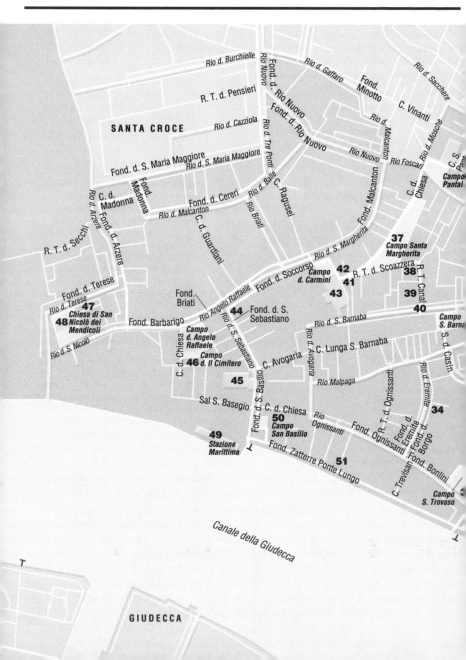

1 Punta della Dogana (Customs Point)

Ships laden with precious cargoes from the Far East stopped here first on arrival in Venice to be examined for customs duties; they would then continue along the Canal Grande and anchor in front of the patrician palazzi, where they would be unloaded. This easternmost point of Dorsoduro was entirely reconstructed beginning in the 1670s as part of a vast plan to design an impressive entrance to the Canal Grande, culminating in the church of **Santa Maria della Salute.** Today the area is rarely crowded, not even with tourists, though in the evening it is a favorite stroll for couples looking for an isolated romantic spot. The **Customs House,** between the extreme tip of the island and **La Salute,** was built in 1677 (northeast wing) and in the 1830s (southwest wing). The 17th-century tower at the tip supports two bronze giants carrying a gold sphere (designed by Bernardo Falcone) representing the world, surmounted by a huge statue of *Fortune* that acts as a wind gauge. Thus the city welcomed its ships with the symbols of its naval power. ♦ Fondamenta Dogana Alla Salute (east of Campo della Salute). Vaporetto stop: La Salute (1)

2 Le Zattere
From the tip of Punta della Dogana all the way to the western end of Venice, the Canale della Giudecca is flanked by an uninterrupted walkway called Fondamenta delle Zattere, or simply Le Zattere. *Zattere* means rafts; and it was to this extended pier

that huge barges once brought their cargoes of supplies from the mainland. The sunny southern exposure of the canal bank makes this a favorite walk for Venetians on mild winter afternoons and on Sunday mornings year-round. Many cafes open onto the street and some have wooden terraces suspended on piles over the water. A cross section of the population can be seen here soaking up the sun, sitting at the cafes, or walking along eating ice cream. The Canale della Giudecca, now congested with boat traffic, still offers some memorable sights: the boats of the **Bucintoro** rowing club going out for practice or the large cruise ships and cargo ships, taller than any buildings in the area, slowly passing by on their way to the **Stazione Marittima** harbor at the bank's western end. Until the 1960s, a small section of the canal was enclosed by a white and blue fence, creating a swimming pool right in the canal's water, where most Venetians learned how to swim. Today the water of the canal is polluted (though it has improved in recent years) and few brave its waters. ♦ Fondamenta delle Zattere (between Punta della Dogana and the Stazione Marittima). Vaporetto stops: Zattere (82, 52); San Basilio (82); La Salute (1)

3 Seminario Patriarcale The building between **La Salute** church and the **Porta della Dogana,** designed by **Baldassare Longhena,** was built in 1670 as a school for children of noble families. In 1817, it became the **Venice Seminary** (previously on the island of Murano). Inside is a 17th-century cloister and the **Pinacoteca Manfrediniana,** a collection of minor works of art mostly from the 16th century. ♦ By appointment only. Campo della Salute 1C (east of La Salute church). 5225558. Vaporetto stop: La Salute (1)

4 Santa Maria della Salute (La Salute)
In the 1630s, to fulfill a vow made during a terrible plague, the city fathers held a competition to design a church in honor of the Virgin of Good Health. The site they had selected for this solemn tribute was of vital importance to Venice, both commercially and aesthetically: It sat at the entrance to the Canal Grande and was visible from almost any point in Venice. **Baldassare Longhena** was then only 26, but his daring project was chosen over those of 11 other competitors. The structure he designed is one of the best examples in Europe of the Baroque concern for large-scale planning (the idea being that a building should not only express its own individual beauty but also should work with the surrounding landscape as a whole). **Longhena** based his design on a circular plan, and set the whole church aboveground on a huge embankment. In order to support the massive structure, the ground had to be reinforced with more than a million wood piles. The dome of the church was supported by buttresses, or volutes, disguised as stone spirals, affectionately referred to by the Venetians as *"orecchioni"* (big ears), and topped by a statue of the *Virgin Mary* dressed as a Venetian admiral. The front of the church, with its imposing staircase and wealth of over 125 statues and other stone decorations, faces the Canal Grande. Behind the dome, **Longhena** built a second, smaller dome flanked by two bell towers, creating an elongated shape from the door to the main altar, as in the **Basilica di San Marco.** It took more than 50 years to build this wonder of European architecture and engineering (**Longhena** died in 1682, five years before completion but one year after the solemn inauguration).

Santa Maria della Salute (La Salute)

In contrast with the festive, exuberant exterior, the interior is sober and reverential. On sunny days, a good deal of light enters the main hall of the church, while the high altar, under the smaller dome, remains shaded and intimate. The six open chapels on the sides of the church correspond to the six secondary facades on the outside. In the first chapel at the right, look for Luca Giordano's *Presentation of the Virgin,* part of a larger cycle of paintings celebrating the Virgin Mary originally planned for the church's interior. The high altar, designed by **Longhena,** surrounds a Greek-Byzantine icon of the Virgin Mary that is very dear to Venetians (it was taken from Crete in 1672 as war booty). At the third altar on the left is a lackluster Titian, *The Descent of the Holy Spirit,* which the artist repainted (unenthusiastically, it appears) after the original was damaged. A small door at the left of the main altar leads to the **Sacristy** (open erratically; admission charge). Inside are three ceiling paintings, *St. Mark Enthroned* (at the altar), and eight medallions depicting the Evangelists and church doctors, all by Titian. On the right wall is *The Marriage at Cana,* usually considered one of Tintoretto's best works. ♦ Campo della Salute. Vaporetto stop: La Salute (1)

5 Campo San Gregorio The church in front of this *campo,* originally built in the ninth century, was renovated in the 15th century and is now used as a laboratory for the restoration of stone monuments. The beautiful apses are visible from the bridge at the back. At the left side, a wall encloses the garden of **Palazzo Genovese,** a Neo-Gothic building dating from 1892 with a facade on the Canal Grande. A few steps farther **(No. 172)** are still-visible remnants of the old **Abbey of St. Gregory** (now privately owned) with its 14th-century cloister. ♦ Campo San Gregorio (west of Campo della Salute). Vaporetto stop: La Salute (1)

6 Traghetto to Santa Maria del Giglio This gondola service to the other side of the Canal Grande will save you from a long detour on foot over the Ponte dell'Accademia or from having to wait for the *vaporetto.* ♦ Calle del Traghetto (on Canal Grande). Vaporetto stop: La Salute (1)

7 Rio Terrà dei Saloni This wide street was created in the 19th century by filling in a canal (*rio terrà* means "land-filled canal"). The building at the corner of Rio Terrà dei Catecumeni **(Nos. 107-108)** was rebuilt by **Massari** in 1727. For many centuries it was a center for the education of non-Catholics who intended to convert, among them Lorenzo da Ponte, Mozart's librettist. The handsome **Palazzetto Costantini (Nos. 70-71)** dates back to the 14th century and still has the original wood beams over the portico. ♦ Between Le Zattere ai Saloni and Rio Terrà dei Catecumeni. Vaporetto stop: La Salute (1)

8 Saloni or Magazzini del Sale (Salt Warehouses) An early source of Venetian wealth was the salt trade. The huge building at **Nos. 258-266** was built in the 14th century to store the salt supplies the city imported from the East. The facades were redesigned in the 1830s, but the enormous storage rooms are still capable of holding 45,000 tons of salt as originally planned. Today they house the boats of a rowing club, as well as temporary art exhibitions, often held in conjunction with the *Venice Biennale d'Arte.* ♦ Fondamenta Zattere ai Saloni 258266 (between Rio Terrà dei Saloni and Fondamenta della Ca' Balà). Vaporetto stop: La Salute (1)

HOTEL
ALLA SALUTE
★ ★

9 Hotel Alla Salute da Cici $ This comfortable, efficiently run former *pensione* is in a great location along a charming canal. More than half of its 50 rooms have private baths. ♦ Fondamenta della Ca' Balà 22228 (between Fondamenta Zattere ai Saloni and Rio Terrà dei Catecumeni). 5235404; fax 5222271. Vaporetto stop: La Salute (1)

10 Hotel Messner $$ Clean, pleasant, and unpretentious, this small hotel has 11 rooms with wonderful windows looking out on a canal. ♦ Madonna della Salute 216 (off Fondamenta della Ca' Balà near Rio Terrà dei Catecumeni). 5227443; fax 5227266. Vaporetto stop: La Salute (1)

11 Cenedese The pieces on display in the elegant two-story showrooms of this firm, one of the oldest and most prestigious producers of Murano glass, range from exquisite objets d'art to affordable objets d'everyday. The facade of the building **(Palazzo Salviati)** is on the Canal Grande. This retailer also has a small showcase shop in **Piazza San Marco (No. 40)** near the **Campanile,** where you can familiarize yourself with a small cross section of their wares. ♦ M-Sa Mar-Oct; M afternoon, Tu-Sa Nov-Feb. Campo San Gregorio 173 (on Canal Grande). 5229998. Vaporetto stop: La Salute (1)

12 Campiello Barbaro This cozy, quiet little square on the bank of a small canal is one of the most charming in all of Venice. The back of **Palazzo Dario** is visible from the bridge, beyond the wall and the small garden. ♦ Between Rio della Fornace and Rio Pietre Blanche near Canal Grande. Vaporetto stop: La Salute (1)

𝕸𝖆𝖗𝖆𝖓𝖌𝖔𝖓 𝖉𝖆 𝕾𝖔𝖆𝖟𝖊

13 Marangon da Soaze In **Campiello Barbaro,** near the gentle fountain, you may hear the tapping of this cabinetmaker laboring in his workshop, whose name comes straight from ancient Venetian dialect and means, roughly, "wood carpenter specializing in frames." In fact, he restores old furniture and produces gilded wood objects. ♦ M-Sa Mar-Oct; M afternoon, Tu-Sa Nov-Feb. Campiello Barbaro 364 (between Rio della Fornace and Rio Pietre Blanche near Canal Grande). 5237738. Vaporetto stop: La Salute (1)

14 Collezione Peggy Guggenheim (Peggy Guggenheim Collection) In 1949, American millionaire Peggy Guggenheim chose the odd, one-story **Palazzo Venier dei Leoni** for her home and her extraordinary collection of 20th-century art. It was actually a fateful coincidence that her modern art collection found itself in this modern palazzo. As the story goes, the noble Venier family, who built the residence, halted construction after completing only the ground floor (begun in 1749), apparently after a rival family moved into a larger palazzo across the Canal Grande and pressured them to stop building lest they block their view. The palazzo remains an oddity on the Canal Grande, though it has slowly acquired a beauty of its own.

The entrance to the museum is graced with an iron and glass grille by Claire Falkenstein (1961). The collection inside highlights works by such artists as Pablo Picasso, Georges Braque, Jackson Pollock, and René Magritte. The garden contains sculptures by Alberto Giacometti, Max Ernst (one of Ms. Guggenheim's husbands), Henry Moore, Jean Arp, and others, along with Guggenheim's tomb. The interior of the palazzo was redesigned as a gallery space for changing exhibitions after the owner's death; it is now run by the Solomon R. Guggenheim Foundation (the art collection first assembled by her uncle). A museum shop/bookstore, recently opened in a separate building behind the garden, displays interesting photos of Guggenheim and her colorful life as a Venetian fixture. At press time there were confirmed plans to open three satellite museum sites in Venice by 1997. ♦ Admission; free Sa after 6PM. M, W-Su. Calle San Cristoforo 701 (on Canal Grande east of Campo San Vio). 5206288. Vaporetto stops: La Salute (1); Accademia (1, 82)

15 Calle delle Mende A walk through the area between this street and Le Zattere (the bank of Canale della Giudecca to the south) is the best way to see why this neighborhood is so dear to foreign lovers of Venice. This is residential Venice at its best. The houses are rarely more than two stories high; frequent, small gardens are visible; and flower pots line most windows. Quite a few locals still live here, but they are gradually being driven out by soaring real estate prices—apartments here now start at 4 million lire a square meter (about $3,000 a square yard). On the **Campiello degli Incurabili,** notice the fading fresco of Venice's skyline by local painter Bobo Ferruzzi. The small streets on both sides of the Rio Terrà San Vio allow access to the buildings between the two canals. At the far end of the *rio terrà* **(No. 460),** a door opens into the former **Convento dello Spirito Santo** (Convent of the Holy Spirit), used today as a high school; visitors are welcome to look at the courtyard and the 16th-century cloister. ♦ Southeast of Campo San Vio. Vaporetto stops: Accademia (1, 82); La Salute (1)

16 Ospedale degli Incurabili The history of this 16th-century building is a chronicle of sadness: It was built for people with incurable diseases (mostly syphilis), then used to house abandoned children, and in the 20th century it became a prison for juvenile delinquents. It now stands semi-abandoned, like many other buildings in Venice, while the city fights over who the future tenants will be: the university (which has more than 30,000 students and only one dormitory with 150 beds), a hospital, the state, district and city offices, the senior citizens, the youth, the rowing clubs. . . . Empty buildings and lots are abundant in town, but as soon as one is assigned to a group, a chorus of protests, strikes, and legal issues is often raised to block the decision. ♦ Fondamenta Zattere allo Spirito Santo 423426 (between Rio della Ca' Balà and Rio Piccolo delle Legname). Vaporetto stops: Accademia (1, 82); La Salute (1)

17 Norelene Nora and Elene sell velvets, silks, and cottons that they hand-print in their recently relocated workshop, using the process invented by Mariano Fortuny at the turn of the century. However, the patterns at this shop are original and inspired by painstaking research into the history of Venetian textiles. The fabrics can be used for clothing and interior decorating. Particularly wonderful are the panels printed with designs inspired by St. Mark's mosaics. ♦ M-Sa Nov-Feb; M afternoon, Tu-Sa Nov-Feb. Calle della Chiesa 727 (east of Campo San Vio). 5237605. Vaporetto stops: Accademia (1, 82); La Salute (1)

18 Galleria di Palazzo Cini This 17th-century palazzo belongs to the Cini Foundation and houses the **Raccolta d'Arte della Collezione**

Vittorio Cini (The Vittorio Cini Art Collection). The 30-plus Tuscan Renaissance paintings here include works by Taddeo Gaddi, Bernardo Daddi, Sandro Botticelli, a Guariento, and a *Madonna* by Piero della Francesca. While the artists may not belong in the pantheon of great Tuscan artists, the paintings bequeathed to the foundation by the Conte Vittorio Cini (who died in 1977) illustrate the collector's eye for minor gems. Every year the collection displays a different masterwork on loan from a major art gallery. ♦ Admission. Hours irregular, usually daily in summer only. San Vio 864 (at Piscina del Forner west of Campo San Vio). 5210755. Vaporetto stops: Accademia (1, 82); La Salute (1)

19 869 It is not by chance that Paula Carraro's shop sits snugly between the **Accademia** and **Peggy Guggenheim** museums: This young artist gives a new spin to the ancient craft of knitting by marrying it with modern art. Her exquisite (and expensive) oversized sweaters in cotton, mohair, and silk depict some of the contemporary world's greatest masterpieces by artists such as Klee, Warhol, Magritte, and Picasso. You can't miss the window display of colorful sweaters—you'll think you've arrived at the Guggenheim! ♦ M-Sa Mar-Oct; M afternoon, Tu-Sa Nov-Feb. Calle Nuova Sant'Agnese 869 (between Campos San Vio and della Carità). 5206070. Vaporetto stop: Accademia (1, 82)

20 Galleria dell'Accademia Venice has Napoleon to thank for this unrivaled catalog of Venetian art housed in the former 15th-century school, church, and convent of **Santa Maria della Carità.** As the little emperor began suppressing Venetian churches and monasteries in the 1800s, he gathered up their works of art and shipped them off to this warehouse of a museum. Return trips to savor the wealth of its 24-room collection, arranged more or less chronologically, will cut fatigue and enhance appreciation of the gallery's attempt to illustrate the development of Venetian art from the 14th to the 18th century. In high season, when the lines can be a nightmare, it is best to arrive at opening time or late in the afternoon.

The museum's newest exhibition space, the **Quadreria** (Picture Room), opened in 1995. It features 88 paintings, most never shown before, including works by Tintoretto and Titian. Access to the room is limited; reservations are required (713498; fax 713487).

The earliest paintings in the museum, displayed in **Room I,** are notable mainly for their Byzantine influence, which is especially evident in Paolo Veneziano's glittering *Coronation of the Virgin with Scenes from the Lives of Christ and St. Francis.* The mastery of the 15th century's Giovanni Bellini, whose favorite subject was the Madonna, is amply represented in **Rooms II, IV,** and **V.** A particular favorite among his paintings here is the restful *Madonna of the Trees* **(Room V).** Hanging nearby is one of the museum's must-sees, Giorgione's brooding secular masterpiece *La Tempesta.* Among the works by early 16th-century artists in **Rooms VI** through **IX,** the most interesting is *Portrait of a Young Man in His Study,* by Lorenzo Lotto **(Room VII).** The heavyweights of the High Renaissance, Tintoretto, Titian, and Veronese, dominate **Rooms X** and **XI.** The latter's *Feast at the House of Levi* **(Room X)** was originally intended to be a treatment of the Last Supper. When the Inquisition objected to the inclusion of dwarfs and Germans in the painting, the artist, in a stroke of genius, avoided redoing the work by simply changing its title. In the same room, Tintoretto's cycle of paintings on the subject of St. Mark (*St. Mark Freeing the Slave, Transport of the Body of St. Mark,* and *St. Mark Rescuing a Saracen*) is another of the museum's major attractions. Nearby is Titian's final work, a *Pietà* that he intended to be mounted above his tomb as an epitaph. Three more masterworks by Veronese (*Madonna Enthroned with the Baptist and Saints Joseph, Francis, and Jerome, The Mystic Marriage of St. Catherine,* and *Ceres Paying Homage to Venice*) are in **Room XI.** Among the highlights of the 18th-century works displayed in **Rooms XII** through **XX** are Giovanni Battista Piazzetta's *Fortune Teller* **(Room XVIA)** and Gentile Bellini's *Corpus Domini Procession* **(Room XX).** As you wander among the paintings in **Room XVII**— scenes of 18th-century Venice by Francesco Guardi, Canaletto, and Pietro Longhi—you may begin to think the city outside has been untouched by time. As fascinating for its detailed depiction of 15th-century Venetian fashion as for its poignant story, Carpaccio's *St. Ursula Cycle* **(Room XXI)** is the most popular of the **Accademia**'s paintings. The story unfolds left to right around the room: Young Ursula is betrothed to the king of England, accepts the condition that the marriage remain unconsummated while she undertakes a pilgrimage in the company of 11,000 virgins, and is eventually martyred outside Cologne. **Room XXIII** is what remains of the original church of **Santa Maria della Carità,** designed by **Bartolomeo Bon** and built between 1441 and 1452. Titian's *Presentation of the Virgin* **(Room XXIV)** should be your last stop before leaving the museum—probably in Madonna overload. ♦ Admission. Daily. Campo della Carità (at Ponte dell'Accademia). 5222247. Vaporetto stop: Accademia (1, 82)

21 Ponte dell'Accademia This "temporary" bridge was built in the 1930s to replace a suspended bridge designed and built in the 1840s by **A.E. Neville.** Its replacement was restored in the 1980s. ♦ Between Galleria dell'Accademia and Campo San Vidal. Vaporetto stop: Accademia (1, 82)

22 Rio Terrà Antonio Foscarini This unusually wide and straight alley, flanked by a few trees, is as close as Venice comes to a boulevard. It was built in 1863 by filling in a canal (hence the *rio terrà*) to facilitate pedestrian traffic to the Accademia Bridge. The building at **Nos. 898-902** houses the **Istituto Cavanis,** a private grammar and high school founded in the 18th century to provide poor children with free education. It's still free, and the quality of education at the school is so high that Venice's upper crust tries to send their children here. Across from the school, the Cavanis Fathers (a small, local monastic order) run an inexpensive hotel during the summer months, usually reserved by Catholic groups, but theoretically open to anyone. ♦ Southeast of Campo della Carità. Vaporetto stop: Accademia (1, 82)

23 Hotel Agli Alboretti $$ Given its proximity to the **Galleria dell'Accademia** (and its easy access to the *vaporetto* stop), this well-run hotel is in demand. Its 22 rooms are comfortable, although some are small and can be dark. ♦ Rio Terrà Antonio Foscarini 882-884 (southeast of Galleria dell'Accademia). 5230058; fax 5210158. Vaporetto stop: Accademia (1, 82)

Adjoining the Hotel Agli Alboretti:

Ristorante Agli Alboretti ★$$ Whether you're staying at the hotel next door or you've just spent an exhilarating day at the **Accademia,** you might want to stop here for a relaxing dinner. The seafood can be pricey, but the pasta dishes make a satisfying, reasonably priced meal. ♦ M-Tu, Th-Su dinner. Rio Terrà Antonio Foscarini 882-884 (southeast of Galleria dell'Accademia). 5230058. Vaporetto stop: Accademia (1, 82)

24 Trattoria Ai Cugnai ★$$ *Cugnai* means brothers-in-law, which makes sense at this crowded, colorful restaurant that is run by a pair of energetic sisters and their husbands. It started out as an inexpensive neighborhood hangout, but word quickly spread (Venetians are always looking for old-time, tourist-free restaurants and cafes), and it has become a favorite on everyone's list. As a result, some of the old spontaneity is gone, in spite of the efforts of the two tireless, down-to-earth sisters. Still rather inexpensive, the restaurant specializes in homemade, unpretentious food such as *spaghetti con vongole* (spaghetti with clams) and homemade gnocchi, and serves a good *prosecco* wine. ♦ Tu-Su lunch and dinner. Piscina del Forner 857 (between Campo San Vio and Galleria dell'Accademia). 5289238. Vaporetto stop: Accademia (1, 82)

25 Pensione Seguso $$ This old-fashioned *pensione*, still run by the Seguso family, is one of very few places in town where half-board—breakfast plus one meal per day—is still required of its guests during high season. (If you know you'll be out for dinner and want to avoid a trip back to the hotel for the noon repast, ask the management if they would prepare a box lunch for you.) Regular guests, many with young children, return again and again for the threadbare charm and comfort and a room with a view over the Canale della Giudecca. All but 10 of the 38 rooms have private baths. ♦ Open *Carnevale* (mid- to late-winter) through November. Fondamenta delle Zattere ai Gesuiti 779 (at Rio di San Vio). 5286858; fax 5222340. Vaporetto stop: Zattere (52, 82)

26 La Calcina $$ This 40-room hotel, home to 19th-century British author John Ruskin while he wrote *The Stones of Venice,* recently underwent a much needed restoration. Request one of the renovated rooms with a view of the canal—it's worth the slightly higher price. There's no restaurant, but you'll find a number of neighboring outdoor pizzerias along the Zattere. ♦ Closed mid-January to mid-February. Fondamenta della Zattere ai Gesuiti 780 (at Rio di San Vio). 5206466; fax 5227045. Vaporetto stop: Zattere (52, 82)

27 Ristorante Alle Zattere ★★$$ This dining spot is best known for its location; it is one of only a few restaurants with a terrace overlooking the Canale della Giudecca. The food is good, though the prices reflect its monopoly over the canal view. In this case, however, location is a good enough reason to stop by for lunch or dinner. On hot summer evenings a gentle breeze blows through the terrace, while rowboats, *vaporetti,* and cruise ships lazily float past. Many Venetians come here and to **Ristorante da Gianni** a few doors down for a good pizza and beer and a respite from their hot apartments. ♦ M, W-Su lunch and dinner. Fondamenta Zattere ai Gesuiti 795 (just east of Chiesa dei Gesuati). 5204224. Vaporetto stop: Zattere (52, 82)

28 Chiesa dei Gesuiti This church (officially named **Santa Maria del Rosario**) and its adjacent monastery were originally built by the Gesuati, a local monastic order different from the Gesuiti (Jesuits). In the 17th century the order collapsed and both the church and the monastery went to the Dominicans, who proceeded to rebuild the church entirely, trusting the project to **Giorgio Massari.** The facade is clearly reminiscent of **Palladio** (whose **Redentore** church is visible across the canal). Both churches are flanked by two bell towers, but the **Gesuiti** is somewhat more imposing. The canal bank and gondola landing were redesigned to harmonize with the new church, although the effect has been somewhat spoiled by the *vaporetto* stop in front.

The interior is one of the masterworks of 18th-century Venice, consisting of a single nave, as in the church of **La Pietà,** with a large chancel behind the altar. Most of the statues are by the ubiquitous and rather uninspiring Giovanni Maria Morleiter; but the paintings are among the best by Tiepolo and Piazzetta. Tiepolo painted the ceiling (1737-39) with his *Institution of the Rosary* (center of ceiling) and with stories from the life of St. Dominick in his *St. Dominick Praying to the Virgin Mary* (near the chancel). Also by Tiepolo is the altarpiece dedicated to the Virgin Mary on the first chapel to the right, while Piazzetta painted *St. Dominick* in the next chapel and a splendid *St. Vincent Ferreri* in the following one (third at the right). More frescoes by Tiepolo are on the inside of the apse. A remarkable Tintoretto adorns the first chapel on the left side: It is a *Crucifixion* dated 1526, said to have been restored by Piazzetta himself. ♦ Fondamenta Zattere ai Gesuiti (at Rio Terrà Antonio Foscarini). Vaporetto stop: Zattere (52, 82)

29 Ristorante da Gianni ★★$$ This restaurant shares the spotlight with **Ristorante Alle Zattere** (see page 144) as one of the only restaurants with a terrace overlooking the Canale della Giudecca. Both the food and service are better here (though if you're in town on a hot summer evening and the place is full, don't hesitate to try its competitor—the breeze is just as pleasant). *Signore* Gianni has been running this place for more than 30 years. Many Venetians fondly remember the days when the canal could only be crossed by gondola (today there is *vaporetto* service), and **da Gianni,** then a seedy wine shop, was a welcome refuge from bad weather. ♦ M-Tu, Th-Su lunch and dinner. Fondamenta Zattere ai Gesuiti 918 (west of Chiesa dei Gesuati). 5237210. Vaporetto stop: Zattere (52, 82)

30 Squero di San Trovaso This small compound, most visible from Fondamenta Nani across the narrow canal, is now a national landmark and probably the most photographed and painted sight in Venice. It is one of three places that still builds and maintains gondolas in Venice using traditional methods. The 17th-century wooden buildings (homes of the owners and hangars for boats) are unusual for Venice but were typical of boat builders. They resemble Dolomite mountain homes, and in fact both the wood for the gondolas and the master carpenters often came from that region. ♦ Campo San Trovaso 1092 (at Fondamenta Bontini). Vaporetto stop: Zattere (52, 82)

31 Liceo Marco Polo The building at **No. 1073** Fondamenta Toffetti (with an 18th-century facade by **Andrea Tirali**), just across the Ponte delle Meravegie, was restored in 1980. Since time immemorial it has housed one of two high schools for classical studies in Venice, attended by children of the upper classes. ♦ Fondamenta Toffetti 1073 (north of Campo San Trovaso). Vaporetto stop: Accademia (1, 82)

Pensione Accademia

32 Pensione Accademia–Villa Meravegie $$ It's rare in Venice to find a *real* free-standing villa, surrounded by a garden and detached from other buildings. This 27-room hotel is just such a rarity. The halls and common areas are reminiscent of a private home, and guests can enjoy break-fast in the canal-side garden. Refurbishing of the rooms was scheduled for completion at press time. Loyal guests keep this hotel booked, so try to make reservations well in advance. There is no restaurant. ♦ Fondamenta Meravegie 1058 (west of Galleria dell'Accademia on Rio della Toletta). 5237846; fax 5239152. Vaporetto stop: Accademia (1, 82)

While the rest of medieval and Renaissance Italy and Europe were competing in jousts and tourneys for social recreation, Venice—with no lists or piazzas to accommodate these early sports—held regattas in the Grand Canal and the *laguna.* Today, more than 100 of them take place every year, the most important being the *Voga Lunga* in May and the *Regata Storica,* held the first Sunday of every September.

". . . an abhorrent, green, slippery city."

D.H. Lawrence

Literary Italy

Cradle of more than a few great Italian writers (Dante in Florence, Alessandro Massoni in Milan), northern Italy has also had its share of expatriate writers-in-residence. The Brownings doted on Florence, Ruskin on Venice, and Stendhal on Milan. The following is a sampler of the wealth of literature on these three cities.

FLORENCE

A Florentine Merchant by Giovanni Caselli (1986, Bedrick) The daily life of Florence is seen through the eyes of an adolescent Russian slave, Zita, who describes her master's household near Florence during the 14th century. Based on the extensive household accounts and letters of Messer Francesco, this title gives great feeling for the period.

The Gardens of Florence (1992, Rizzoli) This volume is filled with photos of Florence's lush greenery and meticulous lawns, along with text about the unique history (dating from the Renaissance) of each garden and the influential families that lived in the palatial structures surrounded by them.

The House of Medici: Its Rise and Fall by Christopher Hibbert (1974, William Morrow and Company) Florence's most influential family provided the world with some of its most colorful statesmen, scholars, art patrons, popes, builders, and soldiers. The story begins in Florence during the Renaissance, with Donatello, Fra Angelico, Michelangelo, and Botticelli working for the Medici; and ends there several hundred years later amid decay and dissoluteness.

VENICE

Death in Venice by Thomas Mann (1928, Alfred A. Knopf, Inc.) On a trip to Venice in search of everlasting beauty, Gustav von Aschenbach, a successful author, becomes aware of his decadent tendencies and finally succumbs to a consuming love. The story is full of symbolism, with frequent overtones from Greek literature.

The Grand Canal (1993, Vendome Press) This photographic and textual survey carries the reader—as if in a gondola—along the famous watercourse, all the while detailing the aesthetic and social history of each building.

Italian Hours by Henry James (1909; reissued 1977, Greenwood Press) In these essays on travels in Italy written from 1872 to 1909, James explores art and religion, political shifts and cultural revolutions, and the nature of travel itself.

Remembrance of Things Past by Marcel Proust (1925; reissued 1981, Vintage Books) Translated from the original French by C.K. Scott Moncrieff and Terence Kilmartin, Proust's long and most important novel is set in part in Venice. The narrator—in his "search for lost time"—analyzes personal relationships, art, and reality. He explores the true meaning of experience, revealing the change it undergoes in one's memory over time.

The Stones of Venice by John Ruskin (1853; reissued 1985, Da Capo Press) The author wrote this critique in response to what he feared would be the destruction of medieval Venice through restoration and neglect. Despite Ruskin's contempt for such buildings as the churches of **San Giorgio Maggiore** and **La Salute,** his magnificent account remains a classic, especially admired for the section on "The Nature of the Gothic."

Those Who Walk Away by Patricia Highsmith (1967; reissued 1988, Atlantic Monthly Press) Ray Garrett convinces the police in Rome that his new bride committed suicide, but his father-in-law, Ed Coleman, believes otherwise. After Coleman's failed attempt at revenge, he heads for Venice; a wounded Ray follows close behind. Their eerie game of cat-and-mouse plays out in the back alleys and narrow canals of Venice.

Watermark by Joseph Brodsky (1992, Farrar, Straus, and Giroux) The meat of this slim collection of memoirs, speculation, and incisive observation is carved out of the laureate poet's winters in Venice.

MILAN

The Charterhouse of Parma by Stendhal (1958; reissued 1992, Alfred A. Knopf, Inc.) Follow the passionate Duchessa Sanseverina through fearful consideration of refuge in many cities, including Florence and Milan.

Duchess of Milan by Michael Ennis (1993, Signet Books) Set in 15th-century Italy, this novel tells the tale of two women who brilliantly match wits and cunning with ruthlessness, at a time when Italy was both dazzling and dangerous.

33 Libreria Alla Toletta This is one of the best bookstores in Venice, with a good section on Venice itself (some books are in English) and an art and photography section that is well worth a look. ♦ M-Sa Mar-Oct; M afternoon, Tu-Sa Nov-Feb. Sacca della Toletta 1214 (off Calle della Toletta). 5232034. Vaporetto stops: Accademia (1, 82); Ca' Rezzonico (1)

34 Trattoria Montin ★★★$$ The entrance to this restaurant is on one of the most attractive canals in Venice. The dining room walls are lined with paintings by Venetian artists, who have patronized the place since the 1940s. When current owner Giuliano Montin was a child, his father ran the trattoria and made it famous, and guidebooks and movies have kept the restaurant popular and the prices high. The food is very good and the atmosphere friendly and informal. Try the *pappardelle* (a kind of large fettuccine), osso buco, and beef filet with green pepper; among the fish dishes, the *branzino* (sea bass) is worth every lira. Service, under the direction of Giuliano's wife, Midi, is very professional. Dine in the huge, wonderful garden in the summer. ♦ M, Th-Su lunch and dinner; Tu lunch. Fondamenta di Borgo 1147 (at Rio delle Eremite). 5227151. Vaporetto stops: Accademia (1, 82); Ca' Rezzonico (1)

Upstairs from Trattoria Montin:

Antica Locanda Montin $ The restaurant also rents out seven rooms upstairs that are among the best bargains in town. Their only inconvenience is the lack of private bathrooms (there are four bathrooms and showers). Four of the rooms have a marvelous view over the canal, with small terraces and beautiful geranium pots. No credit cards accepted. ♦ 5227151

35 Ca' Rezzonico–Museo del Settecento Veneziano (Museum of the Venetian 18th Century) This imposing palazzo, with its main facade on the Canal Grande, was begun by **Baldassare Longhena** in the 17th century and was completed by **Giorgio Massari** in the 18th century. Poet Robert Browning died here in 1889. The museum contains furniture, textiles, and decorative objects one would have seen in a patrician home of the 18th century. On the first of the two "noble floors" (*piani nobili,* as opposed to the higher floors, often occupied by servants), the large ballroom contains furniture by the famous woodcarver Andrea Brustolon. The ceiling of **Room No. 2** has a fresco by Giambattista Tiepolo called *The Marriage of Ludovico Rezzonico and Cristina Savorgnan.* More works by Tiepolo are in **Room No. 6** (*Allegory of Nobility and Virtue,* a ceiling painting) and in **Room No. 8** (*Fortitude and Wisdom,* a canvas). **Room No. 12** is dedicated to Brustolon: The astonishing,

extremely elegant furniture was originally conceived for **Palazzo Venier dei Leoni** (the unfinished building now occupied by the **Guggenheim Collection**). In **Room No. 13,** on the second *piano nobile,* is the large, dramatically attractive *Death of Darius* by Giovanni Battista Piazzetta. **Room No. 14,** adorned by a Tiepolo ceiling *(The Triumph of Zephir and Flora),* is called **Sala del Longhi** because it contains some 30 canvases by Pietro Longhi, a Venetian of the late 18th century who delighted in painting scenes from everyday life *(The Morning Chocolate, The Family Concert).* Nothing illustrates the dramatic changes in Venetian life after the loss of independence better than a comparison between the triumphant Tiepolo ceilings and these intimate, bourgeois interiors. In a totally different vein, hints of decadence are also present in the frescoes by Gian Domenico Tiepolo, son of Giambattista and himself a first-rate painter. They can be seen in **Rooms No. 22** and **23,** where they were placed after being removed from the painter's home on the Venice mainland (Gian Domenico had painted them for his own enjoyment). **Room No. 29** contains a famous small canvas by Francesco Guardi—also a painter of the second half of the century— *Il Ridotto,* which portrays one of the many Venetian gambling casinos. On the third floor is an exhibit of a complete 18th-century pharmacy, restored and moved here after it went out of business in 1909. ♦ Admission. Daily summer; M-Th, Sa-Su winter. Fondamenta Rezzonico 3136 (on Canal Grande at Rio di San Barnaba). Vaporetto stop: Ca' Rezzonico (1). 2410100

36 Ca' Foscari This sumptuous 15th-century Gothic palazzo, one of the most stately on the Canal Grande, was built for Doge Francesco Foscari, one of the most remarkable of the Venetian doges. After he had presided over a tumultuous period in Venetian history, the doge was deposed and his son was exiled. Foscari died in disgrace in his home, which is now the main building of the **University of Venice.** A constant crowd of students and staff move about the building and the courtyard when the university is open— school usually begins in mid-November and ends in mid-May with breaks for Christmas and Easter. ♦ Canal Grande at (Rio di Ca' Foscari). Vaporetto stop: Ca' Rezzonico (1)

37 Campo Santa Margherita Lined with food shops, cafes, and open spaces where mothers take their children to play, this is one of the most charming and lively of Venice's many squares. The large building on the east side **(Nos. 3003-3006)** is now occupied by a supermarket, run by the union of shopkeepers in the neighborhood. On the same side is **Al Capon**, a restaurant and *pensione.* An abandoned church at the northern end is marked by the truncated bell tower. Some of the houses on the *campo* are among the oldest and most attractive in Venice: The one at **No. 2931** (west side) is 13th-century Gothic with original Byzantine elements (such as the 12th-century arch over the main door); a few doors away **(Nos. 2945-2962)** are two 14th-century Gothic houses. ◆ West of Ca' Foscari. Vaporetto stop: Ca' Rezzonico (1)

38 Ristorante L'Incontro ★★$ An authentic and friendly Venetian atmosphere, excellent wine list, and always delicious pasta of the day draw diners to this restaurant. Maybe you'll even catch Paolo, the main waiter, in a good mood. ◆ Tu-Su lunch and dinner. Rio Terrà Canal 3062 (southeast of Campo Santa Margherita off Rio Terrà della Scoazzera). 5222404. Vaporetto stop: Ca' Rezzonico (1)

39 Mondonovo Since *Carnevale* was reintroduced in 1980, hundreds of mask shops have popped up all over Venice. **Mondonovo** is one of the originals, as well as one of the few where masks are still made with artistic care and respect for tradition. Owners Giorgio Spiller and Giano Lovato, well-known nationally and internationally, create their traditional and contemporary masks and other papier-mâché objects in a workshop behind the counter. ◆ M-Sa; no midday closing. Rio Terrà Canal 3126 (southeast of Campo Santa Margherita off Rio Terrà della Scoazzera). 5287344. Vaporetto stop: Ca' Rezzonico (1)

40 Ponte dei Pugni The name, which means Bridge of the Fistfights, comes from an old tradition (now abandoned) which pitted the residents of San Nicolò (a Dorsoduro neighborhood inhabited mostly by fishermen) against those of Castello (mostly **Arsenale** shipbuilders). The champions of both areas used to hold mock fights on the bridge, trying to push their opponents into the water. Four white footprints still mark the starting places of the opposing fighters. ◆ Rio Terrà Canal at Rio di San Barnaba. Vaporetto stop: Ca' Rezzonico (1)

41 Pizzeria Al Sole di Napoli ★$ Its location in one of Venice's most colorful piazzas and its outdoor tables make this friendly, inexpensive pizzeria a favorite hangout on summer evenings. Locals gather here when they don't feel like cooking at home. ◆ M-W, F-Su lunch and dinner. Campo Santa Margherita 3023 (southeast in the *campo*). 5285686. Vaporetto stop: Ca' Rezzonico (1)

Restaurants/Clubs: Red   Hotels: Blue
Shops/❦ Outdoors: Green   Sights/Culture: Black

42 Scuola Grande dei Carmini (Great School of the Carmelites) During the 17th century, the charitable organization of Santa Maria del Carmelo (one of many denominations of the Virgin Mary) had some 75,000 people under its wing. The importance of the building today is tied to the extraordinary number and quality of paintings by Giambattista Tiepolo. Nine of his works adorn the ceiling of the main hall on the second floor. The central one, *The Virgin Mary with the Blessed Simon Stock,* is considered one of the high points in Tiepolo's career. A masterwork by Giovanni Battista Piazzetta, *Judith and Holofernes,* is in the passageway between the **Sala dell'Archivio** and the **Sala dell'Albergo.** ◆ Admission. M-Sa. Rio Terrà Santa Margherita 2616 (southwest of Campo Santa Margherita). 5289420. Vaporetto stop: Ca' Rezzonico (1)

43 Chiesa dei Carmini (Santa Maria del Carmelo) This Gothic church, begun in the 14th century, was modified in the 16th century by raising the central nave (the rose window on the facade was then partly filled). The campanile, by **Giuseppe Sardi,** was added in the 17th century. The rich wood decoration of the church interior also dates from the 17th century. Within the church are two masterworks: In the second chapel on the right is *Adoration of the Shepherds,* one of the last works by Cima da Conegliano; and in the second chapel on the left is *Saint Nicolas, Saint Lucy, Saint John the Baptist, and Saint George Killing the Dragon,* one of the few paintings by Lorenzo Lotto in Venice and much admired for the coastal landscape at the bottom. Behind the church is the convent of the Padri Carmelitani, now used by the **Istituto d'Arte,** which is the main high school for young Venetian artisans specializing in glass, ceramics, and textiles. ◆ Campo dei Carmini (southwest of Campo Santa Margherita). Vaporetto stop: Ca' Rezzonico (1)

44 Fondamenta del Soccorso and Fondamenta di San Sebastiano These two charming streets, running along two canals, lead to the tall, Gothic **Chiesa di San Sebastiano.** Across the canals is **Palazzo Ariani Pasqualigo,** with its remarkable Gothic windows and an outdoor staircase, now a *scuola elementare* (grade school). Northeast of Campo dell'Angelo Raffaele. Vaporetto stop: San Basilio (82)

45 Chiesa di San Sebastiano This 15th-century church contains a wealth of 16th-century works by Paolo Veronese, one of the major painters of the Venetian Renaissance. On the ceiling of the main nave is his *Esther in Front of Ahasuerus, Esther Crowned by Ahasuerus,* and *The Triumph of Mordecai.* The latter painting could be taken as a manifesto of Veronese's ideas about his art: His aim seems to be a kind of high, refined spectacularity, regardless of the nature of the subject (whether religious or, as in the patrician villas, totally secular). The perspectives on the two horses in the foreground, the twisted column, and the top balcony with overlooking ladies are particularly striking. With these paintings, Veronese established himself as the man who could best represent the theatrical, grandiose fantasies of the Venetian nobility in a moment of relentless commercial and political expansion. He also painted the doors to the organ (left wall); the canvas on the main altar (*The Virgin in Glory with Saint Sebastian, Peter, Catherine, and Francis);* the two large canvases in the chancel (*Saint Mark and Saint Marcellino* and his famous *Martyrdom of Saint Sebastian*); the ceiling of the **Sacristy** (this was his first work here); and, visible from a walk over a stair (ask the custodian to accompany you), two frescoes: *Saint Sebastian in front of Diocletian* and another *Martyrdom of Saint Sebastian.* ♦ Campo San Sebastiano (west in the *campo*). Vaporetto stop: San Basilio (82)

46 Ristorante All'Angelo Raffaele ★★$$ This restaurant started as the kind of place where dock workers got drunk and played cards after work. In the 1960s, the proprietors added a few basic dishes to the menu— mostly favorite Venetian fish appetizers such as octopus, cuttlefish, smelts, and sardines— and attracted a different kind of clientele, who ordered the appetizers as whole meals. Along with the new clientele came an expanded menu. Now the backroom card games are history—the space is too valuable—and some of the spontaneity is gone, but the restaurant is still a great place for inexpensive fish dishes. ♦ Tu-Su lunch and dinner. No credit cards accepted. Campo dell'Angelo Raffaele 1722 (south of the *campo*). 5237456. Vaporetto stop: San Basilio (82)

47 Casa dei Sette Camini This 18th-century building, a national landmark, is in need of restoration, but its regularity and striking chimneys give it a simple beauty that transcends its decay. The surrounding neighborhood, once extremely poor, is slowly being renovated as more and more Venetians, lured here by lower prices, are discovering its quiet, old-fashioned charm. ♦ Campiello Tron 1877 (just east of Campo San Nicolò dei Mendicoli). Vaporetto stop: San Basilio (82)

48 Chiesa di San Nicolò dei Mendicoli A restoration in the 1970s uncovered architectural remnants from as far back as the seventh century, making this one of the oldest churches in Venice. The existing structure was built between the 13th and 15th centuries; the magnificent Veneto-Byzantine bell tower dates from the 11th century; and the facade was redone in the 18th century. The interior, unusually welcoming and intimate, is adorned with exquisite 15th-century woodwork. ♦ Campo San Nicolò dei Mendicoli (off Fondamenta della Terese). Vaporetto stop: San Basilio (82)

49 Stazione Marittima South of the **Chiesa di San Sebastiano**, at the western end of the Zattere, is Venice's cruise-ship terminal. The whole area is in bad shape and barely worthy of a modern passenger harbor. Dozens of acres of unattractive and vacant buildings cover the southwest tip of Venice. The city has yet to decide on a plan of action. An equally dismal fate has fallen upon the Mulino Stucky, the strange (for Venice) Neo-Gothic construction looming across the canal from the terminal. The former flour mill, abandoned in 1950, was to become a modern conference center, then a huge youth hostel; even converting the building into condominiums was considered, but no decision has ever been made. The building has fallen apart, the windows have all broken, and the only occupants are the pigeons that fly in and out. ♦ Fondamenta San Basegio (at the western end of Le Zattere). Vaporetto stop: San Basilio (82)

50 Campo San Basilio The building separating the *campo* from the Canale della Giudecca **(Nos. 1511-1522)** is an interesting example of a 17th-century housing development. It was conceived as a rental apartment building (four apartments on each floor). Inside, a small courtyard allows light to enter the back rooms. The triple windows on the third and fourth floors are typical of popular domestic 17th-century architecture. ♦ At the western end of Le Zattere. Vaporetto stop: San Basilio (82)

51 Ristorante Riviera ★★$$ This restaurant may not have a wood terrace over the canal, but the tables set on the banks of the Giudecca are inviting and pleasant. The chef/owner worked at **Harry's Bar** before opening this place, and his training can be seen in the quality of the food and service. The homemade gnocchi, ravioli *con zucca* (with pumpkin) or *di pesce* (with fish), as well as the Venetian specialties, are all delicious. ♦ Tu-Th, Su lunch and dinner; F, Sa dinner. Fondamenta Zattere Ponte Lungo 1473 (between Campo San Basilio and Rio di San Gervasio e Protasio). 5227621. Vaporetto stops: San Basilio (82); Zattere (52, 82)

Bests

Marchesa Barbara Berlingieri
Vice President, Save Venice

Legatoria Piazzesi for special Venetian paperwork.

Bar Al Teatro for cappuccino and the best *zaletti* (delicious traditional Venetian biscuits).

Harry's Bar for a dinner of risotto and all the best types of pasta.

Palazzo Vendramin Calergi on the **Giudecca**— the best view in Venice.

The **Hotel Monaco and Grand Canal** terrace for lunch or dinner in warm weather.

Osteria al Ponte del Diavolo on **Torcello** island— delicious food and atmosphere.

San Polo

While it may not be chockablock with treasures and is often ignored by tourists, San Polo has no shortage of distinguished art and architecture. The **Chiesa dei Frari** and **Chiesa dei Santi Giovanni e Paolo**, for example, rank among the highest achievements of Venetian Gothic style, and the **Scuola di San Rocco** houses a breathtaking array of canvases by Tintoretto. **Campo San Polo** itself—vast, luminous, and elegant—is one of the most beautiful squares in all of Venice. For Venetians, San Polo is the part of town where *real* people live and go about their daily business. The fruit and vegetable market and the nearby fish market still serve shoppers from throughout Venice, who arrive by *vaporetto* to buy their weekly food supplies at prices much lower than in their neighborhood shops. The liveliest street is **Ruga degli Orefici** (commonly called **Ruga Rialto**), parallel to the **Canal Grande** on the west side of the **Ponte di Rialto** (Rialto Bridge). The narrow streets between Ruga Rialto and the Canal Grande are where market merchants used to have their homes and warehouses. In the labyrinth of tiny streets on the other side of Ruga Rialto hide the best wine shops in town: **L'Antico Dolo**, **Ai Do Mori**, and **A le Do Spade**. These are real institutions, still packed with Venetians who stop for an *ombra* (glass of wine) and a *cicchetto* (the Venetian version of tapas) before lunch or dinner. Among the patrons are pensioners, students, teachers, doctors, lawyers, and architects—the latter abound in Venice because of the university's acclaimed school of architecture. Even though the food booths at the Rialto **Mercato della Frutta** (Produce Market) are gradually giving way to stalls selling tourist trinkets, San Polo remains one of the last places where class and money distinctions don't seem to matter, and where the locals simply enjoy their city, perhaps more than any outsider ever could.

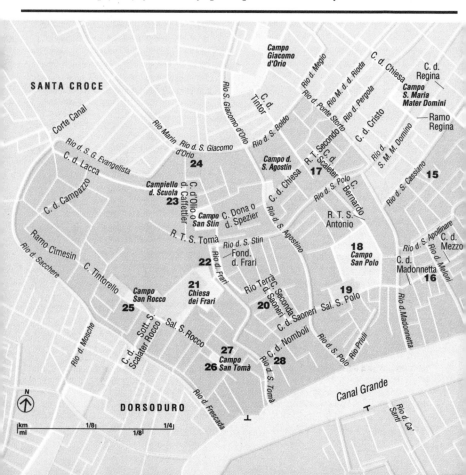

1 Ponte di Rialto (Rialto Bridge) Built at the end of the 16th century, this stone bridge replaced a wooden drawbridge that was too low for ships' masts to pass under. Until the middle of the 19th century, it was the only passage across the Canal Grande and the only link between the three city districts *de citra* (on this side) and the three *de ultra* (on that side). Appropriately enough, the architect's name was **Antonio da Ponte** (no relation of the painter better known as Bassano, nor of Mozart's librettist, Lorenzo da Ponte). Competition for the bridge commission was fierce; proposals by **Michelangelo, Antonio Palladio,** and **Jacopo Sansovino** were all rejected in favor of **da Ponte**'s arcaded design. Perhaps one reason his plan was preferred was his inclusion of shops lining the interior of the bridge. After all, the Rialto was the mercantile center of the city. Today these small stores sell everything from fine gold to not-so-fine machine-made masks. The downstream facade of the bridge is decorated with a high relief of the *Annunciation* by Agostino Rubini. The buildings on the San Marco side, now owned by the city bishopry, are rented as apartments to a few lucky Venetians—lucky because the rental prices are established by a national law, which does not take into account such things as views. On the San Polo side are two Renaissance palazzi, the building to the right (north) is the 16th-century **Palazzo dei Camerlenghi** (Finance Ministry), the ground floor of which once served as a prison. The palazzo to the left (south) housed the **Dieci Savi,** the 10 magistrates in charge of collecting taxes. ♦ Between San Marco and San Polo. Vaporetto stop: Rialto (1, 82)

1 Voltolina T-shirt collectors head straight for this small shop on the Ponte di Rialto, noteworthy for its selective choice of quality T-shirts at reasonable prices (and a particularly good selection for children). There is no shortage of inexpensive T-shirts around town, but most are poorly stamped on thin cottons. This shop's wares are made of high-quality cottons, and many of the available designs are nicely embroidered. The store's personable staff will gladly unfold before you a seemingly endless array of T-shirt possibilities. ♦ M-Sa. Ponte di Rialto 4 (mid-bridge, north side). 5225667. Vaporetto stop: Rialto (1, 82)

2 La Bottega dei Mascheri Amid the produce stands and tourist shops on the San Polo side of the bridge, this mask shop is a standout. Sergio Boldrin's small *bottega* (workshop) has been praised for its high-quality collection of masks—no small feat given the number of mask shops that have cropped up since *Carnevale* was reinstated in 1980. The artisan produces a variety of papier-mâché commedia dell'arte characters as well as court jesters and more contemporary fantasy masks, but their common characteristic is the artistry with which they are lovingly created. ♦ M-Sa, no midday closing. Calle degli Orefici 80 (between Ponte di Rialto and Campo San Giacomo). 5223857. Vaporetto stop: Rialto (1, 82)

3 Mercato della Frutta (Produce Market) Despite the rapid transformation of the rest of the market into a tourist trap, the fresh produce market (also called *Erberia*) is still very much alive at the foot of the Rialto Bridge near the **Pescheria** (Fish Market). ♦ M-Sa. Ruga degli Orefici (northwest of Ponte di Rialto). Vaporetto stop: Rialto (1, 82)

4 Campo San Giacomo During the daytime, it's hard to see the beauty of this little square, crammed as it is with vegetable stands and shabby canopies. But at night the little church, fondly called **San Giacometto** by the locals, evokes a time when human size was more important than imperial magnificence. Its 12th-century portico, once common in front of churches, is one of very few left in Venice. The handsome clock on the bell tower dates back to the 15th century. From the early times of the Republic until the 18th century, this square was the Wall Street of Venice. Here, the modern banking system was first invented: Bankers had their tables on the square or under the nearby colonnade, and they would record transactions in their books, avoiding the transfer of real gold and silver. ♦ Off Ruga degli Orefici. Vaporetto stop: Rialto (1, 82)

5 Rialta This little shop sells necklaces, bracelets, earrings, *Carnevale* masks, and collectors' dolls, all of original design, as are the purses and hats. Some of the glass beads and other materials that make up the designs are antiques from the 1920s and 1930s. ♦ M-Sa Mar-Oct; M afternoon, Tu-Sa Nov-Feb. Ruga degli Orefici 56 (north of Campo San Giacomo). 5285710. Vaporetto stops: Rialto (1, 82); San Silvestro (1)

6 Ruga Vecchia San Giovanni This narrow, busy *ruga* (old Venetian for the French word *rue,* or street) is the main connection between the Rialto and **Campo San Polo.** Until the 1960s it was also the main shopping street for Venetians, as opposed to the Mercerie across the canal in San Marco, where goods and prices were geared toward tourists. But increased tourist traffic in the San Polo–Rialto area is quickly transforming the street. Venetians now tend to avoid it, using a parallel, more intricate path to reach **Campo San Polo** (Calle dei Do Mori to Calle San Mattio to Campiello del Sole: all relatively deserted and totally charming). ♦ Between Ruga degli Orefici and Calle San Polo. Vaporetto stops: Rialto (1, 82); San Silvestro (1)

Venetian Streets

"Wonderful city, streets full of water, please advise," is what humorist Robert Benchley is said to have cabled home on his first visit to Venice. A waterway in Venice is called a *rio,* but even for those streets that are not full of water the visitor to this wonderful city needs some advice, since the names are mostly in dialect and you won't find translations for them in any dictionary. A *calle* is a street. A *stretto* is a narrow passageway. A *sottoportego* is a passage-way or a covered street. A *ruga* (from the French word *rue*) is a street originally running next to a shop or residence, while a *fondamenta* runs alongside a canal, and a *riva* is an important *fondamenta*. A *lista* is a street that runs in front of a former embassy of the Republic and was once a place of diplomatic immunity. A *salizzada* was one of the first paved streets in a parish, while a *rio terrà* is a filled-in canal. A *piscina* is a small, filled-in basin, now acting as a small piazza. The only piazza in Venice is **Piazza San Marco;** what would be called a piazza elsewhere in Italy is known locally as a *campo* or *campiello,* and often has a well in the center. Venice's wells have long since been covered.

7 Trattoria Alla Madonna ★★$$ This is one of the few restaurants in Venice that serve really fresh fish at decent prices. A local favorite, it dates back more than 50 years, and its eclectic clientele keeps it lively. Dine here and you rub elbows with everyone from upper-crust Venetians and Japanese tourists to gondoliers who park their craft on the nearby stretch of the Grand Canal. Try the risottos and the *granseola* appetizer (a type of crab with delicious meat). ♦ M, Tu, Th-Su lunch and dinner. Sotoportego della Madonna 594 (off Riva del Vin). 5223824. Vaporetto stops: Rialto (1, 82); San Silvestro (1)

8 Locanda Sturion $$ This is one of those rare hotels that has Grand Canal views without grand rates. A recent refurbishing of the smart, 11-room establishment includes amenities such as heated towel racks and air-conditioning. There's no elevator, so steady yourself for the three-flight walk up. If you're not lucky enough to procure one of the two rooms on the canal, take solace in a breakfast in the pretty canal-side dining room. ♦ Calle del Sturione 679 (at Riva del Vin). 5236243, fax 5228378. Vaporetto stops: Rialto (1, 82); San Silvestro (1)

Aliani

9 Gastronomia Aliani One of the few take-out delis in town where you can buy fancy food items as well as the traditional roast chicken. ♦ M-Tu, Th-Sa; W mornings. No credit cards accepted. Ruga Vecchia San Giovanni 654 (between Ruga degli Orefici and Chiesa de San Aponal) 5224913. Vaporetto stops: Rialto (1, 82); San Silvestro (1)

10 L'Antico Dolo ★★$ For the time being, this is still an *osteria:* an old-fashioned wine shop where the owner lines the counter with a pot of hot *musetto* (boiled sausage), a pot of *pasta e fagioli* (bean soup), and a few other popular dishes to go with the carefully selected house wines. A few small tables have now appeared in the narrow space, and table service and more ambitious dishes announce the beginning of a transformation. ♦ M-Sa. No credit cards accepted. Ruga Vecchia San Giovanni 778 (between Ruga degli Orefici and Chiesa de San Aponal). 5226546. Vaporetto stops: Rialto (1,82); San Silvestro (1)

11 A le Do Spade ★★$ This is a well-known *bacaro*—a small, homey wine bar/trattoria where *cicchetti* (finger foods) and bonhomie make for an ultra-Venetian experience. Casanova was a regular when this tavern was already 300 years old. Sample the *prosciutto d'oca* (goose ham) or make a selection from the excellent wine list. The regulars—workers from the market and savvy visitors—always

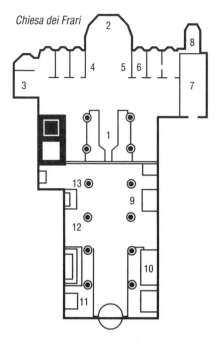

Chiesa dei Frari

Alessandro Vittoria, a 16th-century sculptor who is abundantly represented in Venetian churches. Farther down the aisle is a 19th-century *Monument to Titian* by Luigi and Pietro Zandomeneghi **[10]**. Titian died during a plague and was probably buried here. The monument was first commissioned from Antonio Canova, but was built by the Zandomeneghi, Canova's pupils, after the master's death. It is one of the latest examples of Neo-Classical sculpture in Venice.

In 1827, Canova's plans for the Titian monument were used by a team of his pupils, including the Zandomeneghi, for a monument to Canova himself **[11]**. The statues on the sides of the pyramid's open door represent *The Arts, St. Mark's Lion,* and *Genius.* Although Canova's body is elsewhere, his heart is inside the pyramid in a vase of porphyry. This entire corner of the nave is occupied by an imposing Baroque *Monument to Doge Giovanni Pesaro,* based on plans by **Baldassare Longhena.**

The *Pesaro Madonna* **[12]** was painted by Titian in 1526. Here again the artist broke with some of the most venerated rules in composition and the use of color. The striking perspective of the painting is explained by Titian's attempt to attract the eyes of visitors walking up the aisle from the church's main door; the two gigantic columns in the painting are an ideal continuation of the real columns supporting the church's roof. Nearby is the burial place of yet another member of the Pesaro family, Bishop Jacopo Pesaro **[13]**. ♦ Admission; Sunday 3:30PM-5PM, free. M-Sa; Su afternoon. Campo dei Frari. 5222637. Vaporetto stop: San Tomà (1, 82)

22 Archivio di Stato (State Archives) The **Chiesa dei Frari** opens onto a small square along a canal appropriately called Rio dei Frari. The building to your left as you exit, once part of the large Franciscan monastery attached to the church, has two charming cloisters, one of which is attributed to **Jacopo Sansovino** (inquire at the archive office for permission to visit). Today the building houses what remains of the Venetian Republic, one of the richest, most well-organized archives in the world. The doges carefully conserved all kinds of documents related to the city's government. Some 15 million files—some as much as 10 inches thick—are stored along many miles of shelves. They tell the story of Venice month by month and often even day by day. Ambassadors' letters and international files in the archives have proved invaluable in the study of the history of Europe. A competent and kind staff welcomes dozens of scholars from all over the world every day. ♦ Campo dei Frari 3002 (north corner of square). Vaporetto stop: San Tomà (1, 82)

The chancel contains two important monuments. The *Tomb of Doge Niccolò Tron* **[4]**, on the left wall, was completed by Antonio Rizzo in 1476 and is considered one of the best examples of Venetian Renaissance sculpture. The doge is portrayed standing in the central niche, with Charity and Prudence on either side; he is also sculpted lying on top of his cinerary urn, under a lunette with bas-reliefs of *Christ with God the Father* and *The Annunciation.* Across the chancel is Antonio Bregno's *Monument to Doge Francesco Foscari* **[5]**, one of the greatest Venetian leaders. Completed 20 years before the Tron monument, this work mixes the old Venetian Gothic style with influences of the Renaissance from central Italy.

The first chapel at the right of the altar **[6]** contains a marvelous wood sculpture of *St. John the Baptist* by Donatello.

The **Sacristy [7]** was built in the 15th century with donations from the wealthy Pesaro family, one of the most prominent families in Venetian history. Their presence is obvious in this church. The monument on top of the **Sacristy** door represents Benedetto Pesaro, an admiral in the Venetian navy. The altarpiece in the small chapel off the **Sacristy** is decorated with one of the best paintings by Giovanni Bellini, *Madonna and Child with Four Saints* **[8]**, in the original carved wood frame.

Return through the choir screen to the nave of the church. The statue of *St. Jerome* **[9]** in the right aisle is one of the best works of

23 Scuola Grande di San Giovanni Evangelista (Great School of St. John the Evangelist) The rich and powerful brotherhood named after St. John acquired this property early in the 14th century. In 1478, master **Pietro Lombardo,** one of the first architects and sculptors to introduce the Renaissance in Venice, redesigned the little square on the side of the building and in front of the church. He added the elegant marble portal, decorated with an eagle (the symbol of St. John) and two angels, thus creating one of the first Renaissance environments in town. The brotherhood was housed in the building at the right of the square's entrance (notice the medieval bas-relief *The Virgin and St. John Being Adored by the Brotherhood's Members*). **Giorgio Massari** redesigned most of the interior in the 18th century, but its most interesting feature is the splendid staircase designed and built by **Mauro Codussi** in 1498. The building is not usually open to the general public, although musical performances are held here quite often. ◆ Campiello della Scuola 2455 (just north of Chiesa dei Frari). Vaporetto stop: San Tomà (1, 82).

24 Caffè Orientale ★★$$ The Venetian brothers who took over an old wine shop and transformed it into this stylish restaurant have recently left. The Art Deco look—black lacquer and mirrors—remains though, as does the menu featuring old-time Venetian cooking inspired by Venetian culinary history. Try to reserve a table on the terrace overlooking the canal. When you're through dining, ask to have a gondola called to take you back to your hotel or on further explorations of the city. ◆ T-Su lunch and dinner; Su lunch only. Fondamenta delle Late 2426. 719804. Vaporetto stop: San Tomà (1, 82)

The Venetians are convinced they invented marzipan, explaining that its Latin root, *pan marci* or *pane di Marco* (Mark's bread) refers to a sweet made in honor of the city and Republic's ubiquitous patron saint.

In the heyday of the Venetian Republic, nearly 200,000 people lived in Venice; as many as one in 10 were foreigners. Presently, a realistic estimate of the local population is a mere 60,000 and shrinking.

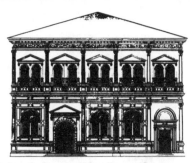

25 Scuola Grande di San Rocco (Great School of St. Roch) Most of the great Renaissance architects of Venice contributed to this remarkable and recently restored building (pictured above), which epitomizes the stylistic trends of that period: The ground floor was started in 1516 by **Bartolomeo Bon,** the middle and top floors were added by **Sante Lombardo** and **Scarpagnino,** and the final touches were contributed by **Gian Giacomo de' Grigi.** Like its neighboring rival at **St. John the Evangelist,** the brotherhood of St. Roch was a powerful association of merchants, storekeepers, and other members of the Venetian bourgeoisie, whose purposes ranged from assisting the poor to redeeming sinners and helping the sick during times of plague. When the brotherhood commissioned Jacopo Tintoretto to decorate the interior of the building, it tied its name forever to one of the most extraordinary cycles of paintings in the history of Venice.

Start your visit on the second floor. A large door on the left side of the **Salone Maggiore** (to be visited later) leads to the **Sala dell' Albergo,** the first room decorated by Tintoretto in 1565. A majestic *Crucifixion* on the back wall sets the tone for the artist's amazing exploits in the composition of figures, in the use of light, and in surprising perspectives. On the ceiling, Tintoretto painted *St. Roch in Glory,* the sample work that helped him win the commission for the whole cycle (among the painters he competed against was Veronese). On the other walls of the room are *Christ in Front of Pilate, Ecce Homo,* and *Christ Carrying the Cross.* Back in the **Salone Maggiore,** the painting immediately to the right of the door is Tintoretto's *Self-Portrait.* The ceiling here consists of 21 canvases on which the artist depicted stories of the Old Testament; the New Testament was illustrated in the large paintings on the walls. On the long wall in front of the staircase are *The Nativity, The Baptism, The Resurrection, The Agony in the Garden,* and *The Last Supper;* in front of the altar are *St. Sebastian* and *St. Roch;* on the entrance wall are *The Temptation of Christ, The Pool of Bathsheba, The Ascension, The Resurrection of Lazarus,* and *The Miracle of the Loaves and Fishes.* The altarpiece, also by Tintoretto, represents *St. Roch in Glory.* Standing on easels on the sides of the altar are an *Annunciation* by Titian and a *Visitation* by Tintoretto; in front of the banisters, also on easels, are two youthful paintings by Giambattista Tiepolo: *Abraham with Angels* and *Hagar Abandoned*. The cycle continues with eight large canvases in the ground floor hall (**Salone Terreno**) that tell stories from the life of the Virgin Mary. These were the last works Tintoretto executed for the brotherhood and were completed when the painter was nearly 70. They are, starting from the left side: *The Annunciation, The Epiphany, The Flight into Egypt, The Slaughter of the Innocents, St. Mary Magdalen, St. Mary of Egypt, The Circumcision,* and *The Assumption.* ◆ Admission. Daily. Campo San Rocco 3054 (west of Chiesa dei Frari). 5234864. Vaporetto stop: San Tomà (1, 82)

26 **Trattoria San Tomà** ★★$$ On the small **Campo San Tomà**, this wonderful neighborhood restaurant with an outdoor garden area serves great pizza, as well as a number of homemade pastas and Venetian specialties.

◆ M, W-Su lunch and dinner. Campo San Tomà 2864A (south of Chiesa dei Frari). 5238819. Vaporetto stop: San Tomà (1, 82)

27 **Argentiere Sfriso** Mario and Giancarlo Sfriso are master artisans who create elegant silver objects in their workshop at the back of this store. Their designs, ranging from expensive vases and trays to affordable souvenir medallions and miniature gondolas, are handmade with ancient tools. ◆ M-Sa Mar-Oct; M afternoon, Tu-Sa Nov-Feb. Campo San Tomà 2849 (south of Chiesa dei Frari). 5223558. Vaporetto stop: San Tomà (1, 82)

28 **Casa di Goldoni** The great Venetian playwright Carlo Goldoni was born here in 1707. The small palazzo now houses the **Istituto di Studi Teatrali** (Institute for Theatrical Studies), with a small museum (temporarily closed—call for update) and a **Theater Library** open to students and scholars. ◆ M-Sa. Calle dei Nomboli 2793 (east of Campo San Tomà). 5236353. Vaporetto stop: San Tomà (1, 82)

Bests

Beatrice H. Guthrie
Director, Save Venice, Inc.

To really enjoy Venice, avoid the heart of the city at peak hours, when it's swamped with zillions of tourists. Visit **San Marco** and **Rialto** early in the morning or late at night, and spend other times discovering out-of-the-way parts of the city.

The **Punta della Dogana** is an ideal place to watch the sun come up. To see it set, go to the **Lido** and take the *vaporetto* back to **San Marco** at twilight.

The Rialto markets are in full swing at 6AM, but "late risers" can come at 8AM and still find it colorful.

If you're spending Christmas in Venice, don't miss the concert in the **Chiesa dei Frari** on Christmas afternoon or the mass in **Basilica di San Marco** (St. Mark's) on Christmas Eve. To walk off Christmas dinner, take the *vaporetto* to the Lido, where you will find millions of shells along the miles of beach.

In August and September, enjoy the outdoor films in **Campo San Polo.**

Have a coffee or gelato in **Piazza San Marco** at midnight to hear the Marangona toll midnight. The bell has been in the **Campanile** so long, no one knows its origin. The resonance is unforgettable, and it rings only at noon and midnight.

My favorite paintings include Carpaccio's *St. George Killing the Dragon* in the **Scuola di San Giorgio degli Schiavoni;** Giovanni Bellini's altarpieces in the church of **San Zaccaria** and in the **Sacristy of the Chiesa dei Frari;** the *Baptism of Christ* in the **San Giovanni in Bragora;** Titian's *Annunciation* in the **Chiesa di San Salvador;** and the many canvases by Veronese that decorate his parish church, the **Chiesa di San Sebastiano.**

Campo San Giacomo dell'Orio, in **Santa Croce,** is hard to find, but worth discovering. So is the

Sant'Apollonia Monastery—the only Romanesque monument in Venice—located behind the **Basilica.**

My favorite Venetian churches are **Chiesa di Santa Maria dei Miracoli,** built in 1489 by **Pietro Lombardo** (its beauty makes it a popular site for Venetian weddings) and **Chiesa dei Gesuiti,** whose Baroque interior is completely decorated with green and white marble carved to resemble draped brocade.

The best view of Venice is from the campanile of **San Giorgio Maggiore.**

No trip to Venice is complete without a boat ride to **Torcello** to see its churches and Byzantine mosaics. For lunch, don't miss the warm seafood salad at **Osteria al Ponte del Diavolo.** The affluent can have a water taxi take them there, wait, and bring them back, but the public ferry that leaves from the **Fondamente Nuove** is more fun. To reach the Fondamente Nuove, take the *No. 52 sinistra* (left) *vaporetto* from St. Mark's through the **Arsenale** (the site of Venice's ancient ship factory, noted in Dante's *Inferno*). At the entrance to the **Arsenale,** don't miss the extraordinary collection of stone lions shipped home by the Venetians from ancient sites in Greece and Turkey.

From one who has made a systematic study, the *gelateria* in **Campo Santa Margherita** has the best ice cream; the best pizzas are at **Trattoria Do Mori** on the **Giudecca** and the **Trattoria San Tomà** in **Campo San Tomà.** The best place for seafood is **Da Fiore,** but it is hidden deep in **San Polo** and it takes a genius with a map to find it. A favorite restaurant is the terrace of the **Hotel Monaco and Grand Canal,** where the world's most charming Venetian, Gianni Zambon, will spoil you. In summer, **Harry's Dolci** on the **Giudecca** provides the **Harry's Bar** menu at a lower price and with the most beautiful view in the world. Finally, the Garden of Eden surely had nothing on the gardens and pool of the **Cipriani Hotel,** but unfortunately this best thing in life does not come free.

Santa Croce

Seven small canals from the **Canal Grande** crisscross toward **Campo San Polo** in Santa Croce, in the center of which is the charming church and *campo* of **San Giacomo dell'Orio**. Part modern, part ancient, Santa Croce is all rather off the beaten track, making it a pleasant place to get away from the crowds snaking through the rest of Venice.

1 Piazzale Roma This busy area is the closest automobiles can come to the historical center around **St. Mark's.** Built in the 1930s when the railroad bridge over the lagoon was enlarged to permit access by car, this redesigned point of entry into Venice radically transformed the city's street system: Peripheral and neglected before, the area immediately became of vital importance. Ever-increasing tourist traffic further contributed to the transformation, creating challenges the city still struggles with. The *piazzale* is a chaotic traffic circle where out-of-town automobiles drive around and around helplessly in search of nonexistent parking places. Many buses unload their cargo of one-day visitors here, where they are assaulted by vendors of postcards, guidebooks, and plastic gondolas. All the streets feeding into the square are lined with souvenir stands, which can make

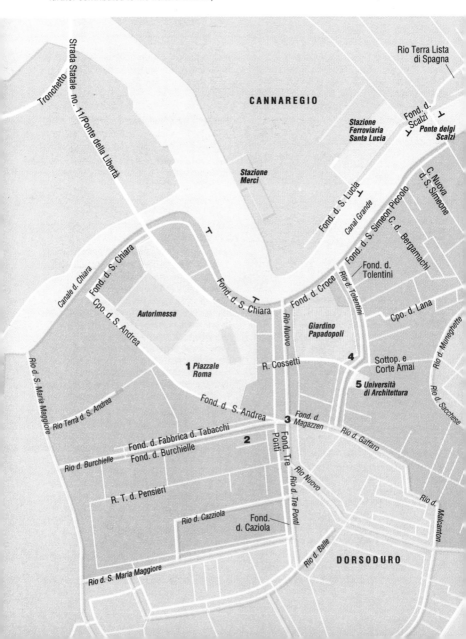

passage into and out of the area difficult on a busy day. Gondoliers, taxi drivers, and middlemen of all sorts offer their services to puzzled newcomers. In 1990 the city approved legislation that attempted to remove the vendors to an artificial island called **Tronchetto** (where additional parking is available); whether it succeeds remains to be seen. The garage at the entrance of the *piazzale* is of some architectural interest since it was one of the first such buildings in Italy. ♦ Vaporetto stop: Piazzale Roma (1, 52, 82)

2 Trattoria Alle Burchielle ★$ The tables along the canal make this restaurant one of the most pleasant in the area around **Piazzale Roma**. Bruno, the owner, knows how to select

his fish at the morning market, one reason the place is a preferred lunch spot of gondoliers and water taxi drivers. Stick to the dishes of the day—including fish appetizers and the spaghetti with seafood. ♦ Tu-Sa lunch and dinner. Fondamenta delle Burchielle 393 (south of Piazzale Roma). 5231342. Vaporetto stop: Piazzale Roma (1, 52, 82)

3 Tre Ponti This bridge—actually a group of three bridges—is one of the most complex and interesting in Venice. It was completed in 1938, when the opening of **Piazzale Roma** made it necessary to dig a new canal to join the Canal Grande with the square's auto-mobile terminal. Although young, Rio Nuovo, as the new waterway is called, is one of the

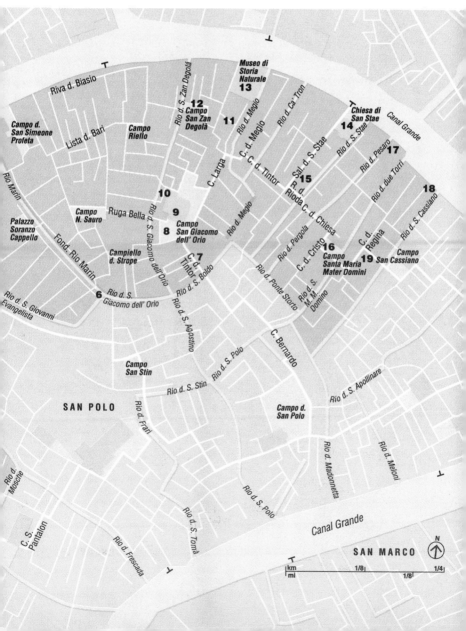

most battered and fragile canals in the city. The relentless traffic of taxis and *motoscafi* (water buses) constantly erodes the building foundations along the banks. Since 1991 long stretches of the canal have been closed to traffic ever more frequently, allowing for the urgent repairs to underwater banks that continue in a frustrating fight against the laws of physics. ♦ Rio Nuovo at Fondamenta di San Andrea. Vaporetto stop: Piazzale Roma (1, 52, 82)

4 Sofitel Venezia $$$ Across the Rio Nuovo from the **Piazzale Roma,** on the outskirts of the **Giardino Papadopoli** (Papadopoli Garden), this recently renovated 95-room hotel combines its quiet location with efficient service. The rooms are attractively decorated in 18th-century Venetian style. The top floor rooms have private balconies with views of the church, square, and the small Rio dei Tolentini. The hotel also has a restaurant. ♦ Giardino Papadopoli 245 (southeast of the garden). 5285394; fax 5230043. Vaporetto stop: Piazzale Roma (1, 52, 82)

5 Università di Architettura (University of Architecture) Like many Venetian institutions, the School of Architecture of the **University of Venice** occupies a former convent. Built in the early 17th century and including a pleasant cloister, it features a main entrance designed in the 1950s by Venetian architect **Carlo Scarpa,** a teacher at the school and an acclaimed contemporary Italian architect. ♦ Campo dei Tolentini 191 (off Fondamenta dei Tolentini). Vaporetto stop: Piazzale Roma (1, 52, 82)

6 Ponte della Late The view is very Venetian from this bridge over the Rio Marin, one of the most charming canals in town, and over the Rio di San Giacomo on the other side of the bridge. Off the south end of the bridge is the pleasant **Caffè Orientale.** ♦ Near Campo N. Sauro (on Fondamenta Rio Marin). Vaporetto stop: Ferrovia (1, 52, 82)

7 Pizzeria Alle Oche ★★$ Word is out on what used to be a well-kept secret: This is one of the best pizza places in Venice, boasting more than 70 varieties and 10 interesting combination salads. Be ready to wait for a table inside or out, either in the rear garden or the small space in front. A choice of 30 beers will make it worth your

while. ♦ Tu-Su lunch and dinner. Calle del Tintor 1552B (south of Campo San Giacomo dell'Orio at Calle delle Oche). 5241161. Vaporetto stop: San Stae (1)

8 Campo San Giacomo dell'Orio Venetians call this campo Da L'Orio after a laurel tree (*lauro* or *lorio*) that supposedly once stood in the square. Daily life in the Santa Croce neighborhood revolves around this square and the nearby **Campo San Zan Degolà.** The local church is run by an active and popular parish priest, who frequently organizes dances, picnics, and other events here. ♦ At the intersection of Calle Larga and Calle del Tintor. Vaporetto stop: San Stae (1)

9 Chiesa di San Giacomo dell'Orio The handsome exterior of this 10th-century church, surrounded by the square on all sides, provides passersby with a variety of views. The main entrance is on the facade along the canal (important worshippers used to arrive by gondola); the bell tower dates from the 13th century, as does the main apse visible at the back; the other entrance was redone in the 14th century. The interior is characterized by a 14th-century wood ceiling that is often noted as exemplary of ancient building techniques: It was built like an inverted ship hull, a familiar process for Venetian carpenters who built more ships than churches. The Crucifix hanging in front of the main altar is by Paolo Veneziano, and was restored to its golden splendor in 1988. ♦ Campo San Giacomo dell'Orio. Vaporetto stop: San Stae (1)

10 Trattoria da Crecola ★★$ There is nothing exceptional about the quality of the food served in this restaurant, but the pizza is good and the location is simply superb—and they offer takeout! The tables are outdoors in the little square in front of **San Giacomo,** right under the medieval bell tower and along a canal. Quiet, charming, and inexpensive, it's no wonder the locals flock here. ♦ M, W-Su lunch and dinner. Campiello del Piovan 1461 (northwest corner of Campo San Giacomo dell'Orio). 5241496. Vaporetto stop: San Stae (1)

11 La Zucca ★$$ "The Pumpkin," opened by a group of women in the early 1970s when the feminism movement was in its nascence, is an informal eatery that has maintained something of a nonconformist atmosphere all these years. The emphasis here is still on good vegetarian cooking, as can be witnessed by the *minestra di zucca e porri* (pumpkin and leek soup) or the lasagna made with radicchio. ◆ M-Sa lunch and dinner. No credit cards accepted. Ponte del Megio 1762 (northeast of Campo San Giacomo). 5241570. Vaporetto stop: San Stae (1)

12 Campo San Zan Degolà There is a magical beauty to this secret spot frequented by locals. The small square, flanked by a narrow canal and adorned with a 10th-century church (the facade was redone in the 18th century), offers escape from the bustle of the city. ◆ North of Campo San Giovanni dell'Orio on Riva de Biasio. Vaporetto stop: San Stae (1)

13 Museo di Storia Naturale (Natural History Museum) The **Fondaco dei Turchi**, the palazzo housing this museum (see "Canal Grande" chapter for a description), is one of the oldest and most unusual in Venice. The best way to appreciate its splendid facade is from the Canal Grande or from the opposite bank. The museum includes the usual exhibitions of animals, plants, and fossils. The highlights are a large dinosaur skeleton found in the Sahara desert in 1973 (the digging was financed and directed by a wealthy Venetian entrepreneur) and the rooms showing animal life in the Venice lagoon. ◆ Admission. Tu-Su. Salizzada del Fondaco dei Turchi 1730 (near Campo San Zan Degolà). 5240885. Vaporetto stop: San Stae (1)

14 Chiesa di San Stae The name is old Venetian dialect for *Sant' Eustachio*. As with most Venetian churches, **San Stae** was remodeled at various times—the original building dates back to the 12th century.

As can be seen from the Canal Grande, the facade, richly decorated with statues, is one of the finest examples of Venetian Baroque. The interior is particularly interesting for art historians because it includes a wealth of paintings from the first half of the 18th century. The artists are not among the most famous (Camerata, Pittoni, Bambini, Balestra), but their work illustrates the process that produced painters like Tiepolo and Piazzetta. Piazzetta himself is represented here on the lower left of the chancel (*The Martyrdom of St. James*), and there is a youthful Tiepolo on the lower right (*The Martyrdom of St. Barthelmy*). Next to the Piazzetta is *St. Peter Freed from Prison* by Sebastiano Ricci, who also painted the chancel's ceiling. Ricci was one of the painters most influential in merging the new trends developed by the Roman Baroque painters with the Venetian tradition of Veronese, thus opening the way to the last great season of painting in Venice. The most significant of his paintings are in the **Carmini Church,** the **San Rocco Church,** and the **Accademia Gallery.** The church is a frequent venue for concerts of Baroque chamber music. ◆ Campo San Stae (on Canal Grande). Vaporetto stop: San Stae (1)

15 Centro degli Studi di Storia del Tessuto e del Costume (Center for the Study of Textile and Clothing History) This unusual center has a large collection of original textiles from the 16th, 17th, and 18th centuries, together with a library that specializes in textiles and antique prints. Scholars and students can identify the material in the library's files and ask for samples to be brought to their tables. ◆ Library: Tu-W, Sa. Salizzada di San Stae 1992 (southwest of Campo San Stae). 721798. Vaporetto stop: San Stae (1)

16 Campo Santa Maria Mater Domini This delightful little campo is bounded on one side by a canal and on the other three sides by small Gothic palazzi that are among the most charming in Venice. **Casa Zane (No. 2172),** in Veneto-Byzantine style, dates back to the 13th century; across from it is **Casa Barbaro (No. 2173),** about a century younger; on the fourth side is **Palazzo Viaro-Zane (No. 2123),** built early in the 14th century (the third floor, in Renaissance style, was added later). The *campo* gives you a glimpse of Venice as it was before the introduction of the Florentine and Roman Renaissance: smaller and more intimate buildings, grace and lightness instead of majestic corpulence. The blacksmith near the bridge works outdoors in the summer; his ancestors are the cause of the smoky grayness of the stones around his shop. ◆ Southwest of Ca' Pesaro on Rio della Pergola. Vaporetto stop: San Stae (1)

Celluloid Cities

Whether they were searching for an airy Renaissance light or brooding Gothic menace, movie directors have long turned to Florence, Venice, and Milan for inspiration. Among the films to take advantage of the unique settings in these three cities are the following:

FLORENCE

Much Ado About Nothing (1993) Directed by and starring Kenneth Branagh, this film tells the tale of Benedick (Branagh) and Beatrice (Emma Thompson) who have sworn never to marry, but are tricked into falling in love with each other anyway. This lively version of Shakespeare's witty and romantic comedy is set and shot entirely in and around an Italian villa in Tuscany.

Paisan (1946) This early Roberto Rossellini and Federico Fellini classic uses six vignettes to depict life in Italy during World War II. The best has an American nurse (Harriet White) searching for her lover in battle-torn Florence.

A Room With a View (1986) This elegant and witty adaptation of the E.M. Forster novel about English mores brings to life an innocent girl (Helena Bonhame Carter), who arrives in Florence with her chaperone (Maggie Smith) to spend time in the city. The well-reared Edwardian girl has her eyes opened to real life and romance, falling in love in the process.

VENICE

The Comfort of Strangers (1990) Natasha Richardson and Rupert Everett star in this bleak and icy tale about a conventional couple on vacation in Venice, where they become involved with mysterious locals (Christopher Walken and Helen Mirren).

Death in Venice (1971) Thomas Mann's slow-moving classic is brought to the screen by director Luchino Visconti. An artist (Dirk Bogarde) is caught up in his life, his loves, his homosexuality, and a continuous search for everlasting beauty. The musical score is by Gustav Mahler, whom Bogarde is made-up to resemble.

Don't Look Now (1973) An arty, gripping Daphne du Maurier occult thriller follows the parents (Julie Christie and Donald Sutherland) of a drowned child through their horror-laden visit to Venice.

From Russia With Love (1963) Starring Sean Connery, the second James Bond film is one of the best. In true 007 style, a highly charged boat chase, with plenty of suspense and action, winds through the waterways of Venice.

Summertime (1955) David Lean directs this lilting film about an American spinster (Katherine Hepburn) vacationing in Venice and falling in love with a married man (Rossano Brazzi).

Venice/Venice (1992) Director Henry Jaglom pretentiously parodies himself, playing a "maverick" American filmmaker at the Venice Film Festival, where a French journalist (Nelly Alard) becomes involved with him. The title refers to Venice, Italy, and Venice, California, where the director also is shown to have a coterie of admirers.

MILAN

All Screwed Up (1973) Lina Wertmuller directs this appealing tragicomedy about various young working-class men and women, and what happens when they move into a Milan apartment.

Miracle in Milan (1951) Vittorio de Sica directs a bitingly comic film, condemning the manner in which displaced Europeans were treated after World War II. Toto the Good (Francesco Golisano) brings cheer to a dreary village of poor people, aided by the old lady—now in heaven—who raised him.

Rocco and His Brothers (1960) In order to make a better life for herself and five sons, a poor farm woman (Annie Girardot) moves to Milan. This engrossing film, directed by Luchino Visconti, portrays their urban experiences.

The Stolen Children (1992) "Il Ladro di Bambini" is the story of a young cop (Enrico Lo Verco) who travels across Italy to a children's home with an 11-year-old girl (Valentina Scalici)—who has been forced to become a prostitute by her mother—and her younger brother (Giuseppe Ieracitano).

17 Ca' Pesaro Early in the 17th century, the wealthy Pesaro family acquired three adjacent buildings on the Canal Grande and asked the fashionable architect **Baldassare Longhena** to create an imposing palazzo. The result is probably the most successful among the Baroque palazzi in Venice. The facade must be seen from the Canal Grande if you are to appreciate its grandeur and elegance. The building changed hands a few times, until Duchess Bevilacqua La Masa, the last owner, donated it to the city in 1889. The water entrance, now little used, is marked by stairs, as if for a building on land. ♦ Fondamenta Pesaro 2076 (east of Campo San Stae on the Canal Grande). 721127. Vaporetto stop: San Stae (1)

Within Ca' Pesaro:

Museo d'Arte Moderna Ca' Pesaro
The street entrance of this palazzo leads to a Baroque courtyard and an 18th-century staircase. The **Museo d'Arte Moderna** occupies the first two floors of the palazzo, one of which was closed for renovation at press time. The bulk of the collection consists of paintings and other works of art chosen from those exhibited at the *Venice Biennale* since its opening in 1895. It's hard to come up with well-known European-centered 20th-century painters who are not represented in this rich collection (although not always by their best works): Vedova, Morandi, Boccioni, De Chirico, Sironi, and Rosai are just a few of the Italians, while painters from other countries include Chagall, Dufy, Kandinsky, Klee, Ernst, and Klimt. ♦ Admission. Tu-Su. 721127

Museo d'Arte Orientale Located in the same palazzo as the **Museo d'Arte Moderna,** this museum was built around the collection of Duke Henry of Bourbon, a tireless traveler and acquirer of Oriental objects. It specializes in Japanese art (particularly armor and swords), but also includes rooms devoted to India, China, and Indonesia. ♦ Admission. Tu-Su. 5241173

18 Hotel San Cassiano $$ In the second half of the 19th century, painter Giacomo Favretto owned this small, handsome, 14th-century palazzo, elements  of which date back to the 11th century. His house has been remodeled into a hotel, though most of the features of the palazzo were lost in the process. The interior now looks more like a comfortable, old-fashioned hotel than an ancient palazzo. A few of the 36 rooms have beautiful Gothic windows overlooking the Canal Grande. This is one of the few hotels in the neighborhood, since most visitors prefer to cluster around **Piazza San Marco.** There is no restaurant. ♦ Calle della Rosa 2232 (on Canal Grande near Campo San Cassiano). 5241768; fax 721033. Vaporetto stop: San Stae (1)

19 Osteria Al Nono Risorto ★★$ This old wine shop was bought and remodeled by the son of Dino Boscarato, one of Venice's great restaurateurs. In keeping with the shop's tradition, the restaurant is very informal, even slightly bohemian. But class with a capital C is evident in the quality of both the food and service—find confirmation in the spicy gnocchi *alla busera* (with scampi in a tomato base). The side garden is heaven in the summer, when it is scented with the perfume of a large wisteria tree. ♦ Tu-Su lunch and dinner. No credit cards. Sotoportego di Siora Bettina 2338 (near Campo San Cassiano). 5241169. Vaporetto stop: San Stae (1)

Bests

Marcella Hazan
Chef/Cookbook Author

The historic open-air fish and produce market at the **Rialto.** Along with the markets in Cagliari and Palermo, it is one of Italy's most thrilling displays of food, replenished daily with produce from the farm islands of the Venetian lagoon and with a dazzling variety of fish pulled in each night from the seemingly inexhaustible Adriatic.

After 11PM, the *No. 1 vaporetto* going up the **Canal Grande** toward **San Marco.** At sunset, the *No. 52 vaporetto* line from the **Fondamente Nuove** to the **Giudecca.**

The **Museo Storico Navale (Naval Museum).**

The **Chiesa di Santa Maria dei Miracoli.**

The astonishing marble interior of the **Chiesa dei Gesuiti.**

Chamber music concerts at the **Vivaldi Church (La Pietà).**

Pizza al fresco at **Bar Al Teatro,** while watching everyone in Venice who has not gone to bed walk by.Saturday lunch at **Da Fiore** (near **Campo San Polo**), the best seafood restaurant in the western world.

Chocolate ice cream at the bar by the **Hotel Cipriani** pool: the most beautiful people in Venice and the darkest, richest chocolate anywhere.

The embankment on the **Giudecca**: the best place in Venice to look at Venice. Sit on a bench and watch the sun setting or take a long, uncrowded walk.

Eleven PM on the Saturday before the third Sunday in July, sitting in a boat anchored in **St. Mark**'s basin, watching the fireworks burst out of the blue-black Venetian night.

CANNAREGIO

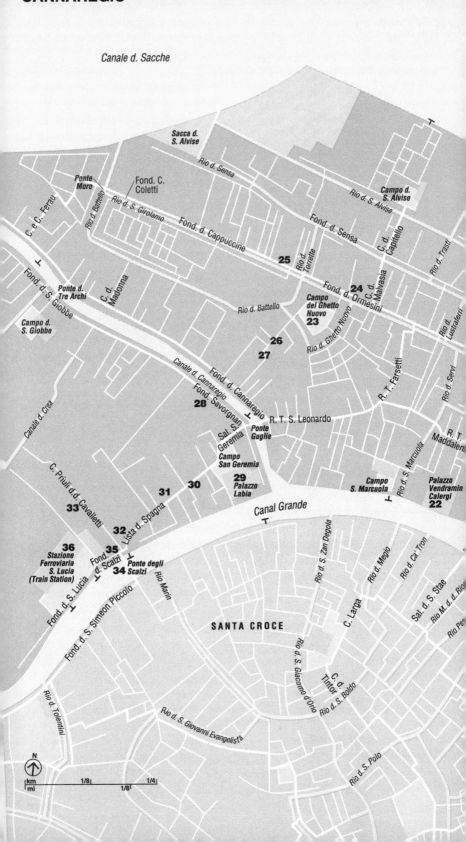

Canale d. Sacche

Sacca d.
S. Alvise

Rio d. Sensa

Ponte
Moro

Fond. C.
Coletti

Rio d. S. Girolamo

Rio d. Battello

C. e C. Ferau

Fond. d. Cappuccine

Rio d. S. Alvise

Campo d.
S. Alvise

Fond. d. Sensa

C. d.
Capitello

Rio d. Trasti

25

Rio d.
Torrette

Fond. d. S. Giobbe

Ponte d.
Tre Archi

C. d.
Madonna

Rio d. Battello

Fond. d. Ormesini

24

C. d.
Malvasia

Campo d.
S. Giobbe

Campo
del Ghetto
Nuovo
23

Rio d. Ghetto Nuovo

Rio d. Lustraferri

26

Rio d. Servi

27

Canale d. Crea

Canale d. Cannaregio

Fond. d. Cannaregio

R. T. Farsetti

Fond. Savorgnan

28

R. T. S. Leonardo

R. T.
Maddalena

Sal. S.
Geremia

Ponte
Guglie

C. Priuli d.d. Cavalletti

Campo
San Geremia

Campo
S. Marcuola

Rio d. S. Marcuola

Palazzo
Vendramin
Calergi
22

31

30

29
Palazzo
Labia

Lista d. Spagna

33

Canal Grande

Rio d. S. Zan Degola

32

36
Stazione
Ferroviaria
S. Lucia
(Train Station)

35

Fond.
d. Scalzi

34

Ponte degli
Scalzi

Rio Marin

C. Larga

Rio d. Meglio

Rio d. Cà Tron

Sal. d. S. Stae

Rio M. d. Rio d.

Fond. d. S. Lucia

Fond. d. S. Simeon Piccolo

SANTA CROCE

Rio d. S. Giacomo d'Orio

C. d.
Tintor

Rio d. S. Boldo

Rio Pe

Rio d. Tolentini

Rio d. S. Giovanni Evangelista

Rio d. S. Polo

N

km
mi

1/8   1/4

1/8

Canale d. Navi

21 Chiesa della
Madonna
dell'Orto

Rio Braso

19

20
Palazzo
Mastelli

C. Larga

Rio d. Madonna d'Orto

Rio d. Muti

Sacca d. Misericordia

ond. d. Misericordia

Rio d. Ca Moro

Rio d. Trapolin Grimani

Rio d. Misericordia

Rio d. Sensa

18 **17**

16
15

Canale d. Misericordia

Rio d. S. Caterina

Fond. Nuove

C. lunga S. Caterina

10 **9**

Rio d. Gesuiti

Strada Nuova

Rio d. Maddalena

Rio d. S. Fosca

Ponte
Pasqualigo

C. d. Racchetta

14

Rio d.
S. Andrea

Rio d. Racchetta

11

Fond. Nuove

Rio d. Noale

Rio d. S. Felice

C. Larga

Doge Priuli

Rio Priuli

Rio d. Ca Dolce

Rio d. Sartori

Fond. Nuove

Ponte
S. Felice

13

Rio d.
Torri

Strada Nuova

12

Rio d. S. Cassiano

8

7

6 Chiesa dei
SS. Apostoli

Rio d. S. Canciano

Fond. d. Mendicanti

Rio d. P. d.
Beccarie

Rio d. SS. Apostoli

Sal. S. Canciano

C. l.
Giacinto Gallina

Campo
Santa Maria
Nova **5**

Rio d. S. Giovanni Grisostomo

4

Sal. d. S. G.
Grisostomo

3

2

Rio d. Miracoli

Rio d. S. Marina

Campo d.
SS. Giovanni
e Paolo

SAN POLO

Ruga d. Orefici

Rio d. Fontego

1

Ponte di
d. Tedeschi

Ponte di
Rialto

CASTELLO

Cannaregio

Except for the **Ghetto** and the bustling **Strada Nuova**, Cannaregio is largely unknown to the average visitor. This may be why the *sestiere* has preserved its ancient characteristics—and characters. Parallel to the lagoon border on the north side are three small canals. It is hard to decide which is more charming or typically Venetian. Houses along them are usually no higher than three stories, bridges are tiny and often made of wood, and life goes on largely oblivious to the activity on Strada Nuova. The canals here run east-west, making them a wonderful place for a stroll at sunset, when a golden light seems to fill the houses, the bridges, the water, and the old wooden boats tied along the banks. Be sure to walk past the church of **Madonna dell'Orto** at sunset, continuing on to the *vaporetto* stop of the same name. It is a lonely stop, with few if any waiting passengers. It sits on the bank of the open lagoon, with **Murano** in front, **Burano** and the terra firma in the distance. The sun sets over the lagoon to the left, and a light sea breeze usually ripples the water. On clear days even the local commuters can't stop gazing at the sight—the most spectacular sunset in Venice.

1 Coin The name has nothing to do with the English word "coin"; it's pronounced *co-'een* and, like Benetton and Stefanel, it is the name of a family of entrepreneurs who expanded out of the Venice area to conquer national and international markets. The largest of the retailer's stores is in Mestre, just across the lagoon bridge from Venice, while other stores are scattered throughout Italy. The Cannaregio branch specializes in clothing and beauty and fashion accessories, and is probably the most elegant of all the store's branches. Venetians are fond of it, and visitors might want to explore it to get an idea of the quality and prices of goods in a middle-to-high-end Italian department store. The third-floor housewares department is particularly worth a peek. ♦ M-Sa Mar-Oct; M afternoon, Tu-Sa Nov-Feb. Salizzada di San Giovanni Grisostomo 5787 (near Campo San G. Grisostomo). 5203581. Vaporetto stop: Rialto (1, 82)

2 Corti del Milion The *Milion* in the name comes from the title of Marco Polo's memoirs of his marvelous journeys to the Far East. In the maze of alleys just east of **Campo San Giovanni Grisostomo**, at **No. 5845** in the Corte Seconda del Milion, is where the famous explorer was probably born in 1254. The house has been modified many times over the centuries, but like the others in this little square, it preserves an unmistakably Byzantine character. Some of the window frames and columns and all of the round bas-reliefs date back to the 11th and 12th centuries. ♦ Corte Prima del Milion and Corte Seconda del Milion (near Campo San G. Grisostomo). Vaporetto stop: Rialto (1, 82)

2 Osteria Al Milion ★★$$ Informal, inexpensive, and well run, this restaurant is popular with Venetians and tourists alike. Some dishes are exactly the same as those you would find in more expensive restaurants. Try the risotto with arugula and shrimp or the filet of dory à la Milion. The house wine is good, too. ♦ M-Tu, Th-Su lunch and dinner. Reservations recommended. No credit cards accepted. Corte Prima del Milion 5841 (near Campo San G. Grisostomo). 5229302. Vaporetto stop: Rialto (1, 82)

3 Chiesa di San Giovanni Grisostomo This late 15th-century church by **Mauro Codussi** lies at the center of a small island defined by the Canal Grande on the west and by three tiny, charming canals on the other sides. This was one of the first areas settled by the founders of the city and one that still maintains traces of its original Byzantine character. The church, however, is pure Venetian Renaissance; the original structure was destroyed by a fire and entirely rebuilt by **Codussi,** the Lombard-born master who changed the face of Venetian architecture by introducing Renaissance models to replace the late-Gothic tradition (see **San Michele, San Zaccaria,** and **Santa Maria Formosa**). The facade has the typical **Codussi** design—a full, round arch on the top with two half-arches on the sides. **Codussi**'s interior is a masterpiece of clarity and simplicity. On the first altar at the right is one of the last and best paintings by Giovanni Bellini: *St. Christopher with St. Jerome and St. Augustine*. The canvas on the main altar is *St. John Chrysostomos with Other Saints* by Sebastiano del Piombo, painted by the artist when he was 25 and just before the pope summoned him to Rome and launched his brilliant career. ♦ Salizzada di San Giovanni Grisostomo (in Campo San G. Grisostomo). Vaporetto stop: Rialto (1, 82)

Restaurants/Clubs: Red   Hotels: Blue
Shops/♥ Outdoors: Green   Sights/Culture: Black

4 Fiaschetteria Toscana ★★★$$$ In spite of the name, which means Tuscan Wine Shop, this elegant restaurant decorated in typical Venetian style specializes in traditional Venetian cooking. Owner Albino Busato is the head of the association of Venetian restaurateurs and a true culinary professional. Service is impeccable, and the wine list is one of the best in town. Although this is also a good choice in Venice for a meat-based menu, begin with the house specialty *gnocchi al pesce* (homemade gnocchi with a light fish sauce). Try not to leave without having tasted the *tarte tartin,* a warm apple cake made daily by the owner's wife, Mariuccia. ♦ M-Su lunch and dinner. Reservations recommended, especially for outside tables. Salizzada di San Giovanni Grisostomo 5719 (in Campo San G. Grisostomo). 5285281. Vaporetto stop: Rialto (1, 82)

5 Chiesa di Santa Maria dei Miracoli The particular charm of this small church, built in 1489, is its location at the crossing of two of the most handsome canals in Venice. One side of the church is covered with precious polychrome marbles and runs directly along the water, creating ever-changing reflections. The facade opens onto a tiny square and an equally small bridge. The creator of this jewel was **Pietro Lombardo,** one of the fathers of the Venetian Renaissance (it is possible that **Mauro Codussi** authored the original plan). Venetian couples love to use this church for weddings: The elegant, cozy interior with its hues of pink, gray, and white, offers a soft, romantic light, while the square in front is a perfect place for guests to arrive and leave on gondolas. ♦ Campiello dei Miracoli (across the canal from Campo Santa Maria Nuova). Vaporetto stop: Rialto (1, 82)

6 Chiesa dei SS. Apostoli The relatively high banks of the islands in this part of Venice made them desirable for early settlers. The foundations of this church date back to the seventh century; however, its present shape is due to a radical renovation in the 17th century. Inside, the first chapel at the right is the **Cappella Corner,** attributed to **Mauro Codussi** and adorned with *The Communion of St. Lucy,* one of Giambattista Tiepolo's best paintings. ♦ Campo dei Santissimi Apostoli (at the eastern end of Strada Nuova). Vaporetto stops: Rialto (1, 82); Ca' d'Oro (1)

7 Locanda ai Santi Apostoli $$$ The Bianchi-Michiel family has lovingly restored its patrician home (parts of it dating to the 15th century) on the Canal Grande and made the third floor into a small and very special hotel. The 11 rooms are tastefully decorated with a choice selection of the family's elegant antiques. Request rooms **8** or **9**—the only two directly on the canal—the view is well worth the additional cost. The second floor is an apartment that can also be rented. ♦ Strada Nuova 4391 (off Campo dei Santissimi Apostoli). 5212612; fax 5212611. Vaporetto stops: Rialto (1, 82); Ca' d'Oro (1)

8 Strada Nuova The **Campo dei Santissimi Apostoli** marks the beginning of this long, wide (for Venice), and unusually straight street. It runs parallel to the Canal Grande from **Santissimi Apostoli** to **Campo Santa Fosca,** crossing two canals and continuing with the relatively wide Rio Terrà Maddalena and Rio Terrà San Leonardo before leading into the Lista di Spagna, which terminates at the train station. The street was designed and built in the 19th century, and it represents one of the few attempts to accommodate pedestrian traffic in Venice. It addressed the problem of connecting the central Rialto and St. Mark's areas with the new train station, which had joined Venice to the mainland for the first time in the city's history. Among the many proposals, the one that was finally chosen was probably the least damaging to the existing urban structure, but it destroyed a large, ancient neighborhood, characterized by tiny alleys and teeming daily life. All buildings that stood in the way of the new thoroughfare were destroyed, and new facades were erected along its perfectly straight, totally un-Venetian sides. The residents showed their disapproval by refusing to call the new street by the name proposed by its builders, calling it Strada Nuova instead, making this the only *strada* (street) in Venice. Today the steady flow of day-trippers arriving by train use the route extensively. The heavy pedestrian traffic toward the Rialto in the morning and toward the train station in the afternoon precipitated the proliferation of souvenir shops, making this the kingdom of Venice T-shirts and plastic gondolas. A few yards away, opposite the Canal Grande, the city remains blessedly deserted and perfectly charming, with the old labyrinth of *calli* (the local word for streets), bridges, and porticoes. ♦ Strada Nuova (west of Campo dei Santissimi Apostoli). Vaporetto stops: Ca' d'Oro (1); San Marcuola (1)

9 Fondamente Nuove The word *fondamente* is used in Venice for the paved banks of the canals and of the open lagoon. The borders of the natural islands were—and still are—reinforced with foundations made of wood poles and stone to prevent erosion by the waves and tides. The long banks called Fondamente Nuove were built in the 16th century as part of a reclamation effort that involved the whole northeastern part of the city. Far from the typical tourist tracks (except for the small part used by *vaporetti* to and from Murano, Torcello, and other islands), they constitute a splendid, although somewhat melancholy, walk, particularly during the long summer evenings. The nearest island visible from here, recognizable by its cypress trees, is San Michele, site of the Venice cemetery. Beyond that is Murano and, in the distance, the slanted bell tower of Burano. On a clear day it is not unusual to see all the way to the mainland and the snow-capped mountains of the Alps. There is a channel along the Fondamente for boat traffic. Beyond the channel, marked by the typical wood poles called *bricole,* the lagoon is not deeper than three feet and motorboats can cross it only at high tide. An hour's walk along the Fondamente is a romantic experience and a way to see the daily rituals of Venetian life—on weekdays, heavy boats pass by, carrying goods to be distributed all over town, while on Sundays and in the evenings, a surprising number of rowboats cross the area, with Venetians doing their equivalent of jogging. Flat-bottomed sailboats, old-fashioned craft with balanced lug sails that are ideal for the flat lagoon waters, are enjoying a Renaissance among Venetians, who now shun polluting powerboats. ♦ East and west of Chiesa dei Gesuiti. Vaporetto stop: Fondamente Nuove (12, 13, 52, 52 sinistra)

10 Chiesa dei Gesuiti When it was readmitted to Venice after a 50-year banishment in 1657, the Jesuit order took over this church, which overlooks the beautiful lagoon toward the cemetery and Murano. The Jesuits then proceeded to rebuild the 13th-century church—according to their well-established standards of grandeur—in the international Baroque style they had successfully experimented with in Rome (Chiesa del Gesù), Paris (St. Paul), and all over Europe. The facade is tall and emphatic, with the Jesuit trademark of columns on two levels. It is topped by Baroque statues with limbs reaching skyward in typical Baroque poses. But the real magnificence is in the interior, which is decorated with a stunning wealth of marble carved to imitate damasks and draperies. White and green marble covers most of the walls, falling in rich folds like real drapery material and creating an effect that, depending on the viewer's taste, could be thought of as marvelous or kitsch. The canvas on the first altar at the right is *The Martyrdom of Saint Lawrence,* a masterwork painted by Titian on his return from Rome (which might explain the Classical architecture in the background, not characteristic of Titian). The painting immediately became famous. Titian himself made a copy of it for Philip II of Spain, and a popular engraving, based on the painting and approved by Titian, soon circulated all over Europe. A cleaning

performed for the Titian exhibition in Venice and Washington, DC, in 1990 brought out the fine details of this nighttime scene, where the only sources of light are the burning coals under the martyr's body and the divine rays breaking through thick, black clouds in the sky. ♦ Campo dei Gesuiti (south of Fondamente Nuove). Vaporetto stop: Fondamente Nuove (12, 13, 52, 52 sinistra)

11 Oratorio dei Crociferi The *Crociferi* were a monastic order that once owned this entire area, including the square in front of the oratory, the church, and the large building at the church's right (originally their monastery). The oratory was an extra chapel. Restored in the 1980s, it contains a cycle of paintings by Palma il Giovane, who is considered the heir of Titian and the best painter of Venetian Mannerism. Palma's works, which mark the passage between the late-Renaissance and Baroque periods, are found throughout Venice. ♦ Admission. F-Su; to confirm schedule, call 5200633. Campo dei Gesuiti 4903-4905 (south of Fondamente Nuove). Vaporetto stop: Fondamente Nuove (12, 13, 52, 52 sinistra)

12 Ca' d'Oro The facade of this splendid 15th-century building by **Matteo Reverti,** universally considered a masterwork of Venetian Gothic, should be seen from the Canal Grande. The facade was recently restored to its original splendid state. In striking contrast with medieval building principles, the Venetian palazzi have light facades made of carved stone, with ample loggias and open spaces between slender columns. Nothing could be further from the austere, almost hostile, appearance of the medieval and Renaissance palazzi of Florence, but the leading Florentine families were constantly fighting each other and needed to build their homes like fortresses, while the Venetian constitution guaranteed peace within the city limits (there are no examples of armed feuds among leading families nor of any popular insurrection during the millennium of the Republic's life). Hence the open loggias, the ample windows, and the very fragility of the Venetian facades—perhaps more an act of faith in the serene Republic than an aesthetic choice.

In the **Ca' d'Oro,** the central part of the facade can be seen as a unique window, made precious by the lacework applied to the stones. Originally the facade was decorated in red and blue and trimmed with gold leaf, which gave the palazzo its name, **House of Gold.** Ironically, the name no longer fits. The restoration stripped the marbel of all its guilt work, as well as the red and blue embellishment. The building changed hands a number of times after it was built in 1440, until it was acquired by a Russian prince who presented it to an Italian ballerina in 1840. Later it passed on to Baron Giorgio Franchetti, who restored it and bequeathed it to the city of Venice. ◆ Calle della Ca' d'Oro 3932 (off Strada Nuova). Vaporetto stop: Ca' d'Oro (1)

In Ca' d'Oro:

Galleria Franchetti The gallery housed in the **Ca' d'Oro** (which will remain open throughout the restoration) was built around a core collection bequeathed to the city by Giorgio Franchetti and reorganized in 1984. On the second floor is an extraordinary collection of early Venetian and Byzantine bas-reliefs in stone, dating from the 11th to 13th centuries. They were used to decorate the facades of public and private buildings, and they exhibit a delightful sense of symmetry and grace. A niche in **Room 1** contains a famous *Saint Sebastian* by Andrea Mantegna. Through the splendid, sunlit ballroom, one can reach the loggia on the Canal Grande and—once the scaffolding is removed—enjoy the view over a long stretch of the canal and of the *Pescheria* (fish market) on the other side. **Room 3** contains medals and bronzes of the Renaissance, and **Room 6** has a fine collection of minor Italian painters, mostly Tuscans. On the third floor, **Room 9** contains *Venus at the Mirror* by Titian, and two remarkable portraits of gentlemen, one by Tintoretto and one by Anthony Van Dyck. Collected in **Room 16** are the few remnants of the frescoes that used to cover the **Fondaco dei Tedeschi** (Germans' Warehouse) on the Canal Grande. Although barely recognizable, they have an emotional impact on art lovers because they are by Giorgione and Titian, who worked almost shoulder to shoulder on the same facade. Other items of interest on this floor include Bernini's preparatory work for his famous fountain on Piazza Navona in Rome, and two Views of Venice by Francesco Guardi. ◆ Admission. Daily. Calle della Ca' d'Oro 3932 (off Strada Nuova). Vaporetto stop: Ca' d'Oro (1)

13 Osteria dalla Vedova ★★$$ Old bare wooden tables, antique furniture, and total informality characterize this most venerable of Venetian *bacari* (taverns). The owners have retained the original atmosphere of a working-class wine bar, with ready-made food available at the counter to accompany the drinks. An eclectic group of wealthy Venetians, gondoliers, and hard-hats frequent the place. The owners speak a little English, and have been serving tourists for years. Upon entering, check the counter for the choice of food, but ask about what's cooking as well—it may be worth sipping your wine for a few minutes while the risottos, spaghetti, or *pasta e fagioli* (pasta and beans) receive their final touches. The official name of the place, written on top of the door, is **Trattoria Ca' d'Oro,** but all Venice knows it as **dalla Vedova** (at the widow's). ◆ M-W, F-Su lunch and dinner. Reservations for large groups. No credit cards accepted. Ramo Ca' d'Oro 3912 (near Ca' d'Oro). 5285324. Vaporetto stop: Ca' d'Oro (1)

14 Trattoria All'Antica Adelaide ★★$$ Also informal, this trattoria lost some of its old charm when Gianni, the owner's son, brought in new wooden tables to increase the seating in the large dining room. But in the summer, dining moves outdoors to a lovely courtyard—a decided advantage over the rival **Osteria dalla Vedova.** Among the many seafood dishes, the grilled *mazzancolle* (jumbo shrimp) is recommended. But the owner, Gianni's mother, is a virtuoso of Venetian cooking, and if money is no object, call her to your table to see what she recommends. ◆ Tu-Su lunch and dinner. No credit cards accepted. Calle della Racchetta 3728 (north of Strada Nuova). 5203451. Vaporetto stop: Ca' d'Oro (1)

15 Fondamenta della Misericordia The name of this canal bank changes five times before ending in the northwest area called Sant'Alvise. A walk along this stretch offers a glimpse of the quiet, old-fashioned charm of the area. ◆ Along the Rio della Misericordia and San Girolamo. Vaporetto stops: Ca' d'Oro (1); San Marcuola (1, 82); Madonna dell'Orto (52)

16 Scuola Nuova della Misericordia The building, unusually tall for this part of town, was designed in 1583 by **Jacopo Sansovino** for a local charitable brotherhood and was never completed. The interior, also by **Sansovino,** has been neglected by the city. For 50 years, until 1990, the hall on the second floor was used as a stadium, with seats for hundreds of spectators right under the decaying 16th-century frescoes. A *fondamenta* along the building's east side leads to the Ponte dell'Abbazia, which has a charming view over the Canale della Misericordia to the open lagoon. ◆ Fondamenta della Misericordia 3599 (at Canale della Misericordia). Vaporetto stop: Ca' d'Oro (1)

17 Chiesa di Santa Maria Valverde The name of this 14th-century church, which means Church of Santa Maria in the Green Valley, was derived from the original landscape of the area, which was probably once covered with vegetable gardens. Secluded as it seems to be on the water's edge, with canals in front and on the right side, this small, delightful church used to be the main chapel for the friars of the abbey of the nearby **Scuola Vecchia della Misericordia**. The facade, designed by **Clemente Moli,** is a remarkable example of elegant, surprisingly sober Baroque architecture. The statue over the portal is not, as one would expect, the portrait of a saint but a monument to Gaspare Moro, the patrician who financed the works on the facade. ♦ Campo dell'Abbazia (on Canale della Misericordia). Vaporetto stop: Ca' d'Oro (1)

18 Scuola Vecchia della Misericordia This charitable association of laymen (connected to the abbey of the same name), was housed in this 15th-century *scuola* (school) along the canal called Rio della Sensa. The late-Gothic facade of the *scuola,* at right angles with the Baroque church of **Santa Maria Valverde,** completes one of the most pleasant little squares in Venice. Today the *scuola* and abbey belong to the city and house one of the most advanced centers for stone restoration in the world. Peep through the small door on the Rio della Sensa to see the large garden, behind which are the sophisticated laboratories where international experts examine stones and marbles from monuments all over the world, studying their composition and figuring out how to preserve them. ♦ Campo dell'Abbazia 3551 (on Rio della Sensa). Vaporetto stop: Madonna dell'Orto (52)

19 Campo dei Mori Four merchants of Arabic origin—and ancestors of the Mastelli family of Arab heritage—had their headquarters in this part of town in the 12th century. The Moors are portrayed, turban and all, in four 13th-century statues (three on the square and one along the canal). ♦ On Fondamenta della Sensa (next to Palazzo Mastelli). Vaporetto stop: Madonna dell'Orto (52)

20 Palazzo Mastelli The Mastelli family—merchants who arrived in Venice in AD 112 from the Peloponnesus—had this palazzo built in the 12th century. Some remnants of the original Byzantine decorations are still visible, but the most admired feature is the large stone camel in a bas-relief on the facade along the Rio della Madonna dell'Orto—a reminder of the origin of the family's wealth in the spice trade. On the same facade, a Gothic balcony sits curiously on top of a Renaissance first floor, in an unusual reversal of history. Look at the palazzo from the *fondamenta* across the canal. ♦ Fondamenta Gasparo Contarini 3527 (near Campo della Madonna dell'Orto). Vaporetto stop: Madonna dell'Orto (52)

21 Chiesa della Madonna dell'Orto This most sober yet pleasing of Gothic churches opens onto a lovely, well-proportioned square along a quiet canal with the same name. The statues in the beautiful niches over the sides represent the 12 Apostles. The five statues at the very top represent the Virgin Mary and the four Evangelists.

Inside this unpretentious 15th-century church is a surprising wealth of first-class paintings painstakingly restored after severe damage by the 1966 floods. At the first altar on the right is one of the most beautiful paintings by Cima da Conegliano, *St. John the Baptist Among the Four Saints,* in which the 34-year-old artist, just after his arrival in Venice from his native village of Conegliano, dared to replace the traditional gold background—or the more recent perspectives of Classical buildings—with a landscape of the beautiful hills where he had grown up. The first altar on the left contains a jewel by Giovanni Bellini, a *Virgin Mary with Child,* which epitomizes Bellini's craft in the painting of Madonnas. On the apse and behind the altar is a group of large canvases by Jacopo Tintoretto, who lived near the church (at **No. 3399** on Fondamenta dei Mori) and is buried inside it, in the last chapel on the right. On the left wall of the chancel is Tintoretto's gigantic *Adoration of the Golden Calf,* a painting strangely and dramatically divided into three horizontal sections. Behind the altar, Tintoretto painted *The Martyrdom of St. Christopher* and *The Apparition of the Holy Cross to St. Peter.* On the right wall is another huge canvas, *The Last Judgment,* with Christ and the Virgin Mary surrounded by angels and saints while a stormy whirlpool carries away the damned souls, with Charon's boat appearing on a background of fire. Tintoretto's *Presentation of the Virgin to the Temple,* on the right side over the door to the last chapel before the chancel, is also dramatically beautiful. ♦ Campo della Madonna dell'Orto. Vaporetto stop: Madonna dell'Orto (52)

22 Palazzo Vendramin Calergi The facade of this 15th-century palazzo facing the Canal Grande was the first great achievement of **Mauro Codussi,** the artist who changed Venetian architecture by abandoning the Gothic tradition for the new Renaissance style popular in Florence and Rome. Richard Wagner lived in this palazzo and died here in 1883. Today it belongs to the city of Venice and is used in the winter for the **Casino,** whose summer home is in a far less impressive modern location on the Lido. (At press time there were plans to relocate the **Casino** to a year-round mainland location easily accessible by car.) From October to early May, gamblers flock to the **Casino,** one of only four allowed on national territory by Italian legislation. A couple dozen roulette tables are installed in the Renaissance rooms, with bets taken from 10,000 lire up; baccarat and blackjack tables are also available. A few water taxis are always stationed at the door at night, ready to take the winners to their hotels or to their cars parked on **Piazzale Roma**—the losers can walk. ♦ Casino: Daily 3PM-3AM. Fondamenta Vendramin 2400 (off Rio Terrà della Maddalena on Canal Grande). 5297111; Casino: 5297111. Vaporetto stop: San Marcuola (1, 82)

23 Campo del Ghetto Nuovo A look at the map shows how perfectly this small island lent itself to housing a community separate from the rest of the city. Heavy gates were built at the end of the only three bridges (traces of their hinges are still visible), and they were closed at sunset and reopened on the following morning. Jews in Venice were confined to this space in the 16th century and were allowed to move out of it only when young Napoleon conquered the Republic in 1797. The "ghetto" in the square's name is derived from *gettare,* old Venetian dialect for to cast in metal, referring to a foundry that was located here. The generic name would spread throughout the world to refer to confined ethnic quarters of a city and later to poor areas. Jews of many nationalities moved to this area, particularly after they were banished from Spain in 1492. They spoke German, Spanish, Italian, and a variety of Asian languages; and though they were accepted as permanent residents, they were often subjected to a series of hard conditions and were under constant threat of expulsion. They were not allowed to own any land or buildings; they could not practice any professions, except to sell used clothes and objects; and at times, to practice medicine; and above all they were obliged to run three pawn shops at impossibly low interest rates—an absolute requirement in order to avoid expulsion and keep the economy of the Republic afloat. The pawn shops took heavy losses, and Jewish communities from all over Europe had to cover their debts to keep them open. The houses on the small island were built around a central square that once housed no fewer than 60 tailors' shops and three moneylenders' offices. As new families came in, extra floors were added to the buildings (some apartment ceiling heights are under six feet!). These "Venetian skyscrapers," some seven, eight, or even nine stories high (and without elevators), can still be seen.

Today the square is a wide and peaceful space, ideal for neighborhood children to play in while mothers watch from their apartment windows. Although a handful of Jewish families still live in the ghetto, only a kosher baker and a couple of souvenir shops remain from the colorful mixture of languages and nationalities that once filled this area. ♦ Entrance on Fondamenta del Connaregio. Vaporetto stops: San Marcuola (1, 82); Guglie (52)

In Campo del Ghetto Nuovo:

Gianfranco Penzo This tiny retail store and workshop is every bit as interesting as the **Museo Ebraico** next door. Senor Penzo, one of the few Jewish artisans still working in the ghetto, painstakingly hand paints scripture-inspired scenes and vignettes onto exclusively produced Murano glass. The result, whether ceremonial or decorative, is an instant heirloom glass or plate. The kindly Signor Penzo spends too much of his workday patiently answering the awe-motivated questions of visitors from around the world, few of whom leave without ordering at least one item to commemorate an upcoming bar mitzvah, wedding anniversary, or merely their visit to Venice's ghetto. ♦ M-F; occasionally Su. Campo Ghetto Nuovo 2895 (southwest side). 716313

Museo Ebraico (Jewish Museum)

Four centuries of Jewish life in the Venice ghetto, including precious books, tapestries, jewels, and sacred articles are displayed in this small museum. The Ghetto's five synagogues can only be visited on a guided tour that leaves the museum every hour, beginning at 10:30AM. ♦ Admission. M-F, Su; closed on Jewish holidays. Campo del Ghetto Nuovo 2902B (east side of *campo*). 715359

Synagogues on the Campo del Ghetto Nuovo Of the five remaining synagogues in this area (there were nine in Napoleon's day), three 16th-century *scuole* opened directly onto this square. Their names reflected the diversity of the population: the **Scuola Grande Tedesca** (Great German Synagogue), the **Scuola del Canton** (Synagogue of the Corner, so-called probably because of its location), and the **Scuola Italiana** (Italian Synagogue). They can be visited during museum hours (see **Museo Ebraico,** above), with a guide provided by the museum. ♦ Campo del Ghetto Nuovo

24 All'Antica Mola ★★$$ This restaurant a few steps from the **Campo del Ghetto Nuovo** used to be an *osteria* (wine shop) strictly for the people of the neighborhood. Transformed into a restaurant in the 1980s, it has kept its old-fashioned character, with large, unpretentious wooden tables, informal service, and reasonable prices. The menu is based on traditional Venetian dishes—try the *baccalà alla Vicentina* (a stew made with the local codfish) or the spaghetti *con caparossoli*, a local clam, served in the shell. ♦ M-Su lunch and dinner. Fondamenta degli Ormesini 2800 (north of Campo del Ghetto Nuovo). 717492. Vaporetto stops: San Marcuola (1); Sant'Alvise (52); Guglie (52)

25 Osteria Al Bacco ★★★$$$ At the end of the handsome Fondamenta degli Ormesini (where it becomes Fondamenta delle Cappuccine) is another former wine shop that is now a well-respected *ristorante*. The atmosphere is still that of an old *osteria*, with uncovered wood tables and wood panels on the walls, but the food (fish and original pasta dishes are the specialties here) is superior. After dinner, take a walk along the canal all the way to **La Misericordia:** The street is quiet—almost deserted—with long rows of boats tied along the canal and frequent bridges. A small detour will take you to splendid sites such as **La Madonna dell'Orto** and the church of **Santa Maria Valverde.** ♦ Tu-Sa lunch and dinner, Su dinner only. No credit cards accepted. Fondamenta delle Cappuccine 3054 (near Campo del Ghetto Nuovo). 717493. Vaporetto stops: San Marcuola (1); Sant'Alvise (5); Guglie (52)

26 Scuola Levantina (Eastern Mediterranean Synagogue) This sephardic synagogue is on a little square outside the original island of the ghetto, on a little piazza called **Campiello delle Scuole.** The exterior was designed in the 17th century, probably by **Baldassare Longhena;** the interior was decorated with astonishingly beautiful wood carvings by Andrea Brustolon, the finest Venetian cabinetmaker of the 18th century. Visits must be arranged at the **Museo Ebraico.** ♦ Campiello delle Scuole 1228 (southwest of Campo del Ghetto Nuovo). Vaporetto stops: San Marcuola (1, 82); Guglie (52)

27 Scuola Spagnola (Spanish Synagogue) This synagogue, also on the **Campiello delle Scuole,** is the largest and most interesting of all the ghetto's synagogues. It was redesigned in the 17th century by **Baldassare Longhena,** and the interior decorations are mostly from the 18th century. Visits must be arranged through the **Museo Ebraico.** ♦ Campiello delle Scuole 1146 (southwest of Campo del Ghetto Nuovo). Vaporetto stops: San Marcuola (1, 82); Guglie (52)

28 Hotel Hespera $$ This romantic, 20-room hotel would cost far more if it were closer to the city's hub; its location on a lazy little canal only enhances its charm. Rooms are of average size but the decor is thoughtfully done, and private, spacious baths are a plus. The hotel's **Il Melograno** restaurant has a few tables outside where meals or an *aperitivo* are offered in warm weather. ♦ Calle Riello 459 (off Fondamenta Savorgnan near Campo San Geremia). 715251; fax 715112. Vaporetto stop: Guglie (52)

29 Palazzo Labia Built by **Andrea Cominelli** in 1720 for the wealthy Labia family, this sumptuous home has three facades: one on the Canal Grande, one on the Canale di Cannaregio, and a third on the **Campo San Geremia.** Legend has it that when the palazzo opened, Signore Labia stood at a balcony and threw precious pieces of silverware into the canal one by one and said, "*L'abbia o non l'abbia, sarò sempre un Labia.*" (Have it or not, I will always be a Labia.) The legend continues that he had ordered sunken nets to be spread underwater, which were later hoisted up to retrieve the family valuables. The interior salons were frescoed by Giambattista Tiepolo. In all, 13 rooms of the *piano nobile* (second floor) can be visited upon request. Today the palace is the Venice headquarters of **RAI,** the Italian radio and television network. Production studios as well as offices were installed in the countless rooms, while the Tiepolo halls are frequently used for meetings and conferences—often with protests from the Art Conservation Department. ♦ Admission. W-F 3-4PM; call to confirm. Campo San Geremia 275 (near Ponte Guglie). 5242812. Vaporetto stops: Guglie (52); Ferrovia (1, 52, 82)

30 Lista di Spagna In the time of the Serene Republic, the Spanish Embassy was on this street (hence its name), at **Palazzo Zeno 168.** Like most embassies, it was far from the city's center, as though to keep foreigners away from the Republic's heart (members of the Venetian nobility were forbidden even to *talk* to representatives of foreign powers, except in an official capacity; in the theaters and casinos, government spies would denounce patricians simply for greeting or nodding to foreign ministers). The Lista is the most un-Venetian of Venetian streets. It is the only part of town where neon signs are allowed, and its proximity to the train station has turned parts of it into a bazaar for cheap souvenirs. ♦ Between Campo San Geremia and train station. Vaporetto stops: Guglie (52); Ferrovia (1, 52, 82)

31 Hotel Amadeus $$$ This handsome hotel is located just 200 yards from the train station. The 63 rooms, some with small terraces, are large and decorated with 18th century–style furniture. The hotel also has a small private garden and two restaurants. The service is impeccable. ♦ Lista di Spagna 227 (east of train station). 715300; fax 5240841. Vaporetto stop: Ferrovia (1, 52, 82)

32 Hotel Bellini $$$ Its location just a stone's throw from the railroad station is not the only appealing feature of this 99-room hotel. Equally attractive is the decor: antique furnishings, silk damask wall covering and draperies, and Murano chandeliers. It also has a sundeck overlooking the Canal Grande and a breakfast room, but no restaurant. ♦ Lista di Spagna 116 (east of train station). 5242488; fax 715193. Vaporetto stop: Ferrovia (1, 52, 82)

33 Hotel Abbazia $$ The only shortcoming of this hotel is its forlorn entrance in a narrow alleyway near the side of the train station. The interior is a pleasant surprise. The building dates from the 19th century when it was a monastery for the monks of the Scalzi church. It was totally renovated in 1988. The 39 air-conditioned rooms with mini-bars and TVs are in striking contrast with one's idea of a monk's cell—they are large (two cells were joined to make each room) and comfortable. Otherwise, the monastery atmosphere has been skillfully preserved, and a large garden allows for relaxation in the warm weather. There is a breakfast room but no restaurant. ♦ Calle Priuli d.d. Cavalletti 68 (east of train

station). 717333; fax 717949. Vaporetto stop: Ferrovia (1, 52, 82)

34 Ponte degli Scalzi When the trains started to arrive in Venice in 1841 during the Austrian occupation, a bridge over the Canal Grande across from the station became a necessity. **A.E. Neville,** a noted builder of iron bridges and the designer of the Accademia Bridge, produced another of his striking creations: a suspended iron bridge (it was his 38th), reminiscent of such structures as the Eiffel Tower and the Brooklyn Bridge. It contrasted sharply with the Venetian aesthetic, and in 1934 the city decided to demolish it (together with the Accademia Bridge), replacing it with the present stone structure by Italian architect **Miozzi.** ♦ Near the train station. Vaporetto stop: Ferrovia (1, 52, 82)

35 Chiesa degli Scalzi The *scalzi* (barefoot friars) are an ancient monastic order that settled in Venice in the 17th century. Their church was designed by **Baldassare Longhena** in a style reminiscent of Roman Baroque; the facade was added by **Giuseppe Sardi** in 1680. The main altar is a Baroque masterpiece, also of Roman inspiration, by Giuseppe Pozzo; the ceiling was originally frescoed by Giambattista Tiepolo, but was destroyed by an Austrian bomb in 1915. A Tiepolo fresco remains in the vault in the second chapel on the right (*St. Theresa in Glory*), and two more, of lesser importance, are in the vault in the first chapel on the left. ♦ Fondamenta dei Scalzi (near the train station). Vaporetto stop: Ferrovia (1, 52, 82)

36 Stazione Ferroviaria (Train Station) The present structure was erected in 1954 to replace the original station, built under Austrian domination in 1841. Officially called the **Stazione Santa Lucia,** it carries the name of the Renaissance church that was demolished to make room for it. A pier where all the main *vaporetto* lines converge is conveniently located down the steps from the station. ♦ Fondamenta di Santa Lucia. Vaporetto stop: Ferrovia (1, 52, 82)

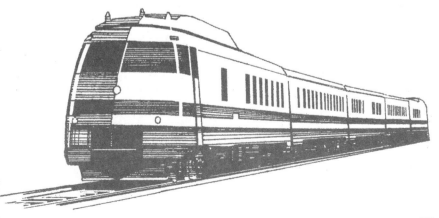

CASTELLO

CANNAREGIO

Fond. d. Mendicanti

20 Campo Santi Giovanni e Paolo

Sal. SS. Giovanni e Paolo

21 Barbaria d. Tole

22

Rio d. Mendicanti

Rio d. Fava

Rio d. S. Marina

Rio d. Piombo

Rio d. Fava

Rio d. Piombo

Rio d. Paradiso

Rio d. Piombo

C. d. Ospedale

Rio d. S. Giovanni Laterano

19

C. Tetta

14 Sal. S. Lio

15 **16**

17 C. d. Paradiso

Rio d. Santa Maria Formosa

12 C. Lunga S. Maria Formosa

13

Campo Santa Maria Formosa

18

11

C. Larga S. Lorenzo

Rio d. Tetta

C. Zen

C. d. Cappucine

C. d. Caffettier

Rio d. S. Giustina

Fond. S. C. S. Francesco

Rio d. S. Giustina

Campo San Francesco d. Vigna

39 San Francesco della Vigna

Campo S. Giustina

Rio d. Fontego

Campo d. Confraternità

Ramo Ponte S. Francesco

Rio d. S. Francesco

Rio d. Lorenzo

Rio d. Pietà

Campo S. Lorenzo

Rio d. S. Severo

Fond. d. S. Severo

Rio d. Guerra

C. d. Bande

Rio d. Santa Maria Formosa

10

Ruga Giuffa

Rio d. S. Maria Formosa

Rio d. S. Provolo

9

8

Rio S. Osmarin

Fond. d. S. Lorenzo

C. d. Madonna

37

Fond. d. Osmarin

Salizzada d. Greci

36

Sal. d. Gatte

Rio d. Scudi

38 C. d. Furlani

C. d. Scudi

Rio dell'Arco

40 Campo Do Pozzi

SAN MARCO

C. d. Canonica

Sal. S. Provolo

C. S. Provolo

6

7

Piazza San Marco

5

Rio d. Palazzo o d. Paglia

C. d. Albanesi

C. C. d. Rasse

4

3

2

1

Riva degli Schiavoni

Rio d. Vin

23

24 Campo San Zaccaria

25

26 **27**

Rio d. Greci

28

29

30

Rio d. Pietà

31 Campo Bandiera e Moro

32 **34**

33

Sal. d. Pignater

C. d. Dose

Sal. d. Greci

C. d. Pestrin

35

Riva Ca' d. Dio

Rio Ca' d. Dio

C. d. Forni

GIUDECCA

N

km
mi

1/8

1/8

1/4

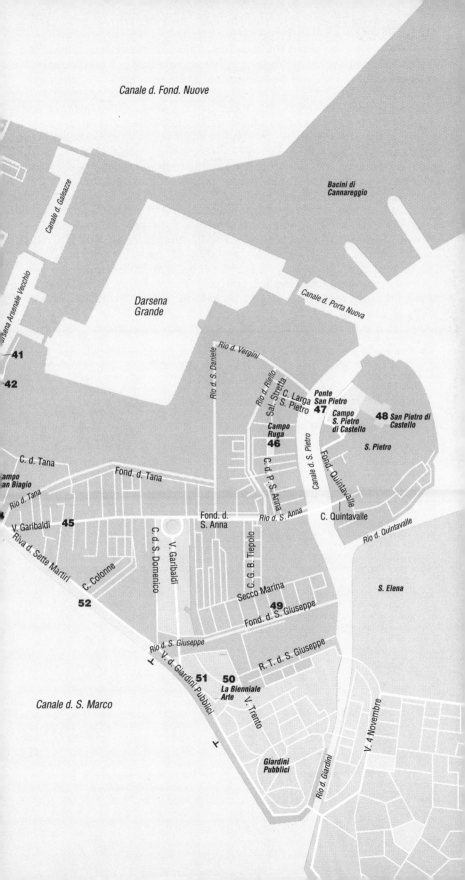

Castello

Castello is the oldest and one of the largest *sestieri* in Venice. More than half of it is taken up by the **Arsenale,** the vast shipyard that once was the main source of the Republic's wealth and military power. The densely populated area around the **Arsenale** was largely built by the old oligarchy to house its workers and sailors. The orderly rows of small homes, often embellished with Gothic arches and windows, around **Campo Do Pozzi** and on both sides of **Via Garibaldi** are examples of farsighted urban planning dating from the 13th century. People on the eastern part of Castello still live a quiet existence. Bakeries, fish shops, and vegetable stands have yet to disappear in favor of shops selling masks or Murano glass, primarily because the train station and parking lots are at the opposite end of town. The neighborhood has nonetheless become an interesting area for dining, with unobtrusive spots like **Al Covo** and **Corte Sconta** drawing food fans away from San Marco. The western part of Castello is rich in palazzi and monuments. It centers around three magnificent squares—**San Zaccaria, Santi Giovanni e Paolo (San Zanipolo),** and **Santa Maria Formosa.** From the narrow midsection of central Castello it is very easy to reach the lagoon, from either the north or south sides. Perhaps that is why the residents are passionate boat lovers, crowding both banks of the canals with their craft, ready to take them to the lagoon islands of **Torcello** and **Sant'Erasmo.**

1 Riva degli Schiavoni and Riva dei Sette Martiri It changes names several times, but by any name this broad walkway is the most splendid embankment in town. The *riva* (bank) extends from **Piazza San Marco** all the way to the eastern end of Venice. On this bank the Slavonians (*Schiavoni*) were allowed to tie their commercial boats (the *Sette Martiri,* or Seven Martyrs, stretch derives its name from an episode of the anti-Fascist civil war, when seven partisans were captured and executed by the Germans). There is no better way to experience the peculiar nature of Venice than by taking this 20-minute walk at sunset. Tourists rarely wander beyond the first 300 or 400 yards of the walk; after that, only locals populate the wide banks along the lagoon. Water buses, private boats, and enormous cruise ships share the water space. At sunset, lights come on atop the wood poles that mark the deep canals in the lagoon flats, while the sun sets magnificently behind **La Salute** church at the Canal Grande's entrance. ♦ Along the waterfront east of Piazza San Marco. Vaporetto stop: San Zaccaria (1, 52, 82)

Restaurants/Clubs: Red   Hotels: Blue
Shops/ ♥ Outdoors: Green   **Sights/Culture: Black**

2 Hotel Danieli $$$$ Set in the 15th-century **Palazzo Dandolo,** this hotel is the most illustrious in Venice and one of a number of CIGA properties recently purchased by ITT Sheraton. Since its opening in 1822 it has hosted countless celebrities, including Honoré de Balzac, Charles Dickens, Gabrielle D'Annunzio, and Richard Wagner. In one of its rooms the French author George Sand started an affair with an Italian physician, who later became her companion, by stroking his foot while Alfred de Musset, her lover at the time, wasn't looking. In 1948 a plain modern annex was added to the hotel, something many Venetians still cannot accept. The suites and waterfront rooms are very comfortable, but some back rooms and those in the annex may not be worth the price. The dramatic hall is 19th-century Neo-Gothic, a curious feature in Venice. It has a piano bar open to non-guests from 10PM to 2AM. Dining or relaxing with a drink on the rooftop restaurant **Terrazza Danieli** is delightful. ♦ Riva degli Schiavoni 4196 (east of Piazza San Marco). 5226480, in the US 800/325.3589; fax 5200208. Vaporetto stop: San Zaccaria (1, 52, 82)

3 Calle delle Rasse The name, meaning "Street of Races," comes from Republican days when international merchants crowded the narrow passageway. Today it's crowded with restaurants. With their open windows filled with fresh fish and live lobsters, these eateries may look very inviting, but diner beware: Bait-and-switch might have you dining on frozen substitutes (although a recent law requires that frozen fish be listed as such). If you still care to eat here, be sure to look at the fine print on the menus—many of the prices are listed per hundred grams rather than per portion. ♦ Between Campo San Zaccaria and Piazza San Marco. Vaporetto stop: San Zaccaria (1, 52, 82)

4 Bar Penasa A popular watering hole for gondoliers, shopkeepers, passersby, and a few tourists in the know. A large variety of *panini* (sandwiches) are displayed at the counter. The spot offers good beer and wine, plus espresso and cappuccino. A set of tables and chairs (not always found in Venice's cafes) offers a welcome respite for walkers. ♦ M-Tu, W-Su 8AM-8PM. No credit cards accepted. Calle delle Rasse 4585 (between Riva degli Schiavoni and Salizzada San Provolo). 5237202. Vaporetto stop: San Zaccaria (1, 52, 82)

5 Sant'Apollonia Monastery The gem of this compound, a former Benedictine monastery, is the 13th-century cloister, restored in 1969. Its Romanesque style is rare in Venice. The stones around the cloister are mostly fragments of decorations from the original **Basilica di San Marco** (9th-11th centuries). On the second floor, the **Museum of Sacred Art** houses a collection of paintings and objects from churches now closed or destroyed. ♦ Admission. M-Sa. Fondamenta Sant'Apollonia (just east of Piazza San Marco). 5529166. Vaporetto stop: San Zaccaria (1, 52, 82)

6 Alfredo Alfredo ★★$ Kitschy fast-food joints are a lire-a-dozen in Venice, but take time to try this exception. Locals are loyal to this popular spot (its eponymous sister-establishment near the **Rialto Bridge** should be avoided) that welcomes snackers and serious eaters alike. Its central location, large menu, and long, nonstop hours, make it a practical choice for lunch or dinner. Many of the 20 reasonably priced "primi" (first courses) are homemade on the premises: lasagna is a perennial best seller, but tourists gravitate to the selection of big "insalatoni" salads with the very un-Italian combinations of sweet corn, mushrooms, tuna, olives, etc. ♦ M-Tu, Th-Su 11AM-2AM. Campo S. Filippo e Giacomo 42 (between Campo San Zaccaria and Piazza San Marco). 5225331. Vaporetto stop: San Zaccaria (1, 52, 82)

7 Anticlea Antiquariato The city is awash with "Venetian pearls," colorful glass beads of all sizes, colors, shapes—and costs. Gianna and her daughter Elena have the best antique collection in this tiny shop, with drawers and drawers arranged according to color, shape, and value. Pick and choose and take them home to string them yourself, or have the owners do it for you. Some of the 18th-century beads were used for trade as far away as Turkey and Africa and have found their way back home. ♦ M-Sa. Closed Monday morning, lunch in winter. Campo San Provolo 4719 (off Salizzada San Provolo west of Campo San Zaccaria). 5286946. Vaporetto stop: San Zaccaria (1, 52, 82)

8 Paolo Brandolisio If you've succumbed to the magic of the gondola, you'll agree that its wooden *forcola* (oarlock) is sculpture. Its smooth twists and turns, each with a different use for propelling and steering the boat, are unique. In the workshop of Paolo Brandolisio this everyday Venetian object becomes nothing less than modern art. The young, congenial Paolo, for years the apprentice and protege of the late master Giuseppe Carli, is the artisan of choice of Venice's most demanding gondoliers. He mounts a small number of his oarlocks to be sold as unique mementos of Venice. ♦ M-Sa. No credit cards accepted. Ruga Giuffa 4725 (off Fondamenta dell'Osmarin). 5224155. Vapotetto stop: San Zaccaria (1, 52, 82)

9 Al Tucano ★★$$ Word is out among the locals, but few tourists know this is a reliably great spot for something as simple as a pizza or as elaborate as a full-course Venetian meal (with a surprising number of meat-based dishes as a concession to non-Venetians). Tony, the amiable owner, is also the talent in the kitchen, regularly releasing delicious pastas and grilled specialties that confirm his dedication to using the freshest ingredients available. He'll guide you through the menu; if available, try the light-as-air homemade gnocchi with *granchio e rucola* (crab meat and tart arugula) or cornmeal polenta served with tiny *schie* shrimp, a local delicacy. ♦ M-W, F-Su lunch and dinner. Ruga Giuffa 4835 (off Fondamenta dell'Osmarin). 5200811. Vaporetto stop: San Zaccaria (1, 52, 82)

10 Biblioteca Querini Stampalia (Querini Stampalia Library) The Querini family was one of the oldest and most powerful in Venice. In 1207 they became lords of Stampalia, an island on the Aegean Sea they conquered for Venice. Among the many branches of the family, the one residing in this early 16th-century palazzo was the richest, although they never provided the city with a doge. The last scion of the family, Count Giovanni Querini, bequeathed the building to the city in 1869 to be used as a public library and art gallery. Between 1959 and 1963, the ground floor was redesigned by the brilliant Venetian architect **Carlo Scarpa.** The second floor is taken up by the library, an extremely important Venetian institution and the only library open in the evening. Generations of college students have prepared for their examinations here, sitting shoulder to shoulder at the ancient tables, ignoring the squeaky floors, the gloomy mythological paintings on the walls, and the sounds of gondoliers serenading tourists drifting in through the giant windows. On the second floor is a *pinacoteca* (art collection) specializing mostly in minor Venetian painters and known for its collection of canvases by 18th-century painter Pietro Longhi representing scenes of Venetian life. It is temporarily closed. ♦ Library: free. Gallery: admission.

Library: M-Sa. Gallery: Tu-Su. Campiello Querini 4778 (south of Campo Santa Maria Formosa). 5225235. Vaporetto stops: San Marco (1, 82); San Zaccaria (1, 52, 82)

11 Santa Maria Formosa *Formosa* means "good looking," with connotations of Junoesque plumpness, as was the Virgin Mary who appeared to a Venetian bishop in AD 639, ordering him to have a church built in her name. The present shape of the church is due to **Mauro Codussi,** the great early-Renaissance architect. It is surprising that there are no saints or prophets on the facade; instead there are statues of gentlemen, obviously not dressed as religious leaders. They are members of the powerful Cappello family, who financed the building of the church. The habit of adorning churches with portraits of donors was common in Venice, contributing to the puzzling mixture of sacred and profane elements so typical all over town. The church's interior, after some incongruous modifications in the 19th century, was restored according to **Codussi**'s plans in 1921. ◆ Campo Santa Maria Formosa. Vaporetto stops: San Zaccaria (1, 52, 82); Rialto (1, 82)

12 Campo Santa Maria Formosa This square, one of the most spacious in Venice, is a real anthology of architectural styles and periods. **Palazzo Vitturi (No. 5246)** is one of the best examples of 13th-century Byzantine architecture; the **Palazzi Donà (Nos. 6123-6126)** include two fine Gothic buildings dating from the 14th century; **Casa Venier (No. 6129)** is a delightful Gothic home from the end of the 15th century; and **Palazzo Ruzzini-Priuli (No. 5866)** is 16th-century Renaissance. Radial streets connect this pivotal square to key neighborhoods in the city such as Rialto and San Marco. It is therefore a busy square, even in the afternoons when the small fruit and vegetable market has closed for the day. ◆ Between Piazza San Marco and Campo Santi Giovanni e Paolo. Vaporetto stops: San Zaccaria (1, 52, 82); Rialto (1, 82)

13 Santa Maria della Fava The name of this church may derive from an ancient food vendor, now long gone, specializing in beans (*fave*), or from the last name of a wealthy

family living nearby. The building is a fine example of Venetian architecture of the 18th century, a time when, in spite of political and economic decay, the Republic was still investing enormous funds in public and private buildings. At least 49 new churches were built in the 18th century, while many others were restored and modified, most often through private contributions by wealthy families. The final plans for this church were drawn by **Giorgio Massari,** the architect of the **Chiesa dei Gesuati** and **Chiesa di Santa Maria della Pietà.** The church contains two masterworks of 18th-century painting: *Madonna with St. Filippo Neri* (1727) by Giambattista Piazzetta (second altar on the left) and *Virgin as a Child with St. Anne and St. Joachim* (1732) by Giambattista Tiepolo (first altar on the right). The former is a product of Piazzetta in his full maturity; the latter is one of the first great works by the young Tiepolo. Together they represent the last great flourishing of Venetian painting. The beautiful 18th-century organ is used every Sunday at 10:30AM to accompany the mass service with Baroque music. ◆ Campo della Fava (west of Campo Santa Maria Formosa). Vaporetto stop: Rialto (1, 82)

14 Canada $ If your legs don't mind the hike to the third-story lobby, ask for one of the two top-floor rooms with wood-beamed ceilings and small terraces. Sitting on a quiet, characteristic *campiello* (small square), the 25-room hotel has modern baths and an attentive, capable management. There is no restaurant. ◆ Campo San Lio 5659 (on Salizzada San Lio). 5229912; fax 5235852. Vaporetto stops: San Marco (1, 82); Rialto (1, 82)

15 Silvia The elegant Signora Silvia and her daughter Francesca discerningly edit the collections of designer names such as Desmo, Missoni, Genny, and Cerrutti to offer a representative assortment of handbags from the season's best. You can rely on the owners' on-the-mark judgment for the best in leather goods from these Italian fashion houses, with a smaller collection of shoes and accessories to complete the fashionable picture. ◆ M-Sa. Salizzada San Lio 5540 (east of Campo San Lio). 5238568. Vaporetto stop: Rialto (1, 52, 82)

16 Salizzada San Lio This rather narrow street leading to or from the Rialto is busy with locals doing their shopping, as it has been since time immemorial. It still has some good examples of early vernacular architecture. The narrow facade next to the arch at **Nos. 5691-5705** is an intact house dating from the 13th or 14th century; and the small palazzo at **Nos. 5662-5672** is from the 13th century (the second-floor window to the right of the arch may belong to the 12th century). Each of the buildings may have consisted of two turretlike dwellings united by a pointed arch. The original windows in both buildings have the typical Byzantine shape (round arches pointed at the top and elongated at the base)—a shape that could naturally evolve into the Gothic arch. ♦ Between Campo Santa Maria Formosa and the Rialto Bridge. Vaporetto stop: Rialto (1, 82)

17 Calle del Paradiso Here you'll find an example of 15th-century urban planning, where grace and functionalism didn't seem to be at odds with one another. The two rows of houses here still have shops on the ground floor. To make the upstairs apartments a bit larger, and to protect the street from rain, the top floors were made to protrude with a typical Venetian feature called a *barbacano;* the ones on this street are original. The Gothic archways at both ends of the street date from the 14th century, and the house on the canal side features Byzantine windows from the 12th century. ♦ West of Campo Santa Maria Formosa. Vaporetto stop: Rialto (1, 82)

18 Osteria al Mascaron ★★$$ Friendly, fun, and informal, this popular wine bar— patronized by students, intellectuals, and a few lucky tourists in the know—serves excellent snacks (*ciccheti*) from the countertop. Good luck finding a free table to enjoy their antipasto, pasta, and entrées. At press time, the owners were about to open a new wine bar to be called **Mascheretta** just a few doors down on the same side of the *calle.* ♦ M-Sa lunch and dinner. Calle Lunga Santa Maria Formosa 5225 (east of Campo Santa Maria Formosa). 5225995. Vaporetto stop: Rialto (1, 82)

19 Ponte dei Conzafelzi The small island in front of this bridge (south side) ends at a house surrounded by water on three sides. The rest of the island is occupied by a former convent, designed by **Andrea Tirali** in 1731 and now used as a high school, located at the opposite end next to the handsome 15th-century Venetian Gothic **Palazzo Cappello,** once famous for its glorious receptions. The facade of the palazzo is visible only from the canals. ♦ Off Calle Lunga Santa Maria Formosa (near Campo Santi Giovanni e Paolo). Vaporetto stop: Rialto (1, 82)

20 Campo Santi Giovanni e Paolo This *campo,* known in dialect as **San Zanipolo,** is the center of an old and active part of the city. It was an important crossroads between the large island to which it belongs (extending northward toward the lagoon, visible from the *campo*) and a group of busy, densely populated islands to the south (centered around **Campo Santa Maria Formosa**).

The north section was reclaimed from the lagoon between the 13th and 15th centuries and used as a site for convents and charitable institutions. Today it is wholly occupied by the Venice hospital, a maze of streets, pavilions, churches, and cloisters where citizens as well as newly hired nurses and doctors easily get lost.

The south section of the *campo,* between the street on the side of the church and the parallel canal (Rio di San Giovanni Laterano), was built in the 13th century for low-income residents, with blocks of homes separated by parallel alleys (the oldest are the late Byzantine buildings on Calle Muazzo, **Nos. 6450-6454**). As always in Venice, quite a few patrician families had their palazzi next to the low-income developments. Among them was **Palazzo Bragadin (No. 6480),** best seen from the bridge across the canal, with land access in an alley off the **Campo Santa Marina.** Here young Casanova lived the best years of his youth under the protection of old Matteo Bragadin, who was convinced that the charming young man knew how to consult the spirits in order to forecast the future. Casanova played a similar trick in Paris on the Marquise d'Urfé, who in turn supported the Venetian adventurer for years, until she was rudely awakened by being conned into a mock death-and-resurrection ritual.

The *campo* is still an important center of local life, with a constant flow of Venetians crossing it in all directions, while in the two spacious cafes, groups of old men kill time playing card games and sipping wine in the afternoon. On the canal at the hospital's side, frequent ambulance launches carry patients to and from the hospital's water entrance. The *pasticceria* (pastry shop) in the *campo* has remained intact since the turn of the century, and the owners proudly serve old-fashioned pastries (most Venetians like the green ones, with pistachio nuts).

The equestrian monument at the center of the *campo* represents Bartolomeo Colleoni, one of the greatest Renaissance *condottieri,* or military heroes, who served Venice for decades until his death in 1475. Colleoni bequeathed most of his considerable wealth to the Republic on the condition that a monument to him be built in front of **San Marco.** The city government agreed, but after his death decided that this *campo* was good enough, perhaps playing on the name of the building at the church's side (**Scuola Grande di San Marco**). While the city fathers may not

have done right by Colleoni on the location, they could not have chosen a better sculptor for the commission: The monument was entrusted to Andrea Verrocchio, who honored the old warrior with one of the most admired monuments in Italy (the statue was cast by his pupil Alessandro Leopardi).

The building at the left of the church and along the canal is the hospital's entrance. Originally it was the entrance of the **Scuola Grande di San Marco** (pictured below). The 15th-century facade was designed by **Mauro Codussi** and sculpted by Pietro Lombardo with his sons Tullio and Antonio. The splendid trompe l'oeil marble statues represent *St. Mark's Lion* (left side) and two episodes from the life of St. Mark (right side). The 15th-century statue by Bartolomeo Bon over the portal represents *Charity*, while the winged lion under the top arch was added in the 19th century to replace the original one, destroyed after the French conquest (1797) along with countless similar mementos of the oligarchic Republic. You can visit the large

hall within the building and—among a crowd of patients and their visitors—study the exhibition of photographs representing the interior of the compound before and after the restorations. You can also explore the compound, but don't be surprised to see patients in pajamas. For visits to the interior of the *scuola* (whose 16th-century halls are decorated with paintings by Palma il Giovane, Palma il Vecchio, and Jacopo Tintoretto's son Domenico) and to the attached convent, ask the hospital doorman. ♦ Northeast of Piazza San Marco. Vaporetto stop: Rialto (1, 82)

21 Santi Giovanni e Paolo (San Zanipolo)
Owned and run by the Dominican friars, this church is one of the largest in Venice, and undoubtedly one of the most beautiful. **Santi Giovanni e Paolo,** built in the 13th and 14th centuries, can properly be called the Pantheon of Venice, because, from the 15th century on, the funerals of the doges were held here, and no fewer than 25 doges were buried here. On the facade, never completed with the planned marble covering, are some of the oldest

Scuola Grande

tombs. Inside the arches on the left side are those of Doge Jacopo Tiepolo and of his son, Doge Lorenzo Tiepolo. The portal was designed by **Bartolomeo Bon** in the second half of the 15th century. The interior of the church is filled with chapels and monuments, and a walk through it is equal to a course in Venetian political and artistic history.

Highlights include:

The **Monument to Doge Pietro Mocenigo**, just inside the entrance to the right, is by Pietro Lombardo, one of the greatest representatives of the early Renaissance in Venice. In this monument, the warlike attributes of the doge are exalted: Six young warriors stand inside the niches, while the bas-reliefs on the sarcophagus illustrate two of his victorious expeditions. The Latin inscription means "the money for this monument came from booty of war." On top of the sarcophagus, Mocenigo appears in full battle dress. This monument is clearly as grandiose as the one erected in honor of Doge Niccolò Tron at the **Frari** church.

Nearby is the **Monument to Marcantonio Bragadin,** attributed to Vincenzo Scamozzi. Inside the urn is *the skin* of General Bragadin, who was flayed alive by the Turks on the island of Cyprus in 1571, after negotiating the free exit of his army. The Turks kept the skin in Constantinople, whence the Venetians stole it. The treacherous flaying is represented in the fresco surrounding the statue.

On the second altar in the right aisle is the recently and beautifully restored *Polyptych of St. Vincent Ferreri* (circa 1465), attributed (incorrectly according to some) to a young Giovanni Bellini.

St. Dominick's Chapel, by **Andrea Tirali,** contains *The Glory of St. Dominick,* a masterwork by the 18th-century painter Giovanni Battista Piazzetta.

The narrative stained-glass window in the right transept was laboriously manufactured in Murano over a period of 50 years (1470-1520) by various master artists, including Cima da Conegliano (who did the Virgin, the Baptist, and St. Peter). The painting on the right side of the back wall of the transept, *St. Anthony Giving Alms,* is one of the few works by Lorenzo Lotto in Venice. The painting reflects Lotto's great interest in the world of the underprivileged; St. Antonio, a Dominican, worked on behalf of the poor in Florence in the 15th century. The social content in the painting is rare in 16th-century Venetian art: Like most of Lotto's paintings, it stands in sharp contrast to the celebrative, grandiose paintings of his contemporaries.

The high altar in the chancel is attributed to **Baldassare Longhena.** Left of the altar is **The Monument to Doge Andrea Vendramin,** a

collective work of the Lombardo family and one of the best funerary monuments of its period. The top frame is missing, and the two *Holy Women* at the sides are replacements for statues of Adam and Eve.

The **Cappella del Rosario** (Rosary Chapel, through a glass door in the left transept) was destroyed by a fire in 1867 that also claimed a masterwork by Titian (*St. Peter Martyr*) and a *Crucifixion* by Tintoretto (a copy of the former can be seen on the second altar in the church's left aisle). On the ceiling, rebuilt in 1932, there are now three canvases by Paolo Veronese (*Annunciation, Assumption,* and *Adoration of the Shepherds*) that were previously in another church and are now a highlight of your visit here. ♦ Campo Santi Giovanni e Paolo. Vaporetto stop: Rialto (1, 82)

22 Santa Maria dei Derelitti The unusual facade of this church was built between 1670 and 1674 by **Baldassare Longhena** as an answer to the equally curious facade built by a rival architect at **San Moisè.** The redundant Baroque decorations were meant as a monument to the wealthy donor, Bartolomeo Cargnoni. The church was connected to the nearby Ospedaletto **(No. 6691),** one of the four orphanages in town where children were given a musical education. (The most famous is **Santa Maria della Pietà,** where Vivaldi worked as choirmaster.) Pasquale Anfossi, the author of countless operas in the 18th century, was a music teacher here, as were Niccolò Porpora and Domenico Cimarosa. Concerts, considered among the best in Europe, were performed in an elegant 18th-century music hall, now part of a nursing home for senior citizens (ask the doorman at the hall next door to the church for permission to visit). ♦ Barbaria delle Tole 6990 (east of Campo Santi Giovanni e Paolo). Vaporetto stop: Rialto (1, 82)

23 Campiello $$ This family-run hotel sits in a tiny piazza (*campiello*) off the prestigious Riva degli Schiavoni. Its 15 rooms are always in demand—air-conditioning, tasteful furnishings, and an English-speaking staff explain why. Breakfast only is served in the restaurant. ♦ Calle del Vin 4647 (west of Campo San Zaccaria). 505764; fax 5205798. Vaporetto stop: San Zaccaria (1, 52, 82)

24 Campo San Zaccaria The church on this typical Venetian square used to belong to one of the richest Benedictine monasteries in town, founded in the ninth century. It was the preferred monastery for daughters of the noble families to join as nuns. The doge used to visit it once a year, on Easter, to commemorate the 12th-century donation by the nuns of a large piece of property to enlarge **Piazza San Marco.** Eight early doges are buried inside. To the right of the church is the facade of an older chapel and the entrance to the monastery, now the headquarters of the Venice *Carabinieri*. The beautiful 15th-century building at the left has been spoiled by the addition of shops on the ground floor. ♦ At the eastern end of Salizzada San Provolo. Vaporetto stop: San Zaccaria (1, 52, 82)

25 Chiesa di San Zaccaria The splendid facade was designed by **Mauro Codussi** between 1480 and 1500. **Codussi** was one of the first architects to break with Gothic tradition in Venice; his facades, widely imitated later, are characterized by a large round arch at the top, supported by two half-arches at the sides. His were among the first arches to be seen in Venice, which in the late 15th century was still attached to the ogee arches of the Gothic tradition. **Codussi** brilliantly covered the existing ninth-century Gothic structure—a central nave with two small side aisles—with a set of stone and marble decorations in pure Renaissance style. The facades of the **Frari** and **Santi Giovanni e Paolo**—which were never finished—give an idea of what **San Zaccaria** looked like before **Codussi's** intervention.

The interior marks an important moment in Venice's art history. It is in this church that Renaissance painting made its first appearance in the city, 100 years after the great Tuscan masters had introduced it to Florence and to the world. To see this ground-breaking work, walk along the right aisle and enter the **Cappella di San Tarasio** (Chapel of Saint Tarasius). The paintings in question are the frescoes on the chapel's apse, painted by Andrea del Castagno, a Florentine master. Their innovative character is made evident by a simple comparison with three polyptychs painted just a year later in the same chapel by Venetian masters (Giovanni and Antonio da Murano, with help from Antonio Vivarini), located at the altar and on the two side walls. Notice how old-fashioned they seem next to Castagno's frescoes.

In 1505, more than 60 years after Castagno created his frescoes, Giovanni Bellini painted one of his best-known altarpieces for San Zaccaria: the *Sacred Conversatione,* on the second altar in the left aisle. This recently restored painting marks a further transition between early Venetian style and the new trends that were to emerge with Giorgione and Titian. ♦ Campo San Zaccaria. Vaporetto stop: San Zaccaria (1, 52, 82)

"Venice is like eating an entire box of chocolate liqueurs at one go."

Truman Capote

Restaurants/Clubs: Red   **Hotels:** Blue

Shops/ ♥ Outdoors: Green   **Sights/Culture:** Black

26 Londra Palace Venezia $$$$ Most of the 65 rooms here have a magnificent view over St. Mark's basin, but some are rather small, and the whole place could use a face-lift. The ground floor lobby is comfortable and quiet; **Les Deux Lions**, the hotel's restaurant, is a popular spot for Venetian and French cooking. ♦ Riva degli Schiavoni 4171 (south of Campo San Zaccaria). 5200533; fax 5225032. Vaporetto stop: San Zaccaria (1, 52, 82)

Pensione Wildner

27 Pensione Wildner $$ This small, comfortable hotel is efficiently run by the friendly Signoria Lidia. The simply furnished front rooms have a great view of the island of **San Giorgio** and the surrounding area, and are worth reserving in advance. The back rooms on the higher floors (there is no elevator) may not be worth the hike, or the price. All 16 rooms have air-conditioning. The hotel's restaurant is a convenient spot for a simple meal or snack when tables move outdoors in warm weather. ♦ Riva degli Schiavoni 4161 (east of Piazza San Marco). 5227463; fax 5265615 (attn: Wildner). Vaporetto stop: San Zaccaria (1, 52, 82)

28 Chiesa di Santa Maria della Pietà This 18th-century church, designed by **Giorgio Massari,** was built for the nearby orphanage (the facade was added in 1906). For centuries, abandoned children were raised in four such institutions in town: La Pietà, I Mendicanti, L'Incurabili, and L'Ospedaletto), where they were taught various professions, among the most important of which was music (the word conservatory originally meant "place where abandoned children are kept"). Soon the children of these institutions became famous throughout Europe for their musical talents, and their concerts were one of the main reasons foreigners visited the city. Many of the great singers of the 17th century were raised in such institutions. Among them was Madama Ferrarese, the first interpreter of

Mozart's *Così fan tutte* and the lover of Mozart's librettist, the Venetian Lorenzo da Ponte. Ferrarese was brought up at I Mendicanti, but she eloped in 1780 to marry a young man from Rome and start a glorious singing career. The young singers and players would perform behind a grille, which made them invisible to the audience. In the 1740s, Jean-Jacques Rousseau obtained permission to visit them in the parlor and was bitterly disappointed by the plain looks of these girls who could sing so celestially. On the tiny alley at the right side of the church was the entrance to the orphanage and the spot where children were abandoned. An inscription in stone, still visible in the alley, promised revenge from earth and heaven against parents who abandoned their children. In the first half of the 18th century, the music teacher at **La Pietà** was the Baroque composer and priest, Antonio Vivaldi. He died before construction of the church—therefore the popular appellation "Vivaldi's church" is not appropriate.

The interior, beautifully restored in 1988 with international funds, was conceived more as a concert hall than as a church. The oval shape, designed with acoustics in mind, encloses an elegant space, with two gilt-iron grilles on the walls. The ceiling is a masterwork by Tiepolo, the *Triumph of Faith.*

Baroque music concerts are performed inside the church throughout the year, but particularly from May through September. Tickets are available in the church foyer, the **Metropole Hotel** next door, and at a number of travel agencies around town. ◆ Daily. Riva degli Schiavoni 4150 (at Calle della Pietà). 917257. Vaporetto stop: San Zaccaria (1, 52, 82)

29 Metropole Hotel $$$ The space now occupied by this hotel was the concert hall where Antonio Vivaldi worked and held his Venice performances. The exterior of the present building is quite simple, but the hotel's halls and 75 rooms are filled with lovely antiques from the owner's private and prodigious collection, and the service is excellent. The view from the front rooms overlooks the lagoon. The lobby's recently opened **Buffet** restaurant is a hit with Venetians, who are unaccustomed to the self-service, all-you-can-eat approach to dining. ◆ Riva degli Schiavoni 4149 (at Calle della Pietà). 5205044; fax 5223679. Vaporetto stop: San Zaccaria (1, 52, 82)

30 Casa di Petrarca (Petrarch's House) This small Gothic building was given by the Republic as residence to the Tuscan poet Francesco Petrarca, who lived here with his daughter from 1362 to 1367. In exchange, he promised to leave to the Republic his rare collection of manuscripts, which became the core of the **Biblioteca Marciana.** (In 1367,

Petrarch moved to Arquà, a country village in the Venetian hills.) The view from the Gothic balcony must have been quite exciting in Petrarch's time: The merchant ships coming from abroad would stop right in front for a salute to the city and for customs duties. The house is closed to the public. ◆ Riva degli Schiavoni 4146 (east of Rio della Pietà). Vaporetto stop: San Zaccaria (1, 52, 82)

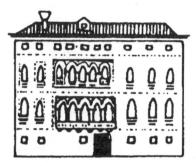

31 Hotel La Residenza $$ Located on the beautiful and quiet **Campo Bandiera e Moro**, this small hotel is in a 15th-century Gothic building with a lovely balcony. Behind the balcony is a large breakfast hall, decorated with original 17th-century stuccos and paintings. Maintenance of the rooms has been negligent, but what the hotel lacks in luxury, it makes up for in drama. Reserve at least one month in advance. ◆ Campo Bandiera e Moro 3068 (north of Riva degli Schiavoni). 5285315; fax 5238859. Vaporetto stop: Arsenale (1)

32 San Giovanni in Bragora Antonio Vivaldi, born in one of the houses on this charming *campo,* was baptized in this eighth-century (rebuilt in 1505) church in 1678. The main altarpiece (*The Baptism of Christ,* 1494) is a masterwork of Cima di Conegliano, one of the first Venetian painters to introduce landscape as a background to figures, thereby breaking with earlier tradition (gold background) and with more recent trends (open loggias or small temples, as in the Bellini at **San Zaccaria**). Cima's birthplace was, not accidentally, in the beautiful Venetian hills, which he portrayed in his paintings much like his contemporary Giorgione, also a native of that area. ◆ Campo Bandiera e Moro (north of Riva degli Schiavoni). Vaporetto stop: Arsenale (1)

33 Al Gabbiano $$ In this area, crowded with mediocre tourist restaurants, this place is an exception—if you can procure an outdoor table. The setting is splendid, with the whole basin in full view. The food is good, but the spot is best for gazing, not grazing. M-Tu, Th-Su lunch and dinner. Riva degli Schiavoni 4120 (near Campo Bandiera e Moro at Calle del Forno). 5223988. Vaporetto stop: Arsenale (1)

34 Al Covo ★★★$$$ Opened in 1986, this restaurant quickly became one of the very best in town, thanks to the combined talents of chef Cesare and his Texan wife, Diane. His passion is for cooking, hers for entertaining and pleasing guests and running a smooth operation. The menu includes all the typical Venetian specialties: homemade pasta and risottos with various fish sauces, shrimp, scampi, and local fish, plus innovative dishes by Cesare, such as an appetizer of fresh fish prepared carpaccio-style. Lunch is a more relaxed meal with a less extensive (and less expensive) menu. ◆ M-Tu, F-Su lunch and dinner. Campiello della Pescaria 3698 (north of Riva degli Schiavoni). 5223812. Vaporetto stop: Arsenale (1)

35 La Corte Sconta ★★★$$$ Chef Claudio, his wife Rita, and his sister-in-law Lucia have been running this restaurant with enormous success for 15 years. In good weather, dining is in an informal but elegant courtyard (*corte*) hidden (*sconta*) in the interior of the building. Most people request the house appetizers (seafood in different styles), followed by the *assaggi* (sampling) of pasta, a taste of three different pasta concoctions. The seafood is excellent and locally caught, a rarity in Venice. Among the house wines is an outstanding *prosecco*—one of the best to be found in town. ◆ Tu-Sa lunch and dinner. Calle del Pestrin 3886 (northeast of Campo Bandiera e Moro). 5227024. Vaporetto stop: Arsenale (1)

36 Trattoria da Remigio ★★$$ One of the few *trattorie* in town where locals still predominate, despite a recent makeover that fancied things up considerably. The homemade gnocchi are wonderful (try them with the gorgonzola sauce or *al pesce*, in a light tomato-based fish sauce); or have the spaghetti *al granchio* (a tomato sauce flavored with crab meat). ◆ M lunch only; W-Su lunch and dinner. Reservations required. No credit cards accepted. Salizzada dei Greci 3416 (east of Chiesa dei Greci). 5230089. Vaporetto stops: Arsenale (1); San Zaccaria (1, 52, 82)

37 Collegio Greco e Chiesa dei Greci This area is the property of the Greek community in Venice, as it has been since 1526. It is the city's largest foreign community and one of its richest. Even today the compound is a small island of Greek civilization in the middle of Venice. Separated from the rest of the town by a grille and a canal, it is quiet and off the tourist track, although no more than five minutes from **Piazza San Marco.** The compound includes the **Museo Dipinti Sacri Bizantini** (Museum of Icons) built by **Longhena** in 1578 (one of the largest collections of Byzantine icons in Western Europe), and the church of **San Giorgio dei Greci** (1539-61), the interior of which is a real triumph of late-Byzantine painting, with gold backgrounds. The bell tower (1592) is, remarkably and dangerously, leaning. ◆ Museum: Admission. M-F. Ponte dei Greci 3412 (at Fondamenta del Osmarin). 5226581. Vaporetto stop: San Zaccaria (1, 52, 82)

38 Scuola di San Giorgio degli Schiavoni The building may look like a church, but it was actually the seat of the brotherhood of the Dalmatian people, also known as Slavonians (*Schiavoni*). It contains nine masterworks by Vittore Carpaccio, himself of Dalmatian descent, painted between 1501 and 1511 to decorate the hall of the building. St. George was the chosen patron of the charitable association; therefore one of the paintings represents *St. George Killing the Dragon*. Two versions of the same scene are sculpted in stone outside the *scuola:* The one on the facade was sculpted in 1552, and the one on the canal side of the building in 1574. (St. George, one of the preferred patrons of warriors, has been removed from the list of Catholic saints because there is no proof he existed.) Two more Carpaccio paintings illustrate episodes from the legend of St. George: the *Triumph of St. George* (second on the left wall) and *St. George Baptizing the King of Libya* (front wall, left side of the altar). An episode from the life of St. Triffon, the second patron of the Slavonians, is painted on the other side of the altar (also by Carpaccio). On the right wall are two episodes from the Gospel and three from the life of St. Jerome (*The Taming of the Lion, St. Jerome's Funeral,* and *St. Jerome in His Study,* also called the *Vision of St. Augustine,* all by Carpaccio). For the first time in Italy, Carpaccio depicted religious and mystical subjects in a real, down-to-earth way (note the animals, trees, and clothes on the people). This reflected a giant step toward the independence of art from religion, which was possible in a city like

Venice, run as it was by active, shrewd, and earth-oriented merchants. ♦ Admission. Tu-Su. Calle dei Furlani (north of Chiesa dei Greci). 5228828. Vaporetto stop: Arsenale (1); San Zaccaria (1, 52, 82)

39 San Francesco della Vigna This Renaissance church is located in an extremely quiet neighborhood, where Venetians go about their daily activity seemingly unaware of being in the middle of a hectic tourist town. The whole area was redesigned from 1525 to 1540 through an ambitious project by Doge Andrea Gritti and architect **Jacopo Sansovino.** It represents a rare example of ancient urban planning. Around the grandiose church, the Gritti residence (**No. 2785**) was rebuilt and later used as the residence of the Pope's ambassador; small houses were demolished to create the **Campo della Confraternità** (right side of the church) and a bell tower similar to the one in **Piazza San Marco** was added. The heavy loggia across the *campo* is a 19th-century addition. The church was carefully designed by **Sansovino** according to rigorous neo-Platonic geometry. The facade was designed by **Andrea Palladio** after **Sansovino**'s death. The interior, sober and solemn, was designed by **Sansovino,** in collaboration with Doge Gritti and an erudite monk, as an embodiment in stone of the *Harmonia mundi* (the order and proportion found by the Humanists in God's planning of the world), and based on multiples of the

number three. In 1535 the side chapels were sold to families of the Venetian nobility, such as Bragadin, Badoer, and Contarini, who vied to tie their names to this monument of Renaissance craft and thought. ♦ Campo San Francesco della Vigna (north of Chiesa dei Greci). Vaporetto stop: Celestia (52 sinistra); San Zaccaria (1, 52, 82)

40 Campo Do Pozzi This *campo* represents small-scale Venice. The square was planned and built in the 14th century as the center of an island surrounded by four canals and adjacent to the **Arsenale.** The island was inhabited by the shipyard's workers, a group of choice craftsmen. All of the houses on the *campo,* except for the one on the south side (rebuilt in 1613), belong to the 14th century; particularly interesting is **Palazzo Malipiero (Nos. 2684-2689).** The wellhead (*pozzo*) at the center was sculpted in 1530 with the figure of St. Martin and gave the square its name. ♦ Northeast of Campo Bandiera e Moro. Vaporetto stop: Arsenale (1)

41 Arsenale Two elegant towers (rebuilt in 1686) mark the water entrance to this astonishingly large compound, the pride of the former Republic and the source of its maritime power. More than 16,000 workers (called *arsenalotti*) could be simultaneously employed here in times of need to build and maintain merchant and wartime vessels. The **Arsenale**'s origins date back to the 12th century, and its fame was already high

Arsenale

at the end of the 13th century, when Dante described its activity in a famous simile in the *Inferno:* The damned souls of corrupt politicians were tormented in Hell by immersion in a lake of boiling pitch, with the devils moving about with pointed forks just like those used by Venetian workers to caulk the hulls of their ships. The **Arsenale** occupies one-fifth of the city's total acreage and is completely surrounded by crenellated walls. It is now a military zone and can be visited only by appointment, with a waiting period of two to three weeks.

Among the precious remnants of the ancient activities are: the **sail factory** (16th century); the **Bucintoro boathouse** (16th century—the Bucintoro was the ship used by the doge for public ceremonies); the slips for construction and maintenance of war galleys (16th century); the **smithies** (ca. 1390); and the astonishing **Corderie** buildings (14th and 16th centuries), which were more than 300 yards long in order to allow the twining of one-piece ropes.

Jobs in the **Arsenale** were coveted and hereditary; the pay was good and the city provided housing for the workers in the surrounding neighborhood. Most of the small homes around the shipyard date back to the 13th and 14th centuries, although many have been modified countless times since.

The land entrance, on the side of the left tower, provides access through a flat bridge over a small canal. The majestic **Portal** was based on a drawing by Jacopo Bellini and built in 1460 by **Antonio Gambello** and is the first example of the Renaissance arch in Venice. The 15th-century winged lion over the arch is attributed to Bartolomeo Bon. The two *Winged Victories* were added in commemoration of a great naval victory over the Turks in the Battle of Lepanto in 1571. Four ancient lions flank the door; the one on the left was taken after a naval victory in Athens at Pireus in 1687 (on its breast, sides, and back it carries a Viking inscription, decoded in the 15th century). The first lion on the right was also taken from Athens the same year. The smaller one on its right, with its elongated body, was taken from the island of Delos and dates back to the sixth century BC. Little is known about the last and smallest of the lions. The *No. 52 (sinistra) vaporetto,* which continues on to the cemetery island of San Michele and to Murano, passes through the **Arsenale,** offering a rare glimpse into its backyard. ♦ Campo dell'Arsenale. Vaporetto stop: Arsenale (1)

"Venice is a paradise for cripples, for a man has no use of his legs here."

Mark Twain

42 Ristorante da Paolo ★★$$ Few restaurants in Venice can boast a better space for outdoor dining than this informal, unpretentious neighborhood eatery. The **Arsenale** gateway is right in front and the quiet Rio dell'Arsenale flows nearby. Savvy tourists have discovered the place, which fills up on summer evenings with colorful residents from this popular neighborhood. The service may not be very professional, but the spaghetti with clams is as good as anywhere else in Venice, and the pizza is prepared to order. At lunchtime the crowd is much smaller, but the place is equally pleasant, with its large umbrellas shading the summer sun. ♦ Tu-Su lunch and dinner. Campo dell'Arsenale (south side of *campo*). 710660. Vaporetto stop: Arsenale (1)

43 Museo Storico Navale (Naval Museum) The building, dating from the 16th century, was originally used by the Republic as a granary. The exhibits include some 25,000 items related to the history of the Italian navy since unification (1861), as well as material collected from the ancient history of the Venetian fleets. There is a large collection of naval cannons from the 16th century on. **Room No. 8** contains interesting models of 18th-century Venetian ships and one of a *fusta,* a 15th-century warship with 224 oars. **Room No. 9** has a splendid model of the last Bucintoro, the ceremonial ship used by the doge. The third floor covers the history and construction of gondolas and other lagoon boats. ♦ Admission. M-Sa 9AM-1PM. Campo San Biagio 2148 (on Fondamenta dell'Arsenale). 5200276. Vaporetto stop: Arsenale (1)

44 Hotel Bucintoro $$ This *pensione*-style hotel is in an unparalleled location on the Riva di San Biagio. Most of the 28 rooms enjoy a lovely view of the lagoon, with the **Giardini Pubblici** (Public Gardens) to the east and **Piazza San Marco** to the west. Service is friendly, the rooms are plain and simply furnished, and breakfast and dinner are served in a functional dining room. There is no elevator, but the stairs are not too steep. It is worth reserving in advance for one of the corner rooms. ♦ Closed December and January. No credit cards accepted. Riva di San Biagio 2135 (at Campo San Biagio). 5223240; fax 5235224. Vaporetto stop: Arsenale (1)

An Affair of the Art

The world-renowned *Venice Biennale* recently celebrated its 100th anniversary. The city's original intention was to celebrate the silver wedding anniversary of King Umberto of Italy and his wife, Margherita of Savoy, by instituting "a biannual national artistic exhibition" in 1893. But it was soon suggested that the exhibition become international, and the inauguration of the *First International Exposition of Art of the City of Venice* was held on 30 April 1895 and attended by the king and queen. Thereafter held from June to September on even years only, the *Biennale* was permanently shifted to odd years in 1993 in order to appropriately celebrate these two inaugural dates.

From the beginning, the *Biennale* has chosen to put forward an unedited and innovative view of art. Among its list of strict regulations, it was decided that no artist would be able to present more than two works, and more important, that these works were not to have been shown before in Italy. Since its early years, international relations have been one of the *Biennale*'s priorities, resulting in the increase of its permanent pavilions in and around the **Giardini Publici** (Public Gardens) from seven in 1914 to 28 today—accommodating the work of artists from more than 50 countries. The international aspect of the *Venice Biennale* remains one of its greatest strengths.

In the 1930s, the well-known Venetian Count Giuseppe Volpi di Misurata dominated the *Biennale*. Through his impetus, the *Biennale* grew and expanded into the multidisciplinary organization that it remains today. The *Music Festival* (today called the *Festival of Contemporary Music*) was founded in 1930; it has premiered the music of Gershwin, Stravinsky, and Cage. The *International Film Festival* (the most important today after Cannes) was also founded under Volpi's aegis in 1932, and became an annual event in 1934. The *International Theatre Festival,* first held in 1934, has recently been suspended, while the popular *Architecture Biennale* was added in 1980 as an autonomous section.

Things change considerably when the *Biennale* is in town. Locals can tell you how the "art" crowd is noticeably different from the "film" crowd. Regardless, a flurry of press and international

celebs—all of whom seem to know each other and live for these reunions—fill all the right hotels and restaurants. If you don't have an embossed invitation and won't be going to any black-tie galas, cheer up. The **Tourist Information Office** (in its new location in front of the **Giardinetti Reali** near the legendary **Harry's Bar**) can give you all the information you need about how to get to the *Biennale* as well as the fringe exhibitions, installations, and performances organized primarily during the opening weeks.

Offshoots of the *Art Biennale,* such as the *Aperto* show, have drawn a growing following by offering the excitement of younger, less-established artists—in a manner, according to many, reminiscent of the *Biennale* before it became what some think is a jaded marketplace for mega-dealers. The **Biennale Archives** are open to the public in the

Palazzo Corner della Regina, which is conveniently located very near the **Ca'Pesaro**'s **Museum of Modern Art** (both are directly on the **Canal Grande**). The museum's small but very selective collection of paintings has been chosen from the *Biennale* since its opening; the host of Italian and international artists represented includes De Chirico, Chagall, Kandinsky, and Klimt.

The **Biennale Organization** is permanently located in **Ca'Giustinian** on **Valle Valleresso,** west of **Piazza San Marco** (5218711).

45 Via Garibaldi This is one of the few areas in Venice where neighborhood life is as it was before the city became a major tourist center. In the morning, a small fruit and vegetable market and a few fish stands are bustling with local shoppers. This colorful street was built by filling a canal, which still flows under its pavement. The whole operation was part of an ambitious project conceived by Napoleon's urban planners during the French occupation (1800-14): They imagined a large and perfectly straight avenue that, like a Paris boulevard, would connect Venice to the mainland, leading right to **La Salute** church. Fortunately, the plan was abandoned with the passage of Venice to Austrian domination (1814-61). ♦ Off Riva dei Sette Martiri east of Campo San Biagio. Vaporetto stop: Arsenale (1); Giardini (1, 52)

46 Campo Ruga Since the 10th century, this *campo* has been the center of a densely populated area. The residential neighborhood of today was built in the 14th and 15th centuries. The buildings at **Nos. 327** and **329** were rebuilt in the 17th century, and they were probably the homes of well-to-do merchants. The wellhead belongs to the 15th century. ♦ Between Calle di Ponte Santa Anna and Salizzada Stretta. Vaporetto stop: Arsenale (1); Giardini (1, 52)

47 Ponte San Pietro Many iron bridges similar to this one were built in Venice in the second half of the 19th century. Flat and unattractive, they were in contrast to those in the rest of the city, and many were later demolished (including the Ponte dell'Accademia and Ponte degli Scalzi). The small lagoon boats, double- and triple-parked along the canal, are witness to the strong ties still existing between the Venetians and the lagoon: Almost every family owns a boat, which it uses almost purely for pleasure—especially on holidays—to go fishing or to reach the popular restaurants that have sprung up on the lagoon islands. ♦ Between Calle Larga San Pietro and Campo San Pietro. Vaporetto stop: Arsenale (1); Giardini (1, 52)

48 San Pietro di Castello The castle (*castello*) that once occupied this island gave its name to the whole *sestiere,* or section of the city. This island was the first to be inhabited when ancient settlers moved from the lagoon island of Torcello to the present Venice in the sixth century, and the church was Venice's cathedral until 1807 (when the title was passed to the **Basilica di San Marco**). The island is like a country village; the families that live in the small houses on the side of the church are undisturbed by the hectic life of the city. The bell tower, now dangerously leaning, was rebuilt in 1596 to plans by **Andrea Palladio.** The interior was totally rebuilt in the 17th century according to Palladian principles. An interesting curiosity is **St. Peter's Chair,** on the right aisle. It was created around the 13th century from an Arab stone; the original inscriptions from the Koran are still visible on the chair's back. ♦ Campo San Pietro di Castello. Vaporetto stop: Arsenale (1); Giardini (1, 52)

49 Ristorante da Franz ★$$$ This restaurant is in the heart of a neighborhood of small, unpretentious homes far from the usual tourist venues. The tables are lined along a quiet and charming canal, a setting that could not be more Venetian. Franz, the owner, has had a lot of experience in fine restaurants, and it shows in the fish dishes served here. No longer as good as it was, this restaurant is too inconvenient for a special trip, but it's a good place to eat if you're in the area. When you're ready to leave, catch a *vaporetto* at the nearby stop **(Giardini),** or take the splendid half-hour stroll to **Piazza San Marco.** Note: The restaurant was closed after a fire at the end of 1995 and at press time its future was uncertain. ♦ M, W-Su lunch and dinner. Fondamenta di San Giuseppe 754 (north of Giardini Pubblici). 5220861. Vaporetto stop: Giardini (1, 52)

50 La Biennale Arte (Venice Art Biennial) The **Giardini Pubblici** (Public Gardens) at the eastern tip of town were designed by Napoleon, who drained a section of marshland to create Venice's favorite park. In 1895 the gardens were designated the home of the *Biennale Internazionale d'Arte,* a large art show planned every second year with the purpose of exhibiting contemporary art from all over the world. Twenty-eight pavilions are now scattered throughout the gardens, representing more than 50 nations. Artists are chosen by committees from their own countries. The *Biennale* is often controversial—and is meant to be so—and always memorable. ♦ June-Sept; odd years only. Zona Giardini (bounded by Rio del Giardini and Via del Giardini Pubblici). 5289327. Vaporetto stop: Giardini (1, 52)

51 Monumento alla Partigiana (Monument to the Partisan Woman) Venetian architect **Carlo Scarpa** designed this unusual, highly moving monument in 1964. It was completed with a bronze statue by contemporary sculptor Augusto Murer. The monument is set on the lagoon's bank at mid-tide level, so that its steps and the statue itself are sometimes immersed at high tide. ♦ Riva dei Partigiani (northwest end of Giardini Pubblici). Vaporetto stop: Giardini (1, 52)

52 Marinaressa The building with two large arches was added in the 1650s at the front of three parallel blocks of houses, built in the 15th century as part of a low-income housing project for sailors who had distinguished themselves. Low-income tenants still inhabit most of the apartments, although the ones in the front show signs of fancy—and expensive—restoration. ♦ Riva dei Sette Martiri 1428-1460 (west of Giardini Pubblici). Vaporetto stop: Giardini (1, 52)

Bests

Samantha Durell
Venice Travel Advisory Service

The best Venetian day possible: Meander through an unknown neighborhood without a map or a guidebook . . . eat where you see good-looking food being served . . . rest on benches in the *campi* beside Venetian residents and talk to them if you can . . . have an espresso here, an aperitivo there . . . let go for a day . . . this is the one you'll remember the rest of your life.

Circle the city at 2AM in an outdoor seat on the *No. 1 vaporetto.* Wonder at a world lost in time, draped now in midnight blue and twinkling lights.

Snacking and grazing is the Venetian way of life and the best way to sample Venetian specialties. Lots of neighborhood bars and restaurants feature *ciccheti* (tidbits of grilled vegetables, fish, and meat).

The **Chiesa Santi Giovanni e Paolo**—the place to be on a sleepy Sunday afternoon when the city shuts down. It is 14th-century Gothic, the size of an airplane hangar, and filled with stone monuments to great Venetian dynasties, the crypts and monuments of 25 doges, Bellini's newly restored *Polyptych*, a Gothic stained-glass window, St. Catherine of Siena's foot, and the unfortunate Bragadin's skin. The jewel of it all is the **Capella del Rosario,** the tiny chapel whose gilded ceiling is graced by four Veronese panels.

I love the antique glass beads and jewelry at **Anticlea Antiquariato:** a jewelbox of a store brimming with the most beautiful trade beads in Venice and an eclectic choice of collectibles, from fabric to furniture to postcards.

Silvia and Francesca Lachin sell elegant leather handbags, shoes and belts in their shop, **Silvia.** This is the best of Italian leather at prices people can afford.

Venetians still make the most beautiful glass—and with their own two hands. From the simplest small objects to the grand, monumental works of art, visit **Marco Polo, Vetro d'Arte.** This is the best showcase in Venice for all the best glass coming off the island of **Murano.** If you decide to take a ride out to Murano, the **Ferro & Lazzarini** factory has a wonderful working furnace, artisans to show you how it is done, and showrooms that glitter and dazzle the eye and the spirit.

The best fresh fish, beautifully prepared and followed by scrumptious desserts, a caring staff, and a warm, friendly ambience is **Al Covo. Fiaschetteria Toscana** also serves wonderful fresh fish, elegant meat and pasta, a fish gnocchi that is world class. **Al Tucano** is a neighborhood place with delicious pasta.

Marilyn Perry
Chair, World Monuments Fund/Art Historian

Sunrise on the lagoon from behind **San Giorgio Maggiore.**

Easter in the Greek church (**San Giorgio dei Greci**).

The midnight bell from the bell tower of **San Marco.**

Biking on the **Lido.**

A box for the opera at the **Teatro La Fenice.**

The flower seller in **Campo Santa Maria Formosa.**

The Titian in the **Chiesa dei Gesuiti.**

Pizza on the **Zattere** waterfront.

The fireworks at the *Notte del Redentore.*

Funghi porchini, radicchio di Treviso alla griggia, prosecco di Conigliano.

The statue of Colleoni in **Campo Santi Giovanni e Paolo** by moonlight.

P.L. Beggiato
Owner, Metropole Hotel

Trattoria Alla Madonna—If you survive the noise, the lights, and the impossible paintings, you will experience what is probably the best fish in Venice (relative to the low prices).

Fiaschetteria Toscana—Nothing to do with Tuscany, but a lot to do with high quality, seriously inventive cuisine, and attentive waiters (I've been there myself 93 times and was disappointed only once).

Harry's Bar (what a bore!)—Go there at 7:30PM just for a drink (the best in town), experience the miraculous transformation of a bar into a restaurant that takes place every day, and, if you have the money and a lack of imagination, stay on for dinner (the standards are monotonously high) and the best pastry in Italy.

Giudecca

The **Canale della Giudecca,** the canal that separates the Giudecca from the rest of Venice, is only 1,000 feet wide, but it is enough to make this island a distinctly autonomous community of some 8,000 residents. There are no bridges over the canal, but *vaporetto* service is regular. Things get a bit complicated in winter, when a thick fog may settle in for hours, making it nearly impossible to get to the island. Traditionally a poor community of fishermen and shipyard workers, the Giudecca is changing rapidly. Next to the modest but welcoming homes of the days of old you will find the most expensive luxury hotel in Venice—the **ALbergo Cipriani**—and an increasing number of fancy restaurants. A walk along the Giudecca canal bank provides one of the most rewarding experiences you can have in Venice—a panoramic view of the city's profile from **Dorsoduro** to **San Marco** is yours for the taking. At night, after a fine dinner at a local restaurant, even waiting for a *vaporetto* to take you back across the beautiful lagoon to **Piazza San Marco** is a delightful experience.

1 Albergo Cipriani $$$$ Located at the end of the Giudecca, this legendary hotel with 93 guest rooms enjoys an incomparable view over **Piazza San Marco** and the lagoon, and is decorated with great sophistication and taste. The garden and the outdoor facilities abound in flowers, and the swimming pool—the only one in Venice—is flanked by an outdoor dining area. In the summer, visitors are welcome to stop in for a luscious poolside buffet lunch. The hotel runs its own complimentary motorboat service to and from **Piazza San Marco**—just ring the buzzer and the handsome wooden launch will arrive in minutes. In 1991 the **Cipriani** opened an extension called **Palazzo Vendramin dei Cipriani** in an aristocratic 15th-century building, where some suites enjoy a splendid view over St. Mark's basin, while others open onto large wooden balconies. It includes nine apartments served by specially appointed butlers. ♦ Giudecca 10 (at eastern end of island). 5207744; fax 5203930.

2 Chiesa del Redentore Designed in 1577 by **Andrea Palladio** and built over a period of 15 years, this church was Venice's way of thanking the Lord for the end of a plague, an event that is still celebrated every year on the second Saturday in July and is called the *Notte del Redentore.* A temporary bridge of linked boats is built over the Canale della Giudecca to allow the traditional pilgrimage to the church. At night, an hour of fireworks over the lagoon attracts enormous crowds from the mainland, while Venetians watch from their boats. The rigorous, Classical harmony of the church's facade was one of **Palladio**'s best inventions and was imitated countless times in Venice and all over Europe. The paintings in the interior chapels illustrate episodes from the life of Jesus, from his birth (first chapel on the right) to the *Crucifixion* (main altar) and the *Resurrection* (on top of the dome). ♦ Campo del SS. Redentore (off Fondamenta San Giacomo). Vaporetto stop: Redentore (82)

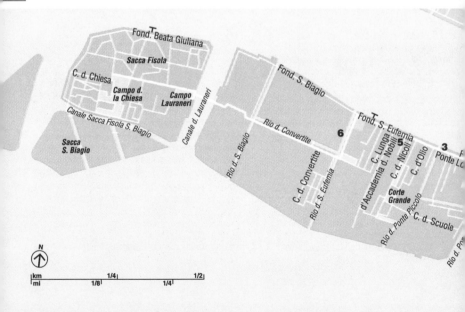

3 Fondamenta Ponte Lungo A walk along this short street gives you a good idea of what the Giudecca used to be like. The homes are modest but pleasant, and quite a few small fishing boats are tied along the canal. The last building at the left houses a rowing club—the keepers are very kind and won't object when visitors ask permission to enter the premises in order to admire the view of the wide lagoon. ◆ Between Rio del Ponte Longo and Rio del Ponte Piccolo. Vaporetto stop: Redentore (82)

4 Ristorante Altanella ★★$$ In warm weather, diners eat surrounded by flowers on a quiet wooden terrace over the Rio del Ponte Lungo. This restaurant is popular with Venetians because of its authentic home-style cooking and affordable prices. Fish dishes are the specialty, particularly those made with less expensive fish such as sardines, octopus, cuttlefish, mussels, and clams—but of course one can have grilled fresh *orata* (dorado, a fish similar to bream) or *branzino* (sea bass). ◆ M lunch; W-Su lunch and dinner. Reservations required. Calle dell'Erbe 264 (off Fondamenta Ponte Lungo). 5227780. Vaporetto stop: Redentore (82)

5 Trattoria Do Mori ★★★$$$ One of many signs of the Giudecca's upgrading was the opening in 1988 of this pleasant restaurant right on the bank of the main canal. The decor is in line with the trattoria tradition: old wood tables, no plastic, and a feeling of the days of old. Chef Fiorella Cicon is fond of Venetian cooking but often ventures beyond its bounds; her pasta is homemade (in the spring, try it with asparagus or artichokes), and her specialties include beef filet *Do Mori* (with nuts, celery, basil, and parsley) and fresh salmon *Do Mori* (sautéed in white wine with seasonal vegetables). ◆ Daily lunch and dinner. Fondamenta del Ponte Piccolo 588 (near Campo Sant'Eufemia). 5225452. Vaporetto stop: S. Eufemia (82)

6 Harry's Dolci ★★$$$ Arrigo Cipriani, owner of the famous (and more expensive) **Harry's Bar,** opened this annex in the early 1980s. It was supposed to specialize in desserts (*dolci*), but it quickly became one of the town's favorite restaurants—Cipriani class at affordable prices. It offers a full restaurant menu, with such unusual additions as club sandwiches. The canopies along the Canale della Giudecca create a beautiful space for dining outdoors, the real reason to come. ◆ M, W-Su lunch and dinner, Nov-Mar. Fondamenta Sant'Eufemia 773 (near Campo Sant'Eufemia). 5208337. Vaporetto stop: S. Eufemia (82)

Bests

John Julius Norwich
Writer and Historian of Venice

Dinner at my favorite restaurant, **Al Covo,** in **Castello.**

The top of the campanile of **San Giorgio Maggiore** at sunset.

A private gondola at night, exploring the swank canals only.

The Carpaccio paintings in the **Scuola di San Giorgio degli Schiavoni.**

The mad windmills in the windows just behind the **Scuola Grande di San Rocco.**

The Bellini altarpiece in **San Zaccaria.** (Five hundred lire lights it up.)

The Virgin behind the altar at **Torcello.**

A drink (or dinner) on the **Hotel Gritti** raft, watching the **Grand Canal.**

The Venetians invented income tax, statistical science, censorship, the gambling casino, the ghetto, and easel painting.

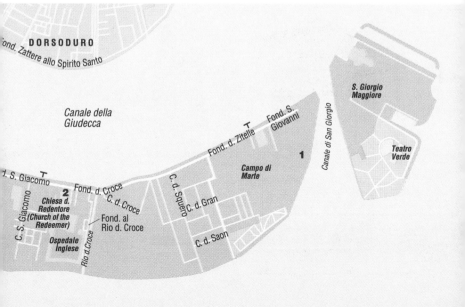

Venetian Islands

San Giorgio Maggiore

The solemn, triumphant sea entrance to the Canal Grande is defined by the **Palazzo Ducale, La Salute** church, and the island of **San Giorgio Maggiore**. The trio creates a majestic stage setting that seems to float on the waters of the lagoon. Architect **Andrea Palladio** was well aware of the overall effect he was creating when he designed the church that is the centerpiece of the island of San Giorgio.

The island was the property of a Benedictine abbey in the 10th century. The monks still occupy a large part of it, sharing the rest with the Fondazione Giorgio Cini, established in 1951 by wealthy Count Vittorio Cini in memory of his son Giorgio, who died in an airplane crash. The foundation (the entrance is near the church, by the boat landing) is one of the most active cultural institutions in Italy. It organizes symposia and conferences and runs three specialized libraries around two splendid cloisters, one of which was designed by **Palladio**. The main staircase was designed by **Baldassare Longhena** in 1644. The libraries—which are open to the general public, well staffed, and never too crowded—are a pleasure to use.

The church of **San Giorgio Maggiore** (founded in the 10th century and reconstructed to **Palladio**'s design

beginning 1565) faces **Piazza San Marco** and the Canal Grande entrance. **Palladio** is at his best in this church—the message is one of quiet, powerful harmony, based on Classical models yet still highly original. The interior contains two paintings by Jacopo Tintoretto, probably his last works: *The Last Supper* (right wall of chancel) and *The Gathering of the Manna* (left wall of chancel). The impressive bronze above the main altar represents *God the Father over the World Supported by the Four Evangelists,* a work by Girolamo Campagna. At the right of the chancel is the entrance to the **Cappella dei Morti** (Chapel of the Dead), with a *Deposition* by Tintoretto. A spiral staircase leads from the chancel to the **Coro Invernale** (winter choir), with *Saint George and the Dragon* by Vittore Carpaccio, painted by the master eight years after his similar work in **San Giorgio degli Schiavoni**. A few of the remaining Benedictine monks meet in the chapel every Sunday at 11AM to sing a mass in Gregorian chant. The general public is welcome. The **San Giorgio** campanile (bell tower), much less crowded than **St. Mark**'s, offers sweeping vistas of the city and the surrounding lagoon. The elevator entrance is in the church's chancel. ◆ Campanile: admission. Daily. (At press time the campanile was temporarily closed for restoration. Call first.) Campo San Giorgio. 5289900. Vaporetto stop: San Giorgio (82)

San Giorgio Maggiore

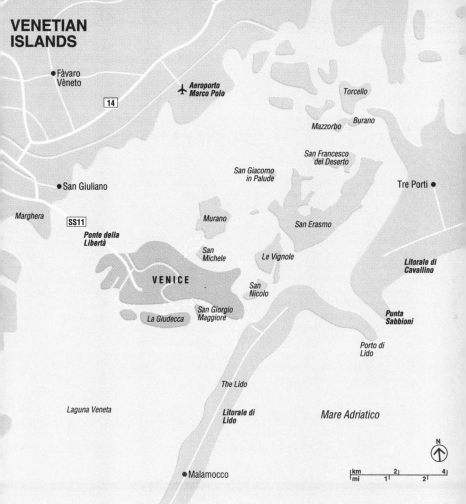

VENETIAN ISLANDS

Fàvaro Vèneto

Aeroporto Marco Polo

Torcello

Mazzorbo

Burano

San Francesco del Deserto

San Giacomo in Palude

Tre Porti

San Giuliano

Marghera

Murano

San Erasmo

Ponte della Libertà

San Michele

Le Vignole

Litorale di Cavallino

VENICE

San Nicolo

La Giudecca

San Giorgio Maggiore

Punta Sabbioni

Porto di Lido

The Lido

Laguna Veneta

Litorale di Lido

Mare Adriatico

Malamocco

N

km
mi

Murano

Less than a mile of water separates Murano from the northern shore of Venice (**Fondamente Nuove**). Transportation is provided by *vaporetto* line *No. 52,* which circumnavigates the whole city of Venice, detouring to circle around Murano as well. It is advisable to board the *vaporetto* at **Piazzale Roma** or at the train station, because the trip to Murano (about a half hour from **Piazzale Roma**) includes some beautiful stretches of the lagoon. From the *piazzale,* the *vaporetto* runs through the colorful **Canale di Cannaregio** to reach the open lagoon at **Sant' Alvise;** then it coasts along the northwestern banks to the Fondamente Nuove, where it heads for Murano. Alternatively, you can board at **Piazza San Marco** (there are two *No. 52 vaporetti;* take the "*sinistra,*" marked by a 52 with a line through it)—the itinerary is equally fascinating, as it cuts through the **Arsenale** and hits the lagoon at the northeastern tip of Venice. Whichever route you choose, you should get off the *vaporetto* at the first stop in Murano (called **Murano Colonna**) and continue the visit on foot.

The island is famous worldwide for its ancient glass factories, many of which offer a chance to see the glass artists at work. Murano's main street (**Fondamenta dei Vetrai**) has been taken over by glass souvenir shops, most of them inexpensive and geared toward tourists. The better factories, however, have their shops in downtown Venice as well, and it has been said repeatedly that prices are no better on Murano than anywhere else in Venice. The major furnaces you should look for are: **Barovier & Toso, Cenedese, Nanson & Moretti,** and **Toso,** all of which have adjacent stores.

Highlights on Murano include:

Museo dell'Arte Vetrario (Museum of Glass Art) The first part of the museum, on Fondamenta Manin 1/C and visible across the canal from Fondamenta dei Vetrai, includes glass objects produced in Murano in the 10th century. To see the second part, continue on Fondamenta dei Vetrai to the bridge called Ponte Vivarini, then make a right turn at Fondamenta Cavour. This part of the museum

contains nearly 4,000 Murano glass objects dating back as far as the 15th century. The 16th-century section is particularly rich in precious goblets, drinking glasses, and painted dishes; the 18th-century section includes some remarkable mirrors.
♦ Admission. Daily. Fondamenta Giustinian 8 (at Fondamenta Cavour). 739586. Vaporetto stop: Murano Colonna (52)

Chiesa di Santa Maria e San Donato

A different Murano from the tourist-oriented glass bazaar awaits you on this corner, just a few steps from the **Museum of Glass Art.** The apse of this church (pictured below), beautifully oriented toward a canal, is a masterwork of Venetian Medieval art—a simple, handsome Romanesque building with subtle Byzantine influences. The grassy square in front of the church adds to the magical medieval feeling. In the interior, the mosaics on the floor date back to the 12th century and have figures of animals, as in the floors of the **Basilica di San Marco.** The splendid mosaic on the inside of the

apse, similar to the one you'll find in Torcello's cathedral, represents the Virgin Mary on a Byzantine-inspired background of gold. The first painting on the left wall represents San Donato and is signed by Paolo Veneziano (1310). ♦ Campo San Donato. Vaporetto stop: Murano Colonna (52)

Busa alla Torre ★★$$ You'll soon get the impression that most Murano restaurants are not much more appealing or reliable than the average glass shop. But once you ferret out the spot where the local *gondolieri* are loyal patrons, eat in peace. Signor Lele runs this unpretentious trattoria with prices to match, where you'll feel welcome to stay even if only for a light lunch. A number of pastas are made regularly, such as the small *gnocchetti al salmone*, or the spaghetti *con pesce e vedura* made with fish and the fresh vegetables of the season (asparagus, zucchini, etc.). Ask about the daily fresh fish specialty, simply prepared *ai ferri* (grilled). ♦ Tu-Su lunch and dinner. Campo Santo Stefano 3 (near vaporetto stop). 739662. Vaporetto stop: Faro (52)

Chiesa di Santa Maria e San Donato

Ferro & Lazzarini The glass-master heavyweights have been manufacturing on Murano for centuries. But if their prices and over-the-top designs are out of your league and the alternative—choosing from among a plethora of poor-quality shops—is overwhelming, where do you go? This well-known furnace and retail store (owned by the Ferro and Lazzarini families since 1927) has its share of touristy trinkets, but it also has a wide selection of good-quality, moderately priced glassware ranging from the traditional to the contemporary.

Lighting fixtures, tabletop "art" glass, drinking glasses, paperweights, and Christmas ornaments can become works of art once rescued from their kitsch-laden environment and safely shipped home. ♦ Daily. No midday closing. Fondamenta Navagero 75 (near vaporetto stop). 739299. Vaporetto stop: Navagero (52)

Burano/San Francesco del Deserto/Torcello

A trip to these three islands is an opportunity to spend a few hours on the quiet landscapes of the lagoon, a totally different environment from the open sea. Public boats depart about every hour from the **Fondamente Nuove.** They are large and comfortable, but in the busy tourist season, you should come in the early morning and leave in the early afternoon to avoid the crowds.

This part of the lagoon is at its best at sunset in the summer—though everyone else seems to know this, too. The lagoon is surprisingly shallow—one could easily walk through it if it weren't for the mud at the bottom. At mid-tide, the depth averages three feet; with the tides it can go as high as five feet or as low as one or lower.

The large public boats run through natural canals marked by the wood poles called *bricole;* a mistake of maneuvering a few yards to either side would cause the boats to run aground in the flats. Smaller craft, however, travel freely, as they have flat bottoms that allow them to move in just a few inches of water.

Burano

Once a fishing community, Burano now depends on tourism for most of its income. Lacemaking was revived on Burano in the 19th century and has turned it into "Lace Island," just as Murano became "Glass Island." Countless shops and stands in the streets and alleys offer all kinds of lace-decorated items—most are machine-made in Spain or Asia, but don't despair, you can still find some handmade, and very costly, items.

In spite of the tourist boom, Burano has maintained the charming character of a small island community. The canals are lined with small lagoon boats, used for fishing and pleasure. It was on one of these boats that the English writer Frederic W. Rolfe, known as

Baron Corvo, spent the last years of his life in the early 1900s working on his novel, *The Desire and the Pursuit of the Whole.* Burano's houses were typically painted in a spectrum of bright colors, apparently to make them easy to identify by fishermen returning home; today the local administration here contributes to the painting by providing guidelines and funding. The best way to enjoy a visit here is to walk along the main street, **Via Galuppi,** taking a few random detours along the side canals—who knows what you'll find. Via Galuppi was named after Baldassare Galuppi, an 18th-century composer who was born on Burano.

Highlights on Burano include:

Ristorante da Romano ★★★$$$
This excellent seafood restaurant at the center of Via Galuppi has a large outdoor dining area. The walls inside are hung with the works of artists who have passed through Burano over the years. The kitchen specializes in fresh fish dishes and fish-based risottos and pastas. Before sitting down to dinner, ask about the boat schedule for your return to the city—the trip back to Venice at night is a memorable experience, but departures are infrequent. ♦ M, W-Sa lunch and dinner; Su lunch. Via Galuppi 221 (near Piazza Galuppi). 730030. Vaporetto stop: Burano (12, 14)

Scuola di Merletti di Burano (Lace School of Burano) For those interested, a visit to the local lace museum provides a historical overview of the craft and its techniques. Outside the museum, dressed in traditional white aprons, lacemakers sit in the sun, exchanging small talk and creating pieces of exquisite lace that can be purchased in the museum store. ♦ Admission. Tu-Sa. Piazza Galuppi. 730034. Vaporetto stop: Burano (12, 14)

San Francesco del Deserto

Near the church of **San Martino** on Burano, a private boat service departs for the small island of San Francesco del Deserto. The island houses an ancient Franciscan monastery (St. Francis is believed to have stopped here on his way back from the Holy Land). The monks offer tours of their lovely little paradise, which includes beautiful gardens and a 13th-century cloister. ♦ Donation. Daily. San Francesco del Deserto. 5286863

On Burano: ". . . an overcrowded little island where the women make splendid lace and the men make children."

Ernest Hemingway

Restaurants/Clubs: Red   **Hotels:** Blue

Shops/♥ Outdoors: Green   **Sights/Culture:** Black

Torcello

After Burano, the *No. 14 vaporetto* continues for 20 more minutes to the neighboring island of Torcello (many visitors get off to tour Burano, then catch one of the next boats to Torcello). This island can also be reached from Venice by a special taxi service available for lunch clients of Torcello's **Locanda Cipriani;** summer departures are every day at noon from the bank near **Piazza San Marco** in front of **Hotel Danieli,** returning at 3:30PM from **Locanda Cipriani.** No service on Tuesday or in winter.

Torcello was the first lagoon island where the mainland population found refuge from barbarian invasions in the fifth century. Although other lagoon areas were sparsely populated at the time, it was with this core of settlers that the city of Venice originated—in the following centuries the Torcello people expanded their settlement to the Rialto area and to the islands around it, gradually abandoning Torcello. It was a long process, and in the meantime this small island had become the civic and religious center of the entire lagoon. The remnants of that period still attract a great number of visitors. Two splendid churches stand side by side on the low, grassy land, surrounded by the lagoon and vegetable gardens of the small community that lives here year-round. The churches date back to the beginning of Venice, exhibiting a remarkable mixture of Byzantine sumptuousness and naïf, almost primitive, imagery. When the area is not filled with tourists, a majestic silence reigns over it—a reminder of the beauty and frailty of all things human. A short walk from the public boat landing along a canal flanked by fields leads to the tiny former main square of Torcello.

Highlights on Torcello include:

Torcello Cathedral

Osteria al Ponte del Diavolo ★★★$$$
This excellent restaurant run by a former manager of the **Locanda Cipriani** specializes in dishes prepared with fresh fish and local vegetables. You'll be taken for a regular if you start with the warm *insalata di frutti di mare* (fresh seafood salad). The restaurant also features outdoor garden seating. ♦ M-W, F-Su lunch. Closed Jan through Feb. Via Chiesa 10-11. 730401. Vaporetto stop: Torcello (14)

Torcello Cathedral The cathedral opens onto a grassy space that used to be the busy center of town, when Torcello had 20,000 residents (today only a few dozen people are permanent residents). An excavation in front of the church shows the foundation of the ancient **Baptistry,** while behind the church stands the 11th-century bell tower, which is sometimes visible from the distant mainland. The cathedral, begun in the seventh century, was reconstructed in 1008 upon the existing structure. Some of the material used in the reconstruction was brought over from early Christian buildings abandoned on the mainland when the barbarians invaded. The interior is reminiscent of the great Byzantine churches of Ravenna. The original 11th-century parts include the capitals, the floor, and the four splendid marble bas-reliefs in the iconostasis. The mosaic *Madonna and Child* in the apse is a masterwork of the 13th century. Of the same period is the famous mosaic on the interior facade, a *Last Judgment* drawn with medieval realism (notice the scene of the *Resurrection of the Dead* and, at the bottom, the *Blessed and the Damned*). Concerts are often held in the cathedral. ♦ Admission. Daily. Piazza del Duomo. 730084. Vaporetto stop: Torcello (14)

Masks, Glass, and Old Lace

Venice, like all major Italian cities that have played a powerful role in history, is home to a number of indigenous crafts that have survived the centuries. Their products make souvenirs that are as authentic today as they were for foreign visitors to the Republic in the past.

Since the reinstatement of *Carnevale* in 1980, the ancient Venetian art of mask making has undergone something of a renaissance. Though the forms are now many and often include the plumes and sequins of cosmic fantasy, there are still a few that would make Casanova feel right at home. The classic mask—the angular white beaklike form that extends over the chin, as depicted in the genre scenes of Pietro Longhi—is called the *bauta* and was once worn by men and women everywhere. Other masks take their cue from the stock characters in the commedia dell'arte (an improvisational comedy style using masks that originated near Venice and traveled from town to town): Pantalone and Il Dottore, the old misers; Arlecchino (Harlequin) and Brighella, the servant buffoons; and Capitano Spaventa, the braggadocio. All the masks are made out of a variety of materials, from the ubiquitous papier-mâché to the original leather and, more recently, ceramic.

Glass has been made in **Murano** since the end of the 13th century, and a furnace or two has always been active, but a 19th-century revival and another rebirth of interest after World War II have kept the fires roaring into modern times. Much of what is hawked on the island and in the city—mass-produced beads and tiny animal figurines—is of little interest, but a few items stand out as authentic or genuinely creative. Chandeliers, mirrors, meticulously replicated goblets, and other classic items from 16th-century Murano—when the industry was at its peak—are among the most appealing objects. Today, a few younger

people—many of them trained as architects or designers, and some of them coming from families of master glassmakers who have handed down the craft for generations—have been adding a welcome breath of fresh air to Venetian glassmaking. A vast array of contemporary designs has appeared, based on simple lines or witty interpretations of traditional forms and deserving of inclusion in the world's museums of modern art. Serious glass buffs or visitors to Venice who intend to buy should make a point of going to Murano's **Museum of Glass Art** (see page 193). A brief visit here will help you separate the sublime from the trash, with which you'll be inundated during your stay.

In the early 16th century **Burano** lace was all the rage among European nobility, even finding its way into Mary Tudor's trousseau. Once its pattern books began to circulate throughout the continent, however, Venetian lacework was soon eclipsed by that of the French, which was nothing more than a good imitation of the Burano art. On the verge of extinction, the industry was revived in the mid-19th century by Paolo Fambri and Contessa Andriano Marcello, and is still producing. While much of what passes for hand-produced Burano lace is imported from Spain or Asia, the industry that put the tiny island on the map survives. Burano's **Scuola di Merletti (School of Lace)** provides local girls with subsidized lessons and the chance to create the intricate stock for the shops on Burano and the even more renowned **Jesurum** in the **Mercerie of San Marco** (see page 136).

ILLUSTRATIONS BY ROLANDO CORUJO

Hotel Excelsior

Santa Fosca This church stands next to the cathedral and is surrounded by a medieval porch with arcades. Across the small grassy square is the **Museo di Torcello** (Torcello Museum), containing archaeological material documenting the Roman presence in the mainland communities bordering the lagoon as well as artifacts from the early Christian period. ♦ Admission. Tu-Sa. Piazza del Duomo. 730761. Vaporetto stop: Torcello (14)

Locanda Cipriani ★★$$$$ Arrigo Cipriani, the founder of **Harry's Bar,** opened this restaurant and tiny hotel in 1946 in a restored 17th-century villa (the operation has since been sold to relatives). His idea was to create a place for a wealthy clientele to spend a restful day or two in total isolation, surrounded by the absolute beauty of Torcello. The large garden and outdoor dining area offer a view of the apse of **Santa Fosca,** and the food and service are very good. The hotel has only four rooms, and at press time there was some question as to whether the place would continue to operate as a hostelry, so call ahead. ♦ M, W-Su lunch and dinner. Closed November through February. Reservations recommended. Locanda Cipriani. 730150; fax 735433. Vaporetto stop: Torcello (14)

San Lazzaro degli Armeni

The small island of San Lazzaro degli Armeni was given to a group of Armenian monks early in the 17th century. The monks installed a printing press

that became famous throughout Europe for the quality of its work. The monastery, **Monastero Mekhitarista,** still runs the island and the press. Their library is exceptionally rich in ancient manuscripts, particularly Armenian. A painting by Giambattista Tiepolo adorns the ceiling of the monastery's entrance hall. ♦ Monastery: admission. Daily 3-5PM. Vaporetto lines No. 10 and 20 connect the island with St. Mark's and the Lido. 5260104

The Lido

Nine miles long and less than a half-mile wide, the Lido is one of two thin, fragile islands that separate the lagoon from the open sea. The other island is called **Pellestrina** and is a continuation of the Lido all the way to the mainland at **Chioggia.** On the side facing the sea, the Lido is an uninterrupted stretch of wide beaches covered with fair-colored sand. For this reason, and because of its proximity to Venice, it became one of the preferred seaside resorts for the European upper classes, beginning in the 17th century. Some of the most luxurious hotels in Italy were built along its shores and are still in business, while the narrow land was built up with villas surrounded by gardens. A special feature of the Lido is that cars are allowed on the limited number of roads, which makes the hotels attractive to visitors who have lots of luggage and prefer to travel by car. A frequent ferry service carries automobiles to and from the **Tronchetto** terminal, near **Piazzale Roma,** while **Piazza San Marco** is a beautiful 15-minute *vaporetto* (no cars allowed) ride away.

Changing into a bathing suit is not permitted in the open on the Lido beaches; you must rent a cabin for a day or a half day. The least expensive area to do this is the **Zona A,** at the immediate left of the **Gran Viale** (very crowded and often noisy). Much more chic—and proportionately more expensive—are the luxury cabins of **Hotel Des Bains** (to the immediate right of the Gran Viale) and of **Hotel Excelsior** (at the end of the seaside walk). Other beach areas offer intermediate prices.

Highlights on the Lido include:

Gran Viale This colorful boulevard is the main street on the Lido, and the way to reach the beaches on foot from the *vaporetto* landings (a 10-minute walk). Most of the outdoor restaurants on both sides of the boulevard cater to tourists looking for a quick bite of pizza and such. There are also a number of places to rent bicycles. Don't miss the wonderful mosaic facade of the **Hotel Hungaria** (on the right, halfway along the Viale), built in 1906. ♦ Vaporetto stop: Santa Maria Elisabetta (1, 6, 52)

Hotel des Bains $$$$ This four-star, 191-room hotel was built in 1900 for the European aristocracy and was made even more famous by Visconti's movie *Death in Venice,* based on Thomas Mann's novel. The interior still has the original Art Deco fixtures. The hotel is surrounded by a large park and includes a swimming pool and an outdoor terrace for lunch. The hotel is part of the CIGA (Compagnia Italiana Grande Alberghi) chain (recently purchased by ITT Sheraton). Free transportation service to and from **Piazza San Marco** is available every half hour for hotel guests (departure is from **Hotel Excelsior**—a couple of minutes by a complimentary minibus). ♦ Early Apr-late Oct. Lungomare G. Marconi 41 (at Gran Viale). 5260201, in US 800/325.3589; fax 5267276. Vaporetto stop: Santa Maria Elisabetta (1, 6, 52)

Hotel Quattro Fontane $$$ This delightful hotel in a villa surrounded by a garden is run with exquisite taste by two highly cultivated sisters, who treat the premises like their own home and the guests like personal friends. All 62 rooms are decorated with antique furniture. The hotel is close to the casino and the film festival and 200 yards from the beach, yet it is perfectly quiet. Dining, available also to outside visitors, is in the garden among the flowers. Transportation to Venice is available every 20 minutes on *vaporetto* and with **Casino Express.** ♦ Early Apr-late Oct. Via delle Quattro Fontane 16 (off Lungomare G. Marconi). 5260227; fax 5260726. Vaporetto stop: Casino (52)

Hotel Excelsior $$$$ This elegant hotel, in a mix of Moorish, Gothic, and Byzantine styles, was built at the turn of the century for the posh clientele of the Lido. It is still the most lavish beachfront hotel in Venice, another jewel in the CIGA chain (recently purchased by ITT Sheraton), with a striking fountain in the main hall and the best of the 184 rooms directly overlooking the beach. Since 1937, in late August and early September, it becomes the headquarters of the jury for the annual *Venice Film Festival* (held across the street), and the list of movie stars who have stayed in its suites is long and dazzling. The **Excelsior** has two fine restaurants, one indoors and one outdoors. ♦ Lungomare G. Marconi 41 (near Via Emo Angelo). 5260201, in the US 800/325.3589; fax 5267276. Vaporetto stop: Casino (52)

Cristallo $$ This family-run hotel is the nicest of its category on the Lido. It has a good location and 24 clean and simply decorated rooms with ceiling fans and modern bathrooms. Parking is available—almost reason enough to stay here if you've arrived by car, especially in the summer months, when access to a private beach a 10-minute walk away is rather alluring. ♦ Gran Viale Santa Maria Elisabetta 51. 5265293; fax 5265615 (attn: Cristallo). Vaporetto stop: Santa Maria Elisabetta (1, 6, 52, 82)

Murazzi The name means "rough walls" and refers to the huge stone and concrete boulders that strengthen the median part of the Lido to protect against erosion. At the end of Lungomare Marconi and just after the **Hotel Excelsior** is this lonely and, in its way, fascinating part of the Lido, a half hour on foot from the main *vaporetto* landing (also accessible by bus). Venetians come here to bathe away from the crowds without having to rent a cabin. Sunset is strikingly beautiful here, as is the walk back to the *vaporetto* if you decide to cross the Lido and walk on the lagoon side. ♦ Vaporetto stop: Casino (52), or bus line *A* or *B* from Santa Maria Elisabetta

Milan Orientation

Milan is the most stylish and open-minded city in Italy. In spite of its rich past, evident in Roman and early-Christian monuments and its excellent art collections, Milan is the most contemporary city in Italy, if not Europe. The center of Italy's (and perhaps the world's) fashion and design industries, Milan is also the country's economic capital (the Milanese insist their city is also the *real* capital) and the locus of Italy's publishing, banking, television, and advertising worlds. Its prosperity ensures the best of everything—shopping and dining included—for travelers in town for business or pleasure.

Chances are visitors will find themselves here for business, but there is still a wealth of attractions for those who come for pleasure—museums, monuments, the world's most famous opera house, **La Scala,** and its most reproduced painting, Leonardo da Vinci's *Last Supper.* From the exquisite antiquities in the **Museo Poldi-Pezzoli** (Poldi-Pezzoli Museum) to the Futurist paintings in the **Galleria d'Arte Moderna** (Modern Art Gallery), Milan spans the ages like no other city in Italy. And though Milan may not be as beautiful as some of its sisters, it is always a delight to find old architecture mixed in with modern glass and concrete palazzi, or to peek into a courtyard to see how the Milanese nobility once lived—and still do.

City code is 2 unless otherwise noted. To call Milan from the US, dial 011-39-2, followed by the local number. When calling from inside Italy, dial 02 and the local number.

Getting to Milan
Airports

Milan has two airports—**Aeroporto della Malpensa** for international flights, and **Aeroporto Linate** for mainly domestic and international carriers. If one is fogged in, planes sometimes land at the other. During particularly heavy bouts of wintertime *nebbia* (fog), arriving flights are commonly rerouted to Turin or Genoa, and passengers are bused to Milan.

Aeroporto della Malpensa

The primary arrival and departure point for international flights, and a major gateway to Italy, **Aeroporto della Malpensa** is 45 kilometers (28 miles) from the city.

Airport Services

Airport Emergencies	40099732
Currency Exchange	40099489
Customs	40099854
Ground Transportation	40099260
Immigration	40099732
Information	74852200
Lost Baggage	74854215
Police	40099732

Airlines

Air France	773821; 800/237.2747
Alitalia	26852; 800/223.5730
British Airways	809041; 800/247.9297
KLM	70003888; 800/374.7747
Lufthansa	58372251; 800/645.3880
TWA	77961; 800/892.4141
United	864831; 800/538.2929

Getting to and from Aeroporto della Malpensa

By Bus

Buses connecting the airport and Milan's **Stazione Centrale** (with a stop at the **Porto Garibaldi** train station) leave every half hour. Tickets cost $7 and are available inside the airport and at the *Agencia Doria* inside the train station. At the airport catch the bus in front of the arrivals terminal (follow signs for **Air Pullman**). In the city the bus departs from the east side of the **Stazione Centrale;** the trip takes about an hour in light traffic.

By Car

The airport is about a one-hour drive to downtown, longer in rush hour. From the airport, follow the signs to the **Autostrada Milano Laghi (A8)** east. Exit at **Piazza Kennedy,** go left (east) on **Viale Alcide de Gasperi** to **Via Renato Serra** and turn right (south). At **Piazzale Lotto,** turn left onto **Via Monte Rosa,** which becomes **Via Giotto.** This connects with **Corso Vercelli** (stay to the right), which becomes **Corso Magenta,** then **Via Meravigli,** and leads to the **Piazza del Duomo.** Most of the downtown area is closed to traffic, except to taxis and vehicles displaying special passes. To get to the airport from **Piazza del Duomo,** simply reverse the route.

Rental Cars

The following rental car agencies have offices at the airport:

Avis 40099375; 800/331.1084

Budget 40099234; 800/472.3325

Hertz 40099022; 800/654.3001

Europcar (National) 40099351; 800/227.3876

By Taxi

Cabs are available at the taxi stand outside the arrivals building, but they are expensive (about $60 at press time). The trip to the city center takes a little less than an hour.

Aeroporto Linate

Milan's second airport, **Linate,** is about eight kilometers (five miles) from town and handles all domestic arrivals and departures as well as some international (though not intercontinental) flights.

Airport Services

Currency Exchange 70200596

Customs 740560

Ground Transportation.............................66984509

Information 74852200

Lost and Found 70102094

Police...70102094

Airlines

Air France.............................773821; 800/237.2747

Alitalia 26852; 800/223.5730

British Airways 809041; 800/247.9297

KLM 70003888; 800/374.7747

Lufthansa 58372251; 800/645.3880

Getting to and from Aeroporto Linate

By Bus

The **STAM** bus service between the airport and

Stazione Centrale in Milan runs every 20 minutes. Tickets can be purchased at the **Agencia Doria** inside the airport or train station. Catch the bus in front of the arrivals building at the airport or on the east side of the train station; the trip between the two takes about 20 minutes in light traffic. Local bus service also connects with the airport. Take the *No. 73* **ATM** bus to **San Babila.**

By Car

To get to the city center, follow the exit signs to **Via Forlanini.** Go west on Forlanini and follow it to the inner circle road near the **Piazza del Duomo.** Note, however, that most of downtown Milan is closed to traffic, except to taxis and vehicles displaying special passes.

Rental Cars

The following rental car agencies have offices at the airport:

Avis 715123; 800/331.1084

Budget 76110234; 800/472.3325

Hertz 70200256; 800/654.3001

Europcar (National) 76110258; 800/227.3876

By Taxi

Taxi service to downtown Milan is available outside the airport arrivals building. At press time, the trip cost about $15 and took about 20 minutes.

Bus Station (Long-Distance)

The city bus terminal is in **Piazza Castello.** A number of bus companies provide service connecting to the rest of Italy.

Train Station (Long-Distance)

Milan's main train station is the **Stazione Centrale** (Piazza Duca d'Aosta, bounded by Via Vitruvio, Via Galvani, and Via Pisani, 675001). When buying a ticket to Milan, make sure the train stops at that station and not at **Lambrate, Porta Genova,** or **Porta Garibaldi,** all stations that are less conveniently located. There's a taxi stand outside the main entrance.

Getting Around Milan

Bicycles

Cycling, although increasingly popular among the Milanese, is not recommended because of the traffic and exhaust fumes.

Buses and Trams

Milan's efficient bus and tram service, **ATM** (875495), runs between 6:15AM and midnight. Tickets are available at most newsstands, tobacconists, and cafes. They must be purchased before boarding the bus (get on at the front or rear doors, as the center one is for getting off), where you validate them in a little orange machine. English is spoken at the main **ATM** information office in the **Duomo** metro station (Piazza del Duomo); other offices are located in the **Cadorna** subway station (Piazza Cadorna near Castello Sforzesco), and **Stazione Centrale** (Piazza

Duca D'Aosta). These offices provide maps and sell day passes good for unlimited travel on the **ATM** system. Maps are also available from the tourist information office (see "Visitors' Information," below).

Driving

Because of the heavy traffic and complicated traffic zones in central Milan, using a car or moped to get around is not recommended. Most of the downtown area is restricted to vehicles with residential passes or taxis.

Parking

Hotels can provide assistance with parking, usually offering discounted rates at nearby facilities. Parking garages are conveniently located in and around the part of downtown that is not closed to traffic, but it is also possible to park on the street. Parking in Disc

MILAN METRO
(Metropolitana Milanese)

MM

Zones (*Zona Disco*, marked in yellow) is limited to one hour and requires a parking permit (*disco*) that is available at any gas station. In Green Zones (*Zona Verde*), parking is prohibited from 8AM to 9:30AM and again from 2:30PM to 4PM; this prohibition does not apply on Saturday afternoon, Sunday, or during the month of August. Towing is frequent, costly, and a major headache, so be sure of the rules before parking a car on the street.

Subway

Construction of Milan's subway, the **Metropolitana Milanese (MM),** started in the 1960s and the system continues to grow. It now consists of three lines operating from 6:15AM to midnight (see map above). Tickets are available at most newsstands, tobacconists, and cafes, as well as in vending machines at individual stations. Subway stops are indicated on the maps in this book with an **MM** .

Taxis

Cabs are plentiful in Milan and the drivers are pleasant. They wait at strategic locations around town (such as the train station, **Piazza del Duomo,** or **Piazza della Scala**), and can be called by dialing 5251, 6767, 5353, or 8585; they can be hailed on the street if their "taxi" sign is lit.

Tours

CIT (Galleria Vittorio Emanuele II, near Piazza del Duomo, 866661) and **American Express** (Via Brera 3, at Monte di Pietà, 77901) offer tours of Milan and excursions outside of the city; they can also help with travel arrangements throughout Italy. **Agenzia Autostradale** (Piazza Castello 1, near Via Dante, 144801161) offers a daily three-hour bus tour of the city, starting at the **Piazzetta Reale.** Tickets can be purchased in most hotels and travel agencies, or on the bus.

Walking

Air pollution and an all-business atmosphere make strolling in Milan less pleasant than walking in either Florence or Venice, but seeing the sights on foot is possible. Most of the major tourist destinations (and some of the best shopping in the world) are in either the **Centro** or **Brera** areas and in easy walking distance of one another.

FYI

Accommodations

Commerce and trade fairs keep Milan's hotels busy year-round, so reservations are always advisable. Since this is a business-oriented town, many hotels offer weekend discounts; don't forget to ask about them.

Climate

The summers in Milan are hot (highs in the 80s Fahrenheit) and very humid, particularly in July and August. The winters are rainy and damp, with occasional heavy fog; low temperatures are in the 30s Fahrenheit. As in most of Italy, the best times to visit the city are in late spring and early fall.

Months	Average Temperature (°F)
January	36
February	40
March	50
April	58
May	66
June	72
July	75
August	74
September	67
October	56
November	45
December	39

Embassies and Consulates

American Consulate Via Principe Amedeo 2/10 (near Via Turati) 290351

Australian Consulate Via Borgogna 2 (near Piazza San Babila)..777041

British Consulate Via San Paolo 7 (near Piazza del Duomo)...723001

Canadian Consulate Via Vittor Pisani 19 (near Stazione Centrale) 67581

Holidays

In addition to the national holidays (see "Northern Italy Orientation") Milan celebrates the feast day of Sant'Ambrose, its patron saint, on 7 December.

Hours

Stores are generally open Monday 3:30 to 7:30PM, and Tuesday through Saturday 9AM to 1PM and 3:30 to 7:30PM. Food shops are open Monday 9AM to 1PM, and Tuesday through Saturday 9AM to 1PM and 4 to 7:30PM. Churches are generally open daily 8AM-1PM and 4-6:30PM. Opening and closing times are listed by day(s) only if normal hours apply; in all other cases, specific hours are given (e.g., 8AM-3:30PM, noon-5PM).

Medical Emergencies

In case of a medical emergency call 7733 or 113. The **Croce Rossa Italia** (Red Cross; Via Pucci 7, near Corso Sempione, 3883) also provides 24-hour emergency assistance.

Money

Change money at **American Express** (Via Brera 3, at Monte di Pietà, 77901), **Banca Cesare Ponti** (Piazza del Duomo 19, 88211), or at any of the principal banks displaying the "Cambio" sign. Banks are generally open Monday through Friday 8:30AM to 1:30PM and again from 3PM to 4PM. Avoid changing money at the airports and train station; the agencies there charge high commissions.

Personal Safety

Pickpockets operate on buses, trams, and crowded subways in Milan. Also, beware of those who prey on weary tourists, especially those getting on and off the airport buses at the **Stazione Centrale.** Exercising some common sense and taking elementary precautions will outwit most bag, camera, and wallet snatchers. Never carry more than you can afford to lose—i.e., keep your passport and larger amounts of cash in the hotel safe or well concealed in a money purse—and don't leave any valuables visible in a rented car.

The nighttime streets of Milan are quite safe, so feel free to venture out to visit the **Duomo** or window shop along **Via Montenapoleone,** but avoid the area around the train station, where light drug dealing occurs.

Pharmacies

There is a 24-hour pharmacy in the **Stazione Centrale,** the **Farmacia Stazione Centrale** (Galleria delle Partenze, Piazzale Duca D'Aosta, 6690735).

Postal Service

The main post office, **Poste e Telecommunicazioni** (Via Cordusio 4, west of Piazza del Duomo, 8692874), is open Monday through Friday 8:15AM to 7:30PM, and Saturday 8:15AM to 12:30PM.

Publications

English-language cultural events listings can be found in *Night & Day Milano,* available in many hotels. Ask for *Milano Mese* at the tourist information office (see "Visitors' Information Office," below). Weekly events listings are also published in the daily newspapers; in *Corriere della Sera* on Wednesday, and in *La Repubblica* on Thursday.

Restaurants

Most restaurants close one or two days a week (the day varies), usually a week or so in August (often the entire month), and between Christmas and New Year's Eve. Lunch is served from 12:30 to 2PM. Peak dinner time is 8:30PM; kitchens close around 10:30PM. Many of the more expensive restaurants in Milan now offer less expensive lunch menus, often at fixed prices. Reservations, while not required, are suggested and may be essential at the most expensive or popular restaurants, particularly when the city is abuzz with one of its many trade fairs. Some dining spots may have an informal dress code, especially in this fashion capital, so be sure to ask when calling for a reservation.

Shopping

Milan is the undisputed capital of modern Italian design—in clothing, architecture, and even humble household objects. In the **Galleria Vittorio Emanuele II** and along the city's most elegant shopping streets, Via Montenapoleone, **Via della Spiga,** and **Via Sant'Andrea** are the names of virtually every designer whose work appears between (or on) the covers of *Vogue, Elle,* and *GQ* (and some that may be there tomorrow). Here, too, are postmodern showrooms for functional but highly designed household and office furnishings, housewares, and gifts.

Visitors looking for something more affordable might want to try shopping outside the trendy Centro and Brera areas, or go to the outdoor market, held every Tuesday morning and Saturday, on **Viale Papiniano** and **Via V. Marcello** in the **Ticinese/Naviglie** area. For antiques, try the **Mercato di Brera,** held on the third Saturday of every month from 10AM to 11PM in and around **Piazza Formentini.**

Street Plan

The heart of Milan is a series of concentric rings (formerly canals) radiating out from the **Piazza del Duomo** and divided into eight neighborhoods: Centro, **Magenta, Parco Sempione,** Brera, **Stazione Centrale, Porta Venezia, Porta Vittoria/Porta Romana,** and **Ticinese/Navigli.**

Telephones

The **SIP/Telecom** office at the **Stazione Centrale** is open daily 8AM to 7:45PM. Telephone calls can be made here using American calling cards or credit cards, or by paying afterward in cash.

Visitors' Information Offices

The offices of the **Azienda di Promozione Turistica (APT)** are extremely helpful and conveniently located near the **Piazza del Duomo** (Via Marconi 1, 809662; fax 72022432) and in the **Stazione Centrale** (Piazzale Duca d'Aosta, 6690432, 6690532). Both are open Monday through Saturday from 8AM to 8PM and on Sunday from 9AM to 12:30PM and 1:30 to 5PM. The **Ufficio Informazioni (Information Office)** in the **Galleria Vittorio Emanuele II** (near Piazza della Scala) is open Monday through Saturday from 8AM to 8PM.

Phone Book

Emergencies

Ambulance	113
Auto Breakdown Service	116
Fire	115
Police Emergency	113
Police Nonemergency	62261
24-hour Medical Service	3883 (Red Cross)

Visitors' Information

Customs	40099854 (Malpensa); 740560 (Linate)
Postal Information	8692874
Taxi	5251, 6767, 5353, 8585
Train	675001

Centro

Milan's Centro, or city center (the densest half is covered here), was enclosed in medieval times by a circular wall and canals, or *navigli*. Although the canals have long since been covered up, the boundaries of Milan's innermost circle are still known as the **Cerchia dei Navigli** or canal ring. Yet apart from the dominating presence of the **Duomo** and the usual scattering of churches, there are relatively few historical sights in the area, and it takes some effort to single them out amid the modern buildings, heavy traffic, and bustling crowds. Among the more noteworthy sights are the spiritual home of the opera world, **La Scala**, and the stately residences wealthy Milanese commissioned during sporadic building booms. Though less genteel, the booms that followed the extensive bombing during World War II were primarily Modernist in style and are predominant in Milan today.

As its Functionalist appearance suggests, the Centro is the heart of Milan's—indeed Italy's—commerce. While most of the business is of little interest to the average visitor, one aspect is of international appeal. Big-name clothing and accessory designers who have made Milan the world's fashion capital have given this small part of the city the largest concentration of status signatures on earth. Most of their wares are dazzlingly displayed on and around the four streets—**Via Sant'Andrea**, **Via Spiga**, **Via Borgospesso**, and **Via Montenapoleone**—collectively known as the **Quadrilatero.** Here the names of the patrician families who built the district's discreet palazzi have been eclipsed by their modern-day designer heirs. As contemporary and trendy as the vision of silks and baubles shining in chic window displays may seem, it evokes the spirit of the medieval mercantile tradition and the outline of the long-gone *navigli* that have permanently inscribed the boundaries of Milan.

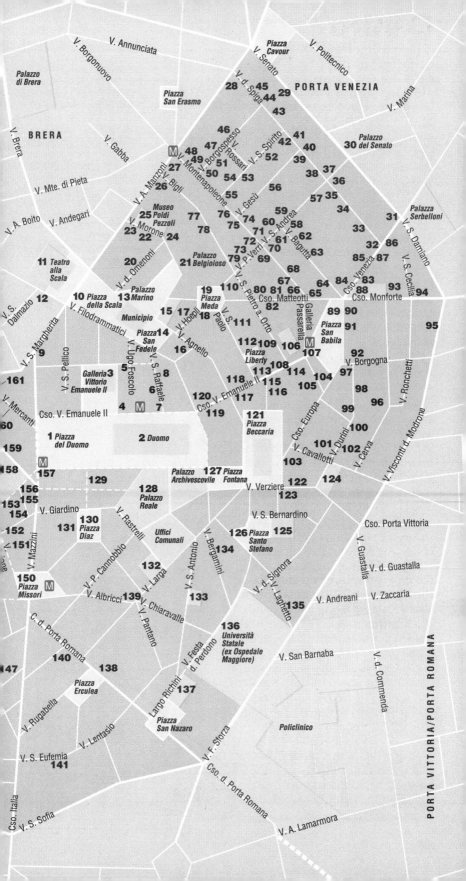

1 Piazza del Duomo The building boom that swept Italy after the country's unification in the 19th century is widely evident in the **Piazza del Duomo.** Part of the site had been the center of Milan's civic life since the Middle Ages, and in the same way that room was made for Florence's **Piazza della Repubblica** and Venice's **Piazza San Marco,** in 1865 a medieval neighborhood was knocked down to expand the space in front of the cathedral. Today the piazza designed by **Giuseppe Mengoni** remains the civic center and roughly the geographical center of Milan, the rings of the city's streets radiating from the vast rectangle of the piazza. Facing the **Duomo** is an equestrian **Monument to Vittorio Emanuele II** (1896, **Ercole Rosa**), the first king of Italy, backed by proud expanses of billboards and neon, making **Piazza del Duomo** an Italian version of Times Square or Piccadilly Circus. The piazza was torn up for years during construction of a new subway line, and now that construction is completed, it's hard to imagine how hordes of people could ever have negotiated the space while it was cluttered with so much equipment. The masses that pass between the monument and the cathedral include Milanese going about their daily business at the usual brisk pace, tourists and schoolchildren gaping at the **Duomo,** strollers and shoppers headed in and out of the **Galleria Vittorio Emanuele II,** determined flocks of Milanese pigeons pecking for a handout, and the occasional pilgrims expressing their faith or seeking peace or prosperity. The piazza is busier than ever underground, now that two of Milan's three subway lines (at the entrances, its "M" emblem, for *Metropolitana Milanese,* unconsciously apes the outlines of the **Duomo**) converge on the spot. ♦ At the intersection of Via Orefici, Via Torino, Via Mazzini, and Corso Vittorio Emanuele II. Subway stop: Duomo (M1, M3)

Duomo

2 Duomo Construction of Milan's bristly cathedral was begun in 1386 under the progressive dominion of Gian Galeazzo Visconti and brought to a hasty conclusion under an impatient Napoleon between 1805 and 1813; however, the bronze portals of its facade were all completed during this century, the southernmost as recently as 1960. Hence the Milanese expression, *lungo come la fabbrica del Duomo* (as long as the building of the **Duomo**), for something that seems interminable. The **Duomo** (see plan at right) is made primarily of white marble from the quarry at Candoglia, opened by Visconti, and white marble is still used to repair it. The marble was first used on the apse, the most beautiful part of the cathedral, built between 1386 and 1447 (with rose windows by Filippino da Modena) in a fairly unadulterated Northern Gothic style. Still more stone was chiseled into a forest of pinnacles and spires sheltering armies of statues, more than 3,000 in all. Take some time to see the trees in the forest and the soldiers in the army—their statues (of saints and sinners, knights and pilgrims, and fanciful gargoyles held up by wild giants) are surprisingly animated and individualistic. Above this display, the Milanese people's beloved *Madonnina* presides serenely from the central spire on the roof. The "little Madonna," an 18th-century gilded-copper statue by Giuseppe Perego, is actually more than 13 feet tall and is considered the protectress of the city. Such ideas may seem quaint for sophisticated Milan, but if you gaze upon the *Madonnina* illuminated at night, when she seems to hover in a golden cloud above the darkness and fog, you may begin to believe.

The facade—a conglomeration of Baroque, Neo-Gothic, and Neo-Classical styles—brings a pout to the mouths of purists. The most interesting of the facade portals is the central one (by **Ludovico Pogliaghi**), depicting the *Life of the Virgin* in a Neo-Gothic style that flows into Art Nouveau. Atop all the doors are 17th-century bas-reliefs designed by Giovanni Battista Crespi (also known as Cerano). Those same purists' mouths drop open in awe when they enter the cathedral and witness its squat and spiny exterior yield to a soaring smoothness inside. Second in the world only to St. Peter's in Rome in its vastness, the interior is filled with row upon row of columns rising into a haze of incense, the heavenly counterpoint to the devilish fog frequently sitting watch outside, while the colors of stained-glass windows blaze through the mist.

More color graces the mosaic marble pavement, designed by Pellegrino Tibaldi in the 16th century and finished in 1940. Works of art are scattered throughout. In the first bay of the right aisle is the *Tomb of Archbishop Ariberto* [1] (numbers refer to floor plan) by

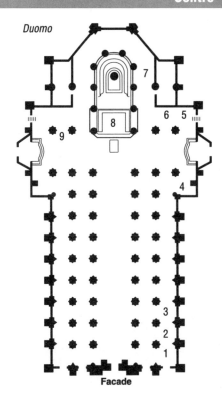

Duomo

Facade

an unknown artist; to its left is a marble slab with the inscription "El principio dil Domo di Milano fu nel anno 1386" (The founding of the Duomo of Milan was in the year 1386), as much proof of the origins of Milan's cathedral as of the obscurity of its dialect. In the second bay [2] are the *Tomb of Ottone Visconti* and the *Tomb of Giovanni Visconti,* both by unknown artists. In the third bay [3] is the *Tomb of Marco Carelli,* also by an unknown artist. Against the west wall of the right transept is the 16th-century *Tomb of Gian Giacomo Medici* [4] by Leone Leoni. On the east wall of the transept is the Renaissance *Altar of the Presentation in the Temple* [5] by Agostino Busti, known as Bambaia. Next to it is a decidedly unidealized 16th-century statue *St. Bartholomew Flayed,* skin in hand, by Marco d'Agrate [6]. The sculptor tried to offset some of his statue's distastefulness by inscribing on it "Non Me Praxiteles sed Marcus Finxit Agrates" (I was not made by Praxiteles but by Marco d'Agrate). The **Ambulatory [7]** contains the 15th-century *Monument to Pope Martin V* by Jacopino da Tradate and the 16th-century *Tomb of Cardinal Mario Caracciolo* by Giacomo da Campione. In the **Presbytery** are a 16th-century high altar and magnificent oak choir stalls [8] by Pellegrino Tibaldi, Camillo Procaccini, and others. In the left transept is the Gothic Trivulzio candelabrum [9]. Just inside the main door is a staircase that leads to the Paleo-Christian excavations beneath the church (admission; Tu-Su). Outside, on either side of the north transept, are the staircase and elevator that lead to the roof (admission; daily), which allows for a close-up view of the architectural details and delightful statuary and pinnacles, as well as the best wide-angle view of the city and its surroundings. If there is no haze or fog, you can see the Alps (including the Matterhorn) and the Appenines across the Lombard plain. ♦ Piazza del Duomo (east side of piazza). Subway stop: Duomo (M1, M3)

3 Galleria Vittorio Emanuele II Through a triumphal arch, the **Galleria** connects the **Piazza del Duomo** to the **Piazza della Scala,** but it is much more than a *galleria,* or passageway. Here, in 1878, **Giuseppe Mengoni** designed the prototypical modern shopping mall: four iron-and-glass covered streets with Neo-Renaissance facades converging on a central piazza topped by an iron-and-glass dome. Though the architect died in a fall from the **Galleria**'s scaffolding a few days before its official opening, his work has lived on with such success that it has become known as *il salotto di Milano* (the drawing room of Milan). Each day thousands of people gather in or pass through the space, so vast that the authorities have draped netting over the entrances to reduce pigeon traffic. One animal is welcome in the **Galleria,** however—the bull depicted in the pavement directly beneath the dome. Stepping on the beast's rather publicly exposed privates is supposed to bring good luck. ♦ Between Piazza del Duomo and Piazza della Scala. Subway stop: Duomo (M1, M3)

Within the Galleria Vittorio Emanuele II:

Caffè Miami The cheery red cordial Campari made its debut here when the cafe was called **Camparino.** Most Milanese still know it by that name, and the cafe retains its original Art Nouveau furnishings, which help make it the most popular such spot in the **Galleria.** ♦ M-Tu, Th-Su 7:30AM-8:30PM. 86464435

Bocca Brusque service and a broad selection of art books distinguish this bookshop, the oldest of many in the **Galleria.** ♦ Daily; no midday closing. 86462321

Bernasconi This is one of the nicest—and most expensive—silversmiths in town, with styles ranging from antique to contemporary. ♦ M afternoon, Tu-Sa. 872334. Also at: Corso Magenta 22 (near Via San Nicolao). 867072. Subway stop for second location: Cadorna (M1, M2)

Restaurants/Clubs: Red   **Hotels:** Blue
Shops/ ♀ Outdoors: Green   **Sights/Culture:** Black

Biffi in Galleria ★★$$ This traditional rendezvous spot for the Milanese serves fine meals in its ground-floor restaurant and upstairs cafeteria, but even better are drinks in its outdoor cafe almost beneath the **Galleria**'s central dome, where you can sample the house cocktail, the "slap," made from grapefruit and pineapple juices with vodka and a splash of curaçao. ♦ M-Sa. Restaurant: noon-midnight; cafeteria: lunch only; cafe: 8AM-midnight. 8057961

Burghy ★$ Despite its name and menu of burgers and the like, this fast-food chain is a thoroughly Milanese phenomenon. Their outlets serve as hangouts for the *paninari* (sandwich eaters) and mall rebels *alla milanese.* Actually, they are less juvenile delinquents than fashion plates, affecting such expensive American dress as Pendleton shirts, Levis, Timberland shoes, Burlington socks, and Ray Ban sunglasses when they (or *mamma*) can afford it. Because of its location at the very center of the **Galleria,** this **Burghy** (one of a dozen or so in the city) is particularly popular. The fare, while standard, isn't bad. The service is faster, and the food is a cut above the other chains in town, such as **Italy & Italy** (which emphasizes design over dining) and **Wendy's** (which consistently serves stale buns and cold fries, and invariably claims its milkshake machines are out of order). ♦ M, W-Su 10AM-midnight. 86460065

CIT The main Milan office of the government-owned **Compagnia Italiana Turismo** travel agency is friendlier and more efficient than other branches in Italy. It is a good place to make travel arrangements and cash traveler's checks because it doesn't charge commissions and accepts credit cards. ♦ M-F (no midday closing); Sa mornings only. 866661

Il Gabbiano This typical *gelateria* offers a full selection of frozen treats in fruity and creamy varieties (which are also used to make *frullati,* or shakes) as well as good, fresh sandwiches. ♦ M-Sa 7:30AM-8PM. 72022411

3 Savini ★★★$$$ There is no better place for a taste of Old Milan than this restaurant, as much a city institution as the **Duomo** or **La Scala.** The Milanese business types who patronize this red-velvet, crystal-chandeliered

restaurant like the international items on the menu, but the surroundings inspire many to order traditional dishes such as *risotto giallo* (a creamy rice dish saturated with saffron, so associated with the city it is known throughout the rest of Italy and abroad as *risotto alla milanese*), *costoletta* (breaded and fried veal cutlet, known elsewhere as *costoletta alla milanese*), or osso buco (roast veal shank, prepared *alla milanese* with a sauce of lemon peel, anchovies, herbs, and spices). There are plenty of variations on the *risotto giallo* theme—it can be ordered plain, *con midollo* (with veal marrow), *con tartufo bianco* (with white truffle), and *al salto* (sautéed into a crisp pancake). At press time, work was being completed to repair damage by a recent fire. ♦ M-Sa lunch and dinner. 72003433

Rizzoli The flagship store of Italy's most internationally known bookstore chain was designed by **Achille Castiglione**. The store is part of a publishing empire that comprises books, magazines, and *Corriere della Sera*, Milan's daily paper and the closest thing Italy has to a national newspaper (along with *La Repubblica*, partially owned by Rizzoli's rival, **Mondadori**). In the basement is the country's largest selection of paperbacks; the non-Italian reader can find guidebooks and books on Italian culture, many of which are in English, on the ground floor. ♦ M-Sa (no midday closing); Su. 8052277

Ricordi Recordings are augmented by videos, books, and sheet music at the main megastore of Italy's best-known music publishers. ♦ M afternoon, Tu-Sa. 86460272

Ufficio Informazione (Information Office) Milan's tourist-information office is so well organized and forthcoming that the first question you want to ask them is, "Am I really in Italy?" Piled high with printed matter and glowing with touch-sensitive video monitors, the material is backed up by a staff of multilingual city employees. The facilities offer information for finding out about current art exhibitions, concerts, plays, and the like. ♦ Daily (no midday closing M-Sa). 809662

4 La Rinascente The success of Milan's longest-established department store is evident in the number of its shopping bags you'll see toted throughout town. This six-floor emporium of quality merchandise is the closest thing in Italy to an American- or British-style department store. A cafe on the top floor called **Cento Guglie** (100 Spires) has an in-your-face view of the **Duomo**. ♦ M afternoon, Tu-Sa; no midday closing. Piazza del Duomo (north side of piazza). 88521. Subway stop: Duomo (M1, M3)

Within La Rinascente:

Bistrot di Gualtiero Marchesi ★★$$$ Adjacent to the cafe, the view of the **Duomo**'s lacy fretwork is more impressive from here,

maybe because the menu is prepared by Senore Marchesi, one of Italy's most renowned chefs. Chic, simple, and considerably less noisy than the eatery next door, you'll sample a seasonal menu here as interpreted by the maestro's hand, without paying the prices of his former restaurant, which was the rage of the culinary world in the 1980s. In addition to choosing à la carte, you might consider the *menu milanese* to experience osso bucco as it was meant to be enjoyed. During store hours take the elevator to the seventh floor; in the evening enter from Via San Raffaele 2. ♦ Tu-Sa lunch and dinner. 877120

5 Primafila ★★$$ This reasonably priced and convenient restaurant and pizzeria serves well-prepared Milanese and Tuscan classics from minestrone, homemade pastas, and various risotto dishes to local gorgonzola cheese. ♦ M-Tu, Th-Su lunch and dinner until 1AM. Via Ugo Foscolo 1 (off Piazza della Scala). 862020. Subway stop: Duomo (M1, M3)

6 Casa Svizzera $$ As efficient as its name implies (it means Swiss house), this no-nonsense, 45-room hotel attracts a loyal business clientele. While it is aesthetically uninteresting, it is conveniently located. There's no restaurant. ♦ Via San Raffaele 3 (between Piazza del Duomo and Piazza della Scala). 8692246; fax 72004690. Subway stop: Duomo (M1, M3)

7 Grand Duomo $$$ A great central location on a quiet side street and courteous service make this hotel popular with upscale business and tourist clientele. Some of the spacious 125 rooms of contemporary design have a view. There is also a well-frequented restaurant offering a Milanese and classic Italian menu. ♦ Via San Raffaele 1 (off Piazza del Duomo). 8833; fax 86462027. Subway stop: Duomo (M1, M3)

8 San Raffaele This little church was commissioned in 1575 by Charles Borromeus, who eventually achieved sainthood himself, on the site of a medieval church. The facade has been attributed to **Pellegrino Tibaldi**, and more recently to **Galeazzo Alessi**. Inside are 17th-century Milanese paintings: *St. Luke and St. Matthew*, by Ambrogio Figino, in the right nave; *Supper at the Jews*, attributed to Caravaggino, on the far wall; *Disobedience of Jonathan*, by Giovanni Battista Crespi (known as Cerano), on the right side wall; and *Dream of Elias*, by Pier Francesco Mazzucchelli (known as Morazzone), on the left side wall. ♦ Via San Raffaele (near Via Ricordi). Subway stop: Duomo (M1, M3)

Berlioz complained that the music at La Scala could not be heard above the noise of the people eating in the boxes during the performances.

9 Caffè Scala ★★$$ This vaguely Viennese-style cafe attracts a definitely Milanese blend of fashion and designer types. It reopened in 1993 after a full restoration. ♦ Tu-Su 7AM-1AM. Via Santa Margherita 14-16 (off Piazza della Scala). 876847. Subway stops: Duomo (M1, M3); Cordusio (M1)

10 Piazza della Scala This piazza, at the northern end of the **Galleria,** is the stage for more Milanese excitement. The piazza's most dramatic moment comes each Saint Ambrose Day, on 7 December, dedicated to Milan's patron saint. The date marks the opening of the opera season at **La Scala** across the street, when a motley crowd gathers to gawk at and sometimes jeer the tanned and bejeweled opening-nighters. In the center of the piazza is a 19th-century statue by Pietro Magni of Leonardo da Vinci, who lived in Milan from about 1482 until 1498 in the service of Ludovico Sforza. ♦ North of the Galleria Vittorio Emanuele II. Subway stop: Duomo (M1, M3)

11 Teatro alla Scala At first glance, the Neo-Classical exterior of one of the world's great opera houses, designed by **Giuseppe Piermarini** (1776-78), seems surprisingly un-grand. Once inside its horseshoe-shaped wooden interior, however, it is easy to imagine the precipitously rising boxes and balconies filled with gentry giving each other the eye, eating, playing cards, carrying on romantic or political intrigues (as they did when Milan was subjugated by Napoleon and the Austro-Hungarian rulers), and occasionally even paying attention to the stage. Among the many works to have premiered here were Vincenzo Bellini's *Norma,* Giuseppe Verdi's *Otello* and *Falstaff,* Amilcare Ponchelli's *Gioconda,* and Giacomo Puccini's *Turandot.* Severely damaged by Allied bombs during World War II, the theater was rebuilt largely thanks to the efforts of Arturo Toscanini, who under Fascism had emigrated to the US, where he raised funds for the reconstruction (1945-46, **Luigi Lorenzo Secchi**). Other kinds of bombs have fallen in the postwar years, since the theater began a policy of introducing less traditional works into its regular repertoire, from Alban Berg's *Wozzeck* to Robert Wilson's production of Giacomo Manzoni's *Dr. Faustus.* Opera season at **La Scala** runs from 7 December to July; concert season is September through November. Though nonsubscription tickets are hard to come by, hotel concierges can often produce them if you sing a convincing enough aria and see to it that their efforts are applauded with palm grease. ♦ M-Sa 10AM-10PM; Su 3-6PM. Via Filodrammatici 2 (at Via A. Manzoni). 72003744. Subway stop: Cordusio (M1)

Within the Teatro alla Scala:

Museo alla Scala An opera fan's Valhalla, this museum contains room after room of operatic memorabilia, a large part of it centering around Giuseppe Verdi. Of more general interest are the bust of tenor Niccolò Taccardini, by neo-classical sculptor Antonio Canova, and objects from ancient Greek and Roman theater, including a Greek drinking vessel covered with scenes from the popular theater. A ticket to the museum will also let you take a peek at the theater. ♦ Admission. M-Sa Nov-Apr; daily May-Oct. 8053418

12 Biffi Scala ★★★$$$ This historic restaurant has been given a light touch in its postmodern decor and menu, though such Milanese classics as *risotto al salto* (crisp fried risotto) and *costoletta alla milanese* (breaded fried veal cutlet) are as deliciously rich as ever. This place is as perfect for a business lunch as it is for an after-**Scala** supper. ♦ M-F lunch and dinner. Via Filodrammatici 2 (at Via Manzoni). 866651. Subway stop: Cordusio (M1)

13 Palazzo Marino Commissioned by the Genoese banker Tommaso Marino, this handsome palazzo is the work of many hands, some heavier than others. The Renaissance facades (dating from 1553) facing Via Marino and **Piazza San Fedele** are by **Galeazzo Alessi,** but the **Piazza della Scala** side dates from 1892 and is by **Luca Beltrami.** From that side you can enter **Alessi's** heavily detailed court-yard, from which you can peek into the ornate **Sala dell'Alessi,** seat of the City Council. City government offices occupy the rest of the palazzo. ♦ Piazza della Scala (northeast in piazza). Subway stop: Duomo (M1, M3)

14 Piazza San Fedele In this small piazza adjacent to the **Palazzo Marino** is Francesco Barzaghi's 1883 *Monument to Alessandro Manzoni,* the Milanese author of *I Promessi Sposi* (*The Betrothed*). ♦ Southeast of Piazza della Scala. Subway stop: Duomo (M1, M3)

15 San Fedele This Jesuit church, begun in 1569 by **Pellegrino Tibaldi,**) has a cupola designed by **Francesco Maria Richini** in 1684 and a Baroque sacristy (also designed by

Richini in 1624-28) containing carved wood by Daniele Ferrari. ♦ Piazza San Fedele (southeast of Piazza della Scala). Subway stop: Duomo (M1, M3)

16 Pellux Luggage, luggage, and more luggage—including the Pellux line of classic leather suitcases in all sizes—is featured here. Attachés are for sale as well. ♦ M afternoon, Tu-Sa. Via Ragazzi del 99 (off Piazza San Fidele). 864104. Subway stop: Duomo (M1, M3)

17 Ravizza Sport This store offers hunting and fishing gear for the Milanese elite as well as leisure wear. ♦ M afternoon, Tu-Sa. Via Hoepli 3 (southwest of Piazza Meda). 8693853. Subway stop: Duomo (M1, M3)

17 Hoepli Milan's famous publishing house of Swiss origin specializes in its own line of technical manuals on practical and obscure subjects such as painting restoration, in addition to books from all over the world. ♦ M-Sa; no midday closing. Via Hoepli 5 (southwest of Piazza Meda). 864871. Subway stop: Duomo (M1, M3)

18 Hotel de la Ville $$$ A great location coupled with service reminiscent of another era are the highlight here. Some of the hotel's 100 rooms are decorated with antiques. ♦ Via Hoepli 6 (southwest of Piazza Meda). 867651; fax 866609. Subway stop: Duomo (M1, M3)

Within Hotel de la Ville:

CANOVIANO

Canoviano ★★★$$$ This restaurant offers sleek eating in a unique and impressive Neo-Classical setting and is especially popular with expense account types. Dishes such as *trittico di pesce al vapore* (steamed fish—whatever's fresh) and *rognoncino trifolato al brandy* (truffled kidney in brandy sauce) speak for the high caliber of this restaurant's offerings. ♦ M-F lunch and dinner; Sa dinner only. 86465215

19 Piazza Meda After dinner at Canoviano, stroll through this piazza, where you'll see Arnaldo Pomodoro's contemporary sculpture *Great Disk.* ♦ East of Piazza della Scala. Subway stop: Duomo (M1, M3)

20 Casa degli Omenoni This "house of the big men" gets its name from the eight caryatid sculptures by Antonio Abondio on the facade. It was designed by **Leone Leoni** in 1565, and since 1929 it has been the headquarters of a private club. ♦ Via degli Omenoni 3 (near Via Caserotte). Subway stop: Duomo (M1, M3)

21 Palazzo Belgioioso This large, stately Neo-Classical palazzo (begun in 1772 by **Piermarino Piermarini**) was built for one of Milan's leading families. ♦ Piazza Belgioioso 2 (northeast of Piazza della Scala). Subway stop: Duomo (M1, M3)

Within the Palazzo Belgioioso:

Boeucc ★★★$$$ A hushed atmosphere prevails at this most beloved of the old-style Milanese restaurants, an excellent place to sample the city's risotto dishes, *costoletta alla milanese* (breaded, fried veal cutlet), and a fine selection of fruits, cheeses, and desserts. Although its name is dialect for hole-in-the-wall, what you'll find here is an elegant, traditional institution. In warm weather it has a few outdoor tables. ♦ M-F lunch and dinner; Su dinner only. 76020224

22 Museo Manzoniano/Casa del Manzoni This unassuming palazzo was home to Alessandro Manzoni from 1814 until his death in 1873. Manzoni was the author of the plodding *I Promessi Sposi,* translated into English as *The Betrothed*—a romantic historical novel written in Tuscan dialect as a nod to Dante, just before the unification of Italy in the 19th century. More important for its politics than as literature, its style is largely derived from Sir Walter Scott; it is required reading for every schoolchild in Italy, and every town in Italy has a street named after the writer. The house is a shrine to the author and contains an exhaustive collection of memorabilia. ♦ Tu-F. Via Morone 1 (near Via A. Manzoni). 86460403. Subway stops: Duomo (M1, M3); Montenapoleone (M3)

23 Peri Miles of exclusive fabrics (from precious Fortuny to Indian and Thai silks) grace this shop, built in the former **Palazzo Crespi,** the rounded facade of which traces the outline of a Roman theater that stood on the spot in ancient times. ♦ M afternoon, Tu-Sa. Via Morone 3 (near Via Manzoni). 8693501. Subway stops: Duomo (M1, M3); Montenapoleone (M3)

24 Giusy Bresciani On display here: lovely millinery (the word comes from Milan, in fact)—from the classical to the very latest—and other fanciful garb for the ladies. Custom orders are taken. ♦ M-F. No credit cards accepted. Via Morone 8 (near Via A. Manzoni). 76002540. Subway stops: Duomo (M1, M3); Montenapoleone (M3)

25 Museo Poldi Pezzoli Gian Giacomo Poldi Pezzoli was a 19th-century nobleman and collector who decorated various rooms of his Neo-Classical palazzo in styles to serve as backdrops for his artworks. Bombed during World War II, the palazzo was subsequently remodeled in accordance with 20th-century exhibition concepts, yet something of the atmosphere of a private collection has been maintained. The ground floor has an 18th-century ceiling fresco by Carlo Innocenzo Carlone. Upstairs are three small rooms, the **Salette dei Lombardi,** with pictures by 15th- and 16th-century Lombard painters. The first has a *Madonna and Child* by Vincenzo Foppa; in the second are Foppa's *Portrait of Giovanni Francesco Brivio, Rest on the Flight to Egypt* by Andrea Solario, and Madonnas by Solario, Cesare da Sesto, and Giovanni Antonio Boltraffio. The **Sala degli Stranieri** has works by Lucas Cranach and other foreign artists. The Rococo-decorated **Saletta degli Stucchi** houses a porcelain collection. The **Salone Dorato,** once decorated in a Renaissance style, was badly damaged during the war but still displays Renaissance works. Among them are the profile *Portrait of a Woman* by Antonio Pollaiuolo, sometimes attributed to his brother Piero (whoever painted her, the bejeweled blond with the charming overbite has now become the mascot of the museum); Piero della Francesca's *St. Nicolas of Tolentino;* Madonnas by Antonio Vivarini, Andrea Mantegna, and Sandro Botticelli; Botticelli's *Lamentation; Grey Lagoon* by Francesco Guardi; and a Pietà by Giovanni Bellini. Adjoining the *salone* is the **Sala Visconti Venosta,** which contains works from the collection of Emilio Visconti Venosta, among them Madonnas by Pinturicchio and Bergognone. Additional rooms are the **Sala degli Orologi,** which houses a collection of clocks; the **Sala Nera,** with six carved walnut doors and paintings and decorative objects; the **Sala dei Vetri Antichi di Murano,** with antique Murano glass; the heavily Neo-Gothic **Gabinetto Dantesco,** intact from the days of Gian Giacomo Poldi Pezzoli; the **Sala del Palma,** so called because of its 16th-century *Portrait of a Courtesan* by Palma Il Vecchio; the **Gabinetto degli Ori,** with a jewelry collection; and finally, other rooms with works by painters from Venice and the Veneto. ♦ Admission. Daily Jan-Mar, Oct-Dec; daily morning Apr-Sept. Via A. Manzoni 12 (near Via Morone). 794889. Subway stop: Montenapoleone (M3)

25 Don Lisander ★★★$$$ Tuscan Giocchino Coppini has mastered the Milanese classics from risotto to osso buco. Select from the sampler menu, which showcases his expertise. A longtime classic Milanese favorite, this lovely, rather formal, restaurant is especially pleasant during the warmer months when tables are placed outdoors overlooking a private garden. ♦ M-F lunch and dinner; Sa lunch only. Via A. Manzoni 12A (near Via Morone). 76020130. Subway stop: Montenapoleone (M3)

26 Poltrona Frau The newer models here at one of the oldest furniture producers in Milan are designed by the likes of Marco Zanuso and Mario Bellini. ♦ M afternoon, Tu-Sa. No credit cards accepted. Via A. Manzoni 20 (near Via

Montenapoleone). 76005646. Subway stop: Montenapoleone (M3)

27 Alle Antiche Armi Antique swords and daggers are the intriguing specialty of this shop. ♦ M afternoon, Tu-Sa. No credit cards accepted. Via Bigli 24 (at Via Manzoni). 76022318. Subway stop: Montenapoleone (M3)

27 Dal Vecchio This old-fashioned silversmith and jeweler has an untarnished reputation for both traditional and contemporary design. ♦ M afternoon, Tu-Sa. Via Montenapoleone 29 (at Via Manzoni). 76008740. Subway stop: Montenapoleone (M3)

27 Grandi Firme As the name implies, designer signatures such as Yves St. Laurent and Guy Laroche can be found here at discounted prices. Not your average bargain basement, however, this elegant store is on the second floor. ♦ M afternoon, Tu-F, Sa afternoon. Via A. Manzoni 26 (at Via Montenapoleone), Second floor. 799240. Subway stop: Montenapoleone (M3)

28 Design Gallery Specializing in contemporary furniture and tabletop design, this gallery has mounted exhibits by Memphis founder Sottsass and other international names such as Alessandro Mendini and Hans Hollein. ♦ M afternoon, Tu-Sa. Via A. Manzoni 46 (at Via Della Spiga), Second floor. 798955. Subway stop: Montenapoleone (M3)

29 Alfio ★★★$$$ Alfio Bocciardi, former owner of **Savini,** now runs one of Milan's most famous restaurants, where a groaning antipasto table leads to good risottos and pastas (spaghetti with caviar is one of the most successful) and on to well-prepared fish and game dishes, supplemented in season with truffles and porcini mushrooms. The most interesting wines are from the Piedmont and Trentino regions. ♦ M-F lunch and dinner; Su dinner only. Via Senato 31 (west of Corso Venezia). 780731. Subway stop: Montenapoleone (M3)

30 Palazzo del Senato Begun in 1608 by **Federico Borromeo** and **Francesco Maria Richini** for the **Collegio Elvetico,** this curved-facaded palazzo now houses the **Archivio di Stato** (State Archives). ♦ Via Senato 11 (near Via Sant'Andrea). Subway stops: San Babila (M1); Montenapoleone (M3)

31 Carlton Senato $$$ Friendly and modern, this primarily business hotel (though what hotel isn't in this town?) is quiet, too. There are 79 rooms total, but the 25 rooms facing pedestrian Via della Spiga are particularly peaceful. The hotel also has a restaurant.

♦ Via Senato 5 (near Corso Venezia).
76015535; fax 783300. Subway stops:
San Babila (M1); Montenapoleone (M3)

32 Prada This stylish shop is one of Milan's
most sought-after venues for ladies' shoes
and accessories. Women's leather goods and
stylish nylon and synthetic accessories are the
most popular items here. Their other items,
such as desk and travel accessories, appeal
to everyone as well. ♦ M afternoon, Tu-Sa. Via
della Spiga 1 (at Corso Venezia). 76008636.
Subway stop: San Babila (M1). Also at:
Galleria Vittorio Emanuele II. 876979. Subway
stop: Duomo (M1, M3); Via Sant'Andrea 21
(near Via della Spiga). 76001426. Subway
stop: San Babila (M1)

33 Crottini This small women's boutique
features big-name designer clothing ranging
from casual to formal wear. ♦ M afternoon,
Tu-Sa. Via della Spiga 3 (at Corso Venezia).
76002677. Subway stops: San Babila (M1);
Montenapoleone (M3)

34 Bulgari This fortresslike Milan branch
protects the heavy-duty jewelry of the Roman
designer. ♦ M afternoon, Tu-Sa. Via della
Spiga 6 (off Corso Venezia). 76005406.
Subway stops: San Babila (M1);
Montenapoleone (M3)

34 Bottega Veneta The much-
imitated hallmark of the
leather goods found here
is buttery-soft hides in
myriad colors worked
into a woven look. ♦ M
afternoon, Tu-Sa. Via della
Spiga 5 (off Corso Venezia).
76024495. Subway stops: San Babila (M1);
Montenapoleone (M3)

34 Miu Miu This is not a pet shop ("miu miu" is
the Italian equivalent of our feline "meow"),
though it is the pet project of Miuccia Prada
(hence the nickname), whose luxury goods
may have proved too expensive for you in her
elegant store next door. The same design
talent applies itself here; the result is still not
throwaway fashion, but the prices are more
approachable and the look guaranteed
Milanese. ♦ M afternoon, Tu-Sa. Via della
Spiga 5 (off Corso Venezia). 76014448.
Subway stops: San Babila (M1);
Montenapoleone (M3)

35 Sharra Pagano Imaginative concoctions of
jewelry in semiprecious and faux gemstones
are featured here. ♦ M afternoon, Tu-Sa. Via

della Spiga 7 (off Corso Venezia). 76002578.
Subway stops: San Babila (M1);
Montenapoleone (M3)

35 Gio Moretti Gio Moretti reigns over Via della
Spiga. His multiple locations along the street
carry top-of-the-line fashions for the whole
family, provided the family fancies Claude
Montana, Gianfranco Ferrè, Gianni Versace,
and the like. ♦ M afternoon, Tu-Sa. Via della
Spiga 4 (off Corso Venezia). 76003186.
Also at: Via della Spiga 6, 76002172 (men's
clothing); Via della Spiga 7, 6571191 (teen's
clothing); and Via della Spiga 9, 780089
(infant's and children's clothing). All between
Corso Venezia and Via Sant'Andrea. Subway
stops (all locations): San Babila (M1);
Montenapoleone (M3)

35 Colombo This store features two floors of
high-fashion leather goods, including some
of the best handbags in Milan. ♦ M afternoon,
Tu-Sa. Via della Spiga 9 (off Corso Venezia).
76000184. Subway stops: San Babila (M1);
Montenapoleone (M3)

36 Cose This is yet another boutique full of well-
selected, of-the-moment designer clothing for
women. ♦ M afternoon, Tu-Sa. Via della Spiga
8 (near Via Sant'Andrea). 76020703. Subway
stops: San Babila (M1); Montenapoleone (M3)

37 Saint Andrew's ★★$$ This popular and
elegant stop for shoppers has the best beef
Wellington in town, as well as a good Italian
menu. The otherwise classic *costoletta alla
milanese* is for some inexplicable reason
called *l'orecchio d'elefante* (elephant ear).
♦ M-Sa lunch and dinner. Via Sant'Andrea 23
(at Via della Spiga). 76023132. Subway stops:
San Babila (M1); Montenapoleone (M3)

37 Trabucco An interesting collection of
beautifully crafted classic and contemporary
jewelry shines here. ♦ M afternoon, Tu-Sa. Via
Sant'Andrea 23 (at Via della Spiga). 76003802.
Subway stops: San Babila (M1);
Montenapoleone (M3)

38 Gianfranco Ferrè Ferrè womenswear
is shown off in a high-tech setting. ♦ M
afternoon, Tu-Sa. Via della Spiga 11 (near Via
Sant'Andrea). 794864. Menswear next door
at: Via della Spiga 13. 76000385. Subway
stops: San Babila (M1); Montenapoleone (M3)

39 Erreuno Choose from three levels of cool
style off the racks of this arbiter of taste: the
ultimate *Erreuno* pret-a-porter line for women;
a slightly less expensive label; and the junior
collection. ♦ M afternoon, Tu-Sa. Via della
Spiga 15 (near Via Sant'Andrea). 795575.
Subway stop: Montenapoleone (M3)

40 Jean Paul Gaultier This fashion-forward
women's clothing is displayed in a far-out
setting designed by the couturier. ♦ M
afternoon, Tu-Sa. Via della Spiga 20
(at Via Gesù). 780804. Subway stop:
Montenapoleone (M3)

41 Diego della Valle This designer combines high and casual style with comfort, making his men's and women's shoes the hottest in Milan. ♦ M afternoon, Tu-Sa. Via della Spiga 22 (near Via Gesù). 76002423. Subway stop: Montenapoleone (M3)

41 Alberto Subert Some of the more portable items in this respected antiques store are the 17th-century *paesini* (little landscapes), made with semiprecious stones. ♦ M afternoon, Tu-Sa. No credit cards accepted. Via della Spiga 22 (near Via Gesù). 799594. Subway stop: Montenapoleone (M3)

41 Adriana Mode One-of-a-kind women's fashion made by Daniela Gerini (daughter of the owner) is the specialty of this shop. ♦ M afternoon, Tu-Sa. Via della Spiga 22 (near Via Gesù). 76008458. Subway stop: Montenapoleone (M3)

42 Krizia Krizia's fanciful womenswear is set off by a stark monochromatic setting. ♦ M afternoon, Tu-Sa. Via della Spiga 23 (near Via Gesù). 76008429. Subway stop: Montenapoleone (M3)

43 Garzanti This bookshop is chock-full of picture books (art, photography, design, fashion) by its namesake publisher and others. ♦ M afternoon, Tu-Sa. Via della Spiga 30 (near Via Santo Spirito). 794222. Subway stop: Montenapoleone (M3)

44 Mauro Brucoli Antiques, including silver objects and Austro-Hungarian–era baubles, are featured in this elegant store. ♦ M afternoon, Tu-Sa. Via della Spiga 46 (at Via Borgospesso). 76023767. Subway stop: Montenapoleone (M3)

44 Nica This shop offers men's and women's footwear in trendy and classic styles. ♦ M afternoon, Tu-Sa. Via della Spiga 42 (at Via Borgospesso). 76006835. Subway stop: Montenapoleone (M3)

45 L'Utile e il Dilettevole This store offers a mix of French and English (therefore very Milanese) country furniture, table linens, and accessories. ♦ M afternoon, Tu-Sa. Via della Spiga 46 (near Via Manzoni). 795044. Subway stop: Montenapoleone (M3)

46 Laura Biagiotti The Biagiotti look in womenswear, featured in her eponymous store, is feminine and luxurious with an emphasis on year-round knits and winter cashmeres. ♦ M afternoon, Tu-Sa. Via Borgospesso 19 (near Via Spiga). 799659. Subway stop: Montenapoleone (M3)

47 Vetrerie di Empoli The Tuscan town of Empoli is known for its rustic, inexpensive green-tinted glass, available here along with more refined breakables. ♦ M afternoon, Tu-Sa. Via Borgospesso 5 (off Via Montenapoleone). 76008791. Subway stop: Montenapoleone (M3). Also at: Via Pietro Verri 4 (near Via Montenapoleone). 76021656. Subway stop: Montenapoleone (M3)

48 Magazzini Cappellini Situated in the courtyard of a historical palazzo, this "warehouse" is the new and only retail outlet for the well-known producers of the Cappellini and Mondo furniture and design collections. Two loftlike floors are divided into the different areas of the house: living room, bedroom, kitchen, bath—each capturing the Milanese design sensibility that made **Cappellini** a forerunner in its field. Choose from sofas to soap dishes and have it all reliably shipped anywhere in the world. ♦ M afternoon, Tu-Sa; no midday closing. Via Montenapoleone 27, Courtyard (near Via Borgospesso). 76003676. Subway stop: Montenapoleone (M3)

48 Galtrucco Tailored menswear by this designer, as well as clothes by such names as Ermenegildo Zegna and Claude Montana, are the highlights in this shop. ♦ M afternoon, Tu-Sa. Via Montenapoleone 27 (near Via Borgospesso). 76002978. Subway stop: Montenapoleone (M3)

48 Tecno This home furnishings showroom features high-design by Centro Progetti Tecno. ♦ M afternoon, Tu-Sa. Via Montenapoleone 27 (between Via Borgospesso and Via A. Manzoni). 76020341. Subway stop: Montenapoleone (M3)

49 Parini This shop carries quality foods, among them such trendy imports as Kellogg's Corn Flakes, but also valued Italian olive oil and dried mushrooms. ♦ M afternoon, Tu-Sa. Via Borgospesso 1 (at Via Montenapoleone). 76002302. Subway stop: Montenapoleone (M3)

50 Bice ★★$$$ This sophisticated trattoria-style restaurant has been in operation for more than 60 years and has an international reputation, with such notables as Giorgio Armani and Gianni Versace drawn to the Tuscan cuisine. Classics such as the barleylike *zuppa di farro* or a hearty *ribollita* (white bean) vegetable soup are the specialties of Signora Bice, the 90-something owner. ♦ Tu dinner only; W-Su lunch and dinner. Via Borgospesso 12 (off Via Montenapoleone). 76002572. Subway stop: Montenapoleone (M3)

51 Sebastian Custom-made shoes for men and women come in a wealth of styles and leathers at this shop. ♦ M afternoon, Tu-Sa. Via Borgospesso 18 (off Via Montena-poleone). 780532. Subway stop: Montenapoleone (M3)

52 Carlo Tivoli The fur flies here, exotically and expensively, but beware of species that customs won't allow back in the US. ◆ M afternoon, Tu-Sa. Via Santo Spirito 26 (near Via della Spiga). 76000833. Subway stop: Montenapoleone (M3)

53 Manzoni $$ Small, pleasant, and quiet, this serviceable 50-room hotel has a prime city-center location. It's a little threadbare and the rooms lack TVs, but it has a venerable charm all its own. There's no restaurant. ◆ Via Santo Spirito 20 (at Via Rossari). 76005700; fax 784212. Subway stop: Montenapoleone (M3)

53 Gulp Texan-born women's wear designer Sam Rey displays a penchant for the unpredictable in his elegant made-to-measure designs. ◆ M afternoon, Tu-Sa. Via Santo Spirito 14 (near Via Rossari). 794903. Subway stop: Montenapoleone (M3)

54 Corrado Irionè Exquisite made-to-measure and ready-to-wear furs are the specialty of this century-old, family-run business. ◆ M afternoon, Tu-Sa. Via Santo Spirito 7 (at Via Rossari). 795630. Subway stop: Montenapoleone (M3)

54 Valentino This is internationally famed women's designer Valentino's Milan shop. The templelike atmosphere here offsets the exquisite ready-to-wear women's fashions of Rome's high priest of design. ◆ M afternoon, Tu-Sa. Via Santo Spirito 3 (near Via Rossari). 76006182. Men's fashion nearby at: Via Montenapoleone 20 (at Via Santo Spirito). 76020285. Subway stop: Montenapoleone (M3)

55 Museo Bagatti Valsecchi After ten painstaking years of restoration, one of Milan's most important cultural monuments and beloved design jewels has finally opened its doors as a decorative arts museum. Thanks to the generosity of the fashion world's Gianni Versace and Gimmo Etro, this Neo-Renaissance palazzo was returned to the glory of its nascent days in the late 1800s when it was built, decorated, and inhabited by two eccentric brothers of an aristocratic Milanese family for whom the museum is named. The brothers bequeathed to the city not only a valuable collection of 16th-century objects and furnishings but the entire contents of their elegant home. ◆ Admission. Tu-Su afternoons. Via Santo Spirito 10 (near Via Rossari). 76006132. Subway stop: Montenapoleone (M3)

56 Four Seasons Hotel $$$$ Their ad campaign reads: "Finally, after 500 years, something sacred has returned to the monastery on Via Gesù: the Guest." What better place than a former cloister on Jesus Street to create this enclave of sheer modern-day luxury? Tastefully renovated to fuse the tranquillity of a 15th-century oasis

with the demands of a 21st-century five-star hotel, this 98-room property is one of the city's newest, most centralized, and most intimate. The **Il Teatro** (dinner only) is appropriately elegant; the **La Veranda** (lunch and dinner) more casually chic. The monks never dreamed of a heaven like this—nor could they have afforded it. ◆ Via Gesù 8 (near Via Montenapoleone). 77088; fax 77085000. Subway stop: Montenapoleone (M3)

57 Fendi The famed Roman sisters' furs are represented here in their Milanese branch, all cleverly cut and some dazzlingly dyed. Clothing and accessories replace them in warm weather. ◆ M afternoon, Tu-Sa. Via Sant'Andrea 16 (near Via della Spiga). 76021617. Subway stops: Montenapoleone (M3); San Babila (M1)

58 Cesare Paciotti Men's and women's shoes, high-styled, yet with a conservative bent and of excellent quality, can be found in this boutique. ◆ M afternoon, Tu-Sa. Via Sant'Andrea 8 (near Via Bagutta). 76001164. Subway stops: Montenapoleone (M3); San Babila (M1)

58 Palazzo Morando Bolognini This 18th-century Baroque palazzo houses three small specialty museums. The **Civico Museo di Milano (Museum of Milan),** through its collection of genre paintings depicting street scenes and popular festivals, will give you an idea of what life was like in the city over the centuries. The 10 rooms of artifacts and photographs in the **Civico Museo di Storia Contemporanea (Museum of Contemporary History)** illustrate the history of the city from 1914 to 1945. The **Civico Museo di Arte Ugo Mursia (Ugo Mursia Museum)** houses the collection of former publishing magnate Ugo Mursia. A great fan of novelist Joseph Conrad, Mursia collected lots of mastheads and other materials related to the sea. ◆ Free. Museo di Milano: Tu-Su. 783797 Museo di Storia Contemporanea: Tu-Su. Museo di Arte Ugo Mursia: Tu-S. Via Sant'Andrea 6 (near Via Bagutta). 76006245; Museo di Arte Ugo Mursi, 76004143. Subway stops: Montenapoleone (M3); San Babila (M1)

> "How glorious that Cathedral is! worthy almost of standing face to face with the snow Alps; and itself a sort of snow dream by an artist architect, taken asleep in a glacier!"
>
> Elizabeth Barrett Browning

59 Giorgio Armani Here you'll find men's and women's clothing made by the reigning king of Italian fashion. Several **Emporio Armani** locations in Milan sell the designer's less-expensive lines. ♦ M afternoon, Tu-Sa. Via Sant'Andrea 9 (near Via Bagutta). 76003234. Subway stops: Montenapoleone (M3); San Babila (M1). Emporio Armani: Via Durini 24, 76003030 (for men and women); Via Durini 27, 794248 (for infants and children). Both near Largo Toscanini. Subway stop: San Babila (M1)

59 Trussardi This store features men's and women's clothing by the designer renowned for his gloves and leather accessories. ♦ M afternoon, Tu-Sa. Via Sant'Andrea 5 (near Via Bagutta). 76020380. Subway stops: Montenapoleone (M3); San Babila (M1)

59 Lo Scarabeo d'Oro This jeweler features unusual creations made from exotic materials such as antique coins and odd metals such as titanium. ♦ M afternoon, Tu-Sa. Via Sant'Andrea 3 (near Via Montenapoleone). 76000547. Subway stops: Montenapoleone (M3); San Babila (M1)

59 Baretto ★★$$ Baretto is a small and sedate place for a refreshing drink or a shopping lunch where, besides oysters and caviar, home cooking (such as *polpettine alla milanese,* or Milanese meatballs) is the order of the day. ♦ M-Sa 10AM-midnight. Via Sant'Andrea 3 (near Via Montenapoleone). 781255. Subway stops: Montenapoleone (M3); San Babila (M1)

60 Guido Pasquali Bring a swatch and get custom-made shoes to match your new outfit. Special sizes are also available, as well as a small collection of elegant ready-made styles. ♦ M afternoon, Tu-Sa. Via Sant'Andrea 1 (off Via Montenapoleone). 76001645. Subway stops: Montenapoleone (M3); San Babila (M1)

60 Sevigne Good china is offered here at better prices than you can find at most shops in the area. ♦ M-Sa. No credit cards accepted. Via Sant'Andrea 1 (off Via Montenapoleone). 76023250. Subway stops: Montenapoleone (M3); San Babila (M1)

In AD 375, Sant'Ambrogio (St. Ambrose), a Doctor of the church and the founder of the Ambrosian Liturgy that is still used in Milan, became bishop of the city. He closed pagan temples and forbade the worship of pagan gods, and his gift of persuasive speech was known far and wide, said to have been as sweet as honey, whence comes the popular use of the word "ambrosia." He is the beloved patron saint of the city, and his feast day, 7 December, is an important and much celebrated holiday that launches the prestigious opera season at La Scala.

60 Marisa Marisa Lombardi's boutique brings together top women's designers, as well as a collection of sweaters made to her specifications. ♦ M afternoon, Tu-Sa. Via Sant'Andrea 1 (at Via Montenapoleone). 7600905. Subway stops: Montenapoleone (M3); San Babila (M1). Also at: Via della Spiga 52 (near Via Manzoni). 76002082. Subway stop: Montenapoleone (M3)

61 Missoni Colorful knits for men and women, especially in sweaters, are the trademark of this designer's boutique. ♦ M afternoon, Tu-Sa. Via Sant'Andrea 2 (at Via Montenapoleone). 76003555. Subway stops: Montenapoleone (M3); San Babila (M1)

62 Bagutta ★★$$ The unique Tuscan cuisine that began when the restaurant was founded by Alberto Pepori in 1926 is still going strong here. This is also still a hangout for writers and other members of the publishing world, and the awarding of the literary prize that originated in this restaurant (it was Italy's first) is still an anticipated annual event in the literary world. ♦ M-Sa lunch and dinner. Via Bagutta 14-16 (between Piazza San Babila and Via Sant'Andrea). 76000902. Subway stop: San Babila (M1)

63 Albrizzi Adalberto Cremonese produces the most chic paper and paper products in Milan. ♦ M afternoon, Tu-Sa. Via Bagutta 8 (off Corso Venezia). 76001218. Subway stop: San Babila (M1)

64 Paper Moon ★★$$ This lively pizzeria has an international reputation. Its *quattro stagioni* (four seasons, made with four kinds of cheese) pizza makes the perfect light lunch after some heavy shopping. ♦ M-Sa lunch and dinner. Via Bagutta 1 (at Corso Venezia). 76022297. Subway stop: San Babila (M1)

65 Palazzo Taverna This handsome, stately palazzo was designed in 1835 by **Ferdinando Abertolli**. Via Montenapoleone 2 (off Corso Matteotti). Subway stop: San Babila (M1)

Within Palazzo Taverna:

Mila Schön Elegant and classic separates for men and women are what designer Mila Schön is best known for, but there are also accessories and leather goods here. ♦ M afternoon, Tu-Sa; no midday closing. 76001803

66 Pederanzi Diamonds are your best friends in this jewelry shop run by two dazzlingly charming brothers. ♦ M afternoon, Tu-Sa. Via Montenapoleone 1 (at Corso Matteotti). 76001728. Subway stop: San Babila (M1)

Design alla Milanese

Fostered by the strongest industrial culture within Italy, design in **Milan** began to develop in the 1930s with such names as **Gio Ponti** and **Ernesto Rogers,** trained architects who applied Bauhaus-influenced and other Modernist principles to their concepts for everyday objects. Following World War II, Milanese design began to take off when the *Triennale* design exhibitions resumed just as Milan became Italy's definitive industrial capital. (An equally important event these days is the *Salone del Mobile,* a furniture trade fair held at the **Fiera di Milano** fairgrounds.) During the postwar period Gae Aulenti, Mario Bellini, Cini Boeri, Rodolfo Bonetto, the Castiglioni brothers (Pier

Giacomo and Livio), Joe Colombo, Vittorio Gregotti, Vico Magistretti, Enzo Mari, Bruno Munari, and Marco Zanuso came into prominence. Many of their efforts were celebrated in the landmark exhibition *Italy: The New Domestic Landscape* at New York's Museum of Modern Art in 1972, which helped establish international recognition for Milanese design. After that, a number of groups popped up, such as Alchymia (whose alchemy derives from such diverse sources as Constructivism and Pop Art) and Memphis (so-called because a record playing the eponymous Bob Dylan song got stuck as its originators were trying to come up with a name for the group, which is known for its deliberately jarring forms and colors). In 1983, the **Domus Academy,** Italy's first postgraduate design school, was founded and helped to institutionalize Milanese design ideology. Lately, the scene has settled into an almost conservative Modernism, but new trends and old polemics should ensure that other tricks are up the Milanese designers' Armani-clad sleeves. Although it can be accessed from afar through the pictures, if not through the often unintelligible words, of such specialized publications as *Domus* and *Modo,* or such general-interest design magazines as *AD, Casa Vogue* (both offshoots of American publications), and *Abitare,* Milanese design is best sampled firsthand in the showrooms concentrated in the heart of the city.

ILLUSTRATIONS BY DIANE DEIESO

66 Fausto Santini This designer boutique has two floors of trendy fashions for men's and women's feet at relatively affordable prices. ♦ M afternoon, Tu-Sa. Via Montenapoleone 1 (at Corso Matteotti). 76001958. Subway stop: San Babila (M1)

66 Fratelli Rosetti Stylish men's and women's shoes are the draw for those who can afford them. ♦ M afternoon, Tu-Sa. Via Montenapoleone 1 (at Corso Matteotti). 760216500. Subway stop: San Babila (M1)

67 Salvatore Ferragamo The revered Florentine shoemaker's foothold in Milan has women's clothing and accessories as well as his stylish women's shoes. ♦ M afternoon, Tu-Sa. Via Montenapoleone 3 (between Corso Matteotti and Via Pietro Verri). 76000054. Subway stop: San Babila (M1). Men's shop at: Via Montenapoleone 21 (at Via

Borgospesso). 70006660. Subway stop: Montenapoleone (M3)

67 Fontana Arte This store offers some of the best one-stop shopping for museum-quality Italian furniture designed by all the famous names, such as Gae Aulenti and Gio Ponti. ♦ M afternoon, Tu-Sa. Via Montenapoleone 3, Second floor (between Corso Matteotti and Via Pietro Verri). 76021089. Subway stop: San Babila (M1)

"The Cathedral is an awful failure. Outside the design is monstrous and inartistic. The over-elaborated details stuck high up where no one can see them; everthing is vile in it; it is, however, imposing and gigantic as a failure, through its great size and elaborate execution."

Oscar Wilde

67 Tanino Crisci Classic footwear for both sexes is the specialty of this shop. ♦ M afternoon, Tu-Sa. Via Montenapoleone 3 (between Corso Matteotti and Via Pietro Verri). 76021264. Subway stop: San Babila (M1)

68 Mario Buccellati Exquisite, delicate jewelry is the draw in this family-run boutique. ♦ M afternoon, Tu-Sa. Via Montenapoleone 4 (between Corso Matteotti and Via Pietro Verri). 76002153. Subway stop: San Babila (M1)

68 Pisa In the display cases of this store you'll find Milan's largest selection of watches and—more affordable—watchbands to fit all major names. ♦ M afternoon, Tu-Sa. Via Montenapoleone 4 (between Corso Matteotti and Via Pietro Verri). 76021998. Subway stop: San Babila (M1). Also at: Via Pietro Verri 9 (near Via Montenapoleone). Subway stop: San Babila (M1)

68 Valeriano Ferrario High-quality shoes for men and women are featured here. ♦ M afternoon, Tu-Sa. Via Montenapoleone 6 (between Corso Matteotti and Via Pietro Verri). 76020928. Subway stop: San Babila (M1)

69 Gucci This is the Milan branch of the legendary Florentine firm, once famous for its loafers but forever updating its look. ♦ M afternoon, Tu-Sa. Via Montenapoleone 5 (between Corso Matteotti and Via Pietro Verri). 76013050. Subway stop: San Babila (M1)

69 Faraone This is Milan's branch of Florence's most famous jeweler. ♦ M afternoon, Tu-Sa. Via Montenapoleone 7A (between Corso Matteotti and Via Pietro Verri). 76013656. Subway stop: San Babila (M1)

69 Larusmiani Classic styling, custom-made or off the rack, is the hallmark of this men's clothing store for those with limitless budgets. ♦ M afternoon, Tu-Sa; no midday closing. Via Montenapoleone 7 (at Via Pietro Verri). 76006957. Subway stop: San Babila (M1). Also at: Corso Vittorio Emanuelle 5 (near Piazza del Duomo). 874865. Subway stop: Duomo (M1, M3)

70 Cova ★★$$$ A well-known traditional stop for pastry in a discreet setting, this cafe/*pasticceria* is frequented by those who work or can afford to shop in this area. Waiters in tails hover over coiffed habituès holding court at the pink lace–covered tables. ♦ M-Sa 8AM-8PM. No credit cards accepted. Via Montenapoleone 8 (at Via Sant'Andrea). 76000578. Subway stop: San Babila (M1)

70 Pirovano This boutique offers made-to-measure and ready-to-wear ladies' evening wear and luxurious fashion accessories. ♦ M afternoon, Tu-Sa; no midday closing. Via Montenapoleone 8 (at Via Sant'Andrea). 76002571. Subway stop: San Babila (M1)

71 Mario Valentino This is the Milanese base for this late leather-goods designer, known for his men's and women's clothing and accessories that come in colorful, high-quality styles. ♦ M afternoon, Tu-Sa; no midday closing. Via Montenapoleone 10 (at Via Sant'Andrea). 798113. Subway stops: Montenapoleone (M3); San Babila (M1)

71 Inès de la Fressange As Karl Lagerfeld's muse and one of the top-paid runway and print models of recent history, Inès had a face that launched a thousand seasons in this fashion-obsessed town. Her infallible choice of the perfect blazer, the indispensable sweater, the classic loafers, and the accessories that pull it all together has met with the same success that put her Paris boutique on the map. ♦ M afternoon, Tu-Sa. Via Montenapoleone 10 (between Via Sant'Andrea and Via Gesù). 76005148. Subway stop: San Babila (M1)

71 Il Salumaio di Montenapoleone After you've shopped until you dropped, stop here for a few delicious gourmet food items, most of which are displayed in the artistic style indigenous to Milan. Choose from the more than 200 cheeses for a nice upscale snack. Takeout only. ♦ M afternoon, Tu-Sa. Via Montenapoleone 12 (between Via Sant'Andrea and Via Gesù). 76001123. Subway stops: Montenapoleone (M3); San Babila (M1)

71 Lorenz This purveyor of fashionable timepieces carries clocks and watches by designers such as Richard Sapper, whose "Static" steel clock won the prestigious *Compasso d'Oro* design award. ♦ M afternoon, Tu-Sa. Via Montenapoleone 12 (between Via Sant'Andrea and Via Gesù). 794232. Subway stops: Montenapoleone (M3); San Babila (M1)

72 G. Lorenzi This shop is on the cutting edge in cutlery, as well as in pipes and housewares such as espresso sets. ♦ M afternoon, Tu-Sa. Via Montenapoleone 9 (at Via Pietro Verri). 76022848. Subway stop: Montenapoleone (M3); San Babila (M1)

72 Venini The famous Venetian glassmaker's Milan branch stocks the firm's complete line of sleek and traditional collectible wares— pricey vases, glasses, decorative plates, and bowls. ♦ M afternoon, Tu-Sa. Via Montenapoleone 9 (at Via Pietro Verri). 76000539. Subway stops: Montenapoleone (M3); San Babila (M1)

72 Gianni Versace This four-story boutique is the fabric-conscious designer's latest outlet for men's and women's clothing. ♦ M afternoon, Tu-Sa. Via Montenapoleone 11 (at Via Pietro Verri). 76008528. Subway stops: Montenapoleone (M3); San Babila (M1)

Ermenegildo Zegna

73 Ermenegildo Zegna Exquisite men's made-to-measure tailoring and ready-to-wear clothing is featured here, with a rich choice of ties and accessories. ♦ M afternoon, Tu-Sa. Via Pietro Verri 3 (between Via Bigli and Via Montenapoleone). 795521. Subway stops: Montenapoleone (M3); San Babila (M1)

73 Manhattan ★$$ Unlike its island namesake, the music at this piano bar/American bar is a romantic combination of Italian and French love songs. The restaurant serves Milanese classics. ♦ Restaurant: M-Sa 6PM-1AM; piano bar: M-Sa 6PM-2:30AM. Via Pietro Verri 3 (between Via Bigli and Via Montenapoleone). 76023566. Subway stops: Montenapoleone (M3); San Babila (M1)

74 Beltrami The focus here is on men's and women's fashion and shoes of the famous chain. ♦ M afternoon, Tu-Sa. Via Montena-poleone 16 (between Via Sant'Andrea and Via Gesù). 76002975. Subway stop: Montenapoleone (M3)

74 Clara Antonini Some of the most reasonable price tags in the area are attached to the womenswear in this boutique. ♦ M-Sa. Via Montenapoleone 16 (between Via Sant'Andrea and Via Gesù). 780788. Subway stop: Montenapoleone (M3)

75 Alexander-Nicolette Conservatively classic shoes for both sexes are sold here. ♦ M afternoon, Tu-Sa. Via Montenapoleone 19 (near Via Gesù). 76001886. Subway stop: Montenapoleone (M3)

76 Lario 1898 This shop has shoes and leather goods for men and women. ♦ M afternoon, Tu-Sa. Via Montenapoleone 21 (between Via Gesù and Via Santo Spirito). 76002441. Subway stop: Montenapoleone (M3)

76 Nazareno Gabrielli Beautiful leather bags and shoes for men and women are featured here alongside diaries, jewelry, and ties. ♦ M afternoon, Tu-Sa. Via Montenapoleone 23 (between Via Gesù and Via Santo Spirito). 76006561. Subway stop: Montenapoleone (M3)

77 I Regali di Nella Longari If you're stumped for a gift and don't have time to shop, trust Nella Longari's exquisite taste in everything from picture frames to tea services. (Her antiques shop is at Via Montenapoleone 23, 782066.) ♦ M afternoon, Tu-Sa. Via Bigli 15 (between Via Pietro Verri and Via Manzoni). 780322. Subway stop: Montenapoleone (M3)

78 Palazzo Bigli-Poni A palazzo (facade 19th century) has occupied this spot since the times of the Sforzas, and it can be seen by stepping into the Bramante-influenced courtyard. ♦ Via Bigli 11 (between Via Pietro Verri and Via Manzoni). Subway stop: Montenapoleone (M3)

79 Etro Milanese par excellence, Gimmo Etro has become known as something of a Paisley (misleadingly called "cashmere" in Italian) King. He swathes furniture and decorative accessories in rich interpretations of this luxury pattern and many others, transforming rooms into romantic homes. The designer's international chain of handsome wood-paneled boutiques began here in Milan, where each of his three stores exudes European elegance and old-world charm. ♦ M afternoon, Tu-Sa. Via Pietro Verri (at Via Bigli). 76005450. Subway stops: Montenapoleone (M3); San Babila (M1). Home-decorating accessories and perfumes at: Via Pontaccio 17 (at Vicoli Fiori), 86461192. Clothing and accessories at: Via Montenapoleone 5 (between Corso Malleotti and Via Pietro Verri), 76005049

79 Cravatterie Nazionali Ties in all fabrics, colors, and patterns are available here for all tastes. ♦ M afternoon, Tu-Sa; no midday closing. Via Pietro Verri 5 (near Via Montenapoleone). 76004208. Subway stops: Montenapoleone (M3); San Babila (M1)

80 Casolari This perfume shop stocks a fine selection of British goods. ♦ M afternoon, Tu-Sa. Corso Matteotti 1 (near Via San Pietro all'Orto). 76021937. Subway stops: Montenapoleone (M3); San Babila (M1)

80 Dom This retailer has the best variety of porcelain, crystal, and silver in the city. ♦ M afternoon, Tu-Sa. Corso Matteotti 3 (near Via San Pietro all'Orto). 76023410. Subway stops: Montenapoleone (M3); San Babila (M1)

Restaurants/Clubs: Red **Hotels:** Blue
Shops/ 🌳 Outdoors: Green **Sights/Culture:** Black

80 Elam Achille Castiglioni designed this showroom for furniture by all the top Milanese designers, including Zanusso and Aulenti. ◆ M afternoon, Tu-Sa. Corso Matteotti 5 (near Via San Pietro all'Orto). 794330. Subway stops: Montenapoleone (M3); San Babila (M1)

81 Sant'Ambroeus After shopping in the area, stop in at this ultrachic place for a pick-me-up, be it tea or Campari accompanied by a delicate pastry or a light snack. A 1930s-style ambience prevails in the tearoom, while the outside area is better for people watching. ◆ M-Sa. Corso Matteotti 7 (near Via San Pietro All'Orto). 76000540. Subway stops: Montenapoleone (M3); San Babila (M1)

81 Alessi This store carries the whole line of its namesake stainless-steel design objects for the home, including the famous tea kettles designed by Aldo Rossi and Richard Sapper. ◆ M afternoon, Tu-Sa. Corso Matteotti 9 (near Via San Pietro All'Orto). 795726. Subway stops: Montenapoleone (M3); San Babila (M1)

82 Enrico Coveri Here you'll find colorful and playful mens- and womenswear by the late Tuscan designer. ◆ M afternoon, Tu-Sa. Corso Matteotti 12 (near Via San Pietro All'Orto). 76005977. Subway stops: Montenapoleone (M3); San Babila (M1)

82 Moroni Gomma This shop's strange specialty is rubber, which comes in boots, coats, containers, and everything else imaginable. ◆ M afternoon, Tu-Sa. Corso Matteotti 14 (near Via Montenapoleone). 76006821. Subway stops: Montenapoleone (M3); San Babila (M1)

82 Martignetti Pearls and coral are the seaworthy specialties of this jeweler. ◆ M afternoon, Tu-Sa. Corso Matteotti 14 (near Via Montenapoleone). 781489. Subway stops: Montenapoleone (M3); San Babila (M1)

83 Neglia All the famous international names in men's clothing are represented in this boutique's nicely chosen selection. ◆ M afternoon, Tu-Sa. Corso Venezia 2 (at Piazza San Babila). 795231. Subway stop: San Babila (M1)

83 Il Vendoro Service is sacrificed for savings at this gold market, where 18-carat gold items come in all varieties. There's a little silver on the side for good measure. ◆ M afternoon, Tu-Sa. Corso Venezia 2 (at Piazza San Babila). 794107. Subway stop: San Babila (M1)

84 Santini ★★★$$$ A contemporary but elegant decor provides the backdrop for Veneto-style cuisine at Japanese tourist–style

prices. Among the specialties are *pasta e fagio* (pasta and beans) and *fegato alla veneziana* (liver and onions). ◆ Tu-Su lunch and dinner. Corso Venezia 3 (near Piazza San Babila). 782010. Subway stop: San Babila (M1)

85 Spazio Romeo Gigli If anyone can fuse the romantic and the cerebral, it is Romeo Gigli, whose feminine interpretation of fashion's ephemeral trends is timeless. ◆ M afternoon, Tu-Sa. Corso Venezia 11 (between Piazza Sar Babila and Via della Spiga). 76000271. Subway stop: San Babila (M1). Also at: G. Gigli (the designer's less-expensive line), Via Palermo 11 (near Via Solferio). 72023864. Subway stop: Lanza (M2)

85 Seminario Arcivescovile (Archbishop's Seminary) A number of architects worked on this building. **Vincenzo Seregni** began it ir 1565; it was taken over by **Pellegrini** in 1577; **Aurelio Trezzi** began the courtyard in 1602, and this was taken over by **Fabio Mangone** in 1608. ◆ Corso Venezia 11 (between Piazza San Babila and Via della Spiga). Subway stop: San Babila (M1)

85 Brigatti Milan's leading sports store is great for standard items or souvenirs such as bicycle shirts, pants, caps, and soccer jerseys, and a few classical items as well. ◆ M afternoon, Tu-Sa. Corso Venezia 15 (between Piazza San Babila and Via della Spiga). 76000273. Subway stop: San Babila (M1)

86 De Padova This very spare designer showroom features the works of leading Italian designers such as Vico Magistretti, as well as the firm's own reproductions, including Shaker-inspired furniture. ◆ M afternoon, Tu-Sa. Corso Venezia 14 (near Via della Spiga). 76008413. Subway stop: San Babila (M1)

87 Casa Fontana Pirovano This rare 15th-century Milanese Renaissance palazzo has been attributed to both **Bramante** and **Bramantino**. ◆ Corso Venezia 10 (near Via della Spiga). Subway stop: San Babila (M1)

88 San Babila The Romanesque basilica that is the namesake of the piazza in which it sits was badly restored in the 19th and 20th centuries. ◆ Piazza San Babila (at the intersection of Corso Venezia and Corso Monforte). Subway stop: San Babila (M1)

89 Piazza San Babila The column in this piazza, designed by **Giuseppe Robecco** in 1626, is surmounted by a lion, symbol of the ancient quarter of Porta Orientale. The outdoor stand in the piazza is known for its inexpensive, well-designed costume jewelry. ◆ At the intersection of Corso Venezia, Corso Monforte, and Corso Vittorio Emanuele II. Subway stop: San Babila (M1)

90 Valextra This store carries a wide assortment of deluxe leather goods—from bags, wallets, and suitcases to desk accessories—at steep prices for discerning gift givers. ♦ M afternoon, Tu-Sa. Piazza San Babila 1 (east in piazza). 76002989. Subway stop: San Babila (M1)

91 Donini *Gin rosa* (pink gin) is just one of the beverages available at this bar/cafe, which also has light sandwiches and ice cream for a quick snack. ♦ M-Sa 7:30AM-8:30PM. Galleria San Babila 4B (east in piazza). 76000461. Subway stop: San Babila (M1)

91 Picowa Kitchen accessories from practical to high-end are featured in this shop. ♦ M afternoon, Tu-Sa. Galleria San Babila 4D (east in piazza). 794078. Subway stop: San Babila (M1)

92 ICF Another imaginative designer showroom, this one features furniture and objects by historic and contemporary Milanese designers. ♦ M-F. Via Borgogna 7 (near Piazza San Babila). 76000583. Subway stop: San Babila (M1)

93 Flos On display here are high-design lighting fixtures. ♦ M afternoon, Tu-Sa. Corso Monforte 9 (near Piazza San Babila). 76003639. Subway stop: San Babila (M1)

93 Artemide This is one of Milan's leading lighting design shops. ♦ M afternoon, Tu-Sa; no midday closing. Corso Monforte 19 (near Piazza San Babila). 76006930. Subway stop: San Babila (M1)

94 Quattrifolio This is yet another high-design lighting fixture store. ♦ M afternoon, Tu-Sa. Via Santa Cecilia 2 (at Corso Monforte). 781498. Subway stop: San Babila (M1)

95 Magnolia This shop has bargain children's clothing galore. The selection is erratic but sometimes includes designer labels such as Missoni. ♦ M afternoon, Tu-Sa. Via Visconti di Modrone 11 (between Via Mascagni and Corso Monforte). 795168. Subway stop: San Babila (M1)

96 Caracalla The Roman baths for which this place is named never had fixtures like this. The bathroom accessories and fixtures here are by leading historic and contemporary designers. ♦ M afternoon, Tu-Sa. Via Cerva 19 (near Via Borgogna). 76002195. Subway stop: San Babila (M1)

97 Simon International Dino Gavina, who went on to found Knoll International, began by producing furniture under the name of Simon International. Other Simon designers on display in this store are Pier Giacomo Castiglioni and Meret Oppenheim. ♦ M afternoon, Tu-Sa. No credit cards accepted. Via Durini 25 (at Via Borgogna). 796322

98 Palazzo Durini This ornate Baroque-style palazzo designed by **Francesco Maria Richini** was built in 1643 for a wealthy Milanese silk merchant. ♦ Via Durini 24 (near Largo Toscanini). Subway stop: San Babila (M1)

Within Palazzo Durini:

Emporio Armani This emporium carries Milanese clothing designer Giorgio Armani's least expensive stylish clothing for men and women. ♦ M afternoon, Tu-Sa. 76003030. Also at: Via Sant'Andrea 9 (near Via Montenapoleone). 76003234 (for men and women). Subway stop: San Babila (M1); Via Durini 27 (near Largo Toscanini). 794248. (for infants and children). Subway stop: San Babila (M1)

99 Franco Maria Ricci FMR's flagship store is stocked with effete publications on esoteric subjects. ♦ M afternoon, Tu-Sa. Via Durini 19 (near Largo Toscanini). 48301524. Subway stop: San Babila (M1)

100 Cassina One of the most spectacular of Milan's design showrooms, this distinguished place carries products signed by Italian designers as well as international names such as Frank Lloyd Wright, Le Corbusier, and Phillippe Stark. ♦ M afternoon, Tu-Sa; no midday closing. Via Durini 18 (near Largo Augusto). 76020758. Subway stop: San Babila (M1)

100 Caffè Moda Durini You might mistake this for an American shopping mall, except that it's full of relatively affordable Milanese-style clothing. ♦ M afternoon, Tu-Sa. Via Durini 14 (near Largo Augusto). 76021188. Subway stop: San Babila (M1)

101 Peppino ★★$$ Tuscan Peppino has been replaced by Alberto Besuti, who has added Apulian chef Gaetano Schiavoni in the kitchen to expand the Milanese-Tuscan standards to include southern specialties such as the tiny ear-shaped pasta called *orecchiette* from Puglia. ♦ M-Th, Su lunch and dinner; F lunch only. Via Durini 7 (near Largo Augusto). 781729. Subway stops: Duomo (M1, M3); San Babila (M1)

101 Joaquin Berao This tiny jewelry store features highly original, almost sculptural, designs. ♦ M afternoon, Tu-Sa. Via Durini 5 (near Largo Augusto). 76003993. Subway stops: Duomo (M1, M3); San Babila (M1)

102 Arcando The exclusive custom-made men's and women's footwear on display here is a tradition dating from 1919. ♦ M afternoon, Tu-Sa. Via Durini 4 (near Largo Augusto). 780791. Subway stops: Duomo (M1, M3); San Babila (M1)

103 B&B With high-tech office and home furniture in a matching setting, this shop boasts exclusive designs by major-league names such as Citterio, Sottsass, and Castiglioni. ♦ M afternoon, Tu-Sa. Corso Europa 2 (in Piazza Beccaria). 76009306. Subway stops: Duomo (M1, M3); San Babila (M1)

104 Fiorucci This boutique features the outrageous clothing and accessories of Elio Fiorucci, whose heyday was in the 1970s. A young crowd still fills the place; most come for the T-shirts. ♦ M afternoon, Tu-Sa; no midday closing. Galleria Passarella 1 (in Piazza San Babila). 76003276. Subway stops: Duomo (M1, M3); San Babila (M1)

105 Benetton This is just one of the myriad shops of the highly successful purveyor of woolen and cotton goods for both sexes. ♦ M afternoon, Tu-Sa. Galleria Passarella 2 (in Piazza San Babila). 796666. Subway stops: Duomo (M1, M3); San Babila (M1)

105 Sisley Benetton's slightly more upscale sister store sells woolen and other goods for the whole family. ♦ M afternoon, Tu-Sa. Galleria Passarella 2 (in Piazza San Babila). 76022454. Subway stops: Duomo (M1, M3); San Babila (M1)

il supermarket dell'informazione

105 Marco This well-stocked newsstand with an international selection is good for a browsing break. In the back and upstairs it's a full-fledged bookstore. ♦ M-Sa 7:30AM-9:30PM; Su 7:30AM-noon. Galleria Passarella 2 (near Piazza San Babila). 795866. Subway stops: Duomo (M1, M3); San Babila (M1)

106 San Carlo al Corso This strangely Pantheon-like church was designed by **Carlo Amati** in the fashionable Neo-Classical style of the mid-19th century. ♦ Piazza San Carlo (off Corso Vittorio Emanuele II). Subway stop: San Babila (M1)

Twenty-five percent of Milan's residences were destroyed or rendered uninhabitable by World War II bombing.

---

107 Zebedia This place has more moderately priced men's shirts (from casual to formal) than you can shake a stick at, with a faithful following of both sexes ♦ M afternoon, Tu-Sa. Corso Vittorio Emanuele II 37B (near Piazza San Babila). 76022078. Subway stop: San Babila (M1)

108 E.E. Ercolesi This is the best place for pens and writing supplies in the city. ♦ M afternoon, Tu-Sa. Corso Vittorio Emanuele II 15 (near Piazza San Babila). 76000607. Subway stop: San Babila (M1)

108 Bocci When you're on the go, come here: this store specializes in luggage and travel accessories in all shapes, sizes, colors, and fabrics. ♦ M afternoon, Tu-Sa. Corso Vittorio Emanuele II 15 (near Piazza San Babila). 76020839. Subway stop: San Babila (M1). Also at: Via San Pietro all'Orto 9 (near Corso Vittorio Emanuele II). 76006926. Subway stop: Duomo (M1, M3)

109 Santa Lucia ★★$$ If you're into Italian celebrity–spotting, this restaurant will be all the more exciting; actors often drop in after the theater to sample the Milanese menu. ♦ Tu-Su lunch and dinner. Via San Pietro all'Orto 3 (near Corso Vittorio Emanuele II). 76023155. Subway stop: San Babila (M1)

110 Linea Lidia Women's shoes of high quality and price are sold here. ♦ M afternoon, Tu-Sa Via San Pietro all'Orto 17 (between Corso Matteotti and Via Pietro Verri). 76021660. Subway stop: San Babila (M1)

110 Pomellato This prestigious Milanese name, synonymous with bold and modern jewelry, also sells table settings, leather goods and men's and women's accessories. ♦ M afternoon, Tu-Sa. Via San Pietro all'Orto 17 (between Corso Matteotti and Via Pietro Verri). 76006086. Subway stop: San Babila (M1)

111 Palazzo Spinola Built between 1580 and 1597 to a design by **Martino Bassi,** this is one of the older residences in the area. Like much of Milan, it was damaged by bombing during World War II, but it was faithfully reconstructed by **Antonio Cassi Ramelli.** ♦ Via San Paolo 10 (near Piazza Liberty). Subway stop: San Babila (M1)

charleston

112 Charleston ★★$ A pleasant spot for a light meal of pizza or a more substantial selection from the regular menu. Many of the pastas are homemade; or skip your first course and go straight for the *pesce spada* (swordfish fillet). ♦ Tu-Su lunch and dinner until 1AM. Piazza Liberty 8 (off Corso Vittorio Emanuele II). 798631. Subway stop: San Babila (M1)

MaxMara

113 MaxMara Ladies love the well-designed, colorful, and superior selection of clothing from casual to business attire for which this Italian chain is famous. Across the street (Corso Vittorio Emanuele II 4, 76000829) is another **MaxMara** shop that sells last season's clothes at a discount. **Max & Co.** (Corso Vittorio Emanuele II 2, 780070) offers a less expensive line for younger clientele. ♦ M afternoon, Tu-Sa. Corso Vittorio Emanuele II 4 (at Galleria de Cristororis). 76008849. Subway stop: San Babila (M1)

114 Mondadori Here you'll find three floors of books sold under the auspices of Italy's largest publisher. It carries not only the Mondadori imprint but many others as well. ♦ Daily 9:30AM-11PM. Corso Dei Servi 11 (at Vittorio Emanuele II). 76005833. Subway stop: San Babila (M1)

115 Il Caffè Ambrosiano ★★$$ Characteristically Milanese (as implied by its name, an adjective loosely used for things typically *milanesi*), this handsome bar/cafe has become a practically 24-hour favorite for a respite in the shadow of the **Duomo.** Down an espresso at the bar in rapid Milanese-style, or linger with breakfast, light lunch, or snacks at the outdoor tables or in the upstairs sitting room. ♦ Daily 6AM-3AM. No credit cards accepted. Piazzetta Pattari 1/3 (on Corso Vittorio Emanuele II). 801004. Subway stops: Duomo (M1, M3); San Babila (M1)

115 Pollini Fashionable footwear for men and women is featured here. ♦ M afternoon, Tu-Sa. Corso Vittorio Emanuele II 30 (near Piazza San Babila). 794912. Subway stops: Duomo (M1, M3); San Babila (M1). Also at: Piazza del Duomo 31 (northeast in piazza). 875187. Subway stop: Duomo (M1, M3)

115 Aldrovandi Conservative men's shoes and more fashionable ladies' footwear are for sale here. ♦ M afternoon, Tu-Sa. Corso Vittorio Emanuele II 30 (near Piazza San Babila). 795962. Subway stops: Duomo (M1, M3); San Babila (M1)

115 Stefanel Benetton's leading competitor offers somewhat jazzier clothing for a slightly younger clientele. This is their new megastore, the largest of 25 locations in Milan alone. ♦ M afternoon, Tu-Sa. Corso Vittorio Emanuele II 28 (near Piazza San Babila). 76006618. Subway stops: Duomo (M1, M3); San Babila (M1)

116 Messaggerie Musicali A huge selection of musical recordings in all forms, Italian and international, as well as music publications, make this Milan's best-loved music store. ♦ Tu-Su (no midday closing Tu-Sa). Galleria del Corso 2 (at Corso Vittorio Emanuele II). 781251. Subway stops: Duomo (M1, M3); San Babila (M1)

117 SEM Fashion chameleons for both sexes, this store offers the latest generic styles at some of the lowest prices in the city. ♦ M afternoon, Tu-Sa. No credit cards accepted. Corso Vittorio Emanuele II 8 (near Piazza del Duomo). 76023892. Subway stops: Duomo (M1, M3); San Babila (M1)

118 Borsalino The Milan outlet of what is perhaps the most famous hatmaker in all of Italy, like their other stores, sells traditional to fashionable headgear for men and women. ♦ M afternoon, Tu-Sa; no midday closing. Corso Vittorio Emanuele II 5 (near Piazza del Duomo). 8690805. Subway stops: Duomo (M1, M3); San Babila (M1). Also at: Galleria Vittorio Emanuele II 92 (at Piazza del Duomo). 874244. Subway stop: Duomo (M1, M3)

FONDATA NEL 1914

119 Fratelli Freni ★$ Stop in for coffee and pastry or some of these Sicilian brothers' artistic marzipan confections of lifelike cacti, watermelons, salamis, or mushrooms. All are made according to recipes they brought here from their native island in 1914. ♦ M-Tu, Th-Su 9AM-midnight. Corso Vittorio Emanuele II 4 (near Piazza del Duomo). 804871. Subway stop: Duomo (M1, M3)

119 Di Bernardi This shop has miles of hosiery and gloves for women, in all colors. ♦ M afternoon, Tu-Sa. Corso Vittorio Emanuele II 4 (near Piazza del Duomo). 872130. Subway stop: Duomo (M1, M3)

120 L'Omm de Preja This ancient stone sculpture (its name is Milanese dialect for *l'uomo di pietra,* or "man of stone") of a Roman emperor stands solemnly amidst the hustle and bustle of the street. ♦ Corso Vittorio Emanuele II (near Piazza S. Carlo). Subway stop: Duomo (M1, M3)

121 Piazza Beccaria The monument in the center of this piazza (a bronze copy of a 19th-century marble by Giuseppe Grandi) is to Cesare Beccaria, an 18th-century Milanese jurist and philosopher, who gave his name to streets and piazzas throughout Italy. ♦ East of Piazza del Duomo. Subway stop: Duomo (M1, M3)

122 Ai Bersaglieri This sculptural monument by Mario Robaudi was dedicated "to the Bersaglieri," Italy's beloved black-plumed, crack military division, which is famed for running, rather than walking, at all times. ♦ Via Verziere (near Via Larga). Subway stop: Duomo (M1, M3)

123 PAB This store sells ladies' made-to-measure clothing for a mature (but not necessarily rich) clientele. ♦ M-Sa. No credit cards accepted. Via Merlo 1 (near Piazza Fontana). 76006142. Subway stop: Duomo (M1, M3)

124 Colonna del Verziere Francesco Maria Richini and son **Domenico**'s column is topped with a statue of *Christ the Redeemer* by 17th-century sculptor Gaspare Vismara. ♦ Largo Augusto (near Via Verziere). Subway stop: Duomo (M1, M3)

124 Jolly President $$$ Offering 260 rooms and thus a better chance of vacancy when accommodations are hard to come by, this is the most central and the most pleasant of this first-class chain's representatives in town. The room decor is unimaginative but modern, the service is attentive and professional, the restaurant is reliable, and the location is great. A businessperson couldn't ask for more. ♦ Largo Augusto 10 (at Via Cavallotti). 7746; fax 783449. Subway stop: Duomo (M1, M3)

125 Santo Stefano Maggiore This imposing church, begun in 1584 by **Giuseppe Meda,** is of historical interest primarily because Galeazzo Maria Sforza was assassinated in its medieval antecedent in 1476. ♦ Piazza Santo Stefano (southeast of Piazza del Duomo). Subway stop: Duomo (M1, M3)

125 San Bernardino alle Ossa This medieval church was worked on by **Andrea Biffi** in 1679, **Carlo Giuseppe Merlo** in 1750, and **Ferdinando Reggiori** in 1937. Its **Cappella Ossario** is bizarrely decorated with human bones and a 1695 fresco of *The Triumph of Souls* by Sebastiano Ricci. ♦ Piazza Santo Stefano (southeast of Piazza del Duomo). Subway stop: Duomo (M1, M3)

126 Piazza Santo Stefano Take a minute to visit this bustling piazza, where you'll see a statue of poet Carlo Porta by Ivo Soli. ♦ Southeast of Piazza del Duomo. Subway stop: Duomo (M1, M3)

127 Piazza Fontana This large expanse is a product of World War II bombing. In the center is a Neo-Classical fountain by Giuseppe Franchi, for which the square is named. ♦ Between Piazza Beccaria and Piazza del Duomo. Subway stop: Duomo (M1, M3)

127 Telerie Ghidoli Textiles and fabrics of all kinds at all prices are the draw here. ♦ M afternoon, Tu-Sa. No credit cards accepted. Piazza Fontana 1. 72022880. Subway stop: Duomo (M1, M3)

127 Palazzo Archivescovile (Archbishop's Palace) The palace of the archbishop has occupied this site since medieval times. The present structure dates from after the sack of Milan by Barbarossa and was rebuilt in 1174. The palazzo's most important addition dates from 1565, when Charles Borromeus, archbishop of Milan, commissioned **Pellegrino Tibaldi** to design its **Cortile della Canonica** (Rectory Courtyard), which has the 19th-century statues *Moses* by Antonio Tantardini and *Aaron* by Giovanni Strazza. The other courtyard, **Cortile dell'Archivescovado,** has statues of *St. Ambrose* and *St. Charles Borromeus* (the archibishop was eventually canonized). The interior of the palazzo, decorated with paintings and tapestries, is no longer open to public. ♦ Piazza Fontana 2 (south side of the Duomo). Subway stop: Duomo (M1, M3)

127 Palazzo del Capitano di Giustizia This imposing building, begun in 1578 by **Piero Antonio Barca,** historically the seat of the Milan court, today houses city offices. ♦ Piazza Fontana (south side of the Duomo). Subway stop: Duomo (M1, M3)

128 Palazzo Reale (Royal Palace) Medieval city offices and, later, residences of the Visconti and Sforza rulers once occupied this site. It reverted to its administrative role under the Spanish and Austrian rulers, the latter of whom commissioned **Giuseppe Piermarini** to transform it into its present aspect, which he did between 1771 and 1778. Sections of **Piermarini**'s extensive palazzo were demolished under Fascist rule to make way for an office building behind it and for the **Arengario** beside the **Piazza del Duomo.** Its Neo-Classical interior was destroyed by bombs during World War II and then refurbished into modern spaces for museums and temporary exhibitions, though the room called the **Sala delle Cariatidi** was left in ruins as an antiwar memorial. ♦ Piazza del Duomo (south side of the Duomo). Subway stop: Duomo (M1, M3)

Within the Palazzo Reale complex:

Museo del Duomo Highlights of the museum include a 15th-century tondo, the *Eternal Father* **(Room I);** a 15th-century marble statue of *Gian Galeazzo Visconti* **(Room II);** 15th-century statues of saints and

Restaurants/Clubs: Red   **Hotels:** Blue
Shops/ ♦ Outdoors: Green   **Sights/Culture:** Black

prophets **(Room III)**; a 14th-century statue of *St. Peter* **(Room V)**; 15th-century statues of *Galeazzo Maria Sforza* and of an angel **(Room VI)**; a Byzantine embossed metal crucifix and a depiction of the Madonna and Child with two angels **(Room VII)**; 15th-century saints **(Room VIII)**; choir stalls **(Room IX)**; 16th-century tapestries and a painting by Jacopo Tintoretto, *Christ at the Temple,* **(Room XI)**; 17th-century sculptural models **(Room XII)**; liturgical objects **(Room XX,** to the left of **Room XII)**; terra-cotta models for the *Madonnina,* the statue atop the **Duomo,** and 18th-century marble statues **(Room XIII)**; 19th-century Neo-Classical sculpture **(Room XIV)**; models of the **Duomo (Room XVI)**; and models of the **Duomo** portals **(Room XVII)**. ◆ Admission. Tu-Su. Piazza del Duomo 14 (south side of piazza). 860358. Subway stop: Duomo (M1, M3)

Civico Museo d'Arte Contemporanea
In its contemporary art museum (known as CIMAC in the acronym-obsessed museum world), as elsewhere, Milan has a loopier view of history than most cities. It expands the commonly accepted definition of contemporary art as beginning after World War II to include Futurism, an avant-garde movement given its name in an article by its leader, Filippo Marinetti, in 1909. At the same time, the museum compresses the definition to comprise only Italian artists. Some of Marinetti's words are remarkably contemporary ("We wish to glorify war. . . "), and where better than Milan to exhibit the works of artists who extolled the virtues of machines and motion before World War I knocked that notion out of them forever. Works by Futurists Umberto Boccioni, Carlo Carrà, Giacomo Balla, and Gino Severini—the highlights of the collection—are on display in **Rooms XXI** and **XXII.** Beyond those, the museum is still the best lesson on the development of 20th-century Italian painting in Italy. Canvases by the Paris-influenced Amedeo Modigliani and Gino Severini **(Room XXIII),** the so-called metaphysical paintings of Giorgio De Chirico **(Rooms XXIV** and **XXV),** and the volumetric landscapes and still lifes of Giorgio Morandi **(Room XXIX)** are among the more internationally recognized works on display. Also represented are those contemporary painters who subscribe to the going zeitgeist that futures are more important than Futurism. ◆ Free. Daily. Piazza

del Duomo 12 (south side of piazza). 62083914. Subway stop: Duomo (M1, M3)

San Gottardo in Corte This medieval church, attributed to **Francesco Pecorari** (1330-36), is noted for its octagonal campanile. The interior, redone in Neo-Classical style, contains a damaged 14th-century Giottoesque fresco of the crucifixion and the Gothic *Tomb of Azzone Visconti* (reconstructed 1930), who commissioned the church. ◆ Via Pecorari (between Via Palazzo Reale and Via Rastrelli). Subway stop: Duomo (M1, M3)

129 Arengario One of these two Fascist-era marble buildings, built in 1939-56 by **Enrico Griffini, Pier Giulio Magistretti, Giovanni Muzio,** and **Piero Portaluppi,** houses the **Ente Provinciale di Turismo (EPT),** where you can pick up maps and information about current events and other activities. ◆ M-Sa (no midday closing), Su. Via Marconi 1 (in Piazza del Duomo). 62083106. Subway stop: Duomo (M1, M3)

130 Piazza Diaz The piazza contains Luciano Minguzzi's sculptural tribute to the *Carabinieri* (one of Italy's police forces, considered by the general public to be much less abstract than the sculpture implies). ◆ South of Piazza del Duomo (west of Palazzo Reale). Subway stop: Duomo (M1, M3)

130 Nepentha Club ★★$$ Up late? Stop in here to dance and dine (champagne, caviar, etc.) amid Milan's most *perbene* (upper-crust) club kids. ◆ 9PM-3AM Tu-Sa dinner. Piazza Diaz (south of Piazza del Duomo, west of Palazzo Reale). 86464808. Subway stop: Duomo (M1, M3)

131 Croff The Rinascente chain owns this great place to get inexpensive and well-designed housewares. ◆ M afternoon, Tu-Sa. Piazza Diaz 2 (south of Piazza del Duomo, west of Palazzo Reale). 862745. Subway stop: Duomo (M1, M3). Also at: Corso Buenos Aires 58 (near Porta Venezia). 29514141. Subway stop: Porta Venezia (M1); Corso Vercelli 10 (between Piazzale Baracca and Largo San Severo). 463373. Subway stop: Conciliazione (M1); Corso XXII Marzo 25 (near Piazzale Cinque Giornate). 733403. Subway stop: San Babila (M1)

The precious real estate surrounding Via Montenapoleone and its offshoots was once the cloistered domain of a number of religious convents. By the late 18th century, they had been all but evacuated by imperial Austrian rulers, leaving behind only the religious names of streets that today boast the city's most expensive stores: Via Gesù, Via Santo Spirito, Via Sant'Andrea.

132 Lirico The largest theater in Milan was designed in 1778 by **Giuseppe Piermarini.** Its interior was renovated in 1939 by **Renzo Gerla** and **Antonio Cassi Ramelli.** ◆ Via Larga 14 (near Via Rastrelli). 866418. Subway stop: Duomo (M1, M3)

133 Sant'Antonio Abate This 14th-century church was rebuilt in the 15th century (from which its campanile dates) and again in the 16th century by **Dionigi Campazzo.** The interior is decorated with 17th- and 18th-century paintings, including *St. Andrew Avellino* by Francesco Cairo, in the second chapel on the right; *Adoration of the Magi* by Pier Francesco Mazzucchelli (known as Morazzone), on the right wall of the transept; *Adoration of the Shepherds* by Ludovico Carracci, on the left wall of the transept; a nativity by Annibale Carracci, on the left wall of the presbytery; and *St. Cajetan* by Giovanni Battista Crespi (known as Cerano). ◆ Via Sant'Antonio (near Largo Richini). Subway stop: Duomo (M1, M3)

134 Beretta At this well-known restaurant-supply warehouse (one of the very oldest stores in Milan, founded in 1800), you can also find industrial-design objects for the home, kitchen, or dining room. ◆ M afternoon, Tu-Sa. Via Bergamini 5 (near Via Larga). 58304131. Subway stop: Duomo (M1, M3)

134 Anaconda This jeweler applies traditional craft techniques to modern designs when fashioning jewelry from semiprecious stones and more unusual materials, such as mother-of-pearl and wood. ◆ M afternoon, Tu-Sa. Via Bergamini 7 (near Via Larga). 58303668. Subway stop: Duomo (M1, M3)

135 Cantina Piemontese ★★$ This old-fashioned trattoria serves traditional Italian fare such as prosciutto and melon, *pasta e fagioli,* (pasta and beans), and a nice selection of cheeses and wines. ◆ M-F lunch and dinner; Sa dinner only. Via Laghetto 11 (off Via della Signora). 784618. Subway stops: Duomo (M1, M3); Missori (M3)

The Duomo was commissioned in 1387 by Galeazzo Visconti III as a votive offering in the hope that God might grant him a male heir. Dedicated to the Virgin Mary—the golden Madonnina that stands as protectress on its highest spire and is beloved by the Milanese—it is the second largest cathedral in Christendom.

"For me, this is the most beautiful place on earth."

Stendhal

Restaurants/Clubs: Red **Hotels:** Blue

Shops/ 🍷 Outdoors: Green **Sights/Culture:** Black

Ospedale Maggiore

136 Ospedale Maggiore Originally built as Milan's main hospital (it still has some administrative offices here), this sprawling palazzo now houses the humanities department of the **Università Statale** (State University), though it is also affectionately known as **Ca' Granda,** Milanese dialect for "big house." Commissioned by Francesco Sforza and begun in 1456 by **Antonio Averulino** (known as **Filarete**), the hospital became a civic project that lasted hundreds of years. Funds were raised privately and publicly, largely through contributions made during the *Festa del Perdono* (from which the street takes its name), held 25 March on odd years.

Filarete's Renaissance plan consists of two sections, each divided into four courtyards and furnished with an elaborate plumbing system connected to the nearby *naviglio,* or canal. The right wing was completed under **Filarete**'s direction; **Guiniforte Solari** continued the construction in a more conservative Gothic style, as seen in the windows of the facade, though the heavy cornice is pure Renaissance. A number of other architects continued the work, adding the Baroque entrance (designed by **Fabio Mangone** and **Francesco Maria Richini**), with 17th-century statues of St. Charles and St.

Ambrose by Gian Battista Bianco and an *Annunciation* by Gian Pietro Lasagna, and doubling **Filarete**'s plan for a central courtyard (also by **Richini**). Heavily damaged during World War II, it was restored by **Piero Portaluppi** and **Liliana Grassi**. ♦ Via Festa del Perdono (between Corso di Porta Romana and Piazza Santo Stefano). Subway stops: Duomo (M1, M3); Missori (M3)

Within the Ospedale Maggiore:

L'Annunziata This 17th-century church has an *Annunciation* by Giovanni Francesco Barbieri, known as Guercino.

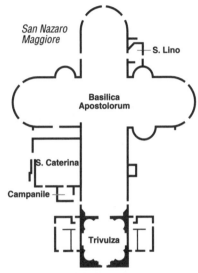

San Nazaro Maggiore

S. Lino

Basilica Apostolorum

S. Caterina

Campanile

Trivulza

137 San Nazaro Maggiore Founded in the fourth century by St. Ambrose, this church was altered through the centuries and restored to its current Romanesque appearance (see floor plan above) after it was bombed in World War II. It contains **Bramantino**'s Renaissance **Cappella Trivulzio**, the octagonal mausoleum of the Trivulzio family (Gian Giacomo Trivulzio was the marshall of Louis XII of France), who lie in black stone sarcophagi in the niches. ♦ Piazza San Nazaro (at Corso di Porta Romana). Subway stop: Missori (M3)

138 NCA Sinigaglia An excellent array of quality housewares, from English and German china to crystal goblets and silver candlesticks, is offered in this store. ♦ M-Sa. Corso di Porta Romana 7 (near Piazza Erculea). 8058590. Subway stop: Missori (M3)

139 Torre Velasca Named after the 17th-century Spanish governor Juan de Velasco, the Torre Velasca (1958, **Studio BBPR**, including: **Gian Luigi Banfi, Lodovico Belgioioso, Enrico Peressutti**, and **Ernesto Nathan Rogers**) is contemporary Milanese architecture at its best: intelligent yet not lacking a sense of humor. Twenty stories of offices are topped with a six-story residential section resting on reinforced-concrete corbels, openly exposed structural elements that refer back to the **Duomo.** The overall effect is wry and impressive, combining the Medieval creepiness of the **Castello Sforzesco** with the delightfully cheap thrills of 1950s space-monster movies. ♦ Piazza Velasca 5 (between Piazza Missori and Ospedale Maggiore). Subway stop: Missori (M3)

140 Magazzini Incendio There are no big-names or designer labels at this busy bargain basement, but there is almost always a big selection of men's and women's quality clothing for Milan's 30-something crowd. You might find cashmere coats, parkas for the great outdoors, Italian-made sweaters; and the price is always right. ♦ M-F (no midday closing), Sa. Corso di Porta Romana 6 (at Via Maddelena). 86451559. Subway stop: Missori (M3)

141 Truzzi The best place in town for made-to-measure men's shirts, with pajamas and suits to boot, if you're in town long enough for a return fitting. ♦ M afternoon, Tu-Sa; no midday closing. Via Sant'Eufemia 21 (off Corso Italia). 861552. Subway stop: Missori (M3)

142 San Lorenzo Maggiore Founded in the fourth century, San Lorenzo is one of the most important churches remaining from Milan's heyday as the capital of the Western Roman Empire. It has maintained its quatrefoil plan despite several remodelings over the centuries that have made it a stylistic hodgepodge of everything from Romanesque to Neo-Classical. Unified only by its immensity, its vast interior is surmounted by the largest cupola of any church in Milan. The most important chapel here is the **Cappella di Sant'Aquilino,** accessible through the atrium on the right as you face the altar (admission). The chapel contains ancient mosaics and a sarcophagus said to hold the remains of Byzantine empress Galla Placidia. Near and dear to the hearts of the Milanese, the church is the site of a particularly elaborate religious procession on 29 January, the feast day of St. Lawrence. ♦ Corso di Porta Ticinese (near Via Molino delle Armi). Subway stop: Missori (M3)

143 Colonne di San Lorenzo Maggiore (Columns of San Lorenzo Maggiore) Perhaps the remains of an ancient temple, these 16 Corinthian columns dating back to the fourth century provide an uncharacteristically Milanese—and rather Roman in both the historic and the contemporary sense—backdrop for spirited soccer games by day and loitering Milanese teenagers by night. A copy of a bronze statue of the Emperor Constantine (who, you'll recall, was responsible for the Edict of Milan in AD 313) imperially oversees it all. ♦ Corso di Porta Ticinese (near Via Molino delle Armi). Subway stop: Missori (M3)

143 Porta Ticinese Medievale Not to be confused with its Neo-Classical counterpart of the same name, this medieval gate dating from the 12th century was built closer to the city center, when Milan's walls held a tighter grip on the metropolis. ♦ Corso di Porta Ticinese (near Via Molino delle Armi). Subway stop: Missori (M3)

144 Palazzo Stampa di Soncino Construction on this palace began around 1534. Residential towers of this sort were once common dwellings for the nobility of northern Italy. ♦ Via Soncino 2 (at Via Torino). Subway stop: Missori (M3)

145 L'Ulmet ★★★$$$ A refined restaurant, built on ancient Roman foundations, it is a favorite of the Milanese. The two dining rooms are decorated in Old Milan style. Refined dishes range from *ravioli d'anatra al burro e timo* (duck-filled ravioli with butter and thyme) and *dorso di coniglio alla Vernaccia* (saddle of rabbit with Vernaccia wine) to a wide selection of mousses (*cioccolata amara*, bitter chocolate; *bianca*, white chocolate; and *caffè*, coffee). ♦ Tu-Sa lunch and dinner. Via Disciplini at Via Olmetto. 86452718. Subway stop: Missori (M3)

146 Fortura This toy store offers international brand names at a 30-percent discount. ♦ M afternoon, Tu-Sa. No credit cards accepted. Via Olmetto 10 (at Via Amadei). 861670. Subway stop: Missori (M3)

147 Profumeria Mario Galli International cosmetics are sold here at a 20-percent discount. ♦ M-F. No credit cards accepted. Via Amadei 11 (at Via Olmetto). 877908. Subway stop: Missori (M3)

148 Standa This long-established department-store chain (modeled on the English store Standard, it was also called **Standard** until foreign words were forbidden under Fascism) is perhaps more down-market than others in the clothing department, but its downstairs section is a good place to get basic home furnishings and grocery items. ♦ M afternoon, Tu-Sa; no midday closing. Via della Palla 2/A (at Via Torino). 866706. Subway stop: Missori (M3)

149 Sant'Alessandro There's a little bit of Rome in this church, which is built on a central plan (like **Bramante**'s and **Michelangelo**'s plan for the Vatican) with a cupola and two domed campaniles. Begun in 1601 on the site of a Romanesque church, Padre Lorenzo Binago's project was carried out by a number of architects, including **Francesco Maria Richini**, and was finished off with a Rococo facade in the 18th century.

The somewhat dark interior is rich in 17th-century works, including the *Beheading of John the Baptist* by Daniele Crespi in the third chapel of the left nave. ♦ Piazza Sant'Alessandro (west of Piazza Missori). Subway stop: Missori (M3)

149 Scuole Arcimboldi This buiding, designed in 1663 by **Lorenzo Binago,** is one of the nicest examples of Baroque architecture in Milan. ♦ Piazza Sant'Alessandro 1 (west of Piazza Missori). Subway stop: Missori (M3)

150 Piazza Missori This piazza displays Riccardo Ripamonti's equestrian monument to Giuseppe Missori (1829-1911), a Russian general who fought for Milan under Garibaldi. Also here are the open-air remains of the Romanesque church of **San Giovanni in Conca**. ♦ At the intersection of Via Mazzini, Corso di Porta Romana, and Corso Italia. Subway stop: Missori (M3)

151 Al Guanto Perfetto The "perfect glove" for men and women can be sought here amid leather creations by the hands of all the top designers. ♦ M afternoon, Tu-Sa. Via Mazzini 18 (near Piazza Missori). 875894. Subway stop: Missori (M3)

152 Latteria Unione ★★$ This is a great place for a quick, light, sit-down lunch of changing daily pasta specials or sandwiches. A few good vegetarian dishes are always available. ♦ M-Sa 11:30-3:30PM. No credit cards accepted. Via Unione 6 (at Via Torino). 874401. Subway stops: Missori (M3); Duomo (M1, M3)

153 Santa Maria presso San Satiro Behind the 19th-century facade of this small complex in the middle of a busy business district is some of Milan's most important Medieval and Renaissance architecture. The site was originally occupied by a basilica that Archbishop Ansperto built to honor St. Satirus, St. Ambrose's brother, in the ninth century. In the 13th century an image of the Madonna in the basilica miraculously bled when it was stabbed; soon after, crowds flocked to the site. To accommodate the pilgrims and commemorate the miracle, the church was enlarged. In 1480, most of the old basilica was demolished, and in its place **Donato Bramante** erected the present Renaissance church. Though in the form of a "T," the church appears to be shaped like a proper cross from the inside, thanks to **Bramante**'s trick of making a perspective relief behind the high altar (where the Madonna is displayed) to create the illusion of a presbytery. Also of note is **Bramante**'s octagonal baptistry (on the right of the nave)—which he originally designed as the sacristy, decorated with a terra-cotta frieze of *putti* (cherubs) and busts of men—made by Agostino de' Fondutis in 1483 following **Bramante**'s designs. Just as interesting are the remains of the medieval **San Satiro,**

accessible through the left transept. Originally thought to have been Archbishop Ansperto's chapel, it contains traces of Byzantine frescoes of saints and of the Madonna and Child, as well as columns topped with early Christian and Romanesque capitals. It is now called the **Cappella della Pietà** because of its 15th-century terra-cotta statue of the Pietà by Agostino de' Fondutis. **Bramante** retained the chapel's Greek-cross shape in its interior, though outside he simplified its lines by enclosing the structure in a cylindrical wall. The 10th-century campanile was also part of the original basilica, and together with the **Campanile dei Monaci** at the basilica of San Lorenzo, served as the prototype for bell towers throughout medieval Lombardy. ◆ Via Torino (at Via Speronari). Subway stops: Missori (M3); Duomo (M1, M3)

154 Casa del Formaggio The Peck food empire's unrivaled cheese store has hundreds of cheeses from throughout Italy (and a few from other countries). Stop in to sample a few. ◆ M afternoon, Tu-Sa. Via Speronari 3 (near Via Mazzini). 800858. Subway stops: Missori (M3); Duomo (M1, M3)

155 Sir Edward $$$ This Anglo-wannabe is the newest of the city's four-star hotels. It is pleasantly small, excellently situated just steps from the **Piazza del Duomo,** and the service is attentive. Its 40 rooms are contemporary in design with a generous use of burnished wood; half have Jacuzzis and one has a sauna. For the business-inclined, the hotel also has a fax machine. There's no restaurant. ◆ Via Mazzini 4 (off Piazza del Duomo). 877877; fax 877844. Subway stops: Missori (M3); Duomo (M1, M3)

156 Fiordipelle Original, well-crafted bags and jewelry can be found here at affordable prices. ◆ M afternoon, Tu-Sa. Via Speronari 8 (off Via Torino). 86460414. Subway stop: Duomo (M1, M3)

157 Galtrucco This store sells elegant fabrics for furnishings and apparel, as well as ready-to-wear clothing for men and women. ◆ M afternoon, Tu-Sa; no midday closing. Piazza del Duomo 2 (at Via Mazzini). 876256. Subway stops: Duomo (M1, M3); Cordusio (M1)

157 Pikenz This Milanese institution's excellent-quality furs are considered a lifetime investment. Its annual sales (January-March) are eagerly awaited because showroom models are discounted as well.

◆ M afternoon, Tu-Sa. Piazza del Duomo 2 (at Via Mazzini). 72003999. Subway stops: Duomo (M1, M3); Cordusio (M1)

158 Savinelli This is the nicest pipe shop in Milan, best appreciated for its own line since 1876. ◆ M afternoon, Tu-Sa. Via Orefici 2 (west of Piazza del Duomo). 876660. Subway stops: Duomo (M1, M3); Cordusio (M1)

159 La Furla Fashionable bags and accessories from the Bologna-based firm are the draw in this boutique. ◆ M afternoon, Tu-Sa. Via Orefici 11 (west of Piazza Cordusio). 8053944. Subway stops: Duomo (M1, M3); Cordusio (M1)

160 Loggia degli Osii This loggia, designed in 1316 by **Scoto da San Gemignano,** is one of Milan's oldest pieces of architecture. It was restored in 1904 and now houses private enterprises. ◆ Piazza Mercanti (west off Piazza del Duomo). Subway stops: Duomo (M1, M3); Cordusio (M1)

161 Palazzo dei Giureconsulti This palazzo, begun in 1561 by **Vincenzo Seregni**, has been much altered through the ages, primarily in the past century, when it was remodeled and sliced up by the city's modern street pattern. ◆ Via Mercanti (near Piazza Cordusio). Subway stops: Duomo (M1, M3); Cordusio (M1)

Palazzo dei Giureconsulti

Magenta

Though much of Magenta lies within the **Cerchia dei Navigli,** or canal ring, which defines the historic center of the city, the most appealing aspect of this part of Milan is the less congested residential quarter centered around **Corso Magenta.** This broad boulevard leads past the original and innermost ring to the second one, known as the **Viali** or **Bastioni,** which traces the city's 16th-century Spanish walls. With sections laid out as recently as the 19th century, the Magenta area abounds with tree-lined streets, boutiques and cafes, and stately apartment buildings. In addition to boasting one of Milan's most prestigious residential neighborhoods, Magenta contains a number of important churches, including **Sant'Ambrogio** (after the **Duomo,** the church most singularly connected with historical Milanese culture) and **Santa Maria delle Grazie** (where one of the most famous works of art in the Western World, Leonardo da Vinci's *The Last Supper,* is housed). Interspersed with a delicious variety of shops and restaurants, the monuments make Magenta one of the most manageable and pleasant places for a boulevardier to sample the more subtle and upscale charms of Milan.

1 Riccardo Prisco This boutique carries a large selection of women's apparel by Prisco and other designers, especially useful for putting together a coordinated and casual working and weekend wardrobe. ♦ M afternoon, Tu-Sa. Via Orefici (at Via Victor Hugo). 878032. Subway stop: Cordusio (M1)

2 Bottega del Maiale This store is the *salumeria* (pork butcher) of **Peck,** whose restaurant and artistic gourmet shops are a mini-empire in the vicinity. ♦ M afternoon, Tu-Sa. Via Victor Hugo 3 (between Via Spadari and Via Orefici). 8053528. Subway stop: Cordusio (M1)

2 Garbagnati In a neighborhood of specialty shops, this one has more gourmet food items than you can shake a breadstick at, including seasonal treats celebrating Christian and Jewish religious traditions. ♦ M morning, Tu-Sa. Via Victor Hugo 3 (between Via Spadari and Orefici). 860905. Subway stop: Cordusio (M1)

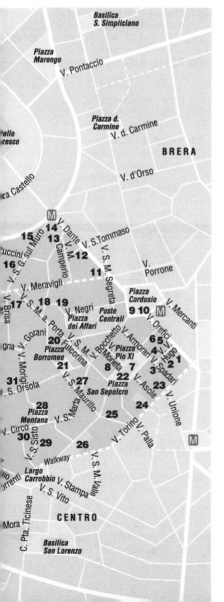

3 Hotel Spadari $$$ Design-conscious, and boasting an excellent location, this small hotel is the embodiment of Milanese style in both its impressive contemporary art collection and its decor, for which it has quickly become an insider's favorite. Service in both the hotel and its fine restaurant is attentive and personalized; there are only 40 rooms, so reserve early. ♦ Via Spadari 11 (at Via Victor Hugo). 72002371; fax 861184. Subway stop: Cordusio (M1)

3 Gastronomia Peck Milan's most famous gourmet shop purveys pasta, meats, pâté, and salads for the most chic office or outdoor picnicking in the city. ♦ M afternoon, Tu-Sa. Via Spadari 9 (near Via Victor Hugo). 860842. Subway stop: Cordusio (M1)

4 Peck ★★★$$$ French chef Daniel Drouaidaine sees to it that the largely business crowd that frequents this bright and bustling restaurant gets some of the most varied yet not-too-unusual fare in the city. Pasta, meat, fish, and dessert are all consistently well prepared (his *paglia e fieno,* a flat-pasta dish, shows that he is one of the few Frenchmen who understands pasta). The two menus (*tradizionale,* or traditional, and *degustazione,* or tasting) and a fine wine list have kept customers coming back for years. ♦ M-Sa lunch and dinner. Via Victor Hugo 4 (between Via Spadari and Via Orefici). 876774. Subway stop: Cordusio (M1)

4 Bottega del Vino Peck's finger foods are washed down here with more than 200 varieties of wine at the "self-service" bar. ♦ M afternoon, Tu-Sa. No credit cards accepted. Via Victor Hugo 4 (between Via Spadari and Via Orefici). 861040. Subway stop: Cordusio (M1)

4 Passerini Gelato time! One of the richest treats at this ice cream parlor is *cioccolato gianduia* (chocolate hazelnut) topped with a generous helping of whipped cream. Have a seat at one of the tables and enjoy. ♦ M-Tu, Th-Su 8AM-10PM. Via Victor Hugo 4 (entrance on Via Spadari). 86464995. Subway stop: Cordusio (M1)

5 Giovanni Galli Outstanding among the confectioner's goodies here are Galli's legendary candied chestnuts and the *paste di mandorle* (almond-paste confections) in fanciful fruit and vegetable shapes. ♦ M afternoon, Tu-Sa. Via Victor Hugo 2 (between Via Spadari and Via Orefici). 86464833. Subway stop: Cordusio (M1)

6 Rosticceria Peck's rotisserie grill is just the place to put together a picnic of plump fowl or spit-roasted meat, with pastas and roasted veggies to round out your meal. ◆ M afternoon, Tu-Sa. Via Cantu 3 (near Via Orefici). 8693017. Subway stop: Cordusio (M1)

7 L'Ambrosiana This institution of higher learning was founded in the early 17th century by Cardinal Federico Borromeo, cousin of St. Charles Borromeus, to further the cause of Roman Catholic orthodoxy through scholarship against the threat of Protestantism. The building, designed by **Lelio Buzzi,** still houses a private foundation associated with the Roman Catholic church. The **Ambrosiana** was once made up of various academies. Of those remaining, the **Biblioteca Ambrosiana** and the **Pinacoteca Ambrosiana** are the most important. ◆ Piazza Pio XI 2 (center of piazza, southwest of Via Spadari). Subway stop: Cordusio (M1)

Within L'Ambrosiana:

Biblioteca Ambrosiana (Ambrosiana Library) Cardinal Federico Borromeo's men combed the civilized world to come up with the core collection of 30,000 books and 15,000 manuscripts for his library, which has since grown to one million volumes and 35,000 manuscripts. Some of its rarer treasures include the *Ilias Picta,* a fifth-century Byzantine manuscript; rare editions of Virgil, Dante, and Boccaccio; and the *Codex Atlanticus,* more than 1,000 pages of technical drawings by Leonardo da Vinci. Its hallowed halls are decorated with sculpture of learned men and wealthy benefactors, among them a bust of Byron by Neo-Classical sculptor Bertel Thorwaldsen. Restoration is under way and scheduled for completion at the end of 1996. ◆ M-F; Sa morning only. 8692987

Pinacoteca Ambrosiana (Ambrosiana Picture Gallery) Originally donated by Cardinal Federico Borromeo to the **Ambrosiana**'s now-defunct fine arts academy (which was transferred to the Brera under Hapsburg rule), this is now the most important art collection in Milan after the **Pinacoteca di Brera** and the **Civici Musei del Castello Sforzesco.** Alas, it will be closed for restoration until the end of 1996, so here's a quick rundown of what you'll be missing (or what to look for if you're lucky enough to arrive post-restoration): Leonardo da Vinci's only portrait in Italy, *Portrait of a Musician;* Caravaggio's only still life in the world, *Basket of Fruit;* works by Botticelli, Ghirlandaio, Titian, and Jan Brueghel; and the huge cartoon or preparatory drawing for Raphael's *School of Athens* fresco in the Musei Vaticani—artistic ambrosia turned forbidden fruit! ◆ Tu-Su. 86451636

8 Gran Duca di York $$ Old-fashioned comfort in 35 tastefully decorated—if not sleek—Milanese rooms at almost old-fashioned prices attracts guests to this handsome 19th-century palazzo. There is no restaurant, but the hotel does have a breakfast room and a bar, and there's also room service for all meals. ◆ Via Moneta 1A (at Piazza Pio XI). 874863; fax 8690344. Subway stop: Cordusio (M1)

9 Banca d'Italia This Beaux Arts building (1907-12) has a somewhat academic look, which makes sense because the architects, **Luigi Broggi** and **Giuseppe Nava,** taught at the **Brera Academy.** ◆ Piazza Edison (southeast of Piazza Cordusio at Via Bocchetto). Subway stop: Cordusio (M1)

10 Piazza Cordusio This piazza, which connects the cathedral to the **Castello Sforzesco,** has a sculpture of Milanese poet Giuseppe Parini by Luigi Secchi and Luca Beltrami. ◆ Between Via Orefici and Via Dante Subway stop: Cordusio (M1)

10 Palazzo della Borsa Another of **Luigi Broggi**'s academic-looking buildings, Milan's old stock market (built in 1898-1901) today houses a large post office. ◆ Piazza Cordusio (south side of piazza). Subway stop: Cordusio (M1)

11 Prenatal The children's clothes this Italian chain carries are bolder and more practical in design than the cutesy-poo stuff inspired by the saccharine side of the Italian character seen in many children's shops. ◆ M afternoon, Tu-Sa. Via Dante 7 (at Via Meravigli). 8692535. Subway stop: Cordusio (M1)

CITTÀ DEL SOLE

12 Città del Sole You'll find high-quality toys of all types here, though the majority are American-made brands. ◆ M afternoon, Tu-Sa. Via Dante 13 (near Piazza Castello). 86461683. Subway stop: Cordusio (M1)

13 American Bookstore English-language books mostly from American publishers—some of which are out of print in their native country—are the specialty of this shop, the largest of its kind in town. ◆ M afternoon, Tu-Sa. Via Manfredo Camperio 16 (at Via Dante). 878920. Subway stop: Cordusio (M1)

14 Santa Maria della Consolazione This church, also called **Santa Maria al Castello** because of its proximity to **Castello Sforzesco,** dates from the 15th century but was completely renovated in the 19th. Inside, in the third chapel on the left, are some nicely decaying frescoes attributed to Daniele Crespi depicting St. Peter Martyr and St. Charles. ♦ Via San Giovanni sul Muro (near Foro Bonaparte). Subway stop: Cordusio (M1)

15 I Quattro Mori ★★$$ Sisto and Lina Arrigoni put a lot of care into their food—the pasta is produced on the premises, the meat and fish are fresh (often personally picked up from the farm or dock by Signor Arrigoni), and the desserts are homemade. The outdoor garden is one of the most pleasant spots in Milan during the warmer months. ♦ Tu-F lunch and dinner; Sa dinner only. Via San Giovanni sul Muro 2 (near Foro Bonaparte). 870617. Subway stop: Cordusio (M1)

16 Vecchia Milano Old Milan, indeed, is what you'll see in the furnishings of this *profumeria,* where cosmetics take second place to Empire-style cabinets and counters as well as frescoed ceilings. ♦ M afternoon, Tu-Sa. Via San Giovanni sul Muro 8 (between Via Puccini and Corso Magenta). 86451669. Subway stop: Cordusio (M1)

17 Marchesi This cafe is a favorite among the local upper crust, who come here to sip Campari or cappuccino in an opulent wood-paneled setting. ♦ Tu-Su 7:30AM-8PM. No credit cards accepted. Via Santa Maria alla Porta 13 (at Corso Magenta). 862770. Subway stop: Cordusio (M1)

18 Santa Maria alla Porta Begun 1652 by **Francesco Maria Richini** and **Francesco Castelli**, this parochial church happens to be a nice little Rococo number (see illustration below). ♦ Via Santa Maria alla Porta (off Via Meravigli). Subway stop: Cordusio (M1)

19 Teatro Romano The fragmented remains of an ancient Roman theater beneath the **Borsa Merci,** or Stock Exchange, are accessible to the public. To see them, contact the **Camera di Commercio,** Via Meravigli 9B, 85151. ♦ Via San Vittore al Teatro 14 (near Via Santa Maria alla Porta). Subway stop: Cordusio (M1)

20 Biscione $$ This small, modern hotel with just 28 rooms is popular with Italian stockbrokers and businesspeople. There's no restaurant, but a continental breakfast is included in the rate. ♦ Via Santa Maria Fulcorina 15 (near Piazza dei Affari). 877288; fax 8056825. Subway stop: Cordusio (M1)

21 Piazza Borromeo This piazza boasts Dionigi Bussola's Baroque statue of Milan's own St. Charles Borromeo, the aristocratic archbishop of Milan. Descendants of the Borromeo family still populate the city today. ♦ On Via San Orsola (between Via Santa Maria Fulcorina and Via San Maurillo). Subway stop: Cordusio (M1)

21 Palazzo Borromeo This lovely 15th-century palazzo has Gothic arches dressed in terra-cotta and, on the ground floor, unusual 15th-

Santa Maria alla Porta

century frescoes depicting games popular at court at the time, such as Tarot. ◆ Piazza Borromeo 7 (off Via San Orsola). Subway stop: Cordusio (M1)

21 Statues For no apparent reason, someone has assembled a group of statues from a Tuscan villa under a portico for all to enjoy. ◆ Piazza Borromeo (off Via San Orsola). Subway stop: Cordusio (M1)

21 Danese One of the mainstays of Milanese design, this shop carries the work of great names such as Achille Castiglioni, Bruno Munari, Enzo Mari, and Angelo Mangiarotti. ◆ M-F. No midday closing. Via Santa Maria alla Porta Fulcorina 17 (near Piazza Borromeo). 86450921. Subway stop: Cordusio (M1)

22 Piazza San Sepolcro It's hard to tell, but Milan's Roman forum once occupied this piazza and the adjacent block, which is now taken up by the **Ambrosiana.** The statue, by Costantino Corti, is of **Ambrosiana** founder Federico Borromeo. ◆ Southwest of Piazza Pio XI. Subway stop: Cordusio (M1)

22 San Sepolcro Founded in 1030, this church has been dedicated to a number of saints throughout the centuries and has been considerably altered architecturally. The most interesting aspect is its 11th-century crypt, which contains a painted terra-cotta sarcophagus decorated with a Pietà that probably influenced the one in **San Satiro.** ◆ Piazza San Sepolcro (southwest of Piazza Pio XI). Subway stop: Cordusio (M1)

23 CIP In this glittery store you'll find rock-bottom prices on rocks of the semiprecious stone and gold-plated costume jewelry variety. ◆ M afternoon, Tu-Sa. Via Torino 22 (near Piazza Santa Maria Beltrade). 860333. Subway stop: Cordusio (M1)

24 San Sebastiano St. Charles Borromeus commissioned **Pellegrino Tibaldi** to design this votive church following the plague of 1576. **Tibaldi**'s circular plan was carried out by a number of architects, the last being **Fabio Mangone,** who completed the project in the early 17th century. The interior is more attractive for its architectural plan than for its art, most of which dates from the 18th to 20th centuries. ◆ Via Torino (near Piazza Santa Maria Beltrade). Subway stop: Cordusio (M1)

After the nationwide bribe-busting expose called "Clean Hands" was launched in February 1992, the term "VIP" took on a new Italian meaning: *visto in prigione* (seen in prison). Thousands of Italian industrialists and politicians under investigation were ushered into Milan's 19th-century San Vittore prison, which was the first outside of England to offer the luxury of individual cells.

25 Papier The fine assortment of paper here is made by the French firm Marie Papier. ◆ M afternoon, Tu-Sa. Via San Maurillo 4 (at Via Torino). 865221. Subway stop: Cordusio (M1)

26 San Giorgio al Palazzo Another ancient church (founded in 750) radically transformed through the ages, this one now displays a Neo-Classical facade (by **Francesco Crose**) fronting a Neo-Classical interior (by **Luigi Cagnola** and **Alfonso Perrucchitti**). In the third chapel on the right are paintings by Bernardino Luini, a *Deposition, Flagellation, Crowning of Thorns,* and *Crucifixion.* ◆ Via Torino (at Piazza San Giorgio). Subway stop: Cordusio (M1)

27 Santamarta 6 ★★$$ Gianni and Dadde add to a regular Milanese menu the robust cooking of Sardinia, rich in *capretti* (roast kid) and *pecorino* (ewe's-milk cheese), and best washed down with a hearty wine such as Doragli, supposedly the strongest table wine in Italy. ◆ M-Sa lunch and dinner. Via Santa Marta 6 (near Via San Maurillo). 86452570. Subway stop: Cordusio (M1)

28 Piazza Mentana The monument here by Luigi Belli is called *To the Garibaldini of Mentana,* commemorating a historic battle led by Giuseppe Garibaldi. ◆ At Via Santa Marta and Via Circo. Subway stops: Cordusio (M1); San Ambrogio (M2)

28 Il Conte Tis ★★$$ A number of restaurants have tried this location—this most recent one might well succeed. Fresh fish and a simple Mediterranean *cucina* are its main draws, along with an elegant, modern decor and live piano music in the background ◆ M-Sa lunch and dinner. Piazza Mentana 8 (near Via Morigi). 860036. Subway stops: Cordusio (M1); San Ambrogio (M2)

29 Civico Studio Museo Francesco Messina (Francesco Messina Studio Museum) Housed in the former church of San Sisto (of remote origin, it was rebuilt in the early 17th century), this museum displays the work of Francesco Messina, a contemporary representational sculptor who works in Milan. ◆ Free. Tu-Sa. Via San Sisto 10 (near Piazza Mentana). 86453006. Subway stops: Cordusio (M1); San Ambrogio (M2)

30 Meazza Only in Milan would you find haute hardware: Shop here for the latest designs in nails, screws, hinges, etc. ◆ M afternoon, Tu-Sa. Via Circo 1 (near Piazza Mentana). 86450961. Subway stops: Cordusio (M1); San Ambrogio (M2)

31 Palazzo Belgioioso Built in the 18th century, this is one of the earliest of the stately residences that helped give this part of Milan its best addresses. ♦ Via Morigi 9 (north of Piazza Mentana). Subway stops: Cordusio (M1); San Ambrogio (M2)

Within the Palazzo Belgioioso:

Pellini Donatelli Pellini designs accessories lines for major runway shows, but here she's on her own with an imaginative collection of beautiful jewelry made of unusual and often inexpensive materials. ♦ M afternoon, Tu-Sa. 72010199. Also at: Via Santa Maria alla Porta 15 (near Piazza dei Affari). 72010569. Subway stop: Cordusio (M1)

32 La Brisa ★★$$ French chef Christian Delemas adds an innovative touch to Milan's restaurant scene. Follow delicate, fresh-made ravioli stuffed with *zucca* (pumpkin) with breast of duck braised with chestnut honey. If you can, hold out for a table either on the glass veranda overlooking a charming inner garden or in the garden itself. ♦ M-F lunch and dinner, Su dinner only. Via Brisa 15 (at Corso Magenta). 86450521. Subway stops: Cordusio (M1); San Ambrogio (M2)

33 Falliva Panizza Well-wrought jewelry gives a touch of originality to traditional shapes in this turn-of-the-century setting. ♦ M afternoon, Tu-Sa. Corso Magenta 5 (at Via Brisa). 804829. Subway stops: Cordusio (M1); San Ambrogio (M2)

33 Bardelli The traditional look in men's and women's executive clothing reigns in this shop. Authentic and imitation Anglo-American fashions, from Burberry-style tartans to Ralph Lauren rep ties, are sold. ♦ M afternoon, Tu-Sa. No credit cards accepted. Corso Magenta 13 (near Via Brisa). 86450734. Subway stops: Cordusio (M1); San Ambrogio (M2)

34 Curiosità Esotiche These exotic curiosities—objects and fabrics from around the world—might not seem so exotic to those who lived through the Third World crafts boom of the 1960s and 1970s, but it's a nice place to pick up an Indian print or brass ashtray for your Milanese friends. ♦ M afternoon, Tu-Sa. Via Nirone 2 (at Corso Magenta). 876693. Subway stop: San Ambrogio (M2)

34 Civico Museo Archeologico (Civic Archaeological Museum) The city's ancient Greek, Etruscan, and Roman archaeological collections are housed i n an evocative Benedictine monastery. Its courtyard appropriately includes two Roman towers from when the city was known as Mediolanum: one square, the other presciently polygonal. The museum's Greek holdings span from examples of third-millennium BC Cycladic statuary through second-century BC vases from Magna

Grecia (the ancient Greek colonies of what is now southern Italy). Etruscan objects include ceramics and a second-century BC sarcophagus from Tarquinia showing a reclining female figure. Artifacts from Roman Milan include first- to third-century AD portrait busts. ♦ Free. Tu-Sa. Monastero Maggiore, Corso Magenta 15 (at Via Nirone). 86450665. Subway stop: San Ambrogio (M2)

35 Palazzo Litta This opulent Baroque palazzo, designed in 1645 by the prolific **Francesco Maria Richini** has a rich Rococo facade by **Bartolomeo Bolli** (1743-60) and no fewer than three indoor courtyards. ♦ Corso Magenta 24 (near Via Nirone). Subway stop: San Ambrogio (M2)

36 Buscemi In this music-lover's paradise, the quiet section sells classical and the livelier portion is devoted to the rest. ♦ M afternoon, Tu-Sa. Corso Magenta 31 (at Largo D'Ancona). 804103. Subway stop: San Ambrogio (M2)

36 Figus Bags and belts here are made by the firm's own artisans: Most are of well-crafted leather, but canvas is available, too. ♦ M afternoon, Tu-Sa. Corso Magenta 31 (at Largo D'Ancona). 86450155. Subway stop: San Ambrogio (M2)

37 Ella This small boutique sells classic women's ready-to-wear and has been especially successful in the blouse department. ♦ M afternoon, Tu-Sa. Via Terraggio 28 (at Piazza Sant'Ambrogio). 867115. Subway stop: San Ambrogio (M2)

38 Profumeria Raimel This shop sells its scents and bath products at one-fifth to one-third off. ♦ M afternoon, Tu-Sa. Galleria Borella (near Piazza Sant'Ambrogio). 875332. Subway stop: San Ambrogio (M2)

39 Pilgio Here you'll find modern-design jewelry in precious and semiprecious metals and stones, some with ethnic twists such as feathers and elephant skin. ♦ M afternoon, Tu-Sa. Via Lanzone 23 (near Piazza Sant'Ambrogio). 86450773. Subway stop: San Ambrogio (M2)

Milan has more than 400 banks and bank branches, and *La Borsa* (the Italian Stock Exchange) is located here and not in the country's capital.

Sant'Ambrogio

40 Pierre $$$ One of the newer small hotels in town (with just 45 rooms), this one prides itself on its combination of high-tech facilities and down-to-earth personal service. Its **Petit Pierre** restaurant is open Monday through Friday. ◆ Via Edmondo De Amicis 32 (near Piazza Resistenza Partigiana). 72000581; fax 8052157. Subway stop: San Ambrogio (M2)

41 Marri A combination of functionalism and sleek design mark the architectural and art supplies that are sold in this shop. ◆ M-F, Sa morning. Via Edmondo de Amicis 47 (near Via Ausonio). 89400800. Subway stop: San Ambrogio (M2)

42 R&G Falzone The piles of women's designer clothing in large sizes here are sold at a 20-percent discount. ◆ Tu-Sa 3-7:30PM. No credit cards accepted. Via Edmondo De Amicis 51 (near Via Ausonio). 89403714. Subway stop: San Ambrogio (M2)

43 Piazza Sant'Ambrogio The square and streets surrounding the church of **Sant'Ambrogio** are most animated on St. Ambrose Day (7 December), when they are transformed into a sprawling outdoor market called *O Bei O Bei*. Of medieval origin, the event takes its name from the cry the vendors use ("Oh beautiful!") to draw attention to their merchandise: everything from cheap snacks and trinkets to antique furniture. The sculpture in the piazza, a monument to the Milanese soldiers of World War I, is by Adolfo Wildt. The column in the piazza is of Roman origin and was probably put in place in medieval times, when Saint Ambrose restored many of the city's monuments. ◆ At Via Lanzone, Via Terraggio, Via Sant'Agnese, and Via Necchi. Subway stop: San Ambrogio (M2)

43 Sant'Ambrogio The brick basilica of **Sant'Ambrogio** was founded on a cemetery in 386 AD by Ambrose, the Bishop of Milan, who later became the city's patron saint. Enlarged in the ninth and 11th centuries, its plan (see top right) became the basis of all Romanesque church architecture in Lombardy. Heavily restored in the 19th century, the church was again restored following bombing during World War II.

The exterior atrium of the church dates from the 12th century. The campanile on the right, called the **Campanile dei Monaci** (Monks' Bell Tower), dates from the ninth century and is the oldest in Milan. The one on the left, called the **Campanile dei Canonici** (Canons' Bell Tower), is from the 12th century. Inside,

religious and other materials, including recordings of chants made in the church, are for sale. Among the most noteworthy works of art are a magnificent pulpit reassembled from 11th- and 12th-century fragments; fifth-century mosaics of Ambrose and other saints in the dome; a richly detailed ninth-century gold-and-silver high altar with a 12th-century ciborium in the sanctuary; more ancient mosaics, reset in the 10th century and restored over the years, in the apse; and a crypt containing a shrine housing the remains of Saints Ambrose, Gervase, and Protasius. A door in the crypt leads to **Bramante**'s unfinished *Portico della Canonica* (dating from 1499), which in turn leads to the **Museo della Basilica di Sant'Ambrogio.** The church museum houses a collection of art and artifacts associated with the long history of **Sant'Ambrogio,** including mosaic and wood fragments, tapestries, frescoes, and a missal that belonged to Gian Galeazzo Visconti. ◆ Admission to museum. M-Sa; Su afternoons only. Piazza Sant'Ambrogio (near Via Lanzone). 86450895. Subway stop: San Ambrogio (M2)

43 Università Cattolica del Sacro Cuore Milan's prestigious private university was founded in 1921, incorporating two cloisters built by **Bramante** in 1498, his last work in Milan. ◆ Largo Gemelli 1 (at Piazza Sant'Ambrogio). 88561. Subway stop: San Ambrogio (M2)

44 Bar Magenta This Art Nouveau bar attracts an artsy New Wave crowd of young people, especially on weekends. ◆ Tu-Su 8AM-2AM. No credit cards accepted. Via Giosue Carducci 13 (at Corso Magenta). 8053808. Subway stop: San Ambrogio (M2)

44 Boccondivino ★★$$ Succulent prosciutto and a mouthwatering selection of regional cheeses from throughout Italy are some of the finer ingredients that make up the menu at

Luigi Concordati's restaurant, which offers a wine-tasting menu as well. ♦ M-Sa lunch and dinner. Via Giosue Carducci 17 (at Corso Magenta). 866040. Subway stop: San Ambrogio (M2)

45 Palazzo Viviani Cova This 1915 palazzo is a unique Milanese example of the fanciful residential architecture of **Adolfo Coppedè**, better known for his work in Rome. This building is an eclectic blend of fortresslike elements with some almost Moorish Romanesque touches. ♦ Via Giosue Carducci 36 (near Via San Vittore). Subway stop: San Ambrogio (M2)

46 Antica Trattoria ★★$$ This small, rustic trattoria is a good place to sample the cuisine of Trieste, exemplified by the fruity wines and rich, strudel-like desserts made under the watchful eye of Grazia Loy. ♦ M-F lunch and dinner, Su dinner only. Via San Vittore 13 (near Via Giosue Carducci). 468355. Subway stop: San Ambrogio (M2)

47 Museo Nazionale della Scienza e della Tecnica Leonardo da Vinci (National Science and Technology Museum) Housed somewhat incongruously in the former Benedictine monastery of San Vittore (which dates from the 11th century, Italy's national science museum was refurbished a few years ago and sings more than ever with the industrial spirit of the city in place of monastic chant. The museum takes its name from a core collection of models of machines and instruments based on drawings by Leonardo da Vinci, each one accompanied by a reproduction of the original drawing and a modern technical drawing of the model. Land, air, and sea machinery for war and peace, as well as a wealth of specialized instruments give insight into the scientific side of Leonardo's genius. After that, you can see what Leonardo and others wrought as you watch the seeds of the Industrial Revolution sprout, grow, and burst forth before your very eyes. Room after room of didactical displays include everything from a medieval jeweler's workshop to printing presses, astronomical instruments, musical instruments, photographic and cinematic equipment, radios, computers, cars, trains, boats, and planes, with a few saints and Madonnas thrown in for good measure (this is the Italian science museum, after all). ♦ Admission. Tu-Su. Via San Vittore 21 (in Piazza San Vittore). 48010040. Subway stop: San Ambrogio (M2)

Within the Museo Nazionale della Scienza e della Tecnica Leonardo da Vinci:

Museo Navale Didattico Comunale (Naval Museum) Some 4,000 pieces are on display in this naval museum, which includes models of Italian ships, as well as exotic and historical vessels from around the world. ♦ Tu-Su. 4817270

48 Carcere di San Vittore Milan's prison (built 1864-79 to a design by **Francesco Lucca**) is laid out in a six-spoked floor plan with an unintentionally whimsical fortresslike entrance. It is one of two Milanese prisons that have been operating at maximum capacity since February 1992, when an unprecedented crackdown on corruption affected thousands of politicians and businessmen. ♦ Piazza Gaetano Filangieri 2 (on Via degli Olivetani). Subway stop: San Ambrogio (M2)

49 La Vetraia di Maria Virginia Bonanni Postwar and contemporary glass objects from vases and ashtrays to dishes and the like are offered in this shop. ♦ M afternoon, Tu-Sa. Corso Magenta 52 (near Via de Togni). 48011512. Subway stops: San Ambrogio or Cadorna (M2)

50 Attilio Nosari Grace This boutique sells well-designed menswear, including off-the-rack suits at competitive prices, and made-to-measure at prices a little less than elsewhere. ♦ M afternoon, Tu-Sa. Via Caradosso 2 (at Piazza Santa Maria delle Grazie). 4818545. Subway stops: San Ambrogio or Cadorna (M2)

51 Casa Donzelli This imaginative Art Nouveau residence (1903-04, **Enrico Donzelli**) is one in a series built in this middle-class residential area. ♦ Via Gioberti 1 (at Via Boccaccio). Subway stops: Conciliazione (M1); Cadorna (M2)

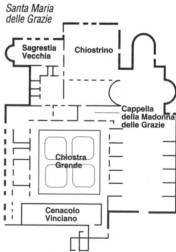

Santa Maria delle Grazie

52 Santa Maria delle Grazie Bramante added the tribune and dome to this Dominican church, the original design for which was by **Guiniforte Solari** (1466-90). In its left nave (see plan above) is the **Cappella della Madonna delle Grazie,** a chapel containing a venerated *Our Lady of Grace* by a 15th-century Lombard painter. The chapel next to it has Paris Bordone's 16th-century painting *Holy Family with St. Catherine of Alexandria.* The

Chiostrino (Cloister) and **Sagrestia Vecchia** (Old Sacristy), are attributed to **Bramante**.
♦ Piazza Santa Maria delle Grazie (at Corso Magenta). Subway stops: Conciliazione (M1); Cadorna (M2)

In the Santa Maria delle Grazie:

Cenacolo Vinciano Even though it is the most famous painting in the world and has been reproduced on everything from calendars to dish towels, it is still possible to look at Leonardo da Vinci's *Last Supper* with a fresh and marveling eye. This is partially because the delicate painting, done at a famously slow pace (between 1495 and 1498), was completely cleaned at an even slower pace and reopened to the public in early 1995. Also, its unexpected movie-screen size is impressive enough to silence the most chattering spectators—well, most of them anyway. We are in Italy, after all. (It has the opposite effect of Leonardo's *Mona Lisa* in the Louvre, which inevitably elicits a chorus of "It's so small!" in various languages.) The first work of the High Renaissance, *The Last Supper* depicts the moment Christ drops the dinner-conversation bomb, "Verily I say unto you, one of you which eateth with me shall betray me" (Mark 14:18). The Savior sits serenely as the apostles, grouped in threes, take it from there, exploding in a flurry of the sort of physical and psychological reaction that fascinated Leonardo. He was also concerned with technique, here experimenting unsuccessfully with tempera on plaster, which started deteriorating in Leonardo's own time and suffered from bad restorations over the centuries. Compare it to the traditional, or *buon fresco,* technique (water-based paint applied to wet plaster) of the *Crucifixion* by Donato da Montorfano on the opposite wall, which was painted in 1495 (Leonardo did the kneeling figures of Ludovico il Moro and family in 1497) and remarkably well preserved. As expansive as it is, *The Last Supper* is also inch-for-inch the most expensive display of art you can see in Italy, the ticket price being as high as admission fees for the entire **Galleria degli Uffizi** in Florence or Musei Vaticani at the Vatican. ♦ Admission. Tu-Su 8AM-2PM. 4987588

53 San Carlo This favorite neighborhood *pasticceria* (pastry shop) is a pleasant place to stop for a cappuccino and croissant. ♦ Tu-Su 7AM-9PM. No credit cards accepted. Via Matteo Bandello 1 (at Corso Magenta). 4812227. Subway stop: Conciliazione (M1)

54 Casa Candiani This is a wonderfully fanciful and eclectic Neo-Renaissance residence by **Luigi Broggi,** one of Milan's leading 19th-century architects. ♦ Via Matteo Bandello 20 (near Corso Magenta). Subway stop: Conciliazione (M1)

55 Biffi ★★$$ This posh patisserie is one of Milan's most traditional tearooms. Its matronly afternoon clientele favors *panettone,* the Milanese citrus-studded cake that dates from medieval days. A variety of tea is offered as well. ♦ Tu-Su 8AM-8PM. No credit cards accepted. Corso Magenta 87 (at Piazzale Baracca). 48006702. Subway stop: Conciliazione (M1)

56 Piazzale Baracca This monument to aviation hero Francesco Baracca is by Silvio Monfrini.♦ At Corso Magenta and Viale Porta Vercellina. Subway stop: Conciliazione (M1)

57 Casa Laugier Antonio Tagliferri (1904-06) used a panoply of stone, brick, cement, and ceramic to build this traditional residence with Viennese Secessionist details. ♦ Corso Magenta 96 (at Pizzale Baracca). Subway stop: Conciliazione (M1)

58 Piazza della Conciliazione The abstract sculpture in this piazza is the 1972 *Gesto per la Libertà* (Gesture for Liberty) by Carlo Ramous. ♦ At Via Ariosto and Via Rasori. Subway stop: Conciliazione (M1)

59 Pupi Solari The owner of this well-trod boutique picks out the best of Milan's top designers in clothing for women, children, and infants. ♦ M afternoon, Tu-Sa; no midday closing. Piazza Tommaseo (off Via Mascheroni). 463325. Subway stop: Conciliazione (M1)

60 Eve Eve sells contemporary-looking fashion handbags as well as shoes, belts, and luggage. ♦ M afternoon, Tu-Sa. Via Mascheroni 12 (at Via Ariosto). 468732. Subway stop: Conciliazione (M1). Also at: Via Solferino 11 (off Via Moscova). 8052931. Subway stop: Moscova (M2)

61 Ariosto $$ This Art Nouveau mansion-turned-hotel offers 54 modernized accommodations in a homey setting. The best rooms overlook the tree-studded courtyard. There's no restaurant. ♦ Via Ariosto 22 (off Via Mario Pagano). 4817844; fax 4980516. Subway stop: Conciliazione (M1)

62 The English Bookshop An excellent destination for nostalgic (or visiting) English speakers or Italians who wish they were, this English-language bookstore stocks everything from fiction and biographies to travel guides and poetry. There's a children's section, too, and a video club with more than 2,000 titles. ♦ M-Sa (no midday closing); Su afternoon. Via Mascheroni 12 (at Via Ariosto). 4964468. Subway stop: Conciliazione (M1)

Restaurants/Clubs: Red   Hotels: Blue
Shops/♥ Outdoors: Green   **Sights/Culture: Black**

63 Gusella This retailer sells tasteful and well-tailored clothes for spoiling your favorite child. ♦ M afternoon, Tu-Sa. Corso Vercelli 14 (near Largo San Severo). 4814144. Subway stop: Conciliazione (M1). Also at: Corso Vittorio Emanuele II, 37B (near Piazza San Babila). 76000118. Subway stop: San Babila (M1)

64 Gemelli Sergio Gemelli selects upscale fashions for the whole family from top-line designers at his eponymous shop. ♦ M afternoon, Tu-Sa. Corso Vercelli 16 (near Largo San Severo). 435595. Subway stop: Conciliazione (M1)

65 Bassetti This local Lombard firm is well-known for its quality bed and bath linens in classic and fashion colors. ♦ M afternoon, Tu-Sa. Largo San Severo 4 (at Corso Vercelli). 435595

66 Coin Well-wrought woolens and men's shirts are among the most eye-catching items in this department store chain, one of Italy's nicest. ♦ M afternoon, Tu-Sa. Corso Vercelli 30 (near Largo San Severo). 48005160. Subway stop: Conciliazione (M1). Also at: Piazza 5 Giornate 1A (at Corso XXII Marzo). 55192083. Subway stop: San Babila (M1); Piazzale Loreto 15 (at Corso Buenos Aires). 2826179. Subway stop: Loretto (M1, M2); Piazzale Cantore 12 (at Viale Papiniano). 58104385. Subway stop: San Agostino (M2)

67 Torrefazione Vercelli The enticing aroma of freshly roasted coffee beans permeates the air in this neighborhood coffee bar. Coffee can be sipped and your choice of beans can be packed to take home as an aromatic gift or souvenir. ♦ M-Sa 6:30AM-8PM. No credit cards accepted. Via Cherubini 2 (at Corso Vercelli). 48005210. Subway stop: Conciliazione (M1)

Bests

Simonetta Brandolini d'Adda
President, The Best in Italy

Milan:

Walking on the **Via della Spiga** as the shops open.

Listening to all the latest news while dining at **Paper Moon.**

Watching the waiters add truffles to the *risotto alla milanese* at **Bice's** and knowing that someone else is paying the bill.

Browsing through the streets around the **Palazzo Brera.**

Florence:

Finding the same good food, menus, waiters, and atmosphere year after year at **Sostanza.**

Driving along the **Viale dei Colli,** watching Florence weave between the hills.

Looking at Florence from the gardens of the **Torre di Bellosguardo.**

Crossing **Ponte Santa Trinita** at sunset when the church bells are ringing.

Browsing through the **Mercato Centrale** (central food market) in **San Lorenzo.**

Watching my children try to choose which ice cream to order at **Vivoli.**

Stopping for a truffle sandwich at **Procacci** on **Via dei Tornabuoni.**

Walking through the **Oltrarno** district, discovering artisans at work on every street.

Having a cool lunch at **Harry's Bar** on a hot summer day.

Watching the colors change on the facade of **San Miniato** from my bedroom window.

Stopping at the church of **Santa Felicità** to see the **Pontormo** again.

Walking through the **Museo de San Marco** and **Museo dell'Opera del Duomo** on an August morning.

Listening to a heavy Florentine accent at work telling jokes.

Venice:

Having lunch outside at **Harry's Dolci** on the **Giudecca** and watching the seagulls dive for pieces of bread.

Walking through the **Pescheria** (Fish Market) at 6AM.

Discovering an empty *campo.*

Enjoying a quiet coffee at **Caffè Florian** in the middle of winter.

Visiting the island of **Torcello** and stepping back into medieval times.

Walking through Venice in January, when the fog has settled in.

Trying to choose which fish to order at **Trattoria Alla Madonna.**

Standing outside on a water taxi while approaching Venice from the airport.

Parco Sempione

At the beginning of the last century, a grandiose project for theaters, meeting halls, government and financial buildings, thermal baths, a customs house, and a Pantheon was conceived for Milan in the area around **Castello Sforzesco**, which Napoleon had occupied with troops and military accoutrements. Called the Foro Bonaparte (Bonaparte Forum) in honor of the French emperor, the project died along with Napoleonic rule in Milan. It remains in name only in the form of the broadly curving avenue called **Foro Bonaparte**, but something of its civic spirit has been revived in the **Parco Sempione**, a public park behind **Castello Sforzesco**. On its grounds are an exhibition pavilion, a public library, a sports arena, an aquarium, a Neo-Classical arch, and an equestrian monument to Napoleon. Of most interest to the visitor is **Castello Sforzesco** itself, which thankfully today is not filled with soldiers but with art—including some of Milan's most important museums, among them the **Civiche Raccolte d'Arte Antica** (Civic Collection of Ancient Art), where Michelangelo's *Rondanini Pietà* is displayed. More than any other park in Milan, **Parco Sempione** provides a pleasant respite from the hustle and bustle of the city, its broad vistas and rambling terrain as relaxing as the occasional surprise of contemporary sculpture is stimulating.

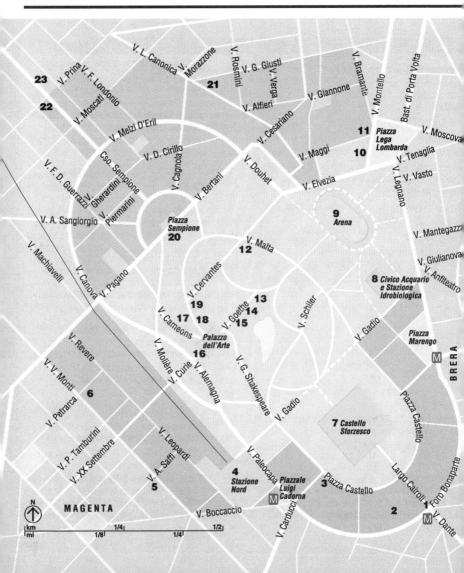

1 Largo Cairoli The confluence of streets in front of **Castello Sforzesco** is dominated by the *Hero of Two Worlds,* Sicilian sculptor Ettore Ximenes' 1895 equestrian monument to Giuseppe Garibaldi. The title refers to Garibaldi's participation in the Uruguayan civil war and his key role in the 19th-century Italian unification movement known as the risorgimento. ◆ At Foro Bonaparte. Subway stop: Cairoli (M1)

2 Teatro Dal Verme This 19th-century opera house designed by **Giuseppe Pestagalli** was the scene of the premiere of Arturo Toscanini's production of Leoncavallo's *Pagliacci,* among other events. It is now used for concerts sponsored by the city. ◆ Largo Cairoli (in Piazza Castello). Subway stop: Cairoli (M1)

3 Castelli Castelli is the showroom of the renowned Bologna-based office furniture design firm whose *Plia* chair is in the collection of New York's Museum of Modern Art. ◆ M-F. No credit cards accepted. Piazza Castello 19 (at Via Carducci). 874789. Subway stop: Cadorna (M1, M2)

4 Stazione Nord This train station, the inside of which was reconstructed in 1956, serves the communities lying to the north of the city. ◆ Piazzale Luigi Cadorna (at Via Paleocapa and Via Boccaccio). 8511608. Subway stop: Cadorna (M1, M2)

5 Seteria del Lago This factory outlet for the nearby silk mills of Como, such as Mantero and Ratti, makes scarves and ties in tasteful Italian and classic English patterns. The store also carries women's blouses, dresses, and shawls and, for men, ascots and shirts in silk and cotton. ◆ M afternoon, Tu-Sa. Via Vincenzo Monti 27 (at Via A. Saffi). 460019. Subway stop: Cadorna (M1, M2). Also at: Corso Buenos Aires 43 (near Piazzale Loreto). 29531531. Subway stop: Loreto (M1, M2)

6 Stivaleria Savoia di Ballini Originally bootmakers to the Italian royal family, the leather workers at this shop now fashion boots and other exquisite equestrian accessories for anyone who can afford them. ◆ M afternoon, Tu-Sa. Via Petrarca 7 (at Via Vincenzo Monti). 463424. Subway stop: Cadorna (M1, M2)

6 Nicol Carmel Maternity clothes à la Milanese, meaning well designed and functional. ◆ M afternoon, Tu-Sa; no midday closing. Via Petrarca 7 (at Via Vincenzo Monti). 4812303. Subway stop: Cadorna (M1, M2)

7 Castello Sforzesco Milan's brick fortress is a 20th-century reconstruction of a 19th-century reconstruction of a 15th-century reconstruction of a 14th-century construction. Originally built by the Visconti family, it takes its name from Francesco Sforza, who in the 15th century commissioned **Giovanni da Milano** to rebuild the castle after it had been sacked by rioting Milanese subjects.

Francesco's son, Galeazzo Maria Sforza, moved the court here and hired Vincenzo Foppa, Cristoforo Moretto, and Benedetto Ferrini to decorate the interior. **Bramante** may have worked on the castle under Ludovico il Moro, who also commissioned Leonardo da Vinci to add some decorative touches. Da Vinci, in fact, became something of a resident court genius.

When the Sforza were replaced by Spanish rulers in the 16th and 17th centuries, the castle was surrounded by heavy bastions in the form of a 12-pointed star to make it an impregnable fortress. With the arrival of Napoleon, the star fell and the castle became a military barracks for years. Its association with despots made the castle a symbol of repression, and proposals called for its destruction following the unification of Italy. Instead it was restored to its approximate appearance under Francesco Sforza and filled with cultural institutions—the civic equivalent of putting a carnation in the gun barrel. The castle was hit heavily during the World War II bombing of Milan, which gave the prestigious architectural firm **Studio BBPR** an opportunity to redesign the museum spaces inside.

Within the Castello Sforzesco:

Civici Musei del Castello Sforzesco (Civic Museums of Castello Sforzesco)
The entrance to the museums is beneath the central tower, the **Torre Filarete**, originally built by **Filarete** in 1452. The expansive main courtyard (concerts are held here in the warmer months) contains remains of various buildings gathered from throughout the city. At its far end is the **Corte Ducale** and the entrance to the **Civiche Raccolte d'Arte Antica (Civic Collection of Ancient Art)**. The first section of this collection is the *Raccolta di Scultura (Sculpture Collection),* which is displayed on the ground floor. In **Room I** is a sixth-century Byzantine marble bust said to be a portrait of the Empress Theodora; **Room II** has the 14th-century *Tomb of Bernabo Visconti* by the sculptor Bonino Campione; **Room VII** is decorated with 17th-century frescoes and tapestries; **Room VIII** has some heavily restored decorations by Leonardo da Vinci; **Room XV** contains the 16th-century *Tomb of Gaston de Foix* by Agostino Busti (called Bambaia) and the highlight of the entire museum, the 16th-century marble sculpture, *Rondanini Pietà,* Michelangelo's last work. (The piece, once part of the collection of the nobel Roman Rondanini family, was bought by the city as a sort of civic status symbol in 1952.) Michelangelo's sculpture is an almost Gothic-looking meditation on death, deeply moving in its abstract, unfinished state.

Upstairs, beyond a huge collection of mostly northern Italian furniture from the 15th to the 18th centuries, is the **Pinacoteca** (Painting Gallery). Highlights here include 15th-century Madonnas by Filippo Lippi, Giovanni Bellini, and Andrea Mantegna (all in **Room XX**). The best of the many 16th-century Lombard paintings here are in **Room XXI**: *The Martyrdom of St. Sebastian* by Vincenzo Foppa, *Madonna* by Foppa, *Pietà* and *The Alms of St. Benedict* by Ambrogio Bergognone, *Noli Mi Tangere* by Bramantino, and *Polyptich* by Cesare de Sesto; also be sure to see *Spring* in the style of Archimboldo **(Room XXIV).** Among the other favorites are the 15th-century *Poet Laureate* by Giovanni Bellini and *Portrait of a Youth* by Lorenzo Lotto **(Room XXV).** From here a loggia leads to the upper floor of the section of the fortress complex called the **Rocchetta.** In it is the **Civiche Raccolte d'Arta Applicata** (Civic Collection of Decorative Art), which includes Chinese porcelain from the seventh to the 18th centuries and Italian majolica from the 15th to the 18th centuries **(Room XXX);** 18th- and 19th-century French and Austrian porcelain **(Room XXXI);** and ivories and precious metal objects **(Room XXXII).**

Downstairs is the **Museo degli Strumenti Musicali** (Musical Instruments Museum), which includes violins by Antonio Stradivarius and Giuseppe Guarnieri **(Room XXXVI).** In the basement of the **Rocchetta** are the prehistoric Lombard and ancient Egyptian holdings of the **Civiche Raccolte Archeologiche** (Civic Archaeological Collections). ♦ Admission. Tu-Su. Piazza Castello (entrance at Largo Cairoli). 72002128/620839400. Subway stops: Cadorna (M1, M2); Cairoli (M1); Lanza (M2)

8 Civico Acquario e Stazione Idrobiologica (Civic Aquarium) Milan's Art Nouveau aquarium (note the statue of *Neptune* by Oreste Labo on the facade), rebuilt after it was destroyed during World War II, contains 38 tanks filled with creatures of the deep. ♦ Free. Tu-Su. Via Gadio 2 (at Via Legnano). 86462051. Subway stop: Lanza (M2)

9 Arena Milan's Neo-Classical sports arena designed by **Luigi Canonica** (1806) in the shape of a Roman amphitheater, has a capacity of 30,000—large enough for small-scale soccer and other sporting events. Contact the Italian State Tourist Office for information about scheduled events. ♦ Entrance on Viale Elvezia (between V. Legnano and V. Dounet). Subway stops: Moscova (M2); Lanza (M2)

10 Vecchia Arena ★★$$ Lino and Mariapia's cozy little restaurant prides itself on its *risotto giallo* (made with saffron) and *risotto al salto* (fried crisp), among other classic Milanese specialties. ♦ Tu-Sa lunch and dinner; M dinner only. Piazza Lega Lombarda 1 (west on piazza). 3315538. Subway stop: Moscova (M2)

Castello Sforza

11 Nuova Arena ★★$$ The heritage of the Egyptian owners of this otherwise nondescript eatery can be sampled in dishes such as *bocconcini al curry con riso pilaf* (curried beef with rice pilaf), adding an unusual (for Milan) twist to an inventive Italian menu. ♦ Tu-Sa lunch and dinner; M dinner only. Piazza Lega Lombarda 5 (west side of piazza). 341437. Subway stop: Moscova (M2)

12 Biblioteca Parco Sempione (Parco Sempione Library) This small branch library has a 1954 abstract cement sculpture called *Grande Motivo,* by Francesco Somaini. ♦ Monte Tordo (at Viale Malta). Subway stops: Cadorna (M1, M2); Cairoli (M1); Lanza (M2)

13 Accumulazione Musicale e Seduta Witty French artist Arman made this 1973 cement-and-metal sculpture. ♦ Viale Goethe (near the Palazzo dell'Arte). Subway stops: Cadorna (M1, M2); Cairoli (M1); Lanza (M2)

14 Teatro Continuo Alberto Burri made this cement and painted-steel sculpture. ♦ Viale Goethe (near the Palazzo dell'Arte). Subway stops: Cadorna (M1, M2); Cairoli (M1); Lanza (M2)

15 Bagni Misteriosi This 1973 sculpture is by the metaphysical artist Giorgio De Chirico. ♦ Viale Goethe (near the Palazzo dell'Arte). Subway stops: Cadorna (M1, M2); Cairoli (M1); Lanza (M2)

16 Palazzo dell'Arte This Modernist building (built in 1932-33 to a design by **Giovanni Murzio**) is also known as the **Triennale,** because it hosts Milan's renowned design exhibition of the same name every three years. At other times it is used to display temporary exhibitions. ♦ Viale Alemagna 6 (at Via Curie). 8900728. Subway stops: Cadorna (M1, M2); Cairoli (M1); Lanza (M2)

17 Torre del Parco This steel-tube tower structure was erected at the same time as the **Palazzo dell'Arte.** It was designed by **Cesare Chiodi, Gio Ponti,** and **Ettore Ferrari.** ♦ Viale Alemagna (northwest of Palazzo dell'Arte). Subway stops: Cadorna (M1, M2); Cairoli (M1); Lanza (M2)

18 Storia della Terra This 1973 abstract sculpture is by Antonio Paradiso. ♦ Viale Guiglielmo Shakespeare (northwest of Palazzo dell'Arte). Subway stops: Cadorna (M1, M2); Cairoli (M1); Lanza (M2)

19 Chiosco Scultura Amelio Roccamonte designed this 1973 abstract sculpture. ♦ Viale Guiglielmo Shakespeare (northwest of Palazzo dell'Arte). Subway stops: Cadorna (M1, M2); Cairoli (M1); Lanza (M2)

20 Arco della Pace (Arch of Peace) This Neo-Classical triumphal arch (1838, **Luigi Cagnola**) is decorated with the sculptures *Chariot of Peace* by Abbondio Sangiorgio and *Four Victories* by Giovanni Putti, personifications of the Po and Ticino rivers by Benedetto Cacciatori and of the Adige and Taglimento rivers by Pompeo Marchesi, and other 19th-century sculptures and bas-reliefs. ♦ Piazza Sempione (between Via Pagano and Via Bertani). Subway stops: Cadorna (M1, M2); Cairoli (M1); Lanza (M2)

21 Europeo $$$ This small (45 rooms), modern hotel is near the park in the heart of Milan's very un-Chinatownlike Chinese district, where only the names on the doorbells indicate the residents' nationalities. There is no restaurant. ♦ Via Luigi Canonica 38 (near Via G. Giusti). 3314751; fax 33105410. Subway stop: Moscova (M2)

22 Former Fascist Headquarters This onetime local headquarters for the Fascist party, designed in 1938-39 by **Gianni Angelini, Giuseppe Calderara,** and **Tito Varisco,** is one of the purest examples of Fascist-era Modernist architecture in the city. ♦ Corso Sempione 25 (near Via Prina). Subway stops: Cadorna (M1, M2); Cairoli (M1); Lanza (M2)

23 Casa Rustici The best example of International Modernist architecture in the city, this apartment building was designed by **Giuseppe Terragni** (1933-35). ♦ Corso Sempione 36 (near Via Prina). Subway stops: Cadorna (M1, M2); Cairoli (M1); Lanza (M2)

After being invited to a 50-course dinner given for the marriage of Violante Visconti to the Duchess of Chirenza in 1368, Friar Galvano Fiamma accused the Milanese of being *magni commestores* (big eaters).

The 19th-century French writer Stendhal lived in Milan for four decades. Before he died in 1842, he requested that his tombstone read "*Arrigo Beyle, Milanese*—lived, wrote, loved."

"Beastly Milano, with its imitation hedgehog of a Cathedral, and its hateful town Italians, all socks and purple cravats and hats over the ear . . . "

D.H. Lawrence

Brera

Named after **Palazzo Brera**—a convent now housing a number of institutions, including the **Pinacoteca di Brera**, one of Italy's finest museums—Brera was until relatively recently one of the most proudly low-rent districts in Milan. Back in the 19th century, **Via San Fermo** was the first neighborhood in Milan expressly developed for public housing, and at the turn of the century it was the center of Milan's bohemian life. Even today the art school within **Palazzo Brera** helps maintain a cafe-society air in the area, though you can be sure its students can't afford to do their shopping in the boutiques that have sprung up on its streets or even at the flea market held on the third Saturday of the month on **Via Fiori Chiari**. There are some elegant sights in this area—a few palazzi on **Via Manzoni**

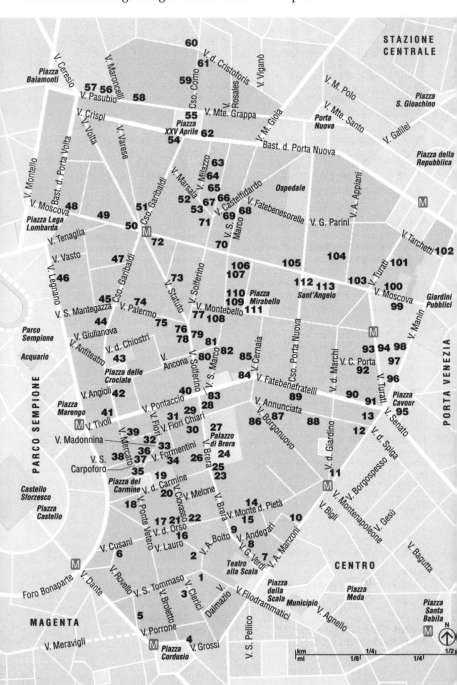

northeast of the world-famous **La Scala** opera house (see Centro chapter)—but the stroller here will find gentrified Brera just as upscale. Whether you are tooling down its cobblestoned streets for shopping and sightseeing by day or stepping out to its bars and clubs by night, Brera is perhaps the single most pleasant neighborhood in Milan.

---

1 Palazzo Visconti Aimi Don't overlook one of the few relatively unchanged 17th-century patrician palazzi in the area. ♦ Via Filodrammatici 10 (near Piazzetta Bossi). Subway stop: Cordusio (M1)

2 Finarte Milan's leading auction house usually has one or two presale showings going on at this space. Call for a schedule of upcoming events. ♦ M afternoon, Tu-Sa. Piazzetta Bossi 4 (at Via Filodrammatici). 877041. Subway stop: Cordusio (M1). Also at: Via Manzoni 38 (near Via della Spiga). 76020436. Subway stop: Montenapoleone (M3)

3 Palazzo Clerici The former residence of Milanese nobleman and statesman Antonio Giorgio Clerici is one of the finest examples of an 18th-century patrician villa in Milan. Though its exterior is typically unostentatious, its granite doorway leads to two courtyards, the second of which features a monumental staircase. The vault above it has a fresco formerly attributed to Giovanni Battista Piazzetta, now to Mattia Bortoloni. Upstairs, in the **Galleria degli Arazzi** (which has lovely 17th-century Flemish tapestries portraying scenes from the life of Moses), is the showpiece of the palazzo, a magnificent frescoed ceiling by Giambattista Tiepolo, his last work in Milan. It depicts the chariot of the sun, driven by Mercury, illuminating the world. Deities of land, sea, and sky are bathed in a beautiful pastel light in this masterpiece of Rococo ceiling decoration. Two other noteworthy rooms in the palazzo are the **Salone degli Specchi** (a mirrored hall) and the **Salottino Dorato** (a small room covered with gold decorations). The palazzo now houses the **Istituto per gli Studi di Politica Internazionale** (Institute for the Study of International Politics), and permission is necessary for a visit. ♦ By appointment only. Via Clerici 5 (near Piazzetta Bossi). 878266; fax 8692055. Subway stop: Cordusio (M1)

4 Mac Borse No, this is not a hamburger chain, but rather a shop that makes stylish bags from the cow's outside. ♦ M afternoon, Tu-Sa. Via Grossi 10 (northeast corner of Piazza Cordusio). 861119. Subway stop: Cordusio (M1)

5 Piccolo Teatro One of Milan's leading cultural institutions since 1947 (the interior was designed by **Marco Zanuso**) presents Italian-language plays, but the strong direction of Giorgio Strehler results in productions that transcend the language

barrier. The **Piccolo Teatro Studio,** a laboratory theater and training center for actors, also presents important productions. ♦ Via Rovello 2 (between Via Dante and Via San Tommaso). 72333222. Subway stop: Cordusio (M1)

6 Rovello ★★$$ The setting is intimate and the pastas are expertly prepared and paired with such inventive ingredients as saffron and salmon. Main courses are equally creative, and desserts—including the house chocolates—are large and sublime. ♦ M-F lunch and dinner; Sa dinner. Via Rovello 18 (at Via Cusani). 864396. Subway stop: Cordusio (M1)

7 Milano Libri In a city where books (like everything else) mean business, it's a treat to walk into Anna Maria and Giovanni Gandini's bookshop. The selection of material on theater, fashion, design, and photography is intelligent, and browsing is actually encouraged. This pleasant shop is the closest thing the city has to a literary scene, and the scene has more style here than anywhere else. ♦ M afternoon, Tu-Sa; no midday closing. Via Giuseppe Verdi 2 (near Piazza della Scala). 875871. Subway stops: Cordusio (M1); Montenapoleone (M3)

8 Suntory ★★$$$ If you have a *lira* (or several) for Japanese food, this is your best bet in town. The menu includes all the standards, sometimes amusingly translated into Italian; an excellent tempura, for example, appears on the menu as *fritto misto*. ♦ M-Sa lunch and dinner. Via Giuseppe Verdi 6 (near Piazza della Scala). 862210. Subway stops: Cordusio (M1); Montenapoleone (M3)

9 San Giuseppe This octagonal church was designed in 1630 by **Francesco Maria Richini.** On the left altar here is a 17th-century canvas depicting the *Marriage of the Virgin* by Melchiorre Gherardini. ♦ Via Giuseppe Verdi (at Via Andegari). Subway stops: Cordusio (M1); Montenapoleone (M3)

10 Sawaya & Moroni Furniture designs by one of the country's hottest up-and-coming design forces are the focus here. Featured in this gallerylike retail showroom, there are designs by the store's owners as well as Luigi Serafini, Don Arad, Jeannot Cerutti, Charles Jencks, Borek Sipek, Michel Graves, Katsuo Shinoara, and others. Look for yearly exhibitions on international design topics. ♦ M afternoon, Tu-Sa. Via A. Manzoni 11 (at Via Andegari). 863951. Subway stop: Montenapoleone (M3)

10 Frette One of Italy's (and the world's) best-known linen shops, **Frette** began just outside of Milan in the town of Monza. Over the past century this shop has graced some of the world's best addresses with its luxurious sheets, towels, bathrobes, and comforters. ♦ M afternoon, Tu-Sa. Via A. Manzoni 11 (at Via Andegari). 864339. Subway stop: Montenapoleone (M3). Also at: Via Montenapoleone 21 (near Via Gesù). 76003791. Subway stop Montenapoleone (M3)

11 Grand Hotel et de Milan $$$$ With enough drama and attention to sumptuous detail to overwhelm the unprepared guest, this hotel attracts an international elite that revels in its 130-year-old history and timeless theatricality. Giuseppe Verdi was its most celebrated guest; also on the roster were Giacomo Puccini, the Duke and Duchess of Windsor, and Gabriele D'Annunzio. Today, high-power, global types and Japanese shoppers fill the 87 painstakingly renovated rooms and the meeting point of the moment, the **Falstaff Bar.** The hotel also has two restaurants: the **Caruso** (named for one of Verdi's most famous interpreters) serves lunch daily and the **Don Carlo** (after the maestro's opera) serves dinner nightly. Precious carpets, inlaid marble pavements, and crystal chandeliers create the ambience of an aristocratic 19th-century palazzo in public rooms and guest rooms alike, masking the amenities of the state-of-the-art technology that makes this the hotel of choice for discerning business travelers. ♦ Via A. Manzoni 29 (at Via Borgonuovo). 723141; fax 86460861. Subway stop: Montenapoleone (M3)

11 Pennisi Not for the penny-pinching, this store offers antique jewelry at all-too-modern prices. Special periods are 18th and 19th centuries, Art Deco, and the 1940s-1950s. ♦ M afternoon, Tu-Sa. Via A. Manzoni 29 (at Via Borgonuovo). 862232. Subway stop: Montenapoleone (M3)

12 Palazzo Borromeo d'Adda The driving force behind this stately 19th-century Neo-Classical residence was architect **Gerolamo Arganini,** who had a hand in shaping the building between 1820 and 1825 before it was again altered. ♦ Via A. Manzoni 39-41 (between Via Montenapoleone and Via della Spiga). Subway stop: Turati (M3)

Within the Palazzo Borromeo d'Adda:

Fiumi At Milan's finest watch and clock shop, timepieces tick and clang in an opulent setting of original turn-of-the-century silks and velvets. ♦ Tu-Sa. 6554370. Subway stop: Turati (M3)

13 Fornasetti An imaginative assortment of objects, from teacups to umbrella stands, designed by one of Milan's foremost such maestri, Piero Fornasetti, are for sale here. Since his death in 1988, his son Barnaba has carried the torch. ♦ M afternoon, Tu-Sa. Via Manzoni 45 (near Piazza Cavour). 6592341. Subway stop: Turati (M3)

14 Banca Regionale Europa Milan's most upscale pawnshop (run by a bank) often holds auction sales of orphaned family furs and jewels. Auctions usually take place between March and May. ♦ Via Monte di Pietà 7 (near Via Brera). 72121337. Subway stop: Montenapoleone (M3)

15 Casa Beccaria Cesare Beccaria, a 17th-century Milanese economist and jurist who is primarily known in Italy as someone streets are named after, was born and died here. ♦ Via Monte di Pietà 6 (near Via Verdi). Subway stop: Montenapoleone (M3)

15 Casa di Risparmio delle Provincie Lombarde The style reference in this 19th-century palazzo designed by **Giuseppe Balzaretto** is that of the imposing palazzi of Renaissance Florence. ♦ Via Monte di Pietà 8 (near Via Verdi). Subway stop: Montenapoleone (M3)

16 Blackout This is the place to find lighting fixtures that reflect the kind of design you've come to expect in Milan. The names in bright lights here include Fontana Arte, Artemide, O Luce, Quattrifolio, Leucos, Lumina, and Traconi. ♦ M afternoon, Tu-Sa. Via dell'Orso 7 (between Via Brera and Via Ponte Vetero). 8056031. Subway stop: Cordusio (M1)

17 Centro Botanico Plants and related products are the root of this shop, where you'll find potpourris, fragrances, and even paper and posters featuring botanical themes. This marketing concept was developed by the enterprising Naj Oleari brothers, whose whimsical fabric designs are featured in another shop in the vicinity. ♦ M afternoon, Tu-Sa. Via dell'Orso 16 (between Via Brera and Via Ponte Vetero). 72001684. Subway stop: Cordusio (M1)

18 Gelateria Toldo This is the cool option for gelato in this neighborhood, with seasonal flavors displayed in two cases—one for fruit, the other for milk-based treats. ♦ M-Sa 7AM-8PM. Via Ponte Vetero 11 (south of Piazza del Carmine). 86460863. Subway stops: Cordusio (M1); Lanza (M2)

Restaurants/Clubs: Red   **Hotels:** Blue
Shops/ ♦ Outdoors: Green   **Sights/Culture:** Black

19 Santa Maria del Carmine This church has been altered several times over the centuries. After a collapse, the original structure, begun in 1400 by **Bernardo da Venezia,** was rebuilt in Gothic style around 1456. Some Baroque additions followed, and it was again remodeled between 1826 and 1839 under the direction of **Giuseppe Pestagalli,** then given a Neo-Gothic facade by **Carlo Maciachini.** The last renovation was done in 1912 by **Ambrogio Annoni.** The art inside, which dates from the 15th to the 19th centuries, is pleasant enough to look at, though historically unimportant. ◆ Piazza del Carmine. Subway stops: Cordusio (M1); Lanza (M2)

la bitta
ristorante

20 La Bitta ★★$$ Dark wood paneling and crisp linen set the scene for Giuseppe Pelliccia's Italian/French restaurant, which features such creations as *gnocchi alle pescatrice* (potato dumplings with seafood). ◆ M-F lunch and dinner; Sa dinner only. Via del Carmine 3 (in Piazza del Carmine). 72003185. Subway stops: Cordusio (M1); Lanza (M2)

21 Galleria Seno A well-designed gallery (lighting by Castiglioni, table by Sottsass) where the works of Albers and Matta, among others, are shown. ◆ Tu-Sa. Via Ciovasso 11 (at Via dell'Orso). 8692868. Subway stops: Cordusio (M1); Lanza (M2)

22 Consolare ★★$$ **La Scala** theatergoers and show folk frequent this recently relocated restaurant, run with great charm by Gianni and Rosanna, whose fresh flowers complement the fresh interpretations of Italian favorites such as *spaghetti al cartoccio con crostacei* (spaghetti with shellfish). ◆ W-Su lunch and dinner; Tu dinner. Via Ciovasso 4 (at Via dell'Orso). 8053581. Subway stops: Cordusio (M1); Lanza (M2)

NAJ-OLEARI

23 Naj Oleari These three Milanese brothers have created an empire based on whimsical fabric designs in patterns ranging from airplanes to eyeglasses for babies, teenagers, and the young at heart, often made into such items as bags and umbrellas. ◆ M afternoon, Tu-Sa. Via Brera 8 (near Piazzetta Brera). 86464988. Subway stops: Cordusio (M1); Lanza (M2); Montenapoleone (M3). Also at: Corso di Porta Ticinese (near Via Vetere). 89409857. Subway stop: San Agostino (M2)

23 Pellegrini This store stocks all sorts of art supplies, as it caters to the students at the nearby **Brera Art Academy.** ◆ M afternoon, Tu-Sa. Via Brera 16 (near Piazzetta Brera). 8057119. Subway stops: Cordusio (M1); Lanza (M2); Montenapoleone (M3)

il diaframma

23 Il Diaframma Lanfranco Colombo runs Milan's first and best photography gallery, showing contemporary and historical work. ◆ Tu-Th 4-7:30PM; Sa 2:30-7:30PM. Via Brera 16 (near Piazzetta Brera). 8056814. Subway stops: Cordusio (M1); Lanza (M2); Montenapoleone (M3)

24 Piazzetta Brera Behind the fence in this little piazza is a monumental sculpture of Francesco Hayez (once president of the **Brera Academy**) by Francesco Barzaghi. ◆ Off Via Brera. Subway stops: Cordusio (M1); Lanza (M2); Montenapoleone (M3)

25 La Forma e Anima della Materia This abstract metal sculpture is by Milanese artist Teodoro Antonio Franz Sartori. ◆ Via Brera (near Via del Carmine). Subway stops: Cordusio (M1); Lanza (M2); Montenapoleone (M3)

26 Palazzo Cusani This opulent palazzo has two rich Rococo facades—one on Via Brera (1715-17, **Giovanni Ruggieri**) and one in the rear (1775-90, **Giuseppe Piermarini**)—making it among the most distinguished residences in the neighborhood. ◆ Via Brera 13-15 (at Via del Carmine). Subway stops: Cordusio (M1); Lanza (M2); Montenapoleone (M3)

27 Palazzo di Brera The present Neo-Classical palazzo is an enlargement of a 14th-century college belonging first to the prosperous Umiliati religious order and later to the Jesuits, who commissioned architect **Martino Bassi** to enlarge it in 1591. It was last expanded in 1651 by **Francesco Maria Richini.** The courtyard, in the tradition of the Jesuit colleges in Rome (Collegio Romano) and Pavia (Collegio Borromeo), has as its centerpiece a monumental bronze statue of Napoleon as the nude god Mars by Antonio Canova. Students at the **Accademia di Belle Arti,** the prestigious fine arts academy within the palazzo, have been known to make use of the statue for less than monumental purposes, draping it with manifestos or spray-painting slogans on it. ◆ Via Brera 28 (between Via Fatebenefratelli and Via Monte di Pietà). Subway stops: Cordusio (M1); Lanza (M2); Montenapoleone (M3)

Behind Napoleon in the Palazzo di Brera complex:

PINACOTECA DI BRERA

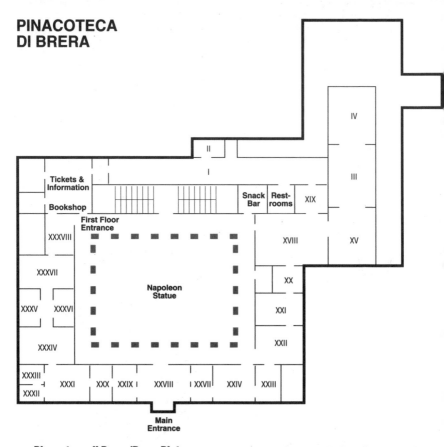

Pinacoteca di Brera (Brera Picture Gallery) As the bronze statue in the courtyard suggests, Napoleon had a monumental role in establishing this gallery's collection. Under his rule, thousands of works of art were confiscated from all over northern Italy and brought to the **Brera,** which has the best collection of northern Italian painting in the world. It is quite extensive, so be prepared for that feeling of faintness from cultural overload called the "Stendhal syndrome," a term that is particularly appropriate here since Milan was the favorite city of the French traveler and connoisseur. The museum is being restored and rearranged; some rooms may be closed, and others may no longer exhibit the works named below. ♦ Admission. Tu-Sa; Su mornings only. 86463501

Highlights of the Brera:

Sala I This long corridor was formerly called the **Corridoio degli Affreschi** because it contained the museum's fresco collection. Today it displays paintings from the museum's modern art collection. Among the important works here are *Head of a Woman* and *Portrait of Moisè Kistling* by Amedeo Modigliani; the Futurist *Rising City* and *Brawl*

in the Galleria by Umberto Boccioni; and the Cubist-influenced *Rhythms of Objects* by Carlo Carrà and *The North-South* by Gino Severini. The gallery also displays three metaphysical paintings by Carlo Carrà: *The Metaphysical Muse, Mother and Son,* and *The Enchanted Room.* These are followed by several still lifes by Giorgio Morandi.

Sala II The 14th-century frescoes of religious subjects in this small room are attributed to Giovanni da Milano, showing that Tuscan painting had begun to influence northern Italian artists by mid-century.

Sala III The next three rooms, along with **Sala XVII,** display the bulk of Napoleon's booty. Their focus is on Venetian painting, with its dramatic use of shimmering light and a warm palette. The genre is introduced spectacularly in **Sala III** with three paintings by the 16th-century painter Paolo Caliari (known as Veronese): *The Last Supper, Christ in the Garden,* and *The Baptism of Christ.* Other important works from 16th-century Venice are Lorenzo Lotto's *Pietà* and Paris Bordone's *Baptism of Christ.* Compare them to the gentler light of the altarpiece by 16th-century Lombard painter Gerolamo Savoldo.

Sala IV The distinct styles of three Venetian Mannerist painters—who, like their counterparts in Florence and Rome, were concerned with manipulating the human figure to often grotesque proportions—may be compared in this room. Here are Veronese's sumptuous *Saints Anthony, Cornelius, and Cipriano;* Jacopo Bassano's gentle *St. Rocco Visiting the Plague Victims;* and one of the most famous paintings in the museum, Jacopo Tintoretto's dramatic *Finding of the Body of St. Mark.* One of four paintings done on the subject of Venice's patron saint for the **Scuola Grande di San Marco** in Venice (the other three are in the **Accademia** in Venice), it depicts the saint halting grave robbers who have discovered his body.

Sala XV This room contains 15th- and 16th-century paintings from Lombardy and Piedmont, including an altarpiece by Vincenzo Foppa.

Sala XVIII This room contains another of the museum's most famous paintings, Andrea Mantegna's gravely foreshortened *Dead Christ,* who lies with his feet in the viewer's face while women grieve in the background. Also on display are canvases by the 15th-century artist Carlo Crivelli, characteristically Venetian in their decorative detail *(Madonna of the Candle)* and richness *(Coronation of the Virgin).*

Sala XIX Two Madonnas and a Pietà by the Venetian Renaissance painter Giovanni Bellini are the highlights of this room.

Sala XX Look for Mantegna's *Madonna with Angels.*

Sala XXI This room contains a number of 15th-century polyptychs, including a particularly impressive one by Gentile da Fabriano.

Sale XXII-XXIII Paintings of the 15th and 16th centuries by artists from Ferrara and Emilia are exhibited here, among them, Francesco Cossa's *St. Peter and St. John the Baptist.*

Sala XXIV: Sala di Piero della Francesca e di Rafaello This room has the two most famous paintings in the museum: 15th-century Tuscan painter Piero della Francesca's severe *Madonna with Saints and Angels Adored by Federico da Montefeltro,* with its attention to architectural detail, and Raphael's delicate *Betrothal of the Virgin,* an early work (1504) showing the influence of his master, Perugino, in its balanced composition.

Sala XXVII Gerolamo Gegna's 16th-century *Madonna and Child with Saints* is the highlight of this room.

Sala XXVIII Dedicated to the Bolognese Carracci family, who painted in the late 16th and early 17th centuries, this room displays *The Canaanite* by Ludovico Carracci, *The Samaritan at the Well* by his cousin Annibale Carracci, and *The Adultress* by Annibale's brother Agostino.

Sala XXIX Dedicated to Caravaggio and his followers, this room is dominated by his subtly dramatic *Supper at Emmaus,* painted in 1606. Caravaggio's spiritual influence can be seen on Battistello Caracciolo's *The Samaritan at the Well,* which was attributed to the master when it was acquired by the museum in 1820.

Sala XXX Among the 17th-century Lombard artists exhibited here are Procaccini, Cerano, and Morazzone.

Sale XXXI-XXXIII Foreign paintings are displayed in these rooms, including a *Last Supper* by Peter Paul Rubens and *Madonna and Child with Saints* by Anthony van Dyck **(Sala XXXI),** a tryptych by Jan de Beer **(Sala XXXII),** and *Portrait of a Young Woman* by Rembrandt **(Sala XXXIII):** all are 17th-century works.

Sala XXXIV A 17th-century *Madonna* by Pietro da Cortona and an 18th-century *Madonna* by Giambattista Tiepolo are here.

Sale XXXV-XXXVI These rooms display 18th-century Italian painting, including Canaletto's *View of the Grand Canal,* Giovanni Battista Piazzetta's *Rebecca at the Well,* and Giovanni Maria Crespi's *A Fair.*

Sale XXXVII-XXXVIII Nineteenth-century Italian paintings are featured in these rooms.

Within the Palazzo di Brera:

Biblioteca Nazionale di Brera (Brera National Library) Founded by Maria Theresa of Austria in 1770, the **National Library** today has more than one million volumes. Among its most notable works is the 11th-century manuscript of St. Ambrose's *Hexaemeron* and the papers of Alessandro Manzoni. ♦ M 1:30-7PM; Tu-Sa 9AM-2PM. 86463484

28 Jamaica ★★$ The 1960s-style decor in this cafe/restaurant (which was founded in 1921) hasn't changed, though the artists and intellectuals who frequented the place at that time have been replaced by fashionable types who've rediscovered Brera. It's a great spot for a simple plate of delicious pasta or salad. ♦ M-Sa 9AM-2AM. Via Brera 32 (off Via Fatebenefratelli). 876723. Subway stop: Lanza (M2)

29 Robertaebasta This well-known antiques store specializes in Empire and Art Deco treasures from Italy and beyond. ♦ M afternoon, Tu-Sa. Via Fiori Chiari 2 (off Via Brera). 861593. Subway stop: Lanza (M2)

30 Franco Sabatelli A very Florentine-looking artisan-type shop that features picture frames in all shapes and sizes, from the 15th century to more modern times. It represents a rare throwback to the workshops that once populated this neighborhood prior to its gentrification. ♦ M afternoon, Tu-Sa. Via Fiori Chiari 5 (off Via Brera). 8052688. Subway stop: Lanza (M2)

30 Decomania Art Deco objects and furniture are all the rage here, with an emphasis on Italian contributions to the movement by Gio Ponti and the like. ♦ M afternoon, Tu-Sa. Via Fiori Chiari 7 (off Via Brera). 86463413. Subway stop: Lanza (M2)

31 Momus Extreme chic reigns in this piano bar/restaurant, where the quality of the people watching often tops that of the food. ♦ M-Sa 8PM-2AM. Via Fiori Chiari 8 (at Vicolo Fiori). 8056227. Subway stop: Lanza (M2)

31 Baldan Enter here for imaginative custom-made jewelry by Maria Grazia Baldan, who works unique antique pieces such as Chinese coins into unusual settings. A move to Via Tivoli 6 is scheduled for late 1996. ♦ M afternoon, Tu-Sa. Via Fiori Chiari 14 (off Via Brera). 86463559. Subway stop: Lanza (M2)

32 Miró American-style 1960s music is revisited and appreciated (if not quite fully understood) at this piano bar/club. ♦ M-Sa 10PM-3AM. Vicolo Fiori 2 (off Via Pontaccio). 876016. Subway stop: Lanza (M2)

33 Poly's This Parisian-style piano bar offers light snacks and sandwiches until midnight. ♦ Daily 9:30PM-2:30AM. Via Formentini 5 (off Via Madonnina). 8053492. Subway stop: Lanza (M2)

34 Club Due Another longtime Brera hangout, this one features live jazz from 10PM-2:30AM. ♦ Via Formentini 2 (off Via Madonnina). 86464807. Subway stop: Lanza (M2)

35 L'Oro dei Farlocchi Very unusual and bizarre gift items, mostly antique British and French curiosities, are this well-known store's stock and trade. ♦ M afternoon, Tu-Sa. Via Madonnina 5 (near Piazza del Carmine). 860589. Subway stop: Lanza (M2)

35 Angela Caputi This is the Milan home of the well-known Florentine jewelry designer, whose fantasy follows the season's fashion. The small boutique carries a bountiful selection of her imaginative costume jewelry. ♦ M afternoon, Tu-Sa. Via Madonnina 11 (near Piazza del Carmine). 86461080. Subway stop: Lanza (M2)

35 Makeup Studio Diego della Palma is the makeup artist of choice in the fashion world. His line of makeup and beauty items, which is popular with American and international models, is sold here. ♦ M afternoon, Tu-Sa. Via Madonnina 15 (near Piazza del Carmine). 8056426. Subway stop: Lanza (M2)

36 Cashmere, Cotton & Silk You'll need no translation to grasp that this men's shop offers highly designed clothing in all the fabrics its name advertises. ♦ M afternoon, Tu-Sa. Via Madonnina 19 (near Piazza del Carmine). 8056426. Subway stop: Lanza (M2)

37 Luisa Beccaria Romantic and sophisticated womenswear (with a new division for babies) by Milanese designer Luisa Beccaria is this shop's specialty. ♦ M afternoon, Tu-Sa. Via Formentini 1 (at Via Madonnina). 86460018. Subway stop: Lanza (M2)

38 Brera You'll find art books galore here. ♦ M afternoon, Tu-Sa. Via Mercato 3 (near Via Tivoli). 865885. Subway stop: Lanza (M2)

39 Idea Bijoux This is a good source for ethnic and costume jewelry and silver. ♦ M afternoon, Tu-Sa. Via Mercato 20 (near Via Tivoli). 876878. Subway stop: Lanza (M2)

39 La Torre di Pisa ★★$$ A fashionable crowd of models, actors, and journalists tuck into the Tuscan food here, including the famous vegetable soup with white beans called *ribollita*. ♦ M-F lunch and dinner; Sa dinner only. Via Mercato 26 (near Via Tivoli). 874877. Subway stop: Lanza (M2)

40 Spelta Fashionable shoes, of the casual but well-made variety, are the featured items here. ♦ M afternoon, Tu-Sa. Via Pontaccio 2 (at Via Solferino). 8052592. Subway stop: Lanza (M2)

40 Lucia Ladies' handbags and men's and women's accessories—fashionable and moderately priced—are yours for the selecting. ♦ M afternoon, Tu-Sa. Via Pontaccio 2 (at Via Solferino). 867708. Subway stop: Lanza (M2)

40 Drogheria Solferino A contemporary men's and women's clothing shop (international threads) is housed in a turn-of-the-century drug store. ♦ M afternoon, Tu-Sa. Via Solferino 1 (near Via Pontaccio). 878740. Subway stop: Lanza (M2)

41 Eclectica From exotic forays and trips across town, Teresa Ginori Conti brings home both ethnic and Milanese objects and furniture whose compatibility is harmonious and surprising. Both antique and new, expensive and downright cheap, the common denominator here is a universal sense of design. ♦ M afternoon, Tu-Sa; no midday closing. Corso Garibaldi 3 (at Via Pontaccio). 876194. Subway stop: Lanza (M2)

42 Al Teatro Cocktails and recorded music welcome a crowd that comes from the theater across the street. ◆ Tu-Su 7AM-2AM. Corso Garibaldi 16 (near Piazza delle Crociate). 864222. Subway stop: Lanza (M2)

San Simpliciano

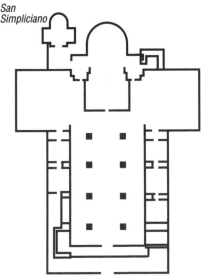

43 San Simpliciano This church (see floor plan above), which dates from early Christian times, was restored to something approximating its original state in the last century. The restoration mainly involved getting rid of the Baroque additions and leaving the meditative impression it imparts today. Even more peaceful is the adjacent convent, whose **Chiostro Grande** (Large Cloister) makes for a pleasant break in the day's activities. ◆ Piazza delle Crociate (north of Via Pontaccio). Subway stop: Lanza (M2)

44 Rossignoli Bicycles, accessories, and nifty racing gear make this a great place to find souvenirs for cycling friends back home. ◆ M afternoon, Tu-Sa. Corso Garibaldi 71 (between Via Giulianova and Via Solera Mantegazza). 804960. Subway stop: Lanza (M2)

45 Al Matarel ★★$$ One of the most beloved of all Milanese restaurants, this place (whose name means crazy) serves definitive versions of the city's specialties, from antipasto to all the risotto dishes and a renowned *cassoeula* (pig's-foot stew). ◆ M-Tu, Th-Su lunch and dinner; W lunch only. No credit cards accepted. Corso Garibaldi 75 (at Via Solera Mantegazza). 654204. Subway stops: Lanza (M2) Moscova (M2)

46 Casa Pacchetti This pleasantly eclectic residence (1903, **Gaetano Moretti**) incorporates architectural elements ranging from the Egyptian to Lombard Renaissance. ◆ Via Legnano 28 (between Via Solera Mantegazza and Via Vasto). Subway stops: Lanza (M2); Moscova (M2)

47 Moscatelli This lovely old *enoteca* (wine bar) has been run for the past few decades by Giuseppe Moscatelli. ◆ Tu-Su 10:30AM-7:30PM, 9:30PM-2AM. Corso Garibaldi 93 (near Largo La Foppa). 6554602. Subway stop: Moscova (M2)

48 G. Asnaghi Conservative, well-designed men's and women's clothes and household linens are offered here at affordable prices. ◆ Closed Sunday, lunch. No credit cards accepted. Via Moscova 68 (near Piazza Lega Lombarda). 6597706. Subway stop: Moscova (M2)

49 Pucci You won't confuse this leather artisan with the Emilio Pucci of psychedelic palazzo pajama fame. Here at his workshop you'll find a complete and varied line of handmade handbags and other canvas and leather goods. ◆ M-F. No credit cards accepted. Via Moscova 60 (near Piazza Lega Lombarda). 6599619. Subway stop: Moscova (M2)

50 Giovanni Battista Piatti This bit of outdoor sculpture by Salvatore Pisani commemorates Milanese inventor Giovanni Battista Piatti. ◆ Largo La Foppa (at Corso Garibaldi). Subway stop: Moscova (M2)

51 Caffè Radetzky ★★$$ This trendy old-style cafe provides the perfect place for whiling away the hours over a newspaper and a plate of oysters. ◆ M-Sa 7:30AM-2AM. No credit cards accepted. Corso Garibaldi 105 (at Largo La Foppa). 6572645. Subway stop: Moscova (M2)

52 Montesi-Garau Owners Grazia Montesi and Raimondo Garau have assembled an enviable collection of everything from Baroque to modern furniture and objects of high Milanese design. ◆ M afternoon, Tu-Sa. No credit cards accepted. Via Marsala 13 (between Via Solferino and Corso Garibaldi). 29002057. Subway stop: Moscova (M2)

53 Effebieffe Anglo and Italian labels on conservative English-style clothing for over-30 men and women golfer-types can be found in this store at reasonable prices. ◆ M-Sa. Via Marsala 7 (between Via Solferino and Corso Garibaldi). 6598069. Subway stop: Moscova (M2)

54 Antonia Jannone The only gallery in Italy dealing exclusively in architectural and theatrical drawings, the designs of Michael Graves, Aldo Rossi, Massimo Scolari, Ettore Sottsass, and others may be perused and purchased here. ◆ M afternoon, Tu-Sa. Corso Garibaldi 125 (near Piazza XXV Aprile). 29002930. Subway stop: Moscova (M2)

54 Panino Giusto Milan's original *paninoteca*—the kind of sandwich shop that revolutionized the natives' eating habits —still makes some of the city's most original sandwiches, and in a much-welcomed (though tiny) nonsmoking atmosphere.

◆ M-Sa noon-1AM. No credit cards accepted. Corso Garibaldi 125 (near Piazza XXV Aprile). 6554728. Subway stop: Moscova (M2). Also at: Piazza Beccaria (east of Piazza del Duomo). 76005015. Subway stop: Duomo (M1, M3)

55 High-Tech One-stop shopping for the kind of design associated with Milan, this place stocks an extensive number of European-designed housewares along with the occasional American kitchen gadget. ◆ M afternoon, Tu-Sa. Piazza XXV Aprile 12 (near Corso Como). 6509515. Subway stop: Moscova (M2)

55 Porta Garibaldi Another Neo-Classical city gate (1826, **Giacomo Moraglia**), this one was marched through by none other than Giuseppe Garibaldi. ◆ Piazza XXV Aprile (near Corso Como). Subway stop: Moscova (M2)

56 Roca's Bar This lively music hangout offers light snacks for grazing and gazing *alla milanese.* ◆ Tu-Su 8AM-2AM. No credit cards accepted. Viale Pasubio 16 (near Via Maroncelli). 6599729. Subway stop: Moscova (M2)

57 Antica Trattoria della Pesa ★★$$ One of the oldest restaurants in the city, it appropriately serves all the Milanese classics— *buseca* (tripe soup), minestrone, *risotto giallo, risotto al salto,* osso buco, *cazzoeula* (pig's foot stew) in a charming old setting. ◆ M-Sa lunch and dinner. Viale Pasubio 10 (near Via Maroncelli). 6555741. Subway stop: Moscova (M2)

58 Piccolo Teatro Fuori Porta ★★$$ Classic Milanese food is served in this new location. Special emphasis is placed on rich desserts such as chocolate mousse and warm zabaglione. ◆ M-Sa lunch and dinner. Viale Pasubio 8 (near Piazza XXV Aprile). 6572105. Subway stop: Moscova (M2)

59 Caffè Novecento ★$$ This favorite watering hole is much frequented by fashion-world denizens, who come here for coffee, cocktails, and snacks. ◆ M-Sa 8AM-2AM. No credit cards accepted. Corso Como 9 (north of Piazza XXV Aprile). 6552090. Subway stop: Moscova (M2)

60 Hollywood Americans in town for the fashion collections flock in numbers to this disco. ◆ Tu-Sa 10PM-3AM; Su 3-6PM. No credit cards accepted. Corso Como 15 (north of Piazza XXV Aprile near Viale Sturzo). 6598996. Subway stop: Moscova (M2)

61 All'Isola ★★$$ Another fabulous fashion-world haunt, this restaurant also serves a Milanese menu with diet-busting desserts like warm zabaglione. ◆ M, W-Su lunch and dinner. Corso Como 10 (north of Piazza XXV Aprile). 6571624. Subway stop: Moscova (M2)

IO·CORSO·COMO

61 10 Corso Como One of Milan's great arbiters of fashion and a trendsetter, Carla Sozzani created this international bazaar of fashion and design in the space that was formerly the boutique of her partner, Romeo Gigli. Come for the experience, if not for the clothes, by Sozzani's private label or the international New Guard such as Vivienne Westwood and Comme des Garcons. A romantic grab bag of accessories and fixtures are all for sale: carpets, sconces, antique buttons, ceramics, artisanal glassware. Don't overlook the gallery upstairs featuring the works of contemporary artists and photographers. ◆ Tu-Sa. Corso Como 10 (north of Piazza XXV Aprile). 29002674. Subway stop: Moscova (M2)

62 Shockin' Club An international crowd of models and advertising people frequent this 1970s-style disco. ◆ Tu-Su until 2AM. No credit cards accepted. Bastioni di Porta Nuova 12 (east of Piazza XXV Aprile). 6595407. Subway stop: Moscova (M2)

63 Galleria Michel Leo Deco plastics and Lalique glass are among the many 20th-century collectibles for sale at this shop. ◆ M afternoon, Tu-Sa. Via Solferino 35 (between Via Marsala and Bastioni di Porta Nuova). 6598333. Subway stop: Moscova (M2)

63 Galleria Paola e Rossella Columbari These sisters sell design objects for home and office from the postwar period onward. They also have their own line of contemporary pieces. ◆ M afternoon, Tu-Sa. Via Solferino 37 (between Via Marsala and Bastioni di Porta Nuova). 29001189. Subway stop: Moscova (M2)

64 Emilio Boffi Stop by the workshop of one of Milan's leading young designers of leather goods. ◆ M afternoon, Tu-Sa. No credit cards accepted. Via Milazzo 6 (between Via Marsala and Bastioni di Porta Nuova). 6592113. Subway stop: Moscova (M2)

64 Giallo ★★$$ Fashionable (with the fashion world) dining here encompasses everything from *pizzettine* (little pizzas) to *costoletta alla milanese* (breaded veal cutlet smothered with melted cheese). ◆ M-Sa dinner. Via Milazzo 6 (between Via Marsala and Bastioni di Porta Nuova). 6571581. Subway stop: Moscova (M2)

65 Cartabolo Not just another paper shop, this small boutique is stocked with gift items crafted with handmade decorative papers with a twist. Young Clara Rota and her partner, Roberta Colombo, take their inspiration from unusual fabrics and exotic textiles that have caught their attention in their travels around the world. ◆ M afternoon, Tu-Sa. Via Solferino 29 (between Via Marsala and Bastioni di Porta Nuova). 6592949. Subway stop: Moscova (M2)

ENOTECA COTTI

dal 1952

66 Enoteca Cotti This is Milan's most famous *enoteca* (wine shop), where a studied selection of great grapes may be tasted and purchased. Expert advice is provided by Signor Cotti. ♦ M-Sa until midnight. No credit cards accepted. Via Solferino 42 (at Via Castelfidardo). 29001096. Subway stop: Moscova (M2)

67 L'Archivolto This is the place to be for the best selection of books on design and architecture in this design- and architecture-obsessed city. Its gallery also holds temporary exhibitions on those subjects. **L'Archivolto**'s next-door design shop carries a variety of highly designed gift items. ♦ Tu-Sa. Via Marsala 2 (at Via Solferino). 6590842. Subway stop: Moscova (M2)

68 Soul to Soul This is not a down-home restaurant, it's the latest of the nocturnal disco pubs in Brera frequented by a handsome mix of local and international youths. The ever-changing music mix l eans toward an Afro-Cuban inspiration—the appropriate background beat for an unpretentious variety of lagers and European beers. You can dance up a storm from 10:30PM to 5AM, or just chat sustained by sandwiches and desserts. ♦ Tu-Su. Via San Marco 33 (at Via Castelfidardo). 6598965. Subway stop: Moscova (M2)

69 Antica Locanda Solferino $ The best choice for inexpensive but stylish accommodations in Milan, this former *pensione* is booked months in advance, so be sure to reserve. The 12 rooms have a lot of character and the staff has a bit *too* much, but the neighborhood is worth the attitude. At press time a thorough renovation was expected to be completed by the middle of 1996. ♦ Via Castelfidardo 2 (at Via Solferino). 6592706; fax 6571361. Subway stop: Moscova (M2)

Within Antica Locanda Solferino:

Solferino ★★$$ The young crowd that frequents this small, cozy restaurant appreciates the inventive menu, which pairs pasta with such things as seasonal vegetables and truffled kidney, and offers various types of carpaccio. There's takeout, too. ♦ M-F lunch and dinner; Sa dinner only. Via Castelfidardo 2 (at Via Solferino). 6599886. Subway stop: Moscova (M2)

70 Bebel's ★$$ What towers there are at **Bebel**'s are pizzas, made in an authentic wood-burning brick oven. More expensive items, such as lobster, are also available. ♦ M-Tu, Th-F, Su lunch and dinner; Sa dinner only. Via San Marco 38 (north of Via Moscova). 6571658. Subway stop: Moscova (M2)

71 L'Amour! ★$ A large cafe where you can stop for the daily plate of pasta. Hope that the fresh *fazzoletti* pasta are on the menu, served in *crema di basilico* (a kind of whipped basil sauce) or *penne sciué sciué* prepared with tomato, mozzarella, basil, and shrimp. ♦ M-Sa dinner. No credit cards accepted. Via Solferino 25 (south of Via Marsala). 6590176. Subway stop: Moscova (M2)

71 La Briciola ★★$$ Another lively place (largely thanks to owner Gianni) forever popular with models and journalists; this one serves a full Milanese menu as well as the highly favored carpaccio (thinly sliced raw beef), here drizzled in extra-virgin Tuscan olive oil. ♦ Tu-Sa lunch and dinner. Via Solferino 25 (south of Via Marsala). 6551012. Subway stop: Moscova (M2)

72 Pavillon ★★$$ Lombard and Piedmontese cuisine is featured here, with risottos and homemade pastas leading the list, which also includes game and truffles in season. ♦ M-Tu, Th-Su lunch and dinner. No credit cards accepted. Via Statuto 16 (near Largo La Foppa). 6552219. Subway stop: Moscova (M2)

73 La Vetrina di Beryl Step into footwear that borrows from and renews historical styles. ♦ M afternoon, Tu-Sa. Via Statuto 4 (near Largo Treves). 654278. Subway stop: Moscova (M2)

74 Enrica Massei A fitting place for up-to-date women to shop for very contemporary clothes and accessories. ♦ M afternoon, Tu-Sa. Via Palermo 8 (at Largo Treves). 6552852. Subway stop: Moscova (M2)

75 Legatoria Artistica The marbleized paper and myriad paper products available here are made on the premises. ♦ M afternoon, Tu-Sa. Via Palermo 5 (at Largo Treves). 72003632. Subway stop: Moscova (M2)

76 Rigolo ★★$$ Always abuzz with a lively crowd of fashion and designer types as well as newspaper journalists from the nearby offices of *Corriere della Sera,* this restaurant serves a long list of ample Italian dishes (homemade ravioli are usually available, and the *costoletta alla milanese* is easily enough for two). It is also one of the few places in town open for Sunday dinner. ◆ Tu-Su lunch and dinner. Via Solferino 11 (at Largo Treves). 86463220. Subway stops: Moscova (M2); Lanza (M2)

77 Argenteria Dabbene Finely crafted silver in jewelry, serving trays, picture frames, and other instant-heirloom gift items will catch your eye here. ◆ M afternoon, Tu-Sa. Largo Treves 2 (at Via Montebello). 6598890. Subway stops: Moscova (M2); Lanza (M2)

78 Koivu This small space chockablock with housewares demonstrates the kind of inventive design Milan is all about. ◆ M afternoon, Tu-Sa. Via Solferino 11 (near Largo Treves). 877328. Subway stops: Moscova or Lanza (M2). Also at: Corso Europa 12 (near Piazza Beccaria). 76020821. Subway stop: San Babila (M1)

79 Controbuffet This is the place to find clever one-of-a-kind gifts such as Avant de Dormir plastic gear (you know, the kind with toy fish and floating palm trees sandwiched inside). ◆ M afternoon, Tu-Sa. Via Solferino 14 (near Largo Treves). 6554934. Subway stops: Moscova (M2); Lanza (M2)

80 Penelopi 3 In addition to lots of well-chosen housewares—from dish towels to Alessi teapots and espresso makers—this shop displays a recent penchant for American country crafts. ◆ M afternoon, Tu-Sa. Via Solferino 12 (at Via Ancona). 6599640. Subway stops: Moscova (M2); Lanza (M2)

CAFE'
STENDHAL

81 Cafe Stendhal ★★$$ Named in honor of the French writer and Milanophile, this trendy restaurant, decorated in a casual French-cafe style, has an elegant menu to match. The *culatello* ham appetizer melts in your mouth. The focus is on dinner, though light meals are served at lunch. ◆ Tu-Su lunch and dinner. Via San Marco (at Via Ancona). 6555587. Subway stops: Moscova (M2); Lanza (M2)

82 Enoteca N'Ombra de Vin This peaceful wine bar provides opportunities not only for sipping and purchasing but also for learning about vintages in its wine appreciation classes. ◆ M afternoon, Tu-Sa. Via San Marco 2 (in Piazza San Marco). 6552746. Subway stops: Moscova (M2); Lanza (M2)

83 Brerarte Like the other important auction houses in Milan, this place usually has a pre-auction viewing or two going on. Call for a schedule. ◆ M afternoon, Tu-Sa. Piazza San Marco 1 (at Via Fatebenefratelli). 6555040. Subway stop: Lanza (M2)

83 Fashion Cafe This modern, unpretentious cafe with outdoor tables is a favorite hangout for all types of fashion models at all hours. ◆ M-Sa 11AM-2AM. Piazza San Marco 1 (at Via Fatebenefratelli). 659823. Subway stop: Lanza (M2)

83 Dilmos Carefully selected furniture and objects by Italy's top designers are displayed in a gallerylike setting. ◆ M afternoon, Tu-Sa. Piazza San Marco 1 (at Via Fatebenefratelli). 29002350. Subway stop: Lanza (M2)

84 San Marco This church, built from the 13th to 18th centuries and restored in the 19th century, contains a number of 14th-century frescoes in the right transept and Cerano's *Baptism of St. Augustine* in the presbytery. ◆ Piazza San Marco (at Via Fatebenefratelli). Subway stops: Turati (M3); Lanza (M2)

85 La Lanterna Clothing, sportswear, and sports equipment are accompanied by agreeable prices, and occasionally agreeable service. ◆ M afternoon, Tu-Sa. Via Cernaia 1A (north of Via Fatebenefratelli). 6555439. Subway stops: Turati (M3); Lanza (M2)

86 Civico Museo del Risorgimento (Risorgimento Museum) The Italian risorgimento—the country's fight for unity during the last century—is little studied outside Italy, but this museum provides a nicely didactic introduction. Even if you're not particularly interested in history, the period costumes and memorabilia are enticingly displayed. ◆ Free. Tu-Su. Via Borgonuovo 23 (off Vicolo Fiori Oscuri). 8693549. Subway stops: Turati (M3); Montenapoleone (M3); Lanza (M2)

87 Claudio Silvestri Various Italian glass collectibles, especially from the 1940s, 1950s, and 1960s are on view here. ◆ M afternoon, Tu-Sa. Via Borgonuovo 26 (near Via Fatebene-fratelli). 6592909. Subway stop: Turati (M3)

88 Via Annunciata 23/1 The architects **Luigi Figini** and **Gino Pollini** defined these modernist apartment buildings (1932-34) as "superimposed villas" because of their modular nature. ◆ East of Via Borgonuovo near Via dei Giardini. Subway stop: Turati (M3)

89 A. Caraceni Suit yourself to some made-to-measure clothing (for both men and women) by the best tailors in Milan. Try to be in town for more than one fitting. ◆ M-Sa. Via Fatebenefratelli 16 (at Corso Porta Nuova). 6551972. Subway stop: Turati (M3)

90 Tanzi Driade One of the choicest retail showrooms for designer furnishings in the city, this store displays designs by all the Italians as well as such international enfants terribles as Philippe Starck. ◆ M afternoon, Tu-Sa. Via Fatebenefratelli 9 (near Piazza Cavour). 29003692. Subway stop: Turati (M3). Also at: Corso Monforte 19 (east of Piazza San Babila). 783697. Subway stop: San Babila (M1)

91 Cavour A wide selection of books in many languages is displayed in style, inviting pleasant browsing. ♦ M afternoon, Tu-Sa. Piazza Cavour 1 (near Via Fatebenefratelli). 6595644. Subway stop: Turati (M3)

91 Cardi Jewelry in the styles of such big names as Cartier and Bulgari is offered here at smaller prices. ♦ M afternoon, Tu-Sa. Piazza Cavour 1 (near Via Fatebenefratelli). 6592495. Subway stop: Turati (M3)

91 Palazzo dei Giornali This Fascist-era building was originally designed by **Giovanni Muzio** for *Il Popolo d'Italia,* the newspaper founded by Mussolini. Today a number of Italian newspapers have offices here. Check out the bas-relief called *Le Origini e lo Sviluppo del Giornale della Rivoluzione* (The Origin and Development of the Revolution's Press) by Mario Sirone at the top. ♦ Piazza Cavour 2 (near Via Turati). Subway stop: Turati (M3)

92 Casa Kit Make yourself at home at this store specializing in well-designed and inexpensive home furnishings. ♦ M afternoon, Tu-Sa. Via Carlo Porta 1 (at Via Turati). 6597916. Subway stop: Turati (M3). Also at: Piazza Risorgimento 10 (east of Piazza Tricolore). 7388419. Subway stop: San Babila (M1)

93 Sinig's The low prices at this home-furnishings store make up for the high-anxiety service. ♦ M afternoon, Tu-Sa. Via Turati 5 (north of Piazza Cavour). 6552125. Subway stop: Turati (M3)

93 Il Discanto This small shop sells ethnic jewelry from around the world as well as antique and exotic fabrics and other accessories. ♦ M afternoon, Tu-Sa. Via Turati 7 (north of Piazza Cavour). 29003557. Subway stop: Turati (M3)

94 Florence Taccani A selection from the miles of majolica here, most of which is Italian in origin (some is from France and Spain), makes a unique and personal gift and travels well in your carry-on luggage. ♦ M afternoon, Tu-Sa. Via Turati 6 (north of Piazza Cavour). 6554025. Subway stop: Turati (M3)

95 Piazza Cavour The piazza and its sculpture (by Antonio Tantardini and Odardo Tabacchi) are dedicated to Count Camille Cavour, the risorgimento politician after whom so many streets and piazzas in Italy are named. ♦ At Via Manin, Via Senato, and Via A. Manzoni. Subway stop: Turati (M3)

On Piazza Cavour:

Porta Nuova This "new gate" dates from the 12th century and is decorated with Roman tomb sculpture from the first century AD. ♦ Piazza Cavour (near Via Senato). Subway stop: Turati (M3)

96 Christie's The Milan outlet for the international auctioneers holds showings and sales with increasing regularity. ♦ M-Sa. Via Manin 3 (northeast of Piazza Cavour). 29001374. Subway stop: Turati (M3)

97 Galleria Milano Modern art and contemporary painting, sculpture, photography, and design are the mixed palette of this gallery. ♦ Tu-Sa. No credit cards accepted. Via Manin 13 (northeast of Piazza Cavour). 29000352. Subway stop: Turati (M3)

98 Spazio Krizia Located in a former stable, the headquarters of the famous designer known for her knits and animal motifs is also used for literary and cultural events. ♦ Via Manin 21 (between Piazza Cavour and Via Moscova). 6596415. Subway stop: Turati (M3)

99 Palazzo Montecatini A model of industrial architecture in its day, this building (1935-38, **Studio Ponti**) was among the first to use such technical tricks as climate control and pneumatic tubes. ♦ Via Moscova 3 (between Via Manin and Via Turati). Subway stop: Turati (M3)

99 Ranieri One of the city's premiere *pasticcerie* (pastry shops), famed for its *panettone ripieno,* the Milanese cake stuffed with creamy filling. ♦ Tu-Sa until 8PM; Su 7AM-1PM. No credit cards accepted. Via Moscova 7 (between Via Manin and Via Turati) 6595308. Subway stop: Turati (M3)

100 Profumeria Leali Brand-name toiletries are sold here at a discount. ♦ M afternoon, Tu-Sa. Via Moscova 10 (between Via Manin and Via Turati). 6552663. Subway stops: Turati (M3); Repubblica (M3)

101 Permanente Società delle Belle Arti Check out this palazzo (1883-85, **Luca Beltrami;** 1951-52, **Achille** and **Piergiacomo Castiglioni**) for the temporary art exhibitions it often houses. ♦ Via Turati 34 (near Piazza della Repubblica). 6551445. Subway stop: Repubblica (M3)

102 Via Manin 33 This residential version of Fascist-era architecture, designed by **Mario Asnago** and **Claudio Vender,** incorporates the reductionist geometric forms of its institutional counterpart, foreshadowing postmodern architecture. ♦ At Via Tarchetti. Subway stop: Repubblica (M3)

103 Ca' Brüta The name of this building (1921-23, **Studio Barelli-Colonnese**) is Milanese dialect for ugly house, an affectionate label attributable to the unusually idiosyncratic decoration on the facade. There's nothing ugly about the courtyard either. ♦ Via Moscova 12 (near Via Turati). Subway stop: Turati (M3); Repubblica (M3)

"Milan . . . has seemed prosaic and winterish as if it were on the wrong side of the Alps."

Henry James

Chic to Chic

Having surpassed Paris as the fashion capital of the world (as the Milanese will be the first to tell you), **Milan** produces fashion that ranges from playful to sophisticated but is always unquestionably stylish.

To a follower of fashion, shopping (or more likely window-shopping, given the prices) in the city's templelike boutiques is equivalent to an art historian's visit to the Louvre. From A to Z, from Giorgio Armani's loose interpretations to Ermenegildo Zegna's highly tailored menswear (not to mention the cerebral romanticism of Romeo Gigli, the animal mascots of Krizia, the colorful knits of Missoni, and the fantasy fashions of Gianni Versace), the roll call of internationally acclaimed designers is the main event for many visitors to Milan. Their shops, often designed by leading architects and designers, are found primarily in and around **Via Montenapoleone.**

During the excitement of spring and fall "Fashion Weeks," Milan appears to be a city that thrives on fashion alone. The spotlight once focused similarly on **Florence,** when the Pitti shows flourished there in the years following World War II, and then on Rome, whose fashion mainstays have long been secured by the couture Valentino empire. Now it is the pret-a-porter *moda italiana* debuted on the runways of Milan that determines hemlines, color combinations, and the status of bell-bottoms—trends that will trickle down ultimately to affect the mode of dressing in Europe, America, and Asia.

Why Milan and not Florence or Rome, or, for that matter, Bologna, Turin, or Palermo? Many Milanesi can still recall too vividly the 15 bombing raids that devastated Milan during World War II. The only blessing was the consequent rebuilding of small, generations-old factories, which turned the city's periphery into a modernized industrial zone. The postwar

Modernist movement encouraged Milan's role as forerunner in the world of fashion as well as furniture and interior design. With a centuries-old patrimony of artisan guilds and the innate sense of design for which Italy has been known since the Middle Ages, the launching of the unrivaled made-in-Italy look in both design and ready-to-wear had a strong evolution behind it; this unprecedented foundation in up-to-date technology was all it needed to take off.

Milan's prime geographic location also influenced its success in the fashion industry. With the wool-producing area of Biella to the west and Como, the silk center of the Western world, 30 miles north, Milan could not have been more strategically positioned. The small Lombard city of Como produces over 80 percent of all Italian silks, representing more than one-third of world production. More important than the statistics is the quality of Como's silk—its most vital credential. The high (and low) priests of fashion turn to Como twice a year for the Ideacomo fabric fair, where the fashion cycle begins. Decisions made there turn up in the world's most discerning wardrobes a year or more later.

Fashion's shift of attention to Milan was inevitable, since it is here that the commercial and industrial interests of the country intersect in an unbridled atmosphere. And one look at how young *Milanesi* effortlessly throw together an indisputably stylish look with studied nonchalance answers the question: "Why Milan?"

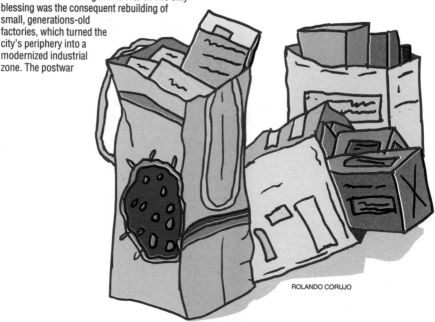

ROLANDO CORUJO

104 Le Cinque Terre ★★$$ Stefano and Elena Galligani have created one of the most upscale seafood joints in town, serving everything from oysters to lobster at their absolute freshest. ◆ M-F lunch and dinner; Sa dinner. Via Andrea Appiani 9 (near Via Moscova). 6575177. Subway stop: Turati (M3); Repubblica (M3)

105 Arform Paolo and Anna Tilche's shop (designed by Paolo, who is trained as an architect) sells a tasteful selection of design objects for home and office, with an emphasis on Scandinavian goods. ◆ M afternoon, Tu-Sa; no midday closing. Via Moscova 22 (at Corso Porta Nuova). 6554691. Subway stop: Turati (M3); Repubblica (M3)

106 Bar Margherita This peaceful nightspot attracts an older jazz crowd and offers a fine selection of grappa, the Italian clear brandy. ◆ M-Sa noon-2AM. Via Moscova 25 (at Via San Fermo della Battaglia). 6590833. Subway stop: Moscova (M2)

107 El Timbun de San Marc This English-style pub serves a mean bean soup. ◆ M-Sa noon-1AM. No credit cards accepted. Via San Marco 20 (at Via Mirabello). 6599507. Subway stop: Moscova (M2)

108 Mirabello Indulge yourself with bed and bath accessories in imaginative patterns and fabrics, including rich silks from the factories of nearby Como. ◆ M afternoon, Tu-Sa. Via Montebello (at Via San Marco). 6599733. Subway stop: Moscova (M2)

109 Raimondo Bianchi Plants are always an appropriate gift for business and other acquaintances in Milan, and this place—considered the best in Milan by many—has some of the most attractive and unusual ones in the city, with high prices to match. ◆ M afternoon, Tu-Sa. Via Montebello 7 (in Piazza Mirabello). 6555108. Subway stop: Moscova (M2)

110 San Fermo ★★$$ Old Milan 19th-century decor provides a backdrop for classic Milanese cuisine, with especially good value on the less-expensive lunch menu. ◆ M-Sa lunch and dinner. Via San Fermo della Battaglia 1 (near Piazza Mirabello). 29000901. Subway stop: Moscova (M2)

111 Caffè Milano ★★$$ Light meals, an array of unusual salads, and pastries are served in an informal and pleasant setting. Adjacent to the restaurant is a handsome stand-up bar and take-out area. ◆ Daily lunch and dinner. Piazza Mirabello 1. 29003300. Subway stop: Moscova (M2)

111 Il Verdi ★★$$ Milan's increasingly American-style eating habits (for better or worse) are in evidence here in one-course meals (called *piatti unici*) of meat, pasta, and salads. ◆ M-F lunch and dinner; Sa dinner. Piazza Mirabello 5. 6590797. Subway stop: Moscova (M2)

112 Piazza Sant'Angelo The highlight of this peaceful piazza is a fountain by realist sculptor Giannino Castiglioni depicting St. Francis of Assisi. ◆ Via Moscova at Corso Porta Nuova. Subway stop: Moscova (M2)

113 Sant'Angelo This church and its adjacent convent were built by the Franciscan brothers to a 1552 design by **Domenico Giunti**. Inside are 16th- and 17th-century frescoes that, while not of outstanding importance in the history of art, provide rather pleasant local interpretations of the stories of St. Francis and other saints. ◆ Piazza Sant'Angelo (Via Moscova at Corso Porta Nuova). Subway stop: Moscova (M2); Turati (M3)

Within Sant'Angelo:

Angelicum This theater/cinema presents plays and films in their original language—usually English. Temporarily closed for renovation. ◆ 29003462, 6592748

Bests

Lorenza de' Medici
Cookbook Author

Milan:

The best shopping in the world and Giorgio Armani clothes. The lovely gardens behind the beautiful homes; the **Museo Poldi Pezzoli**, once a private house; an opera at **La Scala**; a very "in" meal at **Paper Moon** and a creative one at **Aimo e Nadia**; a visit to **Peck** and a morning coffee at **Cova.**

Florence:

Hotel Torre di Bellosguardo, an old villa with the best view of the town and a dream garden, a 10-minute walk from **Palazzo Pitti.** Wandering around **Via delle Campora, Pian dei Giullari, l'Erta Canina,** and **Via San Leonardo. Il Cibreo** for the best food and the **San Lorenzo Market** for a feast of the eye: glorious vegetables, fruits, meats, and, in season, porcini mushrooms.

Venice:

Strolling up and down stairs to reach the more remote squares and narrow byways away from the crowds of **Piazza San Marco,** and around the **Ghetto** to see the synagogues. Eating *altanella alla giudecca,* the tiniest squids with polenta or dry cod fish, at **Antiche Carampane** in **San Polo.** Taking the *vaporetto* across the laguna to **Murano** to admire the glass-blowing and the glass museum, the materials at **Museo Fortuny,** and to buy precious embroidery at **Jesurum.**

Founded in the late 1980s, the Lega Lombarda (Lombardy League) has been seeking greater fiscal autonomy for the industrial north so as not to be bogged down by what it considers the inefficient, scandal-riddled politics of the south. A recent slogan of the league was "Rome makes the taxes, the North pays them, the Mafia pockets them."

Stazione Centrale

On the map, the area around Milan's central train station—**Stazione Centrale**—looks like a fuse connecting the round bomb of the rest of the city, as though the motion-obsessed Milanese Futurists had their hand at urban planning. Indeed, in its own way the station—designed at the same time as the Futurist movement was gaining momentum—glorifies motion and power (and Fascism) as much as the Futurist movement ever did. And the adjacent district, known as the **Centro Direzionale** (Administrative Center), provides more fuel for the explosive

energy of the city. Most visitors arrive at the station from the trains and airport buses that stop there, and many check in nearby at the city's largest concentration of business hotels. Though there is little of more than practical interest in the Stazione Centrale area, the Futurists would have been pleased by the functionalism. Besides the hotels, it bristles with Modernist skyscrapers, including the **Grattacielo Pirelli** (Pirelli Building)—the tallest in Italy—as well as a number of no-nonsense discount outlets. Even its art galleries seem to specialize in the reductionist Italian art of the *arte povera* school.

1 Stazione Centrale Italy's busiest train station was also Italy's longest public construction project—undertaken in 1912 by **Ulisse Stacchini,** the building wasn't completed until 1932. That period coincides with the rise of Fascism in Italy, and Fascism's influence shows in the monumentality of this train station, which rivals anything dreamed up by Nebuchadnezzar. Besides representations of fasces (the bundle of rods with an ax that symbolized the movement), there are a number of other works of art: Giannino Castiglioni's medallions representing *Work, Commerce, Science,* and *Agriculture,* in the entrance hall; Alberto Bazzoni's bas-reliefs, statues, and medallions, in the ticket hall; and Basilio Cascella's ceramic panels with views of Milan, Turin, Florence, and Rome, by the tracks. ◆ Piazza Duca d'Aosta (at Via Vitruvio, Via Galvani, and Via Pisani). Subway stop: Centrale F.S. (M2, M3)

Within Stazione Centrale:

Museo delle Cere (Wax Museum) In the not-unlikely event that your train has been delayed and you're really pressed for entertainment, take heart. Milan's wax museum is right in the station, its motionless dioramas a mocking counterpoint to Italy's train service. Bill Clinton is one of the contemporaries represented, but he can't hold a candle to historical figures such as Napoleon, Albert Schweitzer, and the like. ◆ Admission. Daily 8AM-11PM. 6690495

2 McDonald's $ Somehow the golden arches gleam more stylishly at the granddaddy of all the fast-food restaurants (*fest* as they're pronounced here) in Milan. The place is decked out in chrome and travertine and staffed by personnel uncharacteristically eager, for Italy or for the chain elsewhere in the world. The fast-food concept fits right into Milan's work ethic, so you'll see middle-management types biting burgers right alongside nostalgic American tourists. If you've got a hankerin' for pasta salads, you'll find a salad bar selection here. ◆ Daily 8AM-12:30AM. Piazza Duca d'Aosta 6/8 (northwest in piazza). 66987850. Subway stop: Centrale F.S. (M2, M3)

Restaurants/Clubs: Red   **Hotels:** Blue
Shops/ Outdoors: Green   **Sights/Culture:** Black

3 Excelsior Hotel Gallia $$$$ What the Stazione Centrale is to Fascism, this hotel is to Art Nouveau. Recently refurbished, it is the grandest of Milan's hotels, and its public rooms and banquet facilities provide the majestic setting for power events in Milan. The 250 guest rooms are decorated in pale Postmodern splendor. ♦ Piazza Duca d'Aosta 9 (northwest in piazza). 6785; in US, 800/225.5843; fax 66713239. Subway stop: Centrale F.S. (M2, M3)

Within the Excelsior Hotel Gallia:

Baboon Bar Bartender (or *barman* as the Italians say) Vito Saneramo prides himself on cocktails such as his Kir Royal, Mimosa,

Grattacielo Pirelli

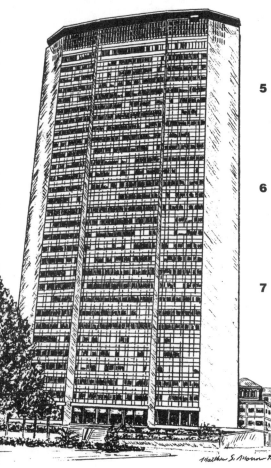

Evelin (pomegranate juice and champagne), and Passion Flower (passion fruit and vodka), served to a loyal, mostly business clientele. ♦ Daily 8AM-1:30AM. 6785

Gallia's Restaurant ★★★$$$ The chic English-language name sets the tone for this spacious and elegant restaurant, where chef Maurizio Campolonghi magnificently prepares a menu that ranges from Milanese classics at lunch to more inventive dishes such as *fiocco di cinghiale con ananas* (wild boar with pineapple) and *branzino farcito al pâté di olive* (bass stuffed with olive pâté) at dinner. ♦ Daily lunch and dinner. 6785

4 Grattacielo Pirelli (Pirelli Building) Designed by a team of eminent architects and engineers (1955-60, **Gio Ponti, Antonio Fornaoli, Alberto Rosselli, Giuseppe Valtolina, Edigio Dell'Orto, Arturo Danuso,** and **Pier Luigi Nervi**), and almost as large as it is high, Italy's tallest skyscraper (127.1 meters, or 417 feet) symbolizes the dynamism of Milan. Built for the Pirelli rubber company, it was sold for 43 billion lire to the Region of Lombardy in 1979 for use as its headquarters. If you'd like to see the view of the city from high atop the pinnacle of the **Pirelli** (illustrated at left), get permission to do so by contacting the Region of Lombardy (Regione Lombardia, Affari Generali, 67651). ♦ Piazza Duca d'Aosta (at Via Galvani). Subway stop: Centrale F.S. (M2, M3)

5 Auriga $$$ This middle-priced, 65-room modern hotel has fairly soundproof double rooms on the busy street side and singles facing a quiet courtyard. The hotel has a breakfast room only, but there's a restaurant across the street. ♦ Via G.B. Pirelli 7 (near Via Fabio Filzi). 66985851; fax 66980698. Subway stop: Centrale F.S. (M2, M3)

6 Porta Rossa ★$$ Chef Checchele features the robust cooking of his native region of Puglia (in southern Italy), with specialties such as the tiny ear-shaped *orecchiette* pasta with broccoli rabe, and roast kid and lamb. ♦ Tu-Su lunch and dinner. Via Vittor Pisani 2 (at Via Locatelli). 6705932. Subway stops: Gioia (M2); Repubblica (M3)

7 Piedra del Sol ★★$$ Simple south-of-the-border (not to mention across-the-Atlantic) dishes are the fare here, accompanied by tequila and live music. This was the first in a chain that now has affiliates in Rome. ♦ Tu-Su lunch and dinner; open until 3AM. Via Cornalia 7 (between Piazza San Gioachino and Via G. B. Pirelli). 6691901. Subway stops: Gioia (M2); Repubblica (M3)

8 Altopascio da Pietro ★★$$ Tuscan cuisine is the specialty of this rustic but elegant restaurant, where Eleanora and Pietro prepare dishes such as *ribollita* (a white bean vegetable soup), ribbons of tagliatelle pasta, and robust roasts. ◆ M-F lunch and dinner; Su dinner only. Via Gustavo Fara 17 (at Via G. B. Pirelli). 6702458. Subway stop: Gioia (M2)

9 Torre Galfa This sleek office skyscraper (designed in 1959 by **Melchiorre Bega**) is so named because it rises from the corner of Via Galvani and Via Gustavo Fara. ◆ Via Gustavo Fara 41 (at Via Galvani). Subway stop: Centrale F.S. (M2, M3)

10 Da Berti ★★$$ Another excellent Tuscan restaurant, this one is run by Enrica Colombi, who also serves dishes such as *bifore alla Berti,* a square pasta accompanied by a sauce of tomato, peas, and rocket (a bitter green). There's also a wine cellar with more than 25,000 bottles of Italian vintages. In summer, you can dine in the lovely garden. ◆ M-Sa lunch and dinner. Via Algarotti 20 (near Via Melchiorre Gioia). 6884158. Subway stops: Centrale F.S. (M2, M3); Gioia (M2)

MILAN

HILTON

11 Milan Hilton $$$$ Milan's 325-room **Hilton** is all you'd expect of the chain; it is as busily efficient as the rest, though less anonymous and more stylish than most, in keeping with the context of the city and the neighborhood. ◆ Via Galvani 12 (between Via Fabio Filzi and Via Copernico). 6983; fax 66710810. Subway stop: Centrale F.S. (M2, M3)

Within the Milan Hilton:

Giuseppe ★★$$$ Dinner at the **Milan Hilton** is less crowded than lunch, with chef Gaspare Alessi preparing especially good risotti and other Milanese and international classics. ◆ Daily lunch and dinner. 6983

12 Madison $$$ A simply decorated modern option on a quiet street, this 100-room hotel serves a substantial American-style breakfast at no extra charge. ◆ Via Gasparotto 8 (near Via Copernico). 67074150; fax 67075059. Subway stop: Centrale F.S. (M2, M3)

13 Gare ★★$$ This is where the *mondo moda* or denizens of the fashion world retreat to for, or after, dinner. Two separate areas—restaurant and disco—are both strikingly outfitted in a Jetson's-like, turn-of-next-century setting. The food is fine (Italian fare with an emphasis on the fresh and natural, with a host of interesting salads for the waif-model community), but don't bother going if you're only interested in grazing, not gazing. The international clientele and music are the draws-of-the-moment. ◆ Restaurant: Tu-Su 8:30PM-3AM. Disco: Tu-Su 11:30PM-4:30AM. Via Ferrante Aporti 37 (at Via Lumieri). 2892922. Subway stop: Centrale F.S. (M2, M3)

14 Diffusione Moda This wholesaler opens to the public on Saturdays (though you can sometimes persuade them to let you in at other times), when women's clothes by such designers as Laura Biagiotti and Krizia are offered at a discount. ◆ M-Sa; no midday closing on Saturday. No credit cards accepted. Via Andrea Doria 44 (near Piazzale Loreto). 6705145. Subway stop: Loreto (M1, M2)

15 Firme Designer signatures, or *firme,* and others appear on discounted clothing for the entire family in this vast selling space. ◆ Monday afternoon, Tu-Sa; no midday closing. No credit cards accepted. Corso Buenos Aires 77 (south of Piazzale Loreto). 66983113. Subway stop: Loreto (M1, M2)

16 El Tropico Latino This coffee bar is popular with a prosperous young crowd and doubles as a great place for tropical cocktails, light Mexican food, and music well into the night. ◆ M-Sa 7:30AM-2AM. No credit cards accepted. Via Ozanam 15 (west of Piazzale Bacone). 201259. Subway stop: Lima (M1)

17 Libreria Buenos Aires At this discount Italian-language bookshop you can pick up the latest translation of American and international best-sellers. ◆ M-Sa, no midday closing; Su afternoon only. Corso Buenos Aires 49 (between Via Ruggero Boscovich and Via Plinio). 29516798. Subway stop: Lima (M1)

In 1529, the Archbishop of Milan gave a 16-course dinner that included caviar and oranges fried with sugar and lemon, 1,000 oysters with pepper and oranges, lobster with citrons, sturgeon in aspic covered with orange juice, fried sparrows with oranges . . . orange fritters, a soufflé full of raisins and pine nuts and covered with sugar and orange juice, 500 fried oysters with lemon slices, and candied peels of citrons and oranges.

18 Hotel Michelangelo Milano $$$$ With 300 rooms, this towering business hotel's high-tech aspect (dozens of TV channels, push-button controls for everything imaginable) lends itself well to Milan's reputation for modern design. ♦ Via Scarlatti 33 (in Piazza Duca d'Aosta). 6755; fax 6694232. Subway stops: Centrale F.S. (M2, M3); Caiazzo (M2)

Within the Hotel Michelangelo Milano:

Bar del David This cocktail lounge has music after 10:30PM and serves a light menu of nouvelle-style Italian food. ♦ Daily 8:30AM-1AM. 6755

Mastro Ghirlandaio ★★$$$ This casual, popular restaurant also serves an unconventional menu of both nouvelle Italian and classic Milanese food. Daily changing fresh fish selections and homemade desserts are as reliable as they are delicious. ♦ Daily lunch and dinner. 6755

19 Florida $$ Convenient for airport and train arrivals and departures, this clean, modern 57-room hotel attracts a loyal European clientele. No restaurant, but there is a breakfast room and room service. ♦ Via Lepetit 33 (between Via Vitruvio and Stazione Centrale). 6705921; fax 6692867. Subway stops: Centrale F.S. (M2, M3); Caiazzo (M2)

20 I Mercanti Housewares of all sorts (from Mikasa to Alessi) are offered here at a 30-percent discount off list price. ♦ M afternoon, Tu-Sa. No credit cards accepted. Via Mauro Macchi 32 (between Via Vitruvio and Via Scarlatti). 6696638. Subway stops: Centrale F.S. (M2, M3); Caiazzo (M2)

21 Grazzini Grazzini sells toys galore, from games to stuffed animals, with a 30-percent discount for members—you can sign up at the cash register. ♦ M afternoon, Tu-Sa. No credit cards accepted. Via Mauro Macchi 29 (between Via Vitruvio and Via Scarlatti). 6691319. Subway stop: Centrale F.S. (M2, M3). Also at: Via Romolo 9 (near Via Liguria). 8370172. Subway stop: Romolo (M2)

22 Atlantic $$$ The 60 pleasant accommodations here cater to a business crowd. ♦ Via Napo Torriani 24 (near Piazza Duca d'Aosta). 6691941; fax 6706533. Subway stop: Centrale F.S. (M2, M3)

23 Flora $$ This hotel's 50 clean and efficient rooms are popular—as such places usually are around here—with a business clientele. ♦ Via Napo Torriani 23 (near Piazza Cincinnato). 66988242; fax 66983594. Subway stop: Centrale F.S. (M2, M3)

24 Mennini $$ This modern 65-room hotel has a lively breakfast room that is popular with its largely Italian clientele. ♦ Via Napo Torriani 14 (near Via Lepetit). 6690951; fax 6693437. Subway stops: Centrale F.S. (M2, M3); Repubblica (M3)

25 Zevrò Zevrò sells clothing for men, women, and children in styles ranging from basic Italian to the ever-popular imitations of British classics. ♦ M afternoon, Tu-Sa. Via Ruggero Boscovich 14/18 (near Via Pisani). 66988151. Subway stops: Centrale F.S. (M2, M3); Repubblica (M3)

26 Profumeria Dorica This store features a nice variety of discount perfumes and cosmetics in major international brands. ♦ M afternoon, Tu-Sa. Via Vittor Pisani 12A (between Via San Gregorio and Via Cappellini). 66983017. Subway stops: Centrale F.S. (M2, M3); Repubblica (M3)

27 Telerie Ginetto You'll find discount fabrics galore here, including a nice selection of linens. ♦ M afternoon, Tu-Sa. No credit cards accepted. Via San Gregorio 48 (at Via Pisani). 66988343. Subway stops: Centrale F.S. (M2, M3); Repubblica (M3)

28 Eugenio Medagliani Milan's best restaurant supply store stocks an astounding variety of pasta and espresso machines, cooking utensils, and the like, and is particularly known for copper pots in every shape imaginable. ♦ M-F. Via San Gregorio 43 (near Via Carlo Tenca). 66981180. Subway stop: Repubblica (M3)

29 Da Lino Buriassi ★★$$ Lino's son Guido now runs this stylish restaurant that serves Italian classics such as *spaghetti con le vongole* (spaghetti with clams) and *filetto con tartufo* (truffled fillet of beef), as well as French-inspired snails and omelettes. ♦ M-F lunch and dinner; Sa dinner only. Via Felice Casati 12 (at Via Lecco). 29523227. Subway stop: Porta Venezia (M1)

30 Sotheby's Italia The Milan branch of this international auction house holds sales of everything from 19th-century paintings to historical design prints. ♦ Call for schedule of viewings and auctions. Via Broggi 19 (near Via Morgagni). 295001. Subway stop: Porta Venezia (M1)

31 Calajunco ★★$$$ The Aeolean Islands off the northern coast of Sicily are the unusual inspiration for much of the menu here. Fish—freshly brought back from the market and not cheap—reigns supreme, but such dishes as fillet of beef and liver with Ala wine nicely round out the menu. ♦ M-F lunch and dinner; Sa dinner only. Via Stoppani 5 (at Via G. B. Morgagni). 2046003. Subway stop: Porta Venezia (M1)

32 Il Sahara ★★$$ As its name implies, this elegant North African restaurant serves the best (and only) couscous in Milan. The hearty fare is complemented by a nice array of teas, beers, and wines. The ambience, too, is in the style of the Middle East, with Turkish rugs and nightly performances of belly dancing. ◆ Tu-Su lunch and dinner. Via Alessandro Tadino 2 (near Piazzale Oberdan). 29400684. Subway stop: Porta Venezia (M1)

33 Lucca ★★$$ This handsome old Tuscan restaurant serves the specialties of Lucca, including *minestra di farro* (a barleylike soup) and *budino di marron glacé* (glazed chestnut pudding). The less expensive, recently added *Bistrot* section serves simpler dishes from the same talented kitchen. ◆ Tu-Su lunch and dinner. Via Panfilo Castaldi 33 (at Via Alessandro Tadino). 29405708. Subway stop: Porta Venezia (M1)

Joia.

34 Joia ★★$$ The subtitle of this popular place, *alta cucina naturale* (natural haute cuisine), says it all. Nicla Nardi and Pietro Leeman have taken the lessons of nouvelle cuisine and applied them to natural foods. The emphasis here is on wholesome ingredients which are presented with panache in tasty pâtés, soups and risotto dishes. The dining rooms are decorated in a modern, elegant style, with black and natural wood furnishings, white linen tablecloths, wood floors, and pale green walls. ◆ M-F lunch and dinner; Sa dinner. Via Panfilo Castaldi 18 (between Via Settala and Via Lazzaretto). 2049244. Subway stop: Porta Venezia (M1)

35 Galleria Christian Stein This art dealer specializes in *arte povera,* a minimalist movement begun in Turin in the mid-1960s and represented here by Mario Merz, Jannis Kounellis, and Michelangelo Pistoletto. ◆ M afternoon, Tu-Sa. Via Lazzaretto 15 (at Via Panfilo Castaldi). 6696637. Subway stops: Porta Venezia (M1); Repubblica (M3)

36 Palace $$$$ This boxy link in the CIGA hotel chain (recently purchased by ITT Sheraton) is 1960s-modern on the outside, Empire on the inside, and a class act through and through, with period prints and 15th century–style furniture in its 212 guest rooms. A costly and elaborate restoration

was completed in 1992. ◆ Piazza della Repubblica 20 (east of piazza). 6336; 800/325.3589; fax 654485. Subway stop: Repubblica (M3)

Within the Palace:

Casanova Grill ★★★$$$ Even in a city where hotel restaurants are actually good, this elegant dining room furnished with antiques is better than the rest. A creative Italian menu by chef Umberto Bettoli features dishes such as *maccheroncini ai fiori di zucca* (macaroni with zucchini flowers) and *fegato d'oca con tartufo nero* (foie gras with black truffles), to the distinct pleasure of Milan's power elite. ◆ Daily lunch and dinner. 29000803

37 Principe di Savoia $$$$ This sprawling hotel is another of Milan's grande dames, its Old World public rooms complemented by the Empire-style guest facilities that are the hallmark of the CIGA chain (recently purchased by ITT Sheraton). As with its sister hotel across the piazza, the **Principe**'s 350 elegant guest rooms were submitted to a thorough and painstaking restoration that was finished in 1992. ◆ Piazza della Repubblica 17 (west side of piazza). 6230; 800/325.3589; fax 6595838. Subway stop: Repubblica (M3)

Within the Principe di Savoia:

Galleria ★★$$$ Milan's newest hotel restaurant has an opulent setting, in which international classics are complemented by well-prepared Lombard specialties such as *risotto giallo* (rice with saffron) and *costoletta alla milanese* (breaded veal cutlet). ◆ Daily lunch and dinner. 6230

38 Piazza della Repubblica This large piazza contains Piero Cascella's low-key 1974 monumental sculpture *Alla Repubblica,* made of stacked stones meant to be walked on and touched. ◆ At Bastioni della Porta Nuova and Bastioni della Porta Venezia. Subway stop: Repubblica (M3)

39 Duca di Milano $$$$ This CIGA-chain hotel (now owned by ITT Sheraton) is smaller and more intimate (99 rooms) than its big sister next door, combining comfortably elegant facilities with a full r ange of business services that make it popular with visiting executives. The **Au Premier** restaurant offers Mediterranean fare. ◆ Piazza della Repubblica 13 (west side of piazza). 6284; 800/325.3589; fax 6555966. Subway stop: Repubblica (M3)

40 Cucine Economiche This Neo-Romanesque edifice by **Luigi Broggi,** in brick and terra-cotta, is surprisingly reminiscent of architecture in America at the time (1886). ◆ Viale Monte Grappa 8 (west of Piazza della Repubblica off Viale Monte Santo). Subway stop: Repubblica (M3)

Parla Italiano?

Relax. Italians don't assume that Americans speak their language. Most are very patient with your possibly flawed attempts, and are generally pleased that you've tried. Here are some basics to get you started. *Buon viaggio!* (Have a good trip!)

Hello, Good-Bye, and Other Basics

Good morning	*Buongiorno*
Good afternoon/evening	*Buona sera*
Good night	*Buona notte*
How are you?	*Come sta?*
Good-bye	*Arrivederci*
yes	*sì*
no	*no*
please	*per favore/per piacere*
Thank you	*Grazie*
You're welcome	*Prego*
Excuse me	*Permesso* (in crowds)/*Mi scusi*
I'm sorry	*Mi dispiace*
I don't speak Italian.	*Non parlo italiano.*
Do you speak English?	*Parla inglese?*
I don't understand.	*Non capisco.*
Do you understand?	*Capisce?*
More slowly, please.	*Più lentamente per favore.*
I don't know.	*Non lo so.*
My name is . . .	*Mi chiamo . . .*
What is your name?	*Come si chiama?*
miss	*signorina*
madame, ma'am	*signora*
mister	*signor/e*
good	*buon/o/a*
bad	*cattivo/a*
open	*aperto/a*
closed	*chiuso/a*
entrance	*entrata*
exit	*uscita*
push	*spingere*
pull	*tirare*
What time does it open/close?	*A che ora apre/chiude?*
today	*oggi*
tomorrow	*domani*
yesterday	*ieri*
week	*settimana*
month	*mese*
year	*anno*

Hotel Talk

I have a reservation.	*Ho una prenotazione.*
I would like . . .	*Vorrei . . .*
a double room	*una camera doppia*
with twin beds	*con due letti singoli*
with a double bed	*con letto matrimoniale*
a quiet room	*una camera tranquilla*
with (private) bath	*con bagno (privato)*
with air-conditioning	*con aria condizionata*
Does that price include . . .	*Il prezzo comprende . . .*
breakfast?	*la prima colazione?*
taxes?	*le tasse?*
Do you accept traveler's checks?	*Accettate i traveler's checks?*
Do you accept credit cards?	*Accettate le carte di credito?*

Restaurant Repartee

Waiter!	*Cameriere!*
menu	*lista, menu*
I would like . . .	*Vorrei . . .*
a glass of . . .	*un bicchiere di . . .*
a bottle of . . .	*una bottiglia di . . .*
a liter of . . .	*un litro di . . .*
The check, please.	*Il conto, per favore.*
Is the service charge included?	*Il servizio è incluso?*
I think there is a mistake in the bill.	*Credo che ci sia uno sbaglio nel mio conto.*
lunch	*pranzo*
dinner	*cena*
tip	*mancia*
bread	*pane*
butter	*burro*
pepper	*pepe*
salt	*sale*
sugar	*zucchero*
soup	*zuppa*
salad	*insalata*
vegetables	*verdure, contorni*
cheese	*formaggio*
egg	*uova*
bacon	*pancetta*
omelette	*frittata*
meat	*carne*
chicken	*pollo*
veal	*vitello*
fish	*pesce*
seafood, shellfish	*frutta di mare*
pork	*maiale*
ham	*prosciutto*
chops (pork)	*costoletta, braciola*
dessert	*dolce*

As You Like It

cold	*freddo/a*
hot	*caldo/a*
sweet	*dolce*
(very) dry	*(molto) secco*
grilled	*alla griglia*
baked	*al forno*
boiled	*bollito/a*
fried	*fritto/a*
raw	*crudo/a*

rare	poco cotto/a
well-done	ben cotto/a
spicy	piccante

Thirsty No More

hot chocolate (cocoa)	cioccolata calda
black coffee	un caffè
coffee with hot milk	cappuccino, caffè latte
milk	latte
tea	tè
fruit juice	succo di frutta
water	acqua
mineral water	acqua minerale
carbonated	gassata
non-carbonated	non gassata
ice	ghiaccio
without ice	senza ghiaccio
beer	birra
red wine	vino rosso
white wine	vino bianco

Sizing It Up

How much does this cost?	Quanto costa?
inexpensive	a buon mercato
expensive	caro/a
large	grande
small	piccolo/a
long	lungo/a
short	corto/a
old	vecchio/a
new	nuovo/a
used	usato/a
this one	questo/a
that one	quello/a
a little	un poco
a lot	molto

On the Move

north	nord
south	sud
east	est
west	ovest
right	destra
left	sinistra
highway	autostrada
street	strada
gas station	stazione di benzina, distributore di benzina
straight ahead	sempre diritto
here	qui
there	là, lì
bus stop	fermata dell'autobus
bus station	stazione degli autobus
train station	stazione ferroviaria
subway	metropolitana
airport	aeroporto
tourist information	informazione turistica
city map	pianta

one-way ticket	biglietto di solo andata
round-trip ticket	biglietto di andata e ritorno
first class	prima classe
second class	seconda classe
smoking	fumare
no smoking	non fumare
Does this train go to . . . ?	Questo treno va a . . . ?
Does this bus go to . . . ?	Quest'autobus va a . . . ?
Where is/are . . . ?	Dov'è/Dove sono . . . ?
How far is it from here to . . . ?	Quanti chilometri sono da qui a . . . ?

The Bare Necessities

aspirin	aspirina
Band-Aids	cerotti
barbershop, hair dresser	barbiere, parucchiere
condom	profilattico
dry cleaner	tintoria
laundromat, laundry	lavanderia automatica/lavanderia
letter	lettera
post office	ufficio postale
postage stamp	francobollo
postcard	carta postale
sanitary napkins	assorbenti igienici
shampoo	shampoo
shaving cream	schiuma da barba
soap	sapone
tampons	assorbenti interni
tissues	fazzoletti di carta
toilet paper	carta igienica
toothpaste	dentifricio
Where is the bathroom/ toilet?	Dov'è il bagno/ la toiletta?
men's room	signori, uomini
women's room	signore, donne

Days of the Week (lowercased in Italian)

Monday	lunedì
Tuesday	martedì
Wednesday	mercoledì
Thursday	giovedì
Friday	venerdì
Saturday	sabato
Sunday	domenica

Numbers

zero	zero
one	uno
two	due
three	tre
four	quattro
five	cinque
six	sei
seven	sette
eight	otto
nine	nove
ten	dieci

Porta Venezia

One of the most exclusive residential neighborhoods in Milan, Porta Venezia is just east of the center of town, sandwiched between the **Cerchia dei Navigli** (the innermost ring) and the **Viali** or **Bastioni** ring built under the Spanish, whose city gates still give many of the neighborhoods their names. Upscale residences can be found on **Via Bellini**, **Via Mascagni**, **Via Mozart**, and **Via Cappuccini**, but even if you don't live in one of them, you can still sample Porta Venezia's gentility by peeking into their courtyards and gardens. If that only whets your appetite for more, some of the patrician palazzi—such as **Villa Reale** and **Palazzo Dugnani**—have been turned into public museums. And if it's gardens you like, visit the broad expanse of the **Giardini Pubblici**—Europe's oldest public park.

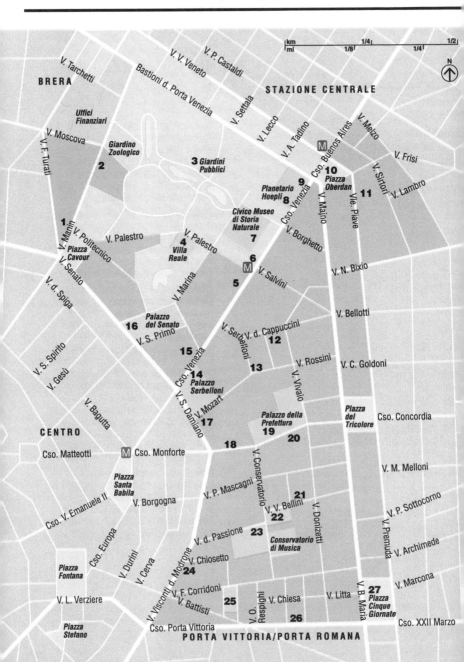

1 Manin $$$ This pleasant hotel has been in the Colombo family for generations. Its 118 rooms are plain but comfortable. The front ones have balconies overlooking the **Giardini Pubblici;** the rear ones are even more peaceful. Service is personal, which accounts for the loyal clientele. The hotel's restaurant is closed on weekends. ♦ Via Manin 7 (northeast of Piazza Cavour). 6596511; fax 6552160. Subway stop: Palestro (M1)

2 Palazzo Dugnani Built in the late 17th century, this patrician residence contains two frescoes of mythological subjects by Giambattista Tiepolo. Via Manin 2 (northeast of Pizza Cavour). Subway stop: Palestro (M1)

Within Palazzo Dugnani:

Spazio Baj Here you'll find a collection of prints by contemporary Italian artist Enrico Baj. ♦ Tu-Su. 62085415

Museo del Cinema e Cineteca Italiana (Cinema Museum and Italian Cinematheque) Displays of cinema equipment and memorabilia are complemented by reconstructions of movie sets. The museum also offers screenings of classic Italian and art films. ♦ Tu-F 3-6PM. 6554977

3 Giardini Pubblici The first public park in Europe (begun in 1783 by **Giuseppe Piermarini,**) the **Giardini Pubblici** was laid out on land confiscated from the suppressed Carcanine and San Diogini religious orders. Its statuary is of little interest; reminiscent of the Civil War statuary in American town squares, it mostly celebrates war heroes in 19th-century monumental style. But the park also has a little zoo and a relaxing cafe, and it offers visitors the chance to take in a bit of fresh air in this hectic city, along with everyone from the *rampanti* (Milanese yuppies) out for *il footing* (jogging) to seniors walking pets and parents out for a *passeggiata* (stroll) with their *bambini.* ♦ Bounded by Corso Venezia and Via Manin, and Via Palestro and Bastioni di Porta Venezia. Subway stops: Palestro or Porta Venezia (M1)

4 Villa Reale Ludovico Barbiano di Belgioioso commissioned this expansive Neo-Classical villa in 1790. Although **Leopold Pollack** designed the villa, the owner designed the English-style garden himself. Napoleon and Josephine lived here for a spell, as did the Austro-Hungarian rulers of Milan. ♦ Via Palestro 16 (enter from Corso Venezia). Subway stop: Palestro (M1)

Within Villa Reale:

Galleria d'Arte Moderna (Gallery of Modern Art) This museum has an exhaustive collection of 19th-century Lombard paintings. Visitors will find nothing surprising among these works, which reflect stylistic changes similar to those that occurred in the rest of Europe: idyllic landscapes, neo-classicism,

Romanticism, and plein air painting. Nineteenth-century paintings from Piedmont, the Veneto, Tuscany (including the *macchiaioli* plein air painters), and Naples are also represented. Upstairs is the **Museo Marino Marini** (Marino Marini Museum), dedicated to the 20th-century Italian sculptor best known for his variations on the horse-and-rider theme; and the **Raccolta Grassi (Grassi Collection),** a rich assemblage of mainly 19th- and 20th-century paintings from Italy and abroad, including some Impressionist and Post-impressionist canvases. ♦ Tu-Su 9:30AM-5:30PM. 76002819

5 Palazzo Castiglioni This is one of the outstanding Art Nouveau palazzi in Italy. Built from 1900 to 1904, its architects, **Ermenegildo Castiglioni** and **Giuseppe Sommaruga,** made the large residence fairly drip with crusty detail. ♦ Corso Venezia 47 (near Via Palestro). Subway stop: Palestro (M1)

5 Civico Padiglione d'Arte Contemporanea (Contemporary Art Museum This museum across from the **Giardini Pubbici** is a temporary exhibition space, usually devoted to contemporary art shows. The museum was closed at press time; it is expected to reopen in late 1996. ♦ Daily; closed last Monday of the month. Via Palestro 14 (enter from Corso Venezia). 784688. Subway stop: Palestro (M1)

6 Palazzo Bovara This Neo-Classical palazzo, designed in 1787 by **Carlo Felice Soave,** served as the French embassy and the office of the French writer Stendhal, who lived and loved in Milan. ♦ Corso Venezia 51 (near Via Salvini). Subway stop: Palestro (M1)

7 Civico Museo di Storia Naturale (Natural History Museum) Designed by **Giovanni Ceruti** in the late 19th century, this was the first structure in Milan built specifically to be used as a museum. Before it was bombed during World War II, it was one of the most important natural history museums in Europe. The reconstructed museum houses an extensive collection of every animal, vegetable, and mineral imaginable, including its own dinosaurs (triceratops, allosaurus, and kritosaurus are the most popular with children). ♦ Tu-Su. Corso Venezia 55 (north of Via Palestro). 62085407. Subway stop: Palestro (M1)

8 Planetario Hoepli Milan's planetarium has a regular program presenting peeks at celestial phenomena to the general public. ♦ Tu-Th; Sa-Su. Corso Venezia 57 (near Piazza Oberdan). 29531181. Subway stop: Porta Venezia (M1)

8 Bar Bianco This Neo-Classical building designed by **Piero Portalupi** dates from 1930 and houses a cafe much appreciated for its outdoor tables in the warm weather and for its hot chocolate in the winter. ♦ Daily 8AM-8PM. Behind the Civico Museo di Storia Naturale and the Planetario Hoepli. Subway stops: Palestro or Porta Venezia (M1)

9 Casa Torre Rasini (Rasini Apartment Building) This Functionalist apartment building, designed by **Gio Ponti** and **Emilio Lancia** in the early 1930s, is one of the few in Milan that takes aesthetics into consideration. ♦ Corso Venezia 61 (near Piazza Oberdan). Subway stop: Porta Venezia (M1)

10 Porta Venezia Twin-colonnaded buildings constitute this gate that was originally part of the walls built under the Spanish, who ruled Milan from 1535-1706. The buildings date from 1827 and were designed by **Rodolfo Vantini.** ♦ Piazza Oberdan. Subway stop: Porta Venezia (M1)

11 Diana Majestic $$$ This Art Deco link in the CIGA hotel chain (recently purchased by ITT Sheraton) is popular with models and others in the fashion trade and show business types, who appreciate its 96 simply decorated rooms. The hotel's garden restaurant offers outdoor dining in warm weather and is enclosed in cooler weather. ♦ Viale Piave 42 (south of Piazza Oberdan). 29513404, 800/325.3589; fax 201072. Subway stop: Porta Venezia (M1)

12 Palazzo Berri-Meregalli This monumental building by **Giulio Ulisse Arata** (1911-14) has an eclectic style embellished with mosaics, a ceiling by Angiolo D'Andrea, sculpture by Adolfo Wildt, and wrought iron by Alessandro Mazzucotelli. ♦ Via dei Cappuccini 8 (near Via Serbelloni). Subway stop: Palestro (M1)

The *milanesi* generally consider themselves better read and more in touch with Northern European and global events than other Italians. This is no surprise, as *Corriere della Sera,* the country's most important newspaper, is based in Milan. So are 20 percent of the nation's publishing houses—15 percent of national book sales take place in Milan's bookshops. For centuries the forerunner in manuscript illumination and printing, Milan continues to lead the world in the printing of high-quality art books.

". . . the beautiful city with its dominant frost-crystalline Duomo . . ."

John Ruskin

13 Oldani This shop has a wide selection of traditional and sporty men's clothing, as well as a smaller section set apart for womens-wear. ♦ Tu-Sa; no midday closing. Via Serbelloni 7 (near Corso Venezia). 76001087. Subway stop: Palestro (M1)

14 Palazzo Serbelloni This imposing Neo-Classical palazzo, built between 1775 and 1793 and designed by **Simone Cantoni,** was home to Napoleon and Josephine Bonaparte when they were in town for a few months in 1796. ♦ Corso Venezia 16 (at Via San Damiano). Subway stops: Palestro (M1); San Babila (M1)

15 Il Girarrosto da Cesarina ★★$$ One of Milan's oldest Tuscan restaurants, this is the place to try *ribollita* (white bean soup) and *bistecca alla fiorentina* (grilled steak drizzled with olive oil). ♦ M-F lunch and dinner; Su dinner only. Corso Venezia 31 (at Via dei Boschetti). 76000481. Subway stops: Palestro (M1); San Babila (M1)

16 Collegio Elvetico This curved palazzo was begun in 1608 by **Fabio Mangone** and completed in 1629 by **Francesco Maria Richini.** Today, it houses the **Archivio di Stato,** or State Archives. In front of it is a sculpture by Joan Miró. ♦ Via Senato 10 (at Via Marina). Subway stops: Palestro (M1); San Babila (M1)

17 Dellera This retailer often offers furs and fur-lined raincoats at discounts of 30 to 50 percent. ♦ M afternoon, Tu-Su. Via San Damiano 4 (at Via Mozart). 796151. Subway stop: San Babila (M1)

18 Studio Casoli This is one of Milan's (and Italy's) best and most followed contemporary art galleries. Its temporary exhibits showcase Italian and international artists. ♦ M-F. Corso Monforte 23 (near Via Conservatorio). 76023238. Subway stop: San Babila (M1)

19 Palazzo della Prefettura Constructed as a religious college between 1779 and 1817, the facade of this palazzo was completed by **Pietro Gilardoni.** ♦ Corso Monforte 31 (between Via Vivaio and Via Conservatorio). Subway stop: San Babila (M1)

20 Palazzo Isimbardi Behind the Neo-Classical facade of this late 15th-century palazzo is *The Triumph of Doge Francesco Morosini,* a grand painting by Giambattista Tiepolo. ♦ Corso Monforte 35 (between Via Donizetti and Via Conservatorio). Subway stop: San Babila (M1)

21 Casa Campanini This **Alfredo Campanini**– designed house (dating from 1904) is decorated in Milanese Art Nouveau in all its splendor. ♦ Via Vincenzo Bellini 11 (between Via Do.nizetti and Via Conservatorio). Subway stop: San Babila (M1)

Santa Maria della Passione

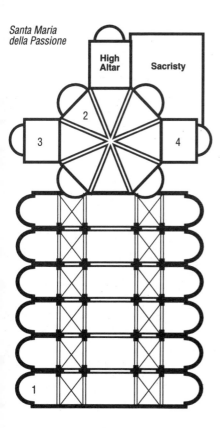

23 Palazzo Archinto This giant palazzo was built between 1833 and 1847 and designed by **Gaetano Besia.** It houses the exclusive **Collegio delle Fanciulle,** a girl's academy founded by Napoleon in 1808. ◆ Via della Passione 12 (at Via Conservatorio). Subway stop: San Babila (M1)

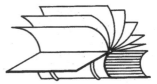

24 Libreria Scientifica Italian books—on science and other subjects—are available here at a 20-percent discount. ◆ M afternoon; Tu-Sa. Via Visconti di Modrone 8 (near Via Chiosetto). 76003734. Subway stop: San Babila (M1)

25 San Pietro in Gessate This Renaissance church (1447-75, attributed to **Pietro Antonio** and **Guinforte Solari**) is noted for its **Cappella Grifi,** which contains 15th-century frescoes of *The Life of St. Ambrose* by Bernardino Butinone and Bernardino Zenale. ◆ Piazza San Pietro in Gessate (at Via F. Corridoni). Subway stop: San Babila (M1)

26 L'Eliografica This trendy store, an architect's dream, sells all types of papers, pens, and drawing materials. ◆ M afternoon; Tu-Sa. Corso Porta Vittoria 29 (near Via Donizetti). 55192093. Subway stop: San Babila (M1). Also at: Via San Nicolao 10 (south of Piazzale Codorna). 8693102. Subway stop: Cadorna (M1, M2)

27 Alle Cinque Giornate Constructed in 1895, this romantic, allegorical monument by Giuseppe Grandi commemorates the period from 18 to 22 March 1848, the five days (*cinque giornate*) during which the Milanese overthrew Austrian rule in the **Castello Sforzesco.** The name *Cinque Giornate* appears on streets and piazzas throughout Lombardy, the same way Garibaldi and Cavour do throughout the rest of the country. ◆ Piazza Cinque Giornate. Subway stop: San Babila (M1)

22 Santa Maria della Passione Second in size only to the **Duomo** in Milan, this church (begun in 1486 and designed by **Giovanni Battagio**) has ample space for the paintings of Daniele Crespi, for whom it is practically a personal museum. The 17th-century Lombard painter expressed the pious ideals of the Counter-Reformation in his series of saints along the nave and especially in his masterpiece, *St. Charles Borromeus Fasting* **[1]**, in the first chapel of the left aisle (see floor plan above). Crespi also painted the organ shutters with *Scenes from the Life of Christ* **[2]**. The left transept **[3]** has a 16th-century *Last Supper* and *Crucifixion,* both by Giulio Campi; in the right transept **[4]** are 15th-century painter Bernardino Luini's *Deposition* and *Christ Rising from the Sepulchre.* In the former monastery next to the church is the **Museo della Basilica di Santa Maria della Passione,** the church museum. The highlight of this collection is series *Christ and the Apostles,* by 16th-century painter Ambrogio da Fossano (known as Bergognone). ◆ Museum: free. M-Su. Via Vincenzo Bellini 2 (at Via Conservatorio). 76021370. Subway stop: San Babila (M1)

Though Milan has extensive and efficient bus and subway systems, its trams are the most entertaining form of public transportation. Typically Milanese in that they are practical rather than touristic, the trams nonetheless have a romantic appeal owing to the original Art Nouveau–era character of the polished wooden seats and dim lighting fixtures in many of them—not to mention the fact that gorgeous models, male and female, often take the trams between their agencies and assignments.

Porta Vittoria/Porta Romana

Like Porta Venezia, the Porta Vittoria/Porta Romana area is sandwiched between the **Cerchia dei Navigli** and the **Viali.** But unlike that high-toned residential neighborhood, the Porta Vittoria/Porta Romana is institutional in nature—with everything from churches and a synagogue to a major hospital. For a rather nondescript part of town, however, it does boast a few surprises—including Italy's first Russian restaurant!

1 **Palazzo Sormani-Andreani** Francesco Croce restructured the preexisting palazzo in 1736. Twenty years later, **Benedetto Alfieri** added the facade facing the garden. Today, the palazzo houses the **Biblioteca Comunale** (Public Library). ♦ Corso Porta Vittoria 6 (at Via Francesco Sforza). Subway stop: Lamarmora (M3)

2 **Palazzo di Giustizia** The Fascist grandeur of this palazzo, designed by **Marcello** Piancentini and **Ernesto Rapisardi** and built between 1932 and 1940, demonstrates that boxy marble buildings weren't invented in the 1960s. ♦ Corso Porta Vittoria (between Via Manara and Via Freguglia). Subway stop: Lamarmora (M3)

3 **Gelateria Umberto** Elio Martinuzzi is the proprietor of this ice-cream parlor, known in the land of tutti-frutti for its sobering vanilla and a select few sorbets, as well as its *taglio di limone reale* (lemon slice served with Champagne). ♦ M-F until 11PM; Sa until 7:30PM. No credit cards accepted. Piazza Cinque Giornate 4 (near Corso Porta Vittoria). 5458113. Subway stop: Lamarmora (M3)

4 **Niki** This store sells flashy women's apparel—from slinky cocktail dresses to fabulous fake furs—at affordable prices. ♦ M afternoon; Tu-Sa. Viale Montenero 78 (near Piazza Cigue Giornate). 5468855. Subway stop: Lamarmora (M3)

ETRO

5 **Etro** This small shop next to the factory that makes luxury home furnishings for Milan's "King of Paisley" is a well-guarded secret. Known for soft materials in opulent, romantic prints and cashmere blends, both used for everything from pillows to throws, you'll also find Etro's elitist sportswear for weekends at the manor—all at close to 50 percent off retail. ♦ M-Sa. Via Spartaco 3 (off Viale Regina Margherita). 55020218. Subway stop: Lamarmora (M3)

6 **Civica Rotonda della Besana** The former cemetery of the **Ospedale Maggiore (Greater Hospital),** this site is surrounded by a Neo-Classical portico designed in 1725 by **Carlo Francesco Raffagno, Attilio Arrigoni,** and **Francesco Croce.** The city has converted it into a pleasant public park. ♦ Daily 9:30AM-7:30PM. Closed last Monday of every month. Via Besana 12 (at Viale Regina Margherita). 5463254. Subway stop: Lamarmora (M3)

7 **Santi Barnaba e Paolo** This Renaissance church (begun in 1558) contains works from the same period, notably a Pietà by Aurelio Luini on the second altar on the right and two paintings illustrating the story of St. Paul and St. Barnabas by Simone Peterzano on the presbytery walls. ♦ Via San Barnaba (at Via Guastalla). Subway stop: Lamarmora (M3)

8 **Tempio Israelitico** Milan's synagogue, in a florid mixture of Romanesque and Arabesque styles, is typical of western turn-of-the-century architecture. It was built from 1890 to 1892 to a design by **Luca Beltrami** and **Luigi Tenenti.** ♦ Irregular hours; call for current schedule. Via Guastalla 19 (at Via San Barnaba). 5512029. Subway stop: Lamarmora (M3)

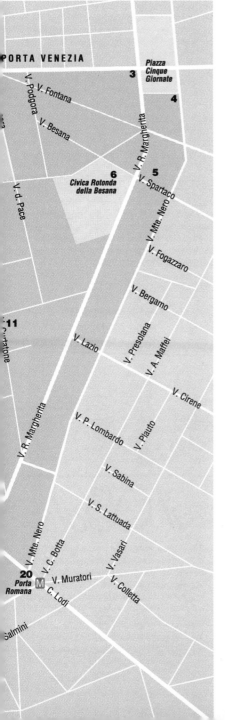

Restaurants/Clubs: Red   Hotels: Blue
Shops/ ♟ Outdoors: Green   **Sights/Culture: Black**

Milanese Morsels

Of all the cities in Italy, Milan offers some of the best quality and widest variety of dining, though it also carries the highest price tag. As the center of the country's food-distribution network, Milan gets the best of Italy's regional ingredients—rice from the north, olive oil and beef from Tuscany, pork and prosciutto from Emilia-Romagna, fish from Sicily, fresh fruit and vegetables, wine, and cheese from throughout Italy—with such locally prized imports as Angus beef and Scotch salmon.

In addition to a vast array of regional Italian restaurants serving everything from creamy Piedmontese specialties to spicy Sicilian dishes (though Tuscan restaurants are by far the most plentiful), Milan boasts a number of places featuring the rich regional cuisine of Milan and the surrounding region of Lombardy. The *primi piatti* (first courses) are numerous. A full Milanese meal might start with such cured meats as *bresaola* (beef) and *salame milanese* (pork salami), followed by an antipasto of *nervetti,* a popular salad made of calf's foot. *Buseca* is a tripe soup; minestrone is a vegetable soup. There are a number of risotto dishes, the most famous being *risotto alla milanese;* its yellow color comes from saffron and it is known locally as *risotto giallo,* or yellow risotto. Almost as popular is *risotto alla certosina,* made with shrimp, freshwater fish, and, occasionally, frogs. Leftover risotto is often made into *riso al salto,* a pancake of risotto sautéed in butter. Another popular dish (as it is in much of northern Italy) is polenta, cornmeal served with a variety of sauces as a first course or as an accompaniment to a main course.

The *secondo piatto* (main course) that is most associated with Milan is *costoletta alla milanese,* veal chops breaded and fried in butter, served with a lemon wedge, and, in the trendier restaurants, topped with tomato and basil. It is usually served with a portion of *risotto giallo* on the side. Other typical main courses are osso buco (braised veal shank) and *rostin negaa* (a veal chop braised in white wine). Desserts include such cheeses as the local blue-veined gorgonzola, the

soft *robiola* and *stracchino,* and the hard and pungent *grana.* Milan's most famous dessert is Christmas *panettone* (though it's increasingly available year-round), a cake studded with citron, raisins, and candied orange peel.

Though the Franciacorta district in Lombardy produces palatable and even acclaimed red and white wines, most Milanese prefer to drink wines from other regions of Italy. Chianti, Barolo, and Bardolino are popular reds; Pinot Bianco and Pinot Grigio (along with the ever-trendy Galestro) are usually preferred among the whites on the list. Milan's restaurants typically have a wide selection of grappas—the Italian aquavit—as after-dinner digestives.

At the other end of the scale, Milan is also known for its proliferation of fast-food outlets, which fit in neatly with the city's hardworking lifestyle. Some of the usual international chains, such as **McDonald's** and **Wendy's,** are here; afficionados of the genre might want to check out the local versions, particularly **Burghy.** Another fast-food phenomenon peculiar to Milan is the *paninoteca,* or sandwich emporium, found all over the city. Much more original and appetizing than the burger joints, the *paninoteche* pride themselves on putting together original combinations that are usually entire meals in themselves and are more substantial than the finger sandwiches called *tramezzini.*

9 Giardino della Guastalla The grounds of this academy have been converted into a pleasant public park filled with venerable trees and decorated with a statuary group depicting Mary Magdelene surrounded by angels. ♦ Via Guastalla at Via San Barnaba. Subway stop: Lamarmora (M3)

10 Policlinico Milan's vast hospital complex was built on land confiscated from the Knights of Malta when religious orders were suppressed. It's a strong example of the sort of postindustrial institutional architecture typical of the late 19th and early 20th centuries. ♦ Via Francesco Sforza (at Via San Barnaba). Subway stop: Lamarmora (M3)

il Sole

11 Il Sole ★★$$ This modern-looking restaurant serves an eclectic cuisine, as well as inventive variations on Italian standards such as *risotto al limone* (lemon risotto). ♦ Tu-Su lunch and dinner. Via Curtatone 5 (near Via A. Lamarmora). 55188500. Subway stop: Lamarmora (M3)

12 L'Acerba II ★★$$ In this upscale postmodern health-food restaurant, the fare is accompanied by the strains of Mozart, and patrons can peruse a selection of magazines and newspapers. The menu favors fresh and light vegetarian dishes such as *melanzane* (eggplant) or *carciofi* (artichoke) *alla parmigiana.* ◆ Tu-Su brunch, lunch, and dinner. Via Orti 4 (at Corso di Porta Romana). 5455475. Subway stop: Lamarmora (M3)

13 Lo Spiffero ★★$$ The varying menu of Betty and Toni Vincenti's pleasant Art Nouveau–style restaurant now centers on a variety of fondues and grilled vegetables, as well as desserts made on the premises. ◆ M-Sa lunch and dinner. Via Orti 1 (at Corso di Porta Romana). 59900279. Subway stop: Lamarmora (M3)

14 Great Perfumery Brand-name toiletries can be found here at bargain prices not implied by the trendy Anglo name. ◆ M afternoon; Tu-Sa. Corso di Porta Romana 57 (near Largo Crocetta). 55180109. Subway stop: Lamarmora (M3)

15 San Calimero This church, which dates from Paleo-Christian times, was redesigned through the ages by the likes of **Bishop Lorenzo** in 490 and **Francesco Maria Richini** in 1609. Unfortunately, a bad restoration in the 19th century stripped the church of most of its interesting features. Some of the older artifacts, including Roman marbles and tombstones, may be seen in the canon's courtyard. ◆ Via San Calimero (near Corso di Porta Romana). Subway stop: Lamarmora (M3)

16 Casa della Meridiana This is one of the first (1924-25) Modernist apartment buildings in Milan (it was designed by **Giuseppe de Finetti,** who was a student of **Adolf Loos**). It takes its name from the sundial painted high up on the facade by Gigiotti Zanini. ◆ Via Marchiondi 3 (at Piazza Cardinal Ferrari). Subway stop: Lamarmora (M3)

17 Yar ★★$$ Natasha Garilskaya opened this, the first Russian restaurant in Italy (now one of only two). Chef Nikolai Yakimov lovingly prepares caviar, smoked sturgeon, borscht, beef Stroganoff, chicken Kiev, and other standards, while Giuseppe Vaccarini takes care of the largely Italian wine list. The spacious dining room has the look and ambience of a St. Petersburg palace—elegant antique lamps, candelabras, and plush red fabrics. The newly added "Bistrot," offering Russian fare at prices below those of the restaurant, attracts a young, hip crowd. ◆ M-F lunch and dinner; Sa dinner only. Via Giuseppe Mercalli 22 (near Corso Italia). 58309603. Subway stop: Lamarmora (M3)

18 Santa Maria Presso San Celso Two of Milan's leading 17th-century painters, Giulio Cesare Procaccini and Giambattista Crespi, decorated the aisles of this church with Mannerist stuccos and frescoes. Construction on it began in 1493 to a design by **Gian Giacomo Dolcebuono;** the facade, designed in 1565 and 1568, is by **Galeazzo Alessi.** Procaccini also painted the *Martyrdom of Saints Nazarius and Celsus* in the fourth bay on the right, which in turn influenced Crespi's *Martyrdom of St. Catherine* in the second bay on the left. Also of interest are Paris Bordone's *Holy Family with St. Jerome* in the right transept; Gaudenzio Ferrari's *Baptism of Christ* and the *Conversion of St. Paul* by Alessandro Bonvicino (called Moretto) in the ambulatory; and *Madonna and Saints* by Ambrogio da Fossano (called Bergognone) in the left aisle. The name of the church translates as "St. Mary next to St. Celsus," because it was built near the restored Romanesque church of San Celso, accessible through a door in the right aisle. ◆ Corso Italia (between Via San Martino and Via Giuseppe Mercalli). Subway stop: Lamarmora (M3)

19 Santa Maria al Paradiso This recently restored church dating from 1590 contains one of only a few low-key examples of Rococo in Milan, namely the altar in the third chapel on the right. ◆ Corso di Porta Vigentina (at Via Quadronno). Subway stop: Lamarmora (M3)

20 Porta Romana This city gate was built in 1598 by **Aurelio Trezzi** in honor of Mary Margaret of Austria, who passed through town from Vienna on her way to marry Philip III of Spain in Madrid. ◆ Piazzale Medaglie d'Oro. Subway stop: Porta Romana (M3)

Bests

Marchesa Barbara Berlingieri
Vice President, Save Venice

Milan:

Ca'Albrizzi, Corso Venezia 29—you can find all sorts of carpets, ceramics, materials, unusual and smart furniture, and decorative objects.

Corso Como 10—a bazaar with everything from books to clothes to English shoes.

Archivolto in Via Marsala—a bookshop specializing in architecture.

Venice:

Legatoria Piazzesi for special Venetian paperwork.

Bar Al Teatro for cappuccino and the best *zaletti* (delicious traditional Venetian biscuits).

Harry's Bar for a dinner of risotto and all the best types of pasta.

Palazzo Vendramin Calergi on the **Giudecca**—the best view in Venice.

The Hotel Monaco Terrace for lunch or dinner in warm weather.

Rosa Salva on the **Campo San Luca**—the best ice cream, marròns glacés, and *liquerizia.*

Osteria Ponte del Diavolo on **Torcello** island—delicious food and atmosphere.

Ticinese/Navigli

Followers of urban renewal (not to mention real estate agents) have for some time had their eye on the adjoining Ticinese and Navigli neighborhoods of Milan. Once a strictly working-class district, the Ticinese has been increasingly settled by *rampanti* (Milanese yuppies), who are attracted to its large, loftlike former warehouses and the charms of the sturdy and always less-affordable *case di ringhiera*—apartment buildings characterized by *ringhiere*, wrought-iron railings that surround the inner courtyards on each floor. The Navigli, also low-rent until recently and with similar architecture, gets its name from the remaining *navigli*, or canals, that run through it (they once connected much of Milan). As romantic as they

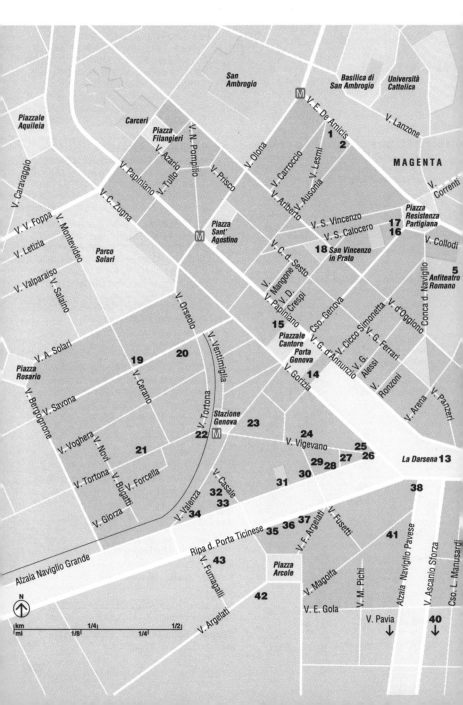

look in the fog and at twilight, the canals have more in common with the gritty Canal St. Martin in Paris than with the well-scrubbed canals of Amsterdam. Still, the entire area—increasingly filled with boutiques and the variety of restaurants and clubs that give Milan its reputation as the home of Italy's liveliest nightlife—is the trendiest in the city and continues to expand as it extends itself beyond the **Viali** toward Milan's third ring, the connecting road called the **Circonvalazione Esterna.** Besides increased property values, gentrification has brought new life to the Ticinese and Navigli districts. This is most evident during the antiques flea market held along the **Naviglio Grande** the last Sunday of every month, and in the nightlife that sparkles along the water well into the wee hours.

1 Bianca & Blu This boutique is the showcase for Monica Bolzoni, whose inventive women's clothing designs are based on cuts and textiles from the 1940s and 1950s. Her romantic apparel and matching accessories have quite a following in Milan. ◆ M afternoon, Tu-Sa. Via Edmondo De Amicis 53 (between Via Ausonia and Via Carroccio). 8361139. Subway stop: San Ambrogio (M2)

2 Franco Fiorentino Men's and women's shoes are the forte of Franco Fiorentino, who makes them in casual and fashionable styles at affordable prices. ◆ M afternoon, Tu-Sa. Via Edmondo De Amicis 51 (between Via Ausonia and Via Carroccio). 89404992. Subway stop: San Ambrogio (M2)

2 Soldati Sas You won't find giveaway prices here, but the markdowns are the biggest you'll ever see on women's clothing by such designers as Valentino, Gaultier, Byblos, and Versace. Prices are slashed even more in their bargain corner. The basement has a somewhat less ample selection of men's clothing. ◆ M-Sa; no midday closing on Saturday. Via Ausonia 14 (courtyard, at Via Edmondo De Amicis). 8373965. Subway stop: San Ambrogio (M2)

3 Sabor Tropical The tropical flavor of this night spot comes from the Caribbean and South American music played in a theatrical setting of toy toucans and the like, and from the Milanese version of umbrella drinks. ◆ Tu, Th-Su 10PM-3AM. No credit cards accepted. Via Molino delle Armi 18 (between Corso Italia and Corso di Porta Ticinese). 58313584. Subway stops: San Ambrogio (M2); Missori (M1)

4 Portnoy Caffè Letterario The high-tech, postmodern trappings of this cafe attract a crowd of literary types and Italian pop singers who come here to enjoy snacks and cocktails. ◆ M-Sa 7PM-midnight. No credit cards accepted. Via Edmondo De Amicis 1 (near Corso di Porta Ticinese). 8378656. Subway stops: San Ambrogio (M2); Missori (M1)

Restaurants/Clubs: Red **Hotels:** Blue
Shops/ Outdoors: Green **Sights/Culture:** Black

5 Anfiteatro Romano Peek into the courtyard of this building to see the surprisingly secret remains of Milan's Roman amphitheater. ♦ Via Edmondo De Amicis 17 (near Corso di Porta Ticinese). Subway stops: San Ambrogio (M2); Missori (M1)

6 Gelateria Ecologica Some of the homemade ecological gelati served in this gleaming and popular spot are: *pistacchio di Sicilia* (Sicilian pistachio), *fico d'India* (prickly pear), and *fragoline di bosco* (wild strawberries). ♦ M-Tu, Th-Su 1PM-midnight, March-July, Sept-Oct. No credit cards accepted. Corso di Porta Ticinese 40 (near Via Edmondo De Amicis). 58101872. Subway stops: San Ambrogio (M2); Missori (M1)

7 Osteria dell'Operetta ★★$$ The menu at this pleasant hangout changes regularly, but fresh pastas, giant Milanese cutlets, and salads are usually among the staples. Performers play live music until 12:30AM. ♦ M-Sa dinner and late-night snacks. Corso di Porta Ticinese 70 (near Via Scaldasole). 8375120. Subway stops: San Agostino (M2); Missori (M1)

8 Panca Men's and women's shoes, some of which are inspired by Ferragamo and Chanel, and many of which are attractive Panca originals, abound in this bargain store. A limited selection can be made to measure for problem feet. ♦ M afternoon, Tu-Sa. Corso di Porta Ticinese 96 (north of Piazza Sant'Eustorgio). 8394543. Subway stops: San Agostino (M2); Missori (M1)

8 Supporti Fonografici Popular with Milan's club set, this shop stocks recordings of New Wave music and beyond. ♦ M afternoon, Tu-Sa. Corso di Porta Ticinese 100 (north of Piazza Sant'Eustorgio). 8372343. Subway stops: San Agostino (M2); Missori (M1)

Sant'Eustorgio

9 Piazza Sant'Eustorgio The column in this piazza is dedicated to St. Peter Martyr, who was born in nearby Verona and is buried inside the church of **Sant'Eustorgio**. ♦ At the intersection of Corso di Porta Ticinese and Viale G. d'Annunzio. Subway stops: San Agostino (M2); Missori (M1)

10 Eliogabalo Stark and dark are the words for the women's clothes sold at bargain prices in this factory outlet. ♦ M afternoon, Tu-Sa. Piazza Sant'Eustorgio 2 (northeast in piazza). 8378293. Subway stops: San Agostino (M2); Missori (M1)

11 Sant'Eustorgio This large Dominican basilica was founded in the fourth century, enlarged in the ninth and 13th centuries, and given a Neo-Romanesque facade in the 19th century (see illustration on page 278). It once housed the relics of the Three Magi, donated by Constantinople's Emperor Constantine and taken to Cologne by Frederick Barbarossa in the 12th century. The **Cappella dei Magi,** and the sarcophagus where the relics were kept, are in the south transept. Of even greater interest is the **Cappella Portinari,** one of the best Renaissance monuments in Milan, accessible from behind the chancel. The chapel was designed for the Medici banker Pigello Portinari by the Florentine **Michelozzo,** who was inspired by **Brunelleschi**'s circle-in-a-square plans for the **Cappella Pazzi** and the **Sagrestia Vecchia** in the churches of **Santa Croce** and **San Lorenzo** in his native city. It is dedicated to St. Peter Martyr, patron saint of Milan's ruling families, who is buried in the elaborate tomb in the center designed by the 14th-century Pisan sculptor Giovanni di Balduccio. The saint's life is depicted in 15th-century frescoes by Vincenzo Foppa, who is probably also responsible for the angels dancing around the dome. For a nominal donation, the sacristan will let you into the **Museo di Sant'Eustorgio** to see numerous reliquaries and paintings connected with the church. From the museum (or from the left nave) you can visit Milan's only in situ Roman and early-Christian cemetery. ♦ Piazza Sant'Eustorgio (north side of piazza). Subway stops: San Agostino (M2); Missori (M1)

12 Porta Ticinese This Neo-Classical city gate (constructed 1801-14) was originally built for the entrance of Napoleon into the city after the Battle of Marengo. Designed by **Luigi Cagnola,** it was also called **Porta Marengo,** a name which, had it stuck, would have made it easier to distinguish this **Porta Ticinese** from the medieval one at the other end of Corso Ticinese. ♦ Piazzale XXIV Maggio (center of piazzale). Subway stop: San Agostino (M2)

13 La Darsena This confluence of three major canals is a great spot for people watching or taking in a toy-boat regatta. ♦ At Piazzale XXIV Maggio. Subway stop: San Agostino (M2)

14 Al Porto ★★$$ This is one of Milan's finest fish restaurants (with first course pasta dishes also based on the sea, such as *bavette con scampi e pomodoro,* a spaghetti-like pasta made with fresh shrimp and fresh tomato). The menu here changes depending on the day's catch (of what husband-and-wife owners Domenico find at the fish market, that is), and the decor is nautical as well. There is also an excellent wine list, primarily consisting of whites, and daughter Barbara makes the desserts on the premises. The glassed-in veranda is a particularly good place to eat in fine weather. ♦ M dinner, Tu-Sa lunch and dinner. Piazzale Cantore (at Corso Genova). 8321481. Subway stop: San Agostino (M2)

15 Pozzi Now here's a wonderful array of gelati: all the old standards, alongside unusual flavors like *tè* (tea), *liquirizia* (licorice), and *pompelmo* (grapefruit). ♦ Tu-Su until 1AM. No credit cards accepted. Piazzale Cantore 4 (at Corso Genova). 8399830. Subway stop: San Agostino (M2)

16 Biffi Terrific variety in men's and women's clothing by many top designers (as well as the shop's own label) draws shoppers from all parts of town. ♦ M afternoon, Tu-Sa. Corso Genova 6 (near Piazza Resistenza Partigiana). Subway stops: San Agostino or San Ambrogio (M2). 8375170. Also at: Via Filzi 45 (near Stazione Centrale). 67072175. Subway stop: Centrale F.S. (M2, M3)

17 Floretta Coen Musil A Milanese institution, this bargain basement (with no fitting rooms) stocks men's and women's designer apparel at a discount. ♦ M-Sa afternoon. No credit cards accepted. Via San Calocero 3 (near Piazza Resistenza Partigiana). 58111708. Subway stops: San Agostino or San Ambrogio (M2)

18 San Vincenzo in Prato The church that has stood on this site since early Christian times has had many uses, among them the production of chemicals while the building was a plant called the **Casa del Mago** (House of the Wizard). Restored to its original Romanesque appearance, it is now a church again—a peaceful pile of brick with a simple interior filled with light. ♦ Via San Calocero (at Via Ariberto). Subway stop: San Agostino (M2)

19 Trattoria all'Antica di Domenico e Maria ★★$$ Domenico Passera prepares Lombard specialties such as *cassoeula* (pig's-foot stew), as well as Spanish paella in an upscale setting. ♦ M-Sa lunch and dinner. Via Montevideo 4 (at Via Savona). 58104860. Subway stop: Genova F.S. (M2)

20 Aurora ★★$$ This is a good place for Piedmontese specialties—from minestrone and a variety of pastas to boiled and roasted meats. Sit in the shaded outdoor garden in the warmer months. ♦ Tu-Sa lunch and dinner. Via Savona 23 (near Viale Coni Zugna). 89404978. Subway stop: Genova F.S. (M2)

21 La Granseola ★★$$$ The ever-changing menu at Rocco Nisi's seafood restaurant (the name means "spider crab" and it's the house specialty) does have one constant—fresh fish prepared in style at reasonable prices. The atmosphere is intimate and romantic—perfect for that late night tête-à-tête. ♦ M-Sa dinner. Via Tortona 20 (near Via Novi). 89402445. Subway stop: Genova F.S. (M2)

22 Osteria dei Binari ★★$$ This sprawling restaurant features crowd-pleasing regional food from various parts of Italy, with an emphasis on Piedmont and Lombardy in both food and wine. *Busecca* (cheese-covered tripe served on bread rounds), game, and grilled meats are all exceptional choices. ♦ M-Sa dinner. Via Tortona 1 (behind Stazione Genova). 89409428. Subway stop: Genova F.S. (M2)

23 La Scaletta ★★$$$ In this small and refined restaurant, Pina Bellini creates grand and refined dishes using such Italian classics as lasagna, ravioli, tripe, foie gras, and saddle of rabbit as her solid starting points. Son Aldo keeps the atmosphere in the dining room hushed without being overly reverent, guaranteeing one of the best meals you'll have in Milan. ♦ Tu-Sa lunch and dinner. Piazza Stazione Genova 3 (east in piazza). 58100290. Subway stop: Genova F.S. (M2)

24 Selfservice dello Scampolo Fabric remnants from various manufacturers at rock-bottom prices are sold here by length as well as weight. ♦ M afternoon, Tu-Sa. No credit cards accepted. Via Vigevano 32 (near Viale Gorizia). 58100866. Subway stop: Genova F.S. (M2)

25 Gambelin Pottery from throughout Italy—terra-cotta, majolica, and the like—can be found here at reasonable prices. ♦ M afternoon, Tu-Sa. No credit cards accepted. Viale Gorizia 30 (at Via Vigevano). 58100880. Subway stop: Genova F.S. (M2)

26 Posto di Conversazione ★★$$ What purports to be a conversation nook turns out to be a comfortable restaurant, serving *crespelle* (crepes), *bistecca* (steak) with a variety of sauces (such as *paprika dolce,* or sweet paprika; *fichi secchi,* or dried figs; and *ginepro,* or juniper), as well as copious salads, well into the night. ♦ Tu-Su dinner. Alzaia Naviglio Grande 6 (off Viale Gorizia). 58106646. Subway stop: Genova F.S. (M2)

27 Vicolo della Lavandaia This tiny street along the *navigli* once had many washer-woman's stands. The only one that remains, a reminder of when cleaner water flowed in the canals and appliance-crazed young professionals had yet to discover the area, is near and dear to the hearts of the old- time residents. ♦ Off Alzaia Naviglio Grande. Subway stop: Genova F.S. (M2)

28 El Brellin Try this small piano bar/restaurant for a late-night drink or a snack after sampling the nightlife along the canal. ♦ M-Sa 10PM-2AM. Vicolo della Lavandaia (off Alzaia Naviglio Grande). 58101351. Subway stop: Genova F.S. (M2)

29 Il Libraccio The bargain books here—many art books and an excellent choice of dictionaries—are not off-putting, as the shop's name (which means "ugly book") might lead you to believe. ♦ M afternoon, Tu-Sa. No credit cards accepted. Via Corsico 9 (off Alzaia Naviglio Grande). Subway stop: Genova F.S. (M2). 8372398. Also at: Via Corsico 12 (across the street); Piazza del Duomo. 72004238. Subway stop: Duomo (M1, M3); Viale V. Veneto (near Piazza della Repubblica). 6555187. Subway stop: Repubblica (M3)

30 Il Discomane This secondhand record shop is especially good for American- and European-label 45s, tapes, and CDs. ♦ M afternoon, Tu-Sa. Alzaia Naviglio Grande 38 (between Via Corsico and Via Casale). 89406291. Subway stop: Genova F.S. (M2)

30 Tornavento This is the place to enjoy an evening of musical standards from such Milanese favorites as Mina (called the Italian Barbra Streisand) and Fred Buongusto (a homegrown Tony Bennett) as interpreted by the cocktail pianist. ♦ Tu-Su 9PM-1AM. Alzaia Naviglio Grande 36 (between Via Corsico and Via Casale). 49405742. Subway stop: Genova F.S. (M2)

31 Santa Maria delle Grazie al Naviglio A typically Italian Neo-Gothic church (1899-1909, **Cesare Nava**) built on the site of a real Gothic church. Inside are eight granite columns that come from the basilica of San Paolo Fuori le Mura in Rome. ♦ Alzaia Naviglio Grande (between Via Corsico and Via Casale). Subway stop: Genova F.S. (M2)

32 Osteria di Via Pre ★$$ The largely Ligurian cuisine served here—meaning pesto sauce, lots of olives, and fried fish—is authentically prepared. The decor features huge blowups amusingly called *gigantografie.* ♦ Tu-Sa lunch and dinner. Via Casale 4 (off Alzaia Naviglio Grande). 8373869. Subway stop: Genova F.S. (M2)

33 Asso di Fiori Osteria dei Formaggi ★★$$ Cheese is the theme of this rustic, yet elegant restaurant furnished with antiques.

Restaurants/Clubs: Red   Hotels: Blue
Shops/ Outdoors: Green   **Sights/Culture: Black**

It comes in all shapes and sizes: melted on pasta, coupled with meat, and sliced up for dessert. ♦ M-F lunch and dinner; Sa dinner. Alzaia Naviglio Grande 54 (at Via Casale). 89409415. Subway stop: Genova F.S. (M2)

34 **Il Montalcino** ★★$$$ Named after the famed wine-producing town in Tuscany, this restaurant prides itself on its wine list. The upscale rustic decor matches the cuisine, mostly Lombard (excellent risottos) but offering other regional specialties (notably Tuscan, which go well with the titular grape) as well. ♦ M-Sa lunch and dinner. Via Valenza 17 (at Alzaia Naviglio Grande). 8321926. Subway stop: Genova F.S. (M2)

35 **Al Pont de Ferr** ★★$$ Near an iron bridge from which it takes its name, this rustic restaurant is a relaxed place to sample simple Milanese cuisine. Only a few dishes are offered daily (or rather, nightly, since it's only open for dinner), such as *pasta e fagioli* (pasta with beans), *cassoeula* (pig's-foot stew), and osso buco, which are reassuringly regular and dependable. ♦ M-Sa dinner. No credit cards accepted. Ripa di Porta Ticinese 55 (between Via Fusetti and Via Paoli). 89406277. Subway stops: Genova F.S. or Romolo (M2)

35 **L'Arcobaleno** One of the best options for gelato right on the *navigli,* with a full selection of cool fruity and creamy treats. ♦ M-Sa until midnight. No credit cards accepted. Ripa di Porta Ticinese 53 (between Via Fusetti and Via Paoli). 89402360. Subway stops: Genova F.S. or Romolo (M2)

36 **Sadler** ★★★$$$ In a flawless, expense-account setting, young chef Claudio Sadler prepares an ever-changing nouvellish cuisine based on luscious regional Italian ingredients, from his zucchini-flower vegetable pâté to delicately presented pheasant and pigeon. Ask for the *gran menu* (full menu) to sample the greatest variety of his wares. ♦ M-Sa dinner. Ripa di Porta Ticinese 51 (between Via Fusetti and Via Paoli). 58104451. Subway stops: Genova F.S. or Romolo (M2)

37 **Warhouse** Despite its bellicose name, this orderly secondhand store is more concerned with the season's trends, selling found fashions from other times. ♦ M afternoon, Tu-Sa. No credit cards accepted. Ripa di Porta Ticinese 49 (between Via Fusetti and Via Paoli). Subway stops: Genova F.S. or Romolo (M2)

38 **Osteria del Pontell** Music videos and occasional live music provide the backdrop for this club, where the snacks include 11 types of *bruschetta,* or toast covered with a variety of tasty morsels. ♦ M, W-Su. No credit cards accepted. Alzaia Naviglio Pavese 2 (at Viale Gorizia). 58101982. Subway stop: Genova F.S. (M2)

39 **Carosello** ★★$$ Design buffs will want to see Milan's newest nightspot for its evocative Middle Eastern atmosphere, curiosity seekers for the design world habitués—those who aren't famous look like they ought to be. Design- and star-gazing aside, you'd do well to visit just for the food: Classic specialties like risotto, homemade pasta, and fresh fish are infused with a sense of the nouvelle and handsomely presented. Find out for yourself why the desserts have become famous in their own right. ♦ Tu- Su 8PM-3AM Via Pietro Custodi 12 (off Via Col di Lana). 58100889. Subway stop: Porta Romana (M3); San Agostino (M2)

40 **Il Torchietto** ★★$$ Owner Sergio Ragazzi is from Mantua, which, although within the region of Lombardy, is nearer to and more influenced by the cuisine of Emilia-Romagna. Thus *culatello* (melt-in-your-mouth ham), boiled and stuffed meats, and sausages are all good choices in this warm, recently renovated restaurant decorated in a modern style with marble columns, soft lighting, and a long bar. ♦ Tu-Sa lunch and dinner. Via Ascano Sforza 47 (at Via Pavia). 8372000. Subway stop: Genova F.S. (M2)

41 **La Magolfa** ★★$$ Another relaxed place with live music where you can sample some Milanese standards, this restaurant offers all the usual risotto dishes as well as osso buco in a glass-enclosed canal-side setting. ♦ M-Sa dinner until 2AM. Via Magolfa 15 (off Alzaia Naviglio Pavase). 8321696. Subway stop: Genova F.S. (M2)

42 **La Topaia** ★★$$ Dine informally on Lombard specialties with a little Ligurian mixed in. Andrea and Anita's menu features numerous risotto dishes, minestrone, and the seafaring *insalata tiepida di polipo* (warm octopus salad). ♦ M-Sa dinner. Via Argelati 46 (at Piazza Arcole). 8373469. Subway stop: Genova F.S. (M2)

43 **Nikken Milano** $$ Appropriately situated in the now-fashionable district, this Japanese property has 92 guest rooms, all decorated in a light, sober elegance. Added attractions here include a small pretty garden and terrace and a restaurant serving Milanese food. ♦ Via Fumagalli 4 (between Via Argelati and Ripa di Porta Ticinese). 58107065; fax 58115066. Subway stop: Genova F.S. (M2)

Called "Mediolanum" by the Romans, Milan was the capital of the Roman Empire from AD 286-402. In AD 313, Constantine the Great signed the Edict of Milan, recognizing Christianity as the official religion of the Empire.

"Milan is a giant, nightmare city."

Dylan Thomas

Additional Milan Highlights

1 Il Salvagente Aptly called "The Lifesaver," this is the original, and still the biggest and best, of Milan's bargain basements, a relatively new concept in Milan. Well organized and spacious, men's and women's clothing (a separate store for children's clothing was recently opened) is divided according to designers, and they are many. Discounts, which are already substantial, are slashed even further during January and June sales. Avoid the masses on Saturdays. ♦ M-Sa; W, Sa no midday closing. Via Fratelli Bronzetti 16 (off Corso XXII Marzo). 76110328. Subway stop: San Babila (M1). Also at: Via Balzaretti 28 (at Largo Usuelli). 26680764 (for children). Subway stop: Piola (M2)

2 L'Ami Berton ★★★$$$ Remigio Bertone was one of the first restaurateurs in town to take an interest in international culinary trends, giving him more experience than most in perfecting such succulent pairings as *lasagnette al pesto e frutti di mare* (pasta with pesto and seafood) and *fegatino con le mele* (liver with apples). The fish dishes here are the most inventive in Milan. Decorated with antiques and a rose and green color scheme, the two linked dining rooms have a tony, elegant atmosphere. ♦ M-F lunch and dinner; Sa dinner only. Via F. Nullo 14 (near Via Carlo Goldoni). 713669. Subway stop: Porta Venezia (M1)

3 Luna Park Varesine Milan's amusement park is close to the center of the city and a little rough around the edges, but it's a great place to take the kids or observe the Milanese version of the same cavorting on merry-go-rounds and roller coasters (called *montagne russe,* or Russian mountains, in Italy). ♦ M-Sa 3-6PM, 9PM-midnight; Su 10:30AM-1PM, 2:30PM-midnight. Via Galileo Galilei 15 (in Piazza San Giochino). 6571149. Subway stop: Repubblica (M3)

4 Botteguccia Richard Ginori This is the factory outlet for the revered Florentine china manufacturer. Prices are attractively low for their entire stock of plates, cups, ovenware, etc., but the major savings are on seconds and the "end of series" remainders. ♦ M-Sa. No credit cards accepted. Via della Pergola 11 (near Piazzale Lagosta). 6887580. Subway stop: Garibaldi F.S. (M2)

5 Cimitero Monumentale While hardly Paris's Père-Lachaise, Milan's extensive cemetery (a conglomerate of five adjoining suburban cemeteries) does contain the remains of Milanese notables such as writer Alessandro Manzoni and intellectual Carlo Cattaneo. Perhaps more interestingly, it is filled with a fanciful assemblage of 19th- and 20th-century funereal sculpture by obscure and less-obscure sculptors such as Giacomo Manzù, Fausto Melotti, and Gio Pomodoro. It is still the final resting place of choice for Milan's leading families, though admission is restricted to those whose ancestors are already buried here. ♦ Tu-Su. Piazzale Cimitero Monumentale (at Viale Certosa). Subway stop: Garibaldi F.S. (M2)

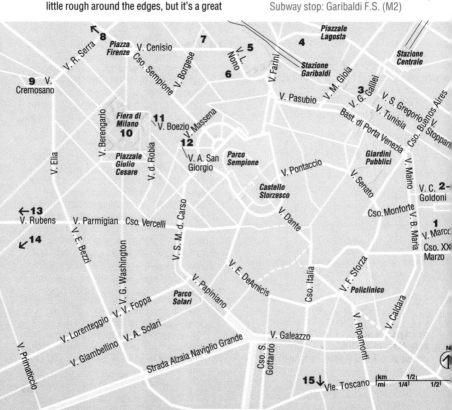

6 Spacci Bassetti Second in size to Bassetti's warehouse-sized factory outlet, this location is slightly more convenient and definitely worth the taxi ride for consumers familiar with the old and respected Lombard manufacturer of high-quality household linens. In addition to discounted seconds and overstock of towels, sheets, and other household items, there's also a large selection of Bassetti goods for close-to-retail prices. ♦ M-Sa; no midday closing. No credit cards accepted. Via Procaccini 32 (off Piazzale Cimitero Monumentale). 3450125. Subway stop: Garibaldi F.S. (M2). Also at: Via Botta 7A (near Piazzale le Libia). 55183191. Subway stop: San Babila (M1)

7 Alfredo Gran San Bernardo ★★★$$$ Opened in 1964, Alfredo Valli's elegant eatery features classic Milanese dishes followed by the city's current dessert trends, chocolate mousse and zabaglione. The restaurant also has an excellent selection of grappa. The dining room has recently been redone in contemporary style. ♦ M-Sa lunch and dinner. Closed January and August. Via Borgese 14 (at Via Cenisio). 3319000. Subway stop: Garibaldi F.S. (M2)

8 Franca, Paola e Lele ★★$$$ Bearing the first names of its owners, this place is homey in everything but price. The *cucina creativa* (creative cuisine) changes according to chef Paola Zanella's whim and what she finds at the market. Usually, you'll find mouthwatering *culatello* ham as an appetizer and a few good game dishes among the pastas and entrées. The chocolate desserts are terrific. ♦ M-F lunch and dinner. Viale Certosa 235 (near Piazza Firenze). 38006238. Subway stop: Lotto (M1 to Molino Dorino)

9 Ribot ★★$$ Named after a famous race-horse (it's near the track of San Siro), this restaurant features many photos of it and similar beasts, and at times seems as busy as the track. Stick with the classics—risotto, grilled and boiled meats, and homemade desserts. ♦ Tu-Su lunch and dinner. Via Cremosano 41 (at Piazzale Stuparich). 33001646. Subway stop: Lotto (M1 to Molino Dorino)

10 Fiera di Milano Italy's most important trade fair was founded in 1920 and opened on its present site in 1923. Dozens of exhibitions (referred to with the odd acronyms the Italians are so fond of, such as MIFED for films and TV) are held regularly each year, the most internationally famous being the fashion and furniture fairs. In 1993, more than 70 specialist fairs were hosted. Like much of Milan, the fairgrounds suffered heavily during World War II bombing, but a number of early structures remain, among them the **Palazzo dello Sport** (1925). Postwar construction includes the **Palazzo delle Nazioni** (1947), the **Emiciclo** (1947-53), the **Padiglione dell'Agricoltura** (1956), and the **Padiglione della Meccanica** (1969). ♦ Largo Domodossola 1 (off Corso Sempione). 49971.

For fair schedules, in the US: 212/459.0015. Subway stops: Fiera Amendola or Lotto (M1 to Molino Dorino)

11 Grand Hotel Fieramilano $$$ Across from the Porta Domodossola entrance to the fairgrounds, this 240-room hotel has amenities such as hair dryers and telephones in the bathrooms and air-conditioning in the warmer months (when you can also have breakfast in the outdoor garden restaurant), making it the hotel of choice for those going to the fair. ♦ Viale Boezio 20 (at Largo Domodossola). 336221; fax 314119. Subway stops: Fiera Amendola or Lotto (M1 to Molino Dorino)

12 Lancaster $$ Also near the fairgrounds, this hotel is a less expensive option. Its smaller size (only 29 rooms) and personal touches such as "Pedro the parrot" at the front desk ensure a regular clientele, which makes reservations a must. Restaurant service available. ♦ Via A. San Giorgio 16 (near Piazza Giovanni XXIII). 344705; fax 344649. Subway stops: Pagano (M1); Buonarotti (M1 to Molino Dorino)

13 Grand Hotel Brun $$$$ This 350-room luxury hotel, located near the racetrack, is virtually a self-contained environment for business travelers. ♦ Via Caldera 21 (near Via Novara). 45271; fax 48204746

Within the Grand Hotel Brun:

Don Giovanni $$$ For years enjoying an excellent reputation as **Ascot**, the arrival of a new French chef brings a new name and a new menu—one highlighted by fresh fish entrees and pasta made on the premises. A good spot for a business lunch or dinner (especially if you are a guest at the hotel). ♦ M-Sa lunch and dinner. 45271

14 Aimo e Nadia ★★★$$$ Aimo and Nadia Moroni have taken their native Tuscan appreciation for wholesome ingredients and put them together in imaginative and ever-changing ways, which makes it impossible to mention specific dishes but pleasantly surprising to try them. Delicate pastries are made in-house by Gabriele Grigolon. ♦ M-F lunch and dinner; Sa dinner only. Via Montecuccoli 6 (at Viale San Gimignano). 416886

15 Hotel Quark $$$$ This is another large (with over 300 rooms), modern and efficient business hotel that's famous for its restaurant, which is under the same ownership as **Don Giovanni** in the **Grand Hotel Brun**. A pool is much appreciated in hot weather, though the hotel closes for the month of August. ♦ Via Lampedusa 11A (at Viale G. da Cermenate). 84431; fax 8464190

Within Hotel Quark:

Pegaso ★★$$$ The menu at this intimate, modern dining room ranges from international specialties to (more interesting) Italian regional dishes such as pastas and truffles, all accompanied by a good selection of wines. ♦ M-Sa lunch and dinner. 84431

Index

Restaurants

Only restaurants with star ratings are listed in the Restaurants index for each city. All restaurants are listed alphabetically in the each city's main (preceding) index. Always call in advance to ensure a restaurant has not closed, changed its hours, or booked its tables for a private party. The restaurant price ratings are based on the average cost of an entrée for one person, excluding tax and tip.

★★★★ An Extraordinary Experience
★★★ Excellent
★★ Very Good
★ Good

$$$$ Big Bucks ($70 and up)
$$$ Expensive ($45-$70)
$$ Reasonable $25-$45)
$ The Price Is Right (less than $25)

Hotels

The hotels listed in the Hotels index for each city are grouped according their price ratings; they are also listed in each city's main index. The hotel price ratings reflect the base price of standard room for two people for one night during the peak season.

$$$$ Big Bucks ($225 and up)
$$$ Expensive ($125-$225)
$$ Reasonable ($90-$125)
$ The Price Is Right (less than $90)

Florence

287

Venice Restaurants

Venice Hotels

Milan Restaurants

Milan Hotels